Early Modern Emotions

Early Modern Emotions is a student-friendly introduction to the concepts, approaches and sources used to study emotions in early modern Europe, and to the perspectives that analysis of the history of emotions can offer early modern studies more broadly.

The volume is divided into four sections that guide students through the key processes and practices employed in current research on the history of emotions. The first explains how key terms and concepts in the study of emotions relate to early modern Europe, while the second focuses on the unique ways in which emotions were conceptualized at the time. The third section introduces a range of sources and methodologies that are used to analyse early modern emotions. The final section includes a wide-ranging selection of thematic topics covering war, religion, family, politics, art, music, literature and the non-human world to show how analysis of emotions may offer new perspectives on the early modern period more broadly.

Each section offers bite-sized, accessible commentaries providing students new to the history of emotions with the tools to begin their own investigations. Each entry is supported by annotated further reading recommendations pointing students to the latest research in that area and at the end of the book is a general bibliography, which provides a comprehensive list of current scholarship.

This book is the perfect starting point for any student wishing to study emotions in early modern Europe.

Susan Broomhall is Professor of Early Modern History at The University of Western Australia and an Australian Research Council Future Fellow attached to the Australian Research Council Centre of Excellence for the History of Emotions. Previous works on emotions include (as editor) *Ordering Emotions in Europe, 1100–1800* (2015), *Gender and Emotions in Medieval and Early Modern Europe: Destroying Order, Structuring Disorder* (2015), *Spaces for Feeling: Emotions and Sociabilities in Britain, 1650–1850*, (2015), *Authority, Gender and Emotions in Late Medieval and Early Modern England* (2015) and, with Sarah Finn, *Violence and Emotions in Early Modern Europe* (2015). Her monograph, *Gender, Emotions and the Dutch East India Company*, is forthcoming from Amsterdam University Press.

Early Modern Themes

Books in the *Early Modern Themes* series are aimed at upper level undergraduate and postgraduate students who are looking more deeply at thematic topics in the early modern period. They combine chapters offering a synthesis of the topic as it stands, the key historiographical debates, and the cutting edge research which is driving the field forward.

Early Modern Things
Edited by Paula Findlen

Early Modern Emotions
Edited by Susan Broomhall

Forthcoming:

Early Modern Childhood
Edited by Anna French

Early Modern Food
Edited by Roderick Phillips

Early Modern Emotions

An introduction

Edited by Susan Broomhall

LONDON AND NEW YORK

First published 2017
by Routledge
2 Park Square, Milton Park, Abingdon, Oxon OX14 4RN

and by Routledge
711 Third Avenue, New York, NY 10017

Routledge is an imprint of the Taylor & Francis Group, an informa business

British Library Cataloguing-in-Publication Data
A catalogue record for this book is available from the British Library

Library of Congress Cataloging-in-Publication Data
Names: Broomhall, Susan, editor.
Title: Early modern emotions : an introduction / edited by Susan Broomhall.
Description: London ; New York : Routledge, [2017] | Includes bibliographical references and index.
Identifiers: LCCN 2016020607| ISBN 9781138925748 (hardback : alk. paper) | ISBN 9781138925755 (pbk. : alk. paper) | ISBN 9781315441368 (ebook)
Subjects: LCSH: Emotions—History.
Classification: LCC BF531 .E33 2017 | DDC 152.409—dc23
LC record available at https://lccn.loc.gov/2016020607

ISBN: 978-1-138-92574-8 (hbk)
ISBN: 978-1-138-92575-5 (pbk)
ISBN: 978-1-315-44136-8 (ebk)

Typeset in Bembo
by Florence Production Ltd, Stoodleigh, Devon, UK

Printed and bound in Great Britain by
TJ International Ltd, Padstow, Cornwall

Contents

Figures *xiii*
Tables *xv*
Acknowledgements *xvi*
Notes on contributors *xviii*
Introduction by Susan Broomhall *xxxvi*

SECTION I
Modern theories and models of emotions 1

I.1 *Emotional community* 3
ANDREW LYNCH

I.2 *Emotives and emotional regimes* 7
TANIA M. COLWELL

I.3 *Affect theory* 10
STEPHANIE TRIGG

I.4 *Performance and performativity* 14
KATIE BARCLAY

I.5 *Materiality* 17
SARAH RANDLES

I.6 *Space and place* 20
KATIE BARCLAY

I.7 *Psychological approaches* 23
SANDRA GARRIDO AND JANE W. DAVIDSON

I.8 *Large data set mining* 27
INGER LEEMANS

SECTION II
Early modern terms, concepts and practices of emotions 31

II.1 *Language of emotions* 33
R.S. WHITE

II.2 *Emotion* 36
PATRICIA SIMONS

II.3 *Humoral theory* 39
DANIJELA KAMBASKOVIC

II.4 *The senses* 42
HERMAN ROODENBURG

II.5 *Pain and suffering* 45
JAVIER MOSCOSO

II.6 *Grammar* 48
ROSS KNECHT

II.7 *Mood* 50
R.S. WHITE

II.8 *Love* 53
DANIJELA KAMBASKOVIC

II.9 *Melancholy* 56
ERIN SULLIVAN

II.10 *Fellow-feeling* 61
KATHERINE IBBETT

II.11 *Sociality and sociability* 64
KATRINA O'LOUGHLIN

II.12 *Holy affections* 67
HANNAH NEWTON

II.13 *The passions* 71
ALEKSONDRA HULTQUIST

II.14 *Contemplation* 74
CHRISTOPHER ALLEN

II.15 *Sensibility* 78
KATRINA O'LOUGHLIN

II.16 *The expressive face* 81
LINDA WALSH

SECTION III
Sources and methodologies for early modern emotions **87**

III.1 *Poetry* 89
DIANA G. BARNES

III.2 *Drama* 92
KATHRYN PRINCE

III.3 *Epistolary literature* 95
DIANA G. BARNES

III.4 *Educational treatises* 99
MERRIDEE L. BAILEY

III.5 *Histories, chronicles and memoirs* 102
ERIKA KUIJPERS

III.6 *Medical sources* 105
ROBERT L. WESTON

III.7 *Economic records* 108
MERRIDEE L. BAILEY

III.8 *Judicial sources* 112
JOANNE MCEWAN

III.9 *Church and parish records* 115
CHARLOTTE-ROSE MILLAR

III.10 *Catholic missionary texts* 118
ANANYA CHAKRAVARTI

III.11 *Letters* 121
CAROLYN JAMES

III.12 *Archives* 124
JAMES DAYBELL

III.13 *Maps* 127
ALICIA MARCHANT

III.14 *Books* 132
STEPHANIE DOWNES

III.15 *Household objects* 135
TARA HAMLING

III.16 *Prints and illustrated broadsheets* 140
CHARLES ZIKA

III.17 *Fantasy figures* 146
MELISSA PERCIVAL

III.18 *Monuments* 151
PETER SHERLOCK

III.19 *Devotional objects* 156
MARY LAVEN

III.20 *Textiles* 161
SALLY HOLLOWAY

III.21 *The body* 165
KAREN HARVEY

III.22 *Gestures* 168
JANE W. DAVIDSON AND ALAN MADDOX

III.23 *Music* 173
ALAN MADDOX AND JANE W. DAVIDSON

SECTION IV
Focus topics for the early modern period **177**

Political realms ***179***

IV.1 *Monarchies* 179
HELEN WATANABE-O'KELLY

IV.2 *Republics* 182
CATHARINE GRAY

IV.3 *Political revolutions* 185
MICHAEL J. BRADDICK

IV.4 *Radical formations* 189
CHRISTINA PETTERSON

IV.5 *Law* 192
DAVID LEMMINGS

IV.6 *Punishment* 195
UNA MCILVENNA

Destructive experiences **199**

IV.7 *Indebtedness* 199
ELISE M. DERMINEUR

IV.8 *War and violence* 202
ERIKA KUIJPERS

IV.9 *Plague* 205
GORDON D. RAEBURN

IV.10 *Domestic violence* 208
RAISA MARIA TOIVO

Life stages **211**

IV.11 *Pregnancy and childbirth* 211
JOANNE BEGIATO (BAILEY)

IV.12 *Childhood* 214
CLAUDIA JARZEBOWSKI

IV.13 *Marriage* 217
KATIE BARCLAY

IV.14 *Death* 220
PETER SHERLOCK

Spaces **225**

IV.15 *Court culture* 225
TRACY ADAMS

IV.16 *Theatre and stage* 228
SAMANTHA OWENS

IV.17 *Church interiors* 230
SING D'ARCY

IV.18 *Battlefields* 235
ALICIA MARCHANT

IV.19 *Civic culture* 238
NICHOLAS A. ECKSTEIN

IV.20 *Village* 242
ELISE M. DERMINEUR

IV.21 *Family and household* 244
KATIE BARCLAY

Intellectual and cultural traditions **248**

IV.22 *Humanism* 248
ANDREA RIZZI

IV.23 *Print media* 251
LUC RACAUT

IV.24 *Antiquarianism* 254
ALICIA MARCHANT

IV.25 *Medicine and science* 257
YASMIN HASKELL

IV.26 *Baroque music* 261
JANE W. DAVIDSON AND ALAN MADDOX

IV.27 *Baroque art* 264
STEPHANIE S. DICKEY

IV.28 *Enlightenment* 269
LAURA MANDELL

IV.29 *Romanticism* 273
R.S. WHITE

Beliefs **277**

IV.30 *Monastic communities* 277
CLAIRE WALKER

IV.31 *The reformations* 280
SUSAN C. KARANT-NUNN

IV.32 *Tolerance* 284
GIOVANNI TARANTINO

IV.33 *Protestant theology* 287
ALEC RYRIE

IV.34 *Witchcraft* — *290*
JACQUELINE VAN GENT

IV.35 *Wonders of nature* — *293*
JENNIFER SPINKS

IV.36 *Racial othering – Jews* — *297*
FRANÇOIS SOYER

IV.37 *Muslim 'others'* — *300*
AUDREY CALEFAS-STREBELLE

The world beyond Europe — ***304***

IV.38 *Global trading companies* — *304*
JACQUELINE VAN GENT

IV.39 *Amerindian and African slaves* — *307*
GIUSEPPE MARCOCCI

IV.40 *Missionary Catholicism* — *310*
PETER A. GODDARD

IV.41 *Protestant global missions* — *313*
JACQUELINE VAN GENT

IV.42 *Colonialism* — *316*
DONNA MERWICK

IV.43 *Theories of empire* — *320*
NICOLE EUSTACE

IV.44 *Indigenous/European encounters* — *323*
MARIA NUGENT

The non-human world — ***327***

IV.45 *Relations with the divine* — *327*
PHYLLIS MACK

IV.46 *The Devil and demons* — *331*
LAURA KOUNINE

IV.47 *Ghosts, fairies and the world of spirits* — *334*
JULIAN GOODARE

IV.48 *Working animals* 337
LOUISE HILL CURTH

IV.49 *Familiars* 340
CHARLOTTE-ROSE MILLAR

IV.50 *Vermin* 343
LUCINDA COLE

IV.51 *Nature* 346
GRACE MOORE

IV.52 *Landscape* 350
ANTHONY COLANTUONO

Select bibliography 355
Index 365

Figures

II.9.1	The all-male frontispiece in Robert Burton's *The Anatomy of Melancholy*	57
II.9.2	Copy of Albrect Dürer's *Melencolia I*	59
II.14.1	Charles Le Brun, *The Queens of Persia before the Feet of Alexander*, also known as the *Tent of Darius*	74
II.14.2	Nicolas Poussin, *Christ and the Woman taken in Adultery*	75
II.14.3	Selection of expressive heads drawn from the paintings of Charles Le Brun. Henry Testelin, *Sentimens des plus habiles peintres*	76
II.16.1	Jean-Baptiste Greuze, *The Angry Wife*	82
II.16.2	Francesco Bartolozzi, after Alexander Cozens, 'Combination of the Features of the Modest', from *Principles of Beauty Relative to the Human Head*	84
III.13.1	Abraham Ortelius, 'Maris Pacifici', *Theatrum Orbis Terrarum*	128
III.13.2	The Cantino Planisphere	130
III.13.3	Pierre Desceliers, World Map, France	131
III.15.1	Wooden bowl from the Mary Rose warship	136
III.15.2	Tin-glazed earthenware mug painted around the rim with '1628 ELIZABETH BROCKLEFIELD'	137
III.15.3	Thomas Mangy, Spoon bearing the arms of the Strickland family and words 'LIVE TO DIE' and 'DIE TO LIVE' on the stem	138
III.16.1	Wolf Traut, *Man of Sorrows and Mater Dolorosa*	142
III.16.2	Cranach Workshop, *The Location and Origin of Monks*	143
III.16.3	*A Wondrous Event that Occurred at Lonnerstadt Five Miles from Nuremberg*	144
III.16.4	Jan Ziarnko, *Description and Depiction of the Witches Sabbath*	145
III.17.1	Rembrandt van Rijn, *An Old Man in Military Costume*	147
III.17.2	Michiel Sweerts, *Man Holding a Jug*	148
III.17.3	Giovanni Battista Tiepolo, *Young Lady in a Tricorn Hat*	149
III.18.1	Monument of Mary Queen of Scots	153
III.18.2	Detail of title-page to Samuel Purchas, *Hakluytus Posthumus or Purchas his Pilgrimes*	154
III.19.1	Religious pendant, probably Spanish	157
III.19.2	Dish, *The Temptation*, Brislington	158

III.19.3 Sampler, Ann Smith, Scottish or English 159

III.20.1 Band of needle lace worked in human hair and possibly horse hair 162

III.20.2 Embroidered flannel blanket used to identify an infant girl admitted on 20 July 1759 163

III.20.3 Ivory silk garters with silver thread 163

III.22.1 *Dolebit*, taken from John Bulwer, *Chirologia, or the Naturall Language of the Hand, with Chironomia, or the Art of Manuall Rhetorique* 169

IV.14.1 The Torre Abbey Jewel, *memento mori* pendant in the form of a skeleton in a coffin, enamelled gold 221

IV.14.2 Funeral of Frederik Hendrik, 1647 223

IV.17.1 Interior of the chapel of the Monastery of Jesus, Aveiro, Portgual 232

IV.17.2 Interior of the Collegiate Church of the Divine Saviour, Seville, Spain 233

IV.17.3 Detail of the lantern in the chapel of Saint Julian, Cathedral of Cuenca, Spain 233

IV.27.1 Gian Lorenzo Bernini, *The Ecstasy of Saint Teresa* 266

IV.27.2 Rembrandt van Rijn, *Civic Guard of District II under the Direction of Capt. Frans Banninck Cocq*, known as *The Night Watch* 267

IV.27.3 Juan de Valdés Leal, *In Ictu Oculi* 268

IV.35.1 Anonymous artist, Luther as the Monk Calf, woodcut, in Arnaud Sorbin, *Tractatus de monstris* 296

IV.52.1 Giorgione and Titian, *Concert Champêtre* 351

IV.52.2 Nicolas Poussin, *Landscape with a Man Killed by a Snake* 352

IV.52.3 Salvator Rosa, *Landscape with the Fable of the Dishonest Woodsman* 353

Tables

III.22.1 Alphabetical Arrangement of Symbolic Letters, from Gilbert Austin's *Chironomia; or, a Treatise on Rhetorical Delivery* 170

Acknowledgements

This volume has benefitted from the financial support and fellowship provided by the Australian Research Council Centre of Excellence for the History of Emotions (project number CE110001011). The Centre has enabled many of the authors to meet and exchange ideas, and to contribute to this work. Colleagues at the Centre's headquarters at The University of Western Australia have provided valuable support and assistance, as well as shared ideas and thoughts on emerging research. I am particularly grateful to Joanne McEwan for her dedicated editorial assistance. I would also like to thank all the participants in this volume for their enthusiasm about this project, their willingness to engage with its core ideas and their patience with its editor.

Publishers' acknowledgements

The Publishers would like to thank the following for their permission to reproduce copyright material: Beinecke Rare Manuscript Library, Yale University; Coram; London Metropolitan Archives; The Mary Rose Trust; The Metropolitan Museum of Art; The National Gallery of Art, London; Staatsbibliothek, Berlin; the Tate Britain; the Victoria and Albert Museum; Zentralbibliothek, Zürich.

Notes on contributors

Tracy Adams received a Ph.D. in French from Johns Hopkins University in Baltimore, Maryland, in 1998. Associate Professor in French at the University of Auckland, New Zealand, she has also taught at the University of Maryland, the University of Miami and the University of Lyon III. She was a Eurias Senior Fellow at the Netherlands Institute for Advanced Studies (2011–12) and an Australian Research Council Centre of Excellence for the History of Emotions Distinguished International Visiting Fellow in 2014. She is the author of *Violent Passions: Managing Love in the Old French Verse Romance* (Palgrave Macmillan, 2005), *The Life and Afterlife of Isabeau of Bavaria* (The Johns Hopkins University Press, 2010) and *Christine de Pizan and the Fight for France* (Penn State University Press, 2014). With Christine Adams, she has just edited *Female Beauty Systems: Beauty as Social Capital in Western Europe and the US, Middle Ages to the Present* (Cambridge Scholars Publishing, 2015).

Christopher Allen is an art critic and historian who graduated from The University of Sydney, held a postdoctoral research position at the Collège de France in Paris (1994–6) and lectured at the National Art School in Sydney for 12 years (1997–2008). He is currently Senior Master in Academic Extension with teaching responsibilities both in Art History and in Classical Greek at Sydney Grammar School. Allen is the author of many works, including *Art in Australia from Colonization to Postmodernism* (Thames and Hudson, 1997), *French Painting in the Golden Age* (Thames and Hudson, 2003) and a new edition of a seventeenth-century art theoretical treatise, *Dufresnoy's De arte Graphica* (Droz, 2005). His latest book, *Jeffrey Smart: Unpublished Paintings 1940–2007* (Australian Galleries) was published in 2008. He was art critic for the *Australian Financial Review* from 2005 to 2008 and since then has been national art critic for *The Australian.*

Merridee L. Bailey is a Senior Research Fellow with the Australian Research Council Centre of Excellence for the History of Emotions at The University of Adelaide. She works on the history of book culture and issues of socialisation and morality in late medieval and early modern England. She has previously published on ideas about virtue and courtesy in fifteenth- and sixteenth-century England, and more recently has begun working on morality and emotions in merchant practices in London. She has published a book on childhood in late medieval and early modern England, *Socialising the Child in Late Medieval England c. 1400–1600* (York Medieval Press, 2012) and has articles and book chapters in *Viator*, *Journal of the Early Book Society* and *The Routledge History Handbook of Gender and the Urban Experience*.

Katie Barclay is an Australian Research Council DECRA Fellow in the Australian Research Council Centre of Excellence for the History of Emotions, The University of Adelaide. She is the author of the double-award winning *Love, Intimacy and Power: Marriage and Patriarchy in Scotland, 1650–1850* (Manchester University Press, 2011), and numerous articles on emotion and family life. Recently she has edited, with Deborah Simonton, *Women in Eighteenth-Century Scotland: Intimate, Intellectual, and Public Lives* (Ashgate, 2013) and is one of the editors of the forthcoming *Routledge History Handbook on Gender and the Urban Experience* (2016).

Diana G. Barnes is a Postdoctoral Fellow at The University of Queensland with research interests in early modern literature and the history of emotions. She has published a book called *Epistolary Community in Print, 1580–1664* (Ashgate, 2013). Her current research includes a book provisionally entitled *The Politics of Civility: Historicising Early Modern Genres*.

Joanne Begiato (Bailey) is a Professor in History at Oxford Brookes University. She specializes in the history of the family, household, marriage and gender. Her publications include *Unquiet Lives: Marriage and Marriage Breakdown in England 1660–1800* (Cambridge University Press, 2003) and *Parenting in England 1760–1830: Emotions, Identity and Generation* (Oxford University Press, 2012). She is currently working on two book projects: *Sex and the Church in the Long Eighteenth Century* with her co-author Professor William Gibson; and *Manly Matters in England 1756–1856*, which uses material culture, materiality and emotions to examine the concept of being manly and its impact on society, culture and men.

Michael J. Braddick is Professor of History at the University of Sheffield. He has published widely on aspects of state formation, political culture and forms of political resistance in early modern England, as well as on the wider history of Britain, Ireland and the British Atlantic World. His most recent publications are *God's Fury, England's Fire: A New History of the English Civil Wars* (Penguin, 2008), and edited collections on *The Politics of Gesture: Historical Perspectives* (Oxford University Press, 2009), *The Oxford Handbook of the English Revolution* (Oxford University Press, 2015) and (with David L. Smith) *The Experience of Revolution in Stuart Britain and Ireland* (Cambridge University Press, 2011). His study of *John Lilburne and the English Revolution* was published in 2016.

Susan Broomhall is Professor of Early Modern History at The University of Western Australia and an Australian Research Council Future Fellow attached to the Australian Research Council Centre of Excellence for the History of Emotions. She is editor of several studies of emotions, including *Spaces for Feeling: Emotions and Sociabilities in Britain, 1650–1850* (Routledge, 2015), *Authority, Gender and Emotions in Late Medieval and Early Modern England* (Palgrave Macmillan, 2015), *Ordering Emotions in Europe, 1100–1800* (Brill, 2015), *Gender and Emotions in Medieval and Early Modern Europe: Destroying Order, Structuring Disorder* (Ashgate, 2015), (with Sarah Finn), *Violence and Emotions in Early Modern Europe* (Routledge, 2015) and is a general editor of the six-volume *A Cultural History of the Emotions* (Bloomsbury) with Jane W. Davidson and Andrew Lynch. Her latest monograph, *Gender, Emotions and the Dutch East India Company*, is forthcoming from Amsterdam

University Press in 2017 and she is now working on a new study, entitled *The Power of Emotions: Catherine de Medici*.

Audrey Calefas-Strebelle earned her Bachelor's and Master's degrees in History from the University of Sorbonne Paris IV and her Ph.D. in French from Stanford University. Her dissertation, entitled '*Têtes de Turcs*: une étude comparée des représentations des grands seigneurs et des Turcs dans la France de l'Ancien Régime', reveals a correlation in modes of representation for two human types that one might expect to have been considered antithetical. She is currently an Assistant Professor in French and Francophone Studies at Mills College, California, and an Honorary Research Fellow in History at The University of Western Australia. Lately she published 'Têtes de Turcs et Grands Seigneurs: Pratique de la violence chez les Turcs et dans l'aristocratie française aux XVIe et XVIIe siècles', in *L'Esprit Createur* (winter 2013), '« Amours dénaturées » et autres débauches, l'homosexualité à la cour du Grand Turc', in *Papers on French Seventeenth Century Literature* 17 (2014) and 'Manipulation de l'image du Turc dans les conflits entre la monarchie et la noblesse à l'aube de l'Ancien Régime', in *Le Verger-bouquet VIII* (2015). She is also writing an essay on maternal love in a collection on three essays under the direction of Michel Serres.

Ananya Chakravarti is Assistant Professor of History at Georgetown University. Previously, she served as the Abdelhadi H. Taher Professor in Comparative Religion and Assistant Professor in the Department of History at The American University in Cairo (2013–15). She received her Ph.D. in 2012 from the University of Chicago and, before moving to Cairo, she was a Max Weber Postdoctoral Fellow at the European University Institute. Her research has focused on Jesuit missions in the early modern Portuguese empire.

Anthony Colantuono received a Ph.D. from The Johns Hopkins University in 1987 and is Professor of Early Modern Italian, French and Spanish art in the Department of Art History and Archaeology, University of Maryland, College Park. He has been a Fellow of the American Academy in Rome (FAAR 1985), Villa I Tatti (2002–3) and the National Endowment for the Humanities (1990 and 2003). His publications address a wide range of interpretative problems in early modern painting and sculpture, especially in the works of Giovanni Bellini, Titian, Caravaggio, Guido Reni, Nicolas Poussin and François Duquesnoy, and in related literary writings from Mario Equicola and Francesco Colonna to Torquato Tasso and Giambattista Marino.

Lucinda Cole is Visiting Associate Professor of English at the University of Illinois Urbana-Champaign. She is author of *Imperfect Creatures: Vermin, Literature, and the Sciences of Life, 1600–1740* (University of Michigan Press, 2016). Her essays on early modern literature have appeared in such venues as *ELH*, *Criticism* and *Journal for Early Modern Cultural Studies*, and those on animal and environmental studies in *The Journal for Critical Animal Studies*, *The Eighteenth Century: Theory and Interpretation* and *Configurations*. With Robert Markley, she is the General Series Editor of 'AnthropoScene' from Pennsylvania State University Press. Her new book-length project explores scavenging and food systems in early modern literature and culture.

Tania M. Colwell is a casual lecturer and Visitor in the School of History at the Australian National University, Canberra, where she teaches medieval and early modern cultural history, including a course on 'Histories of Emotion in Premodern Europe, 1100–1800'. In 2014, she was an Associate Investigator with the Australian Research Council Centre of Excellence for the History of Emotions, a position she retains in an honorary capacity. As well as writing a book on the reception of the French *Mélusine* romances, she has published research on depictions of emotions and gesture in French romance manuscripts and is currently working on 'Beyond Wonder', an exploration of emotions of encounter in late medieval and early modern French ethnographies.

Louise Hill Curth is Professor of Medical History at the University of Winchester. She specializes in early modern English medical history with a particular focus on the health and illness of early modern animals, and is author of *English Almanacs, Astrology & Popular Medicine, 1550–1700* (Manchester University Press, 2007), *The Care of Brute Beasts: A Social and Cultural History of Veterinary Medicine in Early Modern England* (Brill, 2009) and *A plaine and easie waie to remedy a horse: equine medicine in early modern England* (Brill, 2013).

Sing d'Arcy is a Senior Lecturer in Interior Architecture at the University of New South Wales, Australia, having completed doctoral studies in architectural history at The University of Sydney. He was an Associate Investigator with the Australian Research Council Centre of Excellence for the History of Emotions in 2013 and was a visiting scholar at the University of Seville in 2009. His research focuses on the nexus between architecture and music, in particular the role of the pipe organ in architectural space. He has published widely on the historiography of early modern Spanish ecclesiastical architecture as well as regularly publishing on contemporary Australian interior design.

Jane W. Davidson is Deputy Director of the Australian Research Council Centre of Excellence for the History of Emotions and Professor of Creative and Performing Arts (Music) at The University of Melbourne's Faculty of the Melbourne Conservatorium of Music and Victorian College of the Arts. Prior to this, she was Callaway/Tunley Chair of Music at The University of Western Australia and, before that, Professor of Music Performance Studies at the University of Sheffield. She has published extensively, particularly on performance and psychological approaches to music. As a practitioner, she has worked as an opera singer and a music theatre Director, collaborating with groups such as Opera North in UK, Dramma per musica in Portugal and the West Australian Opera Company.

James Daybell is a Professor of Early Modern British History at Plymouth University and a Fellow of the Royal Historical Society. He is author of *The Material Letter in Early Modern England: Manuscript Letters and the Culture and Practices of Letter-Writing, 1512–1635* (Palgrave Macmillan, 2012), *Women Letter-Writers in Tudor England* (Oxford University Press, 2006); editor of *Early Modern Women's Letter-Writing, 1450–1700* (Palgrave Macmillan, 2001), *Women and Politics in Early Modern England, 1450–1700* (Ashgate, 2004) and (with Peter Hinds) *Material Readings of Early Modern Culture, 1580–1730* (Ashgate, 2010), and has written more than 30 articles and essays on the subjects of early modern letter writing, women, gender and politics. He is co-director (with Kim McLean-Fiander, University of Victoria, Canada) of the British Academy/Leverhulme-funded project 'Women's Early Modern Letters Online', co-director (with Svante Norrhem, Lund University) of the AHRC-funded network 'Gender, Politics and Materiality in Early Modern Europe', and with Adam Smyth (Balliol College, Oxford) he edits the Ashgate book series 'Material Readings in Early Modern Culture'. He is currently completing a monograph entitled *The Family and Materials of Memory in Early Modern England*.

Elise M. Dermineur is a Pro Futura Scientia Fellow at the Swedish Collegium for Advanced Study in Uppsala and at Umeå University, Sweden. She received a Ph.D. in History in 2011 from Purdue University, with the thesis 'Women in Rural Society: Peasants, Patriarchy and the Local Economy in Northeastern France, 1650–1789'. This dissertation shows that the experience of women in early modern rural France illustrates some of the ways emerging social practices modified and altered the traditional patriarchal model, thereby adjusting the social practices to the economic and social context while skirting around legal norms. Dermineur's publications include articles published in the *Journal of Social History*, *Journal of Interdisciplinary History*, *Traverse Revue d'Histoire – Zeitschrift für Geschichte* and the *European Review of Contract Law*, among others. Her article titled 'Female Peasants, Patriarchy and the Credit Market in Eighteenth-Century France' was awarded the Ronald S. Love Prize of the Western Society for French History in 2009. Her research interests range widely, from the history of justice and economics to gender and women's history. Above all, she is deeply interested in the study of rural communities in early modern Europe. She currently examines the paradigms of private credit and debt in early modern Europe from 1500 to 1800, with particular reference to French rural communities.

Stephanie S. Dickey received her Ph.D. from the Institute of Fine Arts, New York University, in 1994. She taught at Indiana University from 1995 to 2006 before taking up the Bader Chair in Northern Baroque Art at Queen's University in Kingston, Ontario, Canada. She is the author of numerous publications on Dutch and Flemish art of the seventeenth century, including the book *Rembrandt: Portraits in Print* (Benjamins, 2004). Her research focuses on the art of Rembrandt and his circle, representations of gender and emotion, portraiture as a cultural practice and the history of printmaking. In 2010, she co-edited (with Herman Roodenburg) *The Passions in the Arts of the Early Modern Netherlands*, vol. 60 of the *Netherlands Yearbook for the History of Art*, to which she contributed the article 'Damsels in distress: gender and emotion in seventeenth-century Netherlandish art' (pp. 52–81).

Stephanie Downes is a Postdoctoral Research Fellow at The University of Melbourne. A graduate of The University of Sydney, in 2010–11 she was a British Academy Visiting Scholar at Queen Mary, University of London and a Mayers Fellow at the Huntington Library, San Marino in 2012. She was the Harvard University Bloomfield Fellow in 2014. She has published on Anglo-French manuscript culture, on bilingualism and emotional expression in literature and on the history of emotions and Middle English. With Andrew Lynch, she is the editor of a volume on *Emotions and War: Medieval to Romantic Literature* (Palgrave, 2015).

Her current research fellowship is funded by the Australian Research Council Centre of Excellence for the History of Emotions.

Nicholas A. Eckstein is the Cassamarca Associate Professor of Italian Renaissance History in the History Department at The University of Sydney. His publications include *The District of The Green Dragon: Neighbourhood Life and Social Change in Renaissance Florence* (Leo S. Olschki, 1995), *Sociability and its Discontents: Civil Society, Social Capital and their Alternatives in Late Medieval and Early Modern Europe*, (eds) Nicholas A. Eckstein and Nicholas Terpstra (Brepols, 2009), *The Brancacci Chapel: Form, Function and Setting*, ed. Nicholas Eckstein (Leo S. Olschki, 2007) and, most recently, *Painted Glories: The Brancacci Chapel in Renaissance Florence* (Yale University Press, 2014). He is currently writing a book related to urban space and neighbourhood in the early modern city, and has several articles related to this project forthcoming.

Nicole Eustace is Professor of History at New York University. She is an historian of eighteenth-century British America and the early United States. Her publications include *1812: War and the Passions of Patriotism* (University of Pennsylvania Press, 2012) and *Passion Is the Gale: Emotion, Power, and the Coming of the American Revolution* (University of North Carolina Press, 2008).

Sandra Garrido is an Australian Research Council/National Health and Medical Research Council Dementia Research Development Fellow at the MARCS Institute at Western Sydney University. She completed her Ph.D. at the University of New South Wales and has also worked as a postdoctoral research fellow at the Australian Research Council Centre of Excellence for the History of Emotions and the Melbourne Conservatorium of Music. With a background in both music history and psychology, her work focuses on the use of music for mood regulation and to improve mental health and wellbeing in both historical and modern day contexts. She is a committee member of the Australian Music and Psychology Society, and a member of the editorial board of the esteemed journal *Musicae Scientiae*. She has also previously been a member of the National Committee of the Musicological Society of Australia.

Peter A. Goddard was educated at the University of British Columbia and at Oxford University (D.Phil), and now teaches at the University of Guelph, Ontario. He is an historian of early modern religious culture and works on the religious organizations of the Catholic reformation. He has published articles and entries on Jesuit and Franciscan activity in France and in the seventeenth-century New World. His current work involves reconstructing the evangelical program of the Capuchins, a new branch of the Franciscan Movement that became known for its exuberant and effusive preaching and missionizing in Europe and in non-European mission fields.

Julian Goodare is Reader in History, University of Edinburgh. He is author of *The European Witch-Hunt* (Routledge, 2016, forthcoming). He was Director of the Survey of Scottish Witchcraft, which went online in 2003. His edited books include *The Scottish Witch-Hunt in Context* (Manchester University Press, 2002), *Witchcraft and Belief in Early Modern Scotland* (Palgrave Macmillan, 2008) (co-edited with Lauren Martin and Joyce Miller) and *Scottish Witches and Witch-Hunters*

(Palgrave Macmillan, 2013). With Rita Voltmer and Liv Helene Willumsen, he is currently co-editing *Demonology and Witch-Hunting in Early Modern Europe*.

Catharine Gray is Associate Professor of English at the University of Illinois at Champaign-Urbana. She is author of *Women Writers and Public Debate in Seventeenth-Century Britain* (Palgrave, 2008). In addition to articles on seventeenth-century women writers and politics, she has published essays on military identity, the body politic and Royalist elegy in two recent book collections. These essays are part of her new book project, *Unmaking Britain: Poetry and War in Seventeenth Century Britain*. With Erin Murphy, she is also co-editor of *Milton Now* (Palgrave, 2014), a collection of new essays on the work of John Milton published in honour of Mary Nyquist and Margaret Ferguson's 1987 volume, *Re-membering Milton*.

Tara Hamling is Senior Lecturer in the History Department, University of Birmingham. Her research focuses on the visual arts and material culture of early modern Britain, especially in a domestic context. She is author of *Decorating the Godly Household: Religious Art in Post-Reformation Britain* (Yale University Press, 2010) and editor (with Catherine Richardson) of *Everyday Objects: Medieval and Early Modern Material Culture* (Ashgate, 2010) and (with Richard L. Williams) *Art Re-formed: Reassessing the Impact of the Reformation on the Visual Arts* (Cambridge Scholars Publishing, 2007). Her next book, *A Day at Home in Early Modern England: The Materiality of Domestic Life* (co-authored with Catherine Richardson) is due for publication in 2016 with Yale University Press.

Karen Harvey is Reader in Cultural History at the University of Sheffield. Her work on eighteenth-century Britain explores gender, material culture and the body. She has published several books and articles in these areas, including *The Little Republic: Masculinity and Domestic Authority in Eighteenth-Century Britain* (Oxford University Press, 2012).

Yasmin Haskell, FAHA, is Cassamarca Foundation Chair in Latin Humanism at The University of Western Australia and a Chief Investigator in the Australian Research Council Centre of Excellence for the History of Emotions, in which she leads projects on 'Passions for Learning' and 'Jesuit Emotions'. She is the author of *Prescribing Ovid: The Latin Works and Networks of the Enlightened Dr Heerkens* (Bloomsbury, 2013) and *Loyola's Bees: Ideology and Industry in Jesuit Latin Didactic Poetry* (British Academy and Oxford University Press, 2003), and editor of (inter alia), *Diseases of the Imagination and Imaginary Disease in the Early Modern Period* (Brepols, 2011) and (with Susan Broomhall), 'Humanism and Medicine in the Early Modern Period', special issue of *Intellectual History Review* 18.1 (2008).

Sally Holloway completed her Ph.D. on romantic love at Royal Holloway, University of London in 2013, funded by the Arts and Humanities Research Council. Sally is an Associate Researcher at Historic Royal Palaces and Affiliated Research Scholar at the Centre for the History of the Emotions, Queen Mary, University of London. In 2014 she was a Visiting Fellow of Chawton House Library, and in 2016 an Early Career International Research Fellow at the Australian Research Council Centre of Excellence for the History of Emotions. Sally teaches at Oxford Brookes University and Richmond, The American International University in London.

Aleksondra Hultquist is an Honorary Associate Investigator for the Australian Research Council Centre of Excellence for the History of Emotions, based at The University of Melbourne. She has worked as an Assistant Professor in the United States and a lecturer in Australia. Her work focuses on the literature and culture of the long eighteenth century, especially women writers, and she has published articles in *Philological Quarterly*, *Eighteenth-Century Theory and Interpretation*, and several edited collections. She is a Managing Editor of *ABO: Interactive Journal for Women and the Arts 1640–1830*. She is currently finishing her monograph, *The Amatory Mode,* as well as editing Aphra Behn's *Love-Letters between a Nobleman and his Sister* for the forthcoming Cambridge University Press edition of *The Writings of Aphra Behn*.

Katherine Ibbett is Reader in Early Modern Studies in the School of European Literatures at University College, London. She is the author of *The Style of the State in French Theater* (Ashgate, 2009) and the co-editor of a special issue of *Yale French Studies* on 'Walter Benjamin's Hypothetical French *Trauerspiel*' (2013). She is completing a book on compassion and its failures in early modern France, and with Kristine Steenbergh she is co-editing a volume on compassion across early modern Europe.

Carolyn James is Cassamarca Associate Professor in the School of Philosophical, Historical and International Studies, Monash University. She has edited the letters of the fifteenth-century Italian writer, Giovanni Sabadino degli Arienti and analysed his literary works (Olschki, 1996 and 2002), translated, with Antonio Pagliaro, the late medieval letters of Margherita Datini (Centre of Reformation and Renaissance Studies Toronto, 2012) and is presently working on a monograph entitled *A Renaissance Marriage: Isabella d'Este and Francesco Gonzaga*, to be published by Oxford University Press.

Claudia Jarzebowski is an Assistant Professor at the Department of History at the Free University Berlin and a Partner Investigator at the Australian Research Council Centre of Excellence for the History of Emotions. Her recent research focuses on childhood and emotion in the early modern period. She has held a Distinguished International Visitor Fellowship at The University of Western Australia (2013) and a Feodor-Lynen-Fellowship at the University of Pennsylvania (2007/08). Her recent publications include (edited with Thomas Max Safley) *Childhood and Emotion: Across Cultures 1450–1800* (Routledge, 2013) and 'The Meaning of Love. Incest Discourses in Sixteenth-Century Europe', in David Luebke and Mary Lindemann (eds), *Mixed Matches. Transgressive Unions in Germany from the Reformation to the Enlightenment* (Berghahn, 2014).

Danijela Kambaskovic is a Research Associate with the Australian Research Council Centre of Excellence for the History of Emotions and formerly Assistant Professor, Shakespeare and Renaissance Studies, The University of Western Australia. Her scholarly output includes two scholarly books and numerous articles and research chapters on Shakespeare, Renaissance poetry, the human senses in pre-modern religious, ethical and medical writing and pre-modern treatises on mental health. Her recent edited collection, *Conjunctions of Mind, Body and Soul from Plato to the Enlightenment* (Springer) appeared in 2014. Danijela is also an award-winning poet.

Susan Karant-Nunn is Director of the Division for Late Medieval and Reformation Studies and Regents' Professor of History at the University of Arizona. She has published extensively on ritual, the emotions and gender during the longer Reformation era. Her most recent monograph is *The Reformation of Feeling: Shaping the Religious Emotions in Early Modern Germany* (Oxford University Press, 2010). She is presently at work on the subject of the reformed body. She has served as president of the Sixteenth Century Studies Conference and the Society for Reformation Research, both North American professional organizations.

Ross Knecht is Assistant Professor of English at Emory University and was formerly a Postdoctoral Research Fellow in the Australian Research Council Centre of Excellence for the History of Emotions at The University of Queensland. His work focuses on Shakespeare and early modern literature, with a special interest in the early modern discourse of the passions, the philosophy of language and the history of pedagogy. He is the author of articles in *Comparative Literature* and *ELH: English Literary History* and is currently at work on a manuscript concerning the intersections of passion, grammar and schooling in sixteenth-century literary texts.

Laura Kounine is Lecturer in Early Modern History at the University of Sussex and was previously a Postdoctoral Fellow at the Centre for the History of Emotions, in Berlin. She completed her Ph.D. on 'The Gendering of Witchcraft in Early Modern Württemberg' in 2013 at Clare College, University of Cambridge. In 2014, she was an Early Career International Research Fellow at the Australian Research Council Centre of Excellence for the History of Emotions, based at The University of Melbourne. She is currently revising her thesis for publication. She is co-editor of the forthcoming essay collection on *Cultures of conflict resolution in early modern Europe* (Ashgate, 2016), and co-editor of *Emotions in the History of Witchcraft: Unbridled Passions*, with the 'History of Emotions' series at Palgrave (2016).

Erika Kuijpers is Assistant Professor at the Vrije Universiteit in Amsterdam. She is the author of *Migrantenstad. Immigratie en sociale verhoudingen in 17e-eeuws Amsterdam* (Verloren, 2005). From 2008 to 2013, she worked at Leiden University researching personal memories of the Dutch Revolt, in the VICI research project, 'Tales of the Revolt: Memory, Oblivion and Identity in the Low Countries, 1566–1700'. She co-edited *Memory Before Modernity: Practices of Memory in Early Modern Europe* (Brill, 2013) and is working on a monograph about how early modern witnesses and victims of war dealt with traumatic memories. Her current research entails a pilot project into the computational semantic mining of emotions in early modern texts: 'Embodied Emotions: Mapping Bodily Expression of Emotions from a Historical Perspective'.

Mary Laven is Reader in Early Modern History at the University of Cambridge and a Fellow of Jesus College. Her publications include *Virgins of Venice: Enclosed Lives and Broken Vows in the Renaissance Convent* (Viking, 2002) and *Mission to China: Matteo Ricci and the Jesuit Encounter with the East* (Faber and Faber, 2011). During the period 2013–17, she is co-directing the European Research Council project 'Domestic Devotions: The Place of Piety in the Renaissance Italian Home'.

Inger Leemans is Professor of Cultural History at Vrije Universiteit Amsterdam and Director of ACCESS – the Amsterdam Center for Cross-Disciplinary Emotion and Sensory Studies. Her research focuses on the history of emotions, history of pornography, digital humanities, Dutch literature and cultural economics. She currently works on a cultural history of early modern stock trade. In 2013, Inger Leemans and Gert-Jan Johannes published *Worm en Donder*, a volume on the eighteenth century in the Dutch Language Union Series 'Geschiedenis van de Nederlandse Literatuur' [History of Dutch Literature].

David Lemmings is Professor of History in the School of Humanities at the University of Adelaide and 'Change' Program Leader in the Australian Research Council Centre of Excellence for the History of Emotions. He is the author of *Gentlemen and Barristers: The Inns of Court and the English Bar, 1680–1730* (Oxford University Press, 1990) and *Professors of the Law: Barristers and English Culture in the Eighteenth Century* (Oxford University Press, 2000), editor of *The British and their Laws in the Eighteenth Century* (Boydell Press, 2005) and (with Claire Walker) *Moral Panics, the Media and the Law in Early Modern England* (Palgrave Macmillan, 2009). His latest books are *English Law and Government in the Long Eighteenth Century: From Command to Consent* (Palgrave Macmillan, 2011), and two edited collections, *Crime, Courtrooms and the Public Sphere in Britain, 1700–1850* (Ashgate, 2012) and (with Ann Brooks) *Emotions and Social Change: Historical and Sociological Perspectives* (Routledge, 2014).

Andrew Lynch is a Professor in English and Cultural Studies at The University of Western Australia and Director of the Australian Research Council Centre for the History of Emotions. He has recently published *International Medievalism and Popular Culture*, co-edited with Louise D'Arcens (Cambria, 2014); *Understanding Emotions in Early Europe* (Brepols, 2015), with Michael Champion; and *War and Emotions: Medieval to Romantic Literature* (Palgrave, 2015), with Stephanie Downes and Katrina O'Loughlin. He is a contributor to the forthcoming *Cambridge Companion to Medievalism* (2016).

Phyllis Mack is Professor of History and Women's Studies (Emerita as of June 2015) at Rutgers University. Her most recent publications include *Heart Religion in the British Enlightenment: Gender and Emotion in Early Methodism* (Cambridge University Press, 2008); 'The Senses in Religion: Listening to God in the Eighteenth Century', in A.C. Vila (ed.), *A Cultural History of the Senses in the Age of Enlightenment* (Bloomsbury, 2014); 'Religion and Gender in Enlightenment England: The Problem of Agency', in A. Sterk and N. Caputo (eds), *Faithful Narratives: Historians, Religion, and the Challenge of Objectivity* (Cornell University Press, 2014).

Alan Maddox is Senior Lecturer in Musicology at the Sydney Conservatorium of Music, The University of Sydney, where he teaches early modern music history and coordinates the undergraduate Musicology program. With a background as a professional singer, his main research interests are in early modern Italian vocal music and Australian colonial music, as well as in the intersections between music and the history of emotions, and music in intellectual history. Recent publications include a series of articles on rhetoric in eighteenth-century Italian vocal music, and a study of the role of music in prison reform in the nineteenth-century penal colony on Norfolk Island. He is an Associate Investigator with the Australian Research Council Centre of Excellence for the History of Emotions, a member of the National Committee of the Musicological Society of Australia and consultant musicologist to the Australian Brandenburg Orchestra.

Laura Mandell is Director of the Initiative for Digital Humanities, Media, and Culture and Professor of English at Texas A&M University. She is the author of *Breaking the Book: Print Humanities in the Digital Age* (Wiley Blackwell, 2015), *Misogynous Economies: The Business of Literature in Eighteenth-Century Britain* (University of Kentucky Press,1999), a Longman Cultural Edition of *The Castle of Otranto and Man of Feeling*, and numerous articles primarily about eighteenth-century women writers. Her article in *New Literary History*, 'What Is the Matter? What Literary History Neither Hears Nor Sees', describes how digital work can be used to conduct research into conceptions informing the writing and printing of eighteenth-century poetry. She is Project Director of the Poetess Archive, an online scholarly edition and database of women poets, 1750–1900 (http://poetessarchive.org), Director of 18thConnect (http://18thConnect.org) and Director of ARC (www.ar-c.org), the Advanced Research Consortium overseeing NINES (the Networked Infrastructure for Nineteenth-century Electronic Scholarship), 18thConnect, ModNets (Modernist Networks) and MESA (the Medieval Electronic Scholarly Alliance).

Alicia Marchant is a University Associate in History at the University of Tasmania, where her work focuses on the history of emotions, heritage, narrative and dark tourism. She completed her Ph.D. in Medieval and Early Modern History at The University of Western Australia in 2012, and between 2012 and 2014 was a Research Associate at the Australian Research Council Centre of Excellence for the History of Emotions, based at The University of Western Australia. She is the author of *The Revolt of Owain Glyndŵr in Medieval English Chronicles* (Boydell and Brewer, 2014), and is currently editing a collection provisionally entitled *Historicising Heritage and Emotions: The Affective Histories of Blood, Stone and Land from Medieval Britain to Colonial Australia* (Routledge, forthcoming).

Giuseppe Marcocci is Associate Professor of Early Modern History at the University of Viterbo (Italy). He holds a Ph.D. in History from the Scuola Normale Superiore, Pisa (Italy), and was Visiting Professor at the University of Lisbon (2009) and at the École des Hautes Études en Sciences Sociales, Paris (2013). His publications include numerous entries and articles in international journals, as well as four books: *I custodi dell'ortodossia: Inquisizione e Chiesa nel Portogallo del Cinquecento* (Edizioni di Storia e Letteratura, 2004); *L'invenzione di un impero: Politica e cultura nel mondo portoghese, 1450–1600* (Carocci, 2011); *A consciência de um império: Portugal e o seu mundo, sécs. XV–XVII* (Imprensa da Universidade de Coimbra, 2012); and (with José Pedro Paiva) *História da Inquisição portuguesa, 1536–1821* (A Esfera dos Livros, 2013).

Joanne McEwan is a Research Associate in History at The University of Western Australia and a Research Assistant with the Australian Research Council Centre of Excellence for the History of Emotions. Her research focuses on gender, crime and social and emotional attachments in Britain from the seventeenth to the nineteenth century. She has previously published on lodging arrangements in eighteenth-century London, attitudes towards domestic violence and infanticide in early eighteenth-century Scotland. She is the editor (with Pamela Sharpe) of *Accommodating Poverty: The Housing and Living Arrangements of the English Poor, c. 1600–1850* (Palgrave Macmillan, 2010) and (with Philippa Maddern and Anne Scott) *Performing Emotions in Early Europe* (Brepols, 2017).

Una McIlvenna is Lecturer in Early Modern Literature at the University of Kent. From 2011 to 2014, she was Postdoctoral Research Fellow with the Australian Research Council Centre of Excellence for the History of Emotions, based at The University of Sydney, where she undertook a project on execution ballads in early modern Europe. She has published an article on this research, 'The Power of Music: The Significance of Contrafactum in Execution Ballads', *Past & Present* 229 (2015), 47–89. Her first monograph, *Scandal and Reputation at the Court of Catherine de Medici*, was published by Ashgate in 2016.

Donna Merwick received her Master's degree at DePaul University in 1962. She was awarded a Ph.D. in American Intellectual History from The University of Wisconsin in 1967. From 1969 to 1995, she was a member of the Department of History at The University of Melbourne (Australia), retiring as Associate Professor/Reader in 1995. She is presently a Fellow at the Australian National University, Research School of the Humanities and an Adjunct Associate Professor at Swinburne University, Melbourne. She has written or edited six major publications. Four of these have been in the area of her special research interest, seventeenth-century Dutch New York: *Possessing Albany, 1630–1710: The Dutch and English Experiences* (Cambridge University Press, 1990); *Death of a Notary: Conquest and Change in Colonial New York* (Cornell University Press, 1999); *The Shame and the Sorrow: Dutch-Amerindian Encounters in New Netherland* (University of Pennsylvania Press, 2006). In 2013, she published a biographical study on Peter Stuyvesant, the governor of New York from 1647 to 1664, titled *Stuyvesant Bound: An Entry on Loss Across Time* (University of Pennsylvania Press). This book was awarded the New Netherland Institute's Hendricks Prize in 2015.

Charlotte-Rose Millar is an Associate Investigator and Research Assistant in the Australian Research Council Centre of Excellence for the History of Emotions and is based at The University of Melbourne. Her recently completed Ph.D. examined the role of the Devil and emotion in all extant seventeenth-century English witchcraft pamphlets and is currently under contract with Ashgate. The book will significantly expand the work of the thesis by covering the entire period of state-sanctioned executions (1563–1735). She is the author of eight peer-reviewed articles and book chapters and has been awarded two prizes for her published work.

Grace Moore is a Senior Research Fellow at the Australian Research Council Centre for Excellence in the History of Emotions, based at The University of Melbourne. Her monograph, *Dickens and Empire* (Ashgate) was shortlisted for the NSW Premier's Award for Literary Scholarship in 2006 and she is also the author of *The Victorian Novel in Context* (Continuum, 2012). Grace is at present working on a book-length study of settlers and bushfires, *Arcady in Flames*, while developing a research interest in emotions and the environment.

Javier Moscoso is Research Professor of History and Philosophy of Science at the Spanish Research Council (CSIC), in Madrid. His latest book, *Pain: A Cultural History* (Palgrave, 2012), was previously published in Spanish (Taurus, 2011) and has also been released in French (by Les prairies ordinaires) in 2015. He is the principal investigator of a research group that deals with the history and philosophy of experiences based in Madrid. He has been recently appointed George Lurcy Visiting Professor at the University of Chicago.

Hannah Newton is a social and cultural historian of early modern England, specializing in the histories of medicine, emotions and childhood. Hannah's first book, *The Sick Child in Early Modern England, 1580–1720* (Oxford University Press, 2012), was awarded the European Association for the History of Medicine and Health 2015 Book Prize. From 2011to 2014, Hannah undertook a Wellcome Trust Fellowship at the University of Cambridge and researched for her second monograph, *Misery to Mirth: Recovery from Illness in Early Modern England* (under contract, Oxford University Press). During her Fellowship, Hannah was also Director of Studies for the Department of History and Philosophy of Science at St John's College. Since 2014, she has been based at the University of Reading.

Maria Nugent is Fellow, Australian Centre for Indigenous History, in the School of History, Australian National University. She is the author of *Captain Cook Was Here* (Cambridge University Press, 2009). She co-authored, with Shino Konishi, an entry on Indigenous Australian people's encounters with 'newcomers' (*c.* 1600–1800) in *The Cambridge History of Australia*, vol. 1 (Cambridge University Press, 2013), and is currently involved in a collaborative research project on cross-cultural histories of Australian exploration.

Katrina O'Loughlin holds an Australia Research Council Discovery Early Career Research Award and is based at The University of Western Australia. She is a literary and cultural historian with research interests in eighteenth-century writing, travel and intellectual exchange, particularly among women. She has published on various aspects of Enlightenment and Romantic literature, and her monograph *Women, Writing and Travel in the Eighteenth Century: The Paper Globe* will be published with Cambridge University Press in 2016. Her current research project investigates friendship, or the affective dimensions of literary sociability, in the Romantic period.

Samantha Owens is Associate Professor of Musicology at the New Zealand School of Music, Victoria University of Wellington. Her research is primarily in the field of historical performance practice and performance cultures, focusing particularly on seventeenth- and eighteenth-century European court music. A Fellow of the Australian Academy of the Humanities, she has held visiting fellowships at Clare Hall, University of Cambridge, and at the Martin-Luther-Universität Halle-Wittenberg (as an Alexander von Humboldt Fellow). Recent publications have included an edited book on *Music at German Courts, 1715–1760: Changing Artistic Priorities* (Boydell & Brewer, 2011).

Melissa Percival is Associate Professor in French and Art History at the University of Exeter. She has published widely on topics connected with the human face.

Among her publications are *Physiognomy and Facial Expression in Eighteenth-Century France* (Maney Publishing, 1999), *Physiognomy in Profile: Lavater's Impact on European Culture* (University of Delaware Press, 2005) and *Fragonard and the Fantasy Figure: Painting the Imagination* (Ashgate, 2012). She guest-curated the exhibition *Ceci n'est pas un portrait: figures de fantaisie de Murillo, Fragonard, Tiepolo . . .* at the Musée des Augustins, Toulouse (November 2015–March 2016).

Christina Petterson is a Research Associate at the Religion, Marxism and Secularism Network in the School of Humanities and Social Sciences at the University of Newcastle. She holds a Masters of Theology from Copenhagen University and a Ph.D. in Cultural Studies from Macquarie University, Sydney. Her work, which covers early Christianity and early modern Europe and its colonies, seeks to examine Christianity through the lenses of theology, history and cultural theory.

Kathryn Prince is a theatre historian with a particular interest in early modern drama. Her current work focuses on the intersections of space, bodies, objects and emotions in early modern performance, as well as 'performance' in a broader sense relating to early modern accounts of cross-cultural contact. Her recent publications include *Performing Early Modern Drama Today* (Cambridge University Press, 2013) and *History, Memory, Performance* (Palgrave Macmillan, 2014), as well as articles, book chapters and books on early modern drama in performance from the eighteenth to the twenty-first centuries. She is an Associate Professor at the University of Ottawa in the Department of Theatre, and for part of 2015 was an Early Career International Research Fellow at the Australian Research Council Centre of Excellence for the History of Emotions in Australia.

Luc Racaut is Lecturer in History at Newcastle University (UK). He has published extensively in the field of the history of printing and religious reform during the French Wars of Religion, including *Hatred in Print: Catholic Propaganda and Protestant Identity during the French Wars of Religion* (Ashgate, 2002). He is currently preparing a monograph for Routledge on the history of the body and emotions in the context of the European wars of religion, entitled *The World Inside Out*.

Gordon D. Raeburn completed his Ph.D. at the University of Durham, UK, in 2013. His thesis, 'The Long Reformation of the Dead in Scotland', investigated the changing nature of Scottish burial practices between 1542 and 1856. He is currently a Postdoctoral Research Fellow with the Australian Research Council Centre of Excellence for the History of Emotions, based at The University of Melbourne, and is working on the emotional responses to early modern Scottish disasters and how these emotional responses shaped personal, communal and national identities.

Sarah Randles is an Honorary Research Fellow in the School of Historical and Philosophical Studies at The University of Melbourne and was recently a Postdoctoral Research Fellow in the Australian Research Council Centre of Excellence for the History of Emotions. Her current research project explores the emotions of pilgrimage and sacred place, focusing on the relics and other aspects of material culture of Chartres Cathedral. She has published on medieval and later textiles, the Arthurian legend and on medievalism in Australian architecture.

Andrea Rizzi is an Australian Research Council Future Fellow (2014–18) at The University of Melbourne. He has published on vernacular translators in early Renaissance Italy, courtly culture in Ferrara and Mantua and Italian diplomats and translators at the court of Elizabeth I. His latest book on fifteenth-century Italian translators and their self-fashioning statements will be published by Brepols. Andrea has been a Deborah Loeb Brice Fellow (2011) at the Villa I Tatti Harvard University Center for Italian Renaissance Studies, Florence.

Herman Roodenburg is Professor of Historical Anthropology at the Free University of Amsterdam and a Senior Researcher at the Meertens Institute, also in Amsterdam. A cultural historian, he likes to cooperate with cultural anthropologists and art historians. Among his English publications are *The Eloquence of the Body* (Waanders, 2004) and, as editor, *Forging European Identities, 1400–1700* (Cambridge University Press, 2007) and *A Cultural History of the Senses in the Renaissance* (Bloomsbury, 2014). He is currently finishing a history of the Dutch and their religious emotions (provisionally called *The Crying Dutchman*).

Alec Ryrie is Professor of the History of Christianity at Durham University and co-editor of the *Journal of Ecclesiastical History*. He is author of books including *Being Protestant in Reformation Britain* (Oxford University Press, 2013), *The Age of Reformation* (Longman Pearson, 2009), *The Sorcerer's Tale* (Oxford University Press, 2008) and *The Gospel and Henry VIII* (Cambridge University Press, 2003), and is co-editor, with Tom Schwanda, of *Puritanism and Emotion in the Early Modern World* (Palgrave, 2016).

Peter Sherlock is Vice-Chancellor of the University of Divinity, Melbourne, Australia. His scholarship centres on death, commemoration and memory in early modern European societies, especially the study of monuments as a source for engaging with the past. He is author of *Monuments and Memory in Early Modern England* (Ashgate, 2008).

Patricia Simons is Professor of History of Art at the University of Michigan, Ann Arbor. She is author of *The Sex of Men in Premodern Europe: A Cultural History* (Cambridge University Press, 2011) and co-editor of *Patronage, Art, and Society in Renaissance Italy* (Clarendon Press, 1987). Her numerous entries analysing the visual and material culture of early modern Europe have been published in anthologies and peer-review journals such as *Art History, I Tatti Studies, Journal of Medieval and Early Modern Studies, Renaissance Quarterly* and *Renaissance Studies,* ranging over such subjects as the visual dynamics of desire, secrecy and scandal, female homoeroticism and the visual role of humour.

François Soyer is an Associate Professor in History at the University of Southampton. He is the Author of *Popularizing Anti-Semitism in Early Modern Spain and its Empire. The Centinela contra Judíos of Fray Francisco de Torrejoncillo (1674)* (Brill, 2014) and *The Persecution of the Jews and Muslims of Portugal. King Manuel I and the End of Religious Tolerance (1496–7)* (Brill, 2007).

Jennifer Spinks is Lecturer in Early Modern History at the University of Manchester. Prior to her arrival in Manchester in 2012, she was an Australian Research Council Postdoctoral Fellow at The University of Melbourne, Australia (2009–12), where she worked on a collaborative project with Charles Zika and Susan Broomhall. From 2011 to 2012, she was an Associate Investigator with the Australian Research Council Centre of Excellence for the History of Emotions. Her publications include: *Monstrous Births and Visual Culture in Sixteenth-Century Germany* (Pickering and Chatto, 2009); *Early Modern Women in the Low Countries: Feminizing Sources and Interpretations of the Past* (Ashgate, 2011; co-authored with Susan Broomhall); and *The Four Horsemen: Apocalypse, Death and Disaster* (National Gallery of Victoria, 2012; co-edited with Cathy Leahy and Charles Zika, and accompanying a collaboratively-curated exhibition). She is currently working on a study of wonder books in early modern Reformation and Counter-Reformation northern Europe, supported by an Arts and Humanities Research Council (UK) Early Career Fellowship.

Erin Sullivan is a Senior Lecturer and Fellow at the Shakespeare Institute, University of Birmingham. She has published several articles on early modern sadness and is the co-editor of *The Renaissance of Emotion: Understanding Affect in Shakespeare and His Contemporaries* (Manchester University Press, 2015). Her first monograph, *Beyond Melancholy: Sadness and Selfhood in Renaissance England*, was published by Oxford University Press in 2016.

Giovanni Tarantino is a Research Fellow of the Australian Research Council Centre of Excellence for the History of Emotions at The University of Melbourne, and Editor-in-Chief of *Cromohs*. He is a former Hans Kohn Member of the Institute for Advanced Study in Princeton and Balzan Research Associate at the Scuola Normale of Pisa. He was elected a Fellow of the Royal Historical Society in 2013. Recent publications include: 'Disaster, Emotions and Cultures: The Unexpected Wink of Shiba Kokan (1738–1818)', *Rivista Storica Italiana* 128 (2016); 'The Mysteries of Popery Unveiled: Affective Language in John Coustos' and Anthony Gavín's Accounts of the Inquisition', in Susan Broomhall (ed.), *Spaces for Feeling: Emotions and Sociabilities in Britain, 1650–1850* (Routledge, 2015), pp. 35–51; 'Mapping Religion (and Emotions) in the Protestant Valleys of Piedmont', *ASDIWAL* 9 (2014); *Republicanism, Sinophilia and Historical Writing: Thomas Gordon (c. 1691–1750) and His History of England* (Brepols, 2012).

Raisa Maria Toivo is an Academy of Finland Research Fellow at the Centre of Excellence in History: 'History of a Society, Re-thinking Finland 1400–2000', at the University of Tampere, Finland. She has studied the history of early modern religion, witchcraft, gender and violence. Her publications include *Witchcraft and Gender in Early Modern Society* (Ashgate, 2008) and *Writing Witch-Hunt Histories*, edited with Marko Nenonen (Brill, 2014).

Stephanie Trigg is Professor of Medieval English Literature in the School of Culture and Communication at The University of Melbourne. Her books include *Congenial Souls: Reading Chaucer from Medieval to Postmodern* (University of Minnesota Press, 2002) and *Shame and Honor: A Vulgar History of the Order of the Garter* (University of Pennsylvania Press, 2012). She was also editor of a special issue of *Exemplaria: A Journal of Theory in Medieval and Renaissance Studies* on pre-modern emotions (2014).

Jacqueline Van Gent is an early modern historian at The University of Western Australia and a Chief Investigator with the Australian Research Council Centre of Excellence for the History of Emotions. She has published on Swedish magic, the body and emotions, gender and colonial mission encounters in Australia and the Atlantic, and gender and emotions in the Nassau-Orange family. Her recent publications include: *Magic, Body and the Self in Eighteenth-Century Sweden* (Brill, 2009); with Susan Broomhall (eds), *Governing Masculinities in the Early Modern Period: Regulating Selves and Others* (Ashgate, 2011); J. Van Gent, N. Etherington, P. Brock and G. Griffiths, *The Indigenous Christian Evangelist in British Empire History 1750–1940: Questions of Authority* (Brill, 2015); with Angelika Schaser and Kirsten Rüther, *Gender and Conversion Narratives in the Nineteenth Century. German Mission at Home and Abroad* (Ashgate, 2015); and, with Spencer Young, 'Emotions and Conversion', special issue of *Journal of Religious History* (December 2015). With Susan Broomhall, she will publish *Gender, Power and Identity in the Early Modern Nassau Family, 1580–1814* (Ashgate, 2016) and *Dynastic Colonialism: Gender, Materiality and the Early Modern House of Orange-Nassau* (Routledge, 2016). She edited, with Raisa Maria Toivo, 'Gender, objects and emotions in Scandinavian history', special issue of *Journal of Scandinavian History* (2016). Her current research project concerns the role of emotions in early modern colonial encounters, especially in the context of Protestant missions, East India Companies and early ethnographies.

Claire Walker is a Senior Lecture in Early Modern History at The University of Adelaide. She has written extensively about the post-Reformation English women's religious communities exiled in France, the Southern Netherlands and Portugal. Claire has recently co-edited a collection of entries, *Fama and Her Sisters: Gossip and Rumour in Early Modern Europe* (Brepols, 2015) and she is currently co-writing a monograph, *Governing Emotion: the Affective Family, the Press and the Law in Early Modern Britain*, with Katie Barclay and David Lemmings.

Linda Walsh was until recently Senior Lecturer in Art History at the Open University, UK. She has written teaching texts focusing on art-historical topics ranging from the seventeenth to the mid-nineteenth centuries. Her research publications include work on facial expression and on neoclassicism and romanticism in European sculpture.

Helen Watanabe-O'Kelly has been Professor of German Literature at Oxford University since 1994. Among her books are *Melancholie und die melancholische Landschaft* (Francke Verlag, 1978), *Triumphal Shews. Tournaments at German-Speaking Courts in their European Context 1560–1730* (Gebrüder Mann Verlag, 1992) and *Court Culture in Dresden from Renaissance to Baroque* (Palgrave Macmillan, 2002). She has edited *The Cambridge History of German Literature* (Cambridge University Press, 1997), *Spectaculum Europaeum: Theatre and Spectacle in Europe, (1580–1750)* with Pierre Béhar (Harrassowitz, 1999) and *Europa Triumphans: Court and Civic Festivals in Early Modern Europe* with J. R. Mulryne and Margaret Shewring (Ashgate, 2004). Her most recent book is *Beauty or Beast? The Woman Warrior in the German Imagination from the Renaissance to the Present* (Oxford University Press, 2010). In 2012, she was elected a Fellow of the British Academy. She is the leader of the project 'Marrying Cultures: Queens Consort and European Identities 1500–1800' (www.marryingcultures.eu), which is funded by HERA (Humanities in the European Research Area).

Robert L. Weston is an Honorary Research Fellow at The University of Western Australia. His interests lie in the field of European history of medicine. In 2013, his book *Medical Consulting by Letter in France 1655–1789* was published by Ashgate. He has also published articles and book chapters on issues of gender, masculinity and emotion in later early modern French medicine.

R. S. White, MA (Adelaide), D.Phil (Oxford), is FAHA, Chief Investigator for the Australian Research Council Centre of Excellence for the History of Emotions and Leader of the Centre's 'Meanings' program. He has been an Australian Professorial Fellow and is Professor of English at The University of Western Australia. He has published books and articles on Shakespeare and the Romantics, and among his recent works are *Pacifism in English Poetry: Minstrels of Peace* (Palgrave, 2008), *John Keats: A Literary Life* (Palgrave, 2010) (which has been reissued in paperback), and *Avant-Garde Hamlet: Text, Stage, Screen* (The Fairleigh Dickinson University Press, 2015). He is a past President of the Australian and New Zealand Shakespeare Association.

Charles Zika is a Professorial Fellow in the School of Historical and Philosophical Studies at The University of Melbourne and Chief Investigator in the Australian Research Council Centre of Excellence for the History of Emotions. His interests lie in the intersection of religion, emotion, visual culture and print in early modern Europe. He is the author of *The Appearance of Witchcraft: Print and Visual Culture in Sixteenth-Century Europe* (Routledge, 2007); co-editor of a collection with Cathy Leahy and Jenny Spinks, related to a 2012 exhibition at the National Gallery of Victoria, *The Four Horsemen: Apocalypse, Death & Disaster* (NGV, 2012); and a co-author with Margaret Manion, of *Celebrating Word and Image 1250–1600* (Fremantle Press, 2013).

Introduction

Susan Broomhall

The subject of historical emotions is a growing area of interest and one with which many scholars and students are keen to engage. This presents a need for an introduction to the wide range of current research from scholars primarily of early modern Europe, from varied disciplines, which can offer an entry point to their questions, to the concepts, approaches and sources that currently are, or might be, used in the analysis of early modern emotions, and to the potential perspectives that the history of emotions can offer early modern history more broadly. This volume therefore offers short, accessible commentaries from period experts, which are intended to assist a beginner to history of emotions approaches to begin investigating topics of interest. The aim of the present work is to provide a straightforward and introductory textbook that can help students and scholars to understand the state of the field and allow them to translate and apply its approaches and ideas into their scholarship.

The history of emotions is a burgeoning area of research. Major research centres for the historical study of emotions worldwide have proved a catalyst to the production of carefully-nuanced monographic texts as well as large-scale, collaborative volumes, and indeed to innovative practitioner-based and community-oriented research practices for the humanities. A range of book series with scholarly presses worldwide now captures the current scholarly interest in emotions in history, historical emotions and the emotional practices of specific time periods.

The scholarship on emotions in the early modern period is already vast, stimulated perhaps particularly by the fact that two influential theorists, Barbara H. Rosenwein and William M. Reddy, have grounded their conceptualizations of historical emotional practice in concrete study of medieval and early modern Europe.[1] The breadth of early modern emotion scholarship calls for a student-level text to assist a newcomer to the field to bring together what currently exists, the methodologies by which it has been undertaken to date, potential avenues of future interests and the kinds of findings that these approaches are producing. This text's title 'Early Modern Emotions', makes clear the understanding taken by the contributors – that emotions themselves are cultural and social practices that change over time.[2] We start from the assumption that emotional display and practice are culturally- and historically-specific, and should be understood as expressions of early modern society. The choice of the term 'emotion', however, is entirely pragmatic. It locates the text in the current 'history of emotions' scholarship, and as part of a wider series of such introductory texts that will span other time periods. In doing so, it avoids the dilemma of which of varied emotion terms from the period itself should be given pride of place over others – passions, sentiments, affections among them – each defined by distinct discursive contexts.

The authors of this volume seek to explore therefore what 'emotions' were termed over this 300-year period, how and why such terms changed in use, the discourses in which they were used, the sources in which we can locate emotion terms and evidence of experiences, displays and practices. We explore what emotions did and meant in the social and cultural practice of early modern Europe. It is hoped that this volume will present a useful database for future comparative work with other key periods, such as the medieval and nineteenth century, both periods about which dynamic scholarship has been produced.[3] What is 'early modern' about emotional experiences, terms, practices and display will emerge when we have similar analyses for Europe in other periods. Moreover, to capture the richness and diversity of early modern emotional life requires not just the conventional sources and analytical contributions of historians, but also those of literary, art and music scholars of the period as well. The inclusion of sources and methods of a wide range of disciplines presents challenges for reconciling different scholarly practices and methodologies but also reveals exciting new opportunities for future multi- and interdisciplinary scholarship.

This textbook primarily concerns Western European practices of emotions but also explores emotions created and exhibited through Europe's interactions globally during the period. It keenly awaits comparable volumes analysing other societies worldwide at this period. As the 'early modern', broadly speaking it spans 1500 to 1800, although some entries attend to events and sources slightly beyond these chronological demarcations as is appropriate to their specific topics. The volume entries most commonly concern emotions as human interactions but we also explore the possibilities for considering human relations with material, animal, environmental and supernatural phenomena.

The volume is largely representative of current research trends and questions in early modern emotions research. It is not exhaustive in the coverage of topics that could potentially be analysed in consideration of emotions, but its selection is intended to be exemplary and representative of current study. Some entries are necessarily more speculative than others, reflective of a slimmer basis of extant research, where analysis of emotions constitutes a relatively new perspective for the field. Ultimately, these entries serve as springboards to further thinking produced by individual authors rather than definitive statements of shared approaches. The authors are experts in a wide range of different disciplines that they bring to bear in their contributions. As historians, musicologists, art historians, literary and architectural scholars of the period, they provide coverage of the different ways in which early modern emotions research is currently conducted in various scholarly communities around the globe. The wide range of contributors intentionally showcases the diversity of approaches to the field, the ways in which different kinds of scholars, scholarly disciplines and international scholarly traditions employ emotions to make new interventions.

The entries to follow are categorized into four sections that are intended to assist readers to understand the processes and practices by which history of emotions research is presently conducted. Section I, 'Modern theories and models of emotions', presents key methods, terms and concepts of emotion, considering how they have been, or might be, applied to the early modern period. In Section II, 'Early modern terms, concepts and practices of emotions', the focus turns to particular early modern conceptualizations of, and terms for, emotions that are unique to that time or that have meanings quite distinct from those applied at other periods. In the third section,

'Sources and methodologies for early modern emotions', authors consider a range of potential methodologies for analysis of early modern emotions, and provide examples applied to particular data sets at use in or available for the early modern period.

In the final section of the text, we analyse the impact of history of emotions research for 'Focus topics for the early modern period'. This section reflects upon the potential for historical analyses through the lens of emotions to change how the early modern period is considered more broadly. How do these common topics for discussion in the period shift when emotions are placed in the foreground of analysis? This section is further sub-divided thematically, into 'Political Realms'; 'Destructive Experiences'; 'Life Stages'; 'Spaces'; 'Intellectual and Cultural Traditions'; 'Beliefs'; 'The World Beyond Europe' and 'The Non-Human World'.

Each individual entry includes both key references and several annotated recommendations for further reading on emotions research in that area. The 'Select bibliography' compiles a comprehensive, though not exhaustive, list of current scholarship pertaining to early modern emotions. Finally, a detailed 'Index' to the volume serves an important role in highlighting links across the discussion within individual entries and acts as a significant cross-referencing tool for the volume as a whole.

Notes

1 B.H. Rosenwein, *Emotional Communities in the Early Middle Ages* (Ithaca: Cornell University Press, 2006); Rosenwein, *Generations of Feeling: A History of Emotions, 600–1700* (Cambridge: Cambridge University Press, 2015); W.M. Reddy, *The Navigation of Feeling: A Framework for the History of Emotions* (Cambridge: Cambridge University Press, 2001); Reddy, *The Making of Romantic Love: Longing and Sexuality in Europe, South Asia, and Japan, 900–1200 CE* (Chicago: University of Chicago Press, 2012); an accessible discussion of these and other perspectives from North American historians can be found in N. Eustace, E. Lean, J. Livingston, J. Plamper, W.H. Reddy and B.H. Rosenwein, 'AHR conversation: the historical study of emotions', *American Historical Review* 117, 5 (2012), 1487–1531.

2 For a wider analysis of methodologies for the history of emotions, weighing the anthropological relativist position against the universalism of the neurosciences and other disciplines, see J. Plamper, *The History of Emotions: An Introduction*, (trans.) K. Tribe (Oxford: Oxford University Press, 2015); and emerging work in psychology on social contexts for emotion, B. Mesquita and M. Boiger, 'Emotions in context: a sociodynamic model of emotions', *Emotion Review* 6, 4 (2014), 298–302.

3 For recent comprehensive study of the medieval, see the important collaborative research of Piroska Nagy and Damian Boquet: Nagy (ed.), 'Emotions médiévales', *Critique* (2007); Boquet and Nagy (eds), *Le Sujet des émotions au moyen âge* (Paris: Beauchesne, 2009); Boquet and Nagy (eds), *Politques des émotions au moyen âge* (Florence: Sismel, 2010); Boquet, Nagy and Moulinier-Brogi (eds), 'La Chair des émotions', *Médiévales* 61 (2011); Boquet and Nagy, *Sensible Moyen Age* (Paris: Seuil, 2015); and for the nineteenth century, T. Dixon, *From Passions to Emotions: The Creation of a Secular Psychological Category* (Cambridge: Cambridge University Press, 2003); U. Frevert, C. Bailey, P. Eitler, B. Gammerl, B. Hitzer, M. Pernau, M. Scheer, A. Schmidt and N. Verheyen, *Emotional Lexicons. Continuity and Change in the Vocabulary of Feeling 1700–2000* (Oxford: Oxford University Press, 2014).

Section I

Modern theories and models of emotions

I.1 Emotional community

Andrew Lynch

In the study of early modern emotions, few terms are more widely employed than 'emotional community'. Its popularity stems from several influential books and essays by the historian Barbara H. Rosenwein, but what 'emotional community' means in its different usages can vary considerably. A close look at Rosenwein's formulation and practice of the term is helpful:

> Emotional communities are largely the same as social communities – families, neighborhoods, syndicates, academic institutions, monasteries, factories, platoons, princely courts. But the researcher looking at them seeks above all to uncover systems of feeling, to establish what these communities (and the individuals within them) define and assess as valuable or harmful to them (for it is about such things that people express emotions); the emotions that they value, devalue, or ignore; the nature of the affective bonds between people that they recognize; and the modes of emotional expression that they expect, encourage, tolerate, and deplore.[1]

Roughly speaking, Rosenwein sees the 'communities' she studies as already in existence, but they are revealed and understood as *emotional* communities through her analysis of sets of emotion terms taken from a variety of documentary evidence about them. Her method is partly quantitative, partly qualitative. Always allowing for the skewed social distribution and preservation of surviving sources – we know much less about poor than rich, women than men – she works on the principle that assessing a wide range of materials will offset the potential distortion caused by concentration on a smaller selection. Where possible, she does not rely on only one informant, one narrative, or one genre of writing. In cases where the generic range is more limited, for example in her examination of funerary epitaphs in Gaul, 350–700, she makes a comparative analysis of different locations, distinguishing between their vocabulary choices and emotional emphases.

Rosenwein's overall purpose is to find the historical 'mind-sets' in which past emotions were expressed and understood. In doing so, she does not privilege the 'sincere' or discount the 'banal' in the emotion-related utterances she collects. She looks instead for the testimony they provide of what was emotionally imaginable, or socially normative, in their time and place, and of what emotion concepts were regarded as compatible within the same frame of reference. Her work continues the interest in deliberative and ritualized emotion seen in her earlier collection *Anger's Past*.[2] That interest also underpins her explicit rejection of Norbert Elias's view of a childishly uninhibited middle ages undergoing increasing emotional regulation by the super-ego into modern times.[3] Departing from the idea of emotion as a 'drive' needing 'discharge', she emphasizes the cognitive, relational and culturally constructed nature of emotional understanding and expression.

Accordingly, Rosenwein's view of the emotions' relation to historical change is fine-grained and textually attuned. She takes the view that variations in emotional vocabularies and the rise and fall of emotional styles may indicate longer-term change in the conditions of political and social organization or new dominant ideological influences, but that they may also reflect relatively short-term local occurrences. Changes in forms of emotional expression are treated as occasions for further historical investigation, but a key feature of Rosenwein's approach is that she allows for the simultaneous existence of various emotional communities within the one time and place, and that individuals may inhabit multiple such communities. She explains this through a complex model of emotional 'circles':

> Imagine, then, a large circle within which are smaller circles, none entirely concentric but rather distributed unevenly within the given space. The large circle is the overarching emotional community, tied together by fundamental assumptions, values, goals, feeling rules, and accepted modes of expression. The smaller circles represent subordinate emotional communities, partaking in the larger one and revealing its possibilities and its limitations. They too may be subdivided. At the same time other large circles may exist, either entirely isolated from or intersecting with the first at one or more points.[4]

In practice, Rosenwein's use of the term 'emotional community' is therefore very flexible and covers quite different entities: Christian congregations in particular Gallic cities; the audience implied by the emotional norms of the voluminous writings of Gregory the Great (*c.* 540–604); even a group of just two people – Gregory of Tours (*c.* 538–94) and Venantius Fortunatus (*c.* 530–*c.* 600/09). Rather than operating as a blanket term indicating general likeness, her idea of 'community' is often used to make subtle distinctions of difference in emotional style. So, for instance, although Pope Gregory, Fortunatus and Gregory of Tours all share basic attitudes to heavenly joy and worldly pleasure, Pope Gregory tends to reject family-based emotions in the interests of a greater community of God, while the other two seem quite willing to apply the same emotions to earthly and heavenly objects.

As Rosenwein acknowledges, her use of 'emotional communities' relates in part to Brian Stock's concept of 'textual communities'.[5] Stock employed this term in describing how the spread of literacy activated medieval heretical and reformist groups: 'What was essential to a textual community was not a written version of a text, although that was sometimes present, but an individual, who having mastered it, then utilized it for reforming a group's thought and action'.[6] Stock's textual community seems to resemble an emotional community most especially when its members have reached the stage of 'shared assumptions' about interpretation of their text, 'the textual foundation of behaviour having been entirely internalized'.[7]

An apparent major difference is that Stock concentrates on the role of particular text use (including further oral dissemination of texts) in the formation and functioning of individual groups. Rosenwein, by contrast, analyses patterns of emotion terms in large-scale samples ('dossiers') of the written record of existing 'social communities' such as cities, clerical and monastic circles and courts. She indicates, nevertheless, that these could also be considered as 'textual communities', broadly speaking, for whose members books were 'part of the self', providing intimate models of emotional behaviour and evaluation. If an 'emotional community' can be derived from one man's writings (Pope Gregory's) or from the circulation of works by anonymous writers who probably did not know each other personally, then the constitution of these communities seems as much textual as social, a back-formation from the documents themselves. In her most recent book, Rosenwein discusses early modern English writings on melancholy by Spenser, Shakespeare, Burton and Bunyan simply as 'representative literary works of the period . . . that must have appealed to a wide and literate public'.[8]

Rosenwein's reference to shared 'norms of emotional expression' also gives her emotional communities a relation to the idea of 'emotionology', as put forward by Peter and Carol Stearns: 'the attitudes or standards that a society, or a definable group within a society, maintains toward basic emotions and their appropriate expression'.[9] On the other hand, Rosenwein rejects the Stearns' time-line of growth in emotional control, and is alert to textual factors which contradict or complicate the picture derived from studying emotional prescriptions. That said, it is difficult to treat emotional experience, emotion language and emotional expression as quite separate categories. Rosenwein herself anticipates Jan Plamper's comment that '[e]motional communities could have . . . affinities with Foucault's "discourse", Bourdieu's "habitus" and William Reddy's "emotives"'.[10]

Reddy's 'emotional regimes' are also a related concept: in their 'strict' form these 'require individuals to express normative emotions and to avoid deviant emotions'.[11] Rosenwein speaks occasionally of 'emotion scripts' but sees them as the outcome of a freer process of social interaction and negotiation.[12] To her Reddy's 'emotional regimes' may represent an overly restrictive binarism – 'either one is at court *or* one is in a sentimental refuge'.[13] She prefers to speak of a co-existing variety of emotional 'constellations' or 'sets' which include and exclude, privilege and downplay, particular emotions and versions of emotional life. Even within the one emotional community, she writes, there may be places of both 'suffering' and 'refuge', in Reddy's terms.

Jan Plamper has argued that Rosenwein's own terminology may be 'insufficiently open and radical': 'the boundaries of an emotional community' are 'so porous and transient that one should rather be compelled to move away from the terminology of "boundary" and hence of "community"'.[14] Yet it might be said that this porosity is already accepted within Rosenwein's notion of emotional community on the level of individual practice. Her model of overlapping and non-concentric emotional 'circles', cited above, already weakens the restrictive implications of 'community': she notes 'some people's adaptability to different sorts of emotional conventions as they move from one group to another'.[15] More broadly, the term 'community' suits her fundamental view of emotions as both forms and products of social relations.

One valuable aspect of 'emotional community' is its portability and flexibility; it is equally applicable to a convent, a school of artists, a court, an epistolary network or texts from a military culture. A potential problem stems from the far greater range and quantity of documents from the early modern period in comparison to the earlier medieval era that Rosenwein originally researched. That makes the selection of historical sources used to define 'community' and to track emotional changes – Rosenwein uses the archaeological term 'judgmental sampling'[16] – more controversially directive. How does one decide amongst the many potential 'communities' that might be constructed? The term will perhaps always be most persuasive when it relates strongly to an existing social unit or a specific shared enterprise, but in general the necessity of including emotional commonalities amongst the important factors that both shape and distinguish early modern communities seems indisputable.

Further reading

Karant-Nunn, S., *The Reformation of Feeling: Shaping the Religious Emotions in Early Modern Germany* (Oxford: Oxford University Press, 2010)
—considers how church leaders and preachers of various confessions in the sixteenth and seventeenth centuries used different modes of emotional expression and engagement to shape a communal religious consciousness amongst their followers.

Kuijpers, E., '"O, Lord, save us from shame": Narratives of Emotions in Convent Chronicles by Female Authors During the Dutch Revolt, 1566–1635', in S. Broomhall (ed.), *Gender and Emotions in Medieval and Early Modern Europe: Destroying Order, Structuring Disorder* (Farnham: Ashgate, 2015), 127–46.
—analyses writings by enclosed nuns about their sufferings in the Dutch wars of religion to exemplify communal management of emotions according to available cultural means, including familiarity with various written genres and a shared practice of emotional 'styles'.

Mullaney, S., *The Reformation of Emotions in the Age of Shakespeare* (Chicago: University of Chicago Press, 2015)
—discusses Elizabethan popular theatre 'as a kind of affective laboratory . . . oriented toward the location, exploration and exploitation of those fault-lines and dissonances of feeling that characterized the emotional communities of post-Reformation England'. (69)

Notes

1 B.H. Rosenwein, 'Problems and Methods in the History of Emotions', *Passions in Context: Journal of the History and Philosophy of the Emotions* 1, 1 (2010), online at www.passionsincontext.de/index.php/?id=557, accessed 27 June 2016.
2 Rosenwein (ed.), *Anger's Past: The Social Uses of an Emotion in the Middle Ages* (Ithaca: Cornell University Press, 1998)
3 N. Elias, *The Civilizing Process* (Oxford: Blackwell, 1994)
4 Rosenwein, *Emotional Communities in the Early Middle Ages* (Ithaca: Cornell University Press, 2006), 24.
5 B. Stock, *The Implications of Literacy: Written Language and Models of Interpretation in the 11th and 12th Centuries* (Princeton: Princeton University Press, 1983)
6 Ibid., 90.
7 Ibid., 91.
8 B.H. Rosenwein, *Generations of Feeling. A History of Emotions, 600–1700* (Cambridge: Cambridge University Press, 2015), 254.
9 P.N. Stearns with C.Z. Stearns, 'Emotionology: Clarifying the History of Emotions and Emotional Standards', *American Historical Review* 90, 4 (1985), 813–36, quote 813.
10 J. Plamper, *The History of Emotions: An Introduction*, (trans) K. Tribe (Oxford: Oxford University Press, 2015), 69. See Rosenwein, *Emotional Communities*, 25.
11 W.M. Reddy, *The Navigation of Feeling* (Cambridge: Cambridge University Press, 2001), 125.
12 Rosenwein, 'Problems and Methods', 20.
13 Rosenwein, *Emotional Communities*, 23.
14 Plamper, *The History of Emotions*, 71.
15 Rosenwein, *Emotional Communities*, 25.
16 Rosenwein, *Generations of Feeling*, 12.

I.2 Emotives and emotional regimes

Tania M. Colwell

In 2001 William M. Reddy published *The Navigation of Feeling*, an innovative study in which he formulated an analytical framework for examining historical emotions based around a theory of 'emotives' and 'emotional regimes'.[1] Building upon insights from cognitive psychology, cultural anthropology, speech act theory and his own earlier work, Reddy claimed to offer a new 'politically engaged, and historically grounded', model for exploring emotions that could explain personal and social change.[2] While variously criticized, emotives and emotional regimes offer tools for analysing emotions and historical change in early modern Europe in two key ways. First, they offer a method for exploring the fluid nature of individual and collective emotions at moments within and across time. Second, they provide a framework for understanding how emotions themselves, by their very fluidity, could contribute to historical change within a community.

An emotive is an utterance that characterizes the self and, in limited cases, others in emotional terms. Drawing on speech act theory, Reddy regards emotive phrases such as 'I am pleased' or 'You are sorrowful' as constative or descriptive, but also as performative in that they have the capacity to enact change on the speaking subject or addressee. This claim rests on Reddy's argument that emotion is a dialogue between one's conscious and subconscious thoughts in which numerous sensory inputs are constantly being decoded and translated; it is an automatic and/or learned cognitive position oriented around personal, cultural or societal goals. Emotives are a temporary translation of an emotional position, the very utterance of which loops back into the sensory inputs acting upon one's thoughts. The ongoing dialogue between the emotive, other contemporaneous inputs and one's conscious and subconscious thoughts may confirm or alter one's emotional standpoint. The repetition of particular emotives, such as affirmations of love or loyalty for instance, may intensify an emotional effect and affect over time. However, changing contextual circumstances, such as goal-reorientations, mean that this cannot be predetermined.[3] For Reddy, it is the transformative potential of emotives, their ability to be selected and to act on the speaking subject or the recipient of the emotive, that explains their analytical value as a means of exploring historical change.

An individual's capacity to shape their emotions using emotives provides the opportunity to situate the feeling subject within social collectives. The concept of emotional regimes emerges from the insight gained from cross-cultural anthropological research that emotions are not just constructed or learned, but that they are also 'managed'. Because most communities share broadly interconnected goals, emotions are politically important since they can induce action which may or may not align with social objectives. Thus, Reddy suggests, dominant groups within a society will exercise some control over the types of emotional styles that can be practised.

In effect, they will oversee an emotional regime, defined as a 'set of normative emotions and the official rituals, practices, and emotives that express and inculcate them'; such systems are 'a necessary underpinning of any stable political regime'.[4] Reddy applies his theoretical framework to the French Revolution, exploring sentimentalism's development into a dominant emotional style in (pre-) Revolutionary France, its radical implications during the Terror and subsequent reactionary backlashes towards it. Although criticized for its lack of historical contextualization, and imbalanced source selection and analysis, Reddy's study nonetheless offers a suggestive model for applying emotives and emotional regimes to early modern European history.

Important criticisms of emotives and emotional regimes have included the way they privilege linguistic articulation of emotion over other modes of expression; scholars' consequent reliance on elite textual production for evidence; and the equivalence assumed between emotional and hegemonic political regimes, which typically characterize modern rather than premodern societies. However, Reddy emphasizes that non-verbal expressions, such as physiological or gestural behaviours, when understood as culturally-learned responses, possess the same transformative potential on the performing or receiving subject as linguistic utterances, and so may also be considered emotives.[5] Further, he suggests that 'sensory-rich participatory performances', in which historical subjects are acted upon, can also be scrutinized using emotives and emotional regimes.[6] Reddy's rejoinders expand the analytical lens within which these concepts can be applied to the early modern period, widening the scope of evidence to include rituals, preaching and drama, along with other modes of cultural production intended to cultivate particular emotional styles, such as art, music and dress. Addressing critiques of emotional regimes, Reddy acknowledges that any society hosts various communities, such as those shaped by religious, commercial or familial ties, which each have their own dominant emotional styles. It is when communities 'enforce these styles though penalties such as gossip, exclusion, or demotion, [that] these styles count as "emotional regimes"'.[7] Reddy's qualification regards emotional control and constraint as the coercive features distinguishing an emotional style as a regime, thereby accommodating the variable contours of social bodies and states in premodern Europe.

The defining characteristic of emotives is their performative quality, but we cannot recover how early modern individuals or groups experienced emotion or emotional transformation within a given moment and across time. However, remembering that meanings embedded in particular emotional expressions changed over time, materials produced for both private and public consumption provide fruitful avenues for exploration. Personal sources, such as letters, diaries or sketchbooks for instance, offer important evidence illustrating how individuals could translate and transform their emotions independently of contemporary regimes. Analysis of affective styles using sources intended for public dissemination can uncover in turn how emotional regimes shaped and tried to manage collective emotions. Susan Karant-Nunn, for example, examines how preachers of different denominations in Reformation Germany sought 'to alter religious experience' among their laity through the distinctive use of sermon materials, the removal of vivid art from church interiors and the careful selection of music.[8] By such means, Lutheran and Reformed clerics cultivated affective practices and encouraged a piety that was generated more by emotions from within than stimulated by external referents. Literary and dramatic texts offer rich sources for exploring collective structures of feeling through emotives and performance. The intersection of emotions and power around depictions of the monarch in the history plays by William Shakespeare (1564–1616), notably *Richard II* and *Henry V*, offers scope for exploring the management of emotions of theatre-going communities for political ends that both supported and resisted the rule of Elizabeth I (1533–1603). Importantly, emotional regimes were not restricted to large, public collectives in the early modern period. Families and households were also social and material sites of emotional control as analyses of dynastic art collections, domestic space and correspondence reveal.[9]

Historical crises may furnish powerful case-studies through which to explore the transformative aspect of emotives as influences on both emotional expression and historical change; as Reddy implies, it is when personal or collective emotions and goals conflict with those of the prevailing regime that tensions arise.[10] Nicole Eustace's study of the British colony in pre-Revolutionary Pennsylvania explores historical emotion as a transformative political tool, demonstrating how anger, for example, was shaped into a legitimate conduit for demanding universal rights from the British crown.[11] Such work highlights both the malleability of emotion over time and its capacity to influence change, and offers a constructive model for tracing the fluid nature and influence of emotions on events surrounding, for instance, the 1572 St Bartholomew's Day massacres in France. Ongoing historical events, such as the European witch-trials or the English Civil War, will also reward analysis exploring the influence of emotives and emotional regimes on the momentum of private and popular responses surrounding such phenomena. As scholars progress through the early modern period, a greater array of sources becomes available due to increased publication of political pamphlets, newspapers, plays, sermons, diaries, letters and histories – these materials provide fertile ground for examining how the dynamics of emotional expression produced historical change across premodern Europe.

Reddy's *Navigation of Feeling* was described in 2015 as 'the most important theoretical work dealing with the history of emotion' to date. To an extent, the influence of emotives and emotional regimes is illustrated by their wide application across emotions research in a diminished form to mean simply 'emotion words' and 'norms'.[12] However, this reductive usage obscures the political implications and explanatory value of Reddy's framework. Ultimately, scholars of early modern history, literature and culture will only benefit fully from Reddy's theory and its potential for understanding change between 1500 and 1800 if they maximize the capacity of emotives and emotional regimes to address historical questions about personal and social transformation and emotional power.

Further reading

Eustace, N., *Passion is the Gale: Emotion, Power, and the Coming of the American Revolution* (Chapel Hill: University of North Carolina Press, 2008)

—drawing on Reddy's understanding of emotional expression as a mode of communication with transformative potential, Eustace's analysis of emotional rhetoric in British Pennsylvania demonstrates the fluid yet integral role emotion played in individual and collective assertions of and claims to power in the pre-Revolutionary era.

Singh, J., 'Rereading Emotion and Affect in Shakespeare's *Antony and Cleopatra*', in R. Arab, M. Dowd and A. Zucker (eds), *Historical Affects and the Early Modern Theater* (New York: Routledge, 2015), 97–108.

—applies emotives to analysis of Shakespearean drama to establish how verbal emotional performances fulfil a self-exploratory function that enables characters to navigate tensions created by competing emotional regimes, personal ambitions and shared desires.

Walker, C., 'An Ordered Cloister? Dissenting Passions in Early Modern English Cloisters', in S. Broomhall (ed.), *Gender and Emotions in Medieval and Early Modern Europe: Destroying Order, Structuring Disorder* (Farnham: Ashgate, 2015), 199–214.

—investigates how communities could both adopt and subvert affective practices configuring emotional regimes to create alternate structures of feeling aligned with individual and shared spiritual aspirations.

Notes

1 W.M. Reddy, *The Navigation of Feeling: A Framework for the History of Emotions* (Cambridge: Cambridge University Press, 2001)
2 Ibid., 55.
3 Ibid., 104–5, 111, 322–3.
4 Ibid., 129.
5 Ibid., 107, 331.
6 Ibid., 331.
7 J. Plamper, 'The history of emotions: an interview with William Reddy, Barbara Rosenwein, and Peter Stearns', *History and Theory* 49, 2 (2010), 237–65, quote 243. On Rosenwein's concept of emotional communities, with which regimes are often contrasted, see *Emotional Communities in the Early Middle Ages* (Ithaca: Cornell University Press, 2006).
8 S. Karant-Nunn, *The Reformation of Feeling: Shaping the Religious Emotions in Early Modern Germany* (Oxford: Oxford University Press, 2010), 3.
9 S. Broomhall, 'Renovating Affections: Reconstructing the Atholl Family in the Mid-Eighteenth Century', in S. Broomhall (ed.), *Spaces for Feeling: Emotions and Sociabilities in Britain, 1650–1850* (London: Routledge, 2015), 47–67.
10 Reddy, *Navigation of Feeling*, 122. Also M. Scheer, 'Are emotions a kind of practice (and is that what makes them have a history)? a Bourdieuian approach to understanding emotion', *History and Theory* 51, 2 (2012), 193–220, 218.
11 N. Eustace, *Passion is the Gale: Emotion, Power, and the Coming of the American Revolution* (Chapel Hill: University of North Carolina Press, 2008)
12 J. Plamper, *The History of Emotions: An Introduction* (Oxford: Oxford University Press, 2015), 261, 265.

I.3 Affect theory

Stephanie Trigg

Where do feelings come from? One of the key issues in emotion studies is the relation between feeling, language and the body. This question is often conceived as the relationship between emotion and affect. Terminologies and theories about this relationship abound in the fields of psychology, anthropology, philosophy, cognitive science, psychoanalysis, literary studies, cultural studies and historical studies of all periods. The early modern period is no exception; it is rich in the discourses of passion and feeling, especially around humoral theory and the relationship between body and mind.

There are many starting-points for such inquiries when reading the texts and images of the early modern period: conscious and unconscious actions such as looks and gestures; social and cultural behaviour; the conscious expression and verbalization of emotions and feelings; and the study of contemporary language and terminology used to name emotions, passions and feelings.

The relationship between 'emotion' and 'affect', however, as guiding concepts for historical study, is a difficult one. Each of these terms has a complex genealogy and a contested semantic and conceptual field of reference. 'Emotion' has become the default umbrella term that governs historically-oriented and multidisciplinary studies in the humanities (whether or not the term has currency in the period in question). In this domain, 'emotion' can signify linguistic or non-linguistic expression of feelings, emotions, passions, sentiments and drives, in words, gestures and other social practices. While 'emotion' is the more popular general term, many cultural historians and critics use 'emotion' and 'affect' and their adjectival forms 'emotional' and 'affective' interchangeably, often as a deliberate choice.

There is a strong movement, however, in many areas of contemporary cultural theory, philosophy, psychology and the social sciences to claim a much more specific meaning for 'affect,' as quite separate from conscious or linguistic expression of feeling and emotion. In such usage, 'affect' names the embodied, sensate aspect of mental and emotional activity. 'Affects' or 'affective' feelings are produced independently of, or are less contingent on the discursive mediation of language, and are accordingly often granted a form of ontological priority. But an 'affect' can also refer to a collective or social feeling, such as the 'authority affect' of a politician or public figure who commands attention and respect through their bearing, their clothes, their demeanour and the way they are framed and presented to us, regardless, in some cases, of the words they utter. 'Affects', then, can range from bodily, cerebral or endocrinal activity (a blush, a glance, a tear, a quickening of mental activity or a heartrate) to broader unconscious desires, or the network of forces that drive, motivate and connect minds and bodies with other bodies and bodies in the social world. This concept has a long philosophical history in phenomenology. Brian Massumi, for example, stresses its philosophical genealogy, and its 'irreducibly bodily and autonomic nature,' in the work of Baruch Spinoza.[1]

Like many others, Massumi insists on the difference between affect and emotion:

> It is crucial to theorize the difference between affect and emotion. If some have the impression that it has waned, it is because affect is unqualified. As such, it is not ownable or recognizable, and is thus resistant to critique.[2]

For many scholars in this tradition, affects are often seen as more social and collective in orientation as opposed to emotions.[3] Lauren Berlant insists that the 'shaping of collective affect is therefore quite a different process than the orchestration of political emotion, with lots of convergences and parallel tracks at the same time'.[4] She concludes this interview with these remarks:

> Since affect is about *affectus*, about being affected and affecting, and therefore about relationality and reciprocity as such, affect theory is inevitably concerned with the analysis of collective atmospheres.[5]

This more oppositional meaning of 'affect', a meaning that draws a clear distinction with emotion, has been rejected by several cultural critics. Monique Scheer, for example, advocates the study of emotions as a form of cultural practice that is driven by both mind and body as well as historical traditions and conventions, in a method influenced by Pierre Bourdieu's concept of the social *habitus*. Many historians of emotions are adopting this practice-based model, in part because it allows them to assemble and explore the historical context of fragmentary or partial records of emotional behaviour.[6] But many emotions historians avoid the word and the concept of 'affect' completely. Ruth Leys, for example, is actively critical of many of the premises, methods and practices of affect theory.[7]

It is hard not to suspect that many of these disputes and differences are grounded as much in disciplinary tensions as intellectual ones. And it is clear that the stakes are quite high. From being a somewhat marginal branch of historical studies, the history of emotions has in many institutional contexts become a flagship for dialogue between the humanities, the social sciences and the cognitive sciences, and the opposition between emotion and affect can become quite stark in this context. Where does this leave early modern studies? As in other areas where the history of emotions has made substantial inroads, we must also negotiate our own disciplinary traditions and practices, and our own different starting-points (texts, images, events or practices). Of course, in the case of historical studies, we are restricted to the surviving texts, objects, images and structures around which we reconstruct the history of feeling.

In their important introduction to the 2004 collection, *Reading the Early Modern Passions*, Gail Kern Paster, Katherine Rowe and Mary Floyd-Wilson make some helpful distinctions between the trends of empirical science and those of (historical) cultural studies. Indeed, they are refreshingly candid in their embrace of the liberation of the historical scholar from the 'taxonomic morass' that besets philosophers and psychologists. Writing of the confusing terminology of emotional discourse that survives from the early modern period, 'we see it as providing data to be analysed rather than noise to be filtered'.[8] They are also 'dissatisfied with the linguistic inadvertence of philosophers and psychologists who wish – in vain, we think – to break through the veil of language to prior or nonlinguistic truth about the emotions'.[9] The editors are also keen to emphasize a crucial difference in the historical understanding of the self: early modern emotions are much more overtly social, rather than individual or inward, as privileged by modern culture. They suggest we need to remain alert to social or public feelings and emotions. Consideration of the different cultural frames and expectations around emotions, affects and their representation is an important part of early modern history, and in an ideal world, this would involve looking back for continuities and discontinuities between the medieval and the early modern, as well as between the early modern and the modern. In this regard, Paster, Rowe and Floyd-Wilson are indeed closer to the position of a scholar such as Berlant, who is interested in the collective and social working of affect.

So there are some stark oppositions the early modernist needs to negotiate here: between the methods of the sciences and the humanities; between studies of the present and the past; and indeed, between different kinds of historical sources. Just as we would not want scientists to reject the historical and socially embedded insights of our own cultural research, so too we might develop a more open mind to the work of cognitive theorists. Conversely, it should be acknowledged that early modern culture has its own elaborate mind-body-feeling nexus in the Galenic theory of the humours. Paster, for example, has drawn on Thomas Wright's *The Passions of the Minde in Generall* (1604) to draw out the overlap between animal and human affect in cognitive and emotional behaviours.[10] Cognitive approaches to literature and drama are also developing in early modern studies.[11] The field of affect studies, then, is developing apace. A truly interdisciplinary history of emotions will draw on its insights as it negotiates the world of the emotions and the affects, in the interior, the private and the public lives of early modern people.

Further reading

Drew, D., *The Melancholy Assemblage: Affect and epistemology in the English Renaissance* (New York: Fordham University Press, 2013)

—uses Deleuze and Guattari's model of the assemblage to understand early modern melancholy, drawing on art, literature, philosophy and drama.

Meek, R. and E. Sullivan (eds), *The Renaissance of Emotion: Understanding affect in Shakespeare and his contemporaries* (Manchester: Manchester University Press, 2015)

—moves away from the humoral model of emotion and affect that has dominated early modern studies and reads emotions through cultural context.

Trigg, S., 'Introduction: emotional histories – beyond the personalization of the past and the abstraction of affect theory', *Exemplaria* 26 (2014), 3–15.

—surveys recent critical developments in the study of affect and emotion, and untangles critical usage of these and other terms such as passion, feeling and sentiment.

Notes

1 B. Massumi, 'The autonomy of affect', *Cultural Critique* 31 (1995), 83–109, quote 88–9.
2 Ibid., 88.
3 S. Ahmed, 'Happy Objects', in M. Gregg and G.J. Seigworth (eds), *The Affect Theory Reader* (Durham: Duke University Press, 2010), 29–51, quote 30.
4 L. Berlant and J. Greenwald, 'Affect in the end times: a conversation with Lauren Berlant', *Qui Parle* 20 (2010), 71–89, quote 77.
5 Ibid., 88.
6 M. Scheer, 'Are emotions a kind of practice (and is that what makes them have a history)? a Bourdieuian approach to understanding emotion', *History and Theory* 51, 2 (2010), 193–220, quote 198.
7 R. Leys, 'The turn to affect: a critique', *Critical Inquiry* 37, 3 (2011), 434–72.
8 G.K. Paster, K.Rowe and M. Floyd-Wilson (eds), *Reading the Early Modern Passions: Essays in the Cultural History of Emotion* (Philadelphia: University of Pennsylvania Press, 2004), 6.
9 Ibid., 9.
10 G.K. Paster, 'Melancholy Cats, Lugged Bears, and Early Modern Cosmology: Reading Shakespeare's Psychological Materialism Across the Species Barrier', in Paster, Rowe and Floyd-Wilson (eds), *Reading the Early Modern Passions*, 113–29.
11 M.T. Crane, *Shakespeare's Brain: Reading with Cognitive Theory* (Princeton: Princeton University Press, 2000)

I.4 Performance and performativity

Katie Barclay

Studies of emotion are closely tied to debates on the nature of selfhood and identity. What is the person that feels? What motivates emotion (is it just learned behaviour)? And how is emotion used to create different facets of identity (do emotions make you male or female, Protestant or Catholic, or just human)? Answering such questions has required scholars to not only address models for feeling, but to consider how they relate to the self that emotes. For early modern scholars who often work with selves that are conceived quite differently from the present day, this has perhaps been particularly vital. One model for understanding this relationship is that put forward by performance theorists.

Dramaturgical models of the 'self' were most famously articulated by the anthropologist Erving Goffman who thought that social reality was created through interactions between individuals within 'situations'.[1] In these 'situations', individuals presented the most appropriate version of themselves required to achieve their aim in a particular social context ('a performance'). This might involve putting on the 'right' outfit, saying the 'right' things, gesturing and moving appropriately, and displaying knowledge, education or class as desired by the actor. It also involves emoting appropriately, and Goffman used the example of air hostesses who were trained to be caring, calm and pleasant when working regardless of their personal circumstances or 'feelings'. Here emotion was a form of work. This is not to say that everybody conforms to social norms (some people may play 'the rebel' or 'the goth', for example), but that people wish to display a particular social identity in a particular context, and they do this through their performance. Not every performance is successful; Goffman was aware that people could fail in their presentation of the self – such as when a socially mobile working-class woman did not 'pass' as middle class at university, or when a teenager's act of rebellion brought laughter rather than anger from parents. As people adapted their performances depending on context (such as whether they were at home or at work), individuals in effect had multiple 'selves'.

More recently, Judith Butler developed this model with her concept of 'performativity', where the repetition of culturally normative gestures generates the gendered self.[2] By this, Butler refers to the everyday taught behaviours and actions that people perform unthinkingly, but which signal to others gender and other facets of identity. It extends Goffman due to its denaturalization of the body and emphasizes the ways that even parts of the human performance that appear 'innate' or 'biological', and emotion here is an important example, are performed practices. In many respects, this model is not dissimilar to that proposed by social practice theorists, such as Monique Scheer. The self, and emotion as an act of self, become things that we 'do' and which, through doing, construct identity.

This raises questions about what the 'self' is, and specifically what motivates action and emotion. Goffman provides a model of an autonomous self that sits within the

Western philosophical tradition, and distinguishes between a 'human' self that makes decisions about how to present itself and a 'social' self that is formed through performance, fully recognizing that such distinctions can be blurry in practice. For Butler, 'the self' does not pre-exist its performance, but is constituted through performance. The self is therefore inherently unstable, 'becoming' through action. This actively rejects the idea of an autonomous self and promotes a self that is socially constructed and made through interaction with others. Elizabeth Ermath has attempted to split the difference by modelling a self that pre-exists the 'discursive' (the performance) but that cannot be articulated outside of its performance.[3]

These considerations are important when exploring emotion because they speak to how and why people emote. For Goffman and Ermath, human beings feel in response to material stimuli, but their performance of that emotion is both a learned behaviour and dependent on context. For Butler, Gilles Deleuze and other theorists in that vein, emotion is almost entirely a social phenomenon, with the biological another prop in the performance.[4] Importantly, for all these theorists, emotions are not passive, but active in the construction of identity. Emotions are performed because they 'do something'; they both communicate the self and create it. Moreover, as emotions are performed they become implicated in wider communicative strategies, able to shape the world and not just reflect feeling. This body of work is closely related to, and underpinned by the same theoretical framework as, William M. Reddy's concept of the 'emotive'.[5]

Performance theory is not just useful for helping to understand how emotions work – what it is we study – but has implications for how we work with historical sources to access both emotion and the self. Emotions are created through articulation during a performance. That articulation can happen in writing, in the making of music or art, in verbal expression or played out on the body itself through gesture, countenance or other physical acts. Early modern scholars generally have to work with texts, or other physical artefacts, because they are unable to access the live performance of emotion in the long dead. This has often been viewed as fundamentally limiting for our ability to access the emotion of the historical subject – the source is viewed as the trace or representation of an inner feeling that the historian cannot access. But, if emotion is formed through its articulation (and is not prior to its performance), then surviving textual forms provide a key source of evidence to the making – the performance and so the experience – of emotion in the past. As forms that are implicated in the making of emotion, historical sources are no longer just representations of, but the social practice of, emotion. Susan Broomhall provides an example of this in her work on how the records of charitable establishments are themselves the emotional practices of institutions, conveying their intentions, desires and investments.[6]

This is not to suggest that scholars can access the fullness of the early modern experience of emotion, given that so much of the performance of emotion – like so much human experience – may not have been captured in the historical record. Nor does it deny that historical sources are complex creations, shaped over time, by genre rules, and often incorporating multiple authors in their making. Unpicking whose emotions were in play in any given historical record will likely continue to be an important part of debate and discussion. However, the important contribution of performance theory is enabling us to recognize that these problems are not novel to our interaction with the past. That human beings cannot feel what the other feels, but only experience their performance of emotion in the present, remains a central topic within philosophical debate around the nature of the self and other. For some, this inability to experience what the other experiences creates a fundamental boundary between humans that requires intimacy to be built largely on trust. More hopeful philosophers, such as Deleuze or Hélène Cixous, reject such concerns, seeing the self as reflexive and made through the interaction with the other, unable to exist without it.[7] In both cases, emotion is something that is performed and that we engage with through performance. The difference between our engagement with living individuals and those in the past is only that scholars of the past have more limited sources for accessing that performance.

In essence then, this is a method that challenges the distinction between representation and experience in the historical source. All sources, even fictional accounts, are a product of the experience of the author, for the creation of all textual forms are a form of performance. Representation remains only as the domain that actors draw on in their creation of the self. The historical source then is both a part of the performance of emotion for the creator and, in some instances, a representation that others can draw on in their own future performances. It does not, of course, solve any problems for historians of the 'voiceless', those who left no evidence of their own making (however mediated). But, perhaps, we might have hope, like Cixous and Deleuze, that if the self is formed through interaction with the other then the voices of the voiceless might at least partly be found in the works of those who represent them. Taking this approach, Hannah Newton productively recovers the emotions of dying children in records written by parents, whilst Claire Walker uncovers the emotional investment of nuns through their ritual practices.[8]

Further reading

Miller, N.J., 'Forcible Love: Performing Maternity in Renaissance Romance', in K. Bamford and N.J. Miller (eds), *Maternity and Romance Narratives in Early Modern England* (Farnham: Ashgate, 2015), 137–53.

—explores maternal love as a performative act that reinscribes and reinvents maternal identities in early modern England.

Turner, V., 'Performing the self, performing the other: gender and racial identity construction in the Nanteuil cycle', *Women's History Review* 22, 2 (2013), 182–96.

—part of a special issue on performing the self, uses this theory to rethink medieval selfhood in relation to gender and race, highlighting the porousness of such labels in the period and their significance of medieval society.

Notes

1 E. Goffman, *The Presentation of the Self in Everyday Life* (New York: Anchor Books, 1959)

2 J. Butler, *Gender Trouble: Feminism and the Subversion of Identity* (London: Routledge, 1999)

3 E. Ermath, 'Agency in the discursive condition', *History and Theory* 40, 4 (2001), 34–58.

4 G. Deleuze, *Difference and Repetition* (London: Continuum, 1994)

5 W.M. Reddy, *The Navigation of Feeling: A Framework for the History of Emotions* (Cambridge: Cambridge University Press, 2001)

6 S. Broomhall, 'Beholding Suffering and Providing Care: Emotional Performances on the Death of Poor Children within Sixteenth-Century French Institutions', in K. Barclay, K. Reynolds with C. Rawnsley (eds), *Death, Emotion and Childhood in Premodern Europe* (Houndmills: Palgrave, 2016)

7 S. Renshaw, *The Subject of Love: Hélène Cixous and the Feminine Divine* (Manchester: Manchester University Press, 2009)

, H. Newton, 'Rapt Up with Joy': Children's Emotional Responses to Death in England, 1580–1720', in Barclay, Reynolds with Rawnsley (eds), *Death, Emotion and Childhood*; C. Walker, 'The Bones of a Martyr: Jacobite Ritual in an Early Modern English Convent', in M.L. Bailey and K. Barclay (eds), *Emotion, Ritual and Power in Europe, 1200–1920: Family, State and Church* (Houndmills: Palgrave, 2016)

I.5 Materiality

Sarah Randles

Scholars from a range of fields including archaeology, anthropology, sociology, geography, philosophy, art history and cultural studies have recently begun to consider the range of intersections between human emotions and the material world. As yet, little sustained theoretical work has dealt with the emotions and material culture of early modern Europe, but there is considerable scope for the application of approaches from the archaeology and art history of other periods and places and from contemporary anthropological and philosophical studies of material culture and emotion to be applied to this historical and geographical space.

In her 1999 book, *Bereavement and Commemoration: An Archaeology of Mortality*, Sarah Tarlow used the impetus of her own emotional reaction to gravestone texts to make a case to move beyond subjective empathetic responses to a broader study of emotions in archaeology, despite the difficulties inherent in determining the emotions of the past from material remains.[1] While Tarlow was concerned with the notion of agency in the context of determining motivations for the makers and users of material culture, the anthropologist Alfred Gell used a more expansive notion of agency, ascribing agency not only to humans, but to the items he described as 'art objects'. This class of items is far broader than the typical Western definition of art as something with aesthetic qualities, encompassing, potentially, 'anything whatsoever', including living persons, and describes a wide range of emotional responses to art, including terror, awe and fascination.[2] In Gell's terminology, agency is the art object's ability to *do* something, making it an *index*, allowing it to represent or stand for a *prototype*, and to motivate inferences, responses or interpretations from its *recipients*, those whom it affects, including perhaps those who commissioned the art object. He was concerned with 'things which do duty as persons', extending the human agency of their makers and users.[3] Crucially, Gell did not suggest that indices were self-sufficient, or could act outside of a cultural setting, making it clear that agency was attributed rather than inherent to the object. Gell's theory was expressed in terms of the social effects of indices, but did account for emotional attachments to inanimate objects, as in his example of the little girl who values her doll more highly than her brother. He also allowed for the emotional effects of apotropaic and other supernatural objects, an aspect of this theory which makes it valuable for considering emotional responses to religious and magical objects in the early modern period.[4] Caroline Van Eck has used this approach to consider emotional responses to religious Renaissance statues.[5]

Oliver Harris and Tim Flohr Sørensen affirmed Tarlow's views of the importance of emotions in archaeology, and also drew upon Gell's theory of agency. They developed a more explicit theory of materiality and emotion, using it to examine archaeological material from the Neolithic period, highlighting the importance of working with material culture when there are no documentary descriptions or living witnesses to support the interpretation.[6] Their work emphasized the specific materiality of place as well as of discrete objects. They moved beyond an idea that emotions themselves were 'internal, immaterial phenomena' towards an appreciation that encounters with the material world are 'inherently affective' and an understanding that 'human beings and material things are co-constitutive'.[7] Harris and Flohr Sørensen asserted that emotions themselves are embodied and cannot easily be separated into physical and mental aspects.[8] They further suggested that emotions and materiality exist 'in a continuous, recursive and co-constitutive relationship', that is, that emotions are produced by humans engaging materially with the world, at the same time that emotions produce that engagement.[9]

Harris and Flohr Sørensen proposed several terms to describe the relationship between emotions and materiality. 'Affective fields' denote the relationships between agents, which may be people, places or things, in which something or someone stimulates an emotional response in a causal set of events. Affective fields are dynamic, and may be spread across time and place, so that the emotions experienced within an affective field may vary with circumstances. For example, in the early modern period, the affective field existing between people and relics resulted in radically changing emotional responses at the time of the Reformation. 'Attunement', in contrast, describes the phenomenological experience of being in the world, focusing on the way that bodily movement or material expressions such as clothing disclose emotional states at the same time that they also produce them. Attunement is always material and sensory, specific to time and place and is the means by which individuals can apprehend the emotional states of others. 'Atmosphere' is dependent on a particular co-existence of people, places and things, particularly in architectonic environments. Particular materials may promote atmospheres, which may change as the materials change over time, but different atmospheres may be experienced in the same environment, when it is used for different purposes. Unlike affective fields, atmospheres require human awareness of them.[10]

Harris and Flohr Sørensen's theory differs in that respect from theories of Object Oriented Ontology, in which inanimate objects may have what Jane Bennett described as 'vital materialism' or 'thing power'.[11] She defined this as 'the curious ability of inanimate things to animate, to act, to produce effects dramatic and subtle', including emotional effects.[12] Thing power is relational, but may include relationships between non-human participants, such as bacteria or animals, since it does not require human awareness to be effective. Bennett asserted that things have agency, but explicitly excluded objects invested with supernatural power, a significant category of early modern objects, from her theory.

Sara Ahmed has also been concerned with the materiality of emotions from the perspective of her work in feminist cultural studies. In her 2004 article, 'Affective Economies', she asked how emotions move between bodies, both individual and collective, and suggests that emotions create 'the very effect of the surfaces or boundaries of bodies and worlds'.[13] Like Harris and Flohr Sørensen, Ahmed saw emotions as relational, but rather than situated in either the subject or the object of a relationship, she located emotions in the relational space between them. Ahmed asked the question, not what emotions are, but what they *do*, concluding that they shape both individual and collective bodies, 'through the repetition of action over time'.[14] Ahmed's critique encompasses both literal and metaphorical understandings of emotion and materiality; she points out that an impression can be both an effect on a subject's feelings but also a mark pressed into a literal surface. As well as moving between bodies, emotions have the ability to be 'sticky', aligning individuals with communities and bodily space with social space.[15] Emotions, for Ahmed, work as a form of capital, in which they circulate and are distributed across social as well as psychic fields. This movement of emotion between objects and material signs allows them to accumulate 'affective value' over time, a concept which might be applied to the ways that objects from the early modern period might be interpreted differently from within the context of their time and place and from the perspective of historic distance.[16] Jerónimo Arellano has applied Ahmed's theories of emotions and materiality to an analysis of the Wunderkammer collections of objects from the New World.[17]

Central to all of these theories of emotions and materiality is the idea that emotions exist in a material world, which includes the human body, and that they affect and are affected by it. Material objects may therefore be used as evidence for the emotions of the past, while at the same time the emotional history of an object is necessary to an understanding of its materiality.

However, further consideration needs to be given to specifics of materiality and emotion in early modern Europe, in order to relate the emotional responses of early modern humans to the contemporary objects which they encountered, and to understand how those relationships might change over time and as the result of changes to the social, political or religious environments. While the critical frameworks developed by theorists examining other times and places provide useful entry points to the consideration of early modern materiality and early modern emotions, they also run a risk of failing to be 'attuned' (in Harris and Flohr Sørensen's terminology) to the specific material and emotional circumstances of the period they interpret. There remains therefore a need for theoretical approaches tailored to the materiality and emotions of early modern Europe.

Further reading

Broomhall, S., 'Dishes, Coins and Pipes: The Epistemological and Emotional Power of VOC Material Culture in Australia', in A. Gerritsen and G. Riello (eds), *The Global Lives of Things: Material Culture of Connections in the Early Modern World* (Abingdon: Routledge, 2016), 145–61.

—engages with the emotional effects of objects as they move from one place and culture to another.

Randles, S., '"The Pattern of All Patience": Gender, Agency and Emotions in Embroidery and Pattern Books in Early Modern England', in S. Broomhall (ed.), *Authority, Gender and Emotions in Late Medieval and Early Modern England* (Basingstoke: Palgrave, 2015), 150–67.

—considers the materiality of early modern embroidery, and the way that it could be used to regulate emotional states and to influence relationships.

Van Eck, C., *Art, Agency and Living Presence: From the Animated Image to the Excessive Object* (Leiden: Leiden University Press, 2015)

—extends Gell's anthropological approach to consider emotional reactions to works of art in the early modern period and beyond.

Notes

1 S. Tarlow, *Bereavement and Commemoration: An Archaeology of Mortality* (Oxford: Blackwell, 1999), 20–33.
2 A. Gell, *Art and Agency: An Anthropological Theory* (Oxford: Clarenden Press, 1998), 6–7.
3 Ibid., 16.
4 Ibid., 17–18.
5 C. Van Eck, 'Living Statues: Alfred Gell's *Art and Agency*, Living Presence Response and the Sublime', *Art History* 33, 4 (2010), 643–59.
6 O. J. T. Harris and T. Flohr Sørensen, 'Rethinking emotion and material culture', *Archaeological Dialogues* 17, 2 (2010), 145–63.
7 Ibid., 145–6.
8 Ibid., 146–7.
9 Ibid., 149.
10 Ibid., 150–2.
11 J. Bennett, *Vibrant Matter: A Political Ecology of Things* (Durham: Duke University Press, 2010)
12 Ibid., 6.
13 S. Ahmed, 'Affective economies', *Social Text* 22, 2 (2004), 117–39, quote 117.
14 Ahmed, *The Cultural Politics of Emotion* (New York: Routledge, 2014), 4.
15 Ibid., 4, 90–8.
16 Ahmed, 'Affective economies', 120.
17 J. Arellano, *Magical Realism and the History of the Emotions in Latin America* (Lanham, Maryland: Bucknell University Press, 2015), 16.

I.6 Space and place

Katie Barclay

In recent years, the application of spatial theory to historical records has grown in popularity amongst early modern scholars, particularly for those interested in gender, the household and rethinking the binaries of public and private. There are a number of different models and approaches that can underpin a spatial analysis, but those which have been most influential amongst scholars in the humanities generally formulate space in terms of social relationships. This theory tends to draw heavily on the insights of Henri Lefebvre that space is both constituted by and produces social relations, rather than landscape, architecture and similar locations simply being a stage upon which people act.[1] To fully understand this claim requires a careful use of language. 'Space' for spatial theorists is different from both 'location' and 'place'. 'Location' typically refers to a precise set of coordinates on a map or other material position, such as a house or bridge. 'Place' generally refers to locations that are named and hold the 'symbolic and imaginary investments of the population'.[2] In some contexts, it can be used interchangeably with location, but whereas 'location' may simply be a point on a map, the boundaries of 'place' can be more abstract or undefined. Importantly, 'place' is a social construction – it requires human engagement with location to come into being. For example, place includes cities and towns, which are named and hold particular associations and meanings for large groups. Place might also include a house that holds the specific meaning of 'home' for a particular individual, but not for others. 'Place' typically holds significant emotional investments, including providing a sense of belonging, ownership and identity.

For many scholars, place is a particular type of space. Within this framework, space is understood as a relationship or interaction between the material (physical location, landscape, architecture), the activity and bodies of people in that location, time, and the social norms and cultural meanings attached to all of these. It is a term that captures physical environment, discourse and human behaviour in dialogue, and it only comes into being when that relationship is activated. Space is not static therefore, but is a process, continually being produced in the everyday. Perhaps challenging for early modern scholars, particularly those charting change over time, it is also a concept that resists linearity. Space is not understood as a set of inputs (buildings, people, ideas) that produces outputs (social relations/emotions), but as both in interaction.

For many theorists, this construction of space has been closely tied to performance theory, as it is something that is produced in the making, rather than pre-existing the performance. It is also a model that has sought to take materiality and embodiment seriously, demonstrating how human behaviour is produced in relationship with material conditions and the surrounding environment. A scholarship of emotional geographies pays particular attention to the dynamic interplay between emotion and environment, landscape, topography, distance and boundaries in the production of space. It highlights the ways that, say, the spatial dynamics of the early modern household reinforce particular models for gendered power and the appropriate emotions associated with men and women, or how particular attachments to land acted to strengthen or weaken emotional bonds between family members and to activate particular forms of political activism.[3]

Anthony Giddens suggests that at certain points in history, space and place were interchangeable, but 'space' is important for studies of modernity, which reflect that relationships, and so 'spaces', might be created over distance or digitally, without a strong sense of named 'place'.[4] Early modern historians have provided examples of this in earlier points of history and so retaining the distinction between the two terms remains significant to scholars in all fields.[5] Space is also a useful term when the physical location within the process of space is of less significance in understanding the dynamic, and also in interaction with re-imaginings of place that locate, say, the body or the family as the 'physical location' that holds the symbolic saturation entailed in place. The site of the early modern female body as a space of conquest, a mapped territory or the embodiment of ideas of justice, liberty or nation has been well-charted, for example.[6]

As importantly, understanding place as a form of space has been politically significant. Whereas many claims to place have sought to locate it as a form of representation – a set of static and unchanging ideals – that have been used to reify particular social relationships, attachments and rights in association with geographical locations (some forms of nationalism are a good example), understanding place as space demonstrates the multiple identities that place holds, the porousness of the boundaries of place and the ways that place too is a form of process. Such an approach has been particularly useful for interpreting how migrants integrate into and reform early modern emotional communities, emphasizing the dynamism of community as a relationship.[7]

As can be seen, emotions are increasingly recognized as an important component of 'space'. Emotion is understood by spatial theorists such as Lefebvre to be a social relation constituted through and producing space, so that location, and the way that people interact with it, plays a significant role in what people feel and how they perform such feeling. Studies by urban planners have demonstrated the significance of environment to human behaviour, so that open fields enable different emotional responses from houses when encountering the same stimuli. Emotion plays a role in the production of space, shaping, for example, the safety and security provided by the romantic imaginings of the late eighteenth-century 'home' or the affirmation of masculinity created through the homosocial bonds of the early modern public house. It is also emotion that determines, for example, the meaning of distance, whether it is near or far, bearable or unbearable. Travelling for early moderns was often significantly more fraught, reflected in elaborate leave-taking rituals, given that methods of transportation and communication were slower and more limited than today. The concept of space has also been significant in the metaphorical conceptualization of emotional experience, not least in debates around the growth of ideas of 'interiority' amongst seventeenth-century Puritans. Here 'interior' and embodied emotional experience is articulated in spatial terms, even as it is produced through spatial processes.

Spatial theories have been increasingly important for historians of the early modern world because they have provided a sophisticated model for understanding the operation of power. At its most straightforward, an appreciation for space has enabled us to understand its role in action and so identity and emotion. Doreen Massey, for example, famously observed that domesticity was a 'spatial control, and through that, a social control on identity', arguing that women's association with the home defined where and in what conditions they could exercise power, as well as producing their sense of self and associated behaviours, such as emotional display.[8] In contrast, men's interaction within the space of the home was understood differently and so their access to power was not similarly constricted. This model has been very useful for explaining why, for example, in most periods middle and lower-order men's movements through the same street were seen differently, and, when we take into account time, why it might be acceptable for early modern women to walk the streets during the day, but not after dark. It also helps explain why men and women might have felt different things when placed in the same physical environment; why in eighteenth-century London a woman may have experienced fear on a dark street, but a man, like Samuel Johnson, was invigorated in the same location. Rather than meaning and emotion being attached to the physical environment, it is instead produced in dialogue through human interaction with environment, time and the cultural meanings associated with the different components of the spatial process.

In its emphasis on process, spatial theory has reinvigorated the discussion around 'lines of power', that are so influential in shaping emotional experience and are in turn produced through emotion. Models of gender and class, for instance, traditionally relied on a hegemonic ideal or set of rules against which people and their behaviours were judged, with power flowing in one direction (if occasionally encountering resistance). Spatial theorists emphasize such ideals or boundaries as only one resource in a negotiation of power that is context-specific. For this reason, power is much less stable, but also considerably more flexible and persistent. It helps explain why people succeed in certain context, but not in others, and why such achievements do not always follow traditional social hierarchies. As a dynamic component of human relationships, it also enables emotion to play a significant role in enforcing and disrupting power dynamics, as can be seen in the important uses of emotional display

– from weeping and pleading to kissing and embracing – in negotiating favour at the court of Elizabeth I, activities that in turn reinforced her power as monarch.

Spatial theory enables a more holistic approach to human behaviour that accounts for materiality, ideology, emotion and action in engagement. As such it is particularly useful for early modern scholars of emotion who are required to engage with emotion not only as a biological response but a cultural production. As an emerging methodology, its use by early modern scholars has tended to be focused on the household or the stage; the spatialization of emotion is emerging but has the potential to be applied to a much wider range of situations.

Further reading

Barclay, K., *Men on Trial: Emotion, Embodiment and Identity in Ireland, 1800–1845* (Forthcoming)
—uses the idea of performative space to understand how emotion, identity and power were produced in early nineteenth-century Irish courts, highlighting that emotion was a product of spatial relations as well as culture and biology.

Flather, A.J., *Gender and Space in Early Modern England* (Woodbridge: Boydell and Brewer, 2006)
—first monograph-length work to explore how gender was spatially produced in early modern England, using case studies of a range of 'spaces' from the household to the alehouse.

Notes

1 H. Lefebvre, *The Production of Space*, (trans.) D. Nicholson-Smith (London: Wiley, 1991)
2 D. Birdwell-Pheasant, 'The Home "Place": Center and Periphery in Irish House and Family Systems', in D. Birdwell-Pheasant and D. Lawrence-Zúñiga (eds), *House Life: Space, Place and Family in Europe* (Oxford: Berg, 1999), 105–32.
3 A.J. Flather, 'Space, place and gender: the sexual and spatial division of labour in the early modern household', *History and Theory* 52, 3 (2013), 344–60; K. Barclay, 'Place and power in Irish farms at the end of the nineteenth century', *Women's History Review* 21, 4 (2012), 571–88.
4 A. Giddens, *The Consequences of Modernity* (Cambridge: Polity, 1990), 18.
5 L. Hannan, 'Making space: English women, letter-writing, and the life of the mind, *c.* 1650–1750', *Women's History Review* 21, 4 (2012), 589–604.
6 V. Traub, 'History in the Present Tense: Feminist Theories, Spatialized Epistemologies, and Early Modern Embodiment', in M. Wiesner-Hanks (ed.), *Mapping Gendered Routes and Spaces in the Early Modern World* (Farnham: Ashgate, 2015), 15–54.
7 Barclay, 'Marginal Households and their Emotions: the "Kept Mistress" in Enlightenment Edinburgh', in S. Broomhall (ed.), *Spaces for Feeling: Emotions and Sociabilities in Britain, 1650–1850* (London: Routledge, 2015), 95–111.
8 D. Massey, *Space, Place and Gender* (Cambridge: Polity Press, 1994), 179–80.

I.7 Psychological approaches

Sandra Garrido and Jane W. Davidson

Psychology in the current sense of the word had not yet emerged in the early modern period. The term 'psychology' itself was coined around the sixteenth century, and originally meant a 'study of the soul', rather than a study of the mind and emotions as it is understood today. Discussions about psychological phenomena were approached from a number of perspectives, including naturalist perspectives within which the natural origin of emotions and behaviours were emphasized rather than supernatural or spiritual causes; materialist perspectives based on the premise that matter forms the ultimate reality; mechanistic perspectives that focused on the operation of natural laws of science; vitalism which contended that mechanical processes could not account for the entirety of human experience; and, idealism, or a belief that human experience is a mental construct rather than a material reality.[1]

In the sixteenth century, thought about emotions and their disturbances were influenced by Hippocratic and Galenic theories of humoral temperament and animal spirits. Affective states were often believed to be a result of imbalances of the humours, and a range of affective disorders such as 'splenetic humour' or 'melancholia' were named based on their believed origin in humoral imbalances. However, later in the period, Aristotelian thought came to be gradually categorized as superstition, and humoral accounts declined, as focus shifted to the importance of systematic methodology and the application of the laws of nature to understanding psychological phenomena. There was also increasing interest in individual subjective experience of emotions. Thus the early modern period saw important shifts in thinking that heralded the beginning of modern psychological approaches.

Among the most influential thinkers of the period who shaped these changes was René Descartes (1596–1650). Descartes described the 'passions' as being caused by movements of the animal spirits.[2] He believed control of the emotions to be central to the treatment of both mental and physical illness. However, he also discussed mechanistic explanations of emotions based on learned associations between actions, feelings and thoughts, a perspective that became known as 'associationism'. These arguments are regarded by some modern scholars to have provided the basis for conditioning theories of modern psychology.[3] Descartes also discussed the idea of internal conflicts between passions and rational behaviour, which forms the basic premise of Freudian psychoanalysis.[4]

Descartes also argued that there were six 'primitive passions' and that other emotions were a combination of these principal passions. These ideas are also to be found in modern psychological theory such as in 'discrete emotion models', which argue that all emotions are a combination of a small number of core emotions.[5] These kinds of taxonomies of emotions were common in discussions of the 'passions' among natural scientists of the period, in keeping with the increasing focus on systematic research and classifications.[6]

The seventeenth-century English physician Thomas Willis (1621–75) conducted extensive research along with a group of other scholars from Oxford into the structure of the brain. Willis argued that the animal spirits played an important role in the communication between brain and body. His analysis of the passions and their disturbances were far removed from humoral medicine, arguing that they were the result of mechanistic processes within the brain and nervous system.[7] Similarly, another empiricist, Baruch Spinoza (1632–77), emphasized that the passions followed natural laws and were controllable by reason. He argued that desire, joy and sorrow were the three basic passions or 'affects' and that they motivated different behaviours (Part III, Def. III.11).[8]

Although the work of English philosopher John Locke (1632–1704) did not contain extensive discussion of emotions or the 'passions' specifically, a central concept within his philosophy was that of 'ideas' that encompassed sensation, perception, thoughts, beliefs and the passions.[9] He also took a strongly empirical and associationist stance, attempting to create explanations of psychological phenomena that were similar to Isaac Newton's laws of physics. Several of his concepts are still evident in modern psychological thought, such as his arguments about motivations deriving from an 'uneasiness of desire, fixed on some absent good'.[10] Locke's focus on individual psychological processes also helped shape the modern focus in psychology on individuals.[11] Similarly, David Hume (1711–76) also contended that principles of natural science could explain psychological processes just as Newton's laws explained the functioning of the universe.[12] His central concept was that of 'impressions' that could be simple or complex, and included sensations, passions and reflections.

Divergent perspectives from the period came from romanticist Blaise Pascal (1623–62), who argued that the passions were an integration of thoughts, feelings and bodily responses. Thomas Reid (1710–96) attempted to integrate rationalist and empiricist perspectives, arguing that sensations were the immediate feelings aroused by the senses and were distinct from perceptions and unmediated by thought. However, in general, the early modern period saw an important paradigm shift to a new perspective that reallocated discussions of psychological questions firmly into the realm of the natural world, and away from the idea that humanity enjoyed a special god-like status among living creatures.[13] Thus the nineteenth century saw the emergence of a natural-science approach to psychology that emphasized the physiological systems that give rise to emotions.

Although the roots of modern psychology can be found in the discussion of emotions and the passions in the early modern period, scholars need to remain aware of changing terminology. Seventeenth-century philosophers tended to talk about the 'passions' or 'affect', while in the eighteenth century the term 'sentiment' became more common.[14] None of these terms quite meant what they do in modern psychology, nor did they refer to 'emotion' in the sense that psychologists understand it today. Even the term 'passion' carried a different meaning to its modern-day meaning, often being used to refer to a relatively passive, receptive affective experience, or to an uncontrolled affective response.

At the same time, modern psychological theories and concepts may inform investigations into emotions in the early modern period. For example, models of emotion that define emotion in terms of dimensions such as valence and arousal could prove useful for exploring differences between historical and modern emotional concepts. Such models, like James A. Russell's circumplex model,[15] map all emotions onto a two-dimensional space in terms of whether they are experienced as pleasant or unpleasant (valence), high activation or low activation (arousal). While models such as these are of course regarded as over-simplifications even in modern contexts, they can provide a useful starting point for comparison of emotion concepts across time periods.

Similarly, theories of 'emotion induction' can reveal the differences between culturally-specific emotional responses and those that are more universal, further illuminating how and why people responded to emotional stimuli in various contexts. For example, Patrik N. Juslin *et al* have proposed a number of mechanisms by which music is able to evoke emotional responses in the listener.[16] Their mechanisms include both those that draw on biological mechanisms and those that tap into culturally acquired knowledge. Musical treatises from the early modern period can reveal the compositional and performance techniques that creators and performers of music used to communicate emotions and evoke emotional responses in their audiences. Examining performance traditions from the perspective of our modern understanding of emotion induction mechanisms can help to illuminate the extent to which current concepts of emotion are universal or culturally based.

Other modern research of significance in emotions psychology is that by Michael Boiger and a team of social and cultural researchers in Belgium.[17] This team has investigated sociodynamic models of emotions in which

> emotions are seen as dynamic systems that emerge from the interactions and relationships in which they take place. [The] model does not deny that emotions are biologically constrained, yet it takes seriously that emotions are situated in specific contexts.[18]

Their work has argued that emotions emerge from social interactions and relationships which those emotions then shape and change. These emotions are dependent on the specific social and cultural context in which they emerge. Thus, Boiger's ideas are very similar to those promoted by history of emotions scholars like William M. Reddy.[19]

Modern psychology can also be informed by a consideration of historical perspectives, such as the suggestion by Jane W. Davidson and Sandra Garrido that the use of music in addressing mood disorders in health contexts could benefit from a deeper consideration of individual differences and the possibility of negative impacts that were commonly understood in both Ancient Greek and neo-platonic philosophy.[20] Similarly, Louis C. Charland *et al* argued that understanding historical ideas about the concept of tortuous passions and their capacity to take over the mind and body, could inform approaches to treating anorexia.[21]

Further reading

Charland, L.C. and R.S. White, 'Anatomy of a Passion: Shakespeare's *The Winter's Tale* as Case Study', in S. Broomhall (ed.) *Ordering Emotions in Europe, 1100–1800* (Leiden: Brill, 2015), 197–224.

—uses nineteenth-century and modern ideas about passion to try to elucidate emotional ideas and practices in Shakespeare's *A Winter's Tale.*

Notes

1 R.T.G. Walsh, T. Teo and A. Baydala, *A Critical History and Philosophy of Psychology: Diversity of Context, Thought and Practice* (Cambridge: Cambridge University Press, 2014)

2 *Passions of the Soul* AT XI. (London: J. Martin and J. Ridley, 1650), anonymous translator.

3 Walsh, Teo and Baydala, *A Critical History and Philosophy of Psychology*.

4 For an introduction to Freudian psychoanalysis see T. Gelfand and J. Kerr, *Freud and the History of Psychoanalysis* (Berkeley: Analytic Press, 1992)

5 S.S. Tomkins, *Affect Imagery Consciousness: Volume I, The Positive Affects* (London: Tavistock, 1962)

6 A.M. Schmitter, '17th and 18th Century Theories of Emotions', in E.N. Zalta (ed.), *The Stanford Encyclopedia of Philosophy*, (2014) http:plato.stanford.edu/archives/spr2014/entries/emotions-17th18th/ (accessed 19 April 2016)

7 J. Bos, 'The decline of character: humoral psychology in ancient and early modern medicine', *History of Human Sciences* 22, 3 (2009), 29–50.
8 *Ethics* (1677), (trans) R.H.M. Elwes onlie at www.gutenberg.org/files/3800/3800-h/3800-h.htm, accessed 19 April 2016)
9 *An Essay Concerning Human Understanding* (London, 1689) and M. Billig, *The Hidden Roots of Critical Psychology: Understanding the Impact of Locke, Shaftesbury and Reid* (London: Sage, 2008)
10 (E II.xxi.33, p 252) and L. Berkowitz, *Aggression: A Social Psychological Analysis* (New York: McGraw-Hill, 1962), see also C.L. Hull, 'The conflicting psychologies of learning: a way out', *Psychological Review* 42 (1935), 491–516.
11 Walsh, Teo and Baydala, *A Critical History and Philosophy of Psychology*.
12 *An Enquiry Concerning Human Understanding* (1748) (New York: P. F. Collier & Son, 1909–14)
13 W. Pickren and A. Rutherford, *A History of Modern Psychology in Context* (New York: John Wiley, 2010)
14 Schmitter, '17th and 18th Century Theories of Emotions'.
15 J.A. Russell, 'Affective space is bipolar', *Journal of Personality and Social Psychology* 37, 3 (1979), 345–56.
16 P.N. Juslin, S. Liljeström, D. Västfjäll and L.-O. Lundqvist, 'How Does Music Evoke Emotions? Exploring the Underlying Mechanisms,' in P.N. Juslin and J. Sloboda (eds), *Handbook of Music and Emotion: Theory, Research, and Applications* (Oxford: Oxford University Press, 2010), 605–42.
17 Work in the Center for Social and Cultural Psychology, University of Leuven, Belgium.
18 B. Mesquita and M. Boiger, 'Emotions in context: a sociodynamic model of emotions', *Emotion Review* 6, 4 (2014), 298–302, quote 298.
19 W.M. Reddy, *The Navigation of Feeling: A Framework for the History of Emotions* (Cambridge and New York: Cambridge University Press, 2001)
20 J.W. Davidson and S. Garrido, *My Life as a Playlist* (Perth: University of Western Australia Publishing, 2014)
21 L.C. Charland, T. Hope, A. Stewart and J. Tan, 'The hypothesis that anorexia nervosa is a passion: clarifications and elaborations', *Philosophy, Psychiatry and Psychology* 20, 4 (2013), 375–79.

I.8 Large data set mining

Inger Leemans

Digital emotion research has yet to make history. Until now large data set mining has not been a very active field of research in early modern emotion studies. This is indeed surprising since first, the early modern field has such rich, copyright-free, digitized data sets and second, emotion studies have provided a solid basis for (textual) computational analysis. Moreover, sentiment mining is one of the most active research areas in natural language processing, and the methods and underlying assumptions of sentiment analysis are in urgent need of being tested and improved by the aggregated knowledge from fields such as early modern emotion studies.

Although many early modern researchers work with large sets of digitized data, and many are increasingly trying to reformulate their hermeneutic and quantitative research questions into computational models, historians of emotions tend to choose more traditional methods of research. They have developed emotion lexicons, tracked emotions lost and found, mapped long term (dis)continuities in emotion expression, or analysed affective aspects of visual and material culture, all without making (visible) use of digital data or modes of analysis. In recent textbooks, such as *Doing Emotions History*, digital methods are largely ignored.[1]

Textbooks, however, are only one way to aggregate knowledge. Computational techniques could provide another route to summarize, evaluate and map the large variety of claims about emotional expression, emotion classification and long-term developments produced by the fast expanding field of the history of emotions. Particularly in the field of textual analysis, various computational methods have already been developed that might form a starting point for historians of emotions.

Over the last few decades, many different digital techniques have been developed for sentiment or emotion analysis. These techniques are mainly developed and employed by psychologists, computational linguists, media researchers, political scientists and for business purposes. 'General Inquirer' was one of the first models for content analysis and the classification of textual expressions in binary oppositions; that is, as positive/negative, strong/weak, active/passive, pleasure/pain. Most sentiment-mining programs that were developed later on followed the focus on binary oppositions, classifying sentiments in such terms as positive/negative or in strength, rating from one to five, for example. Some of these programs analyse the sentiment value of whole documents; others, like 'SentiWordNet', measure positive, negative and neutrality over sentences, or over specific genres such as news headlines. Online gateways such as 'TAPoR' present long lists of all the tools available for sentiment mining or other forms of sophisticated text analysis and retrieval.[2]

The term 'sentiment mining', however, especially for emotion historians, could be misleading. 'Sentiment' can indicate any form of subjectivity or appraisal. Sentiment analysis is used, for example, by political scientists or linguists as an equivalent to opinion-mining. Researchers interested in emotion history may be better served by more fine-grained versions of sentiment detection, by 'NLP' (Natural Language Processing) projects that detect specific emotions in text. Until now, these 'emotion mining' projects mainly make use of a limited set of basic emotions (e.g. anger, disgust, fear, surprise, joy, sadness) provided by the psychological research of Paul Ekman and Robert Plutchick.[3] James W. Pennebaker's 'Linguistic Inquiry and Word Count' (LIWC), constructed for analysing depression and well-being in texts, combines sentiment and emotion mining and provides the possibility to relate emotion expressions with other topics and textual information, such as word counts, linguistic dimensions, psychological and biological processes and personal concerns. Semantic taggers like 'WordNet' have various categories in their vocabularies to list emotions, body parts or physical and affective activities and appraisals.[4] 'USAS' (UCREL (University Centre for Computer Corpus Research on Language) Semantic Analysis System) registers emotional actions and states and has a more fine-grained system to identify different levels (in + or -) of serenity/anger, happiness/sadness, fear/bravery, concern/confidence. Some text analysis and visualization environments such as 'DocuScope' have already been tested on early modern texts.

Although these rich and constantly improving and expanding models for sentiment and emotion mining present many possibilities for doing emotion history research, they are also of limited value to historians, since most of them tend to focus on recent text corpora, on born-digital texts, www sites, social media, blogs and short pieces of text such as twitter feeds or customer reviews. They also have a bias for product and consumer analysis or political ideology and focus on analysing subjectivity or opinion. They tend to measure emotions and sentiments in binary oppositions and limit their analysis on a twentieth- and twenty-first-century set of 'basic' emotions.

Finally, many only support analysis of English language texts, or provide translations that have been generated by automatic translation without proper evaluation and adaptation processes. In short, most sentiment-mining programs analyze modern-day texts with current notions of emotions. For historians interested in early modern emotions expressed in complex texts such as encyclopaedias, chronicles, ego-documents or literary texts, this presents a challenge. For historians working in non-English language fields, the situation is even more complex.

In the Netherlands, a research group interested in the embodiment of emotions has started to develop historicized versions of LIWC and WordNetAffect (that can take historical spelling variations in Dutch texts into account) and to develop a completely new 'Historical Embodied Emotions Model' (HEEM), based on a manual annotation of Dutch early modern theatre texts. HEEM is able to detect 37 different emotions in early modern Dutch texts and body parts that are indicated as emotional: the model can make distinctions between hands shaking with anger and 'neutral' hands that are waving. The results might test our twenty-first-century presumptions about basic emotions.[5] This example may underline that manual annotation and algorithmic querying of massive digital corpora can lead to the construction of valid models for historical emotion mining and to historical lexicons of emotions terms. Early modern historians of emotion could make a major contribution to digital research.

The early modern era is particularly promising for this kind of research because it offers large sets of open-access, non-copyright-protected textual data with extensive and reliable metadata, such as Project Gutenberg, Eighteenth Century Collections Online (ECCO), Gallica, Early American Imprints, Folger's Shakespeare collection (www.folgerdigitaltexts.org), German Enlightenment journals, Diderot and d'Alembert's *Encyclopédie* or all the digitized texts in Google Books.[6] Some of these collections have started to provide support for computational analysis, such as the N-Gram browser in Early English Books Online, topic modelling in 'Learned Letters' (ePistolarium), or 'Distant Reading Early Modernity' (DREaM).[7] We could start to conduct digital research into honour and shame in early modern juridical texts, amazement in early modern travel accounts, witness the development of marriage or love in 'Sailing Letters', the sharing of personal feelings in the 'Republic of Letters', or employ the crowd to draw early modern emotional urban maps, following the example of the Stanford University project 'Mapping Emotions in Victorian London'.[8]

Digital research across multilingual text corpora could help to integrate and structure the constantly-expanding knowledge of the history of emotions field and provide new perspectives. It could also help to open up the results of historical research to other scientific fields, such as psychology, linguistics and computer science. Digital history of emotions could help develop historically-layered emotion ontologies that could test or enrich current emotion ontologies, which tend to represent emotions as universal and static. As emotions are so unstable and show so many variations over time, they form an excellent test case for existing models for concept analysis and concept drift.

Hopefully, in a revised reprint of this book, we can present not only various text-mining projects on early modern emotions, but also digital projects on visual and material culture based on the rich collections of the cultural heritage institutes, projects on affective heritage, or network analysis of emotional communities. Digital emotion research could thus combine and help to present the large variety of emotions perspectives from the early modern period.

Further reading

Liu, B., 'Sentiment analysis and opinion mining', *Synthesis Lectures on Human Language Technologies* 5, 1 (2012), 1–167.

—in-depth discussion of the history, the techniques, the uses and problems of sentiment and opinion mining by one of the leading scholars in this field.

Samothrakis, S., and M. Fasli, 'Emotional sentence annotation helps predict fiction genre', *PLoS ONE* 10 (2015): e0141922. doi:10.1371/journal.pone.0141922

—investigates Project Gutenberg fictional texts with Paul Ekman's basic emotions to examine the hypothesis that works of fiction can be characterized by the emotions they portray.

Zwaan, J. van der, I. Leemans and E. Kuijpers, 'HEEM, a complex model for mining emotions in historical text', *IEEE 11th International Conference on eScience* (2015), 22–30.

—describes machine learning aspects of the development of a new model for mining embodied emotions in early modern theatre texts. See https://github.com/NLeSC/embodied-emotions-scripts for the dataset and tools.

Notes

1 P.N. Stearns and S.J. Matt, *Doing Emotions History* (Urbana: University of Illinois Press, 2014)

2 TAPoR (www.tapor.ca)

3 P. Ekman, 'Basic Emotions', in T. Dalgleish and M. Power (eds), *Handbook of Cognition and Emotion* (Chichester: John Wiley, 1999), 45–60. An example of 'basic' emotion mining is A. Acerbi, V. Lampos, P. Garnett and R.A. Bentley, 'The expression of emotions in 20th century books', *PloS one* 8 (2013), 3.

4 C. Strapparava and R. Mihalcea, 'Learning to identify emotions in text', *Proceedings of the 2008 ACM Symposium on Applied Computing* (2008), 1556–60.

5 J. van der Zwaan, I. Leemans and E. Kuijpers, 'HEEM, a complex model for mining emotions in historical text', *IEEE eScience* (2015), 22–30; I. Leemans, J.M. van der Zwaan, I. Maks, E. Kuijpers and K. Steenbergh, 'Mining embodied emotions: a comparative analysis of sentiment and emotion in Dutch texts, 1600–1800', *Digital Humanities Quarterly* (forthcoming).

6 Early English Books Online N-Gram browser (http://earlyprint.wustl.edu); Gallica (http://gallica.bnf.fr); Early American Imprints (www.readex.com/content/americas-historical-imprints); Folger Digital Texts (http://www.folgerdigitaltexts.org); German Enlightenment journals (www.ub.uni-bielefeld.de/diglib/aufklaerung); *Encyclopédie* of Diderot et d'Alembert (http://encyclopédie.eu/index.php/707960516); Googlebooks (http://books.google.com), Project Gutenberg (https://www.gutenberg.org), all accessed 19 April 2016.

7 ePistolarium (http://ckcc.huygens.knaw.nl/epistolarium/); Distant Reading Early Modernity (http://earlymodernconversions.com), all accessed 19 April 2016

8 Travel Accounts (http://digiberichte.de); Sailing Letters (http://www.gekaaptebrieven.nl); Republic of Letters (http://republicofletters.stanford.edu); Mapping Emotions in Victorian London (www.historypin.org/en/explore/victorian-london), all accessed 19 April 2016.

Section II

Early modern terms, concepts and practices of emotions

II.1 Language of emotions

R.S. White

We assume words like 'happiness' and 'sadness' in earlier periods meant the same as today, 'but did they? Have they changed in ways that effectively give them new meanings in our world? This essay will show that many words describing or expressing emotions have in fact changed over time, and their superficial familiarity is misleading. In the term coined by French linguists such words are faux amis or 'false friends', and changes in their meanings often reflect larger changes in emotional definition over time.

The most obvious example is the very word 'emotion' itself, since it did not acquire anything like its modern sense until the later seventeenth century. Occurrences before that took their meaning from the word's roots, ex-motion or 'movement away', and it was most commonly in the sixteenth century used to describe 'political agitation, civil unrest; a public commotion or uprising', a meaning which is now obsolete.

Of course people did have feelings before 1660, but the vocabulary they used to describe them – words like passions, affections, affects, appetites, sensations, humours and sensibilities – were more closely tied with physical processes, since they saw body and mind as inextricably linked. As a result, even these words nowadays have different connotations, since we generally see psychology and physiology as separate realms.

To take the apparently simple examples mentioned above, these days in everyday modern usage 'happiness' is understood as a state of emotional wellbeing that is 'inside' us and can be achieved by taking systematic steps. However, the original meaning of 'hap' was chance or luck, which survives today in 'hapless' meaning unlucky, or 'happenstance' meaning a discovery made by a lucky chance. This may reflect a fundamentally different world view in times when life itself was more contingent on uncontrollable, outer circumstances such as epidemics, making the state of 'happiness' more like a lucky accident than a goal. The phrase in the American Declaration of Independence (1776), 'Life, Liberty and the Pursuit of Happiness', would have had a very different meaning 200 years earlier, when life could be short, liberty at best relative and 'pursuit of happiness' a forlorn and perhaps self-defeating cause. Nobody could 'pursue' something so contingent. The differences must have resulted in subtle and almost invisible understandings of 'happy' love between the sexes in earlier times, amounting to an unexpected and undeserved secular miracle.

Meanwhile, 'sadness' derived from a concept of 'seriousness' rather than necessarily being the opposite of happiness, and as Erin Sullivan has shown, it could also be an extremely dangerous illness potentially leading to suicide – an altogether more acutely worrying state of mind than the one we mean now by 'sadness'.[1] Again, social realities indicate different contexts. In an earlier world where privacy was neither considered desirable nor seen as practical, the sight of a person giving signs of inner distress and avoiding company must have been more alarming than is the case today when we customarily only need 'time off' to be on our own when we are 'sad'.

We use words to describe emotions. But words have histories and they change in meaning over time, either subtly or markedly, and sometimes they become obsolete.

Does this mean the emotions they describe also change or even disappear? Perhaps so, and it takes an effort of lexicographical archeology to find out what people in past times 'felt' when they described their feelings. In conducting such an investigation, the main corpus is documents, especially imaginative literature and drama that are by their nature designed to express and evoke emotional states. However, a shortcut is offered by consulting the monumental *Oxford English Dictionary* (OED), which is essentially a work of historical retrieval of words in the English language. It shows that many 'emotion words' are still in common usage but some have lost or changed their original meanings, such as 'melancholy', 'passion', 'sensible' and 'emotion' itself.

Some changes in language illustrate the earlier 'embodiment' of emotions. Nowadays when we hear news of something unexpected happening, we commonly say we *feel* surprised, or amazed, or astonished, or astounded. We are indicating that a 'feeling' is a cognitive state, existing in the mind rather than experienced on the body. The difference between 'amazed', 'astonished' and 'astounded' is regarded nowadays as negligible, except perhaps in degree of surprise. However, each of these words occurred in medieval and early modern English with significant differences from each other, which in turn suggests that even 'feeling' is not what it is today. 'Amazement' was to be literally a-mazed, lost in a maze, unable to find our way out. The Bastard in *King John* by William Shakespeare (1564–1616) literalizes this meaning: 'I am amazed, methinks, and lose my way/ Among the thorns and dangers of this world'.[2] 'Astonishment' meant to be in a state 'deprived of sensation, as by a blow, stunned, paralysed, deadened', in short, knocked on the head with a stone or 'a-stoned' (the modern 'stoned' is not usually seen as equal to 'astonished', yet it may be the only surviving usage from the original!)[3] One quotation in 1600 is 'A kind of fish [perhaps an electric eel] that hath power to astonish the hands of them that take it'. 'Astounded' comes from the same root. The words come from medieval French, as does 'surprise' itself which then meant something like 'overtaken'. 'Bewilder' was to lose people in a 'wild' place, or as Samuel Johnson (1709–84) defined it in his eighteenth-century dictionary, 'To lose in pathless places, to confound for want of a plain road'. A travel writer in 1790 wrote of 'An unfrequented wood, in which they might probably be bewildered till night'. The *Oxford English Dictionary* gives these meanings as now obsolete and few would associate them with their original.

Another set of words point equally to the way in which emotions could be 'felt' on the body. One meaning of 'affect' in early modern English referred to the way the body registers feelings through, for example, having butterflies in the stomach for anxiety, feeling the hairs on our head prickling for fear and so on. For example, Francis Bacon (1561–1626) in *The Advancement of Learning* titled a chapter, 'How Far the Affects and Humors of the Body do Alter or Work upon the Mind'. Today the word is barely used as a noun, but 'affection' is, though it means something rather different (fondness) from the pre-modern usage, which was richly complex, not necessarily positive, covering feeling as opposed to reason and in this sense probably the closest to our generalized word 'emotions' (whose current sense in English emerged mainly in the eighteenth century). In the King James authorized version of the Bible we find 'For this cause God gave them up unto vile affections' (*Romans* i. 26) which would not mean the same now as in 1611. Likewise, early modern 'humours' were understood as physiological facts relating to particular parts of the body, and, although this meaning is a far cry from our use of 'humorous' (amusing or comic), there is a historical connection that can be traced – a humorous person was one whose behaviour demonstrated an overbalance of a particular bodily fluid (blood, yellow bile, black bile, phlegm) that led to the manifestation of a pronounced temperament (sanguine, choleric, melancholy, peaceful respectively), which was considered incongruous or funny. 'Passion' had several meanings, one primarily religious and another a medical condition indicating an extreme imbalance of a dangerous mental state, analogous to what we would call a neurosis or obsession. Extreme jealousy or unmotivated anger, for example, could be passions that needed medical attention. If we say somebody is 'passionate about football,' we are not suggesting the fan is literally 'fanatic' or ill but simply highly interested. We usually reserve the word to describe sexual love, which again these days is not generally considered an illness.

Many other 'false friends' could be adduced, indicating not only the embodiment of emotions but also, for example, the centrality of religion in early societies. Again, 'passion' is an example, for 'the passion of Christ' had, and still has amongst believers, a specific religious meaning of the final stages in Christ's life leading up to his crucifixion. 'Enthusiasm', until the nineteenth century, was more like a state of being possessed by a god, or supernaturally-inspired, which in the eighteenth century was attached to wild-eyed poets and unorthodox religious or political zealots who were considered dangerous. 'Pity' was originally closer to 'piety', through its root, *pietas*, Latin for 'dutifulness', later merging with Christian thought, as proper devotion demonstrated through compassion for humanity. 'Shame' and its derivatives, like 'shamefaced' and the rarer 'shamefast', today indicate responses to embarrassing secular circumstances, but in earlier times were overwhelmingly associated with religious states.

Many other words that are still used to describe emotions can be seen as 'false friends' when traced back to their historical usages: admiration, confusion, fury, indignation, perturbation, sensibility, wonder, zeal (with its intriguing etymological connection to 'jealous') and many others. It is fascinating to trace their conceptual evolution. But we may have seen enough evidence already to allow us to adapt L.P. Hartley's famous opening sentence in *The Go-Between* (1953) to, 'The past is a foreign country: they *feel* things differently there'.

Further reading

Crystal, D., *Think on My Words: Exploring Shakespeare's Language* (Cambridge: Cambridge University Press 2008)

—explains the term 'false friends' (*faux amis*) in linguistics and provides examples from Shakespeare.

Frevert, U., C. Bailey, P. Eitler, B. Gammerl, B. Hitzer, M. Pernau, M. Scheer, A. Schmidt and N. Verheyen, *Emotional Lexicons: Continuity and Change in the Vocabulary of Feeling 1700–2000* (Oxford: Oxford University Press, 2014)

—offers a broad historical analysis of the language of emotion in the more recent periods, including German, French and English.

White, R.S., '"False Friends": Affective semantics in Shakespeare', *Shakespeare* 8 (2012), 286–99.

—builds on Crystal's account and offers more detailed analysis.

Notes

1 E. Sullivan, *Beyond Melancholy: Sadness and Selfhood in Renaissance England* (Oxford: Oxford University Press, 2016)

2 William Shakespeare, *King John* 4.3.141–2. Quotations from Shakespeare taken from *William Shakespeare: The Complete Works*, ed. Stanley Wells and Gary Taylor, 2nd Edition (Oxford: Clarendon Press, 2005)

3 Unless otherwise indicated, lexical information and explanatory quotations in this article are taken from online *Oxford English Dictionary* (2010): www.oed.com.

II.2 Emotion

Patricia Simons

During the early modern period, the word 'emotion' focused on violence and disruptive motion (including political movements and migration). It was a disorderly, extreme and physical more than psychic quality. By examining its etymology and entry into the English language, we gain a better understanding of the term's initial meaning and ongoing impact.

'Emotion' is based on the Latin verbs *moveo* and *emoveo*, meaning to move out or away, or to dislodge, to stir, to disturb. This notion of physical movement and commotion is embedded in early European vernacular uses, which, even when referring to internal emotional states, inherit the sense that emotions are non-normative and involve disturbance, agitation and change.

Despite its Latin ancestry, the word *emozione* only entered Italian in the early eighteenth century. Nevertheless, in 1579, when the *Oxford English Dictionary* claims 'emotion' was first printed in English ('great stirres and emocions in Lombardye'), it was as the translation of several Italian words. That source, Geffray Fenton's rendition of the history of Italy by Francesco Guicciardini (1483–1540), commonly understood *moto* to signify 'emocion'.[1] According to the contemporary Italian-English dictionary of John Florio (1533–1625), *moto* meant 'a motion, a mooving, a gesture, a wagging, a motion or cause of stirring of any thing, a passion of a mans minde'.[2]

'Emocion' was also what Fenton supplied for such Italian words as *sollevazione* (stirring, provoking, insurrection) and *movimento* (a moving or stirring, the antecedent to what we now mean by political movement). Rome was 'full of feares & emocion' when the populace was 'in grandissima sollevatione & terrore'.[3] Other towns were inclined to 'emocion and insurrection', what Guicciardini called 'grandissimi movimenti'.[4] The sense of 'emotion' as a subjective experience or 'passion' was somewhat evident in its first appearances in English, but overshadowed by a focus on physical movement and active demonstration, usually of a tumultuous and assertive, even militaristic or subversive, kind.

Fenton actually introduced the word to English readers four years earlier, in *Golden Epistles* (London, 1575), a translation of Spanish letters written by Antonio de Guevara (*c.* 1481–1545), though the Englishman relied on a French translation, as he did for Guicciardini's history. Discussing the security of pious vocation in 1541, at a time of religious upheaval and Protestant challenge, the Catholic Guevara drew an analogy between Cain and men who changed faith, being dissolute, inconstant vagabonds who lived in 'sedition and Emotion'.[5] The French phrase was 'sont tousiours esmeuz', from the Spanish 'siempre andan alterados', meaning those who were always changeable and unstable.[6] Rootless, 'wandering prophanly from place to place' and with 'a mind wavering and inconstant seeking change of church', a treasonous, cursed cleric was both in constant motion and unstable in his mind.[7]

Motion was the visible, undeniable evidence of disloyalty and religious change, states that in modern times would be understood instead as primarily interior, invisible and emotional. Writing of religious conviction as though it was a physical state of location and steadfastness, Guevara characterized emotion in terms of perfidious instability. The French word that was later turned into 'sedition & Emotion' was 'esmeuz'. Randle Cotgrave defined 'esmotion' in terms similar to those used by Florio: 'An emotion, commotion, sudden, or turbulent stirring; an agitation of the spirit, violent motion of the thoughts, vehement inclination of the mind'.[8] Nevertheless, a degree of linguistic difference is evident. The Italian version of Guevara's letter underplayed emotion, describing Cain's great betrayal and turning briefly to inquietude but skipping the phrase about changeability, going on with Guevara's following sentence about moving from cloister to cloister, dormitory to dormitory, cell to cell, all physical signs of inconstancy.[9]

Fenton used the word often, occasionally indicating its personal sense. When an Emperor was disturbed by what he perceived to be insufficient support from the Pope, he 'fell into no little emotion & trouble of mind', an adaptation of the Italian observation that his soul was much moved ('commosso molto d'animo').[10] Far more common, though, was the association of the word with war, incursion, insurrection, tumult, trouble and 'stirres', a word Fenton chose with particular frequency, referring to turmoil or incitement. Two reprints each of the *Golden Epistles* (1577, 1582) and the *Historie of Guicciardin* (1599, 1618) further disseminated the word. It continued to appear through the medium of translation, next printed in 1594 within the English version of Louis Le Roy's French compendium, *Of the interchangeable course, or variety of things in the whole world*. There the Tartars had caused a 'great emotion and mutation of humaine things', that is, the word was again about movement, in this case mass migration and physical upturning.[11]

To Florio, however, the more established 'passion' was a better term for our modern sense of 'emotion' perhaps in part because it was endowed with the authority of Thomas Aquinas' thirteenth-century study of the *passiones* of the soul.[12] In 1603 the Anglo-Italian linguist prefaced his English translation of the French essays of Michel de Montaigne (1533–92) by acknowledging that some readers might find terms like emotion 'uncouth'.[13] Dixon has mistakenly understood this to be the first English use of the French term, implying that the coarse nature of the word had to do with its novelty. However, it was already known in English, and Florio named eleven other words that were similarly regarded as somewhat unfamiliar, most of them derived from French.

Florio's aversion may have had something to do with the word's violent and rather plebian connotations, for it usually referred to masses of troops or anonymous people, or disturbances and rebellion amongst the general populace. Furthermore, 'emotion', but also 'passion', pointed to what were considered unnatural, excessive states. Florio defined *passione* as the equivalent of physical disruption, about grief, 'perturbation of minde', or trouble, and also disease that brought the body 'out of temper, being an enemie to the naturall constitution of the bodie'.[14]

Perhaps Florio found the term 'emotion' too loose. The word's capacious portmanteau function is signalled by Fenton's willingness to have it stand many times for several different words employed in his Italian and French sources, or for him to add it for extra emphasis. His 'great stirres and emocions in Lombardye' is a particularly dramatic reading. The Italian referred to far from minor torments, the French to strong actions.[15]

Body language was regarded as a visual and communicative scheme more than a personal or psychic one. Art theory, articulated by authors such as Leon Battista Alberti (1404–72), Leonardo da Vinci (1452–1519) and Gian Paolo Lomazzo (1538–92), stated that movements of the soul were made known by movements of the body.[16] They were adapting the principles of ancient writers like Aristotle, Cicero and Quintilian, who discussed emotion in relation to public address and persuasion, seeking to convince juries and provoke reactions. The word 'emotion' carried with it the fundamental idea of visibility and emphatic communication, for artists, orators and warriors in particular, but it was also a mode of public performance and spectacle at moments like mourning, acclaim or protest. Even as language and habits were modified and augmented over the course of the seventeenth century, with increased or new attention to concepts such as 'the passions', much of the expansion was about more nuanced, acceptable and codified modes of visualization (especially *affetti*) and practice (for example, the delicacy of sentiment).

The association of 'emotion' with a lack of social control or personal management later fostered its link with Romantic rebellion and individual liberty, a heritage still operative today. The observation that someone is 'emotional' ties into these political and cultural assumptions, along with the ongoing influence of the theory Florio reported about physiological balance, for the charge implies that the person is overly excitable or hysterical. Behaviour is considered too feminine, too plebian, too irrational, too unregulated. Rather than a simple, power-ridden duality between mind and body, psyche and corporeality, the history of the word 'emotion' offers the opportunity to consider the interface between neuroscience, history and art history.

That historians and psychologists cannot agree on a common set of feelings that count as emotions indicates the degree to which the terminology and hence social and cultural constructions of the rubric 'emotion' need to be further analysed rather than assumed to refer to a set of universal conditions.

Further reading

Dixon, T., '"Emotion": The history of a keyword in crisis', *Emotion Review* 4, 4 (2012), 338–44.

—overviews the use of the word 'emotion' in English from the seventeenth century, focusing on the nineteenth century.

Montagu, J., *The Expression of the Passions: The Origin and Influence of Charles Le Brun's 'Conférence sur l'expression générale et particulière'* (New Haven: Yale University Press, 1994)

—concentrates on the lecture about expression delivered by a French painter and academician in 1688, but it also surveys earlier artistic theory and provides a useful bibliography.

Rosenwein, B.H., 'Emotion words', in D. Boquet and P. Nagy (eds), *Le sujet des émotions au moyen âge* (Paris: Beauchesne, 2009), 93–106.

—by studying the cultural and philosophical context of various terms used by medieval authors, points out that there is only some degree of overlap with modern notions of 'emotion'.

Notes

1 F. Guicciardini, *La historia d'Italia* (Florence, 1561), 44, 195; G. Fenton (trans.), *The Historie of Guicciardin* (London, 1579), 31, 138.
2 J. Florio, *Worlde of Wordes* (London, 1598), 234.
3 Fenton (trans.), *The Historie of Guicciardin*, 62, 88.
4 Ibid., 135; Guicciardini, *La historia d'Italia*, 190.
5 Fenton (trans.), *Golden Epistles* (London, 1575), 180r.
6 J. de Guterry (trans.), *Les Epistres dorees* (Lyon, 1578), II, 88; A. de Guevara, *Epistolas familiares* (Valladolid, 1541), II, 33v.
7 Fenton (trans.), *Golden Epistles*, 180r.
8 R. Cotgrave, *Dictionarie of the French and English tongues* (London, 1611), s.v. [unpaginated].
9 *Lettere* (Venice, 1591), II, 68 (no translator is given).
10 Fenton (trans.), *The Historie of Guicciardin*, 890; Guicciardini, *La historia d'Italia*, 1199.
11 R. Ashley (trans.), *Of the interchangeable course, or variety of things in the whole world* (London, 1594), 104r.
12 B.H. Rosenwein, 'Emotion words', in D. Boquet and P. Nagy (eds), *Le sujet des émotions au Moyen Âge* (Paris: Beauchesne, 2009), 104–5.
13 J. Florio (trans.), *Essayes* (London, 1603), unpaginated preface.
14 Florio, *Worlde of Wordes*, 261.
15 'Non mediocremente travagliavano', Guicciardini, *La historia d'Italia*, 133; 'remuoit desia bien fort', in J. Chomedey (trans.), *Histoire d'Italie* (Paris, 1568), 36r.
16 For example, L.B. Alberti, *On Painting and On Sculpture*, (ed. and trans.) C. Grayson (London: Phaidon, 1972), 80–3; *Leonardo on Painting*, (ed.) M. Kemp (New Haven: Yale University Press, 1989), 144, 146; G.P. Lomazzo, *Idea of the Temple of Painting*, (trans.) J.J. Chai (University Park: Pennsylvania State University Press, 2013), 73, 102, 155–7.

II.3 Humoral theory

Danijela Kambaskovic

The Latin noun *umor* denotes moisture. Although this meaning has been lost from the modern English noun *humour*, we do not have to go further than its adjectival form, *humid*, to find it again. This helps us conceptualize the fundamental link between the fluids in our bodies and our health and disposition – 'constitution' or 'complection'[1] – which was the crucial medical paradigm of civilized Europe and Asia for almost 20 centuries and the basis for pre-modern medical practice and theories of mind. As humoral theory offers a framework to imagine bodily liquids as causes of emotions and emotional manifestations and behaviours, it is of particular importance for the discipline of the history of emotions.

The origins of the theory are in ancient Greek medicine. Hippocrates (*c.* 450–*c.* 370 BCE) proposed that the human body is governed by four humours: blood (Lat. *sanguis*), yellow bile (Gr. χολη, *chole*), phlegm (Gr. φληγμα, *phlegma*) and black bile (Gr. μελας χολη, *melas chole*). When these humours are in balance, the human body is healthy, and the mind sane; but when one humour begins to dominate, this results in the formation of distinct temperaments, named after the dominant humour ('sanguine', 'choleric', 'melancholic' and 'phlegmatic'), often also associated with various mental and physical disorders. Their symptoms are consistent, and allow for diagnosis and treatment. Galen (129–*c.* 200) posited additional five temperaments (mixtures of the main four), for a total of nine.

Gail Kern Paster has argued that it is impossible for a modern-day reader to fully comprehend the plays of William Shakespeare (1564–1616) without consciously resisting the influence of post-Cartesian abstraction and remembering that the view of emotion as embodied, based on humoral theory, was very real for pre-modern writers and audiences[2]. The link is perhaps a little more obvious in a subgenre of Renaissance drama called 'Comedy of Humours', featuring plays based on comic portrayals of stereotypical (male) characters[3].

Each bodily humour was related to one of the four elements, earth, fire, water and air, and each of those, in turn, was characterized by a unique combination of heat and moisture, also applicable to humours. The element of air, considered warm and moist, was related to blood and the sanguine temperament; fire, warm and dry, corresponded to yellow bile and the choleric temperament; water, cold and moist, corresponded to phlegm and the phlegmatic temperament; and earth, warm and wet, to black bile and the melancholic temperament. The link between elements and bodily humours stood also for the link between the individual with the order within his body and mind (the microcosm) and the natural and political orders (the macrocosm). Poignant illustrations of correspondences between individual and universal disturbances can be found in Shakespeare's plays (see, for example, *Troilus and Cressida*, I, 3; *Macbeth*, II, 4; *Julius Caesar* II, 1; *King Lear*, III, 2).[4]

In his handbook, *The optick glasse of humors* (1607), early modern English proto-psychologist Thomas Walkington (d. 1621) describes sanguine men as tall, sporting a full head of hair and beard 'commonly amber-coloured', 'very affable in speech', gracious and pleasantly witty – good at 'quipping without bitter taunting'. Sanguine men are 'liberally minded' and fiercely loyal, 'chained to the links of true amitie . . . except on a capitall discontent'. On the downside, they are also 'dullards and fooles' without 'a dram of discretion'.[5]

In his *Spiritual physicke to cure the diseases of the soule arising from superfluitie of choler* (1600), John Downame (1571–1652) defines the choleric temperament, caused by an excess of yellow bile, as 'the disease of impaciencie'.[6] In a later treatise focusing on anger (1609), Downame specifies different levels of anger, distinguishes between its 'lawful use' and 'unlawful abuse' and offers – in 10 chapters – various remedies for it, including handy 'remedys to cure anger in others'.[7] Prefiguring modern-day research on psychosomatic illness associated with stress, Walkington and Downame both describe negative physical and mental effects of the condition. As choler 'infectes the veines', Walkington writes, the heat of anger 'shortens the [patient's] life by drying vp the radical moisture'.[8]

The danger of phlegm, on the other hand, lay in its excessive moisture, which was believed to be able to 'extin|guish the naturall heate in man', clog 'the poores of the braine' and hinder 'the course of the bloud, cor|rupting the spirits [and] . . . bringing a morti|fying cold'.[9] Yet a moderate phlegmatic imbalance may have been desirable, since phlegm was thought to be 'of al the humours . . . the best, for it is a dulcet humour . . . changed into the essence of blood . . . and serues especially for the nutriment of . . . the braine'.[10]

Melancholy, caused by an excess of black bile, was the subject of innumerable treatises identifying many sub-types, such as scholar's or lover's melancholy. Melancholic patients were believed to be 'in bondage to many ridiculous passions, ima | gining that they see and feele such things, as no man els can either perceiue or touch' and acting 'with greate timorousnes and sorrow'.[11] The condition was believed to have been accompanied by delusions, compulsive-obsessive behaviours and depressed mood.

Significant treatises specialising in melancholy include *A Treatise of Melancholie* (1586) by Timothie Bright (1551–1615), probably read by Shakespeare, in which pleasure is proposed as an important aspect of treatment. This work addresses carers and servants of the patient as its primary audience, which indicates that Bright associated melancholy with the higher social strata. The trend of glamourizing melancholy emerged when Marsilio Ficino (1433–99), influential fifteenth-century Florentine scholar and Neoplatonist, made the link between melancholy and scholarly genius in his *De Vita Libri Tres* (1489). *The Anatomy of Melancholy* (1621) by Robert Burton (1577–1640) is the most comprehensive theory of melancholy, and describes – in three large tomes – hundreds of types and sub-types of melancholy with relevant treatments. André Du Laurens (1558–1609) sees melancholy as a direct cause of certain physical diseases, as explained in *A Discourse of the Preseruation of the Sight: of Melancholike Diseases; of Rheumes, and of Old Age* (1599); and the *Erotomania or A treatise discoursing of the essence, causes, symptomes, prognosticks, and cure of love, or erotique melancholy* (published 1610, in English 1640) by Jacques Ferrand (1575–*c.* 1630) specializes in love sickness, describes its various symptoms and proposes increasingly bizarre treatments.

The development of scientific knowledge in the seventeenth and eighteenth centuries often uncovered facts which clashed with the humoral theory. Nevertheless, the theory was so deeply ingrained in medical tradition that attempts were repeatedly made to integrate and reconcile it with the new findings. Bloodletting, a medical treatment resulting from beliefs associated with humoral theory, remained the most popular medical procedure used to treat a wide range of physical and mental conditions well into the nineteenth century.

Further reading

Arikha, N., *Passions and Tempers: A History of the Humours* (New York: HarperCollins, 2007)
—a good general historical overview of the humours, from their ancient Greek origin and medieval and early modern heyday to the present-day traces in current health fads.

Lindemann, M., *Medicine and Society in Early Modern Europe* (Cambridge: Cambridge University Press, 1999)
—offering an introduction to health and healing in Europe from 1500 to 1800, is a good general resource.

Trevor, D., *The Poetics of Melancholy in Early Modern England* (Cambridge: Cambridge University Press, 2005)
—a reappraisal of the association between melancholy and life of the intellect, particularly writing.

Notes

1 T. Walkington, *The optick glasse of humors . . . a golden temper wherein the foure complections sanguine, cholericke, phlegmaticke, melancholicke are succinctly painted forth, and their externall intimates laide open . . . by which euery one may iudge of what complection he is* (London, 1607), 58.

2 G.K. Paster, *Humoring the Body: Emotions and the Shakespearean Stage* (Chicago: University of Chicago Press, 2004). William Shakespeare, *The Norton Shakespeare* (gen. ed. S. Greenblatt) (New York: Norton, 1997)

3 Premodern description of temperament in medical treatises and art always relate to men, with the notable (and clearly delineated) exception of greensickness, of maidens and widows caused by the womb's craving for semen, described by Robert Burton in his *Anatomy of Melancholy* (Oxford, 1621)

4 Shakespeare, *The Norton Shakespeare,* (ed.) Greenblatt (New York: Norton, 1997)
5 Walkington, *The optick glasse of humors,* 59–60.
6 John Downame, *Spiritual physicke to cure the diseases of the soule, arising from superfluitie of choler* (London, 1600)
7 Downame, *Foure treatises tending to disswade all Christians from foure no lesse hainous then common sinnes . . . Whereunto is annexed a treatise of anger* (London, 1609)
8 Walkington, *The optick glasse of humors,* 65.
9 Ibid., 61–3.
10 Ibid., 61.
11 Ibid., 69.

II.4 The senses

Herman Roodenburg

Can we leave out the senses when we study the emotions? Clearly, historians can. Over the last decades they started a booming history of the emotions and a booming history of the senses, each with its own conferences, even its own research centres, book series and primers. Were they still with us, early modern scholars would be surprised. For them (and probably for most people living in the sixteenth, seventeenth and eighteenth centuries), to talk about the emotions meant to talk about sensory perception. In this entry I consider three examples, three contemporary domains involved with the emotions, those of physiology, preaching and painting.

As we know from the many painted allegories, early modern people used to distinguish the five senses of sight, hearing, taste, touch and smell. But the paintings only tell half of the story. They also knew such sensory perceptions that we now like to label as proprioception, mechanoreception, nociception and thermoreception. These were all ranged under the sense of touch. In addition, until roughly 1700 most sensory theory still comprised the four or five 'inner senses': the common sense, the fantasy and/or imagination, the estimative forces and the memory. Since Avicenna they were all situated in the brain, in the three ventricles already described by the Roman physician Galen in his *De Usu Partium*.

The common sense was believed to distinguish, coordinate and unify all the sense data coming through the five outer senses. As Aristotle already argued in his *De Partibus Animalium*, through this master sense, the 'sense of sensing', humans could integrate two or more senses into a single mental image. To use his own example, what is simultaneously white and sweet becomes sugar. But the common sense may always err, hence its close cooperation with the fantasy, the imagination and the estimative faculty, which assess all mental images before storing them in the memory, in Galen's third ventricle, at the back of the brain. Various drawings depict this whole inner circuit, including the sensory nerves thought to be involved.[1]

In the sixteenth century, the famous anatomist Andreas Vesalius (1514–64) challenged these Aristotelo-Galenist ideas but neither he nor later scholars, not even René Descartes (1596–1650), came up with a stronger sensory theory. In fact, the older views fitted in perfectly with the period's emotion (or 'passion') theories. As it was phrased by the French physician Ambroise Paré (1510–90), 'For it is first necessary, before wee be moved by any Passions, that the senses in their proper seates, in which they are seldome deceived, apprehend the objects, and strait as messengers carrie them to the common sense, which sends their conceived formes to all the faculties. And then, that each facultie, as a Iudge may a fresh examine the whole matter, how it is, and conceive in the presented objects some shew of good, or ill, to bee desired, or shunned.'[2] In other words, in his physiological views and those of most of his colleagues the emotions were always moulded by the inner senses (Paré's 'faculties'), the common sense in the first place. As Elena Carrera and others point out, this mind-body interaction, the recognition of the emotions as having a cognitive dimension, also qualifies the determinism, frequently assumed by historians of the emotions, of the four bodily humours.[3]

In a classic essay Barbara H. Rosenwein rightly criticized Johan Huizinga (and also early cultural historians such as Marc Bloch, Lucien Febvre and Norbert Elias) for presenting a 'grand narrative' of progressive emotional restraint. Depicting the Middle Ages as a 'convenient foil for modernity', they identified its mental universe with the 'emotional life of a child: unadulterated, violent, public, unashamed'.[4] Dismissing their 'hydraulic' model of the emotions, seeing these as forces always welling up, always striving for release, Rosenwein argued for a cognitivist approach, viewing the emotions as acts of consciousness, comparable to judgements or appraisals, and thus open to historical investigation. As, however, suggested by Monique Scheer, in detaching the emotions from the body, her own approach has its limitations as well.[5] Indeed, it tends to overlook Huizinga's exquisite feel for the late Middle Ages' emotional complexity, its graphic interweaving of the mental, the corporeal and the sensory.

What it may overlook more specifically is the late medieval and early modern interest in *pathopoeia*, the literal 'making' of emotions where there are none. Central to the period's religious practices was the preachers' oratory, their detailed rhetorical techniques to evoke the emotions of the faithful through their outer and inner senses. Especially in their passion sermons, they went to great lengths to realize the believers' sensory and affective immersion in the biblical events. Far from expressing a 'childlike' emotional universe, as argued by Huizinga, both late medieval and early modern pulpit oratory relied on ancient rhetoric and the art of memory. Both priests and ministers wished the faithful to develop the strongest mental images of Christ's suffering or any other biblical event, to have the images lastingly anchored, always open for prayer and meditation, in the memory. Vividness (Gr. *enargeia*; Lat. *demonstratio* or *evidentia*) was the vital rhetorical quality here. When told of the Passion, of Christ's scourging or his crucifixion on Golgotha hill, the audience should have the illusion of presence, of being there and then on the spot, with all their senses alert.[6]

Such working of the emotions through all the believers' senses was still the highest goal in seventeenth-century and much of eighteenth-century preaching, even (and *pace* Max Weber) in the preaching of the English Puritans or the continental Calvinists. Even they, as shown by Debora Shuger, adhered to the 'grand style', the contemporary pulpit style revealing 'a deeply favourable view of the emotions' and always grafted onto sensory 'vividness', on depicting the scriptural events in such an engaging way that, in the words of a widespread Calvinist tract on preaching, 'the listener, carried outside himself, seems to behold the event as if placed in its midst'.[7] Much depended on the priest's or minister's delivery, on his voice, countenance and gestures and on his own emotional involvement, his auto-affection. Often Horace was quoted ('If you would have me weep, you must first feel grief yourself'). Indeed, a weeping audience was often deemed a preacher's highest praise.

A bit surprisingly, most historians of early modern emotions seem to have missed the central importance of affective rhetoric, but so have most church historians, music historians and even art historians. Yet vividness and its crafting of the viewers' emotions through both their outer and inner senses was a standard notion among all painters and sculptors. Rembrandt van Rijn (1606–69), for instance, wrote about *beweechgelickheit*, referring both to the vividness of the motions depicted and to their ability, through this vividness, to touch the heart of the beholder. He was a master of the art, a true 'pathopoios'.

Rembrandt's views have been linked to those of the Dutch philologist Franciscus Junius (1589–1677), whose influential art theory drew heavily on ancient rhetoric and its hammering on vividness. He praised Cicero's notion of *evidentia*, of evoking presence ('as if we were by at the doing of the things imagined') and through such bodily and sensory engagement evoking the emotions. Similarly, Rembrandt's pupil Samuel van Hoogstraten, adopting Junius' insights, argued that painters aiming to rouse the emotions should engage the viewer 'as if he were one of the bystanders'.[8]

Rembrandt himself created such presence by, for instance and most theatrically, depicting swords hanging in mid-air. But that was a modest and far less tactile vividness as that displayed two centuries earlier, in all those blood-soaked images of Christ's agony. The most emotional but also most innovative painter of his time, he even sought to make the viewer hear an absent voice, to hear its mute *beweechgelickheit*, its touching of the heart. Viewing his portrait of the Mennonite preacher Cornelis Anslo and his wife (1641), we notice the celebrated preacher's countenance and gesture. But the true subject may be his wife's hearing and, grasping her handkerchief, her being moved by him.

Further reading

Dickey, S. and H. Roodenburg (eds), *The Passions in the Arts of the Early Modern Netherlands* (Zwolle: Waanders, 2010)

—the first volume to focus on the emotions in Netherlandish painting, it contains several essays discussing issues of affective rhetoric and embodied response.

Quiviger, F., *The Sensory World of Italian Renaissance Art* (London: Reaktion Books, 2010)

—a fine introduction to the senses' primary role in art.

Roodenburg, H. (ed.). *A Cultural History of the Senses in the Renaissance* (London: Bloomsbury, 2014)

—part of a six-volume history of the senses, contains several chapters adopting a historical phenomenology of the senses, the emotions and embodiment.

Notes

1 D. Heller-Roazen, *The Inner Touch: Archaeology of a Sensation* (New York: Zone Books, 2007); F. Quiviger, *The Sensory World of Italian Renaissance Art* (London: Reaktion Books, 2010), 17–19, 105.

2 Cited in E. Carrera, 'Anger and the Mind-Body Connection in Medieval and Early Modern Medicine', in Carrera (ed.), *Emotions and Health, 1200–1700* (Leiden: Brill, 2013), 124.

3 Ibid., 95–146; see also J.R. Solomon, 'You've Got to Have Soul: Understanding the Passions in Early Modern Culture', in S. Pender and N.S. Struever (eds), *Rhetoric and Medicine in Early Modern Europe* (Farnham: Ashgate, 2012), 195–228.

4 B.H. Rosenwein, 'Worrying about emotions in history', *American Historical Review* 107, 3 (2002), 827–36.

5 M. Scheer, 'Are emotions a kind of practice (and is that what makes them have a history?): a Bourdieuan approach to understanding emotion', *History and Theory* 51, 2 (2012), esp. 195–204.

6 H.F. Plett, *Enargeia in Classical Antiquity and the Early Modern Age: The Aesthetics of Evidence* (Leiden: Brill, 2012), 7–10, 115; H. Roodenburg, 'Empathy in the making: crafting the believers' emotions in the late medieval low countries', *BMGN – Low Countries Historical Review* 129, 2 (2014), 42–62.

7 D.K. Shuger, *Sacred Rhetoric: The Christian Grand Style in the English Renaissance* (Princeton: Princeton University Press, 1988), 91; cf. S. Karant-Nunn, *The Reformation of Feeling: Shaping the Religious Emotions in Early Modern Germany* (Oxford: Oxford University Press, 2010); A. Hunt, *The Art of Hearing: English Preachers and Their Audiences, 1590–1640* (Cambridge: Cambridge University Press, 2010), 82–94; A. Ryrie, *Being Protestant in Reformation Britain* (Oxford: Oxford University Press, 2013), 17–26.

8 T. Weststeijn, 'Between Mind and Body: Painting the Inner Movements according to Samuel van Hoogstraten and Franciscus Junius', in S. Dickey and H. Roodenburg (eds), *The Passions in the Arts of the Early Modern Netherlands* (Zwolle: Waanders, 2010), 263–83.

II.5 Pain and suffering

Javier Moscoso

In early modern Europe, physical pain and spiritual suffering were everywhere. They became constitutive elements of private and public life, present in all forms of social practices: from the education of children to conjugal love; from the treatment given to animals to the exercise of political dignity; and from judicial interrogations to healing and mourning practices. It was also at that moment that philosophers began to understand pain as a central phenomenon that originated in the brain. The effects and influence of the 1664 publication *De Homine* by René Descartes (1596–1650) lasted well into the first half of the twentieth century. But while the history of ideas may give some continuity to our subject, the cultural dimension of physical pain and emotional suffering goes far beyond the philosophical or scientific efforts to conceptualize them. This is one of the dilemmas that historians face: the diversity of pain and suffering seems to contradict the unity that, at least in principle, all narratives require.

Early modern suffering experiences, expressions and practices cannot be understood without first taking into consideration the nature of the substances employed to alleviate physical suffering. Well into the mid-nineteenth century, the procedures for palliating acute pain mainly consisted in the ingestion of some substance that was likely to dull consciousness. In the early sixteenth century, only four or five substances with narcotic properties were known, namely, mandrake, cannabis, opium or opium tincture (laudanum) and, of course, alcohol. Along with these, the plethora of alternative popular remedies may give us some indication on the dialectic of hope and desperation that reigned in those days. In the case of toothache, for example, some of the palliative procedures included the use of ointments and spices, principally cinnamon and cloves, as well as hot brandy, laudanum and opium. Some physicians, such as Ambroise Paré (*c.* 1510–90), recommended gargling urine to alleviate the pain, whilst the anonymous author of the *Pious Surgeon* (1654) suggested applying a filling made with vesicant substances. Needless to say, their efficiency in removing pain was limited. The methods of tooth extraction were not much more successful. To alleviate suffering, some surgeons recommended 'wild cat excrement', while the first edition of the *Medicine of the Poor* (1671) treatise considered nicotine spirit or dog earwax to be virtually miraculous remedies. In the eighteenth century, the English surgeon John Hunter (1723–93) suggested that some treatments against pain could act through the application of a stimulus to another part of the body. Thus, 'burning the ear with hot irons has on occasions been an effective remedy against toothache', he wrote.[1] The proliferation of these kind of remedies should be understood within a social logic of hope and resistance. We may also ask to what extent physical pain – and the medical histories for its treatment – was embedded with cultural values and social expectations. In the case of the mother of Louis XIV (1638–1715), Anne of Austria (b. 1601), who died of breast cancer in 1666, the value and intensity of her physical agony were measured against a crucible of religious values and social expectations. Her own understanding of the disease was framed within a religious context. She suffered while she read *The Imitation of Christ*, a devotional book. She had in fact first encountered cancer when she witnessed how some nuns at Val-de-Grâce had died of this disease. From that moment onwards she had been deeply frightened and horrified by this malady, so dreadful to her imagination. On the one hand, the memories of her old weaknesses bolstered her will to suffer; on the other, her sufferings were endured mainly through the acceptance and repentance of her past vanities.

This theatrical form of expressing and experiencing pain has many other different examples. In the case of menstrual pain, treatments such as bloodletting, hot baths, enemas and sedatives were frequently administered, coupled with patience and resignation. Again, pain and fear were counterbalanced by promises and expectations of recovery. Similarly, popular remedies abounded as far as the pains of childbirth were concerned. In some cases, relics and reliquaries were arranged around the room surrounding the birthing mother. In others, a concoction was prepared using the head of a deer. While some women asked for holy water, others drank large quantities of alcohol, which were shared equally between the woman giving birth and the midwives who were present. Early treatises on midwifery allow us to see different social standards regarding the expression or repression on pain depending on social status. While most women were encouraged to cry out their pains, queens and other aristocrats were supposed to bear childbirth pains in silence. Before the arrival of chloroform, their pain was interpreted not only as an inevitable consequence of a natural action, but also as a punishment imposed on women after Eve's expulsion from Paradise. Even after chloroform was incorporated into the process of childbirth in the mid-nineteenth century, arguments were still made against its use under the pretext that it operated against the divine mandate, as was laid down in the Book of Genesis: 'in pain you will bring forth children'.

Although the visualization of physical suffering was not exclusive to early modern Europe, it became a central part of the cultural practices of the period, in a way that is perhaps only comparable to the proliferation of images of extreme pain that have characterized the second half of the twentieth and the beginning of the twenty-first centuries. From the representation of martyrdom to the illustration of cruelty, early modern Europeans had to cope with the gruesome depiction of bodily torments, at times popularized through the printing press. Besides books and pamphlets, related to religious wars or campaigns of colonization, representations of physical violence ranged from wall paintings, frescos and murals to sculptures, miniatures, woodcuts and engravings. On many occasions, these representations were part of a pedagogy of passions, in the sense that they came to inform the mechanisms of their emotional expression and repression. Along with overwhelming presence of the iconographic depiction of the Passion of Christ, the spectacle of suffering within judicial doctrine, political authority, religious struggles and anatomical treatises was expressed repeatedly through a finite set of iconographic elements related to the mutilation, violation and dissection of the body. Despite this diversity, the representation of pain remained faithful to two guiding principles: first, pain was shown as reiterative, monotonous and interminable; second, it was expressed in its greatest and most extreme dimension.

The educational value of pain could be found in judicial and religious practices, where physical and emotional suffering were understood as the proper means to obtain truth or salvation. In some cases, like the iconographic program for the Great Hall in the palace at Binche (in modern-day Belgium), the representation of bodily punishments was meant to serve as a warning for those who rebelled against established order, like the Titans portrayed in the canvasses. From at least as early as the thirteenth century, European legal systems made use of pain and suffering as a way to obtain confessions. Based largely on Roman law, the judicial use of pain was never understood as a form of torture, but as a legitimate way to gain access to the truth.

The search for pain as an instrument for the *Imitatio Christi* also reached a notable level of intensity after the fourteenth century. Even though its origins can be traced to the Low Middle Ages, the deliberate search for pain as a form of theatrically recreating the Passion of Christ lasted well into the early modern period. Giuseppe di Copertino (1603–68), for example, managed to reduce his body to a skeleton through penance. His rigorous sense of existence led him to carry out a systematic and bloody destruction of his body, at times flagellating himself to the bone. Similarly, Francesco di Girolamo (1642–1716) beat himself with such force that he invariably ended up losing a great deal of blood. In Southern Europe, where there is an abundance of works dedicated to penance, the first mystics of the sixteenth century described earthly existence in terms of torment. This is the message contained in the *Agony of the Passage to Death* by Alejo de Venegas (1497/8–1562) in 1537, where life is interpreted as a 'long martyrdom'. An eagerness for pain and suffering can also be found in the *Spiritual Exercises* of Ignatius of Loyola (*c.* 1491–1556), who recommended combining 'interior' penance – the experience of guilt – with three forms of exterior penance: fasting, staying awake and punishing one's own flesh.

The various uses of pain and suffering in these different fields of practice – medicine, education, religion and the judicial system – provide a few examples from which we can gather some preliminary conclusions. First, we should take into account the overwhelming profusion of pain and suffering in early modern Europe. From both a physical and an emotional perspective, pain flooded the private and public lives of early modern citizens: from peasants, to soldiers or to priests, it affected men, women, children and animals alike. Second, many of those painful experiences were represented and understood within a form of theatricality, mainly (but not exclusively) religious, from which those in pain were able to make sense of their own sufferings, and, to a certain extent, cope with them. Finally, both the representation and the experience of pain and suffering in early modern Europe were constructive, in the sense that pain was always meant to serve a purpose, whether it be the recovery of health, the retribution of justice, the search for truth and salvation or the extraction of knowledge.

Further reading

Merback, M.B., *The Thief, The Cross and the Wheel* (London: Reaktion Books, 1999)
—for Merback, the realism of early modern depiction of pain cannot be considered a mere reflection of criminal justice; rather, representation constituted an iconic model with a great deal of pedagogic power.
Moscoso, J., *Pain. A Cultural History* (London: Palgrave Macmillan, 2012)
—considers pain and its history from the late fifteenth to the mid-twentieth century. For Moscoso, there is no suffering that does not entail a social appraisal and, by extension, a form of expression linked to cultural guidelines and expectations.
Silverman, L., *Tortured Subjects: Pain, Truth, and the Body in Early Modern France* (Chicago: The University of Chicago Press, 2001)
—remains the most influential text to date on the uses of pain and torture in early modern Europe.

Note

1 J. Hunter, *The Natural History of the Human Teeth* (1771) (London: W. Spilsbury for J. Johnson, 1803), 150.

II.6 Grammar

Ross Knecht

'A Verbe Passive,' writes John Brinsley (active 1581–1624) in his 1612 grammar manual *The Posing of the Parts*, 'betokeneth passion'.[1] This unusual definition suggests the intersection of two areas rarely associated with one another today but closely related in the early modern period: grammar and emotion. Scholars have identified two points of contact between early modern grammatical practices and the emotions: the first is the role of grammar school pedagogy in the process of early modern subject formation; the second concerns the conceptual links between grammatical and psychological models in pre- and early modern discourse. This entry will review these claims and suggest how they might be synthesized.

To begin with the acculturative role of the grammar school: in recent years, scholars such as Katharine Breen and Lynn Enterline have drawn attention to the way that the grammar school led to the acquisition of a particular *habitus*, an internalized set of habits, dispositions and values that governed one's behaviour in the world. Breen puts it thusly: 'As he acquires the *habitus* of grammar, the student does not merely learn rules but is himself regulated, made regular by the language he studies and the discipline of the classroom in which he studies'.[2] The term *habitus* invokes the sociology of Pierre Bourdieu, who argued that social reproduction and subject formation took place by means of habituated behaviours like those acquired in the schoolroom. But as Bourdieu himself borrowed the term from scholastic philosophy, it also has a basis in the period's own discourses and allows scholars to employ a simultaneously theoretical and historicist approach. Indeed, medieval and early modern schoolmasters frequently associated training in the rules of grammar with the production of orderly subjects in a way that anticipates Bourdieu. And, as Enterline shows, the *habitus* acquired through grammar school instruction had a significant emotional dimension. As the exercises of the schoolroom involved frequent declarations of the love and devotion that the student owed to the master, in addition to the ever-present fear of corporal punishment, the grammar school cultivated dispositions towards ways of feeling as well as ways of acting: 'the school's theatrical forms of corporal and verbal discipline might incline its students towards emotionally charged practices of imitation, personification, and multiple identifications in adult life'.[3]

The second relation between grammar and emotion involves the conceptual links between formal grammatical theory and the historical discourse of the passions. 'Passion', the primary term in the early modern vocabulary of feeling, is derived from the Greek *pathos* via the Latin *passio*. At its most basic, *pathos* simply denoted an instance of passive affection or suffering, a state of being-acted-upon ('passion' is closely related to the word 'passive'). *Pathos* served as a technical term in a variety of disciplines, including metaphysics, ethics, logic, psychology and grammar. It is the last two that concern us here. In ancient psychological theory, *pathos* was a passive state that the soul entered into when subjected to some outside influence; for instance, the soul of a person confronted with a terrifying object would be afflicted with the *pathos* of fear. This sense of the term generally corresponds to what we mean by 'emotion', though it carries a more strictly passive and negative connotation. *Pathos* was also a key concept in ancient grammatical theory: in early Greek grammar, *pathos* was used to describe a mode of inflection equivalent to the passive voice in English. Thus *pathos* was simultaneously a psychological state and a grammatical position, in each case indicating the passive orientation of a subject towards its object.

The association of psychological and grammatical passivity extended from the ancient to the early modern period, and it is for this reason that Brinsley defines a passive verb as that which 'betokeneth passion': the passive verb indicates, and even gives verbal form to, a state of passive affection, including such traditional emotional states as fear, desire, hope and so on. We may even see residual evidence of the association in modern English's tendency to employ the passive voice in expressions of emotion such as 'I am frightened' and 'I am moved'. In addition to this association of passion and the passive voice, grammatical theory from the ancient to the early modern period consistently connected grammatical forms to psychological states. Moods in particular were understood to lend linguistic form to psychological states: the Roman grammarian Priscian, whose views were highly influential in the medieval and early modern period, argues that the moods are *inclinationes animi*, the inclinations of the soul. Thus the imperative mood expresses an inclination to command, the optative a disposition towards hope, and so on. Medieval grammarians such as Thomas of Erfurt (active fourteenth century), who belonged to a school known as the speculative grammarians or *modistae*, developed a complex system in which grammatical forms were derived from states of the soul, which were in turn derived from structures inherent in the world. Thus the entire apparatus of Latin grammar was understood to have a psychological foundation.

While few today would accept the universalism of a scholar like Thomas, the long history of crossings and intersections between psychological and grammatical discourse suggests, in certain cases at least, important links between language and emotion. As the concept of passion was abstracted from passive statements, it makes sense to see those statements as performative rather than referential, manifesting an affective position rather than simply describing it. To declare that one *is frightened* is to orient oneself in particular way, to place oneself in a passive position in regards to an object or situation. Returning to the work of Breen and Enterline, we may see how the exercises and iterative performances of the early modern schoolroom, in which students would rehearse various grammatical forms, might help to cultivate a particular emotional *habitus*. They would not only be trained in ways of speaking, but also in the ways of feeling that coincided with them.

Further reading

Dolven, J., *Scenes of Instruction in Renaissance Romance* (Chicago: University of Chicago Press, 2007)

—artful and sensitive study of the relation between education and literature in the early modern period; its analysis of the early modern concept of 'experience' may be particularly useful to the scholars working in the history of emotions.

Enterline, L., *Shakespeare's Schoolroom: Rhetoric, Discipline, Emotion* (Philadelphia: University of Pennsylvania Press, 2012)

—important recent study that reads Shakespeare's representation of character and emotion in light of the affective pedagogical practices of the grammar school.

Halpern, R., *The Poetics of Primitive Accumulation: English Renaissance Culture and the Genealogy of Capital* (Ithaca: Cornell University Press, 1991)

—landmark Marxist study of English Renaissance culture that was among the first works to address the social role of the grammar school in a contemporary critical idiom; see in particular the first chapter, 'A Mint of Phrases: Ideology and Style Production in Tudor England'.

Notes

1 J. Brinsley, *The Posing of the Parts* (London, 1612), E3r.

2 K. Breen, *Imagining an English Reading Public, 1150–1400* (Cambridge: Cambridge University Press, 2010), 2.

3 L. Enterline, *Shakespeare's Schoolroom: Rhetoric, Discipline, Emotion* (Philadelphia: University of Pennsylvania Press, 2012), 30.

II.7 Mood

R.S. White

'Mood' has a fascinating history, showing how words in the lexicon of emotions may change their meanings over centuries. Nowadays the primary understanding is something like a persisting but eventually passing emotional state explained by an adjective: 'she is in a bad / good mood'. But in pre-modern times there were more specific meanings, some of which fell away over time, while others remained to inform modern usage. It is not to be confused with the term 'mood' used in grammar and logic, which has a different root ('mode'), only tangentially or punningly connected with the emotional sense by ingenious association (the 'imperative mood' delivered in a haughty, commanding tone, the 'subjunctive mood' offered in a quizzical or wondering tone).

Unlike many important 'emotion words' which had classical roots (such as 'passion', 'affect' and 'melancholy'), 'mood' was stolidly Anglo-Saxon and derived from the Germanic languages. In these, such as Old Frisian, Old Dutch, Old Saxon, Old High German and Old Icelandic, the primary meaning of 'mood' used singly was one which is now obsolete, 'courage': 'He hæfde mod micel' ('he had great courage') occurs in the Old English epic *Beowulf*.[1] But it is a form of courage which is out of the ordinary, demonstrating an extreme ferocity and vigour, and in this sense the word could incorporate an intensive state of feeling which bordered on anger. This adds another meaning which has been lost, a specific kind of wrath that makes one courageous in a rash sense: in *The Two Gentlemen of Verona* by William Shakespeare (1564–1616), the 'Second Outlaw' says he has been banished for having killed a man, 'a gentleman / Who, in my mood, I stabbed unto the heart'.[2] This kind of impulsive state of mind, perhaps logically, acquired another consequential association with 'arrogance'. But behind these various applications lay the implication of intensity of feeling driving one to action, so that 'mood' could also refer to passionate outbursts of grief: 'Euer sche cryed wth grete mode' (*Sir Orfeo*). In its origins, then, the word 'mood' indicated an intense state of mind, potentially angry and impelling one arrogantly to acts of violent courage, or motivating equally extreme expressions of sorrow. There are not many 'good moods' to be seen.

The meanings listed above are now more or less obsolete, or at most they could be instanced as specific moods which need more context to explain them. But what gradually came to the fore was a broader sense lying behind the various particular usages. The word described the feeling and thought process behind an action, a mental disposition which could lead to out of the ordinary behaviour. It was not limited to an action in itself, but referred to the state of mind behind a possible range of actions. In this broader sense it could refer to the transitory process of feeling itself as it changes, as opposed to stable, rational thought: 'If thou wolt take into thi mod Reason' ('if you will add to your mood, reason') as John Gower (*c.* 1330–1408) writes in *Confessio Amantis*, and sometimes it was even replaced by 'heart'.[3]

Shakespeare draws on several facets of the word's history when he uses it in a way that is recognizable to modern readers in his Sonnet 93: 'In many's looks the false heart's history / Is writ in moods and frowns and wrinkles strange'. Buckingham in *Richard III* speaks of traitors as 'moody discontented souls' and Gloucester recalls 'in [his] angry mood' stabbing Prince Edward, while Antipholus of Ephesus in *The Comedy of Errors* observes, 'My wife is in a wayward [unpredictable] mood today'.[4] Generally speaking, most of Shakespeare's examples still describe what we would say is a 'bad mood', but not necessarily: in *Julius Caesar* Antony says 'Fortune is merry, / And in this mood will give us any thing', demonstrating also the likely changeability of moods, asserted again by Gower in *Pericles* who says, 'fortune's mood / Varies again'.[5] By about 1600, then, 'mood' had acquired the meaning which is still current, which had always been implicitly present in earlier, more particularized examples, but was now accepted as the core meaning uniting all the others, defined by the *Oxford English Dictionary* as 'A prevailing but temporary state of mind or feeling; a person's humour, temper, or disposition at a particular time'.[6] Moods are also sometimes metaphorically attributed to nature, so that the sea can be calm or turbulent, clouds can be benign or threatening. Reciprocally, weather is assumed to affect human moods.

Perhaps a noticeable difference between 'then' and 'now' is that, whereas in pre-modern times 'mood' could be used on its own and be understandable (courage, anger, arrogance), today it invariably takes specific meaning from an adjectival modifier. Putting this another way, 'mood' needs to be attached to a feeling state to be completed. 'He is in a mood' is assumed to mean 'he is in a gloomy, strange, or negative mood', which assumes or requires some known explanation. For such a resonantly meaningful word, it has become almost evacuated of meaning when used alone, an emotional state without an object, as non-specific as 'emotion' itself. This may account for the plethora of common portmanteau phrases which add some specificity, such as 'mood-altering', 'mood-elevating', 'mood disorder', and 'mood music'. Most of these usages indicate the central characteristic of moods as they are known today, that they *change*. These days, for example in film theory, mood is seen as a precondition of emotion – a pervasive but undirected atmosphere or tone which, when it finds an object to which it can attach itself, becomes a 'goal-oriented' emotion. Mood can be a cue or invitation or prelude to a particularized emotional response.[7] Another significant difference is that in early times moods were not pathologized as medically-caused (unlike passions and melancholy) – it is remarkable that in the huge and encyclopedic account of diseases of the mind composed by Robert Burton (1577–1640), *The Anatomy of Melancholy* (1621), the word 'mood' appears only once in the text, in the context of the frame of mind impelling a generous act. Nowadays, however, moods can in some contexts be considered as serious medical conditions, from adolescent 'moodiness' to severe 'mood disorders' such as bipolar disorder, where the dramatic misfit between the mind's perceptions and the reality around is cause for concern and even intervention.

Further Reading

Rawnsley, C., 'Two Early Modern Usages of "Mood" to mean an Angry or Depressed State of Mind', *Emotions: Australian Research Council Centre of Excellence for the History of Emotions Online Wiki*, http://emotions.arts.uwa.edu.au/wiki/items/show/189

—Examples from Shakespeare of the word 'mood' to designate a feeling of anger or gloomy depression.

The Oxford English Dictionary in 12 volumes, now available online: www.oed.com

—compiled on historical grounds and invaluable in giving early modern meanings and usages of words, browse entries for 'mood' and derivatives.

White, R.S., 'Smiles that conceal, smiles that reveal', *Shakespeare*, 10 (2015), 1–14.

—analyses the ways in which smiling in Shakespeare is an ambiguous indicator of a character's mood.

Notes

1 *Beowulf*, line 1167.

2 William Shakespeare, *The Two Gentlemen of Verona*, 4, 1, 48–9. Quotations from Shakespeare taken from *William Shakespeare: The Complete Works*, (eds) S. Wells and G. Taylor, 2nd ed. (Oxford: Clarendon Press, 2005)

3 John Gower, *Confessio Amantis*, (*c.* 1390) (London: K. Paul and Trench, Trübner, 1900–1), VII, 2301.
4 Shakespeare, *The Comedy of Errors*, 4. 4. 4. www.opensourceshakespeare.org/views/plays/play_view.php?WorkID=richard3&Act=4&Scene=2&Scope=scene
5 Shakespeare, *Julius Caesar*, 3, 2, 1814–15; *Pericles*, 3, 0, 1174–5.
6 *Oxford English Dictionary*, online edition 2010: www.oed.com
7 See G.M. Smith, *Film Structure and the Emotion System* (Cambridge: Cambridge University Press, 2003)

II.8 Love

Danijela Kambaskovic

The pre-modern concept of love was not that of an emotion, but, rather, an intricate system of philosophical thought. In a basic division, love was understood as either gentle – relatable to the Classical notions of *agape* and *caritas*, fuelling the love of one's children, filial love, loyalty to one's feudal master, love of one's neighbour and love of one's country and cultural customs (when not in danger) – or passionate – associated with the notions of *eros* or *passio* – which can be both human and divine. Plato's philosophy of love, which crucially influenced European pre-modern systems of thought about love, concerns the passionate kind.

Plato's famous division of love into the good love – *Urania*, the heavenly Aphrodite – and bad, *Pandemia* or earthly Aphrodite[1] – holds the key to two opposed attitudes to passionate love in pre-modern Europe: one in which it is viewed as a divine force, and the other, as the work of the Devil or an illness. Both rest on the notion of desire, but it is the *quality* of one's desire – its orientation, intensity, object and outcome, as well as one's (in)ability to change it through effort of will – that ultimately determines whether one's love is human or divine, profane or sublime, transient or creative, inappropriate or decorous, sinful or virtuous.

Plato describes love madness (*mania* – a term still in psychiatric use today to indicate a heightened state of mind) using a cluster of key symptoms: restlessness, sleeplessness, pallor, abjection, ceaseless longing.[2] He allocates love madness the highest status amongst the four types of divine madness because of its association with divine inspiration (*enthusiasmos*), an increase in lover's cognitive and creative functions leading to immortal creation, making the suffering meaningful and desirable.[3] By contrast, later, premodern medical treatises on love melancholy all use Plato's symptoms, but with a negative valuation, calling for preventive measures and aggressive treatments.

Plato's works were lost to Europe from after the fall of Rome until the twelfth century, when they were reintroduced via Arabic translations. The positive valuation reached medieval thinkers through Neoplatonist writings. In the fourth and fifth centuries, Macrobius foreshadows Sigmund Freud by interpreting dreams as an allegory of love and divinity, an approach which will be highly influential for the poetry of the Middle Ages. Through the *Roman de la Rose* by Guillaume de Lorris (*c.* 1200–*c.* 1240) and Jean de Meun (*c.* 1240–1305), completed in 1275, Macrobius' idea of using a dream allegory employing symbols which merge the sensual and the transcendent becomes the dominant mode of expression in the period.[4] An early medieval Christian philosophy, probably containing remnants of Platonic philosophy and Paganism, views all love, including sexual love, as a manifestation of the all-pervading love of God through which the Universe is governed.[5]

The desirability of suffering makes passionate love become a civilizing force. Italian poets of the *dolce stil nuovo* argued that love must reside in a noble heart, the notion crucial also to the poetics of courtly love, a European cultural fashion which swept through the continent in the twelfth, thirteenth and fourteenth centuries and inspired writers such as Dante Alighieri (*c.* 1265–1321), Francesco Petrarch (1304–74) and Geoffrey Chaucer (1343–1400). The Platonic concept of inspiration and creative *furor* was also amply theorized, and, as by Plato, favoured over the notion of writerly effort and skill,[6] by many great Renaissance thinkers including Dante, Petrarch, Marsilio Ficino (1433–99), Leone Ebreo (1465–*c.* 1523), Pietro Bembo (1470–1547), Giordano Bruno (1548–1600), Francesco Patrizi da Cherso (1529–97), as well as, in England, Philip Sidney (1554–86).

In the fifteenth century, Florentine Neoplatonists, led by Ficino, wrote commentaries on Plato's work affirming Plato's view of desire as a creative force, but changing it fundamentally by heterosexualizing and desexualizing it. It is impossible to overstate the historical importance of this shift. For Plato, good love is creative and lasting, and base love transient, leaving without a trace; significantly, *both are sexual*. By contrast, for Neoplatonists, good love is virtuous and asexual, while bad love is sexual. Although Ficino explicitly posited that love must be passional in order to qualify as love (*eros,* not *caritas*), he also stipulated that it must be based on two senses only: sight and hearing. Sexual appetite is not love, but lust or frenzy identified with animality, a foolish perturbation of the spirit contrary to love, *rabbia Venerea,* venereal rabies or rabies of Venus. Mario Equicola (1470–1525) went as far as to call it *la spurcitia del coito,* the filth of the coitus.[7] The power of these ideas was such that we still use the expression 'Platonic love' today – but when we use it, we are describing ideas associated with Christian Neoplatonism, not with Plato.

In Plato's thought, the divine beloved is male; by contrast, Neoplatonic beloveds are female. Ficino's Neoplatonism condemns love between men, and attributes to women the power which compels the lover to seek higher forms of beauty. Both Plato's *Pederasteia* and Neoplatonic love are distinguishable from marriage by the focus they place on emotion – not marriage, or procreation – as their main motivator.[8] On the other hand, although Neoplatonism accords the female beloved the same freedom as the male in the previous tradition, her female gender also carries an expectation of submission under the rules of a patriarchal society.[9] The rhetorical aspect of desire – the attempts to win the female beloved by *words* – is a fundamentally Platonic proposal, carried forth, in the premodern period, by the poetry of Petrarch and Petrarchism, a literary vogue which swept across Europe for four centuries, inspiring poets such as Torquato Tasso (1544–95), Pierre Ronsard (1524–85), Étienne Jodelle (1532–73), Thomas Wyatt (1503–42), Sidney, Edmund Spenser (*c.* 1552–99), Samuel Daniel (1562–1619), Michael Drayton (1563–1631) and, of course, William Shakespeare (1564–1616).

Fear of desire is the second most important attitude to passionate love, diametrically opposite to the attitude which idealized it. Andreas Capellanus (*c.* 1155–*c.* 1190),

Bernard de Gordon (1270–1330), Timothie Bright (1551–1615), Jacques Ferrand (1575–*c.* 1630), Robert Burton (1577–1640), Pierre Petit (1617–87) and others catalogue love's torments and devote much attention to cures, often quite bizarre (such as rubbing the patient's genitals with gall of cramp fish, or beating him until he begins to rot). The treatises assume the patient suffering love melancholy to be a man, and describe the condition and treatment accordingly, except in the notable exception of greensickness, – a disturbance caused by the longing of the womb for semen – suffered specifically by women and described by Burton in *Anatomy of Melancholy* (1621).[10]

Christian works on spirituality treat love suffering as lust, one of seven deadly sins, which should be resisted rather than sought. And since the story of Genesis links women's agency in the medieval mind, the joint workings of the medical and theological discourses contribute to love (and women) becoming viewed as a source of danger that virtuous men should avoid. *Diseases of the Soule* (1620) and *Mystical Bedlam, or the World of Mad Men* (1621) by Thomas Adams (1583–1653), *Joy in Tribulation* (1632) by Phineas Fletcher (1582–1650) or *Man's Mortalitie* (1643) by Richard Overton (*c.* 1631–64) all treat erotic desire as the Devil's temptation (in delightful contrast with the poetic discourse of courtly love and Petrarchism, which accord women beatific and salutary powers). As a result, premodern notions of love are never at peace, and love poetry teems with frustration, pain and violence towards the person it purports to adore.

While virtue and honour have always been the fundamental concepts governing 'good' love in European post-Platonic thought, the way this concept is defined has undergone fundamental shifts. Two main cultural shifts emerge in the seventeenth and eighteenth centuries: a more pronounced tendency to equate sexual passion and desire with selfishness, seeking to eradicate, rather than utilize or theorize it,[11] and – most probably in the follow-up of Protestant teachings on companionate marriage – the tendency to regard romantic and passionate loves as pre-requisites for marriage.

Further reading

Altbauer-Rudnik, M., 'Love, madness and social order: love melancholy in France and England in the late sixteenth and early seventeenth centuries', *Gesnerus* 63 (2006), 33–45.

—offers a useful discussion of the impact of treatises on love-madness on society.

Duby, G., *Love and Marriage in the Middle Ages*, (trans.) J. Dunnet (Cambridge: Polity Press, Blackwell, 1994)

—a succinct and perceptive account of the different sets of values governing courtly (romantic) love and marriage in the High Middle Ages.

Reddy, W.M., *The Making of Romantic Love: Longing and Sexuality in Europe, South Asia, and Japan* (Chicago: University of Chicago Press, 2012)

—posits that, in response to religious strictures, European poets, romance writers and lovers devised a vision of love as something quite different from desire.

Notes

1 *Symposium*, 180e; 181 b, c; 183e, 184d, *Phaedrus* 497 b, c. Plato, *Symposium* (trans.) M. Joyce and *Phaedrus* (trans.) R. Hackforth, in *Plato, The Collected Dialogues* (eds) E. Hamilton and H. Cairns, Bollingen Series LXXI (Cambridge: Princeton University Press, 1961)

2 *Phaedrus*, 251d.

3 *Phaedrus*, 265b, *Symposium* 180b and *Phaedrus* 245a.

4 The link between Macrobius and *Roman de la Rose* is expounded by C. Dahlberg, 'Macrobius and the unity of Roman de la Rose', *Studies in Philology* 58, 4 (1961), 573–82.
5 P. Siegel, 'Christianity and the religion of love in *Romeo and Juliet*', *Shakespeare Quarterly* 12, 4 (1961), 164–82.
6 *Phaedrus*, 245b.
7 Mario Equicola, *Libro di natura d'amore*, cited in J.C. Nelson, *Renaissance Treatises on Love* (New York: Columbia University Press, 1955), 70.
8 On the connection between the erotic and the rhetorical, see also L. Enterline, 'Embodied voices: Petrarch reading (himself reading) Ovid', in V. Finuzzi and R. Schwartz (eds), *Desire in the Renaissance: Psychoanalysis and Literature* (Princeton: Princeton University Press, 1994), 120–45.
9 For excellent discussions of this proposal, see S. Vecchio, 'The Good Wife', (trans.) C. Botsford, in C. Klapisch-Zuber (ed.), *A History of Women, Volume II: Silences of the Middle Ages* (Cambridge, Mass.: Harvard University Press, 1992), 105–135, esp. 118–21 and E. Power, *Medieval Women* (1975) (Cambridge: Cambridge University Press, 2000).
10 R. Burton, *The Anatomy of Melancholy Vvhat It Is. Vvith All the Kindes, Causes, Symptomes, Prognostickes, and Seuerall Cures of It. In Three Maine Partitions with Their Seuerall Sections, Members, and Subsections. Philosophically, Medicinally, Historically, Opened and Cut Vp. By Democritus Iunior. With a Satyricall Preface, Conducing to the Following Discourse* (Oxford, 1621), 957–69; see also U. Potter, 'The Trauma of Puberty for Daughters in Godly Households', in M.K. Harmes, L. Henderson, B. Harmes and A. Antonio (eds), *The British World: Religion, Memory, Society, Culture* (Toowoomba: University of Southern Queensland, 2012), 75–86.
11 W.M. Reddy, *The Making of Romantic Love: Longing and Sexuality in Europe, South Asia, and Japan* (Chicago: University of Chicago Press, 2012)

II.9 Melancholy

Erin Sullivan

According to Robert Burton (1577–1640), the great early modern commentator on all things melancholic, the frequent experience of sorrow and dejection was intrinsically connected to the experience of being alive. Citing the Dutch physician Levinus Lemnius (1505–68), he wrote, 'No mortall man is free from these perturbations', and then added himself, 'if he be so, sure he is either a God, or a blocke'.[1] In his epic *Anatomy of Melancholy* (1621), Burton attempted to outline the many anxieties and discomforts that plagued humankind, chronicling the melancholy of scholars, monks, nuns, widows, lovers, the poor, the ambitious, the pious and everyone in between. When the book was first published, it ran to more than 350,000 words, and by its fifth edition 30 years later it had swelled to over half a million. There was always more melancholy to be documented, it seemed, and Burton made it his life's work to try to address the pains of the many people – himself included – who suffered under the condition's heavy shadow.

Burton held that the history of melancholy stretched back to the age of Adam – '*Cain* was melancholy', he claimed – but he also joined several other contemporary writers in suggesting that the condition had become especially common and troubling in what he called 'this crased age of ours'.[2] Both at home and abroad, philosophers, physicians and theologians had commented on the apparent proliferation of melancholic illness in recent years, prompting Burton to go as far as to label it 'an

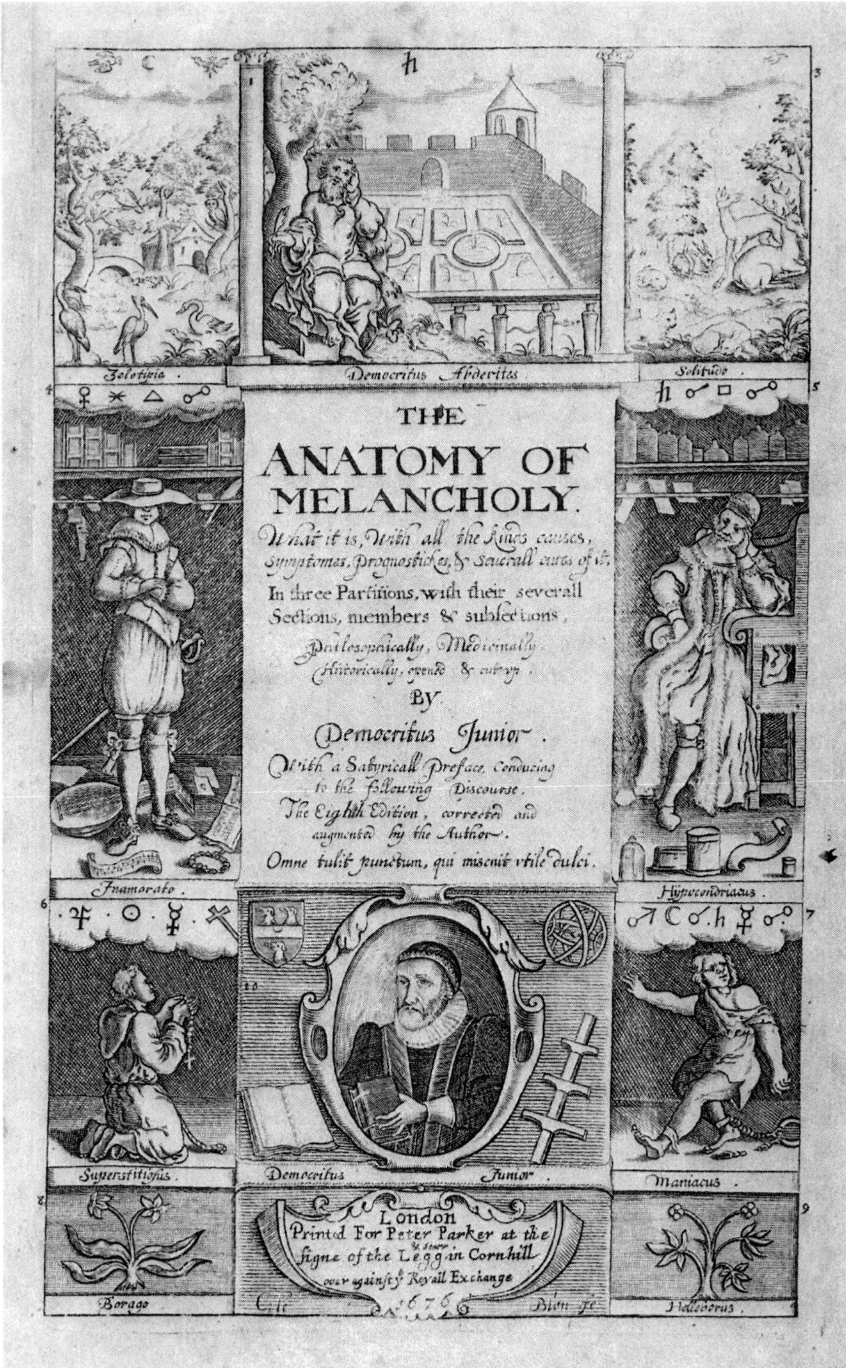

THE
ANATOMY OF
MELANCHOLY.
What it is, With all the kinds causes,
symptomes, prognostickes, & severall cures of it.
In three Partitions, with their severall
Sections, members & subsections,
Philosophically, Medicinally,
Historically, opened & cut up.
By
Democritus Junior.
With a Satyricall Preface, conducing
to the following Discourse.
The Eighth Edition, corrected and
augmented by the Author.
Omne tulit punctum, qui miscuit utile dulci.

London
Printed For Peter Parker at the
signe of the Legg and Star in Cornhill
over against ye Royall Exchange
1676

Figure II.9.1 The all-male frontispiece in Robert Burton's *The Anatomy of Melancholy* (included from 1628 onwards).

Wellcome Library, London.

Epidemicall disease'. At the same time, he and others tended to associate most forms of melancholic anguish specifically with the experience of being a member of the learned elite, and furthermore with being a man. Melancholy might be the eternal 'Character of Mortalitie', he noted, but elsewhere in his tome he also characterized it as a very modern malady brought on by the particular pressures of seventeenth-century political, professional and intellectual life – something that was, for most people at this time, the domain of upper-class men.[3]

But what exactly was melancholy, we might ask, and why did so many people seem to think that it was on the rise in the early modern period? The word itself came from the ancient Greek *μελαγχολία*, which meant, quite literally, 'dark choler' or 'black bile'. As one of the four liquid substances or 'humours' believed to make up the human body, black bile helped constitute a person's well-being or, in less fortunate scenarios, ill-health. When these four humours, which also included blood, phlegm and yellow bile, were well-balanced, then a person's physiology functioned normally and good health ensued. But when this balance slipped and one to two humours started to be produced in excess, then disease followed not only in the body but also the mind and soul. Each humour was thought to be fundamentally connected to certain passions or emotions – melancholy's being sadness and fear – meaning that a change in physiological constitution necessarily provoked a corresponding shift in mental and emotional well-being.

Though physicians stressed that the humours were not good or bad in and of themselves, many still suggested that, of the four, melancholy was the most dangerous. Its cold and dry properties enervated and chilled the body, draining its sufferers of vital energy and turning their minds to sad things. It was sometimes described as the 'dregges' of the blood due to its dark and thick appearance, and though it played an important role in nourishing the liver and spleen, when it became too abundant it clogged the body and clouded the mind, encircling the brain with its black and smoky fumes.[4] According to the English physician Timothie Bright (1551–1615), excessive melancholy 'darken[ed] all the clernesse' of the other humours and 'defile[d] their purenesse with the fogge of [its] slime'. It 'shut up the hart as it were in a dungeon of obscurity', leading to intense sadness, anxiety and even madness.[5]

Given the many illnesses and torments that were associated with this condition, it perhaps comes as a surprise that among certain circles melancholy seems to have been a somewhat fashionable and even aspirational disease. Analysing sixteenth- and seventeenth-century medical case notes, several historians have observed the tendency for patients of a higher social standing to receive melancholic diagnoses more often than the humbly-born, and studies of the condition's representation in contemporary literature and drama have typically reiterated a correlation between melancholic identity and social and cultural privilege. This also meant that this more cultivated form of the condition was frequently a gendered one: given men's greater access to elite institutions of learning, power and wealth, they were more readily associated with such forms of emotive identity, while female melancholy tended to be depicted as more thoroughly disordering, embodied and diseased. Across Europe many illustrious men, such as the poet Torquato Tasso (1544–95), or the patron of the arts Sir William Herbert (1580–1630), sought treatment for melancholy, while on the English stage socially ambitious gentlemen such as Stephano in *Every Man in His Humour* (1598) could be heard asking, 'Am I melancholy enough?'[6]

This link between melancholic illness and elite cultural and social status had its origins in a pseudo-Aristotelian treatise from the fourth century BCE, which asked why it was that 'all those who have become eminent in philosophy or politics or poetry or the arts are clearly melancholics, and some of them to such an extent as to be affected by diseases caused by black bile?'[7] Though the question had gone relatively

Figure II.9.2 Copy of Albrecht Dürer's *Melencolia I*, 1514.
Wellcome Library, London.

unnoticed for the several hundred years that followed, in the fifteenth century the Italian neo-Platonic philosopher Marsilio Ficino (1433–99) generated renewed interest in the possible links between melancholic affliction and intellectual achievement. Perhaps melancholic sorrow and painful introspection led to increased knowledge and even intellectual mastery of the world, he and others suggested – an idea explored by the German artist Albrecht Dürer (1471–1528) in his allegorical depiction of the condition, *Melencolia I* (1514).

It is likely that the tantalizing allure of genius had something to do with the perceived upsurge in melancholic feeling in Burton's times, as perhaps did the many political, religious and intellectual shifts that reshaped life in Europe across the sixteenth and seventeenth centuries. But it is also worth bearing in mind that, despite what Burton might have argued to the contrary, not everyone believed that all forms of sadness and anxiety could be subsumed under the umbrella of melancholy. Even with its profound philosophical and spiritual implications, the condition remained indelibly associated with the workings of the body, and some people chose to express their feelings of dejection and even despair in a way that markedly rejected the language of the humours, as well as subverted the social codings that attended understandings of melancholy.

Distinguishing religious sorrow from melancholic disorder was particularly important for some writers, with Bright, who eventually left medicine to become a clergyman, attesting, 'the affliction of soule through conscience of sinne is quite another thing then melancholy'. While the former was a rational 'sorrow and feare upon cause' – specifically, man's inherent unworthiness before God – the latter was 'a meere fancy' of the mind and body that had 'no ground of true and just object'.[8] Though melancholy was in many cases a powerful and encompassing form of emotive selfhood, for some it brought with it an overly naturalistic understanding of the essence and meaning of sorrow. As a complex malady involving body, mind and soul, it raised fundamental questions about the relationship between physiological, psychological and spiritual experience, prompting the searching and extensive treatment Burton gave it in his ever-expanding *Anatomy*.

Further reading

Gowland, A., *The Worlds of Renaissance Melancholy: Robert Burton in Context* (Cambridge: Cambridge University Press, 2006)

—offers the most authoritative and comprehensive assessment of melancholy in the sixteenth and seventeenth centuries and the ways in which Burton's *Anatomy* consolidated past knowledge while also responding powerfully to the politics and philosophy of its own time.

Schiesari, J., *The Gendering of Melancholia: Feminism, Psychoanalysis, and the Symbolics of Loss in Renaissance Literature* (Ithaca: Cornell University Press, 1992)

—the first to highlight the masculine character of melancholy and examines how this gendering works across a range of European literary texts.

Sullivan, E., *Beyond Melancholy: Sadness and Selfhood in Renaissance England* (Oxford: Oxford University Press, 2016)

—explores how melancholy was not the only form of sadness in the period that helped create powerful experiences of selfhood, and stresses the crucial role literary texts can play in the study of the history of emotion.

Notes

1 R. Burton, *The Anatomy of Melancholy*, (eds) T.C. Faulkner, N.K. Kiessling and R.L. Blair, vol. 1 (Oxford: Oxford University Press, 1989), 248.
2 Ibid., 248, 110.
3 Ibid., 136.
4 T. Elyot, *The Castell of Health* (London, 1595), 14; W. Vaughan, *Directions for Health* (London, 1633), 128.
5 T. Bright, *A Treatise of Melancholie* (London, 1586), 100.
6 B. Jonson, *Every Man in His Humour* (quarto edition) (ed.) D. Bevington, in *The Complete Works of Ben Jonson* (Cambridge: Cambridge University Press, 2012), 2.3.81.
7 Quoted in R. Klibansky, E. Panofsky and F. Saxl, *Saturn and Melancholy: Studies in the History of Natural Philosophy, Religion, and Art* (London: Nelson, 1964), 15–41.
8 Bright, *Treatise of Melancholie*, 187–8.

II.10 Fellow-feeling

Katherine Ibbett

Thomas Hobbes (1588–1679) tells us that '*Griefe*, for the Calamity of another, is PITTY; and ariseth from the imagination that the like calamity may befall himselfe, and therefore is called also COMPASSION, and in the phrase of this present-time a FELLOW-FEELING'.[1] Hobbes clearly sees these three terms – pity, compassion, fellow-feeling – as synonymous, where we today tend to distinguish between pity (sometimes implying a hierarchical relationship) and compassion (a more companionable sharing of suffering). Yet for some early modern writers, these terms were importantly differentiated or supplemented by others – such as sympathy – and made room for various imaginings of ethical and political communities.

Hobbes, writing in the 1640s, was right that fellow-feeling was a 'phrase of this present-time'. Fellow-feeling, and its adjectival and verbal forms (a fellow-feeler, to fellow-feele) were seventeenth-century neologisms, and as Hobbes suggests they were clustered with other terms: the 1604 *Table Alphabetical* by Robert Cawdrey (*c.* 1538–*c.* 1604) gives 'Pitty, fellow-feeling' as the definition for 'Compassion'.[2] The *Oxford English Dictionary* gives the primary meaning of fellow-feeling as 'participation in the feelings of others; sympathy', but usage seems to suggest chiefly a participation in the *sufferings* of others; by the eighteenth century, a secondary sense made room for fellow-feeling as a wider 'community of interest'.[3] Marjorie Garber has shown how, in early modern English, compassion can mean to suffer with *or* to feel on behalf of the sufferer; later, she suggests, compassion took on the feeling 'downwards' that we today call pity and that can carry with it an undertone of contempt, whereas sympathy retains a sense of 'equality or affinity': a fellow-feeling.[4]

Things look a little different in French, where sympathy seems to retain its first and more material sense longer than it does in English; during the seventeenth century it refers chiefly to the complementary properties of two objects. The French usage of 'compassion' begins by presenting it merely as a synonym for pity: the 1606 dictionary of Jean Nicot (1530–1600) pairs the two and adds *commiseration* as a supplement.[5] But dramatic theory starts to separate out the terms by theorizing compassion as the grounds for a theatrical experience grounded in commonality, and towards the end of the century polemical invective turns to pity as an expression of contempt.[6] By 1690, the dictionary of Antoine Furetière (1629–88) has the verb *compatir*, to feel compassion, give the sense 'to live well with someone'; there is a sociability to compassion that is absent from the definition of pity.[7] By the late eighteenth century, compassion implies what is 'human' and its meaning is severed from that of pity.[8]

Hobbes' example suggests that seventeenth-century writers did not tend to make distinctions between different kinds of fellow-feelings. Instead they made firm distinctions between different sorts of *feelers*. Adjectives like 'compassionate' and 'merciful' had often marked the singular and all-powerful emotional domain of God or king; in contrast, the term 'fellow-feeling' allowed writers to explore the proper disposition of human emotions in a very different kind of social organization. But fellow-feeling did not necessarily entail a new social solidarity. Seventeenth-century writers took pains to distinguish between those of their fellows who felt correctly, and those who did not, usually sorting fellow-feelers according to different social types.

Let's return to Hobbes' formulation: we feel pity for others because we fear that what happens to them might also happen to us. This insight stems from Aristotle's *Rhetoric*, where pity is 'a certain pain occasioned by an apparently destructive evil or pain's occurring to one who does not deserve it, which the pitier might expect to suffer himself'.[9] These terms are repeated in the discussion of tragedy in the *Poetics*, provoking vigorous debate in theatrical circles. For many commentators of the period, the observation that pity indicates a concern with the self indicated that pity was a narrow response to suffering, prompted by the self-love central to the thinking of seventeenth-century French moralists as well as figures like Hobbes.

Seventeenth-century writers also imagined a more redemptive fellow-feeling available to particular social types. In *The Passions of the Soul* (1649) René Descartes (1596–1650) proposes a better kind of pity, distinguishing between two kinds of feeling or rather two kinds of *feelers*: whereas for the weak or womanly pity marks a fear for the self, stronger and more 'généreux' minds will feel for others in a more admirable way. Like other neo-stoic writers of the period, Descartes thus inflects fellow-feeling with considerations of gender and social rank. The 'généreux' is a male aristocrat who acts without self-interest. For Descartes, only such a figure can imagine himself beyond fortune and thus take pleasure in a benevolent compassion. Descartes describes this noble emotion as something like the way a spectator feels for the tragic events seen on stage. Theatre is the model for a better-regulated fellow-feeling, in which the nobleman feels for the suffering other with a degree of distance, but never stoops to imagine a similarity between spectator and sufferer.

Eighteenth-century writers continued this enquiry into the theatricality of fellow-feeling, but whereas Descartes extolls the virtue of a pity that recalls theatrical spectatorship, eighteenth-century commentators worried that pity's theatricality made for a more troubling relation to the quotidian. In his *Discourse on Inequality* (1755), Jean-Jacques Rousseau (1712–78) holds pity to be the basis of every social good; its naturalness moderates our tendency to self-love. But in his *Letter to D'Alembert* (1758) he worries that the pity we feel at the theatre might block the emotion that could lead us to act in the wider world.

Whereas the seventeenth century imagined fellow-feeling chiefly in relation to the proper disposition or rank of the self, eighteenth-century writers turned to fellow-feeling as part of a wider exploration of the social bond. The terms of the debate expanded, with sympathy coming to the fore; where compassion spoke only of the sharing of suffering, sympathy could also encompass a feeling for the other across a range of emotions, its meaning narrowing to a sharing of pain only in the twentieth century.

In his *Treatise on Human Nature* (1739–40), David Hume (1711–76) enquires into how it is we come to feel for another and what the social result of such feelings might be. Hume's fellow-feeling is built on resemblance: 'We have a lively idea of everything related to us'.[10] His chief interest is to trace how such an idea comes into our own mind. Hume's investigation into the structures of sympathy addresses not a specific emotion but rather the potential for contagion or communication between selves. Sympathy is a kind of social glue that functions via the imagination. Hume goes on to distinguish between the various terms of fellow-feeling that Hobbes had clustered together: he imagines a form of pity that is similar to dislike, introducing the scornful hierarchy which we today might call pity rather than compassion, and he also dwells on the question of benevolence.

In *Theory of Moral Sentiments* (1759) Adam Smith (1723–90) extolled the compassion felt by the virtuous and vicious alike, imagining it building a larger fellow-feeling at work in human society. For Smith, pity and compassion were broadly interchangeable terms, but sympathy refers to a broader sharing of any emotion, not just a sorrowful one: 'Pity and compassion are words appropriated to signify our fellow-feeling with the sorrow of others, sympathy, though its meaning was, perhaps, originally the same, may now, without much impropriety, be made use of to denote our fellow-feeling with any passion whatever'.[11] Smith was resolute that such sympathy was not selfish.

Accounting for the specificity of these terms and tracing their movement across periods and languages has important consequences. Martha Nussbaum argues that the history of translation of philosophical terms has eroded some of the earliest meanings of words like pity and compassion, and Vivasvan Soni shows how the (mis)translation of Aristotelian pity as sympathy had momentous effects for theories of sentimentalism in eighteenth-century England.[12] Various social theorists have leant heavily on a conceptual distinction between compassion and pity: witness Hannah Arendt who in *On Revolution* (1963) argues that, in dwelling on the singular or particular case, compassion is opposed to the justice inherent to what she calls a 'politics of pity'. Critical models like Arendt's, drawing on eighteenth-century material, have largely dominated the discussion of these terms, and the predominance of scholarship on eighteenth-century sympathy and sentimentalism has obfuscated the particularity of earlier fellow-feeling.

Further reading

Hanley, R.P., 'The Eighteenth-Century Context of Sympathy from Spinoza to Kant', in E. Schliesser (ed.), *Sympathy: A History* (Oxford: Oxford University Press, 2015), 171–98.

—gives an account of eighteenth-century sympathy setting the canonical sympathizers in a broader context.

Ibbett, K., 'Pity, compassion, commiseration: theories of theatrical relatedness', *Seventeenth-Century French Studies* 30, 2 (2008), 196–208.

—describes the significance of the language of compassion in seventeenth-century moral and dramatic theory in France.

Staines, J., 'Compassion in the Public Sphere of Milton and Charles', in G.K. Paster, K. Rowe and M. Floyd-Wilson (eds), *Reading the Early Modern Passions: Essays in the Cultural History of Emotion* (Philadelphia: University of Pennsylvania Press, 2004), 89–110.

—demonstrates the centrality of compassion to new explorations of the public in seventeenth-century England.

Notes

1 T. Hobbes, *Leviathan* (1651), (ed.) R. Tuck (Cambridge: Cambridge University Press, 1996), 43.
2 R. Cawdrey, *A Table Alphabetical* (London, 1604), online at www.library.utoronto.ca/utel/ret/cawdrey/cawdrey0.html, accessed 20 December 2015.
3 *Oxford English Dictionary*, online edition 2010. www.oed.com
4 M. Garber, 'Compassion', in L. Berlant (ed.), *Compassion: The Culture and Politics of an Emotion* (New York: Routledge, 2004), 15–27, esp. 23.
5 J. Nicot, *Thresor de la langue françoyse* (Paris, 1606)
6 On Italian terms, see K. Ibbett, 'Pity, compassion, commiseration: theories of theatrical relatedness', *Seventeenth-Century French Studies* 30, 2 (2008), 196–208.
7 A. Furetière, *Dictionnaire de Trévoux* (Paris, 1704)
8 J.-F. Féraud, *Dictionaire critique* (Marseille, 1787)
9 *The Art of Rhetoric*, (trans.) H.C. Lawson-Tancred (Harmondsworth: Penguin, 1991), chapter 2.8, 163.
10 D. Hume, *A Treatise of Human Nature* (1738–40) (Harmondsworth: Penguin, 1969), 417.
11 A. Smith, *Theory of Moral Sentiments* (1759), (ed.) K. Haakonssen (Cambridge: Cambridge University Press, 2002), 13.
12 M. Nussbaum, *Upheavals of Thought: The Intelligence of Emotions* (Cambridge: Cambridge University Press, 2001), 297–400, esp. 301–303; V. Soni, *Mourning Happiness: Narrative and the Politics of Modernity* (Ithaca: Cornell University Press, 2010), 291–334.

II.11 Sociality and sociability

Katrina O'Loughlin

In the English language, 'sociality' emerges in the late seventeenth century from the medieval French *socialité* to describe 'the state or quality of being sociable' or inclined toward social interaction. In use alongside sociality is the parallel term *sociabilité*, which expresses a particular 'aptitude' for living in society, a disposition toward friendliness and affability. Sociability in the widest contemporary sense then describes those attitudes, practices and emotions that foster a sense of community, with an emphasis on the pleasures and positive affects of such associations. All these connected terms, in their French and English formations, reveal the influence of the post-classical Latin notion of *sociabilitas* – 'the fact of being the same nature or species' – on ideas of community. These are the qualities that make members of a group 'like' each other; the social and affective reciprocities which express and affirm a sense of collective identity.[1]

Two examples of usage from the turn of the seventeenth century alert us, however, to a double register in these terms of social interaction. In 1595, Robert Parsons (1546–1610) represents the 'inclination to liue togeather in company' as an affable preference or choice actively pursued by an individual to join others in company.[2] But in his description of the 'admirable sociabilitie, or configuration of himselfe to popular formes' of Henry VII (1491–1547) some 30 years later, Edmund Bolton (1575–1633) highlights the degree of conformity often required in creating and sustaining sociable bonds.[3] In configuring himself to 'popular formes', Henry makes himself *likeable* to his people by being – or appearing to be – *like* them in key attitudes, values and manners. There is a form of agreement, even orthodoxy, in practices and feelings required to support collective identity.

An important, albeit slippery distinction emerges here between the pleasurable, even playful, associational modes of 'sociability', and the coercive forms of 'sociality' – those social and emotional standards to which individuals must conform to be recognized by their communities – and this is captured in the different resonances of the two terms in English. 'Sociality' is generally displaced in eighteenth-century Anglophone cultures by the term 'sociability' to describe qualities of friendship, companionship and conviviality as positive ideals in British culture. *Sociality* becomes useful then as the broader term that encompasses a complete range (both 'negative' and 'positive') of emotions and practices within social relations, with *sociability* designating those pleasurable social orientations which are specifically valued in the eighteenth century. Sociality describes the prevalent disciplines of social interaction, which typically include behavioural codes, cultural prohibitions and specific emotional regimes: what Keith Wrightson characterizes as the broad 'grid of social relations in local communities'.[4] Within this wider social grid, at any particular moment in history we might distinguish the 'emphatic' sociability of association and affiliation in all its variety of practice – the modes of sociability that Gillian Russell and Clara Tuite describe as 'a form of cultural work' in their own right.[5] Sociality and sociability thus both encompass – in different ways – complex practices of behaviour, language, writing, idiom, manner, disposition and states of feeling, and describe the process of establishing social and emotional communities.[6]

In the early modern period, the associative activities of elite cohorts can be traced to sites such as the court, church and bedchamber (where visitors were received and social business was transacted). New spaces such as literary and learned societies became increasing prominent, while for other pre-modern European communities, taverns, theatres, festivals, public squares and the street continued to shape sociable exchange.[7] It is important to be attentive to both these material locations and conceptual spaces where sociabilities are performed in all historical periods. In the sixteenth and seventeenth centuries for example, one of the most important 'sites' for sociability and feeling is the figurative 'space' of epistolary exchange. Through personal correspondence, coterie circulation of manuscripts, and across the intellectual networks of the early modern 'Republic of Letters', friendship, companionship and intellectual sociabilities were fostered.

There is a significant departure or intensification of meaning after the English Civil War (1642–51) and Restoration (1660), where sociability comes to mark a form of courteous social exchange with new political significance. Some of the richest discussions of sociability as a form of associative practice and identity-formation focus on the seventeenth and eighteenth centuries in Britain and France, at least partly because the ideal and mechanics of sociability becomes a subject of explicit cultural concern and wider discussion at this period. Scottish philosopher David Hume

(1711–76) celebrates a new sociable spirit of 'mutual deference or civility, which leads us to resign our own inclinations to those of our companion, and to curb and conceal that presumption and arrogance so natural to the human mind'.[8] Sociability has here become a set of enlightened social values, a positive endorsement of polite affective relations (as distinct from divisive political passions), and marks the entry of new participants in the political and cultural sphere. Hume, like others, thought that women in particular had an important role to play in this modern reformulation of manners as 'sovereigns of the empire of conversation'.[9]

A shared set of values named 'sociability' thus becomes a conspicuous site for the reshaping of political culture in the eighteenth century by enjoining new social and affective ideals on participants. The *Spectator* cheerfully commends the habit of 'forming ourselves into those little Nocturnal Assemblies, which are commonly known by the Name of Clubs' where men are 'knit together by a Love of Society, not a Spirit of Faction'.[10] As Daniel Gordon has shown, the language and ideas of sociability in Old Regime France also contributed to an emerging social ethos that was neither democratic nor absolutist, but idealized communication, exchange and the private life.[11] Susan E. Whyman's study of the personal papers of the Verney family in late Stuart England likewise demonstrates that 'sociability was a fundamental element of power in a society based upon personal connections'.[12]

Some general patterns in human sociability become obvious over this *longue durée*, practices around eating and drinking, song and dance, conversation, story-telling and literary exchange, and needlework for women. Nonetheless, sociability is also widely and historically variable, dependent on class, gender, geography, religion and other cultural and economic values. Asking about the prevailing sociality or sociability of a period or community thus offers an interesting and important lens for the historian. Whether the court, cloister, village tavern, theatre, coffee house, bedchamber or public street, the nature of sites or spaces where sociable behaviours are performed are highly revealing of the organizing structures of the communities that inhabit them. Sociability is therefore also a key question and resource for the history of emotions: mirth, drollery, good humour, cheer and conviviality are all emotional dispositions contributing to a social alignment of ideas and communal values; even 'negative' feelings like sorrow, pity and sympathy are the foundation of key sociabilities organizing projects such as the abolition of slavery. But quite apart from these particular emotional affinities that often secure social exchange, sociability is an ongoing affective process where relations between people in their various communities constitute a critical space for the development and articulation of shared emotional vocabularies, and an important site of recovery and analysis for historians of emotion.

Further reading

Ahmed, S., 'Sociable happiness', *Emotion, Space and Society* 1 (2008), 10–13.

—a short but suggestive consideration of the sociability of emotions: how social bonds are created and sustained by positive affects that are 'contagious' or shared between individuals.

Brewer, J., *The Pleasures of the Imagination: English Culture in the Eighteenth Century* (London: Routledge, 2013)

—perhaps the seminal account of the emergence of those new spheres of sociability in eighteenth-century England which challenged previous sites of court and church. Highly influential in the subsequent scholarly focus on the history of social and affective relations in Britain.

Broomhall, S. (ed.), *Spaces for Feeling: Emotions and Sociabilities in Britain, 1650–1850* (London: Routledge, 2015)

—explores sociability specifically in terms of the history of emotions by investigating different sites and modes of sociability in the seventeenth and eighteenth centuries.

Notes

1 'sociability, n.', *Oxford English Dictionary*, online at www.oed.com, accessed 3 December 2015.
2 R. Parsons, *A Conference about the Next Succession* (Amsterdam, 1595), I. i. 3, cited in 'sociability, n.', Ibid., online at www.oed.com, accessed 3 December 2015.
3 E. Bolton, *Cities Aduocate* (London, 1629), IV. 43, cited in 'sociability, n.', Ibid., online at www.oed.com, accessed 3 December 2015.
4 K. Wrightson, *English Society 1580–1680* (London: Routledge, 2013), 69.
5 G. Russell and C. Tuite, *Romantic Sociability: Social Networks and Literary Culture in Britain, 1770–1840* (Cambridge: Cambridge University Press, 2006), 5.
6 B.H. Rosenwein, *Emotional Communities in the Early Middle Ages* (Ithaca: Cornell University Press, 2006); Rosenwein, 'Problems and methods in the history of emotions', *Passions in Context: Journal of the History and Philosophy of the Emotions* 1, 1 (2010), 1–32, online at www.passionsincontext.de/index.php/?id=557, accessed 27 June 2016.
7 A. McCue Gill and S. Rolfe Prodan (eds), *Friendship and Sociability in Premodern Europe: Contexts, Concepts, and Expressions* (Toronto: University of Toronto Press, 2014)
8 D. Hume, 'Of the Rise and Progress of the Human Sciences', in *Selected Essays*, (eds) S. Copley and A. Edgar (Oxford: Oxford University Press, 1996), 69.
9 Hume, 'Of Essay Writing', in *Selected Essays*, 3.
10 *The Spectator*, No. 9 (March 10, 1711); J. Addison, *The Spectator*, 8 vols (London, 1712), 1: 48.
11 D. Gordon, *Citizens without Sovereignty: Equality and Sociability in French Thought, 1670–1789* (Princeton: Princeton University Press, 1994)
12 S.E. Whyman, *Sociability and Power in Late-Stuart England: The Cultural Worlds of the Verneys 1660–1720* (Oxford: Oxford University Press, 2002), 4.

II.12 Holy affections

Hannah Newton

The 'holy affections' were a set of special spiritual emotions in early modern Christian culture, which were thought to be imbued with the Holy Spirit.[1] Developed in the writings of the medieval theologians St Augustine of Hippo and St Thomas Aquinas, the holy affections included love for the Lord, praise and thankfulness, and the joyous anticipation of salvation.[2] What was it like to experience these emotions? Why, when and how were they expressed? Drawing on diaries and sermons from seventeenth-century England, I show that the holy affections were often found to be the most exquisite of all human feelings – they saturated the body and soul, filling it with 'heart melting sweetness'. Exploring these delightful experiences helps rebalance our picture of the emotional landscape of early modern Christian culture, which has traditionally concentrated on the gloomier passions of guilt, grief and fear.[3] A wider aim is to demonstrate the value of emotion as a category of analysis in religious history: an investigation of the spiritual feelings of early modern English men and women brings us to a closer understanding of what it was like to be a Christian at this time. The majority of the examples cited here are from Protestant writers, but it is important to note that the holy affections were a Christian, rather than a specifically Protestant, phenomenon.

The holy affections were regarded by religious writers as morally superior to all other emotions. This was because mankind was made to worship and adore God. Isaiah 43, verse 21, states, 'This people have I formed for myself; they shall shew forth my praise'. The elevated status of the holy affections was confirmed by their location in the soul: in classical Christian philosophy, these feelings were envisaged as products of the top part of the soul – the rational soul – as opposed to the middle section, the animal or sensitive soul, which was responsible for all the other passions.[4] The physician and natural philosopher from Somerset, Walter Charleton (1620–1707), explained in his treatise on the passions, 'our love of God, and all other real goods . . . belong only to the *Reasonable* Soul, which . . . [is] seated in a higher sphere . . . looking down . . . upon all tumults, commotions and disorders hapning in the inferior part of man', the sensitive soul.[5] It was within this 'higher sphere' that the Christian's relationship with God was conducted: the holy affections were the soul's chief communications with the Lord, and in turn He made His presence known through the spiritual feelings. Of all the affections, the most important was love for God, on the grounds that 'greatest commandment' in the Bible is to 'love the Lord with all thy heart, and with all thy soul, and with all thy mind' (Matthew 22:37).

The holy affections were supposed to be expressed on a daily basis, but there were certain occasions in life which demanded particularly effusive expressions of these feelings: namely, when God had shown great mercy, such as by healing the sick. Two Bible verses were cited to prove that this was so – the song of David upon his recovery from illness: 'I will extol thee, O Lord, for thou hast lifted me up' (Psalm 30:1), together with Asaph's psalm, 'Call upon me in the day of trouble: I will deliver thee, and thou shalt glorify me' (Psalm 50:15). The duty was described in financial terms – the Lord was owed praise and love in return for His deliverance. The London Presbyterian minister Timothy Rogers (1658–1728), asked his congregation, 'What does the Great God obtain by all his Acts of Bounty . . . but a Revenue of praise? . . . therefore we should be most willing to pay him this easie Tribute'.[6] Praise and thankfulness were also considered to be natural, logical reactions to divine deliverance, stemming from a sense of common courtesy.

Philosophers of both Protestant and Catholic faith taught that the holy affections were exquisite to experience, far more delightful than ordinary emotions or bodily pleasures. The French philosopher Jean-François Senault (*c.* 1599–72) explained in his treatise on the passions, 'the pleasures of the Senses are limited' because the body 'finds no contentment which gives satisfaction to all its senses'. By contrast, the 'pleasures of the soul', the holy affections, 'have no bounds': they 'present themselves all at once' to the soul, enlightening the understanding, will, and memory simultaneously, so that its 'joy is universal'.[7] An analysis of the metaphors that were used to describe the affections confirms that in everyday life, as well as in learned philosophy, these feelings were considered delightful. Upon the recovery of his teenage son John from smallpox in 1669, the Essex puritan minister Ralph Josselin

(1617–83) recorded in his diary, 'I tast[e] love and sweetnes[:] . . . god loves me'.[8] Sweetness was highly prized in early modern culture – in nutrition theory, the sweeter the food the more wholesome it would be to the body, and in Scripture over one hundred references to this quality can be found. Another metaphor that was used in this context involved ravishment. The Northampton attorney Robert Woodford (1606–54) noted that when the Lord did 'heale & Cure' his baby boy in 1637, he experienced 'great & Ravishinge comforts'.[9] Ravishment meant 'to carry away by force', sometimes implying subsequent rape; it was also denoted, 'to fill with ecstasy, [or] intense delight'.[10] These definitions suggest that reciprocal divine love was experienced as a violent pleasure.

Adding to the delight of the holy affections was the belief that they were a 'badge of election'. Thomas Tuke (1580/1–1657), a London conformist minister, declared, 'he that [loves God] may assure himself . . . that hee is . . . in the *ranke* and *roll* of Gods elect; these being infallible tokens . . . of Election, and fore-runners of eternall life'.[11] The enjoyment of the holy affections was also enhanced by the belief that God Himself derived pleasure from hearing the praises. The Presbyterian Suffolk minister, James Steward (1668/9–1753), confirmed that 'the praises of the Saints are sweet Musick, pleasant and delightful Melody in the Ears of the Almighty'.[12] Ultimately, the experience of the holy affections was regarded as the closest thing to heaven on earth, especially when the medium of song was used to express the praise. Humans were 'beginning that blessed Work which we hope to be employed in forever', singing God's praises like the angels in paradise.[13]

Unfortunately, it was not always easy to rouse the spiritual affections, especially during affliction. Despite recognizing that suffering was sent by a loving God for their benefit, Christians often found that the sense of the Lord's anger made it hard to love Him, or to imagine that He loved them in return. An anonymous female relative of Oliver Cromwell confided in her diary in 1701, 'I was under a sevear Fit of the Ston[e], which is a sad Provedence in a double Respect' by reason of the 'great Feare in me, lest the Lord should be angry with me'.[14] In turn, a lack of a sense of divine love was the cause of great concern – it was a sign that the Holy Spirit had left the soul, and could even indicate that damnation would follow.

All was not lost, however. Clergymen taught that affections could be actively 'stirred'. The aforementioned minister, Timothy Rogers, explained,

> This excitation of our selves [to love] is not acquirable by a few cold and transient Thoughts . . . but [by] a continuance of these Acts, arguing and pleading the Case with our Souls, till the Fire of our . . . [love] begin to burn . . . Then will the Holy Spirit cherish our Endeavours.[15]

Loving God was thus an active process, which required sustained effort – only then would the Holy Spirit assist human attempts. The above discussions highlight an ambivalence in Christian understandings of the holy affections: human beings were regarded both as passive receptacles, and as active producers, of these feelings.

To conclude, the holy affections were double joys – not only were they sweet in themselves, but they were also signs of salvation. Such findings may help in small measure to counter the largely negative picture that has dominated historiographical views of early modern Christianity. The value of using emotion as a lens into religious history is twofold: first, by analysing how past faiths made people feel, we can cultivate a greater degree of empathy for religious regimes which, from a modern viewpoint can be hard to fathom. Second, the exploration of early modern expressions of the affections illuminates how the emotions were conceptualised in this era. The affections could be stirred through conscious effort, but they were also sugary morsels that God delivered directly into the believer's soul. This paradox of passivity and activity is a defining feature of early modern emotions.

Further reading

Dixon, T., *From Passions to Emotions: The Creation of a Secular Psychological Category* (Cambridge: Cambridge University Press, 2003), 26–61.

—provides a detailed exposition of the differences between the passions and the holy affections in Christian philosophy, as developed by the medieval Christian philosophers St Augustine of Hippo and St Thomas Aquinas.

Newton, H., *The Sick Child in Early Modern England, 1580–1720* (Oxford: Oxford University Press, 2012)

—about the perception, treatment and experience of childhood illness; chapters 4 and 6 are devoted to the spiritual and emotional experiences of sick children and their parents.

Ryrie, A., *Being Protestant in Reformation Britain* (Oxford: Oxford University Press, 2012)

—the first monograph devoted to the emotional experiences of early modern English Protestants. Seeks to counteract earlier depictions of Protestantism as a fundamentally intellectual, rather than an affective faith; also critiques the deeply negative picture of Protestant emotions presented by others, such as Jean Delumeau.

Notes

1 The holy affections were also known as '*devout* and *religious Affections*': W. Charleton, *A Natural History of the Passions* (London, 1674), 77. My thanks to Thomas Dixon for recommending this treatise.

2 St Augustine, *The City of God,* Books IX and XIV, (trans.) P. Levine (London: Heinemann, 1966); Thomas Aquinas, *Summa Theologiae*, (trans.) The Dominican Fathers (London: Blackfriars, 1964–81), especially Ia.75–83, on 'Man', and Ia.2ae.22–48 on 'The Emotions', 'Pleasure', and 'Fear and Anger'.

3 For example, Jean Delumeau, *Sin and Fear: The Emergence of a Western Guilt Culture, 13th–18th Centuries* (New York: St Martin's Press, 1991), argues that Christian doctrines fostered feelings of fear and guilt in believers.

4 T. Dixon, '"Emotion": The history of a keyword in crisis', *Emotion Review*, 4, 4 (2012), 338–44.

5 Charleton, *A Natural History of the Passions*, 55–6.

6 T. Rogers, *Practical Discourses on Sickness* (London, 1691), 263–4.

7 J.-F. Senault, *The Use of Passions*, (trans.) Henry Carey (London, 1671), 451–2.

8 R. Josselin, *The Diary of Ralph Josselin 1616–1683*, (ed.) A. Macfarlane (Oxford: Oxford University Press, 1991), 547.

9 R. Woodford, *The Diary of Robert Woodford, 1637–1641*, (ed.) J. Fielding (Cambridge: Cambridge University Press, 2012), 190.

10 This is the *Oxford English Dictionary* definition, which is supported by quotations from the early modern period, online at www.oed.com, accessed 12 November 2015.

11 T. Tuke, *The High-Way to Heaven* (London, 1609), 48.

12 J. Steward, *Sacrificium Laudis, or a Thank-Offering* (London, 1699), 15–16.

13 Rogers, *Practical Discourses*, 266.

14 British Library, London, Additional MS 5858, fol. 220v (diary of a female cousin of Oliver Cromwell, 1687/90–1702).

15 Rogers, *Practical Discourses on Sickness*, 175–6.

II.13 The passions

Aleksondra Hultquist

'The passions' were the vocabulary used to define feeling in the early modern period. Philosophical and scientific advances between 1500 and 1800 aided in specifying, diversifying and understanding feeling; thus the Passions moved from religious notions (the Passion, or suffering, of Christ) to psychological, physiological and social conceptualizations. The contemporary term 'emotions' and the early modern term 'the passions' are not directly correlated. Early modern subjects understood the passions to encompass a range of ideas surrounding varied aspects of feeling: political, corporeal, spiritual, intellectual, artistic and emotional. Early modern passions were both public and personal. A helpful analogy might be to think of the modern term 'psychology' and how it underlies post twentieth-century knowledge of mental and physical health as well as both public and private responses to stimuli; the term 'passions' encompasses early modern knowledge of equivalent but not identical phenomena. Much of early modern understanding of the passions was informed by Renaissance humanism and the translations of key studies of the passions by Ancient and early Christian writers, especially Aristotle, Cicero and Seneca, and then Augustine and Thomas Aquinas. The study of the passions was understood to be of paramount importance by many writers for a variety of reasons. It could aid in religious devotion, clarify the causes for and cures of human disease, illuminate certain social and political phenomena and explain personalities and relationships.

Additionally, the vocabulary of the passions was vast. Ideas about emotion in the early modern period were encompassed in words as diverse as affect, appetites, emotion, feelings, passions, perturbations and sentiments. The use of specific terms often indicated allegiances of thought; Stoics, like Immanuel Kant (1724–1804), tended to use the term 'affect'. René Descartes (1596–1650) and the Cartesians who followed him, especially Nicolas Malebranche (1638–1715) and Gottfried Wilhelm von Leibniz (1646–1716), adopted the term 'passions'. These terms, while related, were never interchangeable: to speak of 'affects' or 'sentiments' often connoted calm, useful feelings, while terms like 'passions' and 'appetites' typically referred to raw, unregulated feelings. One must pay attention to specific authors and their use to be sure.

Most writers connected the ideas of the passions to passivity, that is, something acted upon us, something not in our control. The passions were thought to have their own agency, moving from person to person of their own volition, thus providing motivation for action. As David Hume (1711–76) argued, 'intelligent power . . . must be actuated by some passion, which prompts their thought and reflection'.[1] For Descartes the passions were directly linked to action through bodily passions: 'there is no better way to attain to the understanding of our passions, than by examining the difference between the soul and the body, that we may know to which of them each function in us ought to be attributed'.[2]

There were also individual passions. About the middle of the early modern period, writers were concerned about taxonomy of the passions, and many wrote very specifically on macro- and micro-classifications of the passions. In 1649, Descartes counted six basic passions (wonder, love, hatred, desire, joy, sadness) but there were over 30 individual passions such as anger, pity, distaste, regret and emulation that stemmed from these six. Thomas Hobbes (1588–1679) counted into the thirties (*Leviathan*, 1651); Baruch Spinoza (1632–77) referred to about 40, including joy, sadness, love, anger, hate and pride, in his *Ethics* (1677). Some of these passions we recognize today as emotions, like joy or sadness, while others we understand differently, like emulation or curiosity.

The overwhelming goal of passionate discourse in early modern thought was to recognize the passions in order to control them for a greater good, whether that was a closer connection with God, the benefit of self and society, or the regulation of the social order. Many authors believed that reason was the best corrective to passions, but, significantly, the passions were also necessary to intellectual activity and well-being. An absolute absence of any passions, often termed melancholia (also sometimes considered a passion), was destructive and would often be marked by a decline of reason in an individual. Almost all commentators agreed that the passions should be kept in a kind of equilibrium. Positive passion should be encouraged (those that were calm and beneficial to others: joy, sympathy) and negative passions curbed (those that were unruly and destructive: envy, revenge). There were also passions that were ambivalent, such as curiosity and love, and the effects of these passions were often dependent on other early modern factors: the climate of the place in which one lived, one's gender, one's humoral balance or one's tendencies to be particularly receptive to certain feelings. The passions could be regulated through reading, writing, listening to music, changing the diet, praying or undergoing medical procedures. Though harmonizing the passions was a constant preoccupation of early modern theorists, strong passions were also thought to be an asset. Some writers believed in the beneficial uses of powerful, sometimes even uncontrolled passions. For instance, many Christian thinkers believed enthusiastic passions were central to religious doctrine, including Martin Luther (1483–1546); for such thinkers, disinterest and asceticism could be as harmful as extreme enthusiasm.

One of the most influential areas for the early modern discourses of the passions was in the creation and reformation of the social order. Niccolò Machiavelli (1469–1527) for instance in *The Prince* (manuscript 1513, published 1532) determined that the passions of fear and envy provide distinct human motivations that can be manipulated by those in governmental positions: actions were always the result of passions; therefore, it was best for a political leader to utilize those passions that could be relied upon to create political results. Thomas Hobbes' *Leviathan* and *The Elements of Law* (manuscript 1640, publication 1650), *Essay Concerning Human Understanding* (1689) by John Locke (1632–1704) and *The Social Contract* (1762) by Jean-Jacques Rousseau (1712–78) focused on how passions led to the establishment of civil society and how those systems of government might be tweaked to function more efficiently. Other philosophers were concerned with the ways in which the passions supported moral behaviour, and thus improved society as a whole, such as *Characteristics of Men, Manners, Opinions, Times* (1711) by Anthony Ashley Cooper, third Earl of Shaftesbury (1671–1713). For Shaftesbury and the British humanist thinkers he influenced, including Francis Hutcheson (1694–1746) (see *Essay on the Nature and Conduct of the Passions with Illustrations on the Moral Sense* [1728]) and Hume (see *Enquiries concerning*

Human Understanding [1748]), ethical principles of the individual could be cultivated through the recognition of moral passions (usually called sentiments), which would spur the individual to virtuous action.

The basic truths of the understanding of the passions seeped into all literatures of the early modern period. Authors could explore a particular passion in poetry, they could place emotionally volatile characters in particular situations in novels and they could write characters in plays who embodied or were destroyed by their passions. Ben Jonson (1572–1637) used discourses of the humours as shorthand for delineating characters: thus his Volpone, the fox, is wily, choleric and greedy (*Volpone*, 1606). The Libertine plays by Aphra Behn (1640?–89) focused on passionate personalities and the detrimental effects of social restrictions when it comes to expressing passions, such as the character Angelica Bianca in *The Rover* (1677). In his poem *Essay on Man* (1734), Alexander Pope (1688–1744) explored the difference between self and political interests through a discourse of the passions. Sarah Fielding (1710–68), in her novels such as *David Simple* (1744), examined the social benefits of sympathy and sentiment. Rousseau and Mary Wollstonecraft (1759–97) argued textually about the passions in their works, *Julie* (1761) and *A Vindication of the Rights of Woman* (1792), respectively. Rousseau contended that it was women's natural passions that made them passive and Wollstonecraft countered that their lack of a rational education made them bound to their passions. Literature acted as a laboratory for experimenting with and understanding the passions.

As a system of emotional knowledge, the passions were implicated in the physiology, psychology and social constructs of the period. They were central to understanding how and why people as individuals and groups responded to events in the way they did. They were the basis of action and they explained what we might call personalities. The passions are not synonymous with the twenty-first-century concept of the emotions; instead, they are indicative of entire systems of feeling in the early modern world that structured both individual and collective identities and actions.

Further reading

Gross, D.M., *The Secret History of Emotion: From Aristotle's 'Rhetoric' to Modern Brain Science* (Chicago: University of Chicago Press, 2006)

—traces the vocabulary of the passions from classical through contemporary times and is especially rich is details from the early modern period, where he places the beginning of modern conceptions of emotions.

Kahn, V., N. Saccamano, and D. Coli, *Politics and the Passions, 1500–1850* (Princeton: Princeton University Press 2009)

—organized by early modern theorists (Machiavelli through Bentham), and specifically geared to the passions and early modern theories of motivation and civil order.

Paster, G.K., K. Rowe, and M. Floyd-Wilson (eds), *Reading the Early Modern Passions: Essays in the Cultural History of Emotion* (Philadelphia: University of Pennsylvania Press, 2004)

—examines specific vocabularies of the passions and how they manifested in the literature, art, philosophy and culture of the early modern period.

Notes

1 D. Hume, *Four Dissertations, The Natural History of Religion* (London, 1757), Sec. 2, par 5.

2 R. Descartes, *The Passions of the Soul* (London, 1650), Sec 1, par 2.

II.14 Contemplation

Christopher Allen

The representation of the emotions, passions, *moti* or *affetti*, as they are variously known, was recognized as one of the most important functions of painting and sculpture from the beginnings of Renaissance art theory, and assumed a particular prominence in the debates of the French Academy of Painting in the second half of the seventeenth century. Recognizing specific emotions in pictures is not always easy, both because there was originally no fixed repertoire of passions and because pictures are not usually labelled. In the case discussed in this chapter, however, we have both repertoire and labels, as well as a theoretical commentary. But *contemplation* as an emotional category in art remains, as we shall see, somewhat elusive.

The career of Charles Le Brun (1619–90) as a painter could have foundered in 1661 amidst the fall from grace of his patron, the French minister of finance, Nicolas Fouquet (1615–80). By remarkably good fortune, this near-disaster became instead the occasion for his rise to far greater heights as the official painter of Louis XIV (1638–1715). And one picture played a central role in these events, *The Queens of Persia before the Feet of Alexander*, (1660–1) also known as the *Tent of Darius*. Le Brun

Figure II.14.1 Charles Le Brun, *The Queens of Persia before the Feet of Alexander*, 1660–1 (also known as the *Tent of Darius*). h 298 cm × w 453 cm. Salon de Mars, Palace of Versailles.

clearly conceived of this composition, from the outset, as an anthology of significant emotional expressions, particularly among the company of figures who watch the events from within the tent. The women and their attendants are divided between fear and admiration, surprise, confusion and understanding. Each of these states of mind – including, it seems, contemplation – has its own distinctive facial signature.

The idea of a scene in which figures respond variously to the same event reflects the work of Nicolas Poussin (1594–1665), in whose *Christ and the Woman taken in Adultery* (*c.* 1653), for example, the men in the crowd are all shown reacting in different ways to Christ's injunction that the man without sin should cast the first stone. For Poussin, the classical doctrine of expression meant that everything in a picture should convey the meaning of the subject.[1] Under the influence of René Descartes (1596–1650) and his *Les Passions de l'âme* (1649), however, Le Brun came to think of facial expression – as the manifestation of inner emotional states – in a more restricted and mechanical way.[2]

Many of the faces in *The Queens of Persia* are illustrated on a sheet of 12 expressive heads published by Le Brun's close associate Henri Testelin (1616–95) in *Sentimens des plus habiles peintres* (1693).[3] The necessarily quiet and subdued expressions from the *Tent of Darius* are supplemented by more extreme ones, one of which is labelled 'terror' and is drawn from a later Alexander painting, the *Battle of Arbela* (1669). The second of these heads, in the top row – they are all reversed in the printing process – is titled 'La Contemplation'. Others are 'L'Etonnement' (surprise, astonishment), 'La Crainte' (fear), 'L'Inquiétude' (anxiety) and 'L'Abattement' (discouragement).

The print recalls an important lecture on the subject of human passions and their expression especially in the facial features that Le Brun gave, in two parts, at the French

Figure II.14.2 Nicolas Poussin, *Christ and the Woman taken in Adultery*, *c.* 1653, h 122 cm × w 195 cm.

Figure II.14.3 Selection of expressive heads drawn from the paintings of Charles Le Brun. Henry Testelin, *Sentimens des plus habiles peintres*, 1693, following page 25.

© The Metropolitan Museum of Art, New York. Accession Number 68.513.6(6).

Royal Academy of Painting and Sculpture in April and May 1668, published after his death in 1698.[4] For most of the expressions illustrated here we can refer directly to the artist's words, which explain both the nature of the passion and the mechanics of its expression in the human features. But this is not the case for 'contemplation', for none of the passions described in the lecture is given this label. A closer reading of Le Brun's text, however, suggests that we may find that the answer is hidden under another appellation. What Le Brun calls 'Admiration' is not included on Testelin's sheet, but is described as 'the first and most temperate of all the passions, where the heart feels the least agitation'.[5]

The visible manifestations of this 'passion' seem also a plausible match: the face is little changed, the brows are equally raised and the eyes and mouth are gently open. Le Brun's 'admiration', unlike our own, is essentially a suspended state that precedes strong affective responses such as love or hate, desire or fear.[6] According to Le Brun, 'admiration' most easily slips into either 'étonnement', which seems to include surprise, or 'estime', 'vénération' or even 'ravissement', which reveals an affinity with spiritual experience.[7]

What complicates matters, however, is the survival of diagrams and drawings that became the basis for Testelin's printed sheet and, inconveniently, the one printed as 'Etonnement' is here labelled 'Admiration'. The head seems more suited to Le Brun and Testelin's idea of astonishment, as an extreme or sudden form of attention,[8] but

Le Brun's characterization of the stance and gesture of 'Admiration' in the lecture also matches this figure.[9] The figure Testelin labels 'Contemplation', moreover, is here named 'Ravissement' – again an extension of the original 'Admiration', as we see in his accompanying text, which twice uses the term 'contemplation', not as the label for a passion but in relation to forms and degrees of 'Admiration' and 'Ravissement'.[10]

Did Testelin or even Le Brun come to think of 'Contemplation' as the best general term for this 'first of passions'? What is clear, in any case, is that the whole continuum of 'Admiration', 'Etonnement', 'Ravissement' and so on, whether or not subsumed under the label 'Contemplation', was always meant to represent a range of neutral states of attentiveness preceding judgement.[11] They are all essentially distinct from and prior to those passions involving an admixture of will and self-interest[12] that are manifest in the remainder of the figures in the *Tent of Darius*. If there was any deliberate avoidance of the term *contemplation*, it could conceivably be because of its association with the spiritual tradition of Quietism – already mentioned in passing – to which the King was opposed, like all religious movements (most notoriously Jansenism) that departed from strict orthodoxy.

Further reading

Allen, C., Y. Haskell and F. Muecke (eds), *Charles-Alphonse Dufresnoy, De Arte Graphica 1668* (Geneva: Droz, 2005)

—with three introductory chapters and extensive commentary, constitutes a useful introduction to most of the central themes of early modern art theory.

Montagu, J., *The Expression of the Passions: The Origin and Influence of Charles Le Brun's 'Conférence sur l'expression générale et particulière'* (New Haven: Yale University Press, 1994)

—the original scholarly study of the subject and still the most important secondary source.

Notes

1 See C. Allen, Y. Haskell and F. Muecke (eds), *Charles-Alphonse Dufresnoy, De Arte Graphica 1668* (Geneva: Droz, 2005) and C. Allen, *French Painting in the Golden Age* (London: Thames & Hudson, 2003)

2 See C. Allen, 'Painting the Passions', in S. Gaukroger (ed.), *The Soft Underbelly of Reason: The Passions in the Seventeenth Century* (London: Routledge, 1998)

3 Testelin had digested the deliberations of the Academy into 'Tables de Préceptes' on various topics, which he presented to the Academy from 1675 to 1679; they were published in collected form in 1680, and then again in 1693 with essays and plates of illustrations added (*Sentimens* is the seventeenth-century plural of *Sentiment*).

4 J. Montagu, *The Expression of the Passions: The Origin and Influence of Charles Le Brun's 'Conférence sur l'expression générale et particulière'* (New Haven: Yale University Press, 1994), 141–2.

5 Quoted in Ibid., 116.

6 Ibid., 116: 'une suspension de mouvement'.

7 In the spiritual renewal of the seventeenth century, 'contemplation' was associated with the new lay piety of Saint François de Sales as well as with the Quietist movement.

8 Testelin notes that 'l'excès de l'admiration cause l'étonnement'. Montagu, *Expression of the Passions*, 167.

9 Montagu, *Expression of the Passions*, 123.

10 Ibid., 167–8.

11 Its only object is 'neither good nor ill . . . but only to know the thing we admire'. Cited in Ibid., 114.

12 Note the use of the will-terms 'vouloir' and 'volonté' in the characterization of the passions that follow from the initial neutral state of simple attention. Ibid., 113–14.

II.15 Sensibility

Katrina O'Loughlin

The term 'sensibility' has a long history expressing the body's powers of sensation, sensory awareness or somatic perception. This is a condition of sensitivity attaching most closely to the human body, although debates about the emotional sentience of various creatures also became an important feature of eighteenth-century inquiry, the period in which 'Sensibility' as a movement became prominent across Britain and Europe. This sensitivity – even vulnerability – to external stimuli, develops into a desirable personal and social quality. The evolution of sensibility into the literary and philosophical 'Cult of Feeling' in the eighteenth century is highly suggestive for emotions history, because it represents a moment where the nature, historicity and 'fashion' of feeling became widely scrutinized in popular and intellectual debate, and thus perhaps, more than usually visible to scholars of the early modern period.

'What, in your opinion, is the meaning of the word sentimental, so much in vogue amongst the polite', puzzles Lady Bradshaigh (*c.* 1705–85) in a letter to novelist Samuel Richardson (1689–1761), dated 1749: 'Everything clever and agreeable is comprehended in that world . . . I am frequently astonished to hear such a one is a *sentimental* man; we were at a *sentimental* party; I have been taking a *sentimental* walk'.[1] Like Lady Bradshaigh, it is easy to be confused by the popular language of feeling: there is notorious difficulty with the group of terms that cluster closely, but not always clearly, around one another in the literature and culture of the eighteenth century. Like 'sentimental', 'sensibility', 'sympathy' and 'sentiment' appear sometimes to be used interchangeably, and other times with intimations of very distinct meaning.

Reasonably rare before the eighteenth century, 'sensibility' describes an openness or susceptibility to feeling; a primary sensory response of the body to influences outside it, which marks the human subject as fundamentally experiential and sensate. In his influential essay of 1741, David Hume (1711–76) outlines a 'certain Delicacy of Passion, to which some People are subject, that makes them extremely sensible to all the Accidents of Life, and gives them a lively Joy upon every prosperous event, as well as a piercing Grief, when they meet with Crosses and Adversity'. For a person of this 'Sensibility of Temper', Hume suggests, feelings are apt to take 'intire Possession of him'.[2] 'Sympathy' is the term that describes this affective process at work: the mechanism of transfer of feeling to the sensible subject, or the alignment of emotion between people, situations and states. Characterized very often in the eighteenth century as 'fellow-feeling', sympathy – like the third related term of this group, 'sentiment' – implies a collective or collectivizing response that depends on the perception of shared or reciprocated emotion.

It is important to maintain the subtle distinctions developing at this period between the palpable quality of sensibility as a bodily or visceral response to 'external, sensible, objects', and the cognitive processes connected with sentiment, or 'the internal Operations of our Minds, perceived and reflected on by ourselves'.[3] Sensibility is the foundational category of experience or ground on which the discourse of sentiment gets built. 'Sensibility' as a historical epoch, or Foucauldian 'episteme', develops from this new emphasis on sensory experience, growing into a remarkably widespread European literary and cultural movement of the eighteenth century. The Age or Cult of Sensibility names a set of patterns, investments and vocabularies prominent – with curious and significant variations – from the 1730s through to the 1790s. As a movement, Sensibility is often characterized in terms of epistemological contrasts with what came before, particularly early modern science, neoclassicism and Enlightenment rationalism. Inger Brodey suggests for example that in 'direct opposition to classical and Augustan thought, feeling takes the place of reason as the supreme human faculty; feeling rather than reason now provided the only hope of community within the tenets of Sensibility.[4] Jerome J. McGann also emphasizes processes of historical reaction, arguing that the 'momentous cultural shift' named by 'sensibility' and 'sentiment' shaped later movements: 'both romanticism and modernism organized themselves in relation to the traditions of sensibility and sentiment'.[5]

Such epistemic distinctions are appealing – perhaps even inevitable – tools in organizing our understanding of impossibly complex cultural movements. However, in the case of sensibility, this type of oppositional shorthand can obscure the close connections between early modern empiricism and the evolution of sensibility through the shared mechanism of sensory perception. This represents a remarkable shift from a god-centred, to a human-sensed, universe: the emergence of the human as a feeling subject and 'little sensorium'.[6] Jessica Riskin argues that in the French Enlightenment in particular, empiricism was intricately bound up with sensibility, suggesting that in sensibility's formulation of a new mode of 'sentimental empiricism', knowledge and understanding proceeded from a blend of sensory experience and emotion together.[7]

The *Essay Concerning Human Understanding* (1689) by John Locke (1632–1704) is a pivotal moment in the opening of what Northrop Frye describes as this 'new world of sense experience' which, critically, includes feeling.[8] Human understanding, in Locke's account, is drawn from the external sensory world of objects; or 'From EXPERIENCE: In that, all our Knowledge is founded; and from that it ultimately derives itself'.[9] McGann argues that the revolution in philosophy that followed Locke's new approach to ideas as '(literally) sensational forms' radically altered 'the entire culture terrain' of Britain and Europe, and was immediately reflected in a 'linguistic revolution' of a new set of writing practises and cultural conventions we now connect with sensibility.[10] If the forms of the literature of sensibility are the novel, letter and poem, the emblems (according to McGann) are 'the body's elementary and spontaneous mechanisms': tears, blushes, involuntary sighs, swooning and rapid pulse.

But to get even closer to this 'mental habit' of an age, we might turn to Scottish moralist David Fordyce (1711–51), just one of the many who sought to articulate the nature, urgency and moral force of feeling. For the benevolent man, suggests Fordyce:

> His Enjoyments are more numerous, or if less numerous, yet more intense than those of bad Men; for he shares in the Joys of others by Rebound; and every Increase of *general* or *particular* Happiness is a real addition to his own. It is true, his friendly *Sympathy* with others subjects him to some Pain which the hard-hearted Wretch does not feel; yet to give a loose to it is a kind of agreeable Discharge. It is such a Sorrow as he loves to indulge; a sort of pleasing Anguish, that sweetly melts the Mind, and terminates in a Self-approving Joy.[11]

Fordyce's portrait of the sensible 'good Man' reveals the pleasure of feeling, its operation on both 'heart' and 'Mind', and the ideal shaping of the individual in emotional response to his community. Fordyce's language of commerce is also very typical. The vocabulary of exchange, enlargement and value emphasizes both the new moral economy provided by sensibility, and the remarkable currency and transferability of feeling as understood at this period: it moves, nearly contagiously from one subject to another. Passions as almost autonomous forms are reflected in Hume's depiction of the exogenous appearance of his 'own' emotions: 'Hatred, resentment, esteem, love, courage, mirth and melancholy', he writes, 'all these passions I feel more from communication than from my own natural temper and disposition'.[12]

Sensibility thus represents a distinctive emotional repertoire of the late seventeenth and eighteenth centuries in which susceptibility to and the display of feeling become a conspicuous social and personal value. As the language and philosophy of eighteenth-century emotion, sensibility provides a cultural vocabulary for debates about knowledge, understanding and right action, and a mode through which intellectual and popular discussion about the nature and influence of feeling became possible.

Further reading

Goring, P., *The Rhetoric of Sensibility in Eighteenth-Century Culture* (Cambridge: Cambridge University Press, 2005)

—a relatively recent intervention in the discussion of sensibility in the eighteenth century, focuses on the body as an 'eloquent, expressive object', across oratory, theatre and the novel.

Riskin, J., *Science in the Age of Sensibility: The Sentimental Empiricists of the French Enlightenment* (Chicago: University of Chicago Press, 2002)

—moving beyond the study of literary sentiment, examines the impact of new understandings of sensory experience on scientific discourses of the eighteenth century in her study of French sentimental empiricism.

Todd, J., *Sensibility: An Introduction* (London: Methuen, 1986)

—a foundational text for the study of literary sensibility in the eighteenth century, and particularly the gendering of feeling: while these were sensations experienced by both men and women, sensibility's critics associated it with women and effeminacy which required careful management.

Notes

1 *The Correspondence of Samuel Richardson*, (ed.) A.L. Barbauld, vol. 4 (London: Richard Phillips, 1804), 282–3. Italics in the original.

2 D. Hume, 'Essay I. Of the Delicacy of Taste and Passion', in *Essays Moral and Political* (Edinburgh, 1741), 1.

3 J. Locke, *An Essay Concerning Human Understanding* (1689) (London, 1775), 68.

4 I.S.B. Brodey, 'On Pre-Romanticism or Sensibility: Defining Ambivalences', in M. Ferber (ed.), *A Companion to British Romanticism* (Maldon: Blackwell, 2005), 14.

5 J. McGann, *Poetics of Sensibility: A Revolution in Literary Style* (Oxford: Clarendon Press, 1998), 1.

6 I. Newton, *Opticks: or, a Treatise on the Reflections, Retractions, Inflexions and Colours of Light. The Fourth Edition, corrected. Book Three* (London, 1730), 345.

7 J. Riskin, *Science in the Age of Sensibility: The Sentimental Empiricists of the French Enlightenment* (Chicago: University of Chicago Press, 2002), 15.

8 N. Frye, 'Varieties of eighteenth-century sensibility', *Eighteenth-Century Studies* 24, 2 (1990–91), 157–72, quote 160.

9 Locke, *Essay Concerning Human Understanding*, 104.

10 McGann, *Poetics of Sensibility*, 6.

11 D. Fordyce, *The Elements of Moral Philosophy*, Fourth Edition (London, 1769), 264.

12 Hume, *A Treatise of Human Nature* (1739), quoted in A. Pinch, *Strange Fits of Passion: Epistemologies of Emotion, Hume to Austen* (Stanford: Stanford University Press, 1996), 25.

II.16 The expressive face

Linda Walsh

The prototypes of facial expression codified in the seventeenth century by Charles Le Brun (1619–90), Director of the Royal Academy of Painting and Sculpture in Paris, remained dominant in the early part of the eighteenth century and continued to contribute to the education of artists in academies throughout Europe. They studied Le Brun's prototypes of, for example, 'Fear' or 'Wonder', derived in turn from ancient and Renaissance art. These prototypes used different configurations and movements of facial features (eyeballs, eyebrows, mouths and nostrils) to express specific emotions. Many academies ran 'expression' competitions, in which the prize was awarded to the student who represented most effectively the facial expression assumed by a posed model. However, as the eighteenth century progressed, critics and artists began to prefer a less formulaic approach. This was due partly to a new interest in human expressions observed at first hand and in the workings of human feeling, especially through the vogue for 'sensibility' (overtly expressed feeling) that swept through European art, literature and ideas from the 1760s. There was also a growing awareness of the need to adapt the facial expressions of figures in paintings, sculptures and drawings to a diverse range of genres (in the sense of subject categories), each with its own set of aesthetic requirements. As the public for art expanded beyond the previously dominant elite, to include an educated middle class or *bourgeoisie*, more viewers became skilled in interpreting and judging the expression of feeling in social and artistic contexts.

There remained a lack of precision in the eighteenth-century terminology relating to feeling, the terms 'sensibility', 'sensation', 'passion' and 'sentiment' each capable of relating to feeling in general. However, distinctions between different types of feeling became more precise throughout the century and this was reflected in dictionary definitions. 'Passion' became more associated with wilder emotional states; 'sensation' with crude, automatic sensory impressions such as pain and pleasure; and 'sentiment' with feeling that engaged the mind, its powers of reasoning and its moral sense. The eighteenth-century Enlightenment is often characterized as an intellectual movement dedicated to the pursuit of reason, nature (seen as an antidote to an over-sophisticated, artificial and morally suspect society) and moral and scientific progress. This made the expression of the emotions more subtle and complex. Increasingly, Le Brun's prototypes were felt to be too 'mannered' or artificial: artists should observe more closely natural or 'real' facial expressions.

At the same time, artists' approaches to facial expression continued to respect longstanding aesthetic values regarding the appropriateness of the 'tone' or register of a particular style to the subject represented. Le Brun's prototypes had been devised in relation to 'grand manner' history paintings, that is, large canvases representing epic and morally significant narrative scenes taken from the Bible or history. These headed the hierarchy of subject types established by academies of fine art. Less rhetorical expressions were felt to be appropriate for the 'lower' genres of painting, including genre scenes (scenes from everyday life) representing the lives of middle and lower-ranking sections of society. However, some eighteenth-century artists, particularly Jean-Baptiste Greuze (1725–1805), used Le Brun's expressive types in genre scenes. Greuze tried to give such scenes the moral authority previously enjoyed by history paintings. His sentimental (in the sense of 'full of sentiment') genre paintings, representing both tragic and more common scenes of everyday life, drew inspiration from contemporary developments in the theatre. His sketch 'The Angry Wife' (Figure II.16.1) features expressions of intense emotion more traditionally associated with the dramatic genre of high tragedy. In France in particular, Enlightenment authors embraced the theatre as a school of morals. New genres were defined and codified by thinkers such as Denis Diderot (1713–84) who wrote plays known as 'dramas' (*drames*) including 'tearful comedies' (*comédies larmoyantes*, dramatized tales from everyday life) and 'bourgeois tragedies' (*tragédies bourgeoises*, plays with a darker theme). These plays aimed to represent scenes full of emotion that would move the audience to tears, thus improving in a very public (and eventually fashionable) way their moral sensibility. One of the devices commonly used was the stage *tableau* in which figures 'froze' into static positions on stage, as in a painting, and which used exaggerated gestures (of the type that had been popular since ancient Greek theatre) and facial expressions. This vogue passed, however, as did the cult of sensibility as a whole, which was seen increasingly as contrived

Figure II.16.1 Jean-Baptiste Greuze, *The Angry Wife*, eighteenth-century drawing, brush, black and gray wash, heightened with white, over traces of graphite, 52.1 × 64 cm.

The Metropolitan Museum of Art, New York.

and rhetorical, for example in the novels of Jean-Jacques Rousseau (1712–78) and Johann Wolfgang von Goethe (1749–1832). Genre painting as a whole became characterized by the use of more 'natural' facial expressions.

From the time of the ancient Greeks and Romans, the theory of the 'modes' had also influenced artists' choices of expressive motifs. The theory of the modes had been most explicitly developed in music, but was also applied to landscape views, architecture and painting. It was based loosely on the principle of respecting the essential or appropriate 'character' of things. Thus landscapes, historical and genre scenes, could adopt a range of expressive motifs appropriate to their subject, mood and general stylistic tenor. The 'modes' often associated with painting were: the Doric (the firm, grave and severe); the Phrygian (the sharp, quick or astonishing); the Lydian (the dreamy or mournful); the Hypoldian (gentleness and sweetness) and the Ionic (joyfulness). The eighteenth-century thinker Edmund Burke (1729–97) engaged in his 1757 work *A Philosophical Enquiry into the Origin of Our Ideas of the Sublime and Beautiful* in the further theorization of aesthetic categories. The beautiful face (or landscape) should inspire love through its smooth, delicate features; the sublime landscape or historical scene was intended to arouse terror through the use, for example, of stormy skies, rugged mountains or the more violent facial prototypes developed by Le Brun. Both of these aesthetic categories had been theorized from antiquity onwards. In an expanding and diversifying art market, the eighteenth-century art public, nourished by a growing body of critical and theoretical literature, became more adept at recognizing such distinctions. It also became more acceptable to develop subjective interpretations of and responses to works of art, rather than relying on the official explanations and tastes of academies and courts. Less explicit or 'open' facial expressions came to be seen as an invitation to imaginative engagement with a work of art.

Another factor that undermined the dominance of Le Brun's prototypes was the renewal of interest in the 'science' of physiognomics, most notably in the *Physiognomische Fragmente zur Beförderung der Menschenkenntnis und Menschenliebe* (*Physiognomical Fragments to promote the Knowledge and Love of Mankind*), originally published in 1775, by Johann Kaspar Lavater (1741–1801). Whereas the prevailing emphasis in much mid-eighteenth-century art had been on pathognomics or the expression of temporary emotions, physiognomics revived an interest previously expressed in classical and Renaissance thought, as well as in Le Brun's own writings, in the visual markings of the face as signifiers of persistent aspects of character. These were felt by Lavater to convey more truthful, significant insights into an individual's inner life and qualities than signs of transitory emotion.

Stylistic trends also undermined reliance on Le Brun's prototypes. Late-century developments in metropolitan taste led across Europe to a vogue for neoclassicism. This was a diverse movement, but one strain of the paintings, sculptures and buildings within it adopted a more austere, linear and minimalist style derived from the aesthetic theories of Johann Joachim Winckelmann (1717–68) in his *Geschichte der Kunst des Alterthums* (*History of Ancient Art*), published in 1764. Winckelmann's ideal of beauty was derived from the classical, fifth-century BCE ideal of the Greek youth with smoothly curving body and noble, well-proportioned, relatively static facial features, stripped of distracting detail or surface variation. The archetypal neoclassical face and body as represented in much eighteenth-century art, for example in the works of Jacques-Louis David (1748–1825) or John Flaxman (1755–1826) were restrained and dignified in their expressive features and aimed to arouse philosophical meditation as much as emotion. The *Principles of Human Beauty Relative to the Human Head* (1777–8), by Alexander Cozens (1717–86) provided new facial prototypes engraved by Francesco Bartolozzi for artists and viewers interested in this style. These prototypes vary little; such is their conformity to a neoclassical ideal of beauty. They also reflect the new focus on physiognomics. However, an emphasis on more varied and dramatic bodily and facial expression of emotion remained important in much Romantic art of the late eighteenth and early nineteenth centuries.

Figure II.16.2 Francesco Bartolozzi, after Alexander Cozens, 'Combination of the Features of the Modest', from *Principles of Beauty Relative to the Human Head*, 1777–1778, 15: Table IX. Etching on paper, 169 × 140 mm.

Further reading

Barker, E., *Greuze and the Painting of Sentiment* (Cambridge: Cambridge University Press, 2005)
—relates sentimentalism in eighteenth-century French culture, and particularly in the art of Greuze, to contemporary social and economic developments

Montagu, J., *The Expression of the Passions: The Origin and Influence of Charles Le Brun's 'Conférence sur l'expression générale et particulière'* (New Haven: Yale University Press, 1994)
—explains the views of Le Brun on facial expression in the context of seventeenth-century philosophical, aesthetic and scientific ideas.

Walsh, L., 'The expressive face: manifestations of sensibility in eighteenth-century French art', *Art History* 19, 4 (1996), 523–50.
—explores eighteenth-century artists' practices in the representation of emotion in relation to academic training and the codification of genres and 'modes'.

Section III

Sources and methodologies for early modern emotions

III.1 Poetry

Diana G. Barnes

Poetry is a rich source for the history of emotions. Nevertheless, it is not a straightforward documentary source. Realism did not become the dominant form of literary representation until the nineteenth century. Rather, emotion in poetry can have both a symbolic and a literal meaning. Romantic love is by far the most pervasive emotion in early modern poetry, but friendship, grief, patriotism, religious wonder and stoic discipline are recurrent themes bound by conventions of genre, language and affect derived and adapted from classical poetry.

Early modern poets strove to replicate the emotions associated with classical poetry. Ovid's *Heroides*, Virgil's *Aeneid* and *Eclogues*, and Horace's *Odes*, for instance, were widely translated and imitated. Let us consider the example of Ovid's *Heroides* which was adapted by Giovanni Boccaccio (1313–76) and Geoffrey Chaucer (1343–1400) in the fourteenth century; in the sixteenth century it was translated into English by George Turberville (*c.* 1540–97) and into French by Octavien de Saint-Gelais (1468–1502).[1] The process continued through the seventeenth and eighteenth centuries. The *Heroides* represented a *locus classicus* for the emotions – love, desire and heroic fortitude – of oppressed women. Poets admired the emotional force with which Ovid's eloquent heroines complained of their violation at the hands of the heroes of classical legend. They recognized the heroines' passionate complaints as the antithesis of the emotional control intrinsic to the masculine heroic values such as valour and pietas, celebrated in epic poetry. By imitating this emotional pose poets signalled their own relationship to an overbearing tradition. First published in 1559, *The Mirror for Magistrates* was an influential collection of complaints adapted to English history. The 1563 edition included 'Shore's Wife' (1563) by Thomas Churchyard (*c.* 1520–1604). In direct first-person speech Jane Shore, the goldsmith's wife who became mistress to Edward IV (1442–83), relates '[Her] great mischaunce, [her] fall, and heavy state' (l. 5) and offers a moving critique of the abuses of sovereign power which she describes as 'The maiestie that kynges to people beare, / The stately porte, the awful chere they showe' (ll. 78–9). She asks 'Who can withstand a puissant kynges desire?' (l. 89), drawing readers to recognize her plight as symptomatic of the condition of commoners.[2]

During the sixteenth century, poets across Europe sought to give authority to vernacular poetry and abandon slavish imitation of the classics. Pietro Bembo (1470–1547) held up the vernacular poets of the early Renaissance, Francesco Petrarch (1304–74), Giovanni Boccaccio (1313–76) and Dante Alighieri (*c.* 1265–1321), as models.[3] Like Bembo (*Prose della volga lingua*, 1525), Joachim du Bellay (1522–60) (*Défense et illustration de la langue francoyse*, 1549) and Sir Philip Sidney (1554–86) (*Defense of Poetry*, 1595) advocated vernacular language in patriotic terms suggesting that the vernacular poet rejected the overbearing paternalistic legacy of the classics, and pronounced his nation's coming of age. As Edmund Spenser (*c.* 1552–99) demanded 'why a God's name, may not we, as else the Greeks, have the kingdom of our own language'? (*Three Wise and Wittie Letters*, 1580).[4] In defending the literary value of the vernacular they laid down theoretical precepts for poetry.

These precepts are a useful starting point for thinking about the relationship between emotion and poetry during the period. Neither Bembo nor du Bellay and Sidney defined poetry according to technical devices such as rhyme, verse or metre, but rather by the emotional quality of moving its readers.[5] Sidney argued that poetry teaches by impassioning the reader. Whereas the historian must stick to bare facts, the poet's imagination ranges widely and his creations 'may be tuned to the highest key of passion'.[6] Whereas philosophy is obscure and dry, poetry has broad popular appeal. For Sidney this popularity depended upon a light and indirect means of communicating. Whether the poet employs a parodic tone, as Sidney does in his prose romance, *Arcadia* (1590), or a more serious one, as in his sonnet sequence, *Astrophil and Stella* (1591), the emotion portrayed is symbolic rather than literal. Extended metaphors would so delight the reader, that s/he would be drawn, or moved, to recognize truths; this was what Sidney described as 'heart-ravishing knowledge'.[7] Allegory rather than realism governed representation.

When writing of love early modern poets turned to Petrarch. The conventions for representing emotions in poetry are set by genre. In sonnets, the genre for which Petrarch was best known, love is treated as a contradictory state. These lines from the English poet Thomas Wyatt's translation of Petrarch are typical: 'I find no peace and all my war is done; / I fear and hope, I burn and freeze like ice; / I fly above the wind, yet can I not arise, / And naught I have and all the world I seize on'.[8] Here Wyatt (1503–42) gives lyric voice to the psychologically-fraught persona of the lover beset by powerful contradictory sensations. Antithesis heightens the emotional intensity of the love described. Direct speech draws the reader into the lover's anguish. Yet as Arthur Marotti wrote of the sixteenth-century English sonnet craze, the love described by Petrarch and his countless imitators across Europe does not transparently document the poets' love for particular women.[9] Even when the poet hints at the identity of a beloved it may not be firm. Sidney's Stella is not precisely Penelope Devereux, Lady Riche (1563–1607), to whom his engagement was broken, but a means of allegorizing his desire for a position at court in the face of likely failure. Thus poetic representations of love can be instrumental, and for this reason historical context is important to the interpretation of emotions in poetry.

Context does not produce uniform poetic representation of emotion, however. Consider the English Civil War (1642–50). Families and communities suffered grave losses, and were divided by political and religious differences. Poets' responses to this disruptive emotional experience was varied. Some produced elegies grieving the loss, some sought consolation in religious themes and others advocated stoic restraint. These poetic expressions of emotion were bound by both the conventions of genre and political allegiance. Contributors to the royalist collection, *Lachrymae Musarum, The Tears of the Muses; expresst in elegies; written by divers persons of nobility and worth, upon the death of the most hopefull, Henry, Lord Hastings* (1650), for example, used the emotionally-effusive elegiac form to elevate Hastings (1630–49) as a royalist war hero and generate sympathy in royalist readers, and thus bind them together in opposition to the newly established Commonwealth.[10] Writing for his patron the recently retired commander-in-chief of Parliament's New Model Army, Andrew Marvell (1621–76) advocated stoicism. Disavowing the terms of royalist poetics he described 'Tears ([as] watery shot that pierce the mind);/ And sighs ([as] love's cannon charged with wind)'.[11] In these examples emotions and the poetic genres that convey them are inflected with factionalism.

Although early modern poetry is a rich source for the history of emotions, it is important to recognize that its means of communication are symbolic and allegorical. In order to interpret it accurately we must try to identify the generic, linguistic and imitative conventions that govern poetic representations of emotion, and view each poem in its historical and generic context. When early modern poets defined poetry, they stressed its capacity to move its readers, and in doing so they expressed contemporary understandings of passion and restraint which often went without saying. Such defenses offer a valuable tool for decoding the emotional script embedded in poetry and society at large.

Further reading

Clarke, D., '"Formed into Words by your Divided Lips": Women, Rhetoric and the Ovidian Tradition', in D. Clarke and E. Clarke (eds), *This Double Voice: Gendered Writing in Early Modern England* (Houndsmills: Macmillan, 2000), 61–87.

—a reading of the gendering of emotion in poetry.

Marotti, A., '"Love is not love": Elizabethan sonnet sequences and the social order', *English Literary History* 49, 2 (1982), 396–428.

—a good example of the instrumental reading of emotions in literature.

Paster, G.K., K. Rowe and M. Floyd-Wilson (eds), *Reading the Early Modern Passions: Essays in the Cultural History of Emotions* (Philadelphia: University of Pennsylvania Press, 2004)

—sets the terms for analysing what poetry and other literary forms offered the history of emotions.

Notes

1 P. White, 'Ovid's *Heroides* in early modern French translation: Saint-Gelais, Fontaine, Du Bellay', *Translation and Literature* 13, 2 (2004), 165–80; R. Lyne, 'Intertextuality and the female voice after the Heroides', *Renaissance Studies* 22, 3 (2008), 307–23.

2 T. Churchyard, 'Shore's Wife', *The Mirror for Magistrates*, (ed.) L.B. Campbell (New York: Barnes, 1970), 373–86; R. Helgerson, 'Weeping for Jane Shore', *The South Atlantic Quarterly* 98, 3 (1999), 451–76; and on later adaptations see D.G. Barnes, *Epistolary Community in Print, 1580–1664* (Farnham: Ashgate, 2013), 47–71.

3 S. Jossa, 'Bembo and Italian Petrarchism', in A.R. Ascoli and U. Falkeid (eds), *The Cambridge Companion to Petrarch* (Cambridge: Cambridge University Press, 2015), 179–90.

4 E. Spenser and G. Harvey, *Three Proper, and Wittie, Familiar Letters* (1580), in J. Chipps Smith and E. De Selincourt (eds), *The Poetical Works of Edmund Spenser* (London: Oxford University Press, 1912), 611.

5 L. Willet, Introduction, *Poetry and Language in Sixteenth-Century France: Du Bellay, Ronsard, Sebillet*, (trans.) L. Willet (Toronto: Centre for Reformation and Renaissance Studies, 2004), 20, 29.

6 P. Sidney, *A Defence of Poetry*, (ed.) J.A. van Dorsten (Oxford: Oxford University Press, 1966), 35.

7 Ibid., 21.

8 ll. 1–4: T. Wyatt, 'I Find no Peace', in J. Hollander and F. Kermode (eds), *The Literature of Renaissance England* (Oxford: Oxford University Press, 1973), 117.

9 A. Marotti, '"Love is not love": Elizabethan sonnet sequences and the social order', *English Literary History* 49, 2 (1982), 396–428.

10 C. Gray, '*Tears of the Muses*: 1649 and the Lost Political Bodies of Royalist War Elegy', in M.R. Wade (ed.), *Gender Matters: Discourses of Violence in Early Modern Literature and the Arts* (Amsterdam: Rodopi, 2014), 133–54.

11 'Upon Appleton House' (written around 1651, published 1681), ll. 715–16 in A. Marvell, *Pastoral and Lyric Poems 1681*, (eds) D. Ormerod and C. Wortham (Nedlands: UWA Press, 2000). See D.G. Barnes, 'Remembering Civil War in Andrew Marvell's "Upon Appleton House"', in S. Downes, A. Lynch and K. O'Loughlin (eds), *Emotions and War: Medieval to Romantic Literature* (Houndsmills: Palgrave, 2015), 185–202.

III.2 Drama

Kathryn Prince

Drama is, unlike any other genre, acutely interested, perhaps even chiefly interested, in the communication of emotional states. At times, early modern drama might even be considered meta-emotional, preoccupied not only with exploring specific emotions but also with understanding their very nature. *Hamlet* is exceptionally, but not uniquely, exemplary of these emotional and meta-emotional concerns. 'I have that within which passeth show', the visibly melancholy Prince Hamlet tells his recently widowed and freshly married mother in the second scene of *Hamlet*, contrasting Gertrude's apparent cheerfulness with the 'trappings, and the suits of woe' that he wears as an outward manifestation of his grief.[1] Their interaction here is complex, suggesting both that Hamlet believes clothing and behaviour are not reliable guides to emotions and also that in this instance his own 'inky cloak' reflects his inner state.[2] To add another layer of complexity, these lines are delivered by an actor wearing a black costume and audibly sighing, telling another actor, this one an Englishman dressed as a Danish queen, that even though black clothes and audible sighs are precisely the signs that an actor would use to depict grief, in this moment this actor is depicting a character experiencing real grief, a character who is also expressing a mistrust of those very signs that are the only means by which the actor can convey the character's ostensibly real feelings, feelings that this actor is feigning but not in the same way that the actor playing Gertrude is feigning her feelings. If all this is confusing, then it is entirely consistent with the play's themes, since confusion – especially regarding emotions as they are perceived, expressed and received – is one of the chief concerns of *Hamlet*. William Shakespeare (1564–1616), like other early modern dramatists, is acutely aware of the emotions of his characters and of his audience.

Hamlet is a play obsessed with the disparity between a character's inward emotional life and the outward 'actions that a man might play', actions that, the play repeatedly reminds us, are an unreliable guide to feelings.[3] It is also a play obsessed with acting, as Hamlet's advice to the travelling players in Act 3, Scene 2 elucidates when he coaches them in acting techniques that will make their emotions seem more natural. Hamlet later reproaches himself regarding his own grief, the outward manifestations of which contrast so stingily with the copious tears that the player manages to generate for a character who is, after all, only a fiction to him. Feeling emotions and performing them are, in *Hamlet*, two distinct, if related, processes. While this makes Prince Hamlet an early participant in a debate about acting famously expressed by Denis Diderot (1713–84) in his *Paradoxe sur le comédien* (The Paradox of the Actor, written in 1773–7 and published posthumously in 1830), not all commentators on early modern acting are as certain as Hamlet and Diderot that feigned emotions are separable from real ones. Anti-theatrical tracts from the period warn that spectators, moved to tears or to desire by a convincing performance, might be unable to control the physiological consequences of the actors' feigned emotions and be somehow materially harmed by this emotional contagion.[4]

Early modern drama is, in many ways, a mechanism for transmitting emotions, and was seen as such by its detractors as much as by its proponents. The theatre, as Stephen Mullaney has argued, is an affective technology in every period, and the early modern theatre is one of the most sophisticated.[5] The circulation of emotions between character, actor and spectator was a topic of debate and a source of delight across the early modern theatrical world.

Early modern theories about drama draw on Aristotle's concept of catharsis expressed in his *Poetics* and Horace's notion of the edifying and educational functions of literature expressed in his *Ars Poetica*. Sometimes, particularly in England and Spain where the neoclassicism that came to dominate French theatre practice was resisted, they define themselves against these influences. Such is the case with Félix Lope de Vega (1562–1635), the prolific Spanish playwright, who writes in his 1609 treatise *Arte nuevo de hazer comedias en este tiempo* (New art of making plays in this age) that although combining elements of comedy and tragedy violates classical precepts, 'such varied mixtures lead to much delight'.[6]

Recent work on the emotions in early modern drama has begun to contend that certain playwrights have a signature emotional style, something that is certainly discernible in Lope de Vega's characteristic genre-bending. Shakespeare's contemporary John Lyly (1553–1606), Andy Kesson has argued, depicts an unusual degree of emotional volatility in his plays, while Shakespeare himself, R.S. White and Ciara Rawnsley observe, favours complex, mixed emotions to an extent that they can be considered characteristic of his art.[7] Ben Jonson (1572–1637), drawing on the Galenic notion of the humours, derives an entire dramaturgy from an approach to the emotions that he explains in the induction to his 1599 play *Every Man Out of His Humour*:

> Some one peculiar qualitie
> Doth so possesse a man, that it doth draw
> All his affects, his spirits, and his powers,
> In their conflluctions, all to runne one way.[8]

This diversity of emotional practice within the drama of a single country and period suggests that the treatment of emotions is a distinguishing rather than unifying feature among early modern dramatists. Playwrights' theories about drama, for this reason, are probably best considered in relation to their own oeuvre rather than as general rules about practice, or at most in relation to the company with which they were associated, if, as Jacalyn Royce suggests, the Chamberlain's Men, Shakespeare's company, 'transformed the elaborate verse structure and unnatural physical and vocal style that characterized other Elizabethan theatre', developing their own techniques 'more grounded in the variety of language and action of life off the stage'.[9] Jonson's Globe plays, which include *Volpone* (1606) and *The Alchemist* (1610) as well as *Every Man in His Humour* (1598) and *Every Man Out Of His Humour* (1599), do share some family resemblances with Shakespeare's despite their characteristically Jonsonian approach to the humours.

There is, perhaps, more consistency across early modern French drama than English or Spanish because of its emphasis on neoclassical tenets and more codified forms of emotional expression. While the dramatic theories of Pierre Corneille (1606–84) should, like Jonson's and Lope de Vega's, apply only to his own oeuvre,[10] Diderot's *Paradoxe sur le comédien* can be seen as a reflection on the early modern French practice that precedes it, much as Aristotle's *Poetics* can be read as an assessment of Greek tragedy written with the benefit of hindsight. In a treatise that anticipates the psychological acting that would come to dominate the performance of even early modern drama in the twentieth century following the teachings of Konstantin Stanislavki, Diderot argues that the actor is most affecting when not affected by the emotions he performs. An actor whose performance is generated by feelings will be emotionally exhausted, and the performance will be unreliable, while a performance generated by skilful feigning can be sustained and repeated not only over the course of an entire evening but then throughout a production's full run. Approaches to the performance of early modern drama today increasingly turn to non-psychological techniques drawn from physical theatre in order to recapture some of the emotional distance that Diderot recommends, though psychological acting remains dominant as a means of closing historical distance through empathy.[11] Grappling with the challenge of performing early modern emotions today can yield an unusually visceral engagement with the history of emotions both for the actor and for the spectator, one that, even more than the experience of reading dramatic texts, has the potential to highlight both continuities and disruptions between early modern and current emotional practices.

Further reading

Hurley, E., *Theatre & Feeling* (Basingstoke: Palgrave Macmillan, 2010)

—though not focused on the early modern period, Hurley's brief introduction is a provocative starting point for theatre in all eras, considering affect, sensation, emotion and mood as distinct, or at least potentially distinguishable, aspects of the experience of theatrical performance.

Meek, R. and E. Sullivan (eds), *The Renaissance of Emotions* (Manchester: Manchester University Press, 2015)

—brings together an excellent range of approaches to the emotions in the early modern period, situating drama within a rich context of other genres including scriptural exegesis, medical treatises and historical anecdote.

Purcell, S., *Shakespeare and Audience in Practice* (Basingstoke: Palgrave Macmillan, 2013)

—focuses closely on early modern audiences and on the performance of early modern plays for modern audiences.

Notes

1 William Shakespeare, *Hamlet*, 1.2.85, 86. References are to the *Norton Shakespeare*, (eds), S. Greenblatt, W. Cohen, J. Howard and K. Eisaman Maus (New York: WW Norton, 1997)

2 Ibid., 1.2.77.

3 Ibid., 1.2.84.

4 On Renaissance anti-theatricalism, three different perspectives useful for emotions scholars are offered by M. O'Connell's *The Idolatrous Eye: Iconoclasm, and Theater in Early Modern England* (Oxford: Oxford University Press, 2000); L. Levine's *Men in Women's Clothing: Antitheatricality and Effeminization, 1579–1642* (Cambridge: Cambridge University Press, 1994); and J. Howard's *The Stage and Social Struggle in Early Modern England* (London: Routledge, 1994). On emotional contagion, B. McConachie's *Engaging Audiences* (Basingstoke: Palgrave Macmillan, 2008) is an excellent starting point in a growing field.

5 S. Mullaney, 'Affective Technologies: Toward an Emotional Logic of the Elizabethan Stage', in M. Floyd-Wilson and G. Sullivan (eds), *Environment and Embodiment in Early Modern England* (Basingstoke: Palgrave Macmillan, 2006), 71–89.

6 Madrid, 1609. The relationship between Lope de Vega's theories and his plays is discussed in F. Serralta's '¿Un Arte nuevo de deshacer comedias? Sobre algunos autocomentarios en el teatro de Lope', *RILCE. Revista De Filología Hispánica* 27, 1 (2011), 244–56.
7 A. Kesson, '"They that Tread in a Maze": Movement as Emotion in John Lyly', in R. Meek and E. Sullivan (eds), *The Renaissance of Emotion* (Manchester: Manchester University Press, 2015), 177–99; in the same collection, R.S. White and C. Rawnsley, 'Discrepant Emotional Awareness in Shakespeare', 241–63.
8 B. Jonson, *The comicall satyre of euery man out of his humor* (London, 1600)
9 J. Royce, 'Early Modern Naturalistic Acting', in R. Dutton (ed.), *Oxford Handbook of Early Modern Theatre* (Oxford: Oxford University Press, 2009), 477–95, here 480.
10 On the passions in French neoclassical drama, see G. Forestier's *Passions tragiques et règles classiques: Essai sur la tragédie française* (Paris: Presses Universitaires de France, 2003)
11 For a variety of perspectives, see P. Aebischer and K. Prince (eds), *Performing Early Modern Drama Today* (Cambridge: Cambridge University Press, 2012)

III.3 Epistolary literature

Diana G. Barnes

While historians of emotions have recognized that sent letters, or missives, represent a rich documentary source of individuals' emotional lives, they have tended to overlook fictional letters. Epistolary literature is a broad field ranging from epistolary manuals, verse epistle, prose and novels and can circulate in print or manuscript. Whereas 'real' letters are written and read primarily for pragmatic reasons, epistolary literature is designed to entertain, impress or educate readers, and to promote the author. Love and friendship are key emotions in fictional letters, although filial piety, shame and humility are recurrent themes. Historical genre analysis can illuminate the cultural assumptions about emotion invested in the art of letter writing.

The early moderns understood letters as modelling emotions such as love, gratitude or humility, specific to interpersonal relationships. The published fictional letter collections so popular in the early modern period bear a close relationship to civility tracts: in setting forth the rules for exchanges between various social types, letter manuals established conventions for emotional discourse which were readily exploited in literature. Epistolary literature thus provides documentary evidence of a rather hierarchical understanding of emotion operating in this period. The art of letter writing was formulated in epistolary manuals as a quotidian form of writing guaranteed by respected classical antecedents. Both Cicero's letters to his friends (*Ad familiares*, *Ad Atticum*, *Ad Quintum fratrum* and *Ad Brutum*) and Ovid's poetic epistles (*Heroides*) were key to the art of letter writing, and to the development of epistolary literature.[1] Ovid's poetic epistles of classical heroines, *Heroides*, modelled *amore*, or the pain and anguish of love between unequal parties, whereas Cicero's letters modelled *amicitia*, or affection between men who were social equals. Cicero's epistolary oeuvre was the primary *locus classicus* for the early modern epistle, and *amicitia* the dominant emotional mode in prose letters, but Ovidian *amore* also had an influential place in the teaching of rhetoric and letter writing.

When the Italian poet and humanist Francesco Petrarca (1304–74), or 'Petrarch' as he was known by the English, rediscovered Cicero's letters to Atticus and Quintus in 1345, he responded with a passionate letter to the long-dead Roman statesman. Having known Cicero hitherto through his formal public writings, Petrarch was confronted by the intimate portrait of a man beset with human frailties and vanities revealed in his letters.[2] Petrarch described his own letter as 'a lament springing from sincere love and uttered, not without tears, by one of thy descendants who most dearly cherishes thy name'.[3] In it Petrarch developed the fictional premise that the familiar letter was a form so intimate and human as to allow the affective exchange of friendship between reader and writer in spite of the lapse of time. The friendship Petrarch claims is an extension of the affection Cicero portrays in his own letters, but the anguish and tears are inspired by Ovid. Aspiring literati across Europe, including Desiderius Erasmus (*c.* 1466–1536) in the sixteenth century, and Arcangela Tarabotti (1604–52) in the seventeenth, likewise prepared collections of their letters to promote their own intimate familiarity with the classical past *and* their contemporaries.[4]

The letter is both a high literary species of writing and a quotidian and pragmatic mode of communication. The two modes are not worlds apart, however. The standard approach to teaching letter writing was imitation. In the classic Elizabethan pedagogical text, *The Schoolmaster* (1570), Roger Ascham (1515–68) recommended that the student translate Cicero's letters from the Latin into the vernacular and back again to Latin. Ascham made clear that this exercise of double translation would foster friendship both between the student and his master, and the student and Cicero.[5] It also encouraged a habit of adapting emotional templates to new compositions. This affective educational program took place formally within grammar schools and universities, but was disseminated more widely through textbooks and manuals published in English, French, Italian and other European languages from the second half of the sixteenth century. Manuals gave step-by-step instruction in the effective representation of emotion for a variety of interpersonal interactions, ranging from expressing gratitude to a parent, inveighing a master for pay, sympathizing with a friend, establishing trust in order to negotiate trade, chastising a prodigal son or declaring love. Each species of letter employed specific terms to express the emotions fitting the relationship between writer and recipient. These specifications make it clear that the art of letter writing depended not simply upon technical rhetorical know how but also upon familiarity with conventions for emotional exchange.

Letter-writing manuals presented emotional relationships between different kinds of writers in terms that claimed to reflect *real* social relations, but also taught that powerful emotions could be effected rhetorically, and that control over such emotional effects could be deployed strategically.[6] Manuals showed the budding letter writer how to confect an emotion, or adapt the techniques of epistolary fiction to real-life situations. The emotional scenarios rehearsed and popularized in epistolary manuals inspired a variety of new literary forms. The title of *The Secretary of Ladies* (1638), the English translation of the collection by Jacques du Bosq (or Du Bosc) (1600–99) of female friendship letters, pays homage to an earlier prosaic manual, although it is a fictional collection of female friendship letters whose ostensible purpose was not pedagogical. The immensely popular miscellany by Nicholas Breton (Britton or Brittaine) (1545–1626), *A Poste with a Madde Packet of Letters* (1602), on the other hand, copied the manual in portraying a wide variety of letter writers and their letters, using the fiction of the postman's bag to explain the miscellaneous character of the collection.

The prominence of love as a theme for epistolary fiction of the seventeenth and eighteenth centuries testifies to the pervasive influence of Ovid's *Heroides*.[7] Michael Drayton (1563–1631) adapted the Ovidian model to retell the history of England's royal succession through the passions of kings and queens in his collection of verse epistles, *England's Heroical Epistles* (1597). Like its classical precedent, Drayton's poems emphasize the emotion invested in the material letter, highlighting an inky scrawl across the page smudged by the tears of the writer, for example.[8] Drayton also used the Ovidian model to challenge the hegemonic and masculinist account of English history presented in the chronicle histories. Through the laments of women trampled, discarded, entrapped and abused, Drayton highlighted the emotional cost of succession and political intrigue. As in Ovid's *Heroides* the eloquence Drayton gives to his heroines dignifies their emotional experience and the counter-hegemonic histories they recount.

Whereas Drayton accepted that lament and anguish were predominantly female emotions, resulting from women's powerlessness, by the mid-seventeenth century women writers sought to unsettle the gendering of this emotional regime again through the letter. In France, Madeleine de Scudéry (1607–1701) reworked the Ovidian model. Her *Lettres amoureuses de divers autheurs de ce temps* (1641) includes letters of passionate female friendship in the tradition of du Bosq, and also letters in which male rather than female lovers complain of their abandonment and seduction. Scudéry was quick to recognize that the thrice-daily '*petite poste*', which operated in Paris over a three-month period from August 1653, provided a new emotional vocabulary with great literary potential. Now for the first time, a letter writer could maintain anonymity, and epistolary dialogue was more immediate. The collaboratively written manuscript *Chroniques des samedis* is characterized by what Joan DeJean describes as a 'remarkable . . . degree of postal precision'.[9] Scudéry continued to exploit the emotional potential of epistolary form by embedding letters in her lengthy historical novels. As feminist literary critics of the 1980s observe, yearning, entrapment, uncertainty and desire characterize the epistolary novels of the following century.[10]

Samuel Richardson (1689–1761), arguably the most influential novelist of the eighteenth century, began his career with a letter-writing manual. Inspired to expand an epistolary dialogue he had briefly explored there, he went on to write *Pamela; or Virtue Rewarded* (1740) and *Clarissa* (1748), two of the most popular epistolary novels of the period. Richardson's work epitomizes the emotional freight that could be transported from epistolary manual to epistolary novel to prose novel proper. In his preface to *Pamela* Richardson promised 'to paint VICE in its proper colours, to make it *deservedly odious*, and to set VIRTUE in its own amiable light, to make it look *lovely*'. Thus he sought 'to teach the man of *fortune* how to use it; the man of *passion* how to *subdue* it, and the man of *intrigue*, how, gracefully, and with honour to himself, to *reclaim* it'.[11] The epistolary mode utilized by Richardson is critical of this regulation of the passions. Just as for Cicero and Petrarch, the epistolary fiction models appropriate emotional response, while emotions do the work of miraculously collapsing barriers of time, and place, not only between correspondents in the epistolary exchange, but between writer, character and reader.

Epistolary literature is a capacious species of fiction derived from rhetorical theory mixed with prescriptions for civility or proper behaviour. As such it provides a window onto early modern understandings of emotion, in particular, the appropriate expression and bridling of the passions, and the suitability of certain emotions to different social relationships. These values are best exposed by considering epistolary literature as a species of writing governed by rules and conventions that developed over the period.

Further reading

Jardine, L., 'Pedagogy and the Technology of Textual Affect: Erasmus's *Familiar Letters* and Shakespeare's *King Lear*', in J. Raven, H. Small and N. Tadmor (eds), *The Practice and Representation of Reading in Early Modern England* (Cambridge: Cambridge University Press, 1996), 77–101.

—historicist textual analysis of epistolary literature as it developed from classical rhetoric.

Kauffman, L.S., *Discourses of Desire: Gender, Genre, and Epistolary Fictions* (Ithaca: Cornell University Press, 1986)

—desire was a key term in feminist analysis of the 1980s; one of the best examples in relation to epistolary literature.

Darnton, R., 'Readers Respond to Rousseau: The Fabrication of Romantic Sensitivity', in *The Great Cat Massacre and Other Stories in French Cultural History* (New York: Viking, 1984), 215–56.

—a compelling account of epistolary literature's tendency to break down barriers between writer and reader.

Notes

1 J. Bate, *Shakespeare and Ovid* (Oxford: Clarendon Press, 1993)

2 A. Patterson, *Censorship and Interpretation: The Conditions of Writing and Reading in Early Modern England* (Madison: University of Wisconsin Press, 1984), 211–40.

3 *Petrarch's Letters to Classical Authors*, (ed., trans.) M.E. Cosenza (Chicago: University of Chicago Press, 1910), 1.

4 L. Jardine, *Erasmus, Man of Letters* (Princeton: Princeton University Press, 1993), 5, 19–20; M.K. Ray, L.L. Westwater, Introduction to Arcangela Tarabotti, *Letters Familiar and Formal*, (ed. and trans.) M.K. Ray and L.L. Westwater (Toronto: ITER, 2012), 1–40.

5 D.G. Barnes, *Epistolary Community in Print, 1580–1664* (Farnham: Ashgate, 2013), 33–5.

6 L. Magnusson, *Shakespeare and Social Dialogue: Dramatic Language and Elizabethan Letters* (Cambridge: Cambridge University Press, 1999), 61–90.

7 D. Clarke, '"Formed into Words by your Divided Lips": Women, Rhetoric and the Ovidian Tradition', in D. Clarke and E. Clarke (eds), *This Double Voice: Gendered Writing in Early Modern England* (Houndsmills: Macmillan, 2000), 61–87.

8 Barnes, *Epistolary Community*, 47–72.

9 J. DeJean, '(Love) letters: Madeleine de Scudery and the epistolary impulse'. *Eighteenth-Century Fiction* 22, 3 (2010), 399–414, quote 408.

10 P. Kamuf, *Fictions of Feminine Desire: Disclosures of Heloise* (Lincoln: University of Nebraska Press, 1982) and L.S. Kauffman, *Discourses of Desire: Gender, Genre, and Epistolary Fictions* (Ithaca: Cornell University Press, 1986)

11 *Pamela; or, Virtue Rewarded*, (ed.) P. Sabor with an introduction by M.A. Doody (Harmondsworth: Penguin, 1985), 31.

III.4 Educational treatises

Merridee L. Bailey

Early modern educational treatises provide insight into how contemporary pedagogic thinking incorporated physiological theories about emotions into educational theory and practices. These treatises reveal the close attention that was paid to children's temperaments and the complex role education was thought to have in fostering desired emotional states and behaviour. In early modern England the spectrum of printed educational treatises ranges from the humanist writings of Roger Ascham (1515–68), works by schoolmasters like Richard Mulcaster (1531/2–1611) and philosophical texts by John Locke (1632–1704) and Jean-Jacques Rousseau (1712–78). These early modern treatises absorbed, reflected and, in some cases, prompted new ideas about children's passionate temperaments, the role discipline played in encouraging or alternatively stifling learning and, increasingly in the late eighteenth century, children's innocence.

Education would not be organized by nation-states in Europe until the beginning of the eighteenth century, when the desire for a national system of education began to take hold of reformers' minds. In the early modern period educational opportunities therefore developed within schools established by individual charitable bequests, parishes and religious institutions. Despite there being no overarching educational framework, the circulation of printed educational treatises creates a comprehensive surviving archive of sources upon which historians can draw for insight into emotions.

Some of these treatises were intended to deliver theoretical commentary about education but many were written to provide schoolmasters, and sometimes parents, with practical insights into children's learning patterns, their temperaments and popular educational strategies. While these treatises do not represent an educational curriculum as such, they can help historians to understand how early modern educational practices were framed by social-cultural ideas about childhood and emotions. However, this implies a degree of uniformity within contemporary pedagogic theory that overlooks the extent to which early modern pedagogues themselves struggled with the role education and discipline played in curbing or fostering internal and external states. From the sixteenth to eighteenth centuries, the common assumption that children were prone to sudden outbursts of passion, or emotion, meant that childish passions were frequently raised in educational treatises. These passions made children impressionable, inconstant and dangerous. Education could be a tool to quell these passions, ideally leading children towards a more stable emotional state. However, children's more natural and open temperaments could also be lauded. What is clear is that writers and educators paid close attention to the intersection between educational practices and contemporary theories of emotional temperament.

Continental humanism had a significant impact on the trajectory of post-elementary education across Europe from the fifteenth century. The leading humanist pedagogue was Desiderius Erasmus (*c.* 1466–1536) who praised pure and sincere emotions (*affectus*) as a way to attain virtue. Two of Erasmus's most important pedagogical treatises, *De Civiltate Morum Puerilium* (1526) and *Declamatio de Pueris Instituendis* (1529), were concerned with the emotional character and development of young (male) children. Another influential early humanist treatise on education is Roger Ascham's posthumously published *The Scholemaster* (1570). Ascham eloquently made a case for education to be inspired by love and pleasure rather than fear and discipline. These ideas were not in themselves groundbreaking. Ascham's treatise popularized contemporary notions appearing elsewhere in Europe amongst humanist educators, but the almost immediate repute with which his treatise was greeted makes it a central text for understanding the influence of sixteenth-century humanist pedagogy in England.

The late sixteenth-century writings of the grammar schoolmaster Richard Mulcaster have also played a central role in the scholarship about early modern education. Mulcaster viewed laughing and weeping as embodied emotional processes underpinning learning. As was common in pedagogic theory, corporal punishment was cited as a necessary corrective to children's behaviour. However, Mulcaster warned that punishment that appeared to be at the whim of the master would trigger laughter. Ideas based on Galenic humoral pathology are embedded in his explanation of discipline: 'If the maister should beate his boye, and bring no cause why, but that he sought to haue him weepe, so to excercise him to health, and to ridde him of some humours, which made him to moist . . . he might burst out in laughing streight after his stripes'.[1] However, laughter could also serve as a remedy for melancholic students: 'Therfore it must needs be good for them to vse laughing, which haue cold heades, and cold chestes, which are troubled with melancholie, which are light headed by reason of some cold distemperature of the braine'.[2]

Writers like Ascham and Mulcaster tended to work within existing bodies of knowledge about physiology and behaviour, drawing partly on the pseudo-Boethian treatise *De disciplina scholarium* (1230). Other pedagogues across Europe, such as Pietro Paulo Vergerio (1370–1444/5) at Padua, took up similar ideas. However, writers such as Locke have been credited with developing new directions within which children's emotional states and educational practices were conceived. The success of Locke's *Some Thoughts Concerning Education* (1693), reprinted some dozens of times and translated into French, Dutch, German, Italian and Swedish, has ensured that Locke's name has been inextricably linked to changing educational thinking. Yet, the originality of Locke's treatise may be somewhat overstated. A mixture of rationality and close attention to emotional states sums up the Lockean child. Locke's primary concern was the age-old desire to inculcate virtuous behaviour in children; this was to be achieved by mastering self-control from a young age and overcoming children's natural propensity towards wilfulness, which was a common feature of earlier writing. Locke explicitly encouraged tutors and parents to pay close attention to children's unique temperaments and inclinations. Emotional states like shame would help to ensure children understood and internalized mistakes, while esteem and praise would act as emotional inducements for children to better themselves. Children's love of liberty and their pride in independent achievements were central to Locke's views. Curiosity was a 'positive appetite' that would drive children towards learning. However, far more important was the role of rationality. Children were to be treated as rational beings by parents and tutors, a desire which Locke believed was innate to children themselves.

Rousseau's *Emile, Or On Education* (1762) had even more impact on contemporary educational thought across Europe. Rousseau rejected Locke's emphasis on appealing to reason, arguing children would not develop this attribute until their teens. Prior to this, children needed to freely explore the innocent stage of childhood. 'Childhood has its way of seeing, thinking, and feeling which are proper to it', he explained.[3] Rousseau, however, saw children as prone to wilfulness and volatile emotions when he identified them as 'devoured by the most irascible passions'.[4] Rousseau's greatest contribution to educational thinking lay not in any practical exploration of education – Rousseau himself referred to his work as a 'visionary's dreams about education' – but in how he was regarded by later writers and educators as the voice of a more progressive child-centred education.[5]

Emotions were also taught within the grammar curriculum through the emphasis on rhetoric and imitation. Lynn Enterline has revealed how rhetoric taught generations of early modern men to value the transfer of emotion from speaker to audience and trained them in how to create emotional responses in others. Her approach to educational sources combines traditional close reading of material with psychoanalytical approaches, a method of enquiry which opens up questions about emotional oppression, restraint and identity. Here too gender theory plays an important role in understanding early modern masculinity and suggests how careful attention to excavating emotional processes can be used to further our knowledge of gender identity.

To identify the different functions, meanings and values emotions had in early modern educational treatises scholars will first need to explore the ways in which the physiology of emotions was linked to education and when and how this changed towards a social theory of emotions. Identifying continuities and changes in how emotions were theorized will contribute to wider debates about the cultural role of emotions. Scholars can also fruitfully contribute to debates about the reality of educational experiences by identifying fissures between pedagogic theory and practice. Here, the unexpected consequences that theory and practice had on the emotional development of students can be teased out; a direction which Enterline's work proves is of great value. As can be seen here, the need to chart transnational interactions and contact between English and European sources is also required and will allow educational practices to be discussed in relation to wider Continental trends. While ideas about children's emotional states and associated educational practices shifted over time, writers typically assumed that both institutional and textual education primarily related to boys. The need, indeed the desirability, to educate girls was chronically and systematically downplayed. There are, of course, exceptions to this trend. Thomas More (1478–1535) is one, as is the German Ambrosius Moibanus (1494–1554) and, to a lesser extent, Erasmus in some of his writings. Scholars of emotions can expand this field by exploring contemporary thinking about girls' temperaments and questioning the intersection between gender, youth and emotional disposition.

Scholars who examine these texts will be able to fruitfully question the projection of emotions onto children by adults – revealing adult views of emotion and their function, how pedagogic theory took contemporary notions about children's heightened passions, wilfulness and innocence into account, how the pedagogic tool of imitation affected emotions and identity and how ideas about children's emotions were gendered.

Further reading

Bailey, J., *Parenting in England 1760–1830: Emotion, Identity, and Generation* (Oxford: Oxford University Press, 2012)
—an excellent study of the cultural construction of emotional practices associated with parents and children's lives.
Enterline, L., *Shakespeare's Schoolroom: Rhetoric, Discipline, Emotion* (Philadelphia: University of Pennsylvania Press, 2012)
—a rich analysis of Renaissance attitudes towards the passions which is combined with a thorough study of pedagogic theory and practice.

Notes

1 R. Mulcaster, *Positions for the training up of children* (London, 1581), 63.
2 Ibid., 64.
3 J.-J. Rousseau, *Emile, Or On Education*, (trans.) A. Bloom (New York: Basic Books, 1979), 90.
4 Ibid., 87.
5 Ibid., 34.

III.5 Histories, chronicles and memoirs

Erika Kuijpers

In late medieval and early modern Europe an increasingly heterogeneous group of people wrote accounts of their own time. Mostly men but some women as well, religious and lay, people belonging to the urban middle class, learned academics as well as the rural gentry, clerks and schoolmasters, soldiers and craftsmen, all felt a need to keep records of the events they witnessed and remembered. German town archives, even those of small towns, sometimes keep tens, even hundreds, of manuscript chronicles from the early modern period. Although many of them have been published in the nineteenth and twentieth centuries, many more remain unpublished.[1] By their selection of topics chronicles reveal what contemporaries thought worthwhile to record and remember. Chronicles describe the events and circumstances that impacted their lives, that evoked anger, worry or sorrow, but also wonder and joy. The act of chronicling itself can be seen as an act of concern. Quite often the concerns are about disruption, disorder and discontinuity in the existence of local communities.

The activity of chronicling has multiple early medieval origins. Medieval convents had a long tradition of chronicling. Most orders and especially the fifteenth-century Observant movement, recommended the writing of convent histories and caused 'an explosion of scribal activity'.[2] Rather summary texts gradually developed into more extensive history writing – of dynasties, regions, even the whole world. In times of war and religious division but also during the fifteenth-century monastic reforms that encroached deeply on the daily life of the regular clergy, such accounts often implicitly or explicitly reveal their authors' feelings. A second group of medieval chroniclers can be found in the retinue of princes and aristocrats, usually clerics or other men of letters who started chronicling the memorable deeds of dynastic families. From the fifteenth century, ambitious soldiers form another important group of authors. They kept accounts of their services in order to reproduce them in their applications for rewards, pardons or better positions. Contrary to what the term 'memoir' suggests, many military memoirs should be characterized as chronicles of military events rather than autobiographies. Reflections on actions or personal feelings were rarely the subject of such texts.[3] Finally, by the sixteenth century, towns became the most important production centres of lay history writing. In Northern Italy, Southern Germany and Flanders, town secretaries archived town privileges and charters in chronological order and wrote urban histories. While chronicling by town officials evolved into published histories and chorographies by the seventeenth century, the documenting of local events was continued by private initiative and became a widespread urban activity, especially in times of war or political upheaval. Although they usually remained unpublished, they circulated widely and were often copied, edited and expanded by others.

Chronicles seem to have been instrumental in ordering and interpreting the affective turmoil caused by the events in the lifetimes of their authors and readers. Late medieval chronicles typically recorded events in a chronological order without necessarily integrating these into a coherent narrative. Although chroniclers usually followed classical and biblical examples in their structuring and selection of subject matter, soon authors customized these scripts to contemporary needs. Many accounts were produced in times of 'troubles' or 'remarkable occurrences' with the aim of preserving memories of local events and customs, providing facts for future judicial proceedings, or presenting emblems of heroism, good citizenship, devotion and other virtues. Texts that have 'history' in their titles typically exhibit a more consciously-chosen beginning and end, and some reflection about the course of events, making causal connections and adding meaning. Many accounts, however, are difficult to classify. Some had more than one author, and are not consistently written in one style or from the same perspective. Others commence with a recapitulation of significant events in the history of an institution or locality, but subsequently evolve into a more personal narrative of dramatic contemporary events such as war or other disasters. Likewise, memoirs could be turned into a family history by following generations. The level of narrative coherence may thus unexpectedly change in the course of a text.

These sources are useful for students of emotion on three levels: first, analysing semantics, phrasing, emotional expression and description; second, interpreting the selection, omission and structuring of subject matter, the choice of genre, narrative perspective and organization, and third, considering the text as a communicative, mnemonic and emotional object – the social and cultural context of its production, its (intended) use and its afterlife.

First, on the level of verbal expression, chronicles and histories are notoriously terse in style and usually contain little emotional language. Authors believed that they should record facts as they were and without rhetorical flourishes, and they also considered that writing the truth was a matter of the mind, not of the heart. Nonetheless, some emotions as well as their expressions were considered appropriate in many accounts of war and disaster. The most factual reports of political and military events may therefore suddenly be interrupted with a lamentation on the sinfulness of humankind and refer to biblical passages on suffering. Fear of God's punishment should be interpreted as a sign of devoutness in this context. In general, instances of sacrilege and apocalyptic forebodings including omens, plagues, dearth, war and social disorder evoked strong emotions and, as examples of moral decline, emotional expression was legitimate. War accounts typically described fear and sadness among people, but rarely, personal grief or guilt. Chronicles and histories were not texts understood to be about the inner self and even memoirs were rarely intimate or personal in this period. Authors wrote from a collective perspective and usually for an unspecified readership of family, friends or a local community.

By contrast, a category of emotions that can certainly be studied through these sources are those associated with honour and civil pride as well as shame. Threats to justice, privileges, local tradition and symbols of collective honour and pride, such as town walls or belfries, or individual honour such as hats, coats of arms, horses, or the honour of wives and daughters, as well as the virginity of religious women, all evoked very strong emotional reactions. They expressed both fear, agony and indignation, and quite often blaming and shaming is an undercurrent. In the case of loss, feelings of grief and depression are also described.[4] To the modern reader, the rhetoric of lamentations and references to biblical and other literary themes seem impersonal and perhaps even obligatory, yet to contemporaries, these were familiar and meaningful and just as evocative as the commonplaces we use nowadays in more individualized descriptions of what we feel.

Second, even when chronicles scarcely name or describe emotions, the narrative adds to its emotion-triggering effect. For example, in eyewitness reports of dramatic events, a densification in time and the staging of speaking actors, as well as the description of the sensory experiences of the eyewitness, function to increase the emotional effect.[5] Also the enumeration of facts, dry as they seem to the modern reader, can be interpreted as a reaction to disorder and discontinuity, revealing God's providential project. Authors often meticulously chronicle years of hunger and dearth, weather circumstances, plague and natural disaster, until the late seventeenth century, signs from heaven and whales washed ashore. Often an eschatological perspective is quite subtly packed into the historical facts that are registered.

Finally, at a third level, the act of writing a chronicle itself can be studied as part of memory practices and emotional cultures.[6] Although not always explicitly articulated, chronicling was a way of positioning oneself or one's collectivity in time, in space, in society and/or on the road to salvation. Title, address, dedication, motives and of course the selection of topics are all indicative: what motivates the authors, what are their concerns, what do they value or repudiate, what do they get emotional about? The same is true of course for those who copied, edited and preserved these texts for the future.

Further reading

Corens, L., K. Peters and A. Walsham (eds), *The Social History of the Archive: Record Keeping in Early Modern Europe* (Oxford: Oxford University Press, 2016)

—discusses the various ways lay people collected, recorded and ordered the history of their lifetime.

Dale, S. and A. Williams Lewin (eds), *Chronicling History: Chroniclers and Historians in Medieval and Renaissance Italy* (University Park, PA: The Pennsylvania State University Press, 2007)

—case studies exploring the early rise and very rich tradition of urban chronicling by lay people in Italian cities.

Sweet, R., *The Writing of Urban Histories in Eighteenth-Century England* (Oxford: Clarendon Press, 1997) —the first two chapters concern antiquarianism and the chronicling tradition in England.

Notes

1 J.S. Pollmann, 'Archiving the Present and Chronicling for the Future in Early Modern Europe', in L. Corens, K. Peters and A. Walsham (eds), *The Social History of the Archive: Record Keeping in Early Modern Europe* (Oxford: Oxford University Press, 2016)

2 A. Winston-Allen, *Convent Chronicles: Women Writing about Women and Reform in the Late Middle Ages* (University Park: Pennsylvania State University Press, 2004), 11.

3 Y. Noah Harari, 'Military memoirs: a historical overview of the genre from the middle ages to the late modern era', *War in History* 14, 3 (2007), 293–4; Harari, *Renaissance Military Memoirs: War, History, and Identity, 1450–1600* (Woodbridge: Boydell Press, 2004)

4 See E. Kuijpers, 'Expressions of Fear, Counting the Loss: Managing Emotions in War Chronicles in the Netherlands (1568–1648)', in J. Spinks and C. Zika (eds), *Disaster, Death and the Emotions in the Shadow of the Apocalypse, 1400–1700* (Basingstoke: Palgrave Macmillan, 2016), 93–111.

5 Kuijpers, '"O, Lord, Save Us from Shame": Narratives of Emotions in Convent Chronicles by Female Authors during the Dutch Revolt, 1566–1635', in S. Broomhall (ed.), *Gender and Emotions in Medieval and Early Modern Europe: Destroying Order, Structuring Disorder* (Farnham: Ashgate, 2015), 127–45.

6 J.S. Pollmann and B. Deseure, 'The Experience of Rupture and the History of Memory', in E. Kuijpers, J. Pollmann, J. Müller, J. van der Steen (eds), *Memory before Modernity. Practices of Memory in Early Modern Europe* (Leiden: Brill, 2013), 315–29.

III.6 Medical sources

Robert L. Weston

The emotional consequence of illness is a familiar idea to all of us, as has always historically been the case; however, how emotions were expressed and responded to, have varied over time. The manner in which medicine was practiced and the theories which underlay them were quite different in the early modern Europe to those of today, nor were emotions conceived in the same way. To examine these issues, one has to analyse the records of how illness and wellness were understood, and how patients and practitioners reacted to them. The emotions aroused by ill health encompassed anger, fear and shame while the recovery of wellness could be expected to give rise to hope, relief, even joy. Expressions of emotions associated with illness are found in a variety of sources, diaries, personal correspondence, wills, requests for medical advice and the responses to them, and academic texts. These varied sources inevitably result in correspondingly varied rhetoric, depending on the author, the intended readership and their relationship. Treatises were written by physicians and surgeons on the cause and treatments that covered the gamut of disorders from which the population suffered. Many were written for fellow practitioners, others were produced for a wider audience, the medically untrained but literate section of the community. This broader readership represented a significant market, particularly when desperation and fear arose. The value of these works lies in the explanations they offer on the relationship between disease and emotions and contemporary medical theories. Over the period from 1500 to 1800, physicians shifted their thinking on emotions from being a purely physiological phenomenon to one with parallel psychological elements.

The term 'emotion' was not widely used in the early modern period; rather, the terms employed were 'passion' and 'affection'. Amongst the medical fraternity, passion was understood to involve a disturbance, usually called a perturbation, of some part of the body. In this context, when physicians wrote of a 'passion of the liver', this was a specific disorder rather than an emotion. However, when they turned to 'passions of the mind', we are getting close to the modern notion of emotions, even though their understanding of causes was different. For example, in, *Via recta ad vitam longam. Or, A treatise wherein the right way and best manner of living for attaining to a long and healthfull life* (1650), Thomas Venner (*c.* 1609–61) contended that such perturbations could alter the body, and weaken and overthrow the faculties. Later in the period, *First Lines of the Practice of Physic* (1790) by William Cullen (1710–90) not only categorized the passions, but demonstrated how in some circumstances a patient's emotions, such as fear, could be deliberately elevated as a form of therapy.

To examine the way individuals, and those around them, reacted to ill-health, one has to examine a broader set of sources. Thus, Madame de Sévigné (1626–96) described in letters how her own rheumatism affected her emotional state in daily life and, of her distress over the illnesses of her family and friends. Samuel Pepys (1633–1703) diarized a vivid account of his and his wife's fears at the prospect of her undergoing surgery. In this example the actual words clearly indicated their emotional states. However, in some instances, it is in the tone of what is written that indicates emotional arousal; the social class and gender of the writer has to be taken into account when analysing sources.

Another key resource is written medical advice, a practice that dates back to at least the thirteenth century. There are thousands of such records in Dutch, English, French, German, Italian and Latin, mostly as manuscripts. They come in two forms, *consilia,* written advice provided after a physician or surgeon had seen the patient, and *consultations* where a face-to-face encounter had not occurred, and advice was sought and given solely on a written basis. Such requests for help could come from the patient, family members or less expert local practitioners. They concerned both sexes and covered all ages, although instances of sick children are in a minority.

Patients more often commented on their sentiments about what their illness did to their state of mind, than did physicians. At times, emotions were expressed quite explicitly: 'my brain was full of fear and sorrow', at other times it was subtle, like the women whose illness 'has taken away my spirits'.[1] The rhetoric employed was limited by what was socially acceptable. Furthermore, many patients paraphrased the linguistic form used in letters written by physicians. For the most part, the consultant did not even record a patient's emotional state, dealing with what he perceived as a physiological problem by providing a diagnosis, occasionally a prognosis, and therapeutic recommendations.

The exceptions were when the emotional state was related to the cause of the illness. The most vivid descriptions of patients' distress, physical and mental, occurred in cases of melancholia in men, and hysteria in women, common disorders in the early modern period.[2] Thus the Dutch physician Herman Boerhaave (1668–1738) wrote of a patient whose illness was caused by shock:

> prodigiously affrighted by a terrible shock of thunder and lightning, which she looked upon as a judgement, did not recover her fright for some weeks, but was always dull and melancholy, and fell into hysterical fits; which by degrees grew more violent.

Noteworthy here is not simply her derangement, but the moral aspect, that the patient saw the event as a moral judgement.[3] Religion was an important aspect of early modern society, Catholic and Protestant. There had been a traditional view that sickness was God's response to the sins of the patient, or society at large in the case of epidemics. Epidemics were common, some across all of Europe, others of a more localized nature, either way they resulted in fear, often panic, none more so than the plague. After the 1665 plague John Evelyn (1620–1706) wrote in his diary, 'Blessed be God for his infinite mercy in preserving us'.[4] However, expressions of relief or happiness on recovering from sickness that might be expected are rarely encountered, even when death was expected and subsequently avoided. Illness could also be viewed as God testing the faith of the believer. Expressions of emotion were accordingly more common when a patient undertook a pilgrimage or sought out some religious reliquary to pray before, in thanks or to seek a cure.

Death of course led to grief amongst those left behind. Soldier Henri de Campion (1613–63) was disconsolate over the death, from measles, of his first-born, a daughter, a loss he continued to mourn until his own death 27 years later. He wrote 'I have not yet had an hour without I think about it . . . even though there has been more than one [child] that I have lost'. He regarded her not just as a child but as a friend; 'so nice, so agreeable, that from the day of her birth I loved her with a tenderness that I cannot explain'. At the other end of the scale were those disorders that were not life-threatening but which prevented an individual from enjoying their normal lifestyle. There are many instances recorded of individuals suffering from diseases of the eyes and ears which interfered with their everyday lives. The prospect of losing one's sight was fearsome, though, surprisingly, there are few records of the patient's responses when surgical intervention had cured the common complaint of cataracts. Losing the sense of hearing was distressing in the way it disrupted personal relationships. Apart from any physical discomfort, the emotional stress that arose from such disorders was often only alluded to rather than explicitly written.

It was rare for a physician or surgeon to express his own emotions when trying to deal with suffering and pain. That is not to suggest the physicians at the bed-side were immune to feeling for their patients, simply that they seldom recorded them. This could be stoicism, or, as likely, maintaining their authority over the patient. On the other hand, they freely expressed moral outrage when a patient's illness was the result of a dissolute life, such as overindulgence in alcohol or contracting venereal diseases.[5]

The analysis of these varied sources can provide a window into how medical sources articulated emotions in a variety of ways and contexts – scholarly and popular, practitioner and patient. Whilst the experience of disease and ill-health might be thought to be so fundamental as to be chronologically consistent, the manner in which feelings were expressed varied widely through the period as medical ideas and social norms changed.

Further reading

Elmer, P. and O.P. Grell (eds), *Health, Disease and Society in Europe 1500–1800: A Source Book* (Manchester: Manchester University Press, 2004)
—provides examples of primary and secondary sources from across Europe which touch not only on the medicine of the period but also the cultural and social environments in which medicine was practised.
Stolberg, M., *Experiencing Illness and the Sick Body in Early Modern Europe* (Basingstoke: Palgrave Macmillan, 2011)
—describes the changes in patients' and physicians' constructions of psychopathological conditions with time.
Weston, R.L., 'Medical Effects and Affects: The Expression of Emotion in Early Modern Patient-Physician Correspondence', in S. Broomhall (ed.), *Ordering Emotions in Europe, 1100–1800* (Leiden: Brill, 2015), 263–81.
—exemplifies the emotional responses of patients and physicians to illness.

Notes

1 See R. Weston, *Medical Consulting by Letter in France 1665–1789* (Farnham: Ashgate, 2013)
2 There are many contemporary sources and an extensive historiography on these ailments.
3 H. Boerhaave, *Boerhaave's medical correspondence containing the various symptoms of chronical distempers, the professor's opinion, method of cure and remedies: to which is added Boerhaave's practice in the hospital at Leyden, with his manner of instructing his pupils in the cure of diseases* (London, 1745), 11.
4 J. Evelyn, *The Diary of John Evelyn*, (ed.) J. Bowle (Oxford: Oxford University Press, 1983), 206.
5 Weston, 'Epistolary consultations on venereal disease in eighteenth-century France', *French History and Civilization. Papers from the George Rudé Seminar* 3 (2009), 69–79.

III.7 Economic records

Merridee L. Bailey

Early modern economic records have largely fallen outside the scope of scholarly research into emotions. Historians have understandably shied away from supposedly drier source materials, assuming that emotions will be absent from certain bodies of sources. This assumption partly explains the absence of systematic work into the presence of emotions in early modern Europe's economic records and the lack of explicit methodologies to investigate the role emotions have played in historic economic systems. Yet scholars of emotion can turn to a surprisingly varied range of sources to explore the expression, practice and experience of emotion in commercial life across early modern Europe. These sources can be used to identify the distinctiveness of real-world economic practices within which the English and European economy operated. Economic records in the form of merchant account books, journals (or 'daybooks'), merchant letters, diaries and records of debt litigation communicate information about individual commercial actors. Records of institutional commercial life can be found in guild records, banking records, chartered company records, minute books, the archives of the powerful merchant houses, stock ledgers and the records of trading companies such as the East India and South Sea Companies.

Placing economic practices into the wider world of social-political ideas also requires scholars to consider sources beyond the economic domain such as literature, plays and sermons. English literary sources offer insights into English merchant affairs. *The Merchant of Venice* (1596–8) by William Shakespeare (1564–1616) deals explicitly with usurious transactions, but other works such as *Troilus and Cressida* (1602) have also been noted for their preoccupation with value and trade. Shakespeare's contemporaries, such as the playwright Thomas Dekker (*c.* 1572–1632), explored the value of honest labour, stratification in the mercantile community and mercantile aspirations in creative ways, while the genre of the London city comedy frequently included merchant characters and mercantile preoccupations. Similar Continental literary commentary on economic behaviour exists, such as the Dutch *The Great Mirror of Folly* (1720), which appeared after the world's first global stock market collapse and satirized emotions such as greed and competition.

Taken as a whole, these sources testify to the careful recording of credit and debt relationships, household expenditures and risk management by men and women who were involved in small-scale credit transactions, as well as the larger-scale transactions conducted between commercial entities across England, Europe and the Americas. These sources are regularly mined by quantitative economic historians for information about wage and inflation rates, risk management and patterns of commercialization. Social and cultural historians gain insights into social-cultural market practices, the relationship between individualism and reciprocity, interpersonal relationships and, with increasing sensitivity, commerce and gender. However, qualitative historians of early modern markets have been more interested in uncovering the moral and cultural dimensions of market practices than in its emotional side, while most social and cultural historians have been hesitant to add economic dimensions to the study of historical emotional phenomena. As a result, we know very little about how emotion contributed to shaping the cultural and moral environment in which the early modern economy was practised.

Methodological approaches that would help scholars to systematically unpick the emotional dimension of historic economic systems are also in their infancy. An exception to this is Susan J. Matt's work on the emotional style of twentieth-century America, which linked changing emotional codes to growing consumerism.[1] Her work is positioned against economic thinking that posits the universalism of economic instincts, instead showing that certain emotional traits such as envy and the desire for pleasure are needed for particular economic practices (in this case, consumerism) to develop fully, and that these emotional habits are learned processes. Emotions shape, or are implicated in shaping, the trajectory of economic movements.

Two primary obstacles currently hamper scholars from fully integrating economic records into the study of emotions. Quantitative records, such as monetary tallies, records of sales, account books and stock prices appear to offer little obvious scope for investigating the emotional state of the record keeper's mind or the emotional motivations behind decisions to buy or sell particular commodities. However, equally problematic has been the influence of neo-classical economic thinking, along with the later development of behavioural economics, on how emotions and the economic sphere have been broadly conceived. The concept of the 'rational economic man' (*homo economicus*), broadly theorized in the mid-nineteenth century by John Stuart Mill (1806–73) and later codified by commentators of his work, helped modern neo-classical economists to displace emotions from economic life, while in the 1980s behavioural economists reinserted emotions into the economic realm but only by contending that emotions opposed rational thinking. Much of this – largely ahistorical – economic thinking is preoccupied with proving how emotion negatively influences rational economic decision-making. According to these two weighty approaches, emotion is understood as unnecessary to economic practices or as a distraction that modern economic agents can overcome. It is no wonder that the systematic investigation of emotions in historical markets has yet to develop fully. However, history is uniquely placed to show how emotions shape economic behaviour, that economic practices are not ahistorical and, consequently, to offer insights into the role emotions have in modern economic exchanges.

Important groundwork for understanding how emotion might influence historic norms and practices in exchange relationships already exists. At the start of the twentieth century understanding the 'culture of commerce' became one of the principal goals of economic historians. Max Weber, R.H. Tawney and E.P. Thompson recognized that culture – specifically religious culture – influenced not just economic thinking but altered the trajectory of economic practice.[2] More recently, historians such as Craig Muldrew, Margo Finn and Alexandra Shepard have investigated early modern economic practices in social and cultural terms, focusing on merchant exchange relationships, reputation, gender and 'worth', reciprocity and trust.[3] Largely guided by Craig Muldrew's seminal re-examination of the market as a place where cultural meaning and social trust were exchanged, economic historians are increasingly redefining the boundaries of historical market relations by integrating economic behaviour into larger socio-cultural frameworks.

Little attention, however, has been paid to Muldrew's argument that credit in early modern England was understood as having emotional as well as social dimensions. Economic systems are not closed worlds that emotional experiences, behaviours, practises and expressions are unable to penetrate. Conflicts over credit and debt, as well as trading regulations endorsed by civic and guild authorities, had real-life implications for everyone. Emotions like fear, shame, anger, vanity, anxiety, pity and compassion inevitably come into play when individuals are involved in economic conflict with neighbours, in managing risk and uncertainty, or when civic regulations are seen as unfair or punitive.

To explore emotions, scholars need to be attentive to the evidence from merchant letters, account books and legal records that reveal the ways in which merchants and traders themselves articulated ideas about business and financial arrangements in a language that incorporated emotional discourse. Equally vital will be the study of institutional records and philosophical and moral writings about economic practices, and literary sources that articulate a discourse of their own. Barbara H. Rosenwein's methodological approach to language involves the careful exposition of contemporary vocabularies of emotions, and historians can fruitfully draw upon this in the study of economic records.[4] Equally important is acknowledging economic behaviour that once had emotional power, such as esteem, or the desire for honour, which is key to understanding early modern notions of credit but is no longer viewed in the same light as holding emotional meaning. Ute Frevert's work on recovering lost emotions may help economic historians to uncover economically relevant emotions that have fallen from view.[5]

The next step for scholars will be to demonstrate what particular vocabularies tell us about the society in which they appear. This may reveal the existence of unique structural characteristics between emotions and economic practices in particular historic periods or locations, or, habitual patterns which are suggestive of universal behaviour in economic and emotional thinking. Here, much could fruitfully be made by drawing comparisons between English and European records to tease out the nature of the English and European economic experience. Key questions dominating economic history, such as the impact the growing transatlantic trade between Europe and the Americas had on Europe's market economy, the effect of far-reaching commercial networks on risk management and behaviour, the impact commercialization and the gradual movement towards an industrial economy had on individualism, consumerism and the role of desire in shaping economic behaviour, are ones to which historians of emotion can contribute by exploring changing emotional habits and behaviours.

Further readings

Finn, M., *The Character of Credit: Personal Debt in English Culture, 1740–1914* (Cambridge: Cambridge University Press, 2003)

—Finn's willingness to include literature, plays and sermons places economic practices into the wider socio-political world.

Hirschman, A.O., *The Passions and the Interests: Political Arguments for Capitalism before its Triumph* (New Jersey: Princeton University Press, 1977)

—insightful analysis of how the passions were tamed by the promotion of material accumulation; a model study in political economy, the philosophy of emotions and human nature.

Matt, S.J., *Keeping up with the Joneses: Envy in American Consumer Society, 1890–1930* (Philadelphia: University of Pennsylvania, 2003)

—one of the first full-length studies to demonstrate the connection between the history of emotions and consumer capitalism.

Notes

1 S.J. Matt, *Keeping up with the Joneses: Envy in American Consumer Society, 1890–1930* (Philadelphia: University of Pennsylvania, 2003)

2 M. Weber, *The Protestant Ethic and the Spirit of Capitalism*, (trans.) T. Parsons and A. Giddens (London: Unwin Hyman, 1930); R.H. Tawney, *Religion and the Rise of Capitalism* (New York: Harcourt, 1926); E.P. Thompson, 'The moral economy of the English crowd in the eighteenth century', *Past & Present* 50 (1971), 76–136.

3 C. Muldrew, *The Economy of Obligation: The Culture of Credit and Social Relations in Early Modern England* (Basingstoke: Macmillan, 1998); M. Finn, *The Character of Credit: Personal Debt in English Culture, 1740–1914* (Cambridge: Cambridge University Press, 2003); A. Shepard, *Accounting for Oneself: Worth, Status, and the Social Order in Early Modern England* (Oxford: Oxford University Press, 2015).

4 B.H. Rosenwein, *Emotional Communities in the Early Middle Ages* (Ithaca: Cornell University Press, 2006)

5 U. Frevert, *Emotions in History: Lost and Found* (Budapest: Central European University Press, 2011)

III.8 Judicial sources

Joanne McEwan

Judicial records – or official documents produced by the criminal justice system – comprise a substantial but often fragmentary body of extant sources for the study of historical emotions. Created at various points in the legal process, sources such as indictments, depositions and petitions can provide us with insights into the actions and behaviours that particular societies deemed unacceptable, as well as community responses, individual motivations and emotional investments. Social and gender historians have been utilizing these sources since the 1980s. More recently, emotions scholars have also begun to recognize how they can inform us about the emotions experienced and expressed by individuals, and also the expected emotional norms, regimes or styles of various settings. The social and emotional potential of these types of sources has not always been easily reconciled, however, with their official and formulaic nature. Early crime historians were careful to point out the mediated nature of legal sources. They were, for instance, always created in the wake of extraordinary circumstances, especially when they related to serious crimes, and they were always dictated by formal procedure and their purpose within a legal framework. This affected the way they were structured, the information they contained and the kinds of insights we can glean from them. Additionally, while we know a great deal about the legal processes that generated these documents, specific details about exactly how they were created are often lacking. Sources that read like personal narratives – confessions and depositions, for example – were in fact written down by third-party clerks, and this adds a layer of mediation: we do not know if and when the clerk left out certain details he regarded as irrelevant or unimportant, whether he altered phrasing, or whether the narrative was shaped by questions or requests for clarification that were not recorded. We should also not assume that people were not cognizant of the potential consequences of their legal testimony. This, along with other factors, influenced whether they said anything and, if so, how they framed what they said. So long as we keep these limitations in mind, however, legal sources can tell us about emotions in a number of ways.

Scholars have long recognized that each society determines its own criminal code, and that what is deemed unacceptable or illegal at any given time is influenced by the preoccupations of people within those societies, or at least those who exerted influence as legislators. The criminal charges laid out in indictments, then, can tell us about the fears and anxieties of early modern governing bodies. It is not a coincidence, for example, that witchcraft statutes were introduced throughout Europe in the sixteenth century, amidst widespread religious and political turmoil. Similarly, the number of separate property offences in England increased dramatically in the eighteenth century (as part of what came to be known as 'The Bloody Code') precisely *because* of a growing preoccupation among the ruling classes with safeguarding their property. The highly emotive and emphatic, albeit formulaic, language used to describe crimes in indictments often also provides us with insight into the sentiments that the authorities wanted to link with certain behaviours. The wording used to describe child murder in Scotland, for example, routinely included adjectives such as barbarous, heinous, monstrous and unnatural. As records outlining formal criminal charges, indictments can usefully inform our understanding of 'emotional regimes' (the emotions and behaviours deemed acceptable and unacceptable by the authorities) within the society in which they were being laid. But, as documents created with no input from the defendants who were being charged, we must remember that they cannot tell us anything about their actions, emotions or guilt.

The ethos of entire criminal justice systems relied on appealing to certain emotions. In early modern England, for instance, it was thought that the law could be enforced most effectively through terror and example, by executing a select number of men and women in a spectacular manner to instil fear and ensure deterrence from others. The pronouncing of a death sentence in court (and, by extension, official documentation) was consciously retained, even when the judge intended to recommend mercy, in the hope that 'the solemnity of its pronunciation, and the judge's condemnation, would frighten the prisoner into obeying the law in the future'.[1] A system of pardoning developed, which generated records such as official reports about which convicts should be reprieved and individual petitions for mercy. Surviving petitions range from the semi-literate appeals of prisoners to more formal and formulaic documents written by relatives, friends or paid scribes. In a ground-breaking study of French pardoners' letters in 1987, Natalie Zemon Davis argued that petitions need to be viewed as carefully crafted narratives that catered to their specific purpose rather than as objective or truthful reports about the petitioners' circumstances.[2] Reading petitions in this way allows us to appreciate the ways in which the formulaic language and tropes they employ were conscious attempts to evoke particular emotional responses. They drew on notions of family responsibility, for example, to elicit pity.

Depositions, confessions and accounts of trial proceedings (whether transcribed in official minute books or printed in publications such as *The Proceedings of the Old Bailey*) provide us with rare access to the voices of premodern people, albeit in mediated form and under extraordinary circumstances.[3] The explanations provided by defendants shed light on their actions and motives (if they were guilty), and as such can serve as a window into their social and emotional worlds. Drawing on confessions from early modern Germany, for example, Ulinka Rublack has clearly pinpointed fear and shame as reasons why women concealed illicit pregnancies.[4] Confessions are particularly fraught judicial sources. This is especially true when they were secured in judicial arenas that employed torture. When regarded as constructed narratives rather than strictly factual accounts, however, they can give us a sense of the kinds of stories that defendants thought would be plausible, or the ways they tried to justify or make sense of their actions, and the emotions they wanted to convey.

Depositions and testimony from witnesses also offer valuable insights into community attitudes and emotions. As the words of individuals involved in a trial rather than prescriptive legalese, they provide useful perspectives on both the events in question and how emotional regimes were accepted or resisted. Some crimes, especially seemingly victimless ones such as illicit distilling, were tolerated or even enabled within communities. When witnesses were reluctant to testify, as evidenced in affidavits requesting continuances because particular individuals could not be located, or when they found themselves indicted for offering support (harbouring fugitives, beating up excise men), it is clear that people sometimes did not feel the indignation or loyalty to the state that the authorities wanted. In cases of domestic violence, Nancy Tomes has suggested that we can gauge the limits of what local communities regarded as acceptable behaviour from the point at which neighbours were willing to step in.[5] Crime and its prosecution was also increasingly reported in newspapers, but prior to the nineteenth century the message being conveyed was often ambiguous and sometimes blatantly critical of the criminal justice system, suggesting a disjuncture between the emotions and expectations of the authorities and those of the populace.[6]

Social and gender scholars have also recognized the enormous potential of depositions and accounts of courtroom proceedings, when analysed qualitatively, to shed light on the wider emotional engagements, motivations, relationships and investments of individuals. They have usefully gleaned information about neighbourly relations, living arrangements, courtships and economic transactions, for example, from the incidental or background details witnesses provided in court. There is tremendous scope for emotions scholars to expand upon this approach, and also – as historians such as David G. Barrie, Susan Broomhall, David Lemmings and Katie Barclay have begun to do – to analyse the emotional atmosphere or 'style' of the courtroom.[7]

Further reading:

Barrie, D.G. and S. Broomhall, *Police Courts in Nineteenth-Century Scotland*, 2 vols (Farnham: Ashgate, 2014)

—investigates the under-researched summary courts in Scottish cities, including how emotions such as humour or shame were used to shape narratives and influence outcomes.

Davis, N.Z., *Fiction in the Archives: Pardon Tales and Their Tellers in Sixteenth-Century France* (Stanford: Stanford University Press, 1987)

—developed the methodology of reading legal sources as consciously and deliberately framed narratives.

Gatrell, V.A.C., *The Hanging Tree: Execution and the English People, 1770–1868* (Oxford: Oxford University Press, 1994)

—landmark study that examines assumptions about emotion upon which the English system of punishment was based, and argues that attitudes began to shift in the late eighteenth century.

Notes

1 J.M. Beattie, *Crime and the Courts in England, 1660–1800* (Princeton: Princeton University Press, 1986), 431.

2 N.Z. Davis, *Fiction in the Archives: Pardon Tales and Their Tellers in Sixteenth-Century France* (Stanford: Stanford University Press, 1987)

3 T. Hitchcock et al., *The Old Bailey Proceedings Online, 1674–1913* (www.oldbaileyonline.org, version 7.0, 24 March 2012).

4 U. Rublack, *The Crimes of Women in Early Modern Germany* (Oxford: Clarendon Press, 1999)

5 N. Tomes, 'A "torrent of abuse": Crimes of violence between working-class men and women in London, 1840–1875', *Journal of Social History* 11, 3 (1978), 328–45.

6 See P. King, 'Newspaper reporting and attitudes to crime and justice in late eighteenth- and early nineteenth-century London', *Continuity and Change* 22, 1 (2007), 73–112.

7 D. Lemmings (ed.), *Crime, Courtrooms, and the Public Sphere in Britain, 1700–1850* (Farnham: Ashgate, 2013); K. Barclay, 'Singing, performance, and lower-class masculinity in the Dublin magistrates' court, 1820–1850', *Journal of Social History* 47, 3 (2014), 746–68; D.G. Barrie and S. Broomhall, *Police Courts in Nineteenth-Century Scotland*, 2 vols (Farnham: Ashgate, 2014)

III.9 Church and parish records

Charlotte-Rose Millar

Church and parish records have long been recognized as sources that provide vital insights into the history of crime and justice in the early modern period. Their importance to the study of family history and demography is also widely lauded as they allow access to records of births, baptisms, marriages and deaths. But more than providing insights into the ecclesiastical justice system or supplying demographic data, I would argue that these records also allow insight into the emotional worlds of early modern men and women. More so than the criminal courts, church courts heard cases of intimate conflicts, often between family members or neighbours in close village communities. Their focus on sin and morality rather than criminality means that depositions from church courts tell us how early modern people felt about issues of morality, sexuality and sin, and how they reacted emotionally to people in their community who were believed to have transgressed these boundaries. Church courts were a crucial means of justice across Western Europe and, in most judicial areas whose records have been studied, marital and sexual issues accounted for the main business of the lower church courts.[1] This entry focuses on cases of marital and sexual relationships and offers some suggestions as to how we can access both individual and communal emotions within these records.

There are two main ways that church records allow insight into early modern mentalities. The first is at a personal level, in that individual testimonies can allow insight into how people felt about their neighbours, how they dealt with conflict and what emotions these conflicts generated. These testimonies demonstrate what types of emotions were acceptable and in what circumstances, as well as the reaction to those who did not conform to expected modes of emotional behaviour. The second concerns how these same records allow us to build an image of the type of 'emotional community' (thus coined by Barbara H. Rosenwein) that these deponents were living in.[2] We can uncover how a community, as a whole, controlled and regulated emotional behaviour and what types of emotional practices created an emotional community.

Although scholars are cautious about how close we can get to what 'actually' happened through court records, or how accurately these records provide insight into popular mentalities, there is a strong consensus that legal records do allow insight into plebeian opinion. While the form their testimonies took was mediated through ecclesiastical authorities, church courts did allow ordinary men and women to give voice to their thoughts, fears, desires, interests and suspicions. The need to explain that these records have been mediated comes through in nearly all academic work on these accounts. Historians working on women have been particularly vocal about whether we can access female narratives through church records. While Lyndal Roper has claimed that these records allow ordinary women to 'speak', others such as Sara Mendelson and Patricia Crawford have warned that 'while female testimony appears to offer direct access to women's own voices, the historian must be constantly aware that every word spoken by a woman was recorded and edited by male officials'.[3]

Recent work by Frances Dolan has boldly claimed that perhaps we can be less cautious about these records than we have been previously. Surely, she contends, all records are in some way mediated, even if just through self-censorship based on men and women's understanding of what they should and should not say, what they believed was important or what words they thought most appropriate. Given this understanding, Dolan asks whether we can 'recast mediation as collaboration', a collaboration that facilitates expression as much as it occludes it.[4] As Dolan reminds us, being a deponent in a church court was not necessarily an unpleasant experience as many deponents were there voluntarily to share stories about their neighbours. In this context we can access both the 'voices' of these ordinary men and women and learn about their society more broadly. Church records are therefore an extremely rich source from which to study the history of emotions.

One of the primary functions of ecclesiastical courts was the regulation of sexual and marital behaviours. It is notoriously difficult to uncover popular attitudes towards sex and marriage. Although we can access legal and theological condemnations of illicit sex as well as household manuals on proper spousal behaviour and popular printed depictions of happy and unhappy marriages, it is far more difficult to access the voices of ordinary men and women. I would suggest that by studying ecclesiastical records on separation, breach of promise, validity of marriage, adultery and bastardy we can attempt to speculate on how ordinary men and women viewed their marital duties, how they viewed the role of sex in marriage and, importantly, how they felt about their marriages and their other intimate relationships. We can then compare these findings to the modes of sexual behaviour that church courts attempted to enforce across Europe. In ecclesiastical records we hear the voices of the accuser, the accused, the witnesses and the church authorities. We are able to see what emotional expectations each party brought to their relationship, as well as the wider concerns of the community.

These records help us to understand how attitudes towards marriage and sexual relationships were constructed within specific villages or, to use Rosenwein's phrase, specific emotional communities. Rosenwein's theory of emotional communities allows for a person to belong to multiple communities. A deponent could be part of a very small emotional community based around a specific household; but also be part of a larger emotional community based around an entire village or area. In addition, a deponent could identify as being part of a much broader emotional community of Catholics or Protestants, depending on the geographical and chronological circumstances. Each of these communities may have had different ways of regulating and practising emotions. It is through ecclesiastical records that we can access these different layers and attempt to build up a picture of the types of influences that affected ordinary men and women's understanding of how they should act within (and feel about) marital and sexual relationships. We can question how expectations differed across communities and whether individual couples conformed to these expectations. These insights can then be used to compare everyday mentalities toward elite theological and legal attitudes. In cases where a community does not regulate its emotional practices in accordance with new legal or theological attitudes we can illuminate under what conditions and pressures different social groups agree to moderate and regulate their emotional practices; and also the extent to which certain emotional practices and beliefs themselves can be used to withstand concerted attempts at regulating emotion. Church records allow us to listen to the voices of ordinary men and women and understand how they constructed and regulated the role of love and desire in sexual and marital relationships. Combining these intimate records with the documenting of key life stages, such as births, baptisms, marriages and deaths, by church officials as found in parish records allows us a fuller picture of how the Church and ordinary men and women viewed these milestones. By revisiting these records and applying emotions histories and methodologies we can explore individual and communal understandings of emotions, add nuance to existing ecclesiastical and legal histories and attempt to recreate the voices of people who are often overlooked.

Church and parish records have far more to tell us about the early modern world than attitudes towards crime, criminality, immorality or demography. They allow insight into early modern mentalities by demonstrating how ordinary men and women felt about some of the most intimate areas of their lives, but also some of the most public demarcations of their identity and status, as we see from baptisms, marriage and death rites marked by the Church. Not only can they help us to understand individual emotional practices, they can also shed light on how different communities regulated these practices and what sorts of emotions were believed to be acceptable in certain circumstances. Although many historians have used church and parish records to understand the social dynamics of early modern Europe, there is still more to be done on how these records provide access to the emotional dynamics of everyday life. Church and parish records are one of the strongest sources we have for accessing past emotions and for understanding how these emotional practices were formed and how they changed in accordance with community expectations.

Further reading

Brundage, J., *Law, Sex, and Christian Society in Medieval Europe* (Chicago: University of Chicago Press, 1987)

—provides a long history of sexuality and the law in Western Europe and by focusing on the changing role of church courts explains how these records allow insight into sexual and marital practices.

Outwaite, R.B., *The Rise and Fall of the English Ecclesiastical Courts, 1500–1860* (Cambridge: Cambridge University Press, 2006)

—recent study that gives a sense of the crucial role that ecclesiastical courts played in myriad aspects of the lives of early modern English men and women.

Notes

1 J.A. Brundage, *Law, Sex, and Christian Society in Medieval Europe* (Chicago: University of Chicago Press, 1987), 545.

2 B.H. Rosenwein, *Emotional Communities in the Early Middle Ages* (Ithaca: Cornell University Press, 2006)

3 L. Roper, *Oedipus and the Devil: Witchcraft, Sexuality and Religion in Early Modern Europe* (London: Routledge, 1994), 20 and S. Mendelson and P. Crawford, *Women in Early Modern England, 1550–1720* (Oxford: Clarendon Press, 1998), 11.

4 F.E. Dolan, *True Relations: Reading, Literature, and Evidence in Seventeenth-Century England* (Philadelphia: University of Pennsylvania Press, 2013), 118.

III.10 Catholic missionary texts

Ananya Chakravarti

Within the European history of emotions, studies of the early modern Catholic church have centred largely around determining the particular affective regime that characterized Catholicism, as springboard and foil for Protestant emotional cultures.[1] As Andrew Tallon notes, far more than theology, Catholic practice derived from an affective piety marked by an increasing focus on personal emotional experience.[2] This affective culture would be used by Catholic missionaries to challenge their Protestant rivals across Europe, whether through devotional practice or through intellectual exploration of the passions.[3]

The embattled church in this period, however, also extended its reach beyond Europe. The archive of this expansion is both vast and far-flung: in Rome, the holdings of the Congregazione di Propaganda Fide, to which many missionaries reported from across the world, remain woefully underutilized. In Portugal, France and Spain, beyond national archives, historians may mine lesser-known holdings such as the Vanves Jesuit archives or the Academia das Ciências in Lisbon, comprising the library of a former Franciscan convent. State archives of former colonies such as Goa, as well as specialized collections such as the Huntington, the John Carter Brown and the Newbury libraries in the US, devoted to the colonial Americas, contain significant missionary collections.

Just as vast as its geographical reach is the range of materials in this web of archives. Pioneering work by Gauvin Alexander Bailey on Jesuit missionary art, which sought to cement their new faith amongst converts by appealing to sense and sentiment, has already suggested the potential for exploring non-textual artefacts for the history of emotions.[4] Textual sources run the gamut from missionary correspondence, grammars, sermons and confessionals, as well as more elaborate literary texts in non-European languages.

Historians of colonial missions have explored Catholic notions of affect as an evangelical tool in unfamiliar cultural terrain.[5] The real opportunity afforded by this missionary archive, however, lies in constructing the history of emotions at the intersection of two cultural worlds, in which one can discern the voices of indigenous converts.[6]

Yet, precisely because affective piety is an important element in many traditions, how do we discern what distinguishes Catholicism as an affective regime? To see the contours of this challenge, consider the following passage from an early seventeenth-century Marāṭhī religious text:

> To show us low people [*gopāḷ*], cowherds your lotus-feet
> Is that why you have come now to this humble house?
> We are humble cowherds for dumb creatures [*mōnjātī*] with no *bhakti* in the body
> To show us your feet, is that why you have taken birth among these animals?
> . . .

> If only you were already grown a little . . .
> you could have played in the forest . . .
> We would have taken you to play among our assembly.[7]

Without further identifying clues, when read in the original, these verses are exemplary of many of the tropes of Marāṭhī *bhakti* literature of the period. *Bhakti* had spread throughout North India by the fifteenth century, often through the transmission of religious love poetry of poet-saints, who could be male or female, from all castes, or even hail from Muslim families, and often wrote in vernacular languages and not Sanskrit, the traditional language of religious scholarship. The *bhakta* or devotee could therefore circumvent the strictures of religious authority arbitrated by the logic of caste hierarchy, through the cultivation of an intense and personal relationship with the deity and through participation in the broader community of *bhaktas*. *Bhakti* was fundamentally characterized by a tension between intellection and emotion, between the path of knowledge (*jñāna*) and devotion (*bhakti*).[8]

The passage quoted above is deeply reminiscent of the iconography of Kṛṣṇa, drawing upon the biographical details of his upbringing among cowherds. Yet the figure to which the cowherds offer their devotion is in fact the infant Jesus. This retelling of Luke 2:11–20 is found in the *Discurso sobre a vinda de Jesu Christo*, published in Roman script by the English Jesuit Thomas Stephens (1549–1619) in 1617. Written in the *ovī* metre revived and popularized by the great Vārkarī saint Eknāth, a contemporary of Stephens's, the *Discurso* gained almost immediate acclaim, in part due to its superior versification and allusive depth, suggesting indigenous co-authorship. Its reception created the conditions for a tradition of Jesuit writings in Marāṭhī that stretched throughout the seventeenth century.

The collective devotional affect established in the language of *bhakti* in this passage may have theologically significant differences in valence from the perspective of the Christian *padre* and a *bhakti* audience. In the *Discurso*, the social significance of Christ's annunciation to humble cowherds is made clear to the converts, where it is impressed upon a primarily Brahmin audience that the Christian god honours even his low-caste devotees.[9] Thus, *the affect of collective devotion* invoked by the text here has the catechetical purpose of cementing the egalitarianism of the Christian congregation, perhaps best expressed in the ritual of the Eucharist where all converts equally consume the miraculous body of Christ.

Yet the constitution of the *bhakti* public functions quite differently.[10] Here, the *collective performance of affective devotion* (primarily, through the collective singing of devotional songs in *kīrtan*) and the place of the body within that performance is central. This complex set of relationships is expressed beautifully in the words of the saint Eknāth:

> The body is Paṇḍharī, the soul is Viṭṭhal
> Pāṇḍuraṅga resides there all alone . . .
> The company of Vaiṣṇavas has gathered . . .
> The ten senses have gathered in a single group;
> this is their cowherds meal (*gopāḷkālā*)
> I have seen Paṇḍharī in body, people, forest:
> Ekā Janārdan is a Vārkarī.[11]

The parallel between the gathering of the devotees and the coalescing of the 10 senses of the body and mind in devotion is key to the affective regime of *bhakti*, in which, through collective performance, the *bhakta* achieves perfect personal devotion to the deity. The metaphor of the shared cowherds' meal for this parallelism is particularly revealing: in Vedic, *bhakta* referred to a morsel of food and the notion that the deity ingests the worshipper's devotion as food has long literary and philosophical precedent.[12] In this light, the passage from the *Discurso* points to vital distinctions between the affective regimes of Catholicism and Marāṭhī *bhakti*.

What kind of affective regime does such a text establish? Is it 'Catholic'? Should we rather read this within the terms of *bhakti*, particularly given the tradition's own capacious accommodation of saints from ostensibly different religious sects and even faiths within its own boundaries? Moreover, in exploring such a text are we uncovering the history of aesthetic accommodation or the history of emotion – and how may we tell the difference? At the very least, perhaps what this text suggests is the gulf between missionary intention and convert reception, so that the shared non-verbal ground of affect facilitated miscommunication as much as rapprochement.

Readings of such texts that take seriously the indigenous interlocutor of the missionaries, and their affective and cultural worlds are thus useful not solely to elucidate through contrast the particularities of Catholic affective culture. They may very well push us to clarify the conceptual terms via which we do the history of emotions *in general*. It allows us to notice our own biased assumptions grounded perhaps in a Cartesian notion of the body which are by no means universal but which may very well impede our ability to apprehend the history of emotions in non-Eurocentric terms.

Further reading

Chakravarti, A., 'Between *bhakti* and *pietà*: untangling emotion in Marāṭhī Christian poetry', *History of Religions* 55 (2016)

—provides a sustained discussion of distinctions in the affective regimes of Catholicism and Marāṭhī *bhakti*.

Holt, M., 'Errant Hearts: Missionary Melancholy and Consolation in the Spanish Colonial Phillipines', in C. McLisky, K. Vållgarda and D. Midena (eds), *Emotions and Christian Missions* (Basingstoke: Palgrave Macmillan, 2015), 99–122.

—explores the importance of notions of Christian love for early modern Spanish missionaries in the Philippines, and the difficulty of upholding these ideas in an unfamiliar cultural and colonial context.

Pardo, O.F., *The Origins of Mexican Catholicism: Nahua Rituals and Christian Sacraments in Sixteenth-Century Mexico* (Ann Arbor: University of Michigan Press, 2006), 104–30.

—explores the function of nonverbal language within Nahua confessions and the role assigned by the friars to human emotions in new cultural contexts.

Notes

1 S.C. Karant-Nunn, *The Reformation of Feeling: Shaping the Religious Emotions in Early Modern Germany* (Oxford: Oxford University Press, 2010), 15–62.

2 A. Tallon, 'Christianity', in J. Corrigan (ed.), *Oxford Handbook of Religion and Emotion* (Oxford: Oxford University Press, 2008), 111–24.

3 J.R. Fehleison, 'Appealing to the senses: the forty hours celebrations in the Duchy of Chablais, 1597–98', *Sixteenth Century Journal* 36, 2 (2005), 375–96; E. Sullivan, 'The Passions of Thomas Wright: Renaissance emotion across body and soul', in R. Meek and E. Sullivan (eds), *The Renaissance of Emotion: Understanding Affect in Shakespeare and His Contemporaries* (Manchester: Manchester University Press, 2015), 25–44.

4 G.A. Bailey, *Art on the Jesuit Missions in Asia and Latin America, 1542–1773* (Toronto: University of Toronto Press, 1999)
5 M.C. Holt, 'Errant Hearts: Missionary Melancholy and Consolation in the Spanish Colonial Phillipines', in C. McLisky, K. Vållgarda and D. Midena (eds), *Emotions and Christian Missions* (Basingstoke: Palgrave Macmillan, 2015), 99–122; O. Pardo, *The Origins of Mexican Catholicism: Nahua Rituals and Christian Sacraments in Sixteenth-Century Mexico* (Ann Arbor: University of Michigan Press, 2006), 104–130.
6 I. Županov, '"I am a great sinner": Jesuit missionary dialogues in Southern India (Sixteenth Century),' *Journal of the Economic and Social History of the Orient* 55, 2–3 (2012), 415–46.
7 T. Stephens, *The Christian Puránna of Father Thomas Stephens of the Society of Jesus*, (ed.) J.L. Saldanha (Mangalore: Simon Alvares, 1907), 239.
8 K. Prentiss, *The Embodiment of Bhakti* (New York: Oxford University Press, 1999), 25–8.
9 Stephens, *The Christian Puránna*, 240.
10 C. Novetzke, *Religion and Public Memory: A Cultural History of Saint Namdev in India* (New York: Columbia University, 2008)
11 Quoted in R.C. Dhere, *The Rise of a Folk God: Viṭṭhal of Pandharpur*, (trans) A. Feldhaus (Ranikhet: Permanent Black, 2011), 287–8.
12 C. Novetzke, 'Bhakti and its public', *International Journal of Hindu Studies* 11, 3 (2007), 255–72.

III.11 Letters

Carolyn James

The early modern centuries witnessed a dramatic escalation in letter-writing across Europe, as levels of literacy rose, especially among women, postal infrastructure improved and local vernaculars displaced Latin in all but certain categories of official correspondence. Historians have long been alert to the capacity of letters to document the lived experience of social interactions in the past. However, there is now greater awareness among scholars that even the most ordinary and seemingly pragmatic letters are, in some sense, performances. Rather than offering direct, or unmediated, access to an early modern person's interiority, epistolary evidence documents the changing degree to which particular emotions figured in letters, the ways in which feelings were conceptualized and articulated, as well as how interpersonal relationships were negotiated by mail.[1] Most of the scholarly analysis of these themes has been directed at elite correspondence, which survives abundantly in private family collections and state archives throughout Europe. The voices of humble people are more elusive. Nonetheless, they too participated in early modern epistolary culture. Their petitions to charitable institutions, or to wealthy patrons, for example, are extant in substantial numbers. Whether dictated, or written entirely by a scribe on an illiterate person's behalf, these letters constitute an important, if underutilized, resource for understanding how the poor and powerless represented themselves and sought to elicit sympathy from those who could help them.[2]

Gary Schneider's work on English vernacular correspondence between 1500 and 1700 historicizes the epistolary practices of the upper and middling echelons of English society. He argues that in this period people still regarded oral discourse as delivering greater epistemological certainty than letters, since they relied on the visual and bodily cues which accompanied speech to provide evidence of the authenticity of the message and the authority of the speaker. Without tools such as tone, pitch, volume and moments of silence that the voice could deploy, as well as touch and facial expressions which helped to avoid misunderstandings or deceptions, letters were likely to be sources of anxiety. Individuals therefore strove to communicate the sincerity and efficacy of their written words by deploying rhetorical strategies which provided a substitute for their bodily presence.[3]

In an era when most correspondence was penned by secretaries and scribes, due to the physical effort and skill that writing with a quill required, a holograph letter (entirely in a sender's own hand) was at once a mark of respect and a means to amplify and to render more convincing the emotions expressed in the text. It is particularly in family exchanges that we find references to the meanings that contemporaries attached to the physical act of writing. In a letter of March 1490, Isabella d'Este, marchioness of Mantua, (1474–1539) assured her mother, Eleonora of Aragon (1450–1493), that although the latter's usual dictated letters were much appreciated, her holograph missives were 'holy relics'. The paper's contact with Eleonora's body conjured up for the newly married and homesick Isabella a much longed for maternal presence.[4]

Correspondents also sometimes experimented with writing certain passages in dialect to render their characteristic voice more convincingly and so create intimacy, or they might try to capture the cadences of their children's prattle when writing to an absent spouse.[5] Others inserted snippets of hair in the wax that sealed the letter, or used metaphors of the body, especially of the heart, to express love or anxious concern. Isabella d'Este again provides a pertinent example in a dictated letter of April 1490, to her husband Francesco Gonzaga (1466–1519), sent shortly after he embarked on a journey that would keep him from home for several weeks:

> I cannot but be anxious, not only because I am not able to see you every day, but especially since I dwell on the fact that you said, as you left, that you didn't feel very well, which was like a knife in my heart, and I cannot rally until I have news of your Lordship, whom I pray to deign to send news of your health. Please excuse that this letter is not in my hand on the grounds that I am so upset by your departure.[6]

Although here there is a typical example of the bodily metaphors that Schneider analyses in English letters, his insistence that the early moderns always preferred face-to-face communication to letter-writing, may not be entirely borne out in the case of very well educated individuals such as Isabella d'Este, and in contexts such as the city states of Italy, which had long been at the forefront of epistolary innovation. There, late medieval merchants were among the first to adopt straightforward language and a conversational tone in letters that aimed to engender trust and amity between colleagues frequently separated by the itinerant requirements of their businesses.

Like many of her aristocratic peers, Isabella d'Este began learning to write letters that expressed a wide range of emotions from the age of four. Her copy books of correspondence dating from the early 1490s to the 1530s preserve around 16,000 of her out-going letters and attest to her confident, rather than anxious, attitude to articulating and reading emotional subtleties in correspondence. In 1490, Isabella was still physically reticent with her frequently absent husband and relied on letters in the first phase of marriage to lay the emotional groundwork for marital intimacy.[7] Research on other sophisticated letter writers from this period is likely to reveal that Isabella was not alone in preferring to express some emotions by letter, rather than face-to-face. The 'constructive anger' that Linda Pollock has found evidence of in seventeenth-century English correspondence is one such emotion, since letters offered a welcome buffer between antagonists and time for reflection and negotiation.[8]

In the same English context, but a century earlier, James Daybell has found that men were more likely than their wives to express marital love in letters, a finding that is at odds with research on later correspondence, when the opposite is the case. It seems that as women's emotional articulacy rose, they became increasingly adept at expressing themselves in letters and therefore more willing to write about their emotions, especially as the stigma against them asserting their feelings began gradually to dissipate.[9] Letter writers of both genders also continued to find inventive ways to signal emotion more indirectly, through the layout of the page, the size and quality of paper, the use of personal seals as well as other material signs, such as tying a love letter with pretty ribbons, or bordering in black a letter of condolence to enhance the expression of sympathy on the page.[10] We must be sensitive to the meanings of these epistolary signals.

As Susan Broomhall and Jacqueline Van Gent have shown in a number of important essays on the early modern correspondence of the Nassau family, letter-writing created and sustained emotional bonds between individuals dispersed in various parts of Europe and related to each other by different degrees of consanguinity due to the multiple marriages of their parents. When writing to each other, the Nassau took careful account of gender and family hierarchies, observing a strict set of behavioural codes whereby emotions which might be expressed frankly to some relatives had to be suppressed, or were not felt, in relation to others. While particularly intimate connections facilitated the articulation of negative emotions such as envy, anger or annoyance, these feelings were unlikely to be communicated directly to those higher up in the family pecking order.[11] Although the extent to which the Nassau case studies may be extrapolated more widely is not yet clear, the complex relationship between letter-writing and emotions in the early modern European past is beginning fruitfully to inform the methodologies with which we approach this fascinating genre of evidence.

Further reading

Broomhall, S. and J. Van Gent, 'Corresponding affections: emotional exchange among siblings in the Nassau family', *Journal of Family History* 34, 2 (2009), 143–65.

—analyses the behavioural codes which governed the expression of emotions in letters exchanged by members of a prominent European dynasty.

Daybell, J., 'Social negotiations in correspondence between mothers and daughters in Tudor and early Stuart England', *Women's History Review* 24, 4 (2015), 502–27.

—an essential methodological guide that alerts us to the ways in which individuals manipulated conventional epistolary protocols to convey a complex range of emotions and negotiated the changing dynamic of the mother-daughter relationship as it evolved over time.

Schneider, G., 'Affecting correspondence: body, behaviour, and the textualization of emotion in early modern English letters', *Prose Studies* 23, 3 (2000), 31–62.

—analyses the rhetorical techniques that early modern people used to overcome their anxieties about communicating emotions by letter, rather than face-to-face.

Notes

1 L. Pollock, 'Anger and the negotiation of relationships in early modern England', *The Historical Journal* 47, 3 (2004), 567–90.
2 For the use of such evidence, see S. Broomhall, '"Burdened with Small Children": Women Defining Poverty in Sixteenth-Century Tours', in J. Couchman and A. Crabb (eds), *Women's Letters Across Europe 1400–1700* (Aldershot: Ashgate, 2005), 223–37.
3 G. Schneider, 'Affecting correspondence: body, behaviour, and the textualization of emotion in early modern English letters', *Prose Studies*, 23 (2000), 31–62.
4 C. James, 'What's love got to do with it? Dynastic politics and motherhood in the letters of Eleonora of Aragon and her daughters', *Women's History Review* 24, 4 (2015), 528–47.
5 D. Shemek, '"Ci ci"and "Pa pa": Script, mimicry and mediation in Isabella d'Este's letters', *Rinascimento* 43 (2003), 75–91.
6 Isabella d'Este to Francesco Gonzaga, 30 April 1490, from Ferrara, Archivio di Stato, Mantua, Archivio Gonzaga, box 2106, folio 375.
7 James, 'What's love got to go with it?'
8 Pollock, 'Anger and the negotiation of relationships in early modern England'.
9 J. Daybell, *Women Letter-Writers in Tudor England* (Oxford: Oxford University Press, 2006), 227–8.
10 Daybell, 'Material meanings and the social signs of manuscript letters in early modern England', *Literature Compass* 6, 3 (2009), 647–67.
11 S. Broomhall and J. Van Gent, 'Corresponding affections: emotional exchange among siblings in the Nassau family', *Journal of Family History* 34, 2 (2009) 143–65, here 155.

III.12 Archives

James Daybell

The 'archival turn' in early modern studies has meant that scholars treat archives with increasing caution and critical attention, consciously reminded of the roles that archivists and other agents played in 'constructing' archives, which are defined here simply as accretions of records, documents or materials relating to individuals, families, companies, institutions or the state, and which might be preserved privately as well as, for example, by businesses, institutions or public archives at a local and national level. Archives are the very repositories that house many of the different categories of sources commonly interrogated by historians interested in early modern emotions, but generally with little regard given to the nature and composition of these entities. Something of their complexity is indicated by Jacques Derrida's reminder of the 'politics of the archive', that is the relationship of archives to knowledge, power and belief systems, connected as they are to custody, access, preservation (and its antithesis, destruction), classification and the use of materials of memory.[1] Control of the archive at a state, local or even family level was central to the ordering of knowledge, and shaping those paper testimonies of the past that survive to us today. At the most basic level, policies of accession, that is choosing what to keep and what to discard, as well as the motives (conscious and otherwise) that underpinned archival processes, are at the heart of understanding the very essence of the raw materials of history. The constructed nature of historical knowledge as viewed through the lens of archives is thus of import to scholars interested in the history of emotions, in that the very evidence that they study to reconstruct feelings and behaviours in the past was often preserved with specific intentions. Methodologically, my analysis is influenced by material approaches to historicized texts as a way of unpacking and interpreting emotions located in archives and archival forms.

As historians we are increasingly aware of the rhetorical and generic conventions that shaped texts and documents, and Natalie Zemon Davis has encouraged us to pay attention to 'fiction in the archives', in other words, the rhetorical or strategic quality of documentary evidence that further belies its apparent transparency.[2] Ego-documents such as diaries, autobiographies and letters were not direct windows into the emotional lives of their subjects, but prone to literary, linguistic and material conventions that influenced form and meaning. Furthermore, at a meta-level, the survival and preservation of personal or family documents that exposed different emotional states was rarely a reflection of lucky happenstance. This entry considers two main issues: first, the ways in which family archives and archival practices in particular shaped what might be termed their 'emotional memory', in other words to suggest the conscious artificiality of their record-keeping, and the role that emotional considerations motivated the preservation family papers, something akin to the manner by which modern-day memory boxes preserve memorabilia. Second, in contrast to the 'constructed family archive' it sketches the conditions for the 'unadulterated archive', a form of archive that is effectively preserved in historical aspic, and to argue that it is here that one finds the true emotional documents of early modern Europe.

In assembling materials of memory – correspondence, diaries, bibles, receipt books and other personal writings – early modern families throughout Europe were active in forming family archives. While certain families hoarded records, others sought to destroy papers that shed a poor light on the family. In seventeenth-century England, for example, Edward Sackville, fourth Earl of Dorset (1590–1652) burned incriminatory letters in the aftermath of the Civil War (1642–9).[3] The destruction of archival documents in this manner clearly played an important role in constructing family identity and memory. The preservation of records within the household has ordinarily be explained by an archival paradigm associated with property, landholding and titles and the need to provide evidences as proof of right of legal ownership, all of which was bound up with lineage and inheritance. Running alongside (and often connected with) this very pragmatic use of archives was a more personal concern with family, and an emotional impulse to preserve genealogical records as a form of family history, a mode of textual memorialization. Thus, many of the letters of seventeenth-century English gentlewoman Mary Baskerville (d. 1632) were kept in a manuscript miscellany by her son, the antiquarian Hannibal Baskerville (1597–1668). They functioned not only as a material memory of his mother (as examples of letters in her own hand), but also the very paper on which they were penned formed the physical site for her biography, which Baskerville annotated on the reverse sides of the letters.[4] The compiling, selection and ordering of archives in this manner was often deliberate; family correspondence and papers did not automatically gravitate towards muniments rooms, but did so as a result of archival decisions that chose to privilege and preserve. Exemplary of this careful orchestration of family memory is a letter-book in the British Library, entitled 'Lady Petty's Correspondence with her Children, 1684', into which is gathered the correspondence of Lady Elizabeth Petty (*c.* 1636–1708/10), wife of Sir William Petty (1623–87), the natural philosopher and administrator in Ireland, that she wrote to and received from her children.[5] An attempt has been made to reassemble the outgoing letters Lady Petty wrote to her children when she was in Dublin during the period 1684 to 1685, as well as the letters she received in return, including those of her young son Charles (*c.* 1653–96) which are mainly in French, written for educational purposes. In its edited state, the volume – the compilation of which itself is a gesture of affect – acts as a textual memorialization of a mother's relationship with her children.

Active intervention in the ordering of paper memories might thus seek to construct or represent in particular ways the emotional states embodied in an archive. By contrast to these kinds of constructed archives, there are a number of early modern bodies of documents that appear to survive (outwardly at least) in an unadulterated state, in that they were seized or intercepted by the state before their owners could purge or privilege the papers in their custody. Alongside the practical and perfunctory, such collections tend to be more likely to include materials of a more intimate nature. The marital correspondence of the Johnson family based in Calais for the period 1542 to 1552, for example, was gathered by the Privy Council in 1553 to be used as proof in bankruptcy suits in the Admiralty Court;[6] and the Lisle Letters of the 1530s were seized by the crown during the trial of Arthur Plantagenet, Lord Lisle, Lord Deputy of Calais (1461/75–1542), for treason.[7] Perhaps most strikingly in the case of the Lisle letters, the impounding of papers for legal purposes preserved a large cross-section of Anglo-French correspondence representative of a whole range of social and gender relations, including between husband and wife, parents and children, kin, friends and clients, as well as employers and servants. By far the most exciting and still to be fully tapped archive of this nature is the papers of the High Court of Admiralty held at the National Archives in Kew. Amongst its vast archival holdings is a category of document described as 'intercepted mails and papers', which comprises correspondence seized from enemy ships by the English state during the period 1652 to 1811. Not only is this archive effectively in its natural state, but also one of the most remarkable features is that much of this correspondence still remains unopened (some of it intact in its original postbags), since the letters were of course never delivered to their final destinations.[8] A further strength of this archive is that it is not only pan-European, but also transatlantic and global in its reach, and reflective of all kinds of relationships lived at a distance.

In studying the history of early modern emotions – and here particularly the emotional states or relationships as they are expressed, experienced and textualized – this entry is therefore a reminder of the importance of paying attention to archival conditions, which necessarily inform the ways in which we understand and interpret textual traces of feelings and thoughts. As good interdisciplinary early modern scholars, we are schooled to read documents for rhetorical and material meaning, yet arguably less sensitive to the interpretative imperatives of the archive in which such materials reside. The ordering, preserving and even destruction of papers worked to construct family identity and memory; and emotional impulses motivated individuals to acts of memorialization. Alongside these kinds of constructed archives, reside unadulterated archives, which are still intact in their natural state, and arguably record emotional states not confected or eradicated by future generations. Above all, however, I want to suggest that archives broadly defined often represent constructed accumulations of sources of varying types – material as well as textual – and as such consideration of archival practices necessarily conditions the very documentary evidence that we interpret in studying early modern emotions.

Further reading

Ketelaar, E., 'The genealogical gaze: family identities and family archives in the fourteenth to seventeenth centuries', *Libraries & the Cultural Record* 44, 1 (2009), 9–28.

—demonstrates the way in which early modern archives were viewed as a form of cultural patrimony, central in the formation of family identity.

Manoff, M., 'Theories of the archive from across the disciplines', *Libraries and the Academy* 4, 1 (2004), 9–25.

—offers an essential interdisciplinary and theoretical overview of recent research on archives, demonstrating their partial and constructed nature, which shapes history and memory.

Notes

1 J. Derrida, *Archive Fever: A Freudian Impression*, (trans.) E. Prenowitz (Chicago: University of Chicago Press, 1996), 4, note 1.
2 N.Z. Davis, *Fiction in the Archives* (Cambridge: Cambridge University Press, 1987)
3 A.P. Newton (ed.), *Calendar of the Manuscripts of Major-General Lord Sackville, Preserved at Knole, Sevenoaks, Kent, vol. 2, Cranfield Papers, 1534–1612*, Historical Manuscripts Commission, Octavo Series 80 (London: HMSO, 1940), 56.
4 Bodleian Library, Oxford, Rawlinson MS, D 859.
5 British Library, London, Additional MS, 72857: Petty Family Papers.
6 B. Winchester, *Tudor Family Portrait* (London: Jonathan Cape, 1955), 13–14.
7 M. St Clare Byrne (ed.), *The Lisle Letters*, 6 vols (Chicago: The University of Chicago Press, 1981), I, 5.
8 The National Archives, Kew, HCA 30.

III.13 Maps

Alicia Marchant

With their lines and demarcation of geographical spaces, early modern maps do not, at first glance, look particularly conducive sources for the study of early modern emotions. However, maps are visual narratives that display relationships between people and places, and as such are imbued with emotion. Created with emotional purpose and filled with meaningful imagery to encourage particular affective states, maps were a means to communicate and display power and authority, particularly colonization and ownership; maps were intended to be viewed, interpreted, collected and exhibited in both public and private spaces. The emotional states that are associated with maps include wonder, awe, pleasure, pride as well as fear and envy. A history of emotions approach to cartography employs textual, visual and material readings to interpret authorial motivations, social relationships, points of narrative and colour, text and design in and through maps.

Maps are dynamic texts, a heady mix of visual and spatial representations of geospatial and other forms of knowledge. They are both symbolic and practical, and encourage movements in particular ways through the world. Often, in the light of modern cartography, early modern maps (as well as those that preceded them) have been labelled beautiful, but inaccurate and rudimentary. Such perspectives privilege one element of cartography over its other functions, suggesting that the practical aspect of maps is more important than their symbolic meanings. Modern scholars of the history of cartography, especially following the work of David Woodward and Brian Harvey, have come to challenge this tendency, calling for greater historicizing and contextualizing of historical maps and awareness of the social, political and cultural mentalities that produced them.[1] Woodward and Harvey themselves proposed maps to be 'graphic representations that facilitate a spatial understanding of things, concepts, conditions, processes, or events in the human world'.[2] Such a definition allows for expanded understandings of cartography, including considerations of the emotional dimensions.

Early modern cartography evolved and changed over the course of the early modern era, both in terms of its form and its uses. Early modern mapmakers continually found new ways to present the world, which had implications for how viewers of maps envisaged the world and formed connections to it. Mapmakers increasingly had to keep up with demands for detailed and precise geographical representations, whilst simultaneously negotiating past cartographic traditions, particularly medieval spiritual and biblical world views that determined a spatial structuring with Jerusalem at its

Figure III.13.1 Abraham Ortelius, 'Maris Pacifici', *Theatrum Orbis Terrarum*, Antwerp, 1589, photograph by Alicia Marchant.

Courtesy of Reid Library, The University of Western Australia.

centre.[3] Scientific and mathematical innovations altered technical aspects of cartography; new ways of surveying and calculating distances had implications for the composition of maps, which included experiments in how to depict the spherical world in two-dimensional form. Geraldus Mercator (1512–94), a Flemish cartographer and mathematician, produced a new projection in 1569, in which a grid of longitude and increased latitude were drawn across the map. Crucially, this allowed for 'true direction' to be easily worked out by drawing straight lines (rhumb lines) between two points. For the history of cartography Mercator's projection was a critical means of calculating accurate directions for navigators; for the history of emotions, lines on maps were an important expression of the desire to connect places spatially and present them in a logical schema. This mathematical exactness was an instrument of expanding political empires, and a projection of their curiosity and desires into regions that had until recently been *terra incognita*.

Early modern maps increasingly became tools of empire building, and were used to communicate power and authority through such means as producing wonder, fear and awe. Many include military iconography, particularly ships of war, denoting the presence of empire in frontier regions. The *Maris Pacifici* (1589) by Abraham Ortelius (1527–98) (Figure III.13.1) charts the west coast of the Americas for the first time, and displays an image of the Vittoria, the ship of Ferdinand Magellan (*c.* 1480–1521), in full sail, complete with a guardian angel at the front of the boat, and a canon in mid-fire. This ship is a powerful display of empire, containing important religious and military iconography that sought to impress. The Portuguese map compiled around the year 1502 that we today know as the 'Cantino planisphere' (Figure III.13.2) presents a moment of Portuguese empire and expansion; the coast of north-west Africa is dotted with a frontier of Portuguese flags, and a fort with local people outside its walls dominates the region around it. This is a subjugated place, that has been marked out, named, and thereby owned; the indigenous communities, and their naming traditions, are completely sidelined. This image of colonization, like that of Magellan's ship, portrays dominance and submission through iconography and sought to convey the power of European empires in frontier regions through emotions such as fear and awe.

The study of early modern maps and emotions raises exciting prospects for examining and historicizing the relationship between viewing cultures and emotional regimes of the early modern era. The visual tropes on maps were most likely produced to encourage feelings of curiosity, wonderment and awe in the imagined viewer, but also feelings of surprise and fear of the unknown places, strange creatures and peoples frequently illustrated in the map itself, and around the borders. The three maps shown here were all intended for artistic and aesthetic viewing rather than for serious navigational purposes. The strange orientation of the world map of 1550 by Pierre Desceliers (*c.* 1500–58), for instance, suggests that this map was meant to be viewed lying flat upon a table (Figure III.13.3). Viewers would need to be in motion around the map, pointing to a necessary embodied and experiential engagement in order to fully appreciate and read it.

As representations of social constructions and emotional geographies (that is, the way in which people relate to the world), maps offer a vehicle for studying the emotional regimes of the communities that produced them. The structuring and

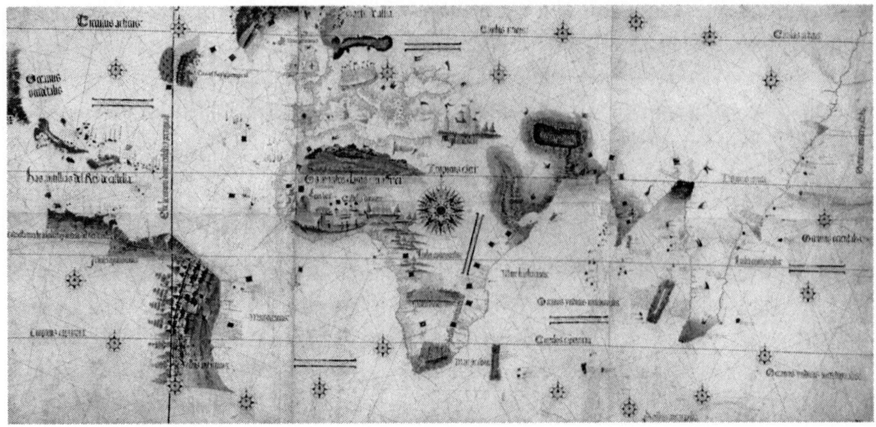

Figure III.13.2 The Cantino Planisphere, 1502, cartographer unknown, vellum, 218 × 102 cm. © Heritage Image Partnership Ltd/Alamy Stock Photo.

imagery of early modern maps communicate ethnocentric (frequently Eurocentric) and gendered affective relationships between the communities that created the maps, and the communities and places depicted on them. Desceliers' 1550 world map contains numerous images and texts that project onto the 'othered' communities of these regions an emotionality that is savage and brutal. In the place that we now know as Australia, there is a scene of great barbarity and savagery with a dog-headed cannibal dissecting one of his kin on a table. The scene is taken directly from the popular travels of Marco Polo (1254–1324), drawing on an ancient repertoire of exotica to reinforce a world-schema in which the centre (Europe) in portrayed as an ordered and civil place of emotional regulation while the peripheral frontiers was one of uncontrolled and unregulated moral and emotional excesses.

Maps likewise narrate a more personal relationship between cartographer and patron(s). Desceliers' map contains the coats of arms of both Henri II of France and the Duke of Montmorency, for whom it was constructed. The homeland of the mapmaker or patron was generally placed centrally, while in the periphery strange creatures and communities were depicted.

While early modern maps are invaluable texts that display emotional relationships between people and places, they were also objects of delight and opulence, and a symbol of an owner's wealth, prestige and knowledge. Maps appear in various works of art and literature for varying effect and affect, such as several of Johannes Vermeer's paintings, including the *Soldier and Laughing Girl* (*c.* 1658) where a map hangs as a lavish, domestic wall decoration. With the advent of printing, owning a map was a greater possibility, although hand-crafted maps remained a highly-prized object throughout the early modern era. The shift from manuscript to print in Europe allowed maps to be accessible to a wider audience than their manuscript counterparts. In 1570 Ortelius produced the *Theatrum Orbis Terrarum*, the first ever collection of maps printed together as a book, forming an atlas. The first edition contained 69 maps, which increased in number for each edition. Ortelius' atlas was to be one

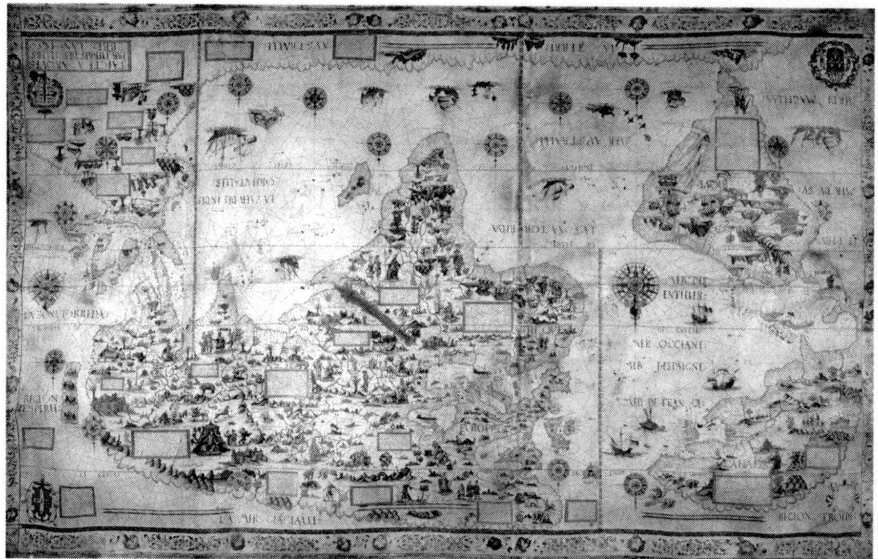

Figure III.13.3 Pierre Desceliers, World Map, France, 1550, vellum, 178 × 219 cm. © 1 Collection/Alamy Stock Photo.

of the best-sellers of the early modern book trade, with an astonishing 7,300 copies sold in Ortelius' lifetime.[4] Such sales are testimony to people's love of maps and desire to own them, and the great pride taken in their ownership.

Maps were also objects of exchange between author and patron, and between libraries, galleries and other spaces. Maps are, to take Sara Ahmed's term, 'sticky objects', materials that hold emotional significance and which accrue emotional value as they oscillate and flow *between* various affective fields.[5] However, value can wane as the colourful history of the Cantino Planisphere illustrates: the Planisphere was smuggled from its point of creation in Lisbon by an Italian diplomat named Alberto Cantino who presented it as a gift to Hercule d'Este, the Duke of Ferrara (1431–1505), in 1502. The map was held in Ferrara and Modena until 1859, when the city was besieged and the map disappeared. It was rediscovered in 1869 by chance by the director of the library at the University of Modena, being used as a screen in a butcher's shop.

Early modern maps are unique sources for research into the history of the emotions. Their multidimensional nature affords numerous avenues though which to explore and historicize the social, visual and technological elements that shaped maps, and indeed that were shaped *by* the maps; as visual narratives with numerous compositional and iconographic elements that sought to produce various feelings, maps offer numerous possibilities for exploring the relationship between visual cultures and emotions. Their material form too allows for discussion of objects and emotions, particularly the communities formed through the creation of the maps, their uses, collection and display. Moreover, maps highlight the ways in which texts can initiate and structure embodied experiences in the world, both actual and imagined.

Further reading

Harley, J.B., *The New Nature of Maps: Essays in the History of Cartography*, (ed.) P. Laxton (Baltimore: The John Hopkins University Press, 2001)

—this important collection, published posthumously, includes Harley's main articles.

Jacob, C., *The Sovereign Map: Theoretical Approaches in Cartography throughout History*, (trans.) T. Conley (Chicago: University of Chicago Press, 2006)

—provides an important scholarly discussion of the history of cartography, and in particular the various elements that make maps.

Notes

1 D. Woodward and J.B. Harley, *The History of Cartography* (Chicago: University of Chicago Press, 1987–98). A total of eight books were produced in this series; Woodward and Harley worked together to produce three books (Volume 1, Volume 2:1 and Volume 2:2.)

2 Woodward and B. Harley, 'Preface', *The History of Cartography, Volume 1: Cartography in Prehistoric, Ancient and Medieval Europe and the Mediterranean* (1987), xvi.

3 E. Edson, *Mapping Time and Space: How Medieval Mapmakers Viewed Their World* (London: The British Library, 1997)

4 P. Binding, *Imagined Corners: Exploring the World's First Atlas* (London: Review, 2003), 282.

5 S. Ahmed, *The Cultural Politics of Emotion* (New York: Routledge, 2004), 11. See also S. Ahmed, 'Affective economies', *Social Text* 22, 2 (2004), 117–39.

III.14 Books

Stephanie Downes

For *Annales* school founder Lucien Febvre, the historical study of both books and emotions was part of the same reconstructive and even mutually informative task.[1] Febvre's highly influential work on the social impact of print during early modernity, *L'Apparition du livre* (*The Coming of the Book*), published posthumously in 1958, explored the *mentalités* (habits of thought) of early modern people in relation to new production technologies.[2] Despite Febvre's perception of the close relationship between emotional and textual cultures in the past, it is only very recently that scholars have begun to consider books and book history as sources for the history of emotions. The study of early modern books – handmade or mass produced – offers new ways of thinking about the broader relationship between material culture and emotional expression during a lengthy period of great social and technological change. The advent of print in the early modern period necessarily affects how we 'read' the book's emotional valencies and its ability to act as a conduit for personal relationships and individual or social emotions. Printed books could provoke new senses of excitement, prestige and pleasure in book ownership among wider social groups, while at the same time, manuscripts themselves took on new significance as alternatives to mass-produced repositories for the written word.

Contemporary debates about books as emotional objects and libraries as spaces for their protection are often predicated on a sense that the emotional or spiritual 'essence' of the physical book is betrayed in modern digital culture. Materials – vellum, parchment and paper – bear the traces of a book's historical existence in relation to those of its makers and handlers. Histories of reading may be able to influence positively our assessment of the emotions associated with (or elicited by) early modern books, helping to deepen our understanding of the early modern book as an object whose production and reception took place within complex emotional as well as social networks. Attention to the 'paratexts' (the text/s surrounding the main text) and margins of early modern manuscript and print, as William H. Sherman observes, helps enrich our sense of the diverse 'places of books in the lives of readers'.[3] The examples given below are drawn from fifteenth- and sixteenth-century England; but might be found in many other times and places.

As an object which exists in both semiotic and physical states simultaneously, the early modern book is a complex historical source. There is an inherent contradiction in seeking to contextualize material culture's relationship to emotion and affect through text, potentially privileging the expression of the written word over the object itself. The representation of books in early modern literature and art further complicates how they might be read as 'signs' of past emotion. The dedications and prefaces of early modern print, for example, set the book in motion in a series of emotional transactions and exchanges in which printers and authors expressed their anxiety about the reception of their work. The first edition of Sir Philip Sidney's *Arcadia*, dedicated to his sister, the Countess of Pembroke in 1590, opens with the author's reference to his own 'idle worke', which, he wrote, 'I fear (like the Spiders webbe) will be thought fitter to be swept away, then worn to any other purpose'.[4] Further exploration of such public performances of emotion may help scholars associate studies of early modern book history and reading practices with textually-oriented histories of emotions.

Indeed in efforts to read the emotional value of the book in the early modern period it is difficult to get away from the various forms of text that seem to define its emotional significance most clearly, such as annotations and marginalia. The inscription of books by hand with particular terms and words – the adjectives 'dear' and 'lovyng' – promises insight into private lives. Analysis of inscribed texts certainly offers one way of accessing the emotional significance of early modern books and their place in the lives of individuals. These approaches are already familiar to historians of early modern book ownership and marginalia, and may be as true of newly produced printed books as of manuscripts during the period – although, interestingly, no study has yet been conducted that explores the potentially different emotional values of manuscript and print. It is, however, clear that books of both kinds might be marked in ways that made them carriers of human relationships, often through successive generations, as in the case of bibles used for recording the names of births and deaths in a given family.

Associating material culture studies more fully with defined histories of emotion, especially in relation to gift-giving, ritual, practice and performance, may thus be productive, but again, textual inscription, whether inside the book itself or in wills and inventories, is key. A manuscript book of hours given by Margaret Beaufort (1443–1509) to her lady-in-waiting, Anne Shirley, possibly on the occasion of her marriage, bears the inscription, in her own hand: 'my good lady Shyrley pray for me that gevythe yow thys booke y hertely pray you / Margaret / modyr to the kynge'.[5]

Margaret's son, Henry VII (1457–1509) also presented a prayer book to his daughter, Margaret Tudor (1489–1541), Queen of Scots, inscribed, 'Remember yor kynde and louyng fader an yor prayers'.[6] Such inscriptions show how books could be perceived as proxies for the giver. In the case of manuscripts, which were often highly durable objects, such associations could be carried through repeated acts of donation: during the later sixteenth, seventeenth and eighteenth centuries, the prayer book Henry presented to his daughter was presented to new recipients, Henry's repeated royal injunctions to 'remember' and 'pray' for the giver symbolically reenacted each time the book was passed on.[7]

But early modern books may also bear traces of their involvement in human emotional lives in non-textually evident ways. Both manuscript and printed psalters were made to be carried close to the body; some so tiny as to be always able to be carried around on the person – recalling Sidney's metaphor of the book as an object that might be 'worn'. In practice they might be kissed, stroked or touched in tactile reading practices which aimed to elicit certain emotional responses in the reader, bringing them closer to God.[8] Surviving manuscript examples bear evidence of this physical 'love' of books, which involved readers' hands and lips as well as their eyes, wearing away certain images and words with repeated contact. Fewer printed copies of such works remain, perhaps for the fundamental reason that they were worn away with use.

Present-day conceptual connections between modern digital reading cultures and those of the early modern era may be of use in connecting book and emotions history, encouraging us to reflect more deeply on the impact of print on the kinds of emotions associated with books and the ways in which they might be expressed. In the examples I have discussed, books are elite objects, predominantly made for and used by the literate classes. This was overwhelmingly the case in the early modern era, although, with print, they became available to other social groups in an unprecedented way. With greater awareness of the changing meaning of the book in the present, the historical study of early modern books may come to bear on both the history of emotions and of text as both a 'social' and an 'emotional' form of media.

Further reading

Rudy, K.M., 'Dirty books: Quantifying patterns of use in medieval manuscripts using a densitometer', *Journal of Historians of Netherlandish Art* 2, 1–2 (2010). www.jhna.org/index.php/past-issues/volume-2-issue-1-2/129-dirty-books

—astonishing analysis of the ways in which medieval manuscripts were handled by readers in the medieval and early modern period – touched, kissed and rubbed in acts of devotion – that suggests the need to pay attention to forms of religious reading practice as emotion ritual.

Sherman, W.H., *Used Books: Marking Readers in Renaissance England* (Philadelphia: University of Pennsylvania Press, 2008)

—a comprehensive study of the place of books 'in the lives of readers' in early modern England, and of particular use to historians in approaching different types of marginalia as evidence of the various forms of social and emotional value attached to the material text.

Notes

1 L. Febvre, 'History and Psychology', in P. Burke and K. Folca (eds), *A New Kind of History: From the Writings of Febvre* (New York: Harper and Row Publishers, repr. 1973); on Febvre and the new history

of emotions, see S.J. Matt, 'Current emotion research in history: or, doing history from the inside out', *Emotion Review* 3, 1 (2011), 117–20.

2 L. Febvre and H.-J. Martin, *The Coming of the Book*, (eds) G. Nowell-Smith and D. Wootton, (trans.) D. Gerard (London: NLB, 1976 [orig. 1958]), 10–11.

3 W.H. Sherman, *Used Books: Marking Readers in Renaissance England* (Philadelphia: University of Pennsylvania Press, 2008), 15.

4 P. Sidney, *The Countess of Pembroke Arcadia* (London, 1590), sig. A3.

5 Cambridge, St John's College MS 264, fol. 12v.

6 Chatsworth House, Hours of Henry VII, fol. 32r.

7 For a history of known owners of the manuscript, see the online description, online at https://chatsworth.org/attractions-and-events/art-archives/art-and-archives-collections/collection/library/the-'hours-of-henry-vii', accessed 25 November 2015.

8 See the work of K.M. Rudy on medieval books, 'Dirty books: quantifying patterns of use in medieval manuscripts using a densitometer', *Journal of Historians of Netherlandish Art* 2, 1–2 (2010), online at www.jhna.org/index.php/past-issues/volume-2-issue-1–2/129-dirty-books, accessed 1 June 2015.

III.15 Household objects

Tara Hamling

Even humble utilitarian objects could be turned to profound uses as part of an early modern tendency to read and treat things in symbolic terms. Catherine Richardson has established how material 'things were good for thinking with in early modern England – the physical form of objects was always a starting point for considering the nature of humanity, its sorrows and joys and the strength and quality of its relationships'.[1] Thus, as well as prompting specific forms of intellectual reflection, everyday things could appeal to a range of emotional responses – love, fellowship, loss, trepidation, hope, pride. Objects were good for thinking and feeling with in the early modern period and the context of the home, the principal site for daily experience and interactions with possessions, is therefore an important area for the history of emotions. It is only when objects are understood and studied as 'things in action'– addressing their forms, uses and trajectories – that we can begin to appreciate in a more nuanced way their significance to people in the past.[2] Alfred Gell's theory of 'distributed personhood' is particularly useful in understanding how crafted objects function as indexes of a person's thoughts and desires, existing simultaneously as material forms and as intentions, to mediate social relationships and influence the behaviour of others.[3]

The domestic household was recognized as the fundamental unit of early modern society. Following the Elizabethan Religious Settlement of 1559, there was also a renewed emphasis on the home as the centre of individual and communal devotional life. There was increased investment in domestic buildings and household goods at the middling levels of society; houses were rebuilt or remodelled to create additional spaces, which were furnished with an expanding range and quality of household fixtures, fittings and wares. It is widely accepted that this material environment reflected the social status and aspirations of householders, but historical scholarship has been hesitant to consider the extent to which it actively shaped everyday experience. This entry considers three categories of evidence for the affective power and value of various household objects. It focuses, first, on the form and appearance of extant domestic artefacts. What can the customization of certain items indicate about their personal and familial significance? Second, it suggests ways of approaching the feelings that could be prompted by some household objects by considering how they were invoked in devotional texts. Third, it considers evidence for emotional ties to objects as expressed in 'personal' testimony.

Household objects include a range of crafted items that were shop-bought, commissioned and handmade. Extant objects representing the latter two categories may contain more information about their original significance because of customization at the point of manufacture but shop-bought items might also be personalized by their owners with the addition of marks. Archaeological finds recovered from the Mary Rose warship, which sank off the south coast of England in 1545, include 60 wooden bowls – unremarkable examples of the most common form of wooden tableware known as 'treen'. But more than half of these bowls have been differentiated by the addition of incised marks to identify ownership by a specific individual.[4] (Figure III.15.1) This suggests a proprietary attachment to a specific, recognizable piece which moves beyond mere utility. One example also contains inverted V marks which have been identified as Marian symbols invoking protection from harm, revealing a sense of trepidation in the face of very real onboard threats from food poisoning and, of course, drowning.[5] Symbolic marks identified as apotropaic in

Figure III.15.1 Wooden bowl from the Mary Rose warship, differentiated with incised marks to identify ownership by a specific individual. By permission of the Mary Rose Trust, no. 82A1712.

Figure III.15.2 Tin-glazed earthenware mug painted around the rim with '1628 ELIZABETH BROCKLEFIELD'.

function have been found on areas of early modern houses associated with storage such as cellars and chests and these protective symbols are also found on thresholds and chimneys; a popular response to the vulnerability of these sources of intrusion or threat.[6]

Commissioned items were usually crafted in more expensive materials by specialized tradesmen and personal information could be incorporated within the design. Examples include furniture such as beds and chests (for example, an elm chest incorporating the carved inscription, 'ELEZABETH LOVELL 1640'[7]) and tablewares (such as the tin-glazed earthenware mug painted around the rim with '1628 ELIZABETH BROCKLEFIELD' (Figure III.15.2) and the tankard with two bands of inscription: 'JAMES & ELIZABETH GREEN ANNO 1630' and 'THE GIFT IS SMALL GOODWILL TO ALL').[8] As these inscriptions suggest, dated items with initials or names were probably bought as gifts associated with baptism, courtship or marriage, to mark and extend the significance of these life stages.

Tablewares had inherent significance as symbols of hospitality and sociability, belonging and community. Incorporating contextual information about specific individuals further enhanced the special quality of these evocative objects, prompting remembrance of significant events and relationships. As well as incorporating names or initials items might proclaim a particular admonitory sentiment, such as the sixteenth-century stoneware drinking mug with a silver-gilt lid engraved with the initials 'PH' and the inscription 'THE TONGE THAT LIETH KILLETH THE SOULE',[9] and the group of spoons made in York *c.* 1670 by craftsman Thomas Mangy with the words 'LIVE TO DIE' and 'DIE TO LIVE' on the stem along with the arms of the Strickland family. (Figure III.15.3) Such *memento mori* inscriptions to prompt spiritual preparation for death were common across a range of domestic surfaces and objects. It is clear from correspondence and journals that the Calvinist doctrine of predestination troubled many believers in seeking surety of their own salvation. Reminders of death on everyday things collapsed the quotidian and the eternal, potentially triggering a range of (mixed) emotions; alarm, apprehension, anxiety, hope, trust. There was also a demand for off-the-shelf items with legends that had more generic application; a skillet for cooking with the text 'LOVE THY NEIGHBOUR' or pottery mugs and jugs with 'FEAR GOD'.[10]

These objects connect forms of thinking and feeling with specific domestic activities, and the use of everyday household things to stimulate mood is also evident in contemporary literature. A thriving market developed for printed guidance on domestic matters including ideals of everyday devotional behaviours. Popular guides to piety supplied a round of prayers and meditations to accompany the daily routine of rising, dressing, eating, keeping company and retiring to bed, with set prayers to accompany material interactions such as lighting candles, washing hands or the feel of bedclothes on the body.[11] While it is impossible to know the extent to which

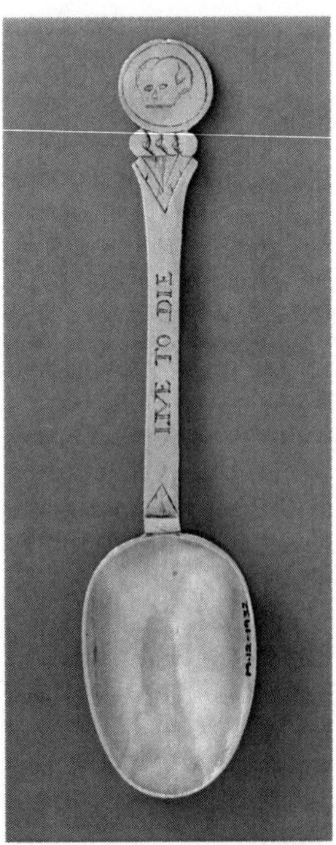

Figure III.15.3 Thomas Mangy, Spoon bearing the arms of the Strickland family and words 'LIVE TO DIE' and 'DIE TO LIVE' on the stem, York *c.* 1670.

ordinary people were influenced by prescription, these texts were bought by a relatively broad public of literate householders and imaginative literature reveals how some authors put such thinking into poetic practice, with meditations on domestic things such as a dusty tablecloth or the movement of bed curtains interpreted as symbols of earthly transience.

Finally, testamentary evidence sometimes provides an additional level of information about the biographies of household things – their histories of acquisition and ownership – which suggests that the context of an object's passage through hands and time carried an emotive charge. Objects given as tokens of affection prior to marriage represented a bond that made the circumstances of the gift and the recipient's response to the item especially meaningful in court proceedings, while testators sometimes went into considerable detail about the previous ownership of goods bequeathed in wills.[12] While indicative of the symbolic weight of exchange, this background information about household items found in depositions and wills reflects legal negotiations and financial, as well as affective, values so can be problematic for study of emotions. However, modifications made to a final object considered here can be understood as a material manifestation of autobiographical life-writing – a genre that facilitated reflection on events and relationships. An earthenware cup in the V&A dating from *c.* 1600 was later embellished, around 1658, with a raised silver mount engraved with an inscription in Latin, which translates as: 'This fragile cup was bought by me in AD 1618 and soon after given to my maternal great-uncle Nicholas Miller Esquire, who, concluding his last day in the year 1621 at the age of 85, bequeathed it to me together with other things worthy of note. Nicholas Miller June 12 An[no] 1658 at the age of 65'.[13] The inscription resembles some testamentary phraseology relating to heirlooms, but in making a permanent change to the form and semiotic capacity of the cup, Nicholas Miller expressed his personal investment in this item, elaborating the relationship between its biography and his own. This kind of material testimony suggests an early modern attachment to certain household objects as tangible, lasting embodiments of familial ties and personal histories and, as with the widespread fashion for memorials in churches, such 'speaking objects' expressed a hope for remembrance.

Further reading

Gaimster, D., T. Hamling and C. Richardson (eds), *The Routledge Handbook of Material Culture in Early Modern Europe* (Abingdon: Routledge, 2016)

—includes various studies of household objects from a range of disciplinary perspectives.

Hamling, T. and C. Richardson (eds), *Everyday Objects: Medieval and Early Modern Material Culture and its Meanings* (Aldershot: Ashgate, 2010)

—an influential collection of essays on early modern material culture; one section deals specifically with 'Emotion/Attitudes towards Objects'.

Hamling, T. and C. Richardson, *A Day at Home in Early Modern England: The Materiality of Domestic Life, c. 1500–c. 1700* (New Haven: Yale University Press, forthcoming)

—a sustained and indepth study of how the middling sorts of early modern England thought and felt about their domestic environment; its decoration, furnishings and goods.

Notes

1 C. Richardson, *Shakespeare and Material Culture* (Oxford: Oxford University Press, 2011), 3.

2 A. Appadurai, *The Social Life of Things: Commodities in Cultural Perspective* (Cambridge: Cambridge University Press, 1986)

3 A. Gell, *Art and Agency: An Anthropological Theory* (Oxford: Clarenden Press, 1998). See T. Hamling, 'To see or not to see?: the presence of religious imagery in the Protestant household', *Art History* 30, 2 (2007), 170–97 and 'Old Robert's Girdle: Visual and Material Props for Protestant Piety in Post-Reformation England', in A. Ryrie and J. Martin (eds), *Private and Domestic Devotion in Early Modern England* (Aldershot: Ashgate, 2012)
4 J. Gardiner with M.J. Allen (eds), *Before the Mast: Life and Death Aboard the Mary Rose* (Portsmouth: The Mary Rose Trust, 2005), 481.
5 The Mary Rose Trust, 82A1712.
6 T. Easton, 'Apotropaic Symbols and Other Measures for Protecting Buildings against Misfortune', in R. Hutton (ed.), *Physical Evidence for Ritual Acts, Sorcery and Witchcraft in Christian Britain: A Feeling for Magic* (Basingstoke: Palgrave, 2015), 39–67.
7 Victoria & Albert Museum numbers: W.31–1926; C.271–1918.
8 Museum of London ID no: A6807.
9 Museum of London ID no: A23406.
10 Museum of Welsh Life, item ref: 98:36. Metropolitan slipware jug, dated 1630, Museum of London ID no: 74.33.
11 T. Hamling and C. Richardson, *A Day at Home in Early Modern England: The materiality of domestic life, c. 1500–c. 1700* (New Haven: Yale University Press, forthcoming)
12 T. Richardson, *Domestic Life and Domestic Tragedy: The Material Life of the Household* (Manchester: Manchester University Press, 2006)
13 V&A Museum No: LOAN:GILBERT.583–2008. Image online at: http://collections.vam.ac.uk/item/O156535/jug-unknown/, accessed 19 April 2016.

III.16 Prints and illustrated broadsheets

Charles Zika

The invention of print using movable metal type in the mid-fifteenth century created new possibilities for the greater circulation not only of literary sources and texts, but also for visual materials.[1] Woodcuts and metal engravings soon began to be used to illustrate books and pamphlets, create broadsheets, and produce single-leaf prints or large multiple-block prints.[2] Printed images enlivened, adorned and embellished all manner of texts; and their use on title pages or as frontispieces made books more attractive and enticed prospective buyers.

Prints as forms of social communication have received focused scholarly attention only in recent decades,[3] and consideration of how they might be used as a source for exploring early modern emotions has been incidental rather than deliberate.[4] However, these seemingly ephemeral sources can provide significant insight into the ways various emotions – belonging, devotion, love, fear, disgust and wonder – influenced the life of early modern European communities, and how such emotions were deployed, shaped and also reproduced through space and time. Artists employed techniques to stimulate devotion or remorse among religious devotees, to galvanize supporters and humiliate enemies, to ratchet up fear, wonder or penitence in response to unusual events, to celebrate political power, and to generate disgust and outrage against threats to the moral and social order. They used prints to move viewers to particular forms of response and action by expressing the emotions of their subjects through facial expressions and gesture, or linking them to particular narratives with which they could readily identify and empathize. Alternatively, artists could associate subjects with objects, situations or actions that were traditionally linked to discourses of shame, disgust or ridicule. They also frequently underlined their aim of arousing eliciting emotion through the use of colour, captions or an appended text.

Some of the earliest prints to be circulated were devotional images. Their function was similar to that of sacred statues, wall paintings and altarpieces: to communicate to the faithful some of the fundamental doctrines, stories and models of the Christian faith, and stimulate devotion to Christ, his mother or the Christian saints.[5] During the Middle Ages, devotional images were most frequently found in illuminated manuscripts, such as picture bibles or Books of Hours.[6] But with the advent of print, relatively expensive images became much cheaper to produce and could now be made available to broader sectors of society, including the illiterate.

Devotional images could be held and gazed upon, touched and even kissed, by individual believers within their own domestic space. They were readily available as illustrations in prayer books or simply as single-leaf woodcuts, often printed together with a prayer for which the devotee could receive an indulgence. Two of the most common devotional images to be reproduced in the first century of print depicted Christ as the Man of Sorrows, surrounded by objects referencing his passion and death; or of Mary, Christ's mother, depicted with swords piercing her heart.

In a woodcut by Wolf Traut (*c.* 1485–1520) (Figure III.16.1), the two figures are brought together, with a text reporting a dialogue between mother and son. The text tells of the suffering, insults and humiliation Christ suffered on account of human sin, and the grief and compassion Mary feels, gazing at the broken body of her son. Mary is clearly the model for viewers, who are encouraged to gaze at Christ's suffering like her, and feel the same grief, compassion and also remorse – a message contained in the large Latin caption: 'Look on me you who pass by, since you are the cause of my sorrow'.

During the religious and political conflicts of the Reformation that overwhelmed much of Europe from the second decade of the sixteenth century, Catholics and especially Lutherans used prints as instruments for propaganda and polemic, weapons to be used in winning new adherents, arousing and galvanizing the fervour of supporters, and ridiculing, humiliating or demonizing enemies.[7] Monks and the papacy, for instance, were routinely ridiculed and insulted by being compared to all manner of animals, monsters and devils.

Some prints, for instance, identified the origin of monks and the pope as the excretions of devils. In one anonymous example (Figure III.16.2), three devils shown seated on the gallows and excreting the mass of monkish bodies below as though into a huge latrine, combines defecation with gallows shame. Such scatological humour was clearly meant to arouse disgust in viewers, and destroy any trust in such putrid and vile creatures, born under the gallows and destined to die on them.

Prints were also critical for a new media genre that proliferated in the second half of the sixteenth and seventeenth centuries: the illustrated news sheet or broadsheet. Most of these news sheets reported on major political and military events, but many reported wondrous or terrifying occurrences, such as comets and eclipses, natural

Figure III.16.1 Wolf Traut, *Man of Sorrows and Mater Dolorosa* (Nuremberg: Hieronymus Höltzel), woodcut, *c.* 1515.

Figure III.16.2 Cranach Workshop, *The Location and Origin of Monks*, woodcut, *c.* 1564.
© bpk/Staatsbibliothek zu Berlin.

disasters like floods, earthquakes and blood rain, or strange deformed births and multiple murders.[8] Visual imagery played a critical role in sensationalizing such events. Artists were able to heighten the emotional pull of these reports by deploying a number of simple visual techniques. One of the most common was to make lavish use of the colour red when describing meteorological disturbances. A fire-like or blood-like red (as it was often described in the text) became a sign of God's anger boiling over, as well as a warning of the imminent shedding of blood and fires of destruction.[9] Another technique – as in the case of a vision that appeared in the sky near Nuremberg in June 1558 (Figure III.16.3) – was to display a dragon in the sky. The dragon attacking a castle with its fiery breath represented a terrifying warning of apocalyptic punishment to be unleashed on society below. Its purpose was to jolt the viewer into a sense of urgency and anxiety, so as to respond with action.

Another common technique of printmakers in eliciting an emotional response from viewers was to create discursive links between the subjects depicted and particular visual motifs and codes that carried with them strong emotional attachments or resonances. Emperor Maximilian (1459–1519), for instance, was one of the first rulers to project his power through prints on paper.[10] Portraits of Maximilian, surrounded by the various symbols of his power – coats of arms, genealogical forbears, familial networks and membership of noble societies – were meant to elicit feelings of confidence and trust in a ruler embodying the most noble virtues and traditions. In contrary fashion, woodcuts depicting lusty devils embracing women, or women shown riding goats through the sky, helped quickly identify these women as witches, diabolical creatures governed by animal lust.

The use of such visual cues to arouse the emotional responses of viewers depends on a recognition of the emotional resonances attached to particular objects depicted. A stronger impact on viewers could be achieved when the emotions of the depicted subjects themselves were represented as the source of their vice or virtue. This is more frequently the case in seventeenth-century prints, which aim to draw viewers into a visualized narrative. We see such techniques being used in representations of Amerindian rituals by Theodor de Bry (1528–98), for instance,[11] and also in several depictions of witches' dances at their sabbaths.

One example of the use of visualized emotion to arouse a strong emotional response on the part of viewers are the two dance scenes depicted in the 1613 etching by Jan Ziarnko (*c.* 1575–*c.* 1628) of a Basque Sabbath (Figure III.16.4). The etching illustrates the *Tableau de l'inconstance* of the French magistrate Pierre de Lancre (*c.* 1533–1631), and the two sets of dancers exhibit the witches' flagrant sensuality and lack of emotional self-control.[12] The thrusting stomachs, full-frontal nudity, spread legs, frizzy hair and jagged, exaggerated movements, all suggest the frenzy of Bacchic orgies described in Lancre's text. The abandonment of emotional control, together with the intense pleasure in unified collective action, is precisely the moral and social threat of witchcraft that the artist was striving to convey. We can only speculate on the

Figure III.16.3 A Wondrous Event that Occurred at Lonnerstadt Five Miles from Nuremberg (Nuremberg: Wolfgang Strauch, 1558), coloured woodcut.

Zentralbibliothek Zürich, Department of Prints and Drawings/Photo Archive, PAS II 1/1a.

Figure III.16.4 Jan Ziarnko, *Description and Depiction of the Witches Sabbath*, etching, in Pierre de Lancre, *Tableau de l'inconstance des mauvais anges et demons* (Paris, 1613), following p. 118.

range of emotional responses – whether disgust, outrage or fear – that Ziarnko's depiction of these witches' emotions would have elicited in viewers. But such images – relatively small and portable in contrast to many other visual media, and in this last case an illustration to an accompanying text – must have worked in the way all but large multiple-block prints did. They spoke directly to individual viewers, rendering the concept of witchcraft truthful through the visual narrative, but also demanding an emotional response to the depiction of intense embodied emotions within the witches themselves.

Further reading

Scribner, R.W., *For the Sake of Simple Folk: Popular Propaganda for the German Reformation* (Cambridge: Cambridge University Press, 1981)

—classic work on popular images in the Reformation; does not consciously focus on emotions, but the emotional power of the imagery and its impact on the viewer underlies much of the study.

Zika, C., 'Violence, Anger and Dishonour in Sixteenth-Century Broadsheets from the Collection of Johann Jakob Wick', in S. Broomhall and S. Finn (eds), *Violence and Emotions in Early Modern Europe* (London: Routledge, 2015), 37–58.

—consciously addresses the ways prints can illuminate our understanding of emotions at particular points of time.

Notes

1 P. Parshall and R. Schoch, *Origins of European Printmaking: Fifteenth-Century Woodcuts and their Public* (Washington: National Gallery of Art, 2005); P. Parshall and D. Landau, *The Renaissance Print, 1470–1550* (New Haven: Yale University Press, 1994)
2 L. Silver and E. Wyckoff (eds), *Grand Scale: Monumental Prints in the Age of Dürer and Titian* (Wellesley: Davis Museum and Cultural Center, 2008)
3 See R.W. Scribner, *For the Sake of Simple Folk: Popular Propaganda for the German Reformation* (Cambridge: Cambridge University Press, 1981); T. Watt, *Cheap Print and Popular Piety 1550–1640* (Cambridge: Cambridge University Press, 1991); C. Zika, *The Appearance of Witchcraft: Print and Visual Culture in Sixteenth-Century Europe* (London: Routledge, 2007); J. Spinks, *Monstrous Births and Visual Culture in Sixteenth-Century Germany* (London: Pickering and Chatto, 2009)
4 An exception is Zika, 'Violence, Anger and Dishonour in Sixteenth-Century Broadsheets from the Collection of Johann Jakob Wick', in S. Broomhall and S. Finn (eds), *Violence and Emotions in Early Modern Europe* (London: Routledge, 2015), 37–58.
5 M. Baxandall, *The Limewood Sculptures of Renaissance Germany* (New Haven: Yale University Press, 1980); J. Chipps Smith, *Sensuous Worship: Jesuits and the Art of the Early Catholic Reformation in Germany* (Princeton: Princeton University Press, 2002)
6 R. Wieck, *Time Sanctified: The Book of Hours in Medieval Art and Life* (New York: G. Braziller, 1998)
7 Scribner, *For the Sake of Simple Folk*
8 W. Harms and A. Messerli (eds), *Wahrnehmungsgeschichte und Wissensdiskurs im illustrierten Flugblatt der Frühen Neuzeit (1450–1700)* (Basel: Schwabe & Co. AG Verlag, 2002)
9 C. Zika, 'Visual Signs of Imminent Disaster in the Sixteenth-Century Zurich Archive of Johann Jakob Wick', in M. Juneja and G.J. Schenk (eds), *Disaster as Image: Iconographies and Media Strategies across Europe and Asia* (Regensburg: Schnell und Steiner, 2014), 49–50, fig. 2.
10 L. Silver, *Marketing Maximilian: The Visual Ideology of a Holy Roman Emperor* (Princeton: Princeton University Press, 2008)
11 The prints of de Bry and his sons are available in G. Sievernich (ed.), *America de Bry, 1590–1634: Amerika oder die Neue Welt: die "Entdeckung" eines Kontinents in 346 Kupferstichen* (Berlin: Casablanca, 1990)
12 *On the Inconstancy of Witches.* Pierre de Lancre's *Tableau de l'inconstance des mauvais anges et demons* (1612), (ed.) G. Scholz Williams (Temple: Arizona Center for Medieval and Renaissance Studies, 2006)

III.17 Fantasy figures

Melissa Percival

Fantasy figures are works of art where a human subject is presented up close to the viewer. They may be based on an actual person, but unlike a portrait, the objective is not to capture a distinct likeness. Instead these paintings experiment with pose, expression, costume and painterly effects. Contextual details are eclipsed by the immediacy of the person: the turn of the head, the arch of a brow, a smile or grimace. By artful persuasion or apparent disregard, fantasy figures elicit the viewer's curiosity, complicity or desire. Artists found a liberating outlet in this type of informal study since they were unconstrained by the requirements of a commission. What originated in the studio found favour with buyers, who appreciated the beauty and mystery of these 'heads' as well as their close connection with the artistic process. Primarily through

Figure III.17.1 Rembrandt Harmensz. van Rijn, *An Old Man in Military Costume*, *c.* 1630–1. Oil on panel, 65.7 × 51.8 cm (25 7/8 × 20 3/8 in.), accession number 78.PB.246. Getty Museum, Los Angeles.

Credit: Digital image courtesy of the Getty's Open Content Program.

the work of Melissa Percival, fantasy figures are starting to be recognized as an important phenomenon in European painting; central to its objectives are the artist's expressive freedom and the frank exploration of human emotions.

The earliest examples of fantasy figures are from sixteenth-century Venice. The mysterious half-length shepherds and musicians by Giorgione (*c.* 1477/8–1510) evoke an erotic pastoral fantasy world with echoes of classical mythology. Titian (*c.* 1488/1490–1576) painted many sensuous, semi-nude females that are fictional hybrids of mythological types, portraits of high-born Venetian women, and studies of models who may have been courtesans. In Rome at the turn of the seventeenth century, Michelangelo Merisi da Caravaggio (1571–1610) innovated with the half-length figure format, squeezing his bodies together and cropping. Caravaggesque figure types – drinkers, musicians and singers, with their colourful anachronistic costumes – were taken north to Utrecht and France by his successors.

In Antwerp from 1609 to 1620, Peter Paul Rubens (1577–1640) produced some 50 head studies, mostly of bearded old men. They were intended as models for his pupils to copy, but after his death these works found their way onto the market, where they were snapped up by buyers. The following decade in Leiden, Jan Lievens (1607–74) and Rembrandt van Rijn (1606–69) began to paint subjects from life, dressed

Figure III.17.2 Michiel Sweerts, *Man Holding a Jug*, *c.* 1660. Oil on canvas, 19 3/8 × 15 3/8 in. (49.2 × 39.1 cm), accession number: 2001.613. Credit: Gift of Herman and Lila Shickman, 2001.

in fantasy costume and strongly illuminated. Their works became known as 'tronies', and rapidly became popular with collectors.[1] Rembrandt used himself as a model, playing with his own features and donning unusual costumes such as plumed hats, medallions and military garb (Figure III.17.1). Rembrandt's pupils and followers made the 'tronie' a significant force in Northern art.

Many fantasy figures depict lower class figures, including children. *Bamboccianti* artists in Rome in the seventeenth century, like Michiel Sweerts (1618–64), produced sensitive and penetrating studies of poor working people (Figure III.17.2). In northern Italy, artists such as Pietro Bellotti (1625–1700) popularized the theme of ragged peasants and other rustic figures. The eponymous vagabonds of Giacomo Ceruti (1697–1767), 'Il Pitochetto', are portrayed with striking dignity and pathos. Spain had its own traditions of beggars and paupers, originating with the earthy tenebrism of Jusepe de Ribera (1591–1652); Bartolomé Esteban Murillo (1617–82) injected his impoverished child subjects with beauty and sentiment.

The fantasy figure took on a more idealized form in Bolognese and Venetian art.[2] Inspired by the elegant and enigmatic half-length genre pieces of Giuseppe Maria Crespi (1665–1747), Ubaldo (1728–1781) and Gaetano Gandolfi (1734–1802) painted a variety of figures, from bearded Asians to brooding females. Rosalba Carriera (1673–1757) and Giambattista Tiepolo (1675–1757) revived the sensuous courtesan

Figure III.17.3 Giovanni Battista Tiepolo, *Young Lady in a Tricorn Hat*, *c.* 1755/1760, oil on canvas, 62.2 × 49.3 cm (24 1/2 × 19 7/16 in.).

Samuel H. Kress Collection 1952.5.77.

type created by Giorgione and Titian; Tiepolo painted a number of female 'teste a capriccio' that openly address themes of disguise and desire (Figure III.17.3).

In eighteenth-century France, the fantasy figures of Jean-Baptiste Santerre (1651–1717), Jean Raoux (1677–1734) and Alexis Grimou (1678–1733) were self-conscious pastiches, produced for a new upwardly-mobile clientele eager to hone their skills of connoisseurship. They used traditional – especially Netherlandish – figure types (musicians, readers, desirable females), formats such as windows and ledges, and experimented with light and brushwork. They also developed a hybrid form of fancy dress – derived from the Caravaggisti, from Rembrandt and from the Venetians. Known as 'Spanish' costume, it became synonymous with the notion of fantasy. The freely executed series of fantasy figures (*c.* 1769) of Jean-Honoré Fragonard (1732–1806), with their ruffs, plumes and dramatic *contrappostos*, are the most daring, exuberant examples of this type of work.

British producers of fancy pictures in the eighteenth century also mediated between tradition and contemporary tastes.[3] The Huguenot artist Philip Mercier (1689–1760) brought a modish French influence with him when he moved to England. Nathaniel Hone (1718–84), Henry Morland (1716–97) and John Opie (*c.* 1716–97) produced sentimentalized versions of kitchen maids, children and beggars. For Joshua Reynolds (1723–92) the fancy picture was a sideline from his position as chief academician and producer of ambitious formal portraits, but it was highly appreciated in elite circles. Thomas Gainsborough (1727–88) was interested in the depiction of figures in a landscape. All these subjects had a strong emotional appeal for art buyers, appearing as whimsical or flirtatious or charmingly serious, craggy old men or pale-skinned children receiving skilfully differentiated attention from the artist's brush.

The fantasy figure has only recently come to be regarded as a distinct category of painting with a pan-European evolution and spread. This is partly a consequence of the varied subject matter and the many different titles given to these works. Also the fantasy figure frequently blurs the boundaries between traditional genres – portraiture, genre painting and allegory – and hence thwarts the distinctions by which we understand the history of art. Yet with its recurring types (courtesans, *bravi*, beggars), and its emphasis on universal human experiences (love, reverie, old age), fantasy figures provide a significant repertoire of early modern period emotions.

There is a close connection between the fantasy figure and the teaching and learning of facial expression. Notable examples are Rubens's studio and Sweerts's drawing academy. Often the people nearest to hand were used as models: family, friends, studio hands or even the artist. Freed from the obligation to make the subject beautiful or noble, the artist constructs a sort of laboratory of the face, fixing on the detail of an eyebrow, of a cheekbone, a flyaway beard, a plethora of wrinkles. The lack of commission means that a range of facial expressions and bodily positions lying outside of social norms is also possible: a grimace or sneer, a peculiar smile. Several artists produced heads in series, seemingly ongoing facial experiments, that were popularized in prints. These include Giambattista Piazzetta (1683–1754), Jean-Baptiste Greuze (1725–1805) and Pietro Rotari (1707–62).

Paradoxically, given the emphasis on expression, fantasy figures are often semiotically weak, and require the viewer to supply missing information. Features are obscured through blank facial expressions, 'closed' poses (such as turned away from the viewer), clothes that conceal the body (a broad-brimmed hat, a veil), shadow or extraneous details that pull attention away from the face, such as jewels, fabric or fur. Many are depicted in a state of intense concentration on a particular task (what Michael Fried has called 'absorption'[4]); but even those who look directly at the viewer can be highly ambiguous. Confronted with a fantasy figure, the viewer participates in an encounter that is both intimate and uncertain. He or she may scrutinize a bit too closely, perhaps too longingly, intruding on the person's 'personal space'. The painting's inscrutability serves to increase the viewer's emotional connection as he or she fills the 'gaps' with hopes and desires.

If traditional interpretations that reinforce social norms can be ascribed to some fantasy figures – such as the sloth of a sleeping servant – then the scarcity or ambiguity of iconographical information, or the displacement of attention towards pose or costume detail, mean that such readings are subtly undermined. Many fantasy figure types come from the margins of respectable society: the *bravo*, a desperado or assassin, the courtesan or whore, the itinerant musician, the gamut of peddlars, beggars and child traders. There is a piquancy to the presence of these exotic or low-life characters in the homes of well-to-do art buyers, maybe adorned by an extravagant piece of costume or 'polished up' by loving attention from the artist's brush. Hence fantasy figures have the propensity to unbind social constraints, to project other models and norms, in short, to imagine society differently.

Fantasy figures lend themselves readily to poetry or fiction, to an imagined encounter with the other. The eighteenth-century term 'fancy' had connotations of whim or sentimentality, with something light and pleasing. Hence a fascination with the trivial and inconsequential can be seen in the innocence of a child, the blush of a young woman's cheek, the angle of a feather, a servant's progress momentarily arrested. An unexplained yearning is found in the 'otherness' of an Arcadian shepherd boy or an exotic turban. That yearning turns to erotic desire when confronted by a beckoning or sleeping woman. These are hybrids of nature and the artist's imagination, transformed through the magic of the brush into living and breathing individuals. They are paintings about not very much, where not a lot happens. Yet the attraction of fantasy figures lies in their capacity to articulate hidden desires and unspoken longing, to valorize the mundane, the bizarre and the overlooked. Awareness of fantasy figures will enable future scholars to reflect on continuities in the portrayal of emotions in the early modern period, on questions of decorum and taste, and on approaches to facial and bodily expression that extend beyond canonical models of expression and physiognomy.

Further reading

Figures de fantaisie du XVIe au XVIIIe siècle, exh. cat. (Toulouse: Musée des Augustins, 2015–16)
—containing an extended version of the above essay, the catalogue provides the first ever synthetic overview of two centuries of European fantasy figures, and features over 80 exhibits.

Percival, M., *Fragonard and the Fantasy Figure: Painting the Imagination* (Aldershot: Ashgate, 2012)
—demystifies Fragonard's famous series of fantasy figures (*c.* 1769) by revealing a common history of poses, typologies and blurred identities in European art.

Notes

1 See D. Hirschfelder, *Tronie und Portrait in der niederländischen Malerei des 17. Jahrhunderts* (Berlin: Gebr. Mann Verlag, 2008)
2 See *Teste di fantasia del settecento veneziano*, exh. cat. (Venice: Palazzo Cini, 2006)
3 See *Angels and Urchins: The Fancy Picture in Eighteenth-Century British Art*, exh. cat. (Nottingham: University of Nottingham, Djanogly Art Gallery / London: Kenwood House, 1998)
4 M. Fried, *Absorption and Theatricality: Genre and Beholder in the Age of Diderot* (Berkeley: University of California Press, 1980)

III.18 Monuments

Peter Sherlock

Early modern Europeans erected monuments to preserve the memory of the dead. Situated in churches or churchyards, they range from humble paving stones bearing a name and a date to sumptuous edifices bearing exquisite effigies. During the sixteenth and seventeenth centuries, monuments presented fresh interpretations of the emotional relationship of the living and the dead. Protestant reformers challenged the idea that the fate of the dead in the afterlife depended on the prayers of the living and placed renewed emphasis on the resurrection of the dead to eternal life. Renaissance humanists – both Catholic and Protestant – revived the ancient concept of fame, promoting the dead as virtuous, heroic examples for the living, deserving of monumental magnificence.

Early modern monuments are designed to convey the idealized beliefs, behaviours and emotions of their patrons and subjects to posterity. There is, surprisingly, very little scholarship on monuments as sources for the history of emotions. Yet a close and deep reading of monuments can reveal how communities chose to represent themselves to the future in response to the rupture of death. This requires attention not only to inscriptions, but also to images, heraldry, architectural form and materials (such as stone, metal, wood, glass or paper). To understand how their messages were produced and received, monuments must be considered within several contexts: patronage and creation; location, including relation to mortal remains and to other monuments; their alteration or destruction over time; the reaction of visitors, tourists and pilgrims; and their dissemination in manuscript, print and art.

Barbara H. Rosenwein provides a methodology for the interpretation of monumental inscriptions as sources for identifying shifts in emotional communities.[1] This entry argues for the fruitfulness of tombs as a source for understanding early modern emotions, following Rosenwein's lead, but moving beyond inscriptions alone to other aspects of monumental culture. It does so through investigation of an exemplary pair of early modern European monuments.

Between 1605 and 1612, James VI and I (1566–1625) erected a pair of monuments at Westminster Abbey to his predecessor Elizabeth of England (1533–1603) and to his mother Mary of Scotland (1542–87).[2] Westminster, the prime location for royal commemoration in the kingdom of England from the eleventh to the eighteenth century, was an influential site with its monuments frequently imitated by the nobility and gentry and visited by European dignitaries and tourists.

The monuments of Elizabeth and Mary attempted to reconcile the dynastic and religious conflicts within James' family and kingdoms by rewriting the past. James decreed that both Elizabeth and Mary would be commemorated at Westminster, bestowing an equality on them in death as heralds of James' reign that they did not enjoy in life. This equality was not empty symbolism. James ordered the disinterment of their bodies so that they might lie in their new tombs. When Mary's corpse was brought from Peterborough to Westminster in 1612, Henry Howard (1540–1614), the Earl of Northampton, wrote with tearful praise of the 'justice of God and the piety of a matchless son'.[3] These regal monuments promoted James' kingship as a source of wonder, ordained by divine justice, providence and personal piety, that unleashed emotional reactions.

The monuments had similar forms, although Mary's was considerably larger than Elizabeth, suggestive of the excess emotional baggage it had to bear in light of her death by the executioner's axe, and perhaps a stronger connection to Catholic piety. Each presented an effigy of the queen under a triumphal arch, an ancient form used to represent victory, celebrating not only the Christian victory over death, but also the victory over life. Mary's effigy lies peacefully with her hands clasped in prayer and her head safely on her shoulders, representing the triumph of her memory and

Figure III.18.1 Monument of Mary Queen of Scots, 1604–1612, Westminster Abbey (view of effigy).

posterity over the violence of her death. (Figure III.18.1) Elizabeth's effigy is adorned with crown, orb and sceptre, displaying her triumph over every adversity to die after forty-five years as a queen regnant. Although both sculptures attempt realism through the depiction of face and costume, the still expressions convey an absence of passion. The effigies represent the belief, taught by both Catholic and reformed Christian doctrine, that the body and soul were separated by death, awaiting reunion at the resurrection to eternal life.

The Latin inscriptions present distinct emotional narratives of their lives and deaths, attempting to command how posterity will remember them. Elizabeth is 'a prince incomparable, endowed with regal virtues above her sex', a 'conqueror, triumpher, the most devoted to piety, the most happy' who 'quietly by death departed' in the 'hope of our resurrection'. In contrast to these calm certainties of Elizabeth's reign and death, Mary's epitaphs focus on the shock of death by execution: 'she was struck down by the axe, a dangerous example to kings'. Furthermore, her death is presented as the cause of anguish to all British subject, who intercede for mercy and vengeance: 'spare us, O God, it is enough, halt these unutterable sorrows . . . may the instigator and perpetrator come hastily to punishment'.[4] Absent from both monuments, however, is the plea for the visitor to pray for the dead that was once omnipresent. Protestant Elizabeth had no need of such prayers, for her virtues in life were evidence of her salvation. Catholic Mary was presented as a martyr, the manner of her death ensuring her soul was in heaven.

James is presented as the unifier and pacifier who transcends not only the virtues of Elizabeth's reign but also the disaster of Mary's death. This is evident in the heraldry on both tombs. The arms on Mary's tomb point to her descent from the Scottish and French royal lines, and the passage of her inheritance to James. Those on Elizabeth's tomb similarly trace the descent of the English crown from the Conqueror, but end with the Stuart line of succession. James' shield, crest and motto 'blessed are the peacemakers' tower over the whole monument, proclaiming the triumph of universal peace in his person and reign and reflecting his belief in his own ability to overcome even religious divisions.

The monuments have been a focus for tourists from the moment of their completion, and new emotional narratives have been added through souvenirs. Printed

Figure III.18.2 Detail of title-page to Samuel Purchas, *Hakluytus Posthumus or Purchas his Pilgrimes* (London, 1625).

Beinecke Rare Book and Manuscript Library, Yale University.

images of Elizabeth's tomb were widely disseminated, a practice portrayed by Thomas Fuller (1608–61) as evidence of the pride and grief of her grateful subjects, 'every parish being proud of the shadow of her tomb; and no wonder, when each loyal subject erected a mournful monument for her in his heart'.[5] In 1625 one image linked her tomb with the death of the late Henry Prince of Wales (1594–1612), demonstrating that death comes for royalty both young and old as it does for all humans. (Figure III.18.2) This image also showed how future generation could use a monument as the backdrop for the projection of emotion, in this case grief, loss and nostalgia for what might have been had Prince Henry lived. In the twentieth century a new inscription was installed at the foot of Elizabeth's tomb to acknowledge the Catholic and Protestant martyrs of the Reformation. By all these means, the wonder and curiosity of visitors is used to direct them to learn the virtues and vices of the past.

Like monuments across early modern Europe, the tombs of Elizabeth of England and Mary of Scotland communicate a world of emotions to viewers. They praise virtue and warn of mortality. They point to the hope of eternal life, both as a reward for pious living and for enduring suffering. They call forth wonder at their magnificence to stimulate attention to their messages. As formal, carefully constructed objects that in the early modern period attempted to control meaning, monuments can obscure emotional impacts. Yet it is precisely because of the controlled nature of their messages that, if read carefully, monuments can tell us much about early modern approaches to emotion and memory. There is much potential for future scholarship to analyse the emotional messages of early modern monuments, to investigate monuments as sites of emotional display, and to explore how such messages and display were affected by differences of gender, religion and status.

Further reading

Llewellyn, N., *Funeral Monuments in Post-Reformation England* (Cambridge: Cambridge University Press, 2001)

—establishes a comprehensive methodology for reading early modern monuments, including attention to their capacity to communicate emotions such as grief and wonder.

Sherlock, P., *Monuments and Memory in Early Modern England* (Aldershot: Ashgate, 2008)

—examines the impact of Reformation and Renaissance on monumental commemoration, arguing that the dominant emotional register of tombs shifted from fear to hope owing to new theologies of the afterlife and a revival of the idea of fame.

Notes

1 B.H. Rosenwein, *Emotional Communities in the Early Middle Ages* (Ithaca: Cornell University Press, 2006), 57–78.

2 P. Sherlock, 'The monuments of Elizabeth Tudor and Mary Stuart: King James and the manipulation of memory', *Journal of British Studies* 46, 2 (2007), 263–89.

3 The National Archives, UK: SP 14/71/16, Earl of Northampton to Viscount Rochester, 10 October 1612.

4 My translation.

5 T. Fuller, *The Church History of Britain* (1655), (ed.) J.S. Brewer (Oxford: Oxford University Press, 1845), vol. 5, 258.

III.19 Devotional objects

Mary Laven

The potential for bringing together the history of the emotions and that of the material culture of religion has as yet been scarcely tapped. This is due in part to the relative novelty of both fields, but it also testifies to the difficulty of recovering the emotional valences of material remains that are often either fragmentary or no longer extant. Archival, literary and physical evidence needs to be carefully interleaved in order to reconstruct lost affective universes. Among studies of the early modern period, much of the work that points the way in this area explicitly addresses the subject of 'popular religion', which has attempted to replace top-down, political or intellectual histories with local, social histories of devotion. The intersection of the material and the emotional in religious cultures is frequently also the intersection between promulgated doctrine and practice on the ground.

Early modern preachers were well aware of the power of material culture to arouse the emotions of their audiences. Two Jesuit missionaries delivering a sermon to the people of Rothenberg in the Upper Palatinate – a community whose allegiance to the true Catholic faith was in doubt – made confident use of their props. While one brandished a large crucifix before the congregation, the other, who wore a noose around his neck and held a skull in his hand, prostrated himself before the crucifix, asking his listeners if they wanted 'to wound again such a loving God'. The performance was irresistible and the villagers shouted back in unison 'No!' According to the Jesuit account, the people 'began to sigh and wail so loudly and furiously that the *patres* had to stop speaking'.[1] The power of objects to arouse sympathy, sorrow, pain and compassion was likewise regularly attested during processions. When a confraternity carried a life-size crucifix through the streets of Seville during the plague year of 1570, accounts celebrated the fact that 'there was not man nor woman old or young who did not weep and cry out for mercy'.[2] On the other hand, statues of saints or reliquaries that had long been revered aroused new feelings of anger and revulsion among certain brands of Protestant. Depending on which side of the theological divide one stood, the breaking up of holy remains, church furnishings or representations of the saints could provoke euphoria or grief.[3] We can therefore see the key role that devotional objects played in the creation and maintenance of 'emotional communities'.[4]

Beyond the charged public arenas of sermon, procession or iconoclastic purge, devotional things played a quieter and less conspicuous role in the emotional lives of early modern Europeans. However, the evidence for their effect is far harder to chart. Written accounts of personal responses to devotional objects are frustratingly sparse, and we therefore need to read the material and contextual evidence that does exist with care and imagination. That said, it is safe to assume that spiritual belongings, owned by individuals, worn on the body and displayed within the home, stimulated the emotions. For example, as illustrated in contemporary rosary manuals, paternoster beads were designed to guide the devout through contemplation of the 'joyous', 'sorrowful' and 'glorious mysteries' of the Incarnation. Triggered by rubbing the

Figure III.19.1 Religious pendant, probably Spanish, *c.* 1600–1625. Enamelled gold and crystal. Height: 5.1 cm.

Fitzwilliam Museum, MAR.M.280–1912.

prayer-beads and reciting the familiar Hail Marys and Our Fathers, the devotee was taken on a roller-coaster ride through the emotions of joy, sorrow and glory. This 'sequencing of emotional effects' (to borrow a phrase that Susan Verdi Webster has applied to the way in which crowds responded to processional sculptures) was achieved in miniature in a stunning three-sided pendant from early seventeenth-century Spain (Figure III.19.1). Measuring 5.1 centimetres from top to bottom, studded with garnets and set in an enamelled gold mount, the pendant features three miniscule scenes enclosed within rock crystal: the Adoration of the Shepherds, the Crucifixion and the Resurrection. While dim light and poor eyesight would often have prevented the owner from 'reading' the images, the distinctive feel of the object when held in the hand would have activated the correct emotional responses.

Small-scale devotional objects also served to create emotional stability: to suppress the extreme emotions of fear, pain and grief and to permit their owners to regain equilibrium. The Dominican author of the *Rosario della gloriosa Maria*, published in

Figure III.19.2 Dish, *The Temptation*, Brislington, *c.* 1680–1700. Diameter 33.4 cm. Fitzwilliam Museum, *c.* 1622–1928.

Venice in 1522, regaled the reader with an assortment of miracle stories in which the faithful had been saved by their devotion to the rosary. One such was the tale of Lucia, a young Spanish noblewoman abducted by infidels. Fourteen or fifteen years old and pregnant by her husband, who had been slain by the Moors, Lucia came to give birth in captivity. It was the feast of the Nativity, and she suffered her labour pains in a barn, surrounded by animals. With no assistance from humans, she took her cord of paternoster beads in her hand and started to say the rosary. Touched by her devotion, the Virgin Mary entered the scene and assumed the role of midwife to the young mother. The 'priest' who then miraculously entered the barn in order to perform the baptism of the new-born child bore a crown of thorns and stigmata.[5] If such miraculous occurrences were exceptional, the instinct of the mother to grip her rosary beads during childbirth was surely very ordinary.

Devotional objects were therefore a source of solace as well as a source of stimulation. We recognize that certain religious things had a protective or amuletic function within the home, but we need to acknowledge their additional role in providing comfort and stability.[6] The ubiquitous presence of representations of the Madonna in homes throughout Catholic Europe is an obvious example: a source of maternal reassurance and love for every occasion.[7] Within Protestant homes, a rich array of moralizing, scriptural and commemorative motifs made their way onto ceramics and other decorative items.[8] Adam and Eve was a favoured theme for the English Calvinist household, as may be seen from the survival of a number of late-

Figure III.19.3 Sampler, Ann Smith, Scottish or English, 1766–1767. Wool canvas, embroidered in polychrome silk.

Fitzwilliam Museum, T.37–1938.

seventeenth and eighteenth-century chargers which represented the Fall (Figure III.19.2). What is striking about these boldly-painted ceramics is that they provoke more cheer than fear. Often presented to couples as wedding gifts, they brought a positive model of marital sexuality into the Protestant home while simultaneously warning men and women of the perils of temptation.

A final example, which also depicts the Fall, is a sampler embroidered by Ann Smith in 1766–7 (Figure III.19.3). Ann's Adam and Eve are reminiscent of the figures who are represented on contemporary English ceramics. Neither they nor their pet snake appear particularly depraved. The two inscriptions speak more clearly of the moral purpose of the textile: at the top, 'Teach me Wisdom Secretly O Lord God That I may run the ways/of thy commandments with great delight. A.S. Began This 1766'; in the middle, 'For as by one mans disobedience many were made sinners; so/by the obedience of one shall many be made righteous'. I want to pause on the one emotion that is expressly referred to here: 'delight'. Here, the sample-sewer draws on her knowledge of Scripture and her visual repertoire of flora and fauna in order to present a calming and approachable account of Original Sin, where the pursuit of an obedient and virtuous life will bring delight – not fear and pain – to the pious.

Further reading

Johnson, T., 'Blood, Tears and Xavier Water: Popular Religion in the Eighteenth-Century Upper Palatinate', in R.W. Scribner and T. Johnson (eds), *Popular Religion in Germany and Central Europe, 1400–1800* (Houndmills: Macmillan, 1996), 183–202.

—a variety of devotional objects are cited in this discussion of the centrality of the emotions to Baroque Catholicism.

Rudy, K.R., 'Kissing images, unfurling rolls, measuring wounds, sewing badges and carrying talismans: Considering some Harley manuscripts through the physical rituals they reveal,' *Electronic British Library Journal* (2011), article 5. www.bl.uk/eblj/2011articles/article5.html

—suggests the potential for looking at material texts – physically marked by the kisses, sweat or tears of their readers – as a source for the history of the emotions.

Verdi Webster, S., *Art and Ritual in Golden-Age Spain: Sevillian Confraternities and the Processional Sculpture of Holy Week* (Princeton: Princeton University Press, 1998)

—on the role of processional objects in the choreography of public and ritualized emotional responses.

Notes

1 T. Johnson, 'Blood, Tears and Xavier Water: Popular Religion in the Eighteenth-Century Upper Palatinate', in R.W. Scribner and T. Johnson (eds), *Popular Religion in Germany and Central Europe, 1400–1800* (Houndmills: Macmillan, 1996), 183–202, quote 193.

2 S. Verdi Webster, *Art and Ritual in Golden-Age Spain: Sevillian Confraternities and the Processional Sculpture of Holy Week* (Princeton: Princeton University Press, 1998), 164–87, quote 174.

3 M. Aston, *Faith and Fire: Popular and Unpopular Religion, 1350–1600* (London: Hambledon Press, 1993), 267–8, for a euphoric account of iconoclasm in England in 1538; P. Johnston and B. Scribner, *The Reformation in Germany and Switzerland* (Cambridge: Cambridge University Press, 1993), 55–7 for a grief-stricken account of iconoclasm in Zurich in 1524.

4 B.H. Rosenwein, *Emotional Communities in the Early Middle Ages* (Ithaca: Cornell University Press, 2006)

5 A. da Castello, *Rosario della gloriosa vergine Maria* (Venice, 1522), fol. 29r–v.

6 On protective qualities, see J. Musacchio, 'Lambs, Coral, Teeth, and the Intimate Intersection of Religion and Magic in Renaissance Tuscany', in S.J. Cornelison and S. Bradford Montgomery (eds), *Images, Relics and Devotional Practices in Medieval and Renaissance Italy* (Tempe, AZ: Arizona Center for Medieval and Renaissance Studies, 2006), 139–56; and T. Hamling, 'To see or not to see? The

presence of religious imagery in the Protestant household', *Art History* 30, 2 (2007), 170–97, especially 191–4.

7 M. Morse, 'Creating sacred space: The religious visual culture of the Renaissance venetian casa', *Renaissance Studies* 21 (2007), 151–84; J. Musacchio, 'The Madonna and Child, a Host of Saints and Domestic Devotion in Renaissance Florence', in G. Neher and R. Shepherd (eds), *Revaluing Renaissance Art* (Ashgate: Aldershot, 2000), 147–64.

8 A. Morrall, 'Inscriptional Wisdom and the Domestic Arts in Early Modern Northern Europe,' in N. Filatkina, B.U. Münch and A. Kleine-Engel (eds), *Formelhaftigkeit in Text und Bild* (Wiesbaden: Reichert Verlag, 2012), 121–38. A. Walsham, 'Domesticating the Reformation: material culture, memory, and confessional identity in early modern England', *Renaissance Quarterly*, 69 (2016), 566–616.

III.20 Textiles

Sally Holloway

Throughout the early modern period, textile objects from garters to gowns provided a fertile site for the negotiation of emotions through the material world. Understanding the emotional 'work' performed by textiles as a source relies upon the interdisciplinary methodologies for studying material culture, considering both objects themselves and how they acquired meaning.[1] This entry will outline some methods and methodologies for uncovering emotional meaning in textiles, considering when and how emotional intent was conferred, and how it can be interpreted by scholars. It will uncover the possibilities offered by garments, accessories and decorative textiles for emotions analysis by exploring their creation, exchange and display in early modern Europe.

Whether the blackwork embroidery popular in the sixteenth century or whitework adorning eighteenth-century muslins, the time invested in creating and embroidering textiles could grant these objects particular emotional value. While objects such as elaborate hangings or quilts can suggest intensive labour in their own right, we are often reliant on supporting sources such as letters and diaries to reveal the time and value accorded particular items. Amanda Vickery has noted that female crafting can be read as both a performance of propriety and service, and a display of affection, contending that it would take 'a heart of stone' to 'deny that a baby's name embroidered on a quilt was a gesture of tenderness'.[2]

The names, mottoes and symbols chosen by women provide pertinent clues for emotions scholars as to the love, hope or defiance that fuelled their creation. In her pioneering work *The Subversive Stitch* (1984), the feminist art historian Rozsika Parker used letters, novels, inventories and extant works to argue that embroidery provided a covert means of power for women. Particular icons held 'specific importance and powerful resonance' for creators. During the sixteenth century, the rose was thought to comfort the heart, while a glove cut in two or cracked mirror symbolized grief.[3] By the eighteenth century, Biblical figures, the senses and seasons had given way to naturalistic and botanical imagery. Embroidering these symbols provided women with a way to work through their emotions as the needle moved through the fabric.

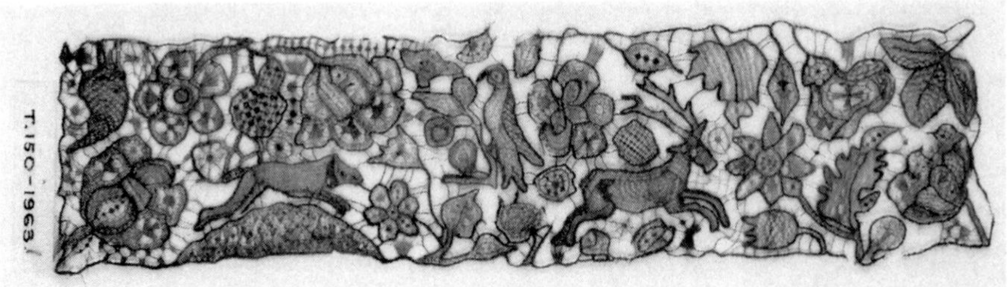

Figure III.20.1 Band of needle lace worked in human hair and possibly horse hair, England, *c.* 1640–80.

The language of symbols is particularly valuable for scholars interpreting the vast number of objects that have been dislocated from their original contexts, leaving no trace of their initial owners or creators.

Particular materials provide further tangible clues. Can the same emotional properties be conferred upon linen and lace? Silk and metallic threads convey wealth and status as well as emotional intent, attested by the longevity of early modern sumptuary laws. Items crafted from hair can be seen to embody more directly the emotions of their creator. In the seventeenth century, accomplished women could create delicate bands of hair lace to literally present part of themselves as a sentimental gift. The example in Figure III.20.1 is likely to have been worn as a bracelet, remaining close to the skin. Hair woven as a material is uniquely corporeal, providing a physical embodiment of love or grief as a lasting relic of the body.

The exchange of textiles is a revealing moment for emotions scholars, whether through the inheritance or giving and receiving of items. Textile gifts were used repeatedly to convey emotional messages in seeking prestige and preferment. In her study of gift-giving at the court of Elizabeth I (1533–1603), Lisa M. Klein has outlined how courtiers offered the Queen a plethora of elaborately embroidered books, cloaks, gloves and dresses. Such items could demonstrate love and fidelity, or profess sorrow after suffering her displeasure.[4] Textiles had a long history as diplomatic gifts, and could be harnessed to secure alliances as embodiments of friendship, hope and good faith. One of the most prestigious gifts from Louis XIII (1601–43) and his successors was a luxury *savonnerie* carpet; their emotional associations were so powerful that many were later burned or had symbols such as *fleurs-de-lys* cut out by Revolutionaries.

Nonetheless, the emotional resonance of textiles extended beyond silken threads. John Styles' landmark exhibition 'Threads of Feeling' at the Foundling Museum in London (2010–11) and Colonial Williamsburg (2013–14) showcased the range of items left as tokens by mothers or cut by clerks at the Foundling Hospital, which continues as the children's charity Coram. Items included infant clothing, ribbons, symbols printed on cottons and linens, and embroidered scraps of fabric.[5] Such textiles could provide an emissary and embodiment of emotions such as love, hope or grief. The fragment of flannel blanket in Figure III.20.2 was preserved to identify a six-week old girl admitted on 20 July 1759. Embroidering the blanket with the initials 'Mb'

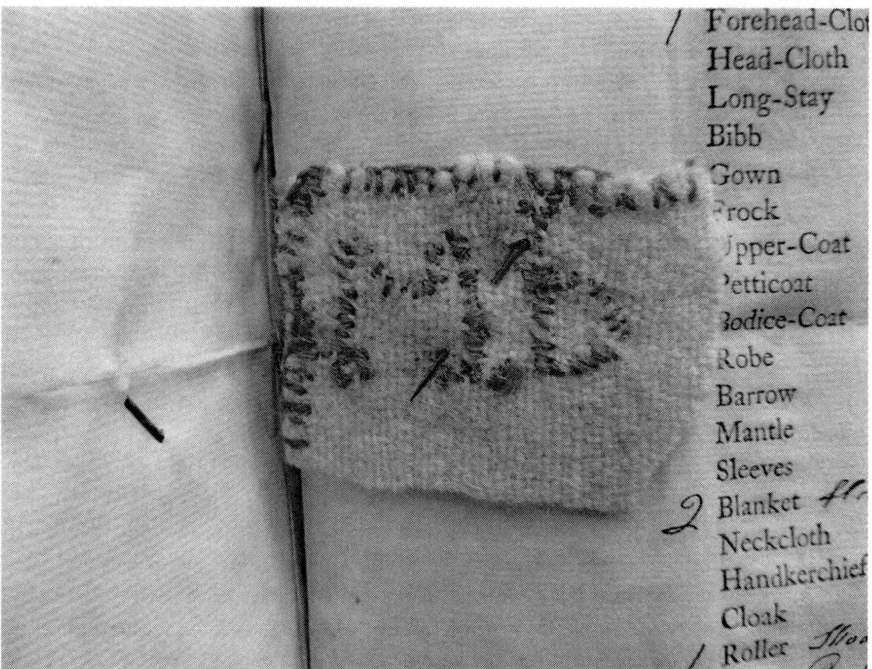

Figure III.20.2 Embroidered flannel blanket used to identify an infant girl admitted on 20 July 1759, no. 13,495, London Metropolitan Archives, A/FH/A/9/1/150.

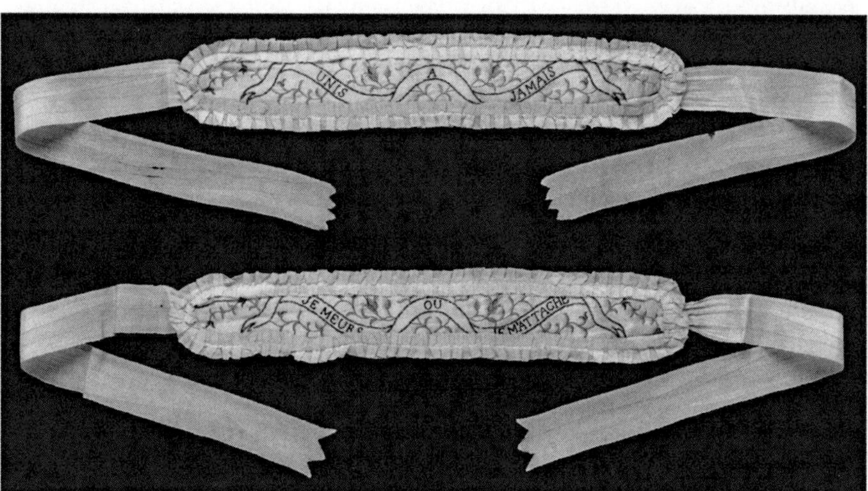

Figure III.20.3 Ivory silk garters with silver thread, France, *c.* 1780.

provided the mother with a way to claim her daughter using her chosen name before they were forced to part.[6] Select tokens also survive from European institutions such as the Ospedale degli Innocenti in Florence and Maagdenhuis in Antwerp, providing precious material evidence of the bond between mother and child.

Courtship involved an intense period of exchange, comprising garters, gloves, handkerchiefs and ribbons, which could be tied with loveknots to enhance their emotional meaning. Throughout the early modern period, such gifts provided a material vocabulary through which to negotiate, cement and intensify romantic relationships. The ivory silk garters in Figure III.20.3 are emblazoned with the phrases 'UNIS A JAMAIS' ('United Forever') and 'JE MEURS OU JE M'ATTACHE' ('I Die Where I Cling'), and are decorated with budding flowers symbolizing a blossoming romance. Garters possessed particular emotional value as they were worn close to the skin, hidden beneath a woman's petticoats. As one pair of Spanish garters teased, 'NO DEBO VERTE' ('I'm not allowed to see you').

Textiles displayed before family, friends and the community could provide a sign of inclusion or badge of shame. Jews in early modern Europe were repeatedly ordered to wear hats or badges in yellow or red to distinguish themselves. The poor were also compelled to display badges as signs they received parish relief, with red and blue badges in England evolving from symbols of honour to humiliation by the end of the seventeenth century.[7] Colour was key in crafting emotional meaning, with a rainbow of hues granted particular symbolic associations. Unfortunately for historians, surviving fabrics are often faded due to light exposure and the use of natural dyes such as madder and indigo made from herbs, roots and vegetables. The tarnishing of metal threads over time also obscures their dazzling appearance by candlelight.

Garments provided an important canvas through which to navigate the rituals of the life-cycle. In her work on textiles in early modern Denmark, Tove Engelhardt Mathiassen has noted how the colour red and metallic threads were often used for infant clothing to symbolize love and protect against evil.[8] Collating and ornamenting the bridal trousseau provided a way for women and their families to channel emotions such as hope and anticipation in the build up to a marriage. At the end of the life-cycle, the display of sombre black, purple or grey textiles during mourning rituals publicly advertized the emotional state of the wearer in the eyes of society.

Textiles could provide a potent means of mediating, negotiating and shaping particular emotional states. By focusing on the creation, exchange and display of items, scholars can glimpse the symbols, rituals and materials from which early modern feelings were woven.

Further reading

Deliberately Concealed Garments Project, www.concealedgarments.org/

—AHRC-funded project led by Dinah Eastop that utilizes caches of hidden or buried garments to analyse a folk practice that was not documented in contemporary texts.

Dolan, A. and S. Holloway (eds), Special Issue: 'Emotional Textiles', *Textile: The Journal of Cloth and Culture* 14, 2 (2016)

—interdisciplinary special issue that is the first to use a range of methodologies to draw out the changing emotional meanings of one type of material.

Styles, J., *Threads of Feeling: The London Foundling Hospital's Textile Tokens, 1740–1770* (London: The Foundling Museum, 2010) and 'Objects of Emotion: The London Foundling Hospital Tokens, 1741–60', in A. Gerritsen and G. Riello (eds), *Writing Material Culture History* (London: Bloomsbury, 2015), 165–72.

—Styles' work on the Foundling Hospital archives provides an exemplar of how textiles can be used to recover emotional experiences.

Notes

1 See K. Harvey (ed.), *History and Material Culture: A Student's Guide to Approaching Alternative Sources* (Oxford: Routledge, 2009)

2 A. Vickery, *Behind Closed Doors: At Home in Georgian England* (New Haven: Yale University Press, 2009), 241.

3 R. Parker, *The Subversive Stitch: Embroidery and the Making of the Feminine* (London: I.B. Tauris, 1984; repr. 2010), 12, 71–8.

4 L.M. Klein, 'Your humble handmaid: Elizabethan gifts of needlework', *Renaissance Quarterly* 50, 2 (1997), 459–93.

5 See Coram, www.coram.org.uk.

6 If a specific token was brought, the billet recording an infant's clothing was usually left blank, although the distinction can sometimes be unclear.

7 S. Hindle, 'Dependency, shame and belonging: badging the deserving poor, *c.* 1550–1750', *Cultural and Social History* 1, 1 (2004), 6–35.

8 T. Engelhardt Mathiassen, 'Protective strategies and emotions invested in early modern Danish Christening garments', in *Textile: The Journal of Cloth and Culture,* Special Issue: 'Emotional Textiles', (eds) A. Dolan and S. Holloway, 14, 2 (2016), 208–25.

III.21 The body

Karen Harvey

In early modern Europe, affect was physical. In seventeenth-century English and French language, for example, 'emotion' referred to movements in or of bodies: individual, social, animal and cosmic.[1] Passions and affections created emotions that were understood to impact upon both the body and the mind. Early moderns understood and experienced emotions as embodied: feelings, moods and desires were rooted in the physiology of the human body. The body is therefore a principal focus for early modern scholars' work on emotions because it directs our investigations to precisely where early modern people believed emotions were generated and experienced. The body is also a universal category common to all and can therefore serve as useful point of comparison to show how factors such as social rank, gender, place and religion affected people's experiences of emotion. This entry surveys some of the more commonly used sources for the history of the body as it relates to the emotions, as well as providing an introduction to the range of methods applied to these sources.

There is no archive of the body. Scholars study the early modern body by drawing on a very wide range of documents: visual, material and textual; official and popular; canonical and ephemeral. Perhaps the most important sources we have to understand the physical basis for the emotions relate to the theory and practice of medicine and health. Printed books allow historians to apply cultural history methods to an examination of the representations and discourse that constituted early modern knowledge about the body and emotions. These sources show how the emotions were an integral part of the physiological system of fluxes and flows, a system that connected the individual human body to the environment around it. Guides to good health promulgated this idea of the emotions as physical movement, one English book describing the 'emotion of the Spirits'.[2] The body was replete with the four humours of black bile, blood, yellow bile and phlegm. Also moving within the body were three kinds of spirit matter: natural spirits (from the liver), vital spirits (from the heart) and animal spirits (from the brain). Emotions were linked particularly to the heart's vital spirits. The heart was a moving organ whose sinking or swelling as a response to emotion affected the body's health in direct ways. Though it would be increasingly seen as a pump, following the work of William Harvey (1578–1657) on circulation published in 1628, the heart was only replaced with the brain as the organ of emotions during the late nineteenth century. Intense emotional experiences could damage the heart and still, in 1793, was one explanation for the death from heart disease of the famous surgeon John Hunter (1728–93).[3]

Sources such as physicians' casebooks, reports and correspondence with patients enable scholars to explore how medical knowledge affected bodily treatment and was applied in other social contexts. The view that emotions moved within the body, producing physical effects such as tears, swellings, pains and discolouration of the skin, was applied in a number of settings. A medical report for a German witch trial of 1652, for example, saw tears as water sent directly from the moved heart; witches, by contrast, could not cry because their hearts were cold and dried up.[4] Patients' letters to the Swiss physician Samuel-Auguste Tissot (1728–97) show the gradual decline of the humoral model and the development of the science of the brain and nervous system in the eighteenth century. His patients adopted the new nervous model and they used emotive language to describe their physical experiences. Describing his abdominal pain to Tissot in a letter of a 1785, Torchon Defouchet referred to his 'embarrassed' stomach.[5] Acquiring wider purchase through the culture of sensibility, nervous science relocated the locus of the emotions. This affected the way that the body was represented and performed.[6] The development of a relaxed and open-mouthed smile in eighteenth-century Paris was an index of changing views of emotions and their outward expression, the cult of sensibility and a focus on natural virtue in particular, as well as developments in dentistry.[7] In characterizing the body as intrinsically 'feeling', nervous science rendered the emotions ever more embodied.

The documents available to early modern scholars can reveal not just how the body was represented but how emotions were experienced physically. For example, descriptions of pain and illness as recorded in individuals' personal writings show the direct connection people felt between their bodily health and feelings. Women in particular attributed non-psychological, physical illness to the emotions of grief, fear and surprise that arose in the context of close interpersonal relationships. In her diary for 1642, Alice Thornton (*c.* 1626–1707) recorded her reaction to seeing her brother's changed appearance following his recovery from smallpox: 'beeing stroke with feare seeing him so sadly used and all over very read [i.e. red], I immediately fell very ill'.[8] Historians' analysis of these rich sources underlines the significance of gender to the history of early modern emotions. Indeed, certain 'diseases of the head, nerves or spirits' were feminized.[9]

Such sources also allow early modern historians access to individuals' physical experiences of emotions in the past. Descriptions of physical suffering could be a proxy for the subject's emotional distress. During her interrogation as part of the investigation into a monstrous birth hoax in 1726, the terms used by Mary Toft (1703–63) to describe her acute and ongoing pain – such as 'uneasie' and 'desperate' – simultaneously expressed her emotional trauma.[10] Historians of the body adopt multiple methodologies but have begun to probe the interaction of culture and social practice with the physical body in order to develop embodied histories. Lyndal Roper has insisted that historians develop tools that acknowledge the 'embodied subjects' of the past, distinguishing within a given historical document an individual's emotional and physical responses to experience from commonly circulating words and images. Such tools allow scholars to study the intertwined 'somatic and emotional experiences' of those embodied subjects.[11]

'The body' is the product of physical, social and cultural processes. As such, it provides a particularly rich locus for interdisciplinary studies of the emotions. The ways in which the body was experienced, managed and represented in early modern Europe can be instructive for our understanding of the emotions. They reveal precisely how, according to early modern people, emotions worked and how emotions impacted in immediate and intimate ways on peoples' lives. A focus on the body, particularly through micro-histories using personal documents, also allows us to observe the relationship between the structures of broader cultural discourses of emotions and the individual agency and experiences of individuals. Finally, attending to the body in the history of emotions is essential if we are to understand how in the early modern period the corporeal and affective were understood and experienced as inseparable.

Further reading

Alberti, F. Bound, *Matters of the Heart: History, Medicine, and Emotion* (Oxford: Oxford University Press, 2010)

—demonstrates the value of a cultural history approach to the body, medicine and emotions, showing how the heart was replaced by the brain between the seventeenth and nineteenth centuries as the idealized seat of the emotions.

Beatty, H., *Nervous Disease in late Eighteenth-Century Britain: The Reality of a Fashionable Disorder* (London: Pickering & Chatto, 2012)

—combines literary sources with medical records, patients' writings and physicians' notes in an instructive exploration of the relationship between the lived experience and changing popular depictions of nervous disease.

Newton, H., *The Sick Child in Early Modern England, 1580–1720* (Oxford: Oxford University Press, 2012)

—shows how the physical and emotional were fused in medical attitudes towards and children's and parents' experiences of child sickness, and demonstrates the importance of age to early modern understandings of the body.

Notes

1 T. Dixon, '"Emotion": the history of a keyword in crisis', *Emotion Review* 4, 4 (2012), 340.

2 G. Hartman, *The True Preserver and Restorer of Health: Being a Choice Collection of Select and Experienced Remedies for all Distempers incident to Men, Women and Children* (London, 1682), 311.

3 F. Bound Alberti, 'Bodies, hearts, and minds: why emotions matter to historians of science and medicine', *Isis* 100, 4 (2009), 798–810.
4 U. Rublack, 'Fluxes: the early modern body and the emotions', *History Workshop Journal* 53, 1 (2002), 7.
5 Quoted in S. Pilloud and M. Louis-Courvoisier, 'The intimate experience of the body in the eighteenth century: between interiority and exteriority', *Medical History* 47, 4 (2003), 464.
6 G.J. Barker-Benfield, *The Culture of Sensibility: Sex and Society in Eighteenth-Century Britain* (Chicago: University of Chicago Press, 1992), 1–36.
7 C. Jones, *The Smile Revolution in Eighteenth-Century Paris* (Oxford: Oxford University Press, 2014)
8 Quoted in O. Weisser, 'Grieved and disordered: gender and emotion in early modern patient narratives', *Journal of Medieval and Early Modern Studies* 43, 2 (2013), 253.
9 W. Churchill, *Female Patients in Early Modern Britain: Gender, Diagnosis, and Treatment* (Farnham: Ashgate, 2012), 179–223.
10 K. Harvey, 'What Mary Toft felt: language, emotions and the body', *History Workshop Journal* 80, 1 (2015), 33–51.
11 L. Roper, 'Beyond discourse theory', *Women's History Review* 19, 2 (2010), 316, 311.

III.22 Gestures

Jane W. Davidson and Alan Maddox

Recent scholarship into early modern emotions, their manifestation and reception in a range of staged contexts, has been informed by research into gesture.[1] Throughout the early modern period, the educated elite was able to learn how to 'perform' emotions by applying a set of codified uses of the voice as well as physical gestures that were learned from detailed treatises on the 'Art of Rhetoric' – itself developed from Ancient Greek culture. Learning rhetoric as a specific set of skills was a crucial requirement of any person who needed to orate: a lawyer, politician, teacher, actor or opera singer. By understanding this art form, we are able to gain crucial understanding about how performers of these gestures looked and sounded, but more particularly, how the emotions themselves were generated through this embodied action. Reading texts, looking at illustrations and experimenting with these materials through practical bodily engagement offer a toolkit to investigate how emotions were practised using gesture.

There were many treatises available, one of note being *La Retorica* (1574) by the Florentine nobleman Bartolomeo Cavalcanti (1503–62). The ideas on the art of delivery link directly to those from Ancient Greece, Cavalcanti noting that it is crucial to recall Demosthenes' saying that there are three essential elements of oration: delivery, delivery and delivery. With this notion well and truly embedded into the mind of the orator, Cavalcanti echoes Cicero's dictum that a poor case has the potential to be made more convincing than a good one if the delivery is just right.

Highly influential throughout the period was the *De arte rhetorica* (On the Art of Rhetoric) by Cypriano Soárez (1524–93), published in 1569 but used, in both original and adapted forms, as the mandated textbook for Jesuit schools throughout the

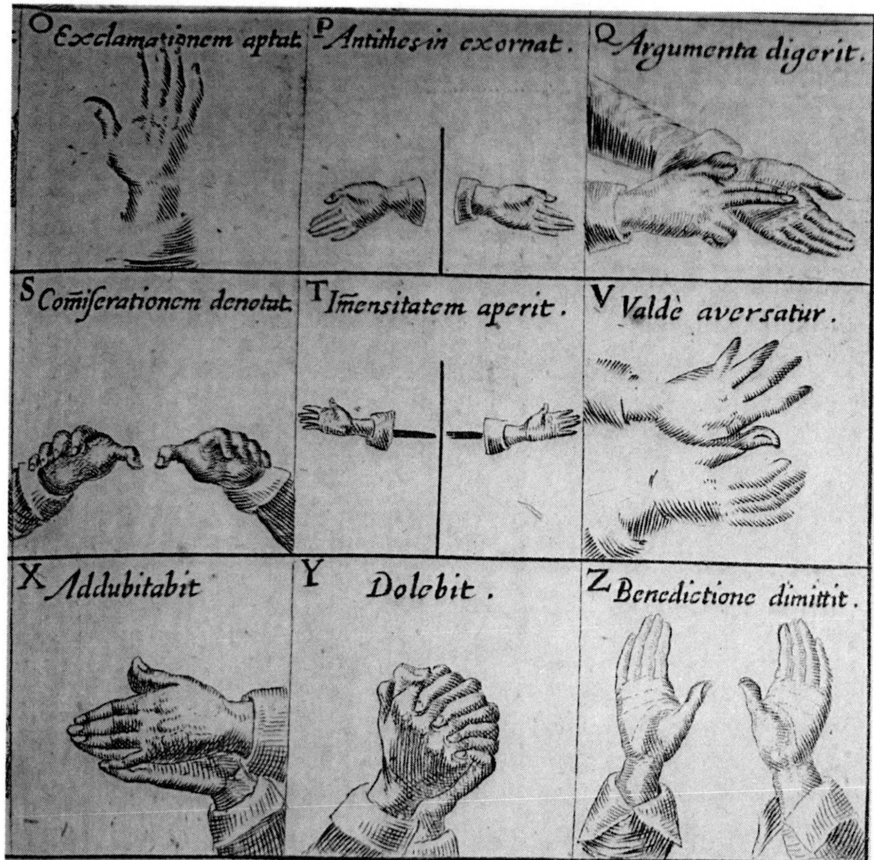

Figure III.22.1 *Dolebit* (grief, suffering), taken from John Bulwer, *Chirologia, or the Naturall Language of the Hand, with Chironomia, or the Art of Manuall Rhetorique* (London, 1644), Part II, 65.

seventeenth and eighteenth centuries. Soárez also drew on classical sources, particularly Cicero and Quintilian, but of particular relevance here, to the 'second Sophistic' authors who placed a very clear emphasis on affect – the orator's ability to influence the emotions of the audience. As late as the 1722 edition of Soarez text, the discussion of delivery begins by defining the elements of classical *pronunciatio*:

> it is agreed that all action is contained in two categories: the sound of the voice and the movement of the body . . . In fact these alone move an audience to the greatest degree, because at the same time the voice has impressed their ears, gestures their eyes, and words their thoughts.[2]

The importance of gesture in the rhetorical art is highlighted further in the words of the anonymous author of the famous treatise on staging and directing from the 1620s or 1630s, *Il corago*:

Alphabetical Arrangement of Symbolic Letters.

	Above the Line. Hands, Arms, Body and Head.							Below the Line Feet.		
	Small Letters relating to the Hand and Arm.									
	1. Hand.	2. Elevation of the Arm.	3. Transverse Position of the Arm.	4 and 5. Motion and Force.	Capital B and double small Letters. Both Arms and both Hands.	Capitals for particular Parts.	Capitals for Head and Eyes.	Small Letters Steps.	Capitals Positions.	Capitals and small; significant Gestures.
A	- - -	- - -	- - -	ascending alternate	applied	- - -	assenting averted	advance	- - -	appealing attention admiration aversion
B	backwards	- - -	backwards	backwards beckoning	both	breast	- - -	- - -	both	
C	clinched	- - -	across	collecting contracted clinching	crossed clasped	Chin	- - -	cross	- - -	commanding
D	- - -	downwards	- - -	descending	- - -	- - -	downwards denying	- - -	- - -	deprecation declaration
E	- - -	elevated	- - -	- - -	encumbered	Eyes	erect	- - -	- - -	encouragement.
F	forwards	- - -	forwards	forwards flourish	folded	Forehead	Forward	- - -	front	fear
G	grasping	- - -	- - -	grasping	- - -	- - -	- - -	- - -	- - -	Grief
H	holding	horizontal	- - -	- - -	- - -	- - -	- - -	- - -	- - -	Horror
I	index	- - -	- - -	inwards	inclosed	- - -	inclined			
K	- - -	- - -	- - -	- - -	a kimbo	- - -	- - -	- - -	kneeling	
L	collected	- - -	- - -	left	- - -	Lips	- - -	- - -	left	Lamentation Listenng
M	thumb	- - -	- - -	moderate						
N	natural inwards	- - -	- - -	noting	enumerating	Nose				
O	outwards	- - -	- - -	outwards						
P	prone	- - -	- - -	pushing pressing	- - -	- - -	- - -	- - -	- - -	Pride
Q	- - -	- - -	oblique	- - -	- - -	- - -	- - -	- - -	oblique	
R	- - -	Rest	- - -	right recoiling repressing rejecting	reposed	- - -	round	retire	right	
S	supine	- - -	- - -	sweep springing, striking shaking	- - -	- - -	shaking aside	start stamp shock	side	shame
T	- - -	- - -	- - -	touching throwing	- - -	- - -	Tossing	traverse	- - -	threatning
U	- - -	- - -	- - -	- - -	- - -	- - -	Uwpards			
V	Vertical	- - -	- - -	revolving	- - -	- - -	Vacancy	- - -	- - -	Veneration
W	hollow	- - -	- - -	waving	wringing					
X	extended	- - -	extended	extreme						
Z	- - -	Zenith								

Table III.22.1 Alphabetical Arrangement of Symbolic Letters, from Gilbert Austin's *Chironomia; or, a Treatise on Rhetorical Delivery* (London, 1806), 366.

> The manner of reciting is of great importance, because something said by a person who knows how to deliver it well and accompany it with gesture will make a much greater impression on the spirits of the listeners and will more easily stir in them the affections of anger, of hatred, of passion, of happiness, and the like. This will not happen when it is simply narrated by someone without gesture or modulation of the voice.[3]

Thus, gesture is a crucial part of action in rhetorical delivery, with affect being at its core.

In texts, gestural codes were explained in depth, one of the most famous books on the topic being the *Chirologia, or the Naturall Language of the Hand,* with *Chironomia, or the Art of Manuall Rhetorique* (1644) by John Bulwer (1606–56). Bulwer emphasizes that gestures originate in natural communication, but are formalized to offer strong signs for interpretation. Developing this idea, Bulwer writes in rhetorical style that the hand offers the 'universal character of reason', suggesting that it contains an inner truth, which is an idea still common in interpretations of body language – a person's gestures and postures show their inner state.[4]

The gestures are described in great detail, and while most were considered to be 'natural' and easily understood by anyone, some were used with particular technical meanings in formal argumentation. For example, 'to apply the Middle-Finger to the Thumbe is the common way of gracing an exordium'.[5] However, any gesture, whether natural or technical, was to be executed elegantly and clearly. For instance, Bulwer continues:

> yet to direct it [the hand gesture described above] as it were towards the left shoulder, and so make it a collaterall action, is nought, but worse, to bring forth the Arme transverse, and to pronounce with the elbow.[6]

The degree of instruction in these treatises shows how clear authors were about the relationship between thought and action. Bulwer offers the following advice:

> To play and fumble with the Fingers in speech is a simple and foolish habit of the Hand, condemned by the ancient Rhetoricians as an argument of a childish and ill-temper'd minde.[7]

There are also comprehensive illustrations of the specific gestures to employ for specific affective outcomes. For example, 'both hands clasped and wrung together is an Action on convenient to manifest griefe and sorrow' (Figure III.22.1).[8]

Chironomia, or, a Treatise on Rhetorical Delivery (1806) by Gilbert Austin (1753–1837) follows very much in the same tradition as Bulwer, so offers excellent insight into the specific gestures in use all the way to the end of the eighteenth century. Austin notes that rhetorical gesture is 'the action and position of all the parts of the body; of the head, the shoulders, the body or trunk; of the arms, hands, and fingers; of the lower limbs, and of the feet'.[9] As a system, the whole body was to be taken over by a particular emotion, thus, the representation of emotions could be standardized through gestures. Principal passions included grief, surprise, terror, anger, contempt, jealousy, aversion or refusal, disparagement, shame and welcome.

Grief, in Bulwer's description, was characterized by gestures in which the hands 'are clasped or wrung in affliction'.[10] Grief was also described as involving the rest of the body in a slow and downward body movement, weeping, wringing one's hands, covering one's face, heaviness of trunk and limbs, and hanging one's head. Such is the degree of detail in cataloguing gestures and their delivery that Austin even provides a system of gestural notation which is shown in the table in Table III.22.1.

Early modern gesture also had to be well timed. The 'stroke' or point at which the gesture was delivered was regarded as crucial to the art of rhetoric and served to illustrate or enforce. It was essential for the orator to deliver the gesture precisely on the accented syllable of the emphasized word, so that the force of the voice along with the gesture's delivery point coordinated to deliver the idea in a lively, distinguished and convincing manner. Dene Barnett and Jeanette Massey-Westropp summarize many of the eighteenth-century sources, dealing with the passions and their embodiment through posture, gestures and movement in the Baroque theatre.[11] The thoroughgoing recreation of early modern systems of theatrical gesture has been a feature of productions by modern directors such as Helga Hill and Benjamin Lazar, providing new insights into the historical vocabulary of emotional expression.

Gestures as rhetorical devices were a vital part of everyday experience. Even for audiences beyond the educated elite, gestures were sources of information; for example, popular theatres and street entertainers would draw on these forms of presentation. We know from watching politicians and pop stars today that such coordinated rhetorical practices continue.[12] Gestures build everyday uses into heightened, codified information toolkits. Though reported from classical Greek times, these practices and codes of gesturing draw heavily upon social and cultural contexts and as such do not remain fixed, with different socio-cultural emphases and developments modifying both style of delivery and something of the content. Indeed, these trends have undoubtedly led to different manifestations according to factors such as gender and national traits, as well as being shaped by personality.[13] Significantly, these transformations are undoubtedly two-directional, with changing everyday comportment feeding back into the development of new rhetorical codes for more formalized performance opportunities and vice versa. Historical and contemporary social science research into human behaviour and social interaction reveals that gestures are important communicators of emotion. Understanding how gestures were codified and used in the early modern period gives us access to important ways of understanding emotions at the time. Reflecting on these historical codes and engaging experimentally with them, we can begin to understand how emotion was practised in the early modern world.

Further reading

Barnett, D. and J. Massey-Westropp, *The Art of Gesture: The Practices and Principles of Eighteenth Century Acting* (Heidelberg: Carl Winter Universitätsverlag, 1987)

—very well-cited source that offered seminal enquiry into gesture, drawing on a wide range of primary source materials.

Kendon, A., *Gesture: Visible Action as Utterance* (Cambridge: Cambridge University Press, 2004)

—comprehensive survey of gesture from historical artefact to contemporary practice, that gives excellent insight into research. The focus is mainly semiotic, linguistic and cultural.

Notes

1 A. Maddox, 'Recitative and the Rhetoric of Speech and Song in Andrea Perrucci's Dell'Arte Rappresentativa (1699)', in K. Nelson and M. Gómez (eds), *A Musicological Gift: Libro Homenaje for Jane Morlet Hardie* (Lions Bay, BC: Institute of Mediaeval Music, 2013), 167–84; G. Richard, '"How to be an emperor": acting Alexander the Great in opera seria', *Early Music* 36, 2 (2008), 181–202.

2 C. Soárez, S.J., *De Arte Rhetorica Libri Tres Ex Aristotele, Cicerone Et Quintiliano Praecipue Deprompti* (Antwerp, 1722), 187–90. Translation by Adam Harris.

3 'From The Choragus, or, Some Observations for Staging Dramatic Works Well', (trans.) M. Murata in L. Treitler and Murata (eds), *Strunck's Source Readings in Music History*, vol. 4: *The Baroque Era* (New York: Norton, 1998), 125.

4 S. Runeson and G. Frykholm, 'Kinematic specification of dynamics as an informational basis for person-and-action perception: expectation, gender recognition, and deceptive intention', *Journal of Experimental Psychology: General* 112, 4 (1983), 585–615.
5 J. Bulwer, *Chironomia* (London, 1644), 104.
6 Ibid., 104.
7 Ibid., 119.
8 Ibid., 55.
9 G. Austin, *Chironomia* (London, 1806), 133.
10 Ibid., 484.
11 D. Barnett and J. Massey-Westropp, *The Art of Gesture: The Practices and Principles of Eighteenth Century Acting* (Heidelberg: Carl Winter Universitätsverlag, 1987)
12 J.W. Davidson, '"She's the One": Multiple Functions of Body Movement in a Stage Performance by Robbie Williams', in A. Gritten and E.C. King (eds), *Music and Gesture* (Aldershot: Ashgate, 2006), 208–26.
13 A. Kendon, *Gesture: Visible Action as Utterance* (Cambridge: Cambridge University Press, 2004)

III.23 Music

Alan Maddox and Jane W. Davidson

Recent years have seen a considerable amount of research on the expression of emotions in early modern music, especially in relation to concepts of musical rhetoric and its associated 'doctrine of the affections'.[1] However, the use of music as a source of information about emotions outside its own domain remains relatively little explored. The ways in which music was understood to express emotion changed significantly throughout the period, and this is reflected in surviving music notation and in treatises and other sources about musical composition and performative practices.

The development of the printing press and a flourishing system of music education in many churches and cathedrals allowed for the training of hundreds of singers and composers across Europe. These musicians were highly sought-after, particularly in Italy, where churches and aristocratic courts hired composers and teachers. A common, unifying musical language emerged in the polyphonic style (a texture in which two or more lines of independent melody weave simultaneously). By the second half of the sixteenth century, the work of composers such as Giovanni Pierluigi da Palestrina (1525/6–94), Orlande de Lassus [Orlando di Lasso] (*c.* 1532–94), Tomás Luis de Victoria (1548–1611) and William Byrd (*c.* 1540–1623) tied polyphony to liturgical function. Working with the same liturgical texts repeatedly, textual constraint led these composers to harness musical techniques to provide subtle, largely melodic effects to give emotional commentary on the words. As a result, the beautiful but rather austere Counter-Reformation style of 'strict' polyphony came to represent the archetypal sound of liturgical music, particularly in Catholic Europe and its dominions. Martin Luther (1483–1546), too, enthusiastically encouraged music in worship, emphasizing its affective power to engage believers, while his fellow reformer Jean Calvin (1509–64) acknowledged music's affective potency just as unequivocally by taking the opposite position, severely restricting the use of music in church, since it has

> a secret and almost incredible power to move our hearts in one way or another. . . . As Saint Paul says, every evil word corrupts good manners, but when it has the melody with it, it pierces the heart much more strongly and enters within; as wine is poured into the cask with a funnel, so venom and corruption are distilled to the very depths of the heart by melody.[2]

As the period progressed, reclamation of ancient Greece and Rome literary and artistic works and aesthetics coincided with the rise of humanism. This led to an extravagant flowering of affective expression in secular music, especially in Italian madrigals of the sixteenth century. Composers such as Cipriano de Rore (1516–65), Luca Marenzio (1553–99) and Carlo Gesualdo (*c.* 1561–1613) pushed the technical resources of polyphony almost to breaking point with increasingly mannerist harmonic devices and melodic 'word painting' figures designed to reinforce every expressive nuance of the poetry.

The ensuing period of music production (*c.* 1600–1750) has retrospectively become labelled as the Baroque period and it has until recently been distilled into a specific canon of works by not much more than a handful of composers. Claudio Monteverdi (1567–1643), Girolamo Frescobaldi (1583–1643), Arcangelo Corelli (1653–1713), Antonio Vivaldi (1678–1741), Alessandro Scarlatti (1660–1725) and his son Domenico (1685–1757) are regarded as vitally important to understanding Italian Baroque music, whereas Jean-Baptiste Lully (1632–87), Marin Marais (1656–1728), François Couperin (1668–1733), and Jean-Philippe Rameau (1683–1764) are seen to reflect the contrasting French style. Key Germans include Michael Praetorius (1571–1621), Heinrich Schütz (1585–1672), Johann Hermann Schein (1586–1630), Samuel Scheidt (1587–1654), Georg Philipp Telemann (1681–1767), George Frideric Handel [Georg Friederich Händel] (1685–1759) and Johann Sebastian Bach (1685–1750); and Henry Purcell (1659–95) is seen as the English representative of the period. It is, of course, a male-dominated hegemonic culture that has its own history of emergence and one that has received considerable criticism in recent study of musical canons and retrospective understandings of musical history.[3] Nonetheless, this canon serves to show common features which subsequent composers and scholars have identified as characterizing the period.

These works share several fundamental philosophical concerns relating to the expression of feeling (or emotion), and are of vital interest in understanding the history of emotions at the time. Musical effects were consciously aimed at the expression of feeling, and focused on dramatic representation of this through the deployment of musical devices such as contrast, with juxtaposition of soft and loud, slow and fast, and solo and ensemble, and so were also characterized by the development of melody and accompanying harmony, rather than the previous style employing many individual lines of polyphony. This change was itself a consequence of a new consciousness of music as a form of rhetoric.

The new 'monodic' style of the seventeenth century was explicitly designed to facilitate a kind of dramatic declamation in music, which above all, had the goal of moving the affections. The idea that the content of the words is to drive affective delivery was promoted to the status of a primary principle amongst the humanist scholars and musicians associated with the neo-Platonic *camerata* of Giovanni de' Bardi (1534–1612) and subsequently Jacopo Corsi (1561–1602) at Florence. It was restated throughout the Baroque period as the highest objective of both spoken oratory and music.

Following the classical Greeks' identification of rhetoric as the art of persuasion for the orator, it became closely related to the development of opera as a powerful tool to develop expressive communication using music. In the words of the humanist Girolamo Mei (1519–94),

> When a musician . . . does not have the ability to bend the souls of listeners to where he wishes, his skill and knowledge may be considered null and vain, because the discipline of music was instituted and counted among the liberal arts for no other end.[4]

The new merger of the expression of feeling in music, with the singer as a powerful 'persuader' is well articulated in the preface to Monteverdi's *Combattimento di Tancredi e Clorinda* from his *Eighth Book of Madrigals* (1638), in which he writes: 'It has seemed to me that the chief passions or affections of our mind are three in number, namely anger, equanimity and humility. The best philosophers agree, and the very nature of our voice, with its high, low and middle ranges, would indicate as much'.[5] The Neapolitan theatre director and opera impresario Andrea Perrucci, too, required that in acting, 'the voice must not always be the same, but must change according to the movements and passions of the soul . . . [W]ith various sounds one seeks to move the affections of the audience'.[6]

The most influential singing teacher of the eighteenth century, Pierfrancesco Tosi (1654–1732) made a particular point of the goal of moving the passions when discussing recitative in the chamber style, which 'according to the opinion of the most judicious, touches the heart more than the others'.[7] Just as the words are calculated to move the passions, so the delivery must skilfully match the passions expressed in order to reinforce their effect on the listener:

> This [kind of recitative] requires a more peculiar skill, by reason of the words which, being for the most part adapted to move the most violent passions of the soul, oblige the master to give the scholar such a lively impression of them that he may seem to be affected with them himself.[8]

It is this new aesthetic that was to dominate the period, impacting on instrumentalists too. Writing in the preface to his volume of keyboard toccatas and partitas in 1614, Frescobaldi, influential organist of St Peter's in Rome, described the manner of performing his organ and harpsichord pieces as being modelled on that of the then new monodic madrigals, in which rhythm was taken flexibly 'according to the affection of the music or the meaning of the word'.[9]

Nearly a century and half after Frescobaldi, the primacy of affective expression in music was equally apparent. One of the most celebrated authors of the era was the flute player and composer Johann Joachim Quantz (1697–1773). His views can be seen to represent ideas of the past as well as to indicate how new trends were developing. Indeed, Quantz informed musicians that the 'orator and the musician have, at bottom, the same aim, . . . namely to make themselves masters of the hearts of their listeners, to arouse or still their passions, and to transport them now to this sentiment, now to that'.[10] With the voice as the model, instrumentalists were asked to imitate the sounds of the singer. Quantz thus disparaged the virtuosity of violinists like the brilliant Italian Giuseppe Tartini (1692–1770) and his imitators who 'seem to have little feeling for the good and true singing style' and conversely advised German instrumentalists to model their playing on 'the good manner of singing'.[11]

Without question, the theoretical writings reveal that aesthetic interest was in moving the affections and that the practice was to use singing and speaking as a model. Indeed, the music historian Claude Palisca identified the objective of expressing the affections as the only characteristic that meaningfully connects the disparate music of the period.[12] We cannot hear them and interpret their emotional meanings in precisely the same ways as listeners did when they were new but sources including music notation, treatises and accounts of performances and audience responses to them provide insights into early modern emotions of a kind that arguably cannot be accessed by other means.

Further reading

Bartel, D., *Musica Poetica: Musical-Rhetorical Figures in German Baroque Music* (Lincoln, Nebraska: University of Nebraska Press, 1997)

—a comprehensive study of the musical devices used by seventeenth- and eighteenth-century German composers, by analogy with the verbal 'figures' of rhetoric, to express the Affections (rationalized emotional states) in music.

Palisca, C.V., *Humanism in Italian Renaissance Musical Thought* (New Haven: Yale University Press, 1985)

—'classic' study of the theoretical sources that provided the intellectual foundation for discussions of music and emotion during the early modern period.

Notes

1 See J. Mattheson (1681–1764) in his *Neu-eröffnete Orchestre* (Hamburg, 1713)

2 Preface to the *Genevan Psalter* (1542) (trans. adapted from that of O. Strunk in L. Treitler (ed.) *Strunk's Source Readings in Music History* (Revised ed., New York: Norton, 1998), 366).

3 S. McClary, *Feminine Endings: Music, Gender, & Sexuality*, 2nd edn (Minneapolis: University of Minnesota Press, 2002); McClary, *Desire and Pleasure in Seventeenth-Century Music* (Berkeley: University of California Press, 2012); S. Cusick, *Francesca Caccini at the Medici Court, Music and the Circulation of Power* (Chicago: University of Chicago Press, 2009)

4 V. Galilei, *Dialogue on Ancient and Modern Music*, (trans.) C.V. Palisca (New Haven: Yale University Press, 2003), 225.

5 P. Weiss and R. Taruskin, *Music in the Western World: A History in Documents*, 2nd edn (Belmont: Thomson Schirmer, 2008), 147.

6 A. Perrucci, *Dell'arte rappresentativa premeditata, ed all'improviso* (Napoli: Michele Luigi Mutio, 1699), 115–16. Translated by A. Maddox.

7 P. Tosi, *Observations on the Florid Song, or, Sentiments on the Ancient and Modern Singers*, (trans.) M. Galliard, 2nd edn (London: n.p., 1743), 68.

8 Ibid., 67–8.

9 G. Frescobaldi, *Toccate e partite d'intavolatura di cimbalo . . . Libro primo* (1615) (Rome, 1637), (pref. and trans.) C. MacClintock in *Readings in the History of Music in Performance* (Bloomington: Indiana University Press, 1979), 133.

10 J.J. Quantz, *On Playing the Flute*, (trans.) E.R. Reilly (New York: Free Press, 1966), 119.

11 Ibid., 324, 342.

12 C.V. Palisca, *Baroque Music*, 3rd edn (Englewood Cliffs: Prentice Hall, 1991), 4–5.

Section IV

Focus topics for the early modern period

Political realms

IV.1 Monarchies

Helen Watanabe-O'Kelly

Since the history of emotions is itself a new topic, it has as yet not been applied to the study of early modern monarchy. This is surprising, since emotions are so central to how early modern monarchies were constituted and understood that we can say that they are the foundation on which monarchy was built. The monarch was God's representative on earth, so the relationship between monarch and subject mirrored that between believer and deity. Just as God loved His people and they had a reciprocal duty to love Him, so the ruler had to exhibit a fatherly love for his subjects and they had to return that love. Just as the believer feared God's righteous anger, knowing that God made the laws and had the power to punish him if he transgressed, so the subject feared the monarch's authority. In 1603 this fundamental relationship was expressed at the coronation of James I of England (1566–1625), the first such ceremony to be held in Westminster Abbey in English: 'Grant Almighty God . . . that he [the king] may be loving and amiable to the Lords and Nobles, and all the faithful Subjects of his kingdom, that he may be feared, and loved of all Men'.[1] The childlike dependency of the subject on the fatherly love of his lord is expressed in 1692 in a panegyric poem for the accession of Johann Georg IV (1668–94) as Elector of Saxony. The Elector is addressed intimately throughout in the German familiar 'Du' form, just as the believer addresses God in prayer, and the poet turns Johann Georg's name into an anagram meaning 'Father Care, bend Thine ear'.[2] He tells the reader that Johann Georg loves his people like a father and that they love him in return, but it seems that Johann Georg is not only their father, he is also their mother, for, in an image sometimes used of Christ, he suckles his people at his breast. Another metaphor for the life-giving power of the monarch depicts him as the sun who gives life, colour and warmth to the world, as the 15-year-old Louis XIV (1638–1715) proclaimed when he appeared in 1653 in Paris in the *Ballet de la Nuit* as the rising sun.[3] Here the proper emotions that the subject must feel are gratitude and awe.

These emotions have a performative power, creating the central contract between sovereign and subject, a contract that is confirmed when the sovereign makes a solemn entry into one of the cities in his realm. He appears before the city gates and formally requests permission to enter. [4] The citizens recognize his authority by presenting him with the keys to the city, which he returns, thereby cementing his relationship with them. He then rides through the city under a series of triumphal arches and other ephemeral structures. The decoration of these arches had to convey the citizens' love and devotion, but it was also often used to remind the ruler of the city's needs and expectations. When the Catholic Habsburg Emperor Charles V (1500–58) made a solemn entry into the Protestant Free City of Nuremberg in 1541 in a period fraught with post-Reformation tension, the 10 triumphal arches and the Gate of Honour gave the Emperor a set of instructions about sparing his subjects, preventing his arrogant nobles from making war, curtailing the power of the Turk and espousing the four cardinal virtues of prudence, justice, courage and temperance.[5] Similar examples could be quoted from many early modern European cities and the more independent they were politically, the more likely they were to speak truth to power.

Joy was another emotion that had to be publicly expressed by the monarch's subjects on certain set occasions and was therefore carefully choreographed. Some monarchs showed themselves aware of this. On the occasion of the betrothal of Louis XIII, King of France (1601–43), to the Spanish princess Anne of Austria (1601–66) in 1612, there was a splendid firework display in Paris, which, according to the official account, evoked the correct response: 'All of Paris is joyful and in triumph'.[6] Louis XIV knew how important this general rejoicing was in creating a bond between monarch and subjects. In his *Memoirs for the Instruction of the Dauphin*, he explained how important lavish court festivities were because they touched and charmed his courtiers, pleased the people and evoked the delight of all his subjects by showing them that he loved the same things that they loved.[7] Another monarch who showed awareness of needing to arouse the emotions of his subject and 'rule over their hearts' was Frederick the Great, King of Prussia (1712–86).[8]

The monarchical system also called for the expression of grief. That too was choreographed by the elaborate mourning rituals for rulers – the impressive funeral procession through the streets which included the dead ruler's riderless horse, the so-called *castrum doloris* or elaborate bier on which the deceased lay in state, the hanging of the church with black fabric, the mourning clothes for the entire court, the funeral orations, the poetry. Not to feel grief and not to be seen to feel grief in a public and physical way was to deny the central relationship between sovereign and subject. The anonymous author of a funeral oration for Elizabeth I (1533–1603) exhibited the correct behaviour when he talked about: 'this floud of teares, that makes his channell through our eyes'.[9] The bald, unemotional language of John Bradshaw (1602–59), the judge at the trial of Charles I, King of England, Scotland and Ireland (1600–49), in January 1649, showed that the bond of mutual love that should have bound Charles to his people had broken down. Once that had happened, it was possible to send him to the scaffold.

The few queens regnant between 1500 and 1800 had to be credited with the same qualities as a male ruler and therefore be accorded the same emotional response. Elizabeth I of England is a good example. If a ruling queen had children, she could be credited in addition with special motherly qualities, for instance, Empress Maria Theresia (1717–80), who bore no fewer than 16 children. The queen consort, on the other hand, played a special role in the emotional economy of the nation. Apart from her obvious duties of bearing sons and of providing her people with a role model of piety and charity, she also had to act as a focus for the emotions of the nation. This can be seen in the official descriptions of princely weddings at the moment of the bride's departure to her new husband's court, when she is depicted as publicly overwhelmed by grief.[10]

Emotions between rulers and subjects may have been reciprocal but they were never equal. In the sixteenth century the love of the subject for the distant and awe-inspiring ruler, who was credited with quasi-divine qualities such as the ability to cure disease by touch, was still linked to feudal notions of fealty. By the eighteenth century, in the age of Enlightenment and sensibility, the subject was expected to love him in a spontaneous and sincere way, which, according to the theorist of courtly ceremonial, Julius Bernhard von Rohr (1688–1742), should have nothing of forced flattery about it.[11] By 1762 Maria Theresia could even be characterized by Joseph von Sonnenfels (1732/33–1817) as the 'noble friend' of her people, a description of an emotional relationship that the sixteenth century surely would not have recognized.[12]

Only by applying the insights of the history of emotions to the study of monarchy can we understand how the emotions constituted and sustained the relationship between the monarch and his people and between the monarch and God. Further research is needed to decode the emotional language which is present but often overlooked in every kind of text from legal documents to occasional poetry and in such art forms as portraiture and opera.

Further reading

Adamson, J. (ed.), *The Princely Courts of Europe. Ritual Politics and Culture under the Ancien Régime 1500–1750* (London: Weidenfeld and Nicholson, 1999)

—provides an excellent fully-illustrated introduction to the study of monarchy across Europe from Spain to Russia. The individual essays are written by leading specialists and there is a helpful introduction by Adamson himself.

Campbell-Orr, C. (ed.), *Queenship in Britain* (Manchester: Manchester University Press, 2002); *Queenship in Europe 1660–1815 – The Role of the Consort* (Cambridge: Cambridge University Press, 2004)

—these two volumes of essays illuminate monarchy from the standpoint of the consort and reveal a lot about the role of the emotions in the monarchical system.

Notes

1 *The Ceremonies, Form of Prayer, and Services used in Westminster-ABBY at the CORONATION of King James the First and Queen Ann his Consort* (London, 1685), 8.

2 Johann Müntzer, *Als der Durchl. Fürst und Herr Herr Johann Georg der Vierdte [. . .] 1691.den 29. Decembr. die unterthänigste Eydes=Pflicht und Erb=Hulddigung in Leipzig allergnädigst annahm* (Leipzig, 1692), no pag.

3 Isaac de Benserade, *Ballet royal de la Nuit, divisé en quatre parties, ou quatre veilles: et dansé par Sa Majesté, le 23 février 1653* (Paris, 1653)

4 In the early modern period Scotland and England are the only territories that have queens regnant. Even Maria Theresia could not be elected Holy Roman Empress in the eighteenth century, though she was crowned king (not queen) of Hungary. The pronoun 'he' is therefore used throughout.

5 *Vonn Römischer Kayerslicher Mayestat Caroli V. Ehrlich einreitten in des Heyligen Reichs Stat Nurmberg den xvi. Februarii.* Anno M.D.XXXXI.

6 Claude Morillon, *Les Feux de Ioye de la France: sur les pompes & magnificences faictes à Paris, pour l'heureuse alliance de son Roy auec l'Infante d'Espagne* (Lyon, 1612), 3.

7 Louis XIV, *Mémoires pour l'instruction du Dauphin* (ed.) P. Goubert (Paris: Imprimerie nationale, 1992), 135.

8 See U. Frevert, *Gefühlspolitik. Friedrich II. als Herr über die Herzen?* (Göttingen: Wallstein, 2012)

9 *Expicedium A Fvneral Oration, vpon the death of the late deceased Princesse of famous memorye, Elizabeth by the grace of God, Queen of England, France and Ireland* (London, 1603)

10 See H. Watanabe-O'Kelly, '"Mit offentlich-ausgebrochenen Liebes=Thränen." How and why early modern festival books depict emotions', *History of Emotions – Insights into Research* (November 2014) www.history-of-emotions.mpg.de/en/texte/mit-offentlich-ausgebrochenen-liebesthranen-how-and-why-early-modern-festival-books-depict-emotions

11 J.B. von Rohr, 'Von der Ehre und Devotion, so die Unterthanen ihrem Landes=Herrn abstatten', in M. Schlechte (ed.), *Einleitung zur Ceremoniel-Wissenschafft der Grossen Herren*, (1733) (Weinheim: VCH, 1990), 724–32.

12 See W. Mauser, 'Maria Theresia. Mütterlichkeit: Mythos und politisches Mandat', in I. Roebling and W. Mauser, *Mutter und Mütterlichkeit. Wandel und Wirksamkeit einer Phantasie in der deutschen Literatur* (Würzburg: Königshausen und Neumann, 1996), 77–87.

IV.2 Republics

Catharine Gray

In a recent critical turn to focus on the affective life of republics, historians and literary critics of the early modern period have begun to analyse political philosophy and literature through the lens of Cartesian science or a new stress on self-interest and security in Renaissance political theory to reveal the role that fear and particularly love played for those writers busily promoting the active 'affective engagement' needed for the voluntary loyalties and participatory politics of republics.[1] As some of these scholars have argued, the politically-precarious nature of republics – outnumbered by monarchies and sometimes short-lived – in fact led to an intensification of debates over the dangers and uses of emotion in the public life of the state.

To introduce these uses, and the importance of the 'political passions' to conceptualizations of the ideal republican state, this entry will offer new, illustrative readings of two very different republican writers, the Italian historian and political philosopher, Niccolò Machiavelli (1469–1527) and the English satirist, polemicist and prophetic poet, George Wither (1588–1667). As other scholars have emphasized, classical republicans such as Cicero promoted love as the affective basis of stable states and civic virtue.[2] While adapting love to their political theories, Machiavelli and Wither turn to the socio-political effects of fear as the key passion that catalyses or coheres classical and godly republics. In doing so, these writers illustrate the very different ways the same emotion could be imagined at the basis of political life, as a means to develop the collective affective disposition or political character best suited to making and re-making the unstable and threatened republican state form.

Though republics rejected dynastic, royal rule and promoted ideals of active civic participation, in early modern Europe they could take a variety of forms, from the federated assemblies and stadholders of the United Provinces to the centralized parliamentary sovereignty of the English Commonwealth. As historians in particular have argued, writers defending the republican form of government often opposed public reason, abstract norms of justice and the collectively-produced regulation of the law to the corrupt wills, emotional excesses and unruly appetites they argued defined the personal politics of monarchy. However, historians and scholars of literature have also demonstrated that those who advocated for republics acknowledged, even embraced, the role of passion in founding and shaping non-monarchal states. In particular, Republican writers argued that constitutional principles cultivated – and thus replicated themselves – in the moral and emotional life of subjects and citizens, so that under the political slavery (as they saw it) of monarchal rule, subjects would themselves become slave-like: politically abject, swayed by self-interest and subject to unruly passions. Conversely the ethos of liberty and habits of public service encouraged by republics would train citizens to value public interests and practice virtuous emotional self-discipline.[3]

Writers explored methods for deploying the passions to particular socio-political ends, promoting them as tools of power or the basis for political renewal. Machiavelli, writing in enforced retirement after the fall of the Florentine republic in 1512, is best known for instrumentalizing fear (and, to a lesser extent, love) as a means for controlling a fickle populace under a single ruler in *The Prince* (1532). However, Machiavelli's defence of the Roman Republic, *The Discourses on the First Ten Books of Titus Livius* (1531), also analyses fear as a force for non-monarchal state unity and revival. According to Machiavelli, fear can unite the state in the face of foreign invasion or attack.[4] More innovatively, fear also aids his argument that republics periodically need to be reborn through a return to their first principles. To avoid what he sees as an inevitable degeneration of governments and their peoples into corruption, Machiavelli counsels that republics should periodically be forcefully returned to their foundational political and legal origins for constitutional renewal. This return is most often accomplished by the 'drastic actions' of an audacious individual or institution, actions that, in Machiavelli's examples, revolve around death – the execution of Lucius Junius Brutus's rebellious sons, for instance, or (in a perhaps wilfully vague example) the deaths of a commission of 10 ambitious law-makers (the *decemviri legibus scribundis*, who were actually forced to abdicate but not executed).[5] The exceptional, extreme nature of these acts renews the republic, he argues, by 'instilling men with that terror and that fear with which they [the republic's governors] had instilled them when instituting' the new state.[6]

Political violence functions here as a mnemonic device, recalling the fear that, Machiavelli implies, helps found new states and then working by punitive threat to delay those states' fall into tyrannical, corrupt license. To endure, therefore, republics must rely on both a classically-inspired virtue (his masculinized and militarized *virtù*) and the manipulation, even self-conscious creation, of emotions. By making the reduction to first principles a return to a politically- and socially-formative passion, Machiavelli situates that passion at the origin and heart of his secular republic. This promotion of a disciplinary fear imposed upon society acts in dynamic tension with his advocacy elsewhere in *Discourses* of an active, productively unruly, populace, whose 'tumults' (or disorderly protests) enable the creation of laws protecting liberty while also holding the nobility in check. Both fear and tumult, however, put audacious action – and its passionate motives and effects – at the centre of a strong, balanced republic. Fear, then, helps Machiavelli imagine the deliberate construction and reconstruction of the forceful but disciplined collective disposition that ideally undergirds, protects and revives a precarious republican state, itself ever teetering on the verge of falling into (tyrannical or royal) corruption.

If Machiavelli stresses fear as a catalyzing, mnemonic and disciplinary force, other defenders of republics emphasize a different role for this passion. One such writer, influenced by Machiavelli, was the prolific English writer, George Wither who, despite his earlier support for constitutional monarchy, published a poetic defence of republican government, *The British Appeals*, in 1651, after the execution of Charles I (1600–49) and the establishment of England as a Commonwealth or 'free state' in 1649.[7] Wither differs from Machiavelli both generically and politically: in place of political philosophy, he offers prophetic poetry; where Machiavelli's republic is secular, even pagan, Wither's is godly, even apocalyptic. For this reason, Wither draws on a different, Biblical and Augustinian, tradition of praise for those passions that can be turned to spiritual ends and condemnation for the stony-hearted Christian who refuses to be moved. In *The British Appeals*, Wither combines celebratory joy at Parliamentary triumph with pious fear at the workings of the almighty Providence enabling it. Wither in fact locates the genesis of the book in the emotional turmoil of 'a Contradicting Passion', bemoaning that he is torn between the competing forces of hope and fear, joy and grief.[8] He argues that what at first seemed a self-destructive contradiction is in fact an emotional and spiritual balance, as one passion counterpoints and moderates its opposite. By tempering joy at Parliamentary triumph with 'filial fear' of God in particular, Wither is able to fuse celebration of the political constitution of the earthly city with proper spiritual humility for the ruler of the heavenly one. Wither's 'Medley' of dynamically contesting and mutually regulating passions offers a model of the ideal emotional and political disposition for every reader to follow.[9] His mixed emotional state, then, becomes the marker of a godly, republican identity that his poetry replicates in others by 'tempring ev'ry Reader'.[10]

Thus, following ancient and humanist theories that poetry could 'move the Reader's passions in various ways', Wither explicitly uses his verse to define and reproduce a political community, through managing and replicating a complex mixture of politically-inflected emotions.[11] Wither's pious passion is an effect of spiritual introspection and a tool for the self-discipline of godly republicans whose personal reform will, in the aggregate, ultimately reform the state. His ecstatic verse, with its similarities to some of the prophetic politics and poetry of John Milton (1608–74), is a long way from Machiavelli's philosophy, which paves the way for the rational, even scientific, analysis of the work of self-interest and fear in state formation that finds its fruition in Thomas Hobbes (1588–1679). Yet for both writers fear is neither spontaneous individual emotion, nor social performance, but a foundational ingredient of the collective affective dispositions that define constitutionally-specific communities.

Early modern studies' current analysis of this mobilization has done much to emphasize the importance of the emotions to republican writers. However, more work remains to be done, perhaps particularly on the sheer range and combination of the emotions that make up the affective 'Medley' of the ideal republican character (beyond fear and love), alongside a consideration of emotion's role in not only the active civic life of republics but also the violently expansionist and military fantasies that sometimes accompanied them. In addition, we might attend to those theories being developed by new materialist critics to consider political passions separately from the self-conscious and self-possessed individual subject of traditional political philosophy, as sites of intersubjective agency and motors of action in their own right that expand our understanding of the collectivity and agency at the heart of republican writing.[12]

Further reading

Kahn, V., *Wayward Contracts: The Crisis of Political Obligation in England, 1640–1674* (Princeton: Princeton University Press, 2004)

—a highly influential and wide-ranging analysis of the language of early modern contract theory that focuses on the role of the wayward passions of fear and love in the turbulent political culture of the second half of seventeenth-century Britain.

Kahn, V., N. Saccamano and D. Coli (eds), *Politics and the Passions, 1500–1850* (Princeton: Princeton University Press, 2006)

—an important collection of essays that focuses on writers such as Machiavelli, Montaigne and Locke to analyse the role of the passions in political theory and subjectivity across a range of topics such as the public's relation to the private, the political production of identity and the disciplining of the body.

Tilmouth, C., *Passion's Triumph Over Reason: A History of the Moral Imagination from Spenser to Rochester* (Oxford: Oxford University Press, 2007)

—a persuasive argument for the increasing importance of the passions to early modern moral and thus political life for a range of literary, philosophical and religious writers, including republicans such as John Milton.

Notes

1 M. Sanchez, *Erotic Subjects: The Sexuality of Politics in Early Modern English Literature* (Oxford: Oxford University Press, 2011), 216. Sanchez analyses the combination of love and (sometimes eroticized) suffering in Renaissance literature on political duty or affiliation.

2 V. Kahn, *Wayward Contracts: The Crisis of Political Obligation in England, 1640–1674* (Princeton: Princeton University Press, 2004), 61. Kahn analyses both love and fear in politics – the latter in particular in relation to Hobbes.

3 On the slavishness induced by monarchy and the variety of European republics, see, for example, M. van Gelderen and Q. Skinner (eds), Introduction to *Republicanism: A Shared European Heritage*, vol. 1 (Cambridge: Cambridge University Press, 2002), 1–6.

4 N. Machiavelli, *The Discourses*, (ed.) B. Crick, (trans.) L.J. Walker (London: Penguin Books, 2003), 2.25, 360.

5 Ibid., 3.1, 385–90.

6 Ibid., 3.1, 388.

7 See D. Norbrook, *Writing the English Republic: Poetry, Rhetoric and Politcs, 1627–1660* (Cambridge: Cambridge University Press, 2000), *passim*.

8 G. Wither, *The British Appeals* (London, 1651), 3.

9 Ibid., 1, 7.

10 Ibid, 47, A4, 8, 7.

11 Wither, *Westrow Revived* (London, 1653), 17.

12 On theories of the 'new materialism' and their interrogation of traditional ideas of political agency, see D. Coole and S. Frost (eds), *New Materialisms: Ontology, Agency, and Politics* (Durham: Duke University Press, 2010).

IV.3 Political revolutions

Michael J. Braddick

By comparison with ideology, collective emotions have occupied a relatively small place in historical explanations of political revolt and revolution. It is clear, however, that collective emotion is an important factor in political mobilization, and the histories of collective action reveal something of that role, although largely incidentally. This chapter does not therefore set out an overview of a mature field of research, but rather to introduce some key issues that historians are beginning to explore.

Over this period the register of political discourse at moments of crisis shifted. Some of the most dangerous rebellions of the sixteenth century were driven by claims about the true religion: for example, the German Peasants War, the Anabaptist revolution in Münster, the Pilgrimage of Grace or the Wars of Religion in France. Such disturbances were not in some essential way 'religious', but the arguments that publicly justified rebellion were strongly inflected by claims about the true religion. Even conflicts that did not originate in religious difference could acquire that patina – for example, the Dutch revolt. By the end of our period serious political conflict was increasingly expressed in different terms, relating to rights and liberties, of abstract civic freedoms – in short, in terms of citizenship. Religious convictions were crucial to the motivation of many American and French revolutionaries, but not to the public justification of their political cause. Religious beliefs remained of fundamental significance to political actors in Napoleonic Europe, but their political claims did not relate directly to the establishment of the true religion.

There seems to have been a shift in what made people angry, fearful or elated. It took place in different ways in different places and at different times but was, cumulatively, clear across the continent and its colonies; it can be broadly summarized as a transition from Reformation politics to Enlightenment politics. There was considerable continuity though in the descriptions of public emotion attached to these crises. Anger, pity, fear and hope remained the key emotional registers referred to by observers in explaining the mobilization of collective political action, despite the shift in the political issues to which these emotional responses were linked. We can trace continuities, for example, in the anger that mobilized attacks on persons and property between the German Peasants War and the French revolution – or the hope that motivated reformers in the English and American revolutions – despite the very different styles of political argument in those crises.[1]

We might think of this as a process by which a timeless repertoire of collective emotional responses 'migrated', as political ideas changed.[2] Fear, for example, can be a source of 'negative integration' as one collective comes to see itself as threatened by another, generating solidarity and through it the capacity for collective action, often of a deeply unpleasant kind. The threat might be real, but seems to be most potent in relation to perceived normative threats posed by an 'Other'. Fear of Catholics in early modern England, for example, seems to have been more powerful in the abstract than in relation to actual Catholic neighbours. It is often conspiracy theories that make the normative threat seem real. We might then trace the migration of that collective emotion as the normative basis of the social order was re-thought. Thus, by the 1790s the English government was more concerned about secular radicals inspired by the French revolution than by Catholics, and that was the terrain in which collective emotions were evoked.

Anger or indignation at injustice, often associated with pity or suffering, has also been a powerful political force in many different historical contexts, helping to mobilize a collective emotional response and driving political change. Lynn Hunt identifies something like this as a crucial aspect of the rise of the human rights movement, for example, starting in the eighteenth century and associated with new means by which people were encouraged to make empathic connections with others.[3] We might see this as an important underpinning of the ideals expressed in the French revolution: pity can be generative of anger or indignation, which demands political change.

Political actors can actively seek to encourage empathetic engagement in order to secure political change. Reformation martyrdom sought to do this for particular confessional issues, at least in a sense – by dramatizing the martyrs' humanity and their suffering, and seeing their fortitude as an expression of the rightness of their cause. This technique might be a means of securing the migration of collective emotional responses. The notion of martyrdom, for example, was secularized by campaigners for other causes in England during the eighteenth century, reflected in the imagery of political suffering: the way, for example, that the Tolpuddle Martyrs (English people who tried to set up labour organizations in the early nineteenth century) or the victims of the Peterloo Massacre were described.

If political crises are often precipitated by anger, fear or pity, they are equally often sustained by hope. As crises unfold charismatic leaders come to be seen as offering the prospect of social and political transformation, or the dispatch of the old regime can be associated with great hopes for the future, as in the celebrated response of William Wordsworth (1770–1850) to the French Revolution: 'Bliss was it in that dawn to be alive, | But to be young was very heaven!'[4] That image, of a sun rising on a new day, is a powerful and recurring one, as is that of spring – political change is figured in a way that resonates with familiar events that have a common emotional association.

From this perspective we might almost assess the strength of a normative value, or of the perceived threat to it, from the strength of emotional responses to such mobilizations. An important question arising from this attempt to trace the migration of emotional responses then is how people seek to evoke collective emotions in relation to particular issues and what determines their success in that.

To address the question this way – or at least exclusively this way – is not adequate, however. Fundamentally, it implies the primacy of reason in the relationship between reason, emotion and experience, a causal relationship that we know to be too simplistic. And this is particularly true of collective emotions, the full complexity of which is coming to be understood. The problem here of explaining change, rather than simply documenting it, might be seen as a variant on a more general challenge in cultural history.

William M. Reddy gives us one very influential way to think about this, exploring the consequences for individuals of the existence of emotional regimes governing the limits of acceptable public expression. The individual costs of this, and the political energy generated by those costs, can be one source of political change.[5] There is perhaps an analogy with Reddy's earlier work on the individual injuries of class, and political alienation. Could we further suggest that changing emotional experience might in itself help explain political conflict? This, again, is the force of Hunt's analysis of the genesis of the human rights movement – that a new capacity for empathetic engagement was crucial for sustaining the collective emotional response that underpins commitment to universal human rights. Historical changes such as this – for example, the spread during the sixteenth and seventeenth centuries of a Tacitean commitment to the restraint of passions, in oneself and in society – may have important things to tell us about the sources and possibilities of political change.[6]

This second approach makes it easier to take account of the changing subjective experience of emotion, and changing collective understandings of the meanings of particular emotions, in understanding political change. Across this period there was significant change in how emotions were understood and expressed, and to treat the issue simply as one of 'migration' is likely to miss important ways in which collective emotions and political life intersect.

Work on this area is not well developed, although the raw materials for analyses of this kind are abundant. Many histories contain commentary on collective emotions – fear, anger, pity and hope in particular – and it might be possible to build up a picture of some of these relationships quite quickly. It is an issue with some topical relevance to many western democracies, where political disengagement from electoral politics is often identified as a problem – emotional disengagement is frequently seen as a (symptom of) failure in political life; the lack of political engagement is frequently characterized as 'apathy'. Given the current state of our knowledge it is difficult to do more than pose the question, about how and when collective emotions can produce political engagement with positive outcomes, but it is an important and timely question to pose.

Further reading

Braddick, M.J. and J. Innes (eds), *Suffering and Happiness in Early Modern England* (Oxford: Oxford University Press, 2016)
—examines the political effects of discourses of suffering and happiness, the public work of emotional language and performance, as opposed to the study of the subjective experience of those emotions.
Hunt, L., *Inventing Human Rights: A History* (New York: W. & W. Norton, 2008)
—offers an important model of how to explore a key ideological development in relation to the development of shared, widely recognized and perhaps collective emotional engagement.
Scheve, C. von and M. Salmela (eds), *Collective Emotions* (Oxford: Oxford University Press, 2014)
—offers the most comprehensive overview of modern research on collective emotions in contemporary life.

Notes

1 Compare, for example, the relevant passages of M.J. Braddick, *God's Fury, England's Fire: A New History of the English Revolution* (London: Allen Lane, 2008) with S. Schama, *Citizens: A Chronicle of the French Revolution* (London: Viking, 1989)
2 Y.-M. Bercé, *Revolt and Revolution in Early Modern Europe: An Essay on the History of Political Violence*, (trans.) J. Bergin (Manchester: Manchester University Press, 1980) is a good overview that could be read this way.
3 L. Hunt, *Inventing Human Rights: A History* (New York: W. & W. Norton, 2008)
4 William Wordsworth, 'French Revolution, as it appeared to enthusiasts at its commencement', reprinted from "The Friend"', lines 4–5 (composed 1805), in *Wordsworth Poetical Works*, (ed.) T. Hutchinson (New Edition, ed. E. de Selincourt, Oxford, 1969), 165–6.
5 W.M. Reddy, *The Navigation of Feeling: A Framework for the History of Emotions* (Cambridge: Cambridge University Press, 2001)
6 R. Tuck, *Philosophy and Government, 1572–1651* (Cambridge: Cambridge University Press, 1993)

IV.4 Radical formations

Christina Petterson

The idea of what constitutes radical is of course tied up with ideas of stability and norm. In the early modern period, ideas of political radicalism could find expression in religious thought and practice. This entry considers the evocation (or not) to emotions in two different radical settings, two in the sixteenth century (Thomas Müntzer and the Münster Rebellion) and one in the eighteenth century (the Moravian Brethren). While the earlier formations have only very recently been in focus of scholars of emotions, the Moravian missions have in the last few years attracted the attention of historians interested in emotions, in part due to their immense archival resources (journals, diaries, ledgers, correspondence, censuses and the like) which date back to the early 1720s. Because this field of radical formations has not yet taken off in emotional studies, the entry seeks to identify the potential for analysis of emotion.

The first is what is known as the 'Radical Reformation' in the sixteenth century and its expression in the works of Thomas Müntzer (*c.* 1489–1525) as well as the actions of the Münster Rebellion. The second formation is a collective known as the renewed Moravian Brethren in the eighteenth century, who belong to what is known as 'Radical Pietism'. As will become clear below, these formations differ in their view of human nature and collectivity, which shows up in their use of emotive language and its relation to their various political goals.

Thomas Müntzer was born around 1489 in the mining town Stolberg, in the Harz region of Germany. He studied at the University of Frankfurt (Oder) in Eastern Germany and graduated in 1512, a Master of Arts and Bachelor of Holy Scripture. He was initially supported by Martin Luther (1483–1546), whom he had met in Wittenberg, Germany in 1518, but after Müntzer's political radicalization following his preaching position in Zwickau in 1520, the two fell out and went their different ways. Müntzer's radicalization increased through encounters with disenfranchized peasants and miners, and came to a head when he led the peasants and miners into the battle of Frankenhausen, where thousands were killed, Müntzer captured and after torture was executed in Mühlhausen on 27 May 1525.

Müntzer's writings burn with the fire of social indignation, and this fire is expressed in scatological and eschatological language and insults such as 'plate-lickers', 'thin-shitters' and 'sack of worms' hurled at his opponents. His writings – sermons, letters, liturgies, manifestos and exegesis – are a tapestry of apocalyptic theology, mystical spirituality and revolutionary politics, interspersed with biblical quotations, references and allusions:[1]

> Go to it, go to it, while the fire is hot! Don't let your sword grow cold, don't let it hang down limply! Hammer away ding-dong on the anvils of Nimrod, cast down their tower to the ground![2]

Müntzer's language, while tremendously affective and intended to rouse, was not an appeal to the individual emotions of the people he addressed, but rather an attempt to carry out a more structural transformation. Hence his use of biblical language was used to heckle and threaten the nobility and the clergy, both of whom he despised as exploiters and oppressors, and to summon the common people in a united battle, as seen in the quote above. The responses to Müntzer were no less virulent and torrential: Luther labelling him a fanatic and naming him the 'villainous and bloodthirsty Prophet',[3] and modern-day Church historians using him as a foil for an anti-socialist agenda.[4]

Another group against whom Luther, as well as the Pope, raged, were the Anabaptists. While there are overlaps with Müntzer and the other radical reformers, it was far from all Anabaptists who participated or condoned the revolts led by the peasants. Combined with the revolts of the Peasants' War, the Anabaptists unsettled Europe from Moravia in the East to the Netherlands in the West, raging through Southern Germany, Tyrol and Switzerland. The most extreme example of the social upheavals that took place during the Reformation period is the so-called Münster Rebellion. In brief, the Münster Rebellion refers to the establishment of the New Jerusalem under the kingship of the Dutch Anaptist Jan van Leiden (1509–36) in 1534 to prepare the way for the return of Christ. The city was besieged for 16 months by an unusual alliance of Protestant and Catholic powers, and fell on 25 June 1535. The three leaders were tortured, executed and their remains placed in cages hung from the steeple of St Lambert's Church in Münster. What is of particular interest in the case of the Münster Rebellion – apart from the apocalyptic fervour and extreme violence of the movement itself and the retaliation – is the emotional response to the Rebellion, from Luther, who was utterly repulsed by the turn of events, up to twentieth-century church historians, who use the events of Münster as a foil for political ideologies from left to right.[5]

Finally, the Moravian Brethren were in the early eighteenth century a motley crew of Moravian peasants, tracing their roots back to the Hussite reformation, and to German aristocrats and peasants. They were founded in 1721 under the leadership of Count Nicolaus Ludwig von Zinzendorf (1700–60), and were regarded as dangerous and radical up until the second half of the eighteenth century. They were also extremely successful missionaries with a global scope, but especially in their missions to North America and Greenland, where their appeal to emotions resonated profoundly with the indigenous populations.[6]

One of the central features of the Moravian Brethren in the eighteenth century is their understanding of union with Christ, which meant that liturgy shaped their everyday lives and social relations. Their community was segregated according to age, marital status and gender, and within these 'choirs' as the groups were called, the members were urged to cultivate a personal union with and experience of Christ, within which they ideally should remain. For the young adult members, the articulation of this union was often in heavily erotic terms – particularly in the period from 1740 to 1760, after which such language and imagery were discouraged and even censored.[7]

A choir, then, was constituted by a group of single men, girls or widowers. Within these groups, the members' relationship to Jesus was expounded corresponding to their status. For example, married women and widows would both, through their experience of sexual intercourse, know of Christ in ways that girls and maidens did not, because the sex they had with their husbands was a foretaste of their union with

Christ. Another function of the choirs was a form of confessional, where members were encouraged to monitor bodily change, movement and arousal in themselves and to lay this at the feet of Christ. This confession of their bodily movements, however small and seemingly insignificant, was connected with a command not to dwell on them in private – because dwelling on such things in private generates 'a sinful emotion'.[8]

The individualization techniques of the Moravian Brethren meant that there was a constant appeal to the emotions of the members, in the liturgies, in the hymnals and in their everyday interaction. The members were constantly encouraged to see themselves in an intimate relation to Christ, and sustain this enthusiasm through their lives. A particularly interesting group of sources are constituted by the so-called funeral (auto)biographies, which were autobiographical texts written by the members (or their choir-siblings) on their early life, conversion, life in the community and finally death. These texts were read aloud at the member's funeral, a tradition that goes back to the early eighteenth century.

The extreme emphasis on emotions as something belonging to the individual, which can be called forth and manipulated towards certain ends is recognizable in the archival material of the Moravian Brethren.[9] It is not, however, a feature of the world-view of Münzer or the Münster Rebellion, even though their language was highly charged and appealed to senses of injustice and apocalyptic passion. Nevertheless, the leaders of the Radical Reformation were able to use religious and apocalyptic imagery to stir and rouse thousands of people to a revolution, while two centuries later, the Moravian Brethren used emotional language within alternative social relations, and created a host of new communities that in time came to live peacefully with the modern state. These differences suggest that with the emergence of a private sphere, and the relegation of religion to this sphere, emotions became a significant element in the forging of the individualized citizens of the modern state.

The field of emotions is incredibly diverse, which is simultaneously its tremendous strength as well as its weakness. It is its strength because it encourages research into seemingly endless geographical, historical and social contexts with insights into stimulating albeit isolated cases. However, a focus on the role and development of emotions over a longer period, say, the *longue durée*, could yield important insights into the changing perceptions of human nature.

Further reading

Atwood, C.D., *Community of the Cross: Moravian Piety in Colonial Bethlehem* (Pennsylvania: Pennsylvania State University Press, 2004)

—although this classic description of emotive nature of the Moravian Brethren in their North American manifestation does not examine emotions as such, its showcase of ritual and practice shows why the Moravians would be an obvious choice for an analysis of emotions.

Goertz, H.-J., *Thomas Müntzer: Apocalyptic, Mystic, and Revolutionary*, (trans.) J. Jacquiery (Edinburgh: T&T Clark, 1993)

—focuses on the pervasive role of the spirit and mysticism in Müntzer's life, and constitutes a valuable source for anyone wanting to engage with this enigmatic figure.

Terpstra, N., *Religious Refugees in the Early Modern World: An Alternative History of the Reformation* (Cambridge: Cambridge University Press, 2015)

—While emotions are not the central analytical category of this book, it constitutes the first steps in applying understandings of emotions to the complex history of period of the reformation.

Notes

1 A. Toscano, 'The Resurrections of Thomas Müntzer', Preface to *Wu Ming presents Thomas Müntzer, Sermon to the Princes* (London: Verso, 2010), vii–xviii.
2 P. Matheson (ed.), *The Collected Works of Thomas Müntzer* (Edinburgh: T&T Clark, 1988), 142.
3 Toscano, *Resurrections*, ix.
4 D. MacCulloch, *The Reformation* (New York: Viking, 2003), 157.
5 R. Klötzer, 'The Melchiorites and Münster', in J.M. Stayer and J.D. Roth (eds), *Brill's Companions to the Christian Tradition*, vol. 6: *Companion to Anabaptism and Spiritualism, 1521–1700* (Leiden: Brill 2006), 218–19.
6 J. Van Gent, 'Sarah and her sisters: letters, emotions, and colonial identities in the early modern atlantic world', *Journal of Religious History* 38, 1 (2014), 71–90; Van Gent, 'The burden of love: Moravian conversions and emotions in eighteenth-century Labrador', *Journal of Religious History* 39, 4 (2015), 557–74; C. McLisky, '"A hook fast in his heart": Emotion and "true Christian knowledge" in disputes over conversion between Lutheran and Moravian missionaries in early colonial Greenland', *Journal of Religious History* 39, 4 (2015), 575–94.
7 P. Peucker, 'Selection and destruction in Moravian archives between 1760 and 1810', *Journal of Moravian History* 12, 2 (2012), 170–215.
8 On the choirs and the speeches, see C. Petterson, '"Gar Nicht Biblisch!" Ephesians, marriage, and radical pietism in 18th century Germany', *Journal for the Bible and its Reception* 1, 2 (2014), 191–207.
9 See Van Gent, 'Gendered Power and Emotions: The Religious Revival Movement in Herrnhut in 1727', in S. Broomhall (ed.), *Gender and Emotions in Medieval and Early Modern Europe: Destroying Order, Structuring Disorder* (Farnham: Ashgate 2015), 233–47.

IV.5 Law

David Lemmings

The administration of justice is a promising site for the study of emotions, although lawyers and legislators have usually regarded courts as places for the containment of feeling by the authorities; and up until recently legal historians have neglected emotion for the superficial logic of doctrinal development, as expressed in professional law reports. Certainly, emotions were fundamental to law and justice in early modern England, where unlike most of the rest of Europe, the adversarial trial endured. This was most apparent in the criminal courts, where there were few lawyers before the middle of the eighteenth century and trials consisted of 'rambling altercations' between victims and accused. In these circumstances anger, hatred and vengeance were the principal currency of the laymen and laywomen who dominated the exchange. Witnesses, jurors and spectators expressed their feelings about the alleged crimes and their perpetrators, while it was left to the judge to act as referee and to apply the 'artificial reason' of the law. Of course lawful punishment involved the expression of emotions too, especially where it involved public execution. Condemned offenders were encouraged to demonstrate that they were appropriately penitent, but in the eighteenth century capital punishment often degenerated into riotous carnival, whereby brazenly unremorseful prisoners appealed to the crowd as counter-cultural heroes. By contrast, in late modern England and its former colonies the adversarial trial was represented as the preserve of professional lawyers, who strictly controlled the expression of emotions by the application of rules that associate justice with equity and cool reason. And, where it survived, capital punishment was normally administered by officials advised by criminologists and doctors, behind closed doors that excluded emotional communication with the crowd. In England the history of trial and punishment is therefore arguably a story of professionalization conquering the emotions in the name of the rule of law.

Or is it? Public exemplary punishment and public trials have always depended on evoking and shaping emotions to achieve the desired outcomes and to legitimize justice proceedings, while much of the business of justice is about unravelling and adjudicating conflicts grounded in emotional exchanges. This entry will focus on two main areas of continuity and change in law and emotions. First, it will consider emotions in the judgement seat (ranging from righteous anger to lachrymose sympathy), and changing emotional styles in courtrooms ('majesty', 'theatre' and 'counter-theatre') taking particular account of the progressive 'lawyerization' of the courts in England. Second, it will address representations of law and justice in the press, considering the 'mediatization' of law and order, and attending to moral panics, the treatment of sensational trials, and policing.

Despite the ideal of law as the application of reason, in the flesh experienced judges always represent and express emotions appropriate to their role and the particular expectations of contemporary culture. This kind of legal regulation draws on a variety of emotional performances: such as majesty (awe of the state, best expressed in the elaborate 'theatre' of the courtroom and judicial dress); anger and vengeance (solemn expressions of sovereign punishment); disgust and shaming (representing and shaping emotions to legitimize verdict and sentence); and mercy and compassion (attending to offenders' emotional states in mitigation, expressing sorrow at death). In England the judge's role in the theatre of courtroom emotions became more muted with the progressive intervention of lawyers, but they were still required to display the appropriate feelings, and there are accounts of eighteenth- and nineteenth-century judges weeping when pronouncing sentence.

While the 'counter-theatre' of crowd participation in court (ranging from significant body language, and meaningful looks and gestures, to audible comments by the crowd) seems to have been largely muzzled, and even jurors were also silenced by 'lawyerization', studying the behaviour of the lawyers in front of them also shows that part of the trial's core business remained appealing to emotions, both subtle and not so subtle. Thus, at the trial of the shoemaker Thomas Hardy (1752–1832) for treason in 1794, the defence counsel Thomas Erskine (1750–1823) represented himself as a champion of English sympathy and patriotism by insisting 'I feel for the care of humanity; . . . if this man is deprived of life, all that remains of our boasted constitution is lost for ever'.[1] Indeed in press accounts of sensational trials commentators applied contemporary 'feeling rules' (expectations of appropriate emotional performance) to weigh defendants' culpability and shape their readers' opinions about the justice of verdicts. For example Catherine Hayes (1690–1726), on trial for murdering her husband in 1726, was supposedly outed by her insincere emotions, for on a public viewing of her husband's severed head she 'pretended to faint', and this was reported in the press as evidence of her bad character.[2] In fully-lawyerized trials, jurors were expected to make similar judgements about emotional sincerity when assessing the performances of lawyers, as well as witnesses; and in 1794 one of the prosecuting counsel at the trial of Hardy attempted to brand Erskine's hyperbolic style of defence as artfully meretricious.[3] Certainly, the easy associations made between authenticity, truth and the proper expression of feelings therefore meant that large doses of emotional judgement continued to inform the rule of law.

As these accounts show, emotional judgements also shaped the representation of law and justice in the press. 'Mediatization' of the public sphere in eighteenth-century England exposed the public to more emotionally coloured and radically selective accounts of crime, just as direct lay participation in justice proceedings was diminishing with the intervention of lawyers. The realities conveyed by the press were mixed and messy. On the one hand it has been suggested that the proliferation of newspaper and pamphlet accounts of crime, trials and punishments from the late seventeenth century meant that the English public was more susceptible to moral panics about crime, especially in the ever-growing metropolis of London. Certainly, newspaper accounts of London crime concentrated on the most violent offences, pamphlets bemoaned 'the increase of robbers', and these fears about the growth of crime and disorder frequently resulted in demands for governing authorities to crack down, either by passing new penal legislation or by increased severity in sentencing and the administration of death. The press did not speak with one voice, however, and besides panics about law and order, there were also many accounts of crimes and trials that showed understanding and even sympathy for defendants, as well as victims of crime. For example the genteel Mary Blandy (1719–52), tried and executed for the murder of her father by poison at Oxford in 1752, inspired expressions of pity and respect, as well as disgust. After considering a printed version of the trial the *Covent Garden Journal*, published by the novelist-magistrate Henry Fielding (1707–54), printed a letter which evinced compassion for Blandy, based on her witnesses' insistence that she had been 'an affectionate, dutiful, respectful Child'. An unscrupulous lover who coveted her fortune apparently led her astray, and this was presented as evidence that women's unstable emotions were easily overcome by affected tenderness and flattery. Whether Blandy or her lover was most culpable, the lesson was that crime depended on a backstory of moral corruption, and such an explanation may have been reassuring for readers concerned about the apparent increase in violent crimes perpetrated by anonymous villains, as constructed by a multitude of newspaper accounts.[4] Fielding knew very well that effective policing and administration of justice depended on management of the public's emotions. Around this time he was conducting a sustained newspaper campaign wherein 'Justice Fielding' assumed the proportions of a law and order champion who was intent on rooting out crime and vice on the streets of London, with the aid of his own band of brave thief-takers, progenitors of the 'Bow Street Runners'. So just as some penal legislation was inspired by appeals to collective fear and disgust, justice also required that the public should have confidence in the legal authorities. So in early modern England, although processes, styles and agents were shifting, the business of law and justice was shot through with emotion.

To date the history of emotions has had relatively little influence on the history of law in early modern Europe. These examples from the administration of justice in England suggest that the study of emotions can reveal fresh layers of meaning associated with 'the rule of law', both at the level of individuals and communities; and may help to explain historical continuity and change.

Further reading

Bandes, S.A. (ed.), *The Passions of Law* (New York: New York University Press, 1999)
—asks very broad questions about the role of emotions in the administration of justice and provides models of research, which may be usefully applied, to early modern Europe.

Lange, B., 'The emotional dimension in legal regulation', *Journal of Law and Society*, 29, 1 (2002), 197–225.
—provides a stimulating discussion of legal regulation and emotional 'processes', which opens new perspectives by applying sociological theory.

Lemmings, D. and C. Walker (eds), *Moral Panics, the Media and the Law in Early Modern England* (Basingstoke: Palgrave Macmillan, 2009)
—a series of case studies that investigate the management of collective emotions through analysis of the 'media' in early modern England.

Notes

1 *Morning Post*, 3 Nov. 1794.
2 *A Narrative of the Barbarous and unheard of Murder of Mr. John Hayes*, 2nd edn (London, 1726), 10, 24–5.
3 *General Evening Post*, 30 Oct. 1794.
4 *Covent Garden Journal*, 10 Mar. 1752.

IV.6 Punishment

Una McIlvenna

Punishment in the early modern period was explicitly designed to inspire a range of strongly felt emotions, and scholars have long attempted to understand the motivations and feelings of those who ordered, carried out, suffered and witnessed the often painful, bloody, and shaming punishment of convicts. Although more attention is usually given to execution, punishment should be viewed as a continuous spectrum of penalties from which judges could select the exact degree of appropriate punishment. Whatever the ruling, all punishments involved a display of the criminal who would make a public confession of their sins before the sentence was carried out.

There was also a variety of emotions that the spectacles of these punishments were expected to engender in both spectators and convicts. The 1532 German legal code known as the *Constitutio Criminalis Carolina* specified that women convicted of infanticide should be buried alive and impaled 'in order that their fear may be the greater'.[1] Lesser crimes that merited only the pillory could see the convict wearing a *Schandmaske* or 'mask of shame'.[2] Execution ballads that sang the news of crime and punishment often employed the first-person voice of the condemned criminal, whose admission of fear, remorse and shame as she awaited her impending death was designed to instil both compassion and fear in listeners. The ballad in the voice of Judith Brown, convicted of murdering her mistress and burned alive in 1684, achieves this by describing her emotions at her imminent punishment, and ends with a typical warning to her spectators:

Alas! you may behold
my sad and dismal doom,
Both hands & heart, and e'ry part,
in flames you'l see consume.
To you that come to see,
a woful sinners fall,
O let those cruel flames now be,
a warning to you all.[3]

The rationale behind the public nature of punishment was that crimes were a sin on the community that all members should be involved in expiating. They did this by attending the 'drawing' of the victim from the prison to the punishment site, pelting victims in the pillory and pulling on the legs of hanging victims to speed up the death. They could also participate in a more metaphysical sense, praying and meditating on the fate of the convict, and performing ballads and verse that broadcast news of the events.

Pain, fear and horror, experienced by both prisoners and spectators, were felt by the legal authorities to act as visual deterrents against sin and crime, as powerful an argument for the death penalty in the period as retribution. The traditional sentencing formula for hanging in southern Germany and Switzerland specified that the body should remain hanging on the gallows so that 'others shall witness his punishment as a fright and a warning'.[4] But it was the emotion of shame that played a central role in public punishment, integrally linked as it was with early modern ideas of honour. Shame in the early modern period was instead closer in meaning to the term 'infamy'. One's honour was inextricably bound up with the honour of one's family, which meant that physical disfigurements such as branding and dismemberment were a social stain not just on the convict but also his family, and that the shame of capital punishment had lasting social repercussions for surviving family members beyond the lifetime of the executed criminal. The manual for a Bolognese lay confraternity of comforters, who devoted themselves to helping condemned prisoners prepare for their executions, contains one chapter titled 'Which deals with how the shame of public execution should be disparaged', although the manual's repeated focus on this emotion reveals how significant a factor it was for the condemned.[5]

With this in mind, each method of punishment was finely calibrated to exact a specific degree of shame. The concept of honour was dictated by social rank and so, while punishments were designed to fit the crime, they also differed according to the convict's social status. In accordance with Roman law, it was believed that the amount of time spent in connection with the weapon of death was in direct proportion to the shame incurred by the criminal. Thus, swift decapitation by the sword or axe was reserved in many countries for the nobility, while those lower down the social scale were left to slowly strangle to death by a hempen rope.

Shame was also linked to the natural elements: to perish by air (as when left to rot on the wheel), by fire (as when burned at the stake), by water (as when drowned), or by earth (as when buried alive), were all considered more shameful by both legal authorities and onlookers than the quick blow of a hand-crafted sword, itself linked with images of chivalry.[6] Upon death, this shame would be transferred to the family of the condemned, who would suffer ostracism and abuse because of the specific method by which the criminal had been punished. The stigma conferred on relatives was so great that in his speech to the newly-formed *Assemblé nationale* in December 1789, the French physician Joseph-Ignace Guillotin (1738–1814) proposed six articles in favour of the reformation of capital punishment, of which Article 3 proposed that 'The punishment of the guilty party shall not bring discredit upon or discrimination against his family'.[7] The subsequent transformation of capital punishment to the same brief act of decapitation for all, regardless of rank or criminal deed, followed by burial of the corpse, did away with the centuries-old stigma of shame being transferred onto the surviving kin.

A papal decree of 1312 allowed convicted prisoners the sacrament of confession before their death, which thereafter profoundly changed the status of the condemned for spectators. If visibly repentant, the prisoner could play the role of exemplar, about to enter heaven after his ordeal. The punishment ritual, with its explicitly religious overtones, was thus intended to evoke compassion in the spectators for one who was suffering in the same way as the Christian martyrs had done. Edward Jackson, executed for treason at Tyburn in 1684, was said by the Ordinary of Newgate to have uttered on the scaffold such 'Heavenly Expressions, with such Passion, Loudness, and Earnestness, that he melted Hundreds of Spectators into Tears'.[8] By contrast, if the prisoner was clearly unrepentant, contemporaries were always deeply troubled by what they perceived as a soul presumably on its way to Hell. When Henry Cuffe, executed in 1601 for his role in the plot of Robert Devereux, Earl of Essex (1565–1601), was openly defiant on the scaffold, declaring his innocence, he was interrupted multiple times by shocked listeners. One official cried,

> "O! how dare you decline from the good example of the penitent death your Lord made, that now go about to justify yourself? You must confess your sin, and make satisfaction to the world that you are justly condemned, that you may the better deserve forgiveness for this your foul and traitorous fact, both of God and the Queen."[9]

The special status of the condemned, on a transition between the earthly life and the afterlife, is likely to be the reason for the widespread folk beliefs in the magical powers of the blood, body parts and clothing of the recently executed. It also explains the popularity of songs and prose confessions in the first person voice of the convict; such first-person accounts promoted a compassionate view of the condemned and acted as a powerful deterrent, urging listeners and readers to shun sin so as to avoid the same fate.

The rise of a culture of sensibility in the eighteenth century led to a belief among elites that visually witnessing the physical punishment of others was emotionally unacceptable for those who were 'properly elevated'. The introduction of the guillotine in France in 1792 was intended to address the growing dissatisfaction with the ubiquity of executions, the cruelty of execution techniques, capital punishment's inefficacy as a deterrent, and – most importantly – the inequality inherent in using different execution methods for criminals of different social status. Enlightenment ideals created an intellectual and emotional climate that transformed centuries of beliefs around the public, communal nature of punishment. Instead of a system in which each member of the community was involved in the expiation of sin through a range of punishments that reflected and reinforced social hierarchies, the growing belief in the rights and dignity of the individual decreed that such public display of a person's shame and humiliation was 'cruel and unusual' punishment.

The highly sensationalized reporting of early modern executions has therefore proved to be a productive source for emotions research. However, while some work has been done on dishonour and the role of the executioner for France and the German lands, we still need a more precise understanding of the role that shame played in early modern punishment rituals. Given the communal nature of punishment in the early modern period, further analysis is warranted on the performativity – of convicts, officials and spectators – during these often lengthy and detailed rituals.

Further reading

Dülmen, R. van, *Theatre of Horror: Crime and Punishment in Early Modern Germany*, (trans.) E. Neu (Cambridge: Polity, 1990)

—remains seminal in the field for its attention to the methods, rationales and outcomes of the execution ritual in the German lands.

Friedland, P., *Seeing Justice Done: The Age of Spectacular Capital Punishment in France* (Oxford: Oxford University Press, 2012)

—valuable for its interrogation of the motives behind the eagerness with which spectators flocked to public executions, and how the revolution in sensibilities spelled the end of public punishment.

Gatrell, V.A.C., *The Hanging Tree: Execution and the English People 1770–1868* (Oxford: Oxford University Press, 1996)

—examining how attitudes to execution in England evolved over the eighteenth and nineteenth centuries, is valuable for its use of sources from a range of social levels, particularly those which allow us insight into the emotions of the lower classes.

Notes

1 Cited in R. Evans, *Rituals of Retribution: Capital Punishment in Germany 1600–1987* (Oxford: Oxford University Press, 1996), 31.

2 Evans, *Rituals of Retribution*, 54.

3 *THE / Unfaithful Servant; / AND / The Cruel Husband. / Being a perfect and true account of one Judith Brown, / who together with her Master Iohn Cupper, conspired the Death of her Mistris, his / Wife, which accordingly they did accomplish in the time of Child-bed, when she lay / in with two Children, by mixing of her Drink with cruel Poyson; for which Fact / she received due Sentence of Death at the late Assizes in the County of Salop, to be / Burned; which was accordingly Executed upon the Old Heath near Shrewsbury, on / Thursday the Twenty-first day of August, 1684* (London, 1684)

4 Cited in R. van Dülmen, *Theatre of Horror: Crime and Punishment in Early Modern Germany*, (trans.) E. Neu (Cambridge: Polity, 1990), 96.

5 *The Art of Executing Well: Rituals of Execution in Early Modern Italy* (ed.) N. Terpstra (Kirksville, MO: Truman State University Press, 2008), 212.

6 Evans, *Rituals of Retribution*, 57.

7 P. Friedland, *Seeing Justice Done: The Age of Spectacular Capital Punishment in France* (Oxford: Oxford University Press, 2012), 218–24.

8 *Old Bailey Proceedings Online*, online atwww.oldbaileyonline.org, version 7.2, accessed 7 December 2015, *Ordinary of Newgate's Account*, May 1684 (OA16840526)

9 *Calendar of State Papers, Domestic Series of the Reign of Elizabeth 1601–1603*, vol. CCLXXIX, 25. (March 13 1601) 'Speech of Mr. Cuffe at his execution for treason'; Document Ref.: SP 12/279 f.35

Destructive experiences

IV.7 Indebtedness

Elise M. Dermineur

'The first quarter of the twenty-first century will witness "an emotional revolution" in the field of behaviour studies', predicted Jon Elster in 2001.[1] His prediction turned out to be only partially true. Yet, scholars from the disciplines of the social sciences, such as economics, political science and philosophy, among others, have only recently recognized the significant role played by emotions in economic phenomena, and in particular in economic change. The critical function of emotions in these processes, which should not be understood as the main causal vector but rather as part of a complex set of various factors, now complements the rational theory approach and sheds light on the decision-making process and choices of agents. But to date, only a handful of early modernists have focused on the role of emotions in economic exchange and economic change for their period. The notions of indebtedness and credit relations, in particular, have increasingly begun to attract the attention of scholars: debt and credit were embedded in society and reached agents in real lives, as Karl Polanyi first suggested decades ago.[2] In early modern Europe, credit and debt relations, as embodiments of social and power relations, triggered a wide range of emotions, affective rhetoric and gestures, the norms of which were shared within the community, and their use and display informed its members on the current health of relationships between community members.

Emotions triggered by indebtedness are to be found in the civil and criminal court records and in particular in testimonies. Testimonies recorded at the local court, indeed, shed light not only on the emotional relationship of the debtor and creditor but also on the affective rhetoric and gestures used by agents and its evolution over time. It must be borne in mind that these testimonies might have suffered the alteration and standardization of the authorities – especially in the eighteenth century – when it came to the rhetoric and presentation of the statements.

In early modern Europe, credit and debt were the two most essential features of economic exchange. Warding off temporary shortages in the cycle of agrarian economic activity constituted the primary function of credit in traditional societies. Credit represented an essential financial tool for millions of Europeans, either to sustain their investments or to make ends meet. Such a system of exchange has always existed.[3] In early modern Europe, however, the notion of moral economy governed most of the local monetary transactions that took place between agents. Moral economy refers to a system of exchange in which fairness, justice, cooperation and moral accountability predominated over any other concern. Its implementation and efficiency proved to be highly operative in small communities where strong cooperation among its members, high endogamy, strong familial and solidarity ties prevailed.[4] Recently, the historian Laurence Fontaine, following the path set by E.P. Thompson, has become one of the first scholars to refer to a moral economy for the early modern period, showing the mechanisms of charity and solidarity at work in traditional communities, when it came to credit, and highlighting its social dimension.[5] She recognizes the vital importance of credit in early modern Europe, as she points to the emerging figure of the *Homo creditus* in the seventeenth century, illuminating the fundamental significance of credit to economic practice but also, and above all, to social relations throughout Europe – and the mutually formative impact they had on each other.

In early modern traditional communities, agents borrowed and lent to each other in an almost hermetic sphere in full knowledge of each other's financial capacity and resources. Agents resorting to such a local credit market shared beliefs, norms and emotional palettes regarding the meaning of their actions. In this form of exchange, the moral economy was loaded with a set of moral values, ethical norms and emotions in which solidarity, cooperation and charity played a critical role for both the debtor and the creditor. In order to be able to borrow money, borrowers had to have good credit – in the figurative sense – and this was often more important than their actual assets. Having credit often equalled having a good reputation.[6] Through this 'moral' credit, borrower and lender established a relation of trust in which the debtor's honour constituted the main guarantee of repayment. In case of non-repayment, on the other hand, the credit capital of the debtor became strongly affected and potentially prevented further transactions with the same creditor, but also with other potential creditors. In small communities, indeed, the news of a default spread among the agents and acted as a coercive mechanism. To recover their capital, lenders often entered into a long negotiation process with their debtors. Some of these negotiations were carried out in the public eye and bore a critical emotional charge.

But asking for justice at the local court to seek repayment in case of default constituted the last resort available, and the most extreme, confirming a breach in the moral contract between the debtor and the creditor. Judicial testimonies available are filled with affective rhetoric and gestures and inform us not only of the emotional norms and beliefs shared by the agents in the community but also on the use and manipulation of emotions. Indeed, as plaintiffs and defendants resorted to a third party in the public eye – the court – both rhetoric and gestures became standardized, understood and shared by the whole community, but it was also a performance displayed in the public sphere asserting social status within the community. The resort to the court notified the whole community of an existing conflict where the law court played a role in publicizing emotions.[7] The ultimate resort to court often underlined a complex relationship between the agents where hatred, spite, resentment, envy, fear and contempt were expressed through insults and specific vocabulary and gestures. Other complex emotions such as humiliation, shame and statements about the meaning of friendship and love, often lurked at the surface of the testimonies. In any case, the action to press charges and to bring the conflict into the public arena pushed the parties to expose their grievances, mediate and solve the issue. Additionally, the resort to court to enforce the repayment of a debt ruled, in most cases, for the seizing of the debtor's assets – if any were available – and his bankruptcy. (Imprisonment for indebtedness had slowly regressed and was no longer the norm in the seventeenth and eighteenth centuries.) A hope to recover the capital invested, however, was often low on the part of the creditor. Judicial litigation, then, often served another purpose in which humiliation, intimidation and honour found echo. Finally, one must note that the emotions triggered by this step varied according to the gender and the marital situation of the agents, who acted according to a predefined social framework in which all played their own part.

In the course of the early modern period, and most specifically in the second half of the eighteenth century, economic development, characterized by substantial growth, notably thanks to improvements emerging in a period of proto-industrialization and boosts in agricultural output, required more capital and financial exchange for further investments, engendering growing indebtedness. Additionally, the development of a market economy, accompanied by a greater monetization of exchanges and a subsequent dramatic decrease in bartering, witnessed the development of a local credit market where investment, with the assurance of profit, progressively replaced one based on norms of fairness. The moral economy no longer prevailed. In early modern France, I have observed that a group of new investors, from the bourgeoisie, socially and often geographically strangers to the local community, began to extend credit and demanded not only stronger guarantees to secure their investments but also set rigid deadlines for repayment. As a result, not only did their saving capacity flood the local credit market and the number of loans increased, causing greater indebtedness, but their exigency towards repayment also changed the moral and emotional norms traditionally experienced by ordinary debtors and creditors, witnessing a sharp increase in non-repayment judicial litigation.[8]

The change brought about by growing indebtedness in the eighteenth century had a tremendous impact on the relationship between lenders and borrowers, not only in terms of the economic balance, but also in the way the interaction of those on the credit market was affected. Indebtedness, indeed, did affect the fabric of the entire community itself. As the pattern of the moral economy was challenged, the distress of agents triggered by indebtedness led to the invention of new affective rhetoric and gestures and to new kinds of social relations within the community, where the gap in power relations and social status widened and where individualist values emerged. Research on emotions triggered by indebtedness remains embryonic so far and limited to a few existing studies. More research on this topic will not only lead to a deeper exploration of early modern emotions in general but will also shed light on the correlation between finances and emotions.

Further reading

Fontaine, L., *The Moral Economy: Poverty, Credit, and Trust in Early Modern Europe* (New York: Cambridge University Press, 2014)

—analyses the nexus of poverty, debt, solidarity and trust in early modern Europe with special reference to the concept of moral economy.

Graeber, D., *Debt: The First 5,000 Years* (Brooklyn: Melville House, 2011)

—explores the historical dimension of debt with particular emphasis on its impact on the social fabric throughout the ages and across various communities.

Lord Smail, D., *The Consumption of Justice: Emotions, Publicity, and Legal Culture in Marseille, 1264–1423* (Ithaca: Cornell University Press, 2003)

—a pioneering work that focuses on the display of emotions in the public eye through the analysis of medieval court records.

Notes

1 J. Elster, *Proverbes. Maximes. Émotions* (Paris: Presses universitaires de France, 2003), 173 (my translation).
2 K. Polanyi, *The Great Transformation: The Political and Economic Origins of Our Time* (Boston: Beacon Press, 2001)
3 See for instance D. Graeber, *Debt: The First 5,000 Years* (Brooklyn: Melville House, 2011)
4 See in particular, J.C. Scott, *The Moral Economy of the Peasant: Rebellion and Subsistence in Southeast Asia* (New Haven: Yale University Press, 1977)
5 L. Fontaine, *The Moral Economy: Poverty, Credit, and Trust in Early Modern Europe* (New York: Cambridge University Press, 2014); E.P. Thompson, 'The moral economy of the English crowd in the eighteenth century', *Past & Present* 50 (1971), 76–136.
6 See C.H. Crowston, 'Credit and the metanarrative of modernity', *French Historical Studies* 34, 1 (2011), 7–19.
7 See D. Lord Smail, *The Consumption of Justice: Emotions, Publicity, and Legal Culture in Marseille, 1264–1423* (Ithaca: Cornell University Press, 2003); A.L. Capern, 'Emotions, Gender Expectations and The Social Role of Chancery, 1550–1650', in S. Broomhall (ed.) *Authority, Gender and Emotions in Late Medieval and Early Modern England* (Basingstoke: Palgrave, 2015), 187–209.
8 For a discussion on new investors in the credit market in the eighteenth century, see E.M. Dermineur, 'Trust, norms of cooperation and the rural credit market in eighteenth-century France', *Journal of Interdisciplinary History* 45, 4 (2015), 485–506.

IV.8 War and violence

Erika Kuijpers

How did people experience and remember their feelings of fear and hope, hatred and belonging, grief and joy, honour and shame in times of war? A growing body of literature explores the experience of war from the perspective of the civilian eyewitness or victim based on contemporary accounts such as chronicles, diaries and letters and retrospective texts such as memoirs and histories. In the German language area important work has been done on accounts of the Thirty Years War by the Research Group 'Self-Narratives in Transcultural Perspective'.[1] The Irish 1641 Depositions Project demonstrates that testimonies used in court are an important source of personal accounts.[2] Pleas for pensions, charity or rehabilitation can also be rich sources for emotional memories.[3] However, few historians working on war experience also work on emotions in a more systematic way. In that respect the work of especially Susan Broomhall and Andreas Bähr is pioneering in the field.[4] Both work on a wide range of source material yet underline that the context and genre of personal testimonies and memories of war and violence shape the expression of emotions. Especially distressing experiences, of which the memories evoke grief, fear or anger, need elaborate narrative styling to allow for their expression as well as a clear communicative goal. Which emotions can and will be voiced depends of course on the identity and position of the author but just as important is what is to be gained by testifying. Reasons sometimes mentioned by the authors are love of truth, honour at stake, accounting of injustice or material losses that should be recovered or compensated for.

In general, sixteenth- and seventeenth-century ego-documents lack the reflective introspection that characterizes so many of their modern counterparts. Their authors do not write about their own very personal feelings, such as guilt or shame, and relatively little about grief for personal loss. Instead they often describe collective experiences and shared emotions. When the miseries of war are concerned authors lament the evilness of the violators or the enemy, moral decay, material losses and the disruption of social unity. Nonetheless we assume that the writing of memory essentially functioned as it does today: creating identities by connecting oneself to a meaningful and shared past.

Emotions related to war and violence are embedded in social practices of groups or communities and can also be studied through non-textual cultural artefacts. It is not self-evident for collective memory practices to develop after episodes of extreme violence.[5] Many peace agreements literally stipulated 'oblivion'. Moreover, while heroes are soon recognized, victimhood is much more complicated to talk about as it often comes with shame and loss of honour. Memories of humiliation, violence and pain can hamper the reconstruction of communities, and the recovery of both social relations and personal identities. Victimhood could be experienced as the result of failure, sin or weakness, and thus create feelings of shame and guilt. Early modern rape victims rarely testified because of their own or their family's shame. Besides, it was often highly problematic to produce evidence.[6] References to the occurrence of sexual crimes derive from hearsay and victims remain anonymous.

Printing presses typically fed the animosity between warring parties. The French wars of religion coincided with a pamphlet war that was increasingly hateful, feeding fear and hate for the enemy by extensively describing and imagining the cruelties and atrocities committed by the other party.[7] During the Dutch Revolt that broke out in 1568 and subsequently the Thirty Years War, the format of picturing atrocity was copied and further elaborated.[8] Violence also played a central role in the shaping of martyrdom of confessional groups in this period. The many published Catholic, Calvinist and Mennonite martyrologies of the seventeenth century were abundantly illustrated with images of killings, torturing and executions. Such images turned victims of violence into heroes, evoked both awe, admiration and sympathy and fed religious identity formation of persecuted minorities.[9] Beside, news prints of war and violence also seem to have appealed to a market for the sensational.[10] Stories and images of war and violence in their turn shaped personal memories. Through the media and through collective practices individuals learnt what and how to feel about war and violent events.

The dominant emotions that may serve as examples for this process are fear and grief, often framed in providential terms. The experience of both could be interpreted as a test. The reference to historical and biblical examples would help to find modes for narrating these experiences and behave appropriately. Early modern Christianity offered many examples of how suffering could be seen as meaningful, deepening faith and spiritual growth. In accounts of sacks and massacres two other topical narratives figure frequently as well, the one stressing individual or collective heroism, the other emphasizing the innocence of the victim and the inhumane cruelty of the aggressor. As such, they do not only describe fear and awe but rather try to evoke these emotions in their intended readership. In both categories religious interpretations offered additional significance. Many accounts feature spectacular escapes that can often be interpreted as resulting from divine providence or mere moral superiority.[11]

The emotions attached to honour are perhaps of an even greater personal concern to most authors who wrote war memoirs and histories. Narratives of war always added to the honour of the author, or aimed to restore it. Even the steadfastness in times of suffering described by both religious and lay authors added to their honour and that of their community. Authors who suffered loss of honour, however, being accused of treason, cowardice, heresy, dishonesty or corruption, wrote apologetic texts that usually blame others or external factors for their failure or for being falsely accused. Feelings of guilt – other than the abstract and general 'we have sinned' – do not occur in sixteenth- and seventeenth-century chronicles or memoirs. Honour and shame are emotions deeply connected to the communal identity of the earliest modern writers of war.

In the late seventeenth and eighteenth centuries the character of warfare changed dramatically. Increasingly wars were fought in battles of an ever larger scale. The civilian population experienced these at a distance, through the media. They still suffered, but indirectly: they bore the immense costs of the war and lost their sons, brothers and fathers. New emotional narratives helped to make sense of the lethal warfare of the developing nations states: love of the fatherland, self-sacrifice, new dimensions of masculine honour in the political and military arena.[12] In the Revolutionary Era, however, war directly re-entered the lives of civilians.[13]

Further reading

Broomhall, S., 'Reasons and identities to remember: composing personal accounts of religious violence in sixteenth-century France', *French History* 27, 1 (2013), 1–20.

—analyses a series of personal accounts of violence during the French Wars of Religion, suggesting that the context in which such accounts were produced determines what emotions will or can be articulated in them.

Downes, S., A. Lynch and K. O'Loughlin (eds), *Emotions and War: Medieval to Romantic Literature* (Houndmills: Palgrave Macmillan, 2015)

—explores how literature records, remembers and recreates war and war's emotions in many forms, from the Middle Ages to the era of Romanticism.

Kuijpers, E., 'Expressions of Fear, Counting the Loss: Managing Emotions in War Chronicles in the Netherlands (1568–1648)', in J. Spinks and C. Zika (eds), *Disaster, Death and the Emotions in the Shadow of the Apocalypse, 1400–1700* (Basingstoke: Palgrave Macmillan, 2016)

—discusses the various emotions expressed or described in accounts of violent events in the Dutch Revolt in the late sixteenth century and shows that they mainly serve to strengthen collective identities and enhances resilience in post-war situations.

Notes

1 C. Ulbrich, K. von Greyerz and L. Heiligensetzer (eds), *Mapping the 'I': Research on Self-Narratives in Germany and Switzerland* (Leiden: Brill, 2014); H. Medick and B. Marschke, *Experiencing the Thirty Years War: A Brief History with Documents* (Boston: St. Martin's Press, 2013); G. Mortimer, *Eyewitness Accounts of the Thirty Years' War 1618–1648* (Basingstoke: Palgrave, 2002)

2 E. Darcy, A. Margey and E. Murphy (eds), *The 1641 Depositions and the Irish Rebellion* (London: Pickering & Chatto, 2012); see also their portal: '1641 Depositions', http://1641.tcd.ie/.

3 See M. Stoyle, 'Memories of the maimed': The testimony of Charles I's former soldiers, 1660–1730', *History* 88, 290 (2003), 204–26.

4 S. Broomhall, 'Disturbing Memories. Narrating Experiences and Emotions of Distressing Events in the French Wars of Religion', and A. Bähr, 'Remembering Fear. The Fear of Violence and the Violence of Fear in Seventeenth-Century War Memories', in E. Kuijpers, J.S. Pollmann, J. Müller and J. van der Steen (eds), *Memory before Modernity. Practices of Memory in Early Modern Europe* (Leiden: Brill, 2013), 251–67, 269–82.

5 S. Broomhall, 'Reasons and identities to remember: composing personal accounts of religious violence in sixteenth-century France', *French History* 27, 1 (2013), 1–20; E. Kuijpers and J.S. Pollmann, 'Why Remember Terror? Memories of Violence in the Dutch Revolt', in M. Ó Siochrú and J. Ohlmeyer (eds), *Ireland: 1641: Contexts and Reactions* (Manchester: Manchester University Press, 2013), 176–96.

6 P.H. Wilson, *Europe's Tragedy. A History of the Thirty Years War* (London: Penguin, 2010), 790; P. Roberts, 'Peace, ritual, and sexual violence during the religious wars', *Past & Present* 214, (suppl 7) (2012), 75–99; Broomhall, 'Reasons and Identities to Remember', 15.

7 L. Racaut, *Hatred in Print: Catholic Propaganda and Protestant Identity during the French Wars of Religion* (Farnham: Ashgate, 2002); P. Benedict, *Graphic History: The Wars, Massacres and Troubles of Tortorel and Perrissin* (Geneva: Droz, 2007); E. Herdman, 'Theatricality and obscenity in graphic histories of the wars of religion', *Early Modern France* 14 (2010), 91–113.

8 J. van der Steen, *Memory Wars in the Low Countries, 1566–1700* (Leiden: Brill, 2015); J. Theibault, 'The rhetoric of death and destruction in the Thirty Years War', *Journal of Social History* 27, 2 (1993), 271–90; H. Medick, 'The Thirty Years War as Experience and Memory: Contemporary Perceptions of a Macro-Historical Event', in L. Tatlock (ed.), *Enduring Loss in Early Modern Germany: Cross Disciplinary Perspectives* (Leiden: Brill, 2010), 25–49; D. Lederer, 'The myth of the all-destructive war: Afterthoughts on German suffering, 1618–1648', *German History* 29, 3 (2011), 380–403.

9 B.S. Gregory, *Salvation at Stake: Christian Martyrdom in Early Modern Europe* (Cambridge, MA.: Harvard University Press, 1999)

10 B. Roeck, 'The Atrocities of War in Early Modern Art', in J. Canning, H. Lehmann and J. Winter (eds), *Power, Violence and Mass Death in Pre-Modern and Modern Times* (Aldershot: Ashgate, 2004), 129–40; B. Sandberg, '"To Have the Pleasure of This Siege": Envisioning Siege Warfare During the European Wars of Religion', in A. Terry-Fritsch and E.F. Labbie (eds), *Beholding Violence in Medieval and Early Modern Europe* (Farnham: Ashgate, 2012), 143–62.

11 Kuijpers, 'Expressions of Fear, Counting the Loss: Managing Emotions in War Chronicles in the Netherlands (1568–1648)', in J. Spinks and C. Zika (eds), *Disaster, Death and the Emotions in the Shadow of the Apocalypse, 1400–1700* (Basingstoke: Palgrave Macmillan, 2016)

12 C. van der Haven, 'Patriotism and bellicism in German and Dutch epics of the Enlightenment', *Arcadia: Zeitschrift Für Vergleichende Literaturwissenschaft*, 47, 1 (2012), 54–78; M.A. Favret, *War at a Distance: Romanticism and the Making of Modern Wartime* (Princeton: Princeton University Press, 2010); P. Shaw, *Suffering and Sentiment in Romantic Military Art* (Farnham: Ashgate, 2013)

13 G. Lefebvre, *The Great Fear of 1789: Rural Panic in Revolutionary France*, (trans.) J.A. White (Princeton: Princeton University Press, 2014); L. James, *Witnessing the Revolutionary and Napoleonic Wars in German Central Europe* (Basingstoke: Palgrave, 2013)

IV.9 Plague

Gordon D. Raeburn

The emotions related to the plague have been little studied to date, although there has been a certain interest from the perspective of art history. This does not mean that the subject has been ignored entirely, however. Samuel K. Cohn, Jr. has touched upon emotions in recent work on the plague, and my own current research deals with emotional reactions to the plague in the early modern period.

The plague was a common occurrence in early modern Europe, unsurprisingly spreading fear, terror and panic whenever and wherever outbreaks occurred. People attempted to isolate themselves, both individually and communally, from the effects and spread of the disease. Villages, towns and cities closed themselves off from their neighbours. Travel and trade were tightly controlled, with the threat of violence and death for those who transgressed the measures taken against the spread of the plague.

On occasion national borders were closed in often unsuccessful attempts to spare the nation as a whole from the ravages of plague.[1] Such a desire was often heightened by the fact that throughout Europe foreigners were sometimes suspected of intentionally spreading the plague across international borders. Whilst many tried to prevent the plague from coming to them, others took another approach, with fear leading them to flee from outbreaks to areas perceived to be safe – predominantly in the countryside – away from denser populations. In Scotland in 1584, the young James VI (1566–1625) fled to his castle at Stirling from rumours of plague at Perth, leaving his servants behind for fear that they may have been infected.[2] Across Europe those who were unfortunate enough to contract the plague were removed from the towns and cities to camps on the outskirts in order to prevent the further contamination of the area. On occasion the normal methods of burial had to be abandoned in favour of mass graves, as the sheer numbers of the dead, coupled with the ever-present fear of infection, overwhelmed the usual processes and locations for the disposal of the dead, who were frequently buried where they had died. Humans, however, were not the only perceived vector for plague; animals too were considered a threat. Popular culture now presents rats as being the most feared animal in early modern plague outbreaks, but in reality cats and dogs were also blamed for the spread of the disease, and as a result were frequently massacred, with examples from Scotland, England, the Netherlands, Italy and Spain. In Sweden stray pigs were to be killed.

Clearly the presence of plague throughout Europe provoked strong emotional reactions in the populace. Fear was a very understandable reaction. Théodore Beza (1519–1605), the French reformer and successor to Jean Calvin (1509–64) in Geneva, believed that fear of the plague and a desire to flee was an eminently sensible reaction, and that those who chose such a route were not to be judged harshly. Indeed, during an outbreak of plague in Geneva in 1543 Calvin himself refused to attend to the infected, viewing himself as indispensable to the city and the Church. Only Sebastian Castellio (1515–63) undertook such duties in the city.[3] But this fear on occasion led to isolationism, the oppression of the poor and vagrant, and violence, both spontaneous and institutionalized. All of these were, of course, everyday occurrences in the early modern period, but during plague they were heightened. It is certainly unlikely that either Calvin or Beza, despite their personal attitudes towards the plague, would have approved of the Kirk Session in Carnock, Perthshire, which attempted to prevent all strangers from entering the church during an outbreak in 1645.[4] In addition to fear, grief and anger were also common reactions to the spread of plague. Communities always mourn their dead, but in times of plague, when the dead were being buried in the aforementioned plague pits, emotional reactions to death could be stronger. Protestant teaching emphasized that the manner of burial had no impact upon the soul's ultimate destination, but to the community at large such a burial could indicate the loss of communal identity, as the ownership of death is central to such notions. And fear and grief frequently resulted in anger, with violent protests against those seen as harbouring the infected, or having introduced the plague into previously clean locations. Indeed, protests and riots were seen throughout the period and the continent, from Edinburgh to Moscow.

Yet emotions such as these were not only the result of the plague. It was also believed that the plague was itself a product of excessive emotions, and that these emotions could also affect the outcome and duration of the sickness. Perhaps surprisingly it was not just emotions perceived as negative that could be the cause of plague or could affect its outcome. A doctor in Piedmont, Italy, claimed that those who were excessively happy were far more likely to die from the plague than those who were overly sad. He believed that the humours were overheated by too much laughter.[5] Against this, however, others believed that it was those of melancholic humour who would take longer to heal, if they survived at all.[6] It would appear that unrestrained emotions of any variety had the potential to induce or incubate the plague.

The ultimate source of the plague, however, was believed to have been the wrath and punishment of God inflicted upon a world of sinners.[7] The only methods by which God's wrath could be appeased were prayer, fasting and repentance. Of course, such actions could be and occasionally were performed on behalf of others, such as national calls for fasting in Scotland in the 1620s through to the 1660s on behalf of England, when England was suffering from plague, yet Scotland was not. These were clearly emotional appeals to God for forgiveness from those not afflicted on behalf of fellow Christians who were; national boundaries were not always obstacles to sentiment and compassion. The issue of whether or not God's reaction to the sinfulness of the world was emotional is best left for another discussion, but it is clear that this led to emotional reactions to plague in countries and communities throughout Europe, ranging from fear and resulting attempts at isolationism to compassionate calls to God on behalf of the afflicted of other countries.

In terms of the engagement of the history of the emotions with the study of early modern plagues we are presently at somewhat of a turning point, with several studies, including my own, currently being undertaken. As such, there is still scope for further work, and such studies may investigate, for instance, the impact of various emotions upon the persecution of specific groups or individuals, or possibly a study of the effect of the more 'positive' emotions used to combat the infection as a counterpoint to the more prevalent work on the 'negative' emotions surrounding the plague.

Further reading

Alberti, F. Bound (ed.), *Medicine, Emotion and Disease, 1700–1950* (Basingstoke: Palgrave Macmillan, 2006)

—brings together historians of the emotions with historians of medicine to produce a useful collection of essays relating to emotions and disease more broadly in the early modern period and beyond.

Cohn, Jr., S.K., *Cultures of Plague: Medical Thinking at the End of the Renaissance* (Oxford: Oxford University Press, 2010)

—touches upon the impact of the plague upon emotions, and the impact of emotions upon the plague and is a valuable entry point into the subject.

Notes

1 See, for example, the 1644 order to close the border to travellers into Scotland during the outbreak of plague in the north of England. See National Records of Scotland (NRS), PA7/3/87. Similarly, in the mid- to late-sixteenth century ships from Gdansk were forbidden from entering ports in Scotland and Northern England. See *Extracts from the Records of the Burgh of Edinburgh*, vol. 3 (Edinburgh: Printed for the Scottish Burgh Records Society, 1875), 181–2, 263.

2 R. Chambers (ed.), *Domestic Annals of Scotland, from the Reformation to the Revolution*, vol. 1 (Edinburgh: W. & R. Chambers, 1858), 155.

3 T. Beza, *A Learned Treatise of the Plague: Wherein, the two Questions: Whether the Plague be Infectious, or no: And Whether, and how farr it may be shunned of Christians, by going aside? are resolved* (London, 1665), 11, 17–18, 19; S. Zweig, *The Right to Heresy: Calvin against Castellio*, (trans.) E. and C. Paul (London: Cassell, 1951), 234.

4 D. Beveridge, *Culross and Tulliallan, or Perthshire on Forth*, vol. 1 (Edinburgh: William Blackwood and Sons, 1885), 210.

5 S.K. Cohn, Jr., *Cultures of Plague: Medical Thinking at the End of the Renaissance* (Oxford: Oxford University Press, 2010), 268.

6 James I, *Medicines Against the Pest, or an Advice Set Down by The Best Learned Physick within the Kingdome of England* (Edinburgh, 1645), 17.

7 G. Skeyne, *Ane Breve Descriptiovn of the Pest Qvhairin the Cavsis, Signis and sum speciall preseruatioun and cure thairof ar contenit* (Edinburgh, 1568), sig. A.2r.

IV.10 Domestic violence

Raisa Maria Toivo

Domestic violence breaks the most fundamental emotional expectations that exist. At the same time, domestic violence forces other emotions in the place of the expected and accepted ones. Therefore it should not be surprising that the history of at least some forms of domestic violence – spousal violence and violence towards children or even infanticide – has been among the first fields of history where emotions is by now established as a useful conceptual tool. On these topics, there is enough scholarship to form a common platform for historical discussion. On other areas of domestic violence, there is less work, and, for example elderly abuse or parent abuse are only currently gaining a place in the field.

It is the starting point of this collection that emotions change in time, place and culture. What is meant by 'domestic', 'family' and 'household' change as well, together with the concept of violence. In the early modern period, 'domestic', 'family' and 'household' comprised more than the modern nuclear family, even in north-western Europe where the nuclear family has traditionally been considered the main form of household. Even in these areas, some households would include grandparents, or unmarried and sometimes married aunts or uncles living in a semi-dependent position, and many households included also servants and other workforce, apprentices and journeymen. These people stood on various steps of overlapping hierarchical ladders, and this influenced what was considered as violence or legitimate discipline or even affection between them.

According to scholars such as Katie Barclay or Joanne Begiato (Bailey), early modern domestic violence was understood in the conflicting context of prescribed ideal emotional relationships – all the more important because domestic relationships between household or family members were presented as the mirror of all relationships in society – and accepted hierarchical violence in patriarchal society where the duty of husbands, parents, masters and mistresses to discipline their wives, children and workforce respectively was a part of love understood as a mutual obligation to protect and discipline or obey and honour.

The legally- and religiously-backed cultural expectations across Europe that love was expressed through patriarchal discipline can be thought of as forming an emotional regime, where a degree of violence was accepted and even expected in order to uphold masculine and family or kin honour. As long as violence stayed within accepted boundaries and relationships, it could be tolerated, if not accepted. However, as explained by Philip Grace, the need for discipline already meant that the ideal of education through love and good example had failed. Disciplinary violence against wives, children and servants could be an extreme attempt at enforcing the emotional regime and the need to share certain values and expressions. When violence could not be legitimized – when it was considered excessive and caused permanent damage or when it went against the hierarchy of the family or household structure – it clarified where emotional expectations or ways of expressing emotion were no longer shared.

On the other hand, violence by adult children towards (elderly) parents, by wives against husbands and by servants against masters was, in the early modern emotional regime, met only with negative connotations. This was a crime that went against all social and emotional hierarchies and, through contemporary analogies between the household and the political realm or the divine order, it was also a crime against the King, God and social order.

Various studies on British skimmington or charivaris and other shaming rituals for husbands who allowed themselves to be beaten by their wives together with emerging studies by Raisa Maria Toivo or Jonas Liliequist on parent abuse in the northern Europe that reveal how parental provocation and bad parenting were referred to as mitigating circumstances in court trials for parent abuse, show how blaming the victim enters the picture on the level of more informal emotional communities such as households, neighbour groups and courts of law.[1] Studying the emotions surrounding this kind of violence may help us better understand victimization even today. These studies also point out how qualified the early modern theoretical patriarchal authority really was, and how, on the emotional level, authority had to be earned and legitimized. The smaller emotional communities of households, villages and kin groups have been, in various studies, shown to have met domestic violence with more fluid values and more situational expectations than the theoretical ideals of each society suggested.

When early modern violence or related emotional cultures are studied, it is usually much easier to approach these from the point of view of severe (often lethal) physical violence. The source material on less grave physical violence is more sporadic, and the material on emotional violence and negligence can be difficult to find although it does exist in, for example, some ego-documents, diaries and letters. Negligence, a form of emotional violence towards children can sometimes be discerned in, for example, Swedish court records, where parents are sometimes reprimanded for not taking care of the upbringing, education and discipline of their children, and in some cases even ordered to spank their children in the presence of a court official.[2] Such a court order was a rare intervention in the patriarchal power within the family, and points to the need to find a way to correct and uphold domestic hierarchy.

Research on emotional and domestic violence faces problems of conceptualization. Domestic violence is a phenomenon which many people find difficult to pinpoint today. If conceptualizing violence was, in the early modern period, different from today, naming the related emotions was even more difficult. Court records in particular often discuss events and actions rather bluntly, hoping to distance rather than engage or transport emotion. Emotive cues have to be read from actions and performances rather than vocabulary used. Moreover, early modern people may have lacked words to describe the conflicting and confused emotions involved in domestic violence in an even greater degree than do people today. To compensate for this, fantasy narratives of supernatural attacks, witchcraft, elves or demonic possession turning some violent and making others suffer inexplicable pain may have served to describe what could not otherwise be described or even fully believed. Attacks by witches often describe pressing or choking as well as magical ammunition. In a Finnish household from 1693, for example, a dying young man testified that his brother-in-law was magically choking him. Later on, it was testified against the same brother-in-law that he frequently fought with his sister-in-law, and he was formally charged with having hit and kicked his parents-in-law, all living in the same household. The events were certainly connected, and once conceptually pinpointed, the man was described as violent towards all household members, except for his wife and children. There is no way of telling if this was because he was not violent towards his nuclear family, or if violence towards his own wife and children was thought of as legitimate or at least outside the public interest of court records. The fear and anxiety caused by domestic violence could also be expressed in physical pain and ailment, understood as effects of witchcraft or other supernatural influence.[3]

Historians of emotion have used contexts of domestic violence and vice versa to the extent that we have a steady starting point from which to look at the conflicting emotions related to patriarchal concepts of love-as-duty, masculine honour and authority in early modern culture and society. Nevertheless, even these topics are far from exhausted: there is need for more comparison and nuance. Moreover, forms of domestic violence other than spousal violence or disciplinary violence are less studied in general and in terms of emotions. The emotions-approach to these may open up new avenues of thinking about the connection of masculinity, authority and honour, as well as the community boundaries and limits of shared emotional codes and expectations.

Further reading

Bailey, J., *Unquiet Lives. Marriage and Marriage Breakdown in England, 1660–1800* (Cambridge: Cambridge University Press, 2003)

—presents a good starting point for studying the history of spousal violence.

Barclay, K., *Love, Intimacy and Power: Marriage and Patriarchy in Scotland, 1650–1850* (Manchester: Manchester University Press 2011)

—investigation of emotional correspondence and rhetoric in marriage that opens up emotional codes and expectations in spousal violence.

Grace, P., *Affectionate Authorities: Fathers and Fatherly Roles in Late Medieval Basel* (Aldershot: Ashgate, 2015)

—Grace's recent work includes a discussion of discipline as fatherly, patriarchal love.

Notes

1 R. Toivo, 'Parent-abuse in early modern Finland: structures and emotions', *Journal of Family History* 41, 3 (2016), 255–70; J. Liliequist, '"The Child Who Strikes His Own Father or Mother Shall Be Put to Death": Assault and Verbal Abuse of Parents in Swedish and Finnish Counties 1745–1754', in O. Matikainen and S. Lidman (eds), *Morality, Crime and Social Control in Europe 1500–1900* (Helsinki: Finnish Literature Society, 2014), 19–42.

2 S. Katajala-Peltomaa and R. Toivo, 'Tila ja hoivan käytänteet keskiajalla ja uuden ajan alussa', *Historiallinen aikakauskirja* 108, 1 (2010), 15–28.

3 R. Toivo, 'Parent-abuse in early modern Finland'.

Life stages

IV.11 Pregnancy and childbirth

Joanne Begiato (Bailey)

Pregnancy and childbirth stirred powerful emotions in parents, families and communities in a period of high infant mortality. It is thus surprising that such emotions have been neglected by historians investigating these common experiences. This entry therefore assesses existing scholarship with emotions in mind to suggest new avenues for research and draws on my own research on the emotions surrounding Georgian parenting and pregnancy.[1] The most dominant individual and familial feelings were apprehension, fear and pain, hope, joy and gratitude. For much of the period medical intervention was limited to difficult births, but by the later eighteenth century medical practitioners were taking over elite women's childbirth from midwives in Britain. This changed landscape of birth created cultural anxieties about man-midwives as sexual predators, since their role meant they touched women's sexual organs.[2] All these feelings shaped perception and experience, and exploring pregnancy and childbirth through the lens of emotions thus offers new insights into their history.

Medical practitioners used the mother's emotional state to aid understandings of conception, pregnancy and birth, and as a way of gathering information about the invisible unborn child. For them, maternal emotions were active agents in the health of the foetus because, as Ulinka Rublack observes, they envisaged that external experiences transformed into inner experiences that affected mother and child.[3] For example, although explanations for the woman's role in conception differed, most medical writers argued that mothers influenced the growth of the embryo 'through their nutrition, actions, and emotions' during pregnancy and birth.[4] In seventeenth-century Germany, Christophe Volter considered that a foetus could be damaged by a mother's violent laughter, along with vigorous activities or excessive eating. In the eighteenth century Denis Diderot (1713–84) explained that parents' state of mind at conception determined the well-being of the child.[5] Maternal feelings could be deadly. In early modern Germany, it was not only foetal problems or accidents that resulted in miscarriage, but also shock or withheld anger. François Mauriceau (1637–1709), a French surgeon man-midwife, noted in his 1688 treatise that extreme fits of anger could provoke a miscarriage.[6]

Mothers' emotions and thoughts were also understood to negatively impact upon the development of the unborn foetus. The determining factor was maternal imagination, whereby a pregnant woman's thoughts or encounters with various phenomena would mould the embryo; providing an explanation for birth defects. In many instances emotions were conceptualized as the bridge between the immaterial thought and the material damage upon the foetus.[7] Typically it was fear, disgust or surprise that caused the damaging thoughts. In 1659 a Stuttgart woman explained that her child was born with one foot and without genitals because on her way to market she had been severely shocked by seeing a lame beggar. In late fifteenth-century Nuremberg the town council issued an ordinance instructing beggars to hide their malformed limbs to protect pregnant women and their offspring.[8]

Some societies understood maternal emotions as facilitating or hindering birth. In 1657, following three still-births, the wife of a Neckarhausen marksman was imprisoned for 10 days and fined. Evidence brought against her included that during labour she sat '"stiff as a stick", as if the birth did not matter to her'.[9] Her lack of obvious feelings was considered suspicious, a view informed by both religion and understandings of the body. As inheritors of Eve's curse, women were expected to travail through the pain of childbirth where suffering facilitated the child's safe delivery. Women who did not conform could be considered ungodly, killers or possessed by the Devil. In medical terms, stagnant or suppressed emotions, blocked perhaps by envy or hatred, were a 'clog' that hindered successful labour and birth. Again anger was particularly dangerous for pregnant women. It was understood to either cause the blood to flow rapidly, causing convulsions, or to reduce its flow leading to a 'clog' where the accumulated blood, it was feared, would endanger the foetus. In early modern Germany, for example, it was considered that anger would cause a hot flow of blood which would damage the embryo's cells, in contrast to shock which would starve the foetus because it directed blood away from it.[10]

Fear and pain were intimate features of childbirth given the risk of maternal and infant damage and mortality.[11] Religious faith was thus bound up with mitigating the dread and suffering of labour and delivery. Judith Aikin demonstrates that devotional texts and prayers were produced by male theologians and pastors for women to utter in early modern Lutheran Germany. These associated mothers' suffering with their sex's punishment for Eve's transgression. Although maternal suffering was seen as part of God's plan, the message of divine chastisement could augment women's fear. Some devotional texts were less punitive. The handbook for pregnant women (1683) written by Aemilie Juliane, the Countess of Schwarzburg-Rudolstadt (1637–1706), for example, included prayers in which God delivered pregnant women from 'fear, terror, anxiety, and suffering' rather than punishing them.[12] These negative emotions could even offer personal agency to mothers. Seventeenth-century providential thinking linked danger to deliverance and thus for women such as Alice Thornton (*c.* 1626–1707), an English gentlewoman, the fear of pain was re-conceptualized as a test of faith. In enduring, Thornton envisaged her emergence from labour as proof of her virtue and purity.[13]

The emotional aspects of pregnancy and childbirth were not unremittingly negative. Analysing the emotions discussed in family correspondence in relation to pregnancy reveals a focus on anticipation and apprehension, with repeated combinations of words about the passage of time and physical change. For example, the discussion of size could be an acceptable way for mothers to express and share the anxiety of pregnancy. Bessy Ramsden referred to both size and timing in the 1770s: 'I am at a loss to say when to expect the fatal moment . . . I am such a monster in size; and indeed I am under great apprehensions I shall drop to pieces before I am ready for the little stranger'.[14] Thus the metaphor of weight conveyed physical and emotional oppression. This emotional vocabulary built bonds between spouses and between them and family members, bridging the difficult transitions from one phase of life to another, and helping neutralize the fear of the arrival of an unseen 'stranger'.[15] Women also used the various emotions associated with pregnancy and birth to construct female authority and make demands or challenge patriarchal authority. For example, the correspondence of Catherine de Medici (1519–89) with the Spanish court about her daughter Elisabeth de Valois (1545–68), queen of Spain between 1559 and 1568, constructed her legitimate authority to direct her daughter's care during childbearing through knowledge of the intertwined health and emotional well-being of pregnancy and childbirth.[16]

It is misleading to see pregnancy and birth as wholly driven by emotions of apprehension, fear and anxiety. Gratitude and joy were also defining feelings for parents in print culture and life-writings. Aemilie Juliane's thanksgiving prayer for women to use during pregnancy declared: 'My heart is joyful in the Lord' at being blessed with a child.[17] Far more explicit research is needed on the role of emotions in pregnancy and childbirth, both from medical practitioners' perspectives and parents' experiences. It is clear that emotions were intrinsic to their handling, management, treatment and endurance. It is as yet unknown, however, how far changing interpretations of emotions as physiological and cognitive phenomena influenced medical understandings of pregnancy, miscarriage and labour, or the ways in which people expressed their feelings about them.

Further reading

Cody, L., *Birthing the Nation: Sex, Science, and the Conception of Eighteenth-Century Britons* (Oxford: Oxford University Press, 2005)

—while this history of midwifery does not take an emotions approach, it offers insights into the relationship between identities, scientific knowledge and emotions.

Evans, J., and C. Meehan (eds), *Perceptions of Pregnancy from the 17th Century to the 20th Century* (Basingstoke: Palgrave, 2016)

—offers novel interdisciplinary insights into changing understandings and experiences of pregnancy and birth and thus allows some consideration of the role emotions can play in their investigation.

Notes

1 J. Bailey, *Parenting in England 1760–1830: Emotions, Identities, and Generation* (Oxford, Oxford University Press, 2012); J. Begiato (Bailey), 'Breeding a "little stranger": Managing Uncertainty in Pregnancy in Later Georgian England', in J. Evans and C. Meehan (eds), *Perceptions of Pregnancy from the 17th Century to the 20th Century* (Basingstoke: Palgrave, 2016)

2 A. Wilson, *The Making of Man Midwifery* (London: University College Press, 1995)

3 U. Rublack, 'Pregnancy, childbirth and the female body in early modern Germany', *Past & Present* 150, 1 (1996), 86.

4 L. McTavish, 'Reproduction, *c.* 1500–1700', in S. Toulalan and K. Fisher (eds), *The Routledge History of Sex and the Body 1500 to the Present* (Abingdon: Routledge, 2013), 362.

5 Rublack, 'Pregnancy, childbirth', 95; M. Terrall, 'Maternal Impressions: Conception, Sensibility, and Inheritance', in Terrall and H. Deutsch (eds), *Vital Matters: Eighteenth-Century Views of Conception, Life and Death* (Toronto: University of Toronto Press, 2012), 110.

6 Rublack, 'Pregnancy, childbirth', 86; McTavish, 'Reproduction', 355.

7 McTavish, 'Reproduction', 362; Terrall, 'Maternal Impressions', 112.

8 Rublack, 'Pregnancy, childbirth', 95, 96.

9 Ibid., 91.

10 Ibid., 91–4.

11 S. Howard, 'Imagining the pain and peril of seventeenth-century childbirth: travail and deliverance in the making of an early modern world', *Social History of Medicine* 16, 3 (2003), 367–82.

12 J. Aikin, 'Gendered theologies of childbirth in early modern Germany and the devotional handbook for pregnant women by Aemilie Juliane, Countess of Schwarzburg-Rudolstadt (1683)', *Journal of Women's History* 15, 2 (2003), 51.

13 Howard, 'Imagining the pain and peril of seventeenth-century childbirth', 367, 370, 377.

14 A. Vickery, *The Gentleman's Daughter: Women's Lives in Georgian England* (New Haven: Yale University Press, 1998), 100.

15 Begiato (Bailey), 'Breeding a "little stranger"'.

16 S. Broomhall, '"Women's little secrets": defining the boundaries of reproductive knowledge in sixteenth-century France', *Social History of Medicine* 15, 1 (2002), 1–15.

17 Aikin, 'Gendered theologies of childbirth', 52.

IV.12 Childhood

Claudia Jarzebowski

When it comes to children, emotions are not too far away. This insight, however, requires careful historicization of how views on childhood and emotions are interrelated in early modern history.[1] Until recently, the history of childhood has been written as a history of on-going improvement, simply assigning abuse, poverty and emotional neglect to premodernity. During the last two decades, however, historians of all epochs have contested these assumptions. Early modern historians play a key role in this shift of paradigms since their sources regarding children allow for a new perception of children in history in general.

The history of childhood commenced with a study by French historian Philippe Ariès.[2] He made two major claims. First, the Renaissance was to be seen as the fundamental precondition to nurture a formerly unknown notion of childhood as a valuable and distinct phase in one's life. According to Ariès, this notion gained more and more attention in scholarly discourse across Europe and eventually merged with eighteenth-century approaches that declared children as raw material shaped by socialization and education. The invention of pedagogy was emblematically displayed in the influential book by Jean-Jacques Rousseau (1712–78) about the coming-of-age of a boy, *Emile* (1762). Second, Ariès coined the now-famous term 'little adults' as a synonym for early modern children – implying that children would come to their parents' mind only after they had reached the age of reason and could be assigned work and household duties. This, however, has led a whole branch of scholarship to assume that children had been neglected in general.

Alongside Ariès' basic layout, scholars of all kinds began to develop their own 'histories of childhood', upholding a picture of history as a reservoir of child abuse and emotional neglect.[3] It is important to understand that this was neither Ariès' intention nor do his sources allow for statements such as Lloyd DeMause's contention that the further we go back in history, the more abusive to children were societies. As one can see, emotions and emotional neglect of children, in regard to the centuries of premodernity, are a basic assumption in this view.

Why were these assumptions so successful? Whereas psychologists-turned-historians such as DeMause left out any primary source studies, historians such as Edward Shorter presented research regarding infant mortality and nursing in south-western France as indicators of emotional neglect.[4] In both respects, argued Shorter, early modern children were clearly disadvantaged compared to modern children of the Western world. The high infant mortality caused parents to contain themselves from emotional bonding to their newborns and babies until they had survived infancy and reached a somewhat more secure age of about five to seven years. As a strong sign of emotional neglect Shorter took the random finding that a significant number of mothers in early modern France had their children nursed by alien wet nurses. Shorter (and those who followed his arguments) assumed that, according to modern habits, these mothers in the past gave their children away because they did not feel attached to them and would never feel attached to them since so many died during their early infant years. Shorter's interpretation of his solidly executed research was predominantly based on 1970s assumptions about the newly re-acquired value of breastfeeding. It lacks, however, historical contextualization. Why should early modern mothers not love their wet-nursed children? Interpretation changes as we look at the situation through the lens of early modern societies.

As we now know, wet nurses came to children's homes much of the time and stayed with families as a live-in-nurse. Wet-nursed children were therefore not given away. In addition, if we take into account scholarly discourse on early child education, conducted by theologians such as Desiderius Erasmus (*c.* 1466–1536), we learn that wet nurses were considered as sober-minded as the milk they provided was considered pure and healthy. To engage a wet nurse can thus be perceived as a sign of special care rather than of emotional neglect.[5] Medical opinions were deeply supportive of this view.[6] Maternal milk was suspected to be solidly impure until about eight weeks after a woman had given birth, since blood, milk and semen (male and female) were widely considered to be simply different compounds of the same fluid.[7] Ideally, however, the milk given to a child contained no traces of blood (or semen, whose occurrence in the milk shortly after a baby's delivery was less probable). So turning to a wet nurse in order to provide one's child with pure and healthy milk and thus increase its chances to survive made absolute sense to the people in early modern history. So, within 20 years of scholarship, wet-nursing had shifted from being an indicator of emotional neglect to being an expression of parental care and bonding. The history of childhood has since seized emotions as a genuine topic of interest.

The task deriving from this fundamental shift in perceiving childhood and children in history is to flesh out the broader argument with primary sources. But rather than finding new sources, it has proved most productive to re-read the sources at hand. Funeral sermons for children, for example, have long been viewed as an example of texts lacking emotions because they were allegedly very similar, displaying no individual child or mourning. It is, however, a modern expectation to have parents mourn excessively over the death of their own child. Early modern emotional regimes instead demanded constraint and modesty. The emotions stirred by the death of one's child were not allowed to exceed the love to God one carried in one's heart. In other words, the death of a child was also perceived to be upsetting and devastating in the early modern period. Religion and the belief in God's will as righteous and all-knowing helped to overcome parental devastation and to accept what eventually would prove to be better for the child: life in heaven instead of on earth. After all, according to Protestant mourning manuals, God took what was His in the first place, since children were considered to be a loan from God, handed to worldly parents only to grow up but never wholly leaving their spiritual family.

Historians have discovered that children were subjected not only to parental love reverberating the love of God and fulfilling emotional norms, but also to severe legal and social violence. For example, children were subjected to the death penalty in early modern France, Switzerland and Germany. How does that fit into a picture of children being the gift of God's love to the world? The spiritual immunization of a newborn took place through baptism. Once a child was baptized it was considered to be safe, in Catholicism more than in Protestantism. Protestants were expected to believe in a child's goodness through its conception as an act of God's will. Parents of both confessions, however, did not rely on that rather intellectual approach and had their weak or even stillborn newborns baptized in their homes (emergency baptism) throughout the eighteenth century. This gap between Church officials and popular belief pertains to a basic ambiguity of a child. The child itself was supposed to overcome this ambiguity through faithful and modest behaviour.

Children who did not behave in this way, children who became for all kinds of reasons conspicuous in their communities, were likely to be perceived as a threat to social order. In times of deep crisis, such as during the Thirty Years War (1618–48), children were often orphaned, inclined to linger around in the streets, and cling to other people on the margin. With no homes and in neighbourhoods suffering from bad harvests and war, these children lost their hold and some of them became suspects of witchcraft. As such they were exposed to torture and at times also to death penalty. These children were considered to be evil, to have changed sides. In the eyes of State and Church officials and sometimes of their neighbours and family, too, they had irrevocably become the victims of Satan in the world. This strict handling, however, did not pass uncontested and can be assigned to specific patterns of crisis, in regard to region and time. Emotions such as fear play a key role in this. Children could spark love as much as they could release fear.

And what about children's emotions? Only recently have historians attempted to retrace their emotional attitudes and feelings. One way to reconstruct children's emotions is to reconstruct the normative and social frames of emotional conduct. A second option asks historians to re-read sources such as court minutes recording children's voices creatively. A third way focuses on self-narratives such as memoirs or letters of parents who would take down memories of their children's behaviour, hopes and fears. However, these sources cannot be considered authentic but present us with a view of what children were supposed to feel or how children were supposed to express their emotions.[8] It can, however, no longer be doubted, that children had feelings, and were surrounded by emotions and different bonding practices.

The introduction of emotions to the history of childhood has steered historians' attention more to children as actors. Children come to the fore as subjects of history. This new focus enables us to understand their various, at times contradictory ways of perceiving and shaping their environment as a valuable addition to the history of emotions from the margins, as children have not been seen as subjects of history before they became graspable as emotional actors. This is inestimably important in order to conceptualize emotions as feelings and as modes of interaction.

Further reading

Dekker, R., *Childhood, Memory and Autobiography in Holland: From the Golden Age to Romanticism* (London: Macmillan, 2000)

—a leading piece in the field, taking on the intricate subject of how to re-voice children from their written legacies.

Maddern, P., 'How Children Were Supposed to Feel, How Children Felt. England, 1350–1530', in C. Jarzebowski and T.M. Safley (eds), *Childhood and Emotion across Cultures 1450–1800* (London: Routledge, 2014), 121–41.

—offers a far-sighted concept of how to relate children and emotions to each other by including normative attitudes as pathways into emotional practices, and establishes a long-lasting methodological paradigm new to the field.

Roper, L., '"Evil imaginings and fantasies": Child-witches and the end of the witch craze', *Past & Present* 167 (2000), 107–39.

—offers a well-reasoned explanation for this variant of the witch craze that deserves attention within the history of emotions in relation to psycho-historical approaches.

Notes

1 C. Jarzebowski and T.M. Safley, 'Introduction', in Jarzebowski and Safley (eds), *Childhood and Emotion across Cultures 1450–1800* (London: Routledge, 2014), 1–13.

2 P. Ariès, *L'enfant et la vie familiale sous l'ancien régime* (1962); *Centuries of Childhood: A Social History of Family*, (trans.) R. Baldick (New York: Vintage, 1962)

3 L. DeMause, *The History of Childhood* (New York: Psychohistory Press, 1974), 1–73.

4 E. Shorter, *The Making of the Modern Family* (New York: Basic Books, 1975)

5 Erasmus, 'De pueris statim ac liberaliter instituendis declamatio' (1529), in *Opera omnia Desiderii Erasmi Roterodami: recognita et adnotatione critica instructa notisque illustrata*, (eds) F. Akkerman, G.J.M. Bartelink, J. Bloemendal, J. Domański, C.L. Heesakkers, H.J. de Jonge, M.L. van Poll-van de Lisdonk, J. Trapman, vol. 1, no. 2 (Amsterdam: North-Holland, 1971), 21–78.

6 I.K. Ben-Amos, 'Reciprocal bonding: parents and their offspring in early modern England', *Journal of Family History* 25, 3 (2000), 291–312.

7 T. Phaire, *The Boke of Chyldren* (1544/5), (eds) A.V. Neale and H.R.E. Wallis (London: E. & S. Livingston Ltd., 1955)

8 P. Maddern, 'How Children Were Supposed to Feel, How Children Felt. England, 1350–1530', in Jarzebowski and Safley (eds), *Childhood and Emotion,* 121–41.

IV.13 Marriage

Katie Barclay

Across the early modern period in Europe, marriage held particular social significance and as a result, it has been a topic of particular interest for scholars. Moreover, from the outset, the history of marriage has been inseparable from the history of emotions. The act of getting married was understood to signal a key shift in identity. For many, and particularly in Reformed Europe, it was a central point in the making of adulthood. The marriage ceremony marked the point that individuals left behind their youth and was a ritual that incorporated them as full members of their local community. In some contexts, it was a precondition for entry into other social and political roles.

In many parts of Western Europe, it signalled the creation of a new household or the transfer of property from one generation to the next. In early modern Pre-Reformation and Catholic Europe, marriage was a sacrament that enabled the sanctification and moral perfection of Christians, partly by protecting them from the sin of sexual immorality. Yet, whilst losing its sacramental quality, even in Reformed Europe marriage was vested with particular social importance, as a contract whose terms were determined not by man but by God. As a result, many parts of Europe, both Catholic and Protestant, placed limits on its dissolution. After the Council of Trent (1545–63), the Catholic Church confirmed the indissolubility of marriage, while a number of Protestant states affirmed the right to divorce and remarry within their laws as a marker of their alternative reading of its sacramental qualities.

That emotion played an important role within marriage has long been recognized by modern historians, for whom marriage cannot be divested from its relationship with 'love'. Within the contemporary West, the right to marry *for* love has been deeply implicated in constructions of freedom and individual rights. In much of the early historiography of the 1960s and 1970s, that many early modern people (like those today) weighed love as only one amongst a number of important motivations for marriage meant that their marriages were viewed as 'low affect' and people's investments in individual members of their family (as opposed to 'the family' as a supra-organization) was relatively low. This was explained by historians as being caused both by a high mortality rate, that made emotional investments in people psychologically challenging, and by the 'harsh conditions of life' that required early modern people to prioritize pragmatic, economic decision-making over affective connections.

Historians such as Lawrence Stone and Edward Shorter recognized that love was an important cultural concept within early modern society, as evidenced by its important role in literature and art, but thought that it played a relatively small role in people's private lives.[1] Moreover, because love was closely tied to ideas of democratic freedom and equality, many early historians of marriage felt that inequality within marriage (notably the patriarchal model provided by all the mainstream early modern churches) was incompatible with love, with love becoming a dynamic force for neutralizing imbalances of power. For historians in this historiographical tradition, it was not until the eighteenth century, or for some even later with industrialization, that economic conditions and changing cultural values provided the opportunity for individuals to prioritize love in their marital relationships, an opportunity that also transformed the nature of the power relationship between husband and wife.

Almost from the outset, an alternative historiography developed challenging ideas around the 'low affect' family by providing ample evidence of people's emotional commitments to their families found in a rich body of letters, diaries and similar 'narratives of the self'.[2] Rather than focusing on declarations of love, however, much of this evidence was built on displays of grief at the death of loved ones, with historians assuming that grief and love were closely related. During this period, feminist historians also challenged the idea that love neutralized patriarchal power, noting that even in the present day love had not reduced inequalities of power between men and women within marriage.[3] They made the important observation that even violent relationships could be 'loving', allowing for a rethinking of the role violence played within the family. The challenge to rethink the relationship between love and power also led to a growth in work on sexual jealousy and expressions of anger within marriage.

As this suggests, the role of emotions within marriage was a lively field before new methodologies from the history of emotions were applied to the topic. Yet the history of marriage has been transformed and invigorated by the new scholarship on emotion. First, new work on the relationship between emotions and patriarchal power not only demonstrated that love and inequality co-existed within marriage, but that love was a vital force in ensuring the operation and continuation of patriarchy.[4] Love and power worked together. Second, a consideration of the role of emotions in building communities and collectives has enabled a much more nuanced understanding of how the marriage ceremony invests people within their communities.[5] As early modern understandings of love and marriage had clear communal dimensions, emotional investments in a spouse also invested people in wider social structures; love (and other emotions) became a tool for enforcing social order.

Third, the range of emotions related to family life has opened up, with consideration not only given to love or sexual jealousy, but the complex emotional domain at play in human relationships.[6] The concept of 'intimacy' has been particularly fruitful as a framework for exploring how living closely together affects human interactions, power relationships and feeling. The relationship between the family and the economic has been re-evaluated, so that economic, or indeed any domain of, choices are no longer 'unemotional' to be situated alongside, but not part of, 'love'. This collapsing of categories has been incredibly fruitful in allowing marital relationships to be re-evaluated and rethought, whilst the role that emotion plays in maintaining, as well as destabilizing, power has enabled the feminist promise that 'the personal is political' to be evidenced and explored. Fourth, as historians have focused on what particular emotions mean and do, the way that the emotional relationship of marriage changes over time has come to the fore.[7] Marriage may have been a 'life stage', but it was one that could last for much of a person's life. A consideration of what love means has also required greater consideration to be given to the intersections of marriage with the age of the married parties, age of children of the relationship, stage in career, composition of the household and length of the marriage itself. That the flush of first love may not last is an old adage, but love could also become deeper, more intimate and more interesting over time; as could the many other emotions within marriage. Recognizing this has destabilized marriage as a 'stage' to a dynamic relationship between two or more people over time.

The overall outcome is that marriage is back on the historical agenda as a relationship that is key to understanding the nature of the early modern experience; no longer relegated to a single chapter in textbooks on the history of women, but now viewed as a domain that was vital not only to men and women but to understanding community and political life. As a result, there is plenty of work still to be done.

Further reading

Barclay, K., *Love, Intimacy and Power: Marriage and Patriarchy in Scotland, 1650–1850* (Manchester: Manchester University Press, 2011)

—the first monograph-length work to apply the new methodologies from the history of emotion to the field of marriage and is particularly significant for its re-articulation of patriarchal power in emotional relationships.

Reddy, W.M., *The Making of Romantic Love: Longing and Sexuality in Europe, South Asia, and Japan, 900–1200* (Chicago: Chicago University Press, 2012)

—Reddy's controversial claim that romantic love can be found across space and time centres this text at the heart of the debate on emotions in marriage.

Notes

1 L. Stone, *The Family, Sex and Marriage in England 1500–1800* (London: Weidenfeld and Nicolson, 1977); E. Shorter, *The Making of the Modern Family* (London: Collins, 1976); R. Trumbach, *The Rise of the Egalitarian Family* (Oxford: Academic Press, 1978)

2 K. Wrightson, *English Society 1580–1680* (London: Hutchison, 1982), 92.

3 B. Taylor, 'Feminists versus Gallants: Manners and Morals in Enlightenment Britain,' in S. Knott and Taylor (eds), *Women, Gender and Enlightenment* (Houndmills: Palgrave, 2005), 38.

4 K. Barclay, *Love, Intimacy and Power: Marriage and Patriarchy in Scotland, 1650–1850* (Manchester: Manchester University Press, 2011)

5 K. Barclay, 'Intimacy, Community and Power: Bedding Rituals in Eighteenth-Century Scotland', in M.L. Bailey and K. Barclay (eds), *Emotion, Ritual and Power in Europe, 1200–1920: Family, State and Church* (Houndmills: Palgrave, 2016); N. Eustace, '"The cornerstone of a copious work": love and power in eighteenth-century courtship', *Journal of Social History* 34, 3 (2001), 518–45.

6 R.K. Rittgers, 'Grief and consolation in early modern Lutheran devotion: the case of Johannes Christoph Oelhafen's *Pious Meditations on the most sorrowful bereavement* (1619)', *Church History* 81, 3 (2012), 601–30; C. Jarzebowski, 'The Meaning of Love: Emotion and Kinship in Sixteenth-Century Incest Discourses', in D. Luebke and M. Lindemann (eds), *Mixed Marriages: Transgressive Unions in Germany from the Reformation to the Enlightenment* (Oxford: Bergahn Books, 2014), 166–83.

7 Barclay, 'Intimacy and the life-cycle in the marital relationships of the Scottish elite during the long-eighteenth century', *Women's History Review* 20, 2 (2011), 189–206.

IV.14 Death

Peter Sherlock

In early modern Europe, death was understood as the separation of body from soul, an unavoidable crisis for individuals and communities. Described as the dissolution of the self, death brought earthly passions to an end, yet the moment of death was so powerful it was the ultimate metaphor for internal feeling, deployed in early modern descriptions of sexual climax. For the dead, the afterlife could be represented as an eternal emotional state, ranging from infernal torment to heavenly joy. Early modern responses to death and dying therefore constituted a rich resource of emotional languages. Scholarly treatments of death have focused on topics from the demography and topography of death to the impact of religious reformation on funerary ritual and beliefs about the afterlife, but only recently have they directly examined the emotions.

Two elements were critical to the emotions of death. First was the passion and death of Christ himself. Early modern Christians were exhorted to contemplate the passion of Christ to prevent temptation from the Devil and to maintain the right state of mind.[1] For Catholics, the five actions of the dying Christ on the cross provided a template for imitation on the deathbed, while for Protestants, following Martin Luther (1483–1546), the focus on the sufficiency of Christ's death required a response of sorrow for sin, gratitude for salvation and love of God and neighbour.[2]

Second was the ideal of the good death, promoted in extensive literature on the *ars moriendi*. This demanded life-long preparation for death, whether at home in one's old age, in sudden sickness, on the battlefield or at the martyr's stake, and necessitated formation of the correct emotional state. *Memento mori* such as the sixteenth-century Torre Abbey jewel assisted elite men and women to contemplate death (Figure IV.14.1). The idealization of the good death could cause anxiety, lest actual behaviour fell short of the desired outcome at the critical moment. Such anxiety was acutely felt by those who believed that the state of mind at the moment of death was a prime determinant of salvation. William Shakespeare (1564–1616) has Hamlet reveal this complex of emotions when he chooses not to murder his uncle on the grounds that he is at prayer and would therefore proceed directly to heaven if killed at that moment.[3]

For Protestants, the good death was characterized by the assurance of salvation won through divine mercy, an assurance which overcame the fear of judgement to eternal damnation on account of sin. Reformed Protestant experiences of death required the decedent to wrestle with and overcome the temptation to despair.[4] Early modern Protestants continually referred in sermons and deathbed accounts to the experience of despair in death, when Satan attacked the soul of the dying in its last

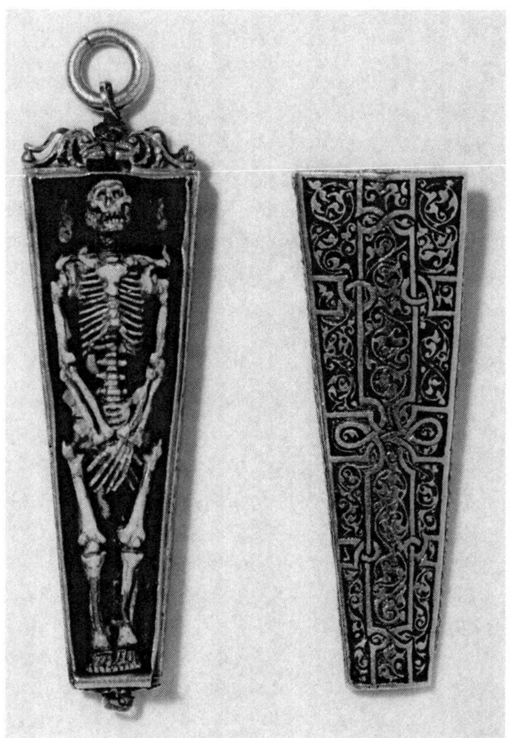

Figure IV.14.1 The Torre Abbey Jewel, *memento mori* pendant in the form of a skeleton in a coffin, enamelled gold, England, *c.* 1540–50.

moments, and the dying might echo Christ's cry on the cross, 'why have you forsaken me?' Despair could lead to doubt, exposing righteous faith as self-delusion. As John Donne (1572–1631) wrote in his *Holy Sonnets*:

Despaire behind, and death before doth cast
Such terrour, and my feeble flesh doth waste
By sinne in it, which t'wards hell doth weigh.[5]

The abhorrence of despair and its association with damnation was revealed nowhere more starkly than in the universal Christian condemnation of suicide. For Protestants, the only way to combat despair was through study of the scriptures and prayer, so that assurance would triumph. For Catholics, application of the sacraments provided the way at the critical moment. In both cases, lifelong preparation was demanded.

Paradoxically, Protestants also emphasized joy and hope as emotional responses to death. Craig Koslofsky has argued that these were critical aspects of Christian death rituals, used to order and guide the emotions of the living. Thus Luther could exclaim after the death of his daughter Magdalena (1529–42) that 'I am joyful in spirit but I am sad according to the flesh'.[6] Confident in his daughter's testimony concerning her justification, her premature death was not only the cause of grief but also a test of Luther's convictions about salvation as revealed in his *Sermon on Preparing to Die* (1519) which concludes with the injunction to thank God 'with great joy in our heart' for Christ's victory over death.[7]

For those who outlived the decedent, grief was predominant among the emotions, yet was problematized in early modern Europe. Ralph Houlbrooke describes English Protestant expressions of fellowship as one method to 'hold grief at bay', citing examples of the dying inviting their companions to join them in a final convivial drink or leaving money to provide a meal for the poor.[8] Such habits emphasized the significance of communal support to the good death, whether in the measured expression of grief or of solidarity in the face of breach. A good death also required the moderation of grief. On his deathbed, George Herbert (1593–1633) told his wife and nieces to cease weeping and take to prayer for 'nothing but their lamentations could make his death uncomfortable'.[9]

Humanist culture as developed in fifteenth-century Florence and spread across Europe praised the exercise of restraint in public rituals of mourning, containing emotion within strictly regulated ceremonial order to affirm the continuity of power and authority (Figure IV.14.2). For male statesmen at least, intimate expressions of grief and sorrow were to be reserved for the world of literary exchange.[10] Desiderius Erasmus (*c.* 1466–1536) promulgated the idea that grief, an unruly passion, should be curbed by stoic reason, in imitation of the ancients, and by the later sixteenth century the concept of melancholy as the subdued contemplation of death was widespread in elite culture.[11] Grief might find formal, enduring expression in epitaphs and elegies that imitated ancient examples but were also capable of incorporating early modern theology. Mourning was appropriate, provided it was not self-serving, and was meant to lead variously to reform of one's own life, prayers for the souls of the dead or tearful joy at the fate of the redeemed.[12]

A key methodological challenge for scholars of death is how to apprehend the emotional experience of dying, mediated as it is through records left by the living.

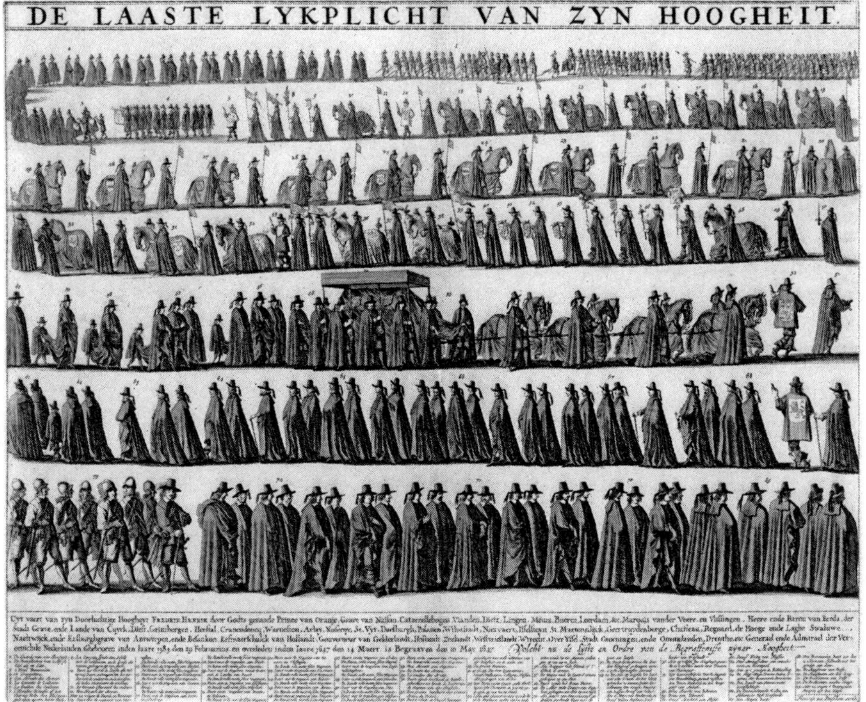

Figure IV.14.2 Funeral of Frederik Hendrik, Prince of Orange (1584–1647), 1647, anonymous, Francoys van Beusekom, 1647.

To overcome this, scholarly literature on death and early modern emotions has relied heavily on close reading and rhetorical analysis of three literary sources: treatises on the art of death, sermons on dying and accounts of deathbed experiences such as spiritual biographies or funeral sermons.

There is considerable scope to advance understanding of early modern emotional landscapes through use of the many other sources exploited in recent scholarship on death, including liturgical and dramatic texts, wills and testaments, monuments and other ecclesiastical furnishings, spaces associated with death such as hospitals and graveyards and visual arts. Rebecca McNamara and Una McIlvenna argue that emotional responses to death are historically and contextually specific. They call for more detailed, nuanced studies of death that take account of the emergence of new methodologies for the historical study of emotions.[13] This reflects the lack of attention to the actual emotional experience of death in early modern Europe, in contrast to extensive treatment of the literature on how emotions were meant to be managed. A key area for further study is how emotions were understood in relation to the afterlife in a time of profound religious change, not only to understand how changing beliefs could affect emotional expression, but also to investigate early modern conceptualizations of the emotional landscape of the afterlife itself.

Further reading

Houlbrooke, R., *Death, Religion, and the Family in England, 1480–1750* (Oxford: Clarendon Press, 1998)
—provides a comprehensive overview of death in early modern England, drawing on a wide range of sources and includes attention to shifts in the emotional responses to death across the Reformation.

Karant-Nunn, S.C., *The Reformation of Feeling: Shaping the Emotions in Early Modern Germany* (Oxford: Oxford University Press, 2010)
—analyses the language of feeling used by sermons about death and dying in early modern Germany with attention to confessional differences, providing a unique study of the emotional response of Catholics, Lutherans and Calvinists to death, and creating a methodology for future studies.

Wunderli, R. and G. Broce, 'The final moment before death in early modern England', *Sixteenth Century Journal* 20, 2 (1989), 259–75.
—seminal article that succinctly traces a wide range of early modern responses to the moment of death, including anxiety, despair, grief and hope, using case studies from a wide range of source materials.

Notes

1 A. Reinis, *Reforming the Art of Dying: The* ars moriendi *in the German Reformation (1519–1528)* (Aldershot: Ashgate, 2007), 36–9.
2 S.C. Karant-Nunn, *The Reformation of Feeling: Shaping the Emotions in Early Modern Germany* (Oxford: Oxford University Press, 2010), 251.
3 R. Wunderli and G. Broce, 'The final moment before death in early modern England', *Sixteenth Century Journal* 20, 2 (1989), 259–75, here 259–60.
4 A. Ryrie, *Being Protestant in Reformation Britain* (Oxford: Oxford University Press, 2014), 460–8.
5 Ibid., 465.
6 C. Koslofsky, *The Reformation of the Dead: Death and Ritual in Early Modern Germany, 1450–1700* (Basingstoke: Macmillan, 2000), 153–4.
7 Reinis, *Reforming the Art of Dying*, 255.
8 R. Houlbrooke, *Death, Religion, and the Family in England, 1480–1750* (Oxford: Clarendon Press, 1998), 191.
9 Ibid., 193.
10 S. Strocchia, *Death and Ritual in Renaissance Florence* (Baltimore: Johns Hopkins University Press, 1992), 106–20, 212–14.
11 Houlbrooke, *Death, Religion, and the Family*, 223, 226–7.
12 J. Scodel, *The English Poetic Epitaph: Commemoration and Conflict from Jonson to Wordsworth* (Ithaca: Cornell University Press, 1997), 86–112.
13 R.F. McNamara and U. McIlvenna, 'Medieval and early modern emotional responses to death and dying', *Parergon* 31, 2 (2014), 1–10.

Spaces

IV.15 Court culture

Tracy Adams

Contemporary writings about early modern court life – letters, memoirs, ambassadors' reports, fiction – emphasize the supreme importance of concealing one's inner feeling behind a blandly pleasant face. Therefore, they are a rich source for historians of the emotions. In the first book of *The Book of the Courtier* (1528) by Baldassare Castiglione (1478–1529), Count Ludovico idealizes the ability to showcase one's natural gifts (*grazia*) without visible effort (*sprezzatura*, often translated as 'nonchalance'). 'I find one universal rule concerning [grace]', he observes,

> which seems to me worth more in this matter than any other in all things human that are done or said: and that is to avoid affectation to the uttermost and . . . to practise in everything a certain nonchalance that shall conceal design and show that what is done and said is done without effort and almost without thought.[1]

Those unable to mask their effort, their 'art', found their 'credit' destroyed and themselves held in 'small esteem'.[2] Successful courtiers exploited this discrepancy between interiority and appearance, deciphering and working the emotions of their rivals.

This perspective on emotions can be traced to Aristotle's *Rhetoric*. Available in Latin translation from the end of the fifteenth century, the *Rhetoric* became part of the humanist enterprise to teach young men to use discourse to effect civic reform. But most importantly for the history of the emotions, in the second book, the philosopher discusses 'feelings that so change men as to affect their judgements' and shows how these can be induced and manipulated by the skilful orator.[3] Coinciding with a gradual shift in mentality manifested in various ways – as a movement from subject defined by social relations to one defined by a sense of interiority, from gift-giving to money culture, from ritual to theatre, from flat to three-dimensional perspective, from mystery to history, from transubstantiation to representation, but, which following William Egginton, can be imagined as a more basic shift in spatiality, from real presence to theatricality – translations of the *Rhetoric* and other treatises on oration offered ways of thinking, self-consciously, about how to use emotions to accomplish goals. As Egginton writes, the subject described by René Descartes (1596–1650) is evidence of 'a new way of experiencing the self in space, a way of experiencing that depends on the ability . . . to distinguish actors from characters and the space of one from that of the other'.[4] The court was a stage and individuals were players. At court, the prince and the courtiers performed. Jonas Barish notes that '[t]he prince is advised to cultivate a pattern of appearances which may or may not correspond to the truth about himself, but which serve the tactical ends of rule'.[5] Courtly society became a sort of police state, 'a certain governmental, religious, and familial system of authority shored up by a newly elaborated set of norms of emotional expression known as "civility"', which reached its apogee under Louis XIV (1638–1715).[6] Although the French Revolution brought court life to a temporary halt, what William M. Reddy calls the 'Flowering of Sentimentality' had already begun to dismantle its emotional foundations early in the eighteenth century. The value of sincerity came to replace that of duplicity; the individual's inner emotions began to be nourished and considered more important than surface qualities.

The emotional life of early modern European courtiers has received increasing attention over the past decade.[7] But despite the recent explosion of scholarship in the history of emotions overall scholars of court emotions continue to feel the influence of German sociologist Norbert Elias. Although recent scholars like Jeroen Duindam and Robert van Krieken have critiqued and refined Elias' major ideas, his corpus remains the starting point for scholars working on court emotions.[8] Forced to flee Nazi Germany, Elias did not become well-known until the late 1960s. Two of his major works, *The Civilizing Process* (first part translated into English in 1969, the second in 1982) and *The Court Society* (translated into English in 1983), have been especially influential among historians of emotion. In contrast with the focus on how nation-states developed out of royal courts prevalent in the early to mid-twentieth century, Elias was interested in the emotions that undergirded the exercise of power along with the ritualistic practices that engendered those emotions in individuals. He was particularly interested in the genesis of the court society of Louis XIV, which he saw as the prototype for other European courts. His fundamental insight was that an important shift occurred sometime between the sixteenth and late seventeenth centuries, such that responsibility for the management of individual bodies at court began to shift from external to internal control. He called this the 'civilizing process', describing the development in his German work as the creation of a particular 'habitus', although in English the term has been translated in various ways. The 'habitus' of course is central to much recent discussion of the emotions, particularly in scholarship following from sociologist Pierre Bourdieu's works. For Elias, refinements in sexual behaviour, bodily functions, table manners (he was very interested in etiquette books) and forms of speech and, more generally, the lessening of violence that was characteristic of early modern European court life resulted in a new habitus, one in which restraint was internalized. Individuals began, instinctively, to police themselves. Or, to state the process in psychological terms, increasingly elaborate networks of social connections led individuals to develop the self-perception that Sigmund Freud later identified as the super-ego and, therefore, to the privileging of appearance over interiority that characterized the emotional life of courtly society. For Elias, bourgeois society developed in contrast with this schema, privileging the inner life over outer appearance, although it appropriated the manners of court society.

Some scholars have criticized Elias (along with Freud) for assuming what has been described as a 'hydraulic' model of emotion, that is, the conception of emotions as 'drives', as seething impulses that must be controlled by social practices. He has also been criticized for his belief that human nature has made progress over time, graduating from a childlike state of inability to control oneself during the Middle Ages to a mature state of self-control. For this reason, Barbara H. Rosenwein explains, recent scholars of the history of emotions have been 'qualified' in their endorsement of Elias. His 'pervasive practice of speaking of the "primitive" and "childlike" emotional life of the Middle Ages . . . was one that few scholars in the 1980s and after could swallow'.[9] Elias has also been challenged by medievalists like C. Stephen Jaeger who locate the beginning of the civilizing process much earlier and, in Jaeger's case, in the episcopal courts of Germany rather than the royal court in France. Moreover, Jaeger argues that 'courtesy' is the instigator rather than product of the civilizing process. Civilization, he writes, 'is a social order in which the warrior class and the intellectual/artist/artisan class are won for the cause of society . . . [they] willingly place their arts in its service, and regard this service as an ideal'.[10] In contrast with Elias' sociological vision of the 'civilized' individual as the product of social conditioning, Jaeger's historical approach seeks the educations that 'civilize' individuals.

Nonetheless, Elias' idea that historians cannot fully understand how court life was organized and, consequently, how early modern governments worked unless they understand the interdependent emotional regimes that produced both rulers and the ruled has gained wide acceptance. No one would deny that Elias' work founded the study of court emotions. Moreover, it seems fair to see it as the genesis for studies on the political emotions of the early modern period more broadly speaking.

Further reading

Elias, N., *The Court Society*, (trans.) E. Jephcott (New York: Pantheon, 1983)
—focuses on the court of Louis XIV, which Elias sees as the most 'absolute' of contemporary court societies.
Elias, N., *The Civilizing Process: Sociogenetic and Psychogenetic Investigations*, (trans.) E. Jephcott (Oxford: Blackwell, 2000)
—traces the history of the process by which manners and non-violence became internalized, giving rise to what Elias calls the 'civilised habitus', and, with *The Court Society*, continues to serve as the reference point for studies of court emotions.

Notes

1 B. Castiglione, *The Book of the Courtier*, (trans.) L.E. Opdycke (1928; reprint Mineola, NY: Dover, 2003), 35.
2 Ibid.
3 Aristotle, *Rhetoric*, online at http://classics.mit.edu/Aristotle/rhetoric.2.ii.html, pt 1, accessed 19 April 2016).
4 W. Egginton, *How the World Became a Stage: Presence, Theatricality, and the Question of Modernity* (Albany: State University of New York Press, 2003), 6.
5 J.A. Barish, *The Antitheatrical Prejudice* (Berkeley: The University of California Press, 1981), 96.
6 W.M. Reddy, *The Navigation of Feeling: A Framework for the History of Emotions* (Cambridge: Cambridge University Press, 2001), 147.
7 To mention just three, see F. Ricciardelli and A. Zorzi (eds), *Emotions, Passions, and Power in Renaissance Italy* (Amsterdam: University of Amsterdam, 2015); J.R. Snyder, *Dissimulation and the Culture of Secrecy in Early Modern Europe* (Berkeley: University of California Press, 2009); J.-P. Cavaillé, *Dis/simulations. Religion, morale et politique au XVIIIe siècle. Jules-César Vanini, François La Mothe Le Vayer, Gabriel Naudé, Louis Machon et Torquato Accetto* (Paris: Champion, 2002)
8 For Duindam, see especially *Myths of Power: Norbert Elias and the Early Modern European Court* (Amsterdam: Amsterdam University Press, 1995). R. van Krieken's most concise discussion of Elias can be found in 'Norbert Elias and Emotions in History', in D. Lemmings and A. Brooks (eds), *Emotions and Social Change: Historical and Sociological Perspectives* (New York: Routledge, 2014), 19–42.

9 See B.H. Rosenwein, 'Controlling Paradigms', in Rosenwein (ed.), *Anger's Past: The Social Uses of an Emotion in the Middle Ages* (Ithaca: Cornell University Press, 1998), 238.

10 C.S. Jaeger, *The Origins of Courtliness: Civilizing Trends and the Formation of Courtly Ideals, 930–1210* (Philadelphia: University of Pennsylvania Press, 1985), 12.

IV.16 Theatre and stage

Samantha Owens

Scholars working in the field of early modern theatre studies have begun only quite recently to explore the question of emotions in any depth, despite the long-acknowledged importance of the passions to theatrical productions of the time. When visiting Hamburg in 1727, the Englishman Thomas Lediard (1685–1743) attended a performance of the opera *Sancio* by Georg Philipp Telemann (1681–1767) during which he was particularly struck by a touching farewell between a king and his (soon-to-be-executed) queen. In later describing this 'tender scene', Lediard especially praised the composer's setting of the last three words of the couple's duet, '*noch einmal fahrewol*', (once more farewell), noting that it showed 'exquisite Skill and Judgment . . . with Music perfectly adapted to the Subject' and thereby providing 'the Actors all the Opportunity they could wish to display their Skill, and the Audience a sufficient Time to indulge that noble Passion, which the preceding Incidents raised'.[1] Telemann was far from alone in the emphasis he placed on the passions when composing his theatrical works; indeed, early modern theorists generally agreed that the expression of the affects was a central aim of all staged entertainments, including plays, operas, ballet and a host of other hybrid forms (such as the German *Singballett* or the French *comédie-ballet*).

For not only were the passions considered to be of fundamental importance to drama, but the perceived power of the union of text and music to move the passions had been key to the creation of opera during the latter decades of the sixteenth century. A number of theorists, including Claude-François Ménestrier (1631–1705) (*Des ballets anciens et modernes*, 1682), also believed that dance was an art form equally capable of producing the same effects.[2] The theatrical stage was therefore seen by some – among them Daniel Heinsius (1580–1655) (*De tragica constitutione*, 1611) and René Descartes (1596–1650) (*Les passions de l'âme*, 1649) – as 'a kind of training hall' for the passions, in which performers and audience were able to experience specific emotions prior to encountering them in real life.[3] It is also worth noting, however, that in some cases it was believed that theatrical representations of the passions could be too powerful and thus 'apt to corrupt the soul of those in the audience', not least when 'seasoned with unwholesome melodies'.[4]

Given the centrality of the passions to the early modern stage, theatrical productions have much to tell us about the cultural history of specific emotions, as well as revealing contemporary understandings of the emotions more generally. While the dearth of surviving records can make research in this area challenging – very few relevant reviews, letters or diaries have survived – play texts, music scores, material objects, treatises on acting, musical performance and dance, as well as iconographical, architectural and archival sources of various kinds all offer significant evidence. Many scholars working in this area rightly stress the importance of investigating historical understandings and conventions concerning the emotions through the analysis of contemporary philosophical treatises and other related material.[5]

The prominence of rhetorical theory in the early modern period meant that rhetorical figures adapted to individual art forms played a key role in the theatrical representation of the emotions. Playwrights, librettists, composers, choreographers, stage designers and performers all drew regularly upon rhetorical principles to assist in the expression of particular affects. In music, for example, most composers' choices concerning tempo, rhythm, harmony or text setting were guided by their affective properties. When writing an aria for the despotic overseer Osmin in his *Singspiel, Die Entführung aus dem Serail* (1782), for example, Wolfgang Amadeus Mozart (1756–91) selected the tonality of successive sections very carefully to reflect Osmin's increasing rage, but without offending his listeners, since 'passions, whether violent or not, must never be expressed to the point of exciting disgust . . . even in the most terrible situations'.[6] The performers themselves were, of course, equally charged with making critical choices concerning their expression of the passions. Early modern treatises on acting provide fascinating evidence regarding appropriate intonation, facial expressions, postures or gestures for actors seeking to portray specific emotions – see, for example, the chapter on how to express 'the various Passions' in *A General View of the Stage* (1759) by Thomas Wilkes (d. 1786) – while treatises on music performance cover such crucial topics as the affective choice of tempo or the appropriate addition of ornamentation.

Not surprisingly then, applied performance studies form an important strand of research in this field, as seen in the increasing number of practical investigations into the 'affectiveness' of historically-informed styles of acting, dancing and musical performance. Consideration of spatial aspects is similarly critical, with different performing spaces having the capacity to influence the expression of individual passions through such parameters as acoustics, the nature of theatre lighting and stage machinery or the size and layout of the stage. A further critical factor to consider is the audience itself, with a number of recent studies examining the role of the emotions in the early modern theatre from the perspective of a performance's spectators.[7] How did audience members experience the passions represented on the stage and in the orchestra pit (from overtly embodied reactions – laughter, tears, hissing – to more private, controlled emotional engagement)? And how, in turn, did their responses impact upon the performers? Whatever the methodology employed – from more traditional textual-based studies to investigations employing arts practice-based research methods – the ever-increasing amount of scholarship undertaken in this field that deals directly with the emotions indicates that the rich potential offered by these approaches is progressively being explored.

Further reading

Hoxby, B., 'Passions', in H.S. Turner (ed.), *Early Modern Theatricality* (Oxford: Oxford University Press, 2013), 556–86.

—covering dramatic criticism and poetry, together with staged performance, Hoxby's recent survey argues convincingly that the passions were fundamental to early modern conceptions of drama.

Risi, C., 'Performing Affect in Seventeenth-Century Opera: Process, Reception, Transgression', in D. Symonds and P. Karantonis (eds), *The Legacy of Opera: Reading Music Theatre as Experience and Performance* (Amsterdam: Rodopi, 2013), 79–101.

—explores the fascination of early modern theorists and composers of opera with affect, in an essay that draws upon specific modern productions of seventeenth-century opera that seek to engage audiences on an emotional level.

Steenbergh, K., 'Emotions and Gender: The Case of Anger in Early Modern English Revenge Tragedies', in J. Liliequist (ed.) *A History of Emotions, 1200–1800* (London: Pickering and Chatto, 2012), 119–234.

—in a study focused specifically on anger through a close reading of contemporary fictional texts, Steenbergh challenges the widely-held perception that the early modern era was characterized by increased emotional control.

Notes

1 Anon., *The German Spy* (London, 1740), 99.

2 See E.R. Welch, 'Constructing universality in early modern French treatises on music and dance', in R. Ahrendt, M. Ferraguto and D. Mahiet (eds), *Music and Diplomacy from the Early Modern Era to the Present* (New York: Palgrave Macmillan, 2014), 103–23.

3 B. Hoxby, 'Passions', in H.S. Turner (ed.), *Early Modern Theatricality* (Oxford: Oxford University Press, 2013), 560.

4 L.A. Muratori, *Della perfetta poesia italiana* (Modena, 1706) cited in J.E. Pontara, 'Music as Wonder and Delight: Construction of Gender in Early Modern Opera through Musical Representation and Arousal of Emotions', in J. Liliequist (ed.), *A History of Emotions, 1200–1800* (London: Pickering & Chatto, 2012), 95.

5 See, for example, I. van Elferen, 'Affective discourse in German Baroque text-based music', *Tijdschrift voor Musizietheorie* 9, 3 (2004), 218–19.

6 Letter to his father, 26 September 1781, in E. Anderson (ed. and trans.), *The Letters of Mozart and His Family*, 3rd Edition (London: W. W. Norton, 1989), 770.

7 For example, M. Steggle, *Laughing and Weeping in Early Modern Theatres* (Aldershot: Ashgate, 2007) and A.P. Hobgood, *Passionate Playgoing in Early Modern England* (Cambridge: Cambridge University Press, 2014)

IV.17 Church interiors

Sing d'Arcy

Architecture and interiors are perhaps the most material of all material culture. Structure, form, space and detail are governed by the physicality of environmental and temporal conditions, rendering the conception and condition of the spatial arts a particularly complex one. In order to address this complexity, research into architectural and design history has often simplified the contexts of analysis into one based purely on observable formal characteristics; in other words, that of style. Whilst students of the built environment may be able to list the canon replete with the names of architects, date sets and their associated periodization or recognize flash cards of Roman churches, the filtering out of non-visible components leaves a very thin presence – literally often just the façade – in relation to understanding a communal venture that has interacted with successive generations and cultures in a physical, psychological and temporal sense. This is particularly relevant to interior spaces that contain the activities of quotidian existence and whose inherently complex legacy negates the simplistic reduction of conventional architectural historiography.

This period saw the globalization of the church and its architecture across oceans, continents and cultures. From Bergamo to Bogota, new churches were constructed and old spaces were re-modelled at an unprecedented pace. Within these sacred interiors the Roman Catholic cult was implanted, renovated and enacted. If the church interior is seen primarily as a vehicle for the celebration of liturgical rite, rather than a discrete historical artefact, it becomes apparent that an analysis of the early modern church interior must recognize the importance that emotions played in the conception, configuration, realization and reception of these spaces. In many regards, utilizing the lens of 'emotion' to view the church interior during this span permits a reading that allows an intelligibility of the evolution of both the formal design characteristics that physically configure the spaces and the philosophies that shaped them.

The development of the church interior was conditioned by the philosophies, ideals and dogmas of the Catholic Reformation. These systems took material form in the new spatial, visual, performative and experiential modes that demanded a more direct, effective and powerful affect on the emotions of those who engaged and operated with the sacred interiors – both the laity and the ordained. The Roman Catholic Church was in a position of battle in terms of its spiritual mission as well as its temporal influence. The colonization of the Americas and Asia by the Luso-Hispano powers presented an evangelical mission on a trans-continental scale. Similarly, in Europe the termination of the Christian 'reconquest' of Spain in 1492 presented the need for catechism and conversion with populations closer to home. Beyond the need of capturing new souls, the Church was simultaneously trying to stem the loss of its adherents to Protestantism. It was recognized that the emotions all humans possessed were a universal trait that subjugated cultural differences, and were therefore an effective means of communication and control across the multi-continental stage upon which Catholicism operated.

The reforms of Trent and its reinforcement and renovation of rites and practices required a response from the ecclesiastical spaces that were to accommodate the renewed and globalized Church. These operated on the communal level as well as the individual, attempting to exploit the differing emotional responses associated with each type of interaction. The exploitation of the emotions through design was to operate in a similar manner as the rhetorical devices of the sermon; that is, to teach and strengthen the doctrines of the Church whilst simultaneously delighting the recipient in the act. Theatre, music, art and dance were also brought into the church, colluding in a synthesized artificial interior environment that through performance transported the ears, eyes and souls of largely illiterate congregations to an altered emotional state. The interior of the church was in essence, refashioned into a form of *theatrum sacrum* replete with actors, scenery, machines and music, and, unlike the theatre, it was free and open every day of the year.

The celebration and adoration of the Eucharist was central to the re-visioning of church interiors. Whereas the fifteenth and early sixteenth century had experimented with centralized church spaces in reference to sacred geometry, the longitudinal nave

Figure IV.17.1 Interior of the chapel of the Monastery of Jesus, Aveiro, Portgual. The interior was commenced in the late sixteenth century and completed in the eighteenth. The view is toward the high altar. António Gomes and José Correia, 1725–29.

Image by author.

found favour again after Trent. This provided strong axial focus to the high altar and reinforced the importance of the Eucharist as central to celebration of the Mass (Figure IV.17.1). Visual accessibility, physical proximity and emotional connectivity to the Eucharistic rite was prioritized over the separation of the clerical reserve, or over abstract geometric considerations. Thus, whilst the demarcation between the lay and ordained was still physically present and marked, the laity was brought much closer to the bodily presence of Christ. Along a similar vein, the sacramental chapel became a common feature that was added to or integrated within church interiors. These intimate spaces allowed for an individual to have a direct and personal access to the Eucharist in reserve and encouraged an alternate means of emotional engagement with Catholic dogma in an extra-liturgical context.

The Catholic Reformation also resulted in the active encouragement of hagiographic veneration. This saw the remodelling of extant chapels, as well as a proliferation of new spaces with their associated retables. The design of altarpieces and their surrounding environments shed much of the former multipartite narrative structure in favour of a reduced centralized image framed by a theatrical architectural scaena. Adherence to architectural rules was abandoned in favour of visual magnificence and novelty (Figure IV.17.2). This design tactic focused the attention of the devotee on the easily understood narrative of a particular aspect of the saint's life, concentrating the emotional attention and hence intensifying the experience. In general, the symbolism within the interior schema of churches became more accessible and direct, even exaggerated, in order to ensure its reception and subsequent intelligibility by the masses (Figure IV.17.3).

Figures IV.17.2 Interior of the Collegiate Church of the Divine Saviour, Seville, Spain. The current interior configuration dates from the late seventeenth-century reconstruction of the church. The view is toward the high altar (Cayetano de Acosta, 1770–1774) and, in the right transept, the chapel of Our Lady of the Waters (Eugenio Reciente and José Maestre, 1722 and 1756).

Image by author.

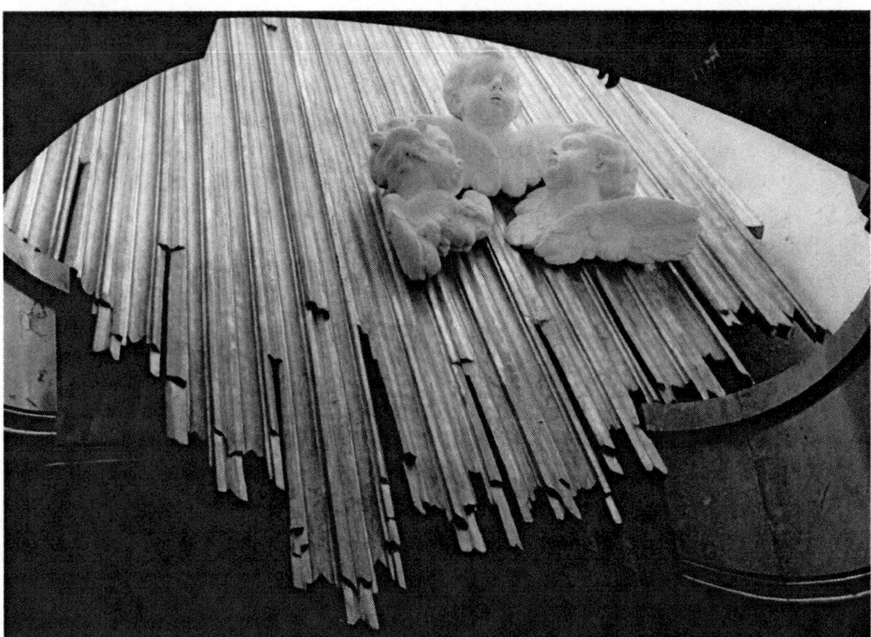

Figures IV.17.3 Detail of the lantern in the chapel of Saint Julian, Cathedral of Cuenca, Spain (Ventura Rodríguez, 1752).

Image by author.

The importance of music as an integrated part of the celebration of the liturgy also led to the increased protagonism of the pipe organ as a design element within the church interior. These fusions of music and architecture often competed with the high altar in terms of prominence and cost. It was the ability for these instruments to liminally transform the rites taking place and emotionally direct the congregation through auditory means that made the organ such a valued element of music making architecture.

Whilst music may have been utilized to transform the sonic environment of an interior instantaneously, the interior itself was also subject to change through the use of ephemeral constructions and decorations. Throughout the seventeenth and eighteenth centuries ephemera was deployed to mark important events such as the death of monarchs or the canonization of saints, as well as the great feast days of the liturgical calendar. Giant monuments were erected in the space of weeks or even days, typically occupying large areas of the internal area, which deliberately disrupted the normal perception, experience and operation of the space. They were built of humble materials such as painted cloth and timber, but disguised to appear as noble stone. They were festooned with rich fabrics, silverware, sculpture and paintings and illuminated by thousands of candles. The scale and brilliance of these temporary structures were designed to impress and overwhelm the viewers with a collective catharsis of celebration or mourning as well as with sentiments of admiration and wonder for the commissioning patrons and designers. The emotional potential of the monuments was further emphasized by the fleeting temporality inherent in these constructions.

By the middle of the eighteenth century the momentum of the Catholic Reformation had dissipated and a questioning of the temporal influence of the Church was beginning to occur, even in Catholic strongholds such as Spain and Bourbon Italy. With this reflection also came a critique of the supposed 'excesses' found within ecclesiastical interiors. Extreme emotional engagement elicited through design and performance was now viewed as indecorous, irrational and irresponsible. Reformers of the eighteenth and nineteenth centuries saw that faith – and therefore its material manifestation – should be expressed through religious sobriety and architectural frugality.

Architectural and design history is gradually beginning to recognize the importance of the history of emotions as a means of investigating and writing about the past. As we have come to know more about the archaeological and archival aspects of spaces, their patrons, designers and builders, attention is now focussing towards the emotive reasons and reactions within the contexts of spatial histories. Particularly in relation to ecclesiastical interiors further research into the performative function of liturgical spaces and the inseparable role that emotions played in this will only further enhance a more complete understanding of the spaces and emotions that were enacted within.

Further reading

Bailey, G., *The Spiritual Rococo: Decor and Divinity from the Salons of Paris to the Missions of Patagonia* (Farnham: Ashgate, 2014)

—covers wide geographic and cultural reach, from its home in France through to the Spanish and Portuguese Americas. Of significance in relation to the study of emotions and ecclesiastical space Bailey focuses on the interior – in particular the notion of décor – and its complex relationship with religion and emotions in the second half of the eighteenth century.

Hall, M. and T. Cooper (eds), *The Sensuous in the Counter-Reformation Church* (New York: Cambridge University Press, 2013)

—in relation to architectural space and emotions, the 'senses' are central vehicles for the choreographing of affect. The compilation of works within this book provide insight into recent research into the role of the sensual in the Counter Reformation as well as the debates around emotions in art and architecture that followed on from the reforms of the Council of Trent.

Maravall, J., *Culture of the Baroque: Analysis of a Historical Structure* (Manchester: Manchester University Press, 1986)

—seminal work in terms of understanding the 'reasons' behind the material cultures, political actions and social paradigms of the seventeenth and eighteenth centuries. In particular, Maravall presents the argument from the Spanish position which gives counterbalance and nuance to our understanding of how the arts and architecture were conscripted as emotional weapons in the war of persuasion and pacification waged on the urban masses.

IV.18 Battlefields

Alicia Marchant

Battlefields are dotted throughout the European early modern landscape, the results of numerous wars and rebellions enacted for political, social and religious reasons. Engagement with these sites of death, massacre and violence induce a range of emotional states, both at the time of the battle itself and through later commemorative practices and historiography. The emotions that are invoked range from pain, grief, displacement, anger, and sadness and horror at the atrocities, to senses of pride and joy at the documented role of the battle in nation building and the cults of heroes. The diversity of emotions associated with battlefields speak to differences between the actual physical and emotional experiences of war, and its later reportage and promotion for political and religious purposes. When considered within a framework of the history of emotions, questions related to the personal and individual emotional costs of engagement with the battlefield spaces, and the potential for trauma to resonate through family and other communities are raised. It also prompts the re-evaluation of how battlefields and war are discussed and memorialized within national narratives, highlighting elements of political and religious propaganda.

Battlefields have received remarkably little attention in the field of the history of emotions, despite their status as sites of inherently emotive experience at the time of battle and in its subsequent recollection. Though military historians have debated whether battle experience is best understood from written sources by focusing on small group actions or from an 'eye of command', this discussion has had remarkably little to say about the emotive aspects of warfare. Spatial theory, performance theory and heritage studies all provide exciting avenues for future scholarship into battlefields and emotions, to consider how people engage with, and are directed to engage with, sites of battle.

As Frédéric Mégret suggests, a battlefield is 'as much an *idea* as it is a space' and it is therefore important to consider how and why social, emotional and moral frameworks determined understandings of the dimensions of battlefield spaces through the social actions that occur within them.[1] It is in this space that various acts of violence and atrocities were performed which would be deemed quite unacceptable if enacted outside the battlefield space. Immediately after the Battle of Culloden (1746), the British troops led by William, Duke of Cumberland (1721–65) gained notoriety for amongst other things, pursuing Scots outside of the battlefield. In a letter written four years after the battle the Reverend George Innes (fl. 1750) of Forres notes that after the battle finished,

> The most shocking part of this woeful story is yet to come – I mean the horrid barbarities committed in cold blood after the battle was over . . . A little house into which a good many of the wounded had been carried was set on fire about their ears, and ev'ry soul in it burnt alive.[2]

The post-battle atrocities have dominated the cultural memory of the battle of Culloden for years, and notions of unfairness and grief at the events are still a prominent narrative. Such emotions regarding this battle are evident in the language of a range of sources such as diaries, letters, and official records of the events as well as stone memorials that have been on the site since 1881.

Early modern battlefields were spaces of social and cultural encounters, with battles occurring between various European nations, as well as with nations outside of Europe. Battles outside of Europe were often in the interests of empire building, such as the Battle of Ollantaytambo (1537) between the Spanish and Incan empire. As embodied encounters with an 'other' they are intrinsically emotive experiences and sites of performances of one's own emotional investment in a cultural identity. Battlefield spaces were, moreover, microcosms of sociality and social organization; the main military operations were directed by gentlemen of the higher nobility, while a greater part of the physical work was conducted by individuals of lower social standing. The battlefield was also a space in which the nobility sought to perform heroic acts of chivalry and gallantry, to win membership in a range of military orders, such as the French *Ordre Royal et Militaire de Saint-Louis* (1693). Battlefields, then, were spaces dominated by the actions and emotions of men. Women's engagement with battlefields were for the most part limited to medical and other caring duties, although women were often caught up in sieges and battles in urban centres, often with dire consequences.[3] Women did commonly accompany early modern armies on campaigns, and in so doing risked violence. As sites for early modern emotional exploration, battlefields prompt questions regarding how and why men and women engaged differently with battlefields, and the role that gender has in shaping the space.

Early modern battlefields were hothouses of emotions. Paradoxically, it was a place in which emotional regulation and discipline was practised, while at the same time it was a space of violent engagements which demanded emotional excesses, and in particular anger and hate. These two extremes were actively invoked through a range of strategies employed to channel motivation and encourage bravery including emotionally-charged depictions of the enemy to justify killing and to instil feelings of honour at self-sacrifice. There was, then, a sense that emotions such as courage, pride, and extreme anger and rage which was a necessary trait in a warrior were considered right when performed in the battlefield space, whereas cowardice, fear and even compassion were wrong.

One bourgeoning avenue of research stimulated by a history of emotions theoretical framework involves analysis of embodied and sensory experiences of the battlefield space. The meaning and significance of soundscapes, visuality and other sensory elements have contributed to understandings of the multidimensional experience of battle, and the affective states generated by such elements as colours, uniforms, (such as the English red uniform), drums, flags and iconography.[4] These elements were actively used to generate feelings of fear amongst opposition members, and were part of strategies of combat.

Post-battle, the scars of engagement had implications both physically and emotionally on those who participated. The horrors of battle increased alongside developments in firearms and military technologies, which had significant implications for how soldiers were hurt, how battles were fought and the degree to which soldiers had physical and personal engagement with the enemy. The trauma of war could resonate for generations, with many soldiers enduring great pain for years after the battle, as well as disabilities and illnesses.[5] Moreover, the emotionally charged nature of the battlefield and general horror of war led to all sorts of post-battle psychological traumas. How such traumas were understood and treated in early modern Europe raises a myriad of avenues of research into the history of emotions, and particularly questions how we today can access and study these.[6]

While battlefields were sites of trauma and suffering, they are also celebrated places linked to notions of nation-building. Battlefield spaces were remembered and commemorated, as well as hidden and forgotten in personal as well as national narratives. Culloden, as well as other Scottish battlefield sites such as Flodden (1513) which is over the current English border, have long been entangled with notions of national independence and freedom from overlordship, particular English overlordship. Scottish battlefields, like those of other nations, are imbued with national memory and significance within national hegemonic narratives of Scotland and Scottish national identity.

Battlefields are emotional landscapes, shaped by emotions such as pride and nostalgia that determine how and why the space is commemorated and recognized as heritage. Battlefields were frequently engaged with, used and inhabited after the battle. The performance of remembering and commemorating through such actions as anniversary processions and building stone markers, encourage feelings of melancholy and sadness at the event, through embodied and experiential engagement with the sites of battles that have long ceased.

Battlefields offer numerous avenues for further innovative scholarship in the history of emotions. As multifaceted sites of engagement and experience, early modern battlefields were physical and experiential spaces in which violence was enacted through emotionally-charged acts. Various textual and material sources provide testimony to the experience of the early modern battlefield, and it is through these sources that the emotions of battle and its aftermath remain to be explored.

Further reading

Kuijpers, E. and C. van der Haven (eds), *Battlefield Emotions 1500–1850: Practices, Experience, Imagination* (Basingstoke: Palgrave Macmillan, forthcoming)

—applies an innovate, interdisciplinary approach to the topic of early modern emotions and battlefields. The introduction, by Kuijpers and van der Haven, is a particularly important contribution to the field.

Downes, S., K. O'Loughlin and A. Lynch (eds), *Emotions and War: Medieval to Romantic Literature* (Basingstoke: Palgrave Macmillan, 2015)

—The introduction (entitled 'War as Emotion: Cultural Fields of Conflict and Feeling') is of particular interest, discussing both the scholarly benefits and difficulties in tackling the topic of emotion, violence and war in the medieval and early modern era.

Notes

1 F. Mégret, 'War and the vanishing battlefield', *Loyola University of Chicago International Law Review* 9, 1 (2011), 133.

2 Letter to Rev. Robert Forbes, 27 February 1750, in G. Bruce and P.H. Scott (eds), *A Scottish Postbag: Eight Centuries of Scottish Letters* (Edinburgh: The Saltire Society, 2002), 38.

3 J.A. Lynn II, *Women, Armies, and Warfare in Early Modern Europe* (Cambridge: Cambridge University Press, 2008)

4 X. Guillaume, R.S. Anderson and J.A. Vuori, 'Paint it black: colours and the social meaning of the battlefield', *European Journal of International Relations* (2015), 1–23.

5 M. Stoyle, 'Memories of the maimed: the testimony of Charles I's former soldiers, 1660–1730', *History* 88, 290 (2003), 204–26.

6 See for instance, E. Kuijpers and J.S. Pollmann, 'Why Remember Terror? Memories of Violence in the Dutch Revolt', in M. Ó Siochrú and J. Ohlmeyer (eds), *Ireland 1641: Contexts and Reactions* (Manchester: Manchester University Press, 2013), 176–96; E. Kuijpers, 'The Creation and Development of Social Memories of Traumatic Events. The Oudewater Massacre of 1575', in M. Linden and K. Rutkowski (eds), *Hurting Memories: Remembering as a Pathogenic Process in Individuals and Societies* (London: Elsevier, 2013), 191–201.

IV.19 Civic culture

Nicholas A. Eckstein

Only very recently have scholars treated emotion as a phenomenon susceptible to systematic historical analysis. One reason that it took so long for this to happen was the tenacious Western prejudice that portrayed emotions as inherently irrational. A related factor was that emotions could not be factored into allegedly more 'intellectual' topics – such as politics – that were the traditional focus of historians until well after the middle of the twentieth century.[1] A further complication was the question whether emotions were universal and whether, therefore, conclusions about one society could be applied to others. One can see Richard Trexler wrestling with this issue in an article of 1975, in which he interpreted the diary of a Florentine merchant named Giovanni Morelli (1371–1444). In 1407, Giovanni memorialized a long nocturnal prayer-vigil that he mounted at home in front of an image of Christ's Deposition on the anniversary of his son's tragic death from a fever. At one point, fixing his eyes on the figure of Mary as she cradled her dead son, Giovanni did not merely empathize with her grief as a parent, he shouldered the blame for it. He knew beyond all doubt that as a sinful Christian he was responsible for Christ's sacrifice and, by extension, for Mary's anguish. Trexler ruminated on the respective limitations of psychologists, who in his opinion attempted to assimilate historical evidence to 'pathologies they have encountered in their offices', and of historians afraid to generalize beyond their own areas of specialization.[2]

We would not find it difficult to describe the emotion to which another fifteenth-century Florentine, Carlo Martelli, gave vent during his private devotions. Weeping before an image of the Crucifixion, he expressed what we might call 'reverent pity'.[3] At the opposite extreme are savage emotions expressed in the context of public mob violence. In 1342, a lower-class Florentine crowd demanded that Walter of Brienne (*c.* 1304–56), who had been acting as a tyrant, hand over his hated Conservator of Justice, Guglielmo d'Asciesi, and d'Asciesi's recently knighted 18-year-old son, Gabriele, whom the crowd detested even more than the father because of his habit of torturing citizens. After seizing the son, the 'enraged' rioters cut him to pieces in the piazza in front of his father, and then did the same to the father: 'Some carried a piece on a lance or sword throughout the city. And there were those so cruel and bestial in their fury that they ate the raw flesh'.[4] Here we do not have to guess the emotions because the chronicler who narrated the events as a witness, Giovanni Villani (*c.* 1280–1348), has named them.

The question is what the early modern historian should do with examples like these. Scholars in the humanities have been divided by the methods that they should use to identify and interpret emotions.[5] There is little point in addressing emotions unless we treat them as contingent on the circumstances in which they appear. Certainly, emotions relate partly to innate cognitive processes that precede culture,[6] and they are a feature of every period and society. But we must not delude ourselves that by some act of empathy we can experience the emotions felt by the members of a culture that is not our own. Morelli is a good cautionary example. One notices that he made a point of explaining how he focused his eyes on specific elements of the painting of the Deposition – Mary's anguished face, the wounds on Christ's body – and how he treated them as visual cues for extravagant outpourings of grief:

> my eyes turned to the right side of the true Crucifixion, where looking towards the foot of the cross I caught sight of His pure, saintly blessed Mother, whom I saw full of the greatest pain and the greatest sadness . . . And this meditation caused me such anguish and pain, that I believed in truth that my soul would depart from my body.[7]

This, however, is not a spontaneous expression of unchecked emotion. In writing his account, and probably also while enacting the vigil itself, Giovanni consciously followed established contemporary practice, manipulating imagery and scriptural knowledge in the manner recommended by contemporary preachers, and in contemporary devotional manuals such as the popular fourteenth-century *Meditations on the Life of Christ*. There is no question that Giovanni's grief-stricken guilt was genuine, but it was also calculated and purposive. To regard it as intrinsically 'private' or 'personal' is to miss the extent to which individual emotions in this period could be structured by contemporary religious norms, and the practical ends – redemption of one's soul in this case – that they could serve.

This point is particularly well made by reference to early modern riots. Savage violence and emotion do not necessarily equate to lack of structure or the absence of intentionality on the part of the actors and their audience. In Naples in 1585, a lower-class mob publicly humiliated and stoned Giovan Vincenzo Storace, one of several elected officials judged to have betrayed the people by raising the price of bread. One contemporary account reported that the protesters

> cut out [Storace's] intestines, his heart, and the other internal organs, which were cut up into little pieces that they avidly divided among themselves. . . . They said to the onlookers that they wanted to eat the pieces in various proper ways, but also some of them bit into the raw flesh, inhumanly sucking the blood.[8]

If this narrative was fiction, the story could have been read as a coded reference to the inherently chaotic, bestial proclivities of the lower classes and the threat that they represented to the established order. But if the story is true, we need to consider the possible intentions of the crowd. As Edward Muir has noted, vilification, public humiliation and theatrical butchering of the victim's corpse are key elements of vendetta, which in turn forms part of a symbolic language of honour and shame.[9] By transforming the object of hatred into a freshly slaughtered carcass, the crowd effected a symbolic transaction. While the victim was dehumanized and dishonoured, the protagonists enhanced and increased their honour and power, actual and symbolic.

These examples show clearly that the historian needs to do more than attempt to identify early modern emotions by assimilating them to the standard categories of our own emotional lexicon. Villani's reference to 'enraged citizens' does not enlighten us to the meaning or purpose of the crowd's anger. We also need to do more than attempt a Geertzian 'thick description' that purports to uncover the 'authentic' symbolic meaning of a particular emotion.[10] Our own thinking about what emotions are is predetermined by inherited patterns of Western thought.[11] One solution is to recognize that, as different as they might seem, the emotional states exhibited by Giovanni Morelli and the putative cannibals of Naples may both be treated as means to achieve a desired end. In each case, they triggered a sequence of ritualized behaviours whose significance and purpose were clearly understood by the protagonists. Neither were these emotions merely triggers for what was to follow: Giovanni's grief and the rage of the crowd were essential stages of the performances to which they belonged. Without them, neither was possible.

William Caferro has recently examined military insults by which besieging armies humiliated the populations of towns that they encircled. Caferro interprets them as elements in a binary dialogue of honour and shame and suggests that that the narrowly military context in which they have been seen may itself be an anachronism.[12] Indeed, as William M. Reddy's recent work eloquently demonstrates, the history of emotion has reached the point at which it may help to rewrite, or at least question, accepted chronologies of European modernization itself. The history of emotion offers the opportunity to retrace and reconstruct the genealogy of feelings with which we are all too familiar, such as the dangerous and frequently bewildering accesses of misogynistic hatred that continue to erupt in our so-called 'developed' twenty-first-century society. In helping to explain, and perhaps to ameliorate, such troubling phenomena, the history of early modern emotion may do more than shed new light on the past; it may also render a valuable service to the present.

Further reading

Eckstein, N.A., *Painted Glories: The Brancacci Chapel in Renaissance Florence* (New Haven and London: Yale University Press, 2014), chapter. 3.

—explores the social and religious culture of pious emotion in fifteenth-century Florence, and explains how this culture informed both the production and public reception of early renaissance visual art.

Lansing, C., *Passion and Order: Restraint of Grief in the Medieval Italian Communes* (Ithaca: Cornell University Press, 2008)

—lays bare the mutually informing relationship between emotion and statecraft in the medieval commune, and reveals how male political elites imposed public order by restraining extravagant public expressions of ritualized grief, typecasting them as effeminate.

Muir, E., *Mad Blood Stirring: Vendetta and Factions in Friuli during the Renaissance* (Baltimore: Johns Hopkins University Press, 1993)

—although more than 20 years old, remains the definitive analysis of the cultural context that makes sense of the violent emotions described in the present essay.

Notes

1 B.H. Rosenwein, 'Worrying about emotions in history', *The American Historical Review* 107 (2002), 821–2.

2 R.C. Trexler, 'In search of father: the experience of abandonment in the recollections of Giovanni di Pagolo Morelli', *History of Childhood Quarterly* 3, 2 (1975), 228: 'Such specialized dissection of past experience can cut us off from both an appreciation of Morelli's transcendental human qualities and his historical specificity'.

3 See D.V. Kent, *Cosimo de' Medici and the Florentine Renaissance: The Patron's Oeuvre* (New Haven: Yale University Press, 2000), 155; N.A. Eckstein, *Painted Glories: The Brancacci Chapel in Renaissance Florence* (New Haven: Yale University Press, 2014), 113–14.

4 Cited in M. Phillips, 'Machiavelli, Guicciardini, and the tradition of vernacular historiography in Florence', *The American Historical Review* 84, 1 (1979), 90.

5 On the many conceptual and methodological pitfalls, see W.M. Reddy, *The Navigation of Feeling: A Framework for the History of Emotions* (Cambridge: Cambridge University Press, 2001)

6 Ibid., 13.

7 Giovanni di Pagolo Morelli, *Ricordi*, (ed.) V. Branca (Florence: Le Monnier, 1956), 484–5.

8 E. Muir, 'The Cannibals of Italy', *Syracuse Scholar* 5 (1984), 7–8.

9 Muir, 'Cannibals', 11; Muir, *Mad Blood Stirring: Vendetta and Factions in Friuli During the Renaissance* (Baltimore: Johns Hopkins University Press, 1993), part 3.

10 C. Geertz, 'Thick Description: Toward and Interpretive Theory of Culture', in *The Interpretation of Cultures: Selected Essays by Clifford Geertz* (New York: Basic Books, 1973), 3–30.

11 Reddy, *The Navigation of Feeling*, 15; Rosenwein, 'Problems and methods in the history of emotions', *Passions in Context: Journal of the History and Philosophy of the Emotions* 1/1 (2010), online at www.passionsincontext.de/index.php/?id=557, accessed 27 June 2016.

12 W. Caferro, 'Honour and Insult: Military Rituals in Late Medieval Tuscany', in S.K. Cohn, Jr., M. Fantoni, F. Franceschi and F. Ricciardelli (eds), *Late Medieval and Early Modern Ritual: Studies in Italian Urban Culture* (Turnout: Brepols, 2013), 183–209.

IV.20 Village

Elise M. Dermineur

In 1688, in his well-known work *Les Caractères*, Jean de La Bruyère (1645–96) labelled rural dwellers 'wild animals' (*les animaux farouches*).[1] Peasants have indeed been depicted as violent, backward and incapable of feelings such as compassion, love and other sentiments, their emotions often reduced to simplistic shortcuts, and grossly reduced to bestial savagery. The violent and spectacular peasant uprisings in the Middle Ages and the early modern period, such as the *Jacquerie* (1358), the German Peasants War (1525), the uprisings of the *croquants* and *nu-pieds*, to name a few, widely contributed to the spread of this narrow image of peasant violence, rusticity, bestiality and greed not only in traditional historiography but also in contemporary depictions of rural dwellers, such as that of La Bruyère. Discourses and visual supports of all kinds represented angry and fearless peasants dangerously armed with pitchforks, and insisted on the difference between the 'wild animals' with the rest of the civilized strata of society.[2] And yet, peasants' emotions in the early modern period constituted a set of complex and interrelated feelings, sentiments, gestures and norms that shaped societal relations and regulated everyday life, and which cannot be reduced to the convulsions of the occasional uprisings. The historians of the *Annales* school were pioneers in the examination of peasant mentalities and offered a broader palette of peasant interaction.[3] However, their contributions to the examination of peasant emotions, while important, remains incomplete and did not reveal all the complexities, depth and texture of such feelings. Their approach, both interdisciplinary and conveyed at a micro level, still remains valuable and promising for the study of peasant emotions. But this history largely remained to be written.

In early modern Europe, the village referred to a physical place but also to a group of people living together, often related by blood, most likely knowing each other, and where various layers of social, legal, economic and emotional norms shaped accordingly the behaviour, gestures and rhetoric of rural dwellers, and where individual and collective emotions were nurtured and expressed both within the household but also within the community as a whole. Incidentally, popular culture and peasant emotions were intrinsically linked and both often shared the same codes and beliefs.

The village was not only a place where people lived together but was above all a place where they worked, exchanged, and socialized together in a hermetic and endogenous sphere. Social proximity and social reproduction engendered shared beliefs and norms among the villagers. Within the village itself, places such as local institutions (the local court, the notary's office for instance), or other social organizations (the church) and gathering places (the wash house, mill, inn, for example) played an important role in the display, emphasis and manipulation of certain emotions as villagers interacted there in the public eye. Peasants adapted certain of their emotions to these places and their specific audience, but also to social norms existing within their community. The significance of agents' actions in public settings had a strong impact on their reputation and honour, valuable and valued qualities for their daily interactions with others. Within the village community, the social hierarchy also bore a set of emotional norms and gestures specific to each group according to their sex, age and to their social position. The household and its organization, whether nuclear, extended, joint or stem families, affected the social status of each member and by extension, its members' social interactions and behaviour.

Religious beliefs shared by the villagers also bore a set of emotional norms, rhetoric and behaviour. The Reformation, in particular, brought important changes regarding shared religious beliefs but also regarding the challenge of traditional rites and religious identities. The emergence of Protestantism in the sixteenth century often divided community members, engendering religious tensions and violence where strong emotions were often displayed.[4] Additionally, the village was also a place where the sacred, the profane and popular culture met and collided, prompting shared beliefs among community members.[5] Close contact with nature, especially, engendered beliefs and superstitions, often founding its roots in a strong and ancient popular culture shared by the whole community and which had its own emotional codes. Alain Cabantous, for instance, has recently shown how the night triggered various myths, legends, fantasies, beliefs and emotions in the early modern period.[6] This was not specific to the early modern period, as emotions triggered by forests or animals, for example, can be found at many times. On the other hand, events such as the witch craze witnessed a dramatic set of violent feelings and emotions and were particular to the early modern period.

Finally, it is important to note that particular attention must be devoted to changes over time. The weight of ancestral traditions has often given an impression of immobility regarding peasant mentalities before the nineteenth century.[7] But legal and economic changes, such as the state building process or the development of the market economy, among others, not only affected the village structure and administration but also household structures, and by extension the affective responses of the peasants to such changes. This is an area still to be investigated.

Peasants very seldom wrote self-narratives. In order to study peasant emotions, one must turn to other sources. The civil and criminal records in particular prove to be excellent source material, 'pulses of daily life', as Jean-Michel Boehler labelled them.[8] The judicial testimonies, especially their semantics, reveal the affective rhetoric and the wide range of gestures. These documents cover excesses and misbehaviour and reveal much about anger, resentment, jealousy, envy and honour among other emotions. Love, empathy, fear and the like often also lurk at the surface of those documents. Emotions in rural communities in early modern Europe had social and economic functions and followed rules and norms invented and moulded by the peasants themselves, not imposed from above, and are revealed by the judicial documents. Attention must be paid however to the legal and institutional changes affecting local courts in the second half of the eighteenth century; state building processes could impose new legal norms in which standardization tended to suppress the colourful words of the villagers to replace it with more technical and uniform terminology.[9] The microhistorical approach in the analysis of such sources appears to be the most efficient for examining peasant emotions, but much more work needs to be done regarding the emotions of rural dwellers.

Further reading

Le Roy Ladurie, E., *Montaillou: The Promised Land of Error*, (trans.) B. Bray (New York: George Braziller, 2008)

—masterful survey of a medieval rural community that reveals a host of details regarding aspects of villagers' intimate and daily lives.

Sabean, D.W., *Power in the Blood: Popular Culture and Village Discourse in Early Modern Germany* (Cambridge: Cambridge University Press, 1988)

—through the examination of several case studies focusing on rural popular culture, highlights the complexity of peasants' beliefs, behaviours and affective responses.

Notes

1 J. de La Bruyère, *Les Caractères* (1688) (Paris: Le Livre de Poche, 1976).
2 P. Freedman, 'Peasant Anger in the Late Middle Ages', in B.H. Rosenwein (ed.), *Anger's Past: The Social Uses of an Emotion in the Middle Ages* (Ithaca: Cornell University Press, 1998), 171–90.
3 Among the numerous rural monographs, see especially E. Le Roy Ladurie, *Montaillou, village occitan de 1294 à 1324* (Paris: Folio, 2008)
4 N.Z. Davis, 'The rites of violence: religious riot in sixteenth-century France', *Past & Present* 59, 1 (1973), 51–91.
5 D.W. Sabean, *Power in the Blood: Popular Culture and Village Discourse in Early Modern Germany* (Cambridge: Cambridge University Press, 1988)
6 A. Cabantous, *Histoire de la nuit: XVIIIe – XVIIIe siècle* (Paris: Fayard, 2009)
7 G. Bouchard, *Le Village Immobile – Sennely En Sologne au XVIIIè siecle* (Paris: Plon, 1971)
8 J.-M. Boehler, *Une société rurale en milieu rhénan: la paysannerie de la plaine d'Alsace (1648–1789)* (Strasbourg: Presses Universitaires de Strasbourg, 1995)
9 J.C. Scott, *Seeing like a State: How Certain Schemes to Improve the Human Condition Have Failed* (New Haven: Yale University Press, 1999)

IV.21 Family and household

Katie Barclay

Under Philippe Ariès' now very controversial schema of change in family life over the early modern period, 'the family' was something created through affective ties and particularly through the intimacy and privacy of sharing household space during the eighteenth century.

> In the world of sentiments and values, the family didn't count previously as much as lineage . . . [Lineage] extended to the ties of blood without regard to the emotions engendered by cohabitation and intimacy. The line was never gathered together within a common space, around a single courtyard. In contrast, the sentiment of family is tied to the house, to the government of the house, to life in the house.[1]

Previously, he believed, people had an investment in 'lineage' – in blood connections and family name – but that the bonds of lineage were looser and demanded less 'emotion' from its members. The lineage family was marked by broad sociability in large households, where rooms were shared and multi-purpose, and privacy was unimportant. Since the publication of his work in the 1960s, historians have sought to nuance this story, highlighting the emotional investments that families had in each other before the eighteenth century, complicating how the early modern family understood and defined privacy and its relationship to intimacy, and demonstrating both the relationship between lineage and 'place' (particularly land) and that an investment in it did not disappear in the eighteenth century. Yet, for all its flaws, Ariès' theory captured an important tension in how the family is understood and interpreted: where is the boundary between the household and the family and what difference does emotion make? Moreover, if 'the sentiment of family is tied to the house', what difference does household space make to this story?

The ways that space, broadly defined, shapes our experience of emotion has perhaps been better encapsulated in histories of the family and household than in many other areas. The emotional connections that tied people together, whether non-relatives living in one household or blood kin spread across distance, have been emphasized by historians seeking to explain early modern constructions of social order and its ability to imagine often diverse individuals as 'friends' and 'family'.[2] Sharing a household space across much of early modern Europe was understood to create family, incorporating not just those related by blood but also servants, apprentices, lodgers and other non-kin who lived under one roof. Such families ideally (but not always in practice) shared a patriarch, who ensured social discipline within the home and, through the household, the wider community. In return, he provided love and care for 'his family', guaranteeing not only the effective operation of the household but that patriarchal power would not be abused. This was a relationship that at its most perfect relied on emotion to reduce tyranny and ensure social harmony. Across the period, people also recognized the intimacy that sharing a household created between its members, emotional bonds that could destabilize traditional power hierarchies (and not just soften them), even leading to inappropriate (often sexual) connections.

Some families worried more about this than others, and such anxieties came to the fore more in some historical periods than other. The eighteenth century was such a moment, as philosophers across Europe attempted to 'scientifically' explain the nature of the familial bond. For some philosophers, the family was created through blood and biology, an innate natural instinct to ensure the survival of the species. For others, it was the intimacy of living together, of sharing a space, especially from a young age, that created the emotional ties of family life. It was perhaps this sentiment that Ariès found so compelling within his own research.

Yet, whilst sharing a space was understood to create connections, moving apart was not always expected to dissolve such bonds. This created networks of family that extended outwards over geographical space and resulted in the formation of multiple homes for the early modern traveller. Early demographic work on the Western European family noted that most people lived in nuclear households (that is husband, wife and children), plus sometimes servants.[3] Extended kin households were relatively unusual, not least because a high mortality rate ensured that families remained small, and were more typical in Eastern Europe. Newer work has complicated this picture, not only across time, occupation and region, but in the life-cycles of families.[4] A late age of marriage allowed many newlyweds to start out married life in the parental home, but to lose their parents relatively early in their relationship, leaving a nuclear household for a generation until a new set of children married. Moreover, a closer look at servants complicates distinctions between kin and non-kin with large numbers of 'servants' working for siblings, cousins and in wider family networks.[5] The clustering of families within geographic areas is also suggestive that household boundaries were fluid.[6] In such contexts, blood ties were not bound to particular households but extended beyond them, highlighting the multiple layers of kinship that could operate in these communities. Here blood, name and lineage could act as ties that created emotional connections over geographic space – a kinship created not through close intimacy, but through an imaginative investment in particular understandings of family.

How the family defined itself (whether through blood or household or friendship) had implications for its operation. A family defined through the household was also defined by its practices. How household space, and the objects within it, was used, and the anticipated emotions arising from such use, shaped emotional dynamics within the family. Some communities were highly attuned to the symbolic use of space, ensuring that placement at the table, the working of land or movement through particular rooms was widely understood to carry particular meaning, not least love and affection. Here the use of space and place played a dynamic role in the making of emotion. For families who defined themselves through blood connection, family might be established through the sharing of gifts, resources or household members. The emotional connections of family became embedded in wider social and economic activities. Most families defined themselves across multiple domains, ensuring that how the family was made was complex, changing and dependent on context. Yet, if we can speak of universals in the early modern family, it seems apparent that 'family' was something that people held a strong investment in; in many contexts, family was a significant component in self-definition, and was strongly implicated in not only the making of identity but also future life choices and outcomes. As such, it was an institution that society and individuals cared deeply about.

Despite increasing recognition of the role of emotion, and particularly intimacy, in shaping family ties, the implications of this for household structures is still being developed, often clustered in work on colonial intimacies that seek to interrogate cross-racial household dynamics. In an early modern European context, the potential for emotion to transform understandings of the household is suggestive in work on loyalty as emotion between master and servants; on anger in shaping household dynamics; and on affection in tempering hierarchies. It is now time to broaden these studies to a wider range of households and to think further about the complex interplay of emotion in family and household life.

Further reading

Barclay, K., 'Gossip, Intimacy and the Early Modern Scottish Household', in C. Walker and H. Kerr (eds), *Fama and Her Sisters: Gossip in Early Modern Europe* (Turnhout: Brepols, 2015), 187–207.

—highlights how the role of gossip in creating intimacy between servants shored up the power of the employer.

Broomhall, S. (ed.), *Emotions in the Households, 1200–1900* (Basingstoke: Palgrave Macmillan, 2008)

—the essays in this collection investigates the role of emotion in a range of household relationships.

Tadmor, N., *Family and Friends in Eighteenth-Century England: Household, Kinship and Patronage* (Cambridge: Cambridge University Press, 2001)

—this classic work highlights the important role of the household in defining the family.

Notes

1 P. Ariès, *L'Enfant et la vie familiale sous l'Ancien Régime* (Paris: Plon, 1960), 239, (trans.) in S. Pucci, 'Snapshots of family intimacy in the French eighteenth century: the case of *Paul et Virginie*', *Eighteenth-Century Culture* 35 (2008), 89–118.

2 N. Tadmor, *Family and Friends in Eighteenth-Century England: Household, Kinship and Patronage* (Cambridge: Cambridge University Press, 2001)

3 P. Laslett, 'Family, kinship and collectivity as systems of support in pre-industrial Europe: a consideration of the 'nuclear-hardship' hypothesis', *Continuity and Change* 3, 2 (1988), 153–75.

4 C. Lundh, 'Households and families in pre-industrial Sweden', *Continuity and Change* 10, 1 (1995), 33–68.

5 I. Bull, 'Inheritance in family business: the "long" merchant family: problems concerning generation change', *Scandinavian Journal of History* 27, 4 (2002), 193–210.

6 M. Chaytor, 'Household and kinship: Ryton in the late sixteenth and early seventeenth centuries', *History Workshop Journal* 10, 1 (1980), 25–60.

Intellectual and cultural traditions

IV.22 Humanism

Andrea Rizzi

Broadly, the term 'humanism' describes the cultural program of a community of European intellectuals who, in the course of the fourteenth, fifteenth and sixteenth centuries, nurtured a strong interest in ancient Latin and Greek languages and cultures. They trained in the art of writing effectively in classicizing Latin, and used this skill in politics, philosophy, history and science. By discovering, reading and translating ancient texts, these thinkers reassessed cultural and political thought of their time. Humanists practised rhetoric in order to unleash, control or suppress their emotions and the emotions of their intended audiences: for instance, budding speakers practised the composition of emotionally charged speeches of praise and vituperation. Through these exercises, students learned to express and react to emotion through the use of language. The recent studies of early modern emotions examined here have brought to light humanist theories of emotions, and rhetorical practices concerned with emotions. Humanists' contribution to Western theories of emotion cannot be overestimated, but the 'real' emotions caused or cured by humanist texts will always remain unattainable. Historians and literary historians need to engineer new methodologies that will overcome the obvious rift between written language and emotions.

The humanist art of writing and speaking effectively and eloquently brought its practitioners social and political acclaim. Because their career and reputation was often threatened by competition and the whims of their patrons or rulers, humanists often engaged in bitter debates entailing base attacks and counter attacks. The invectives of Desiderius Erasmus (*c.* 1466–1536) and Martin Luther (1483–1546) against their detractors are perhaps the most notable examples of this vituperative writing.[1] Such violent exchanges were also fuelled by strong beliefs in certain values and ideas, but also by arrogance and ambition.

Early modern humanists – an enduring and pan-European group of professionals of the pen – have been described as a 'textual community' in the sense that they all shared ideas, education and presuppositions by means of Latin texts.[2] Their strong interest in ancient knowledge exposed them to the importance of moral philosophy and ancient and Christian theories of emotions. In their examination of ancient theories of emotions, humanists faced two main contrasting approaches: on the one hand, Stoicism rejected emotions as a vice to be extirpated, advocating reason as the quality controller of human affections. According to this view, passions are the result of wrong reasoning.[3] On the other hand, the Peripatetic moral philosophy took a moderate line, and accepted emotions as natural while also calling for a temperate degree of passion: Aristotle declared that virtuous people have emotions at the 'right times, with reference to the right objects, towards the right people, with the right aim, and in the right way'.[4] This moderate way was more popular with humanists as it allowed them to deal with their lives' shortcomings and tragedies, but very often humanists adopted elements of both philosophies.

In the third Book of his *De anima et vita*,[5] Juan Luis Vives (1493–1540) took inspiration from an impressive range of ancient, early Christian and medieval sources to offer one of the most comprehensive humanist analyses of the physiology and psychology of emotions. In Vives' text there is a demarcation between 'emotion' and 'passion': they are both motions of the soul, but the former is light while the latter is strong. This distinction is important as it helps Vives and his fellow humanists to differentiate not only between positive and potentially negative emotions, but also between different kinds of writing and public speaking. Emotions, Vives explained, are natural reactions to how people judge impressions or 'images'. A married couple, he recounted, starts crying as soon as they imagine losing their only child.[6] This is an important feature of the art of persuasion employed by humanists: evoking powerful images through writing or speech triggers emotions. Eliciting emotions by eloquence was in effect a way to move audiences towards a reaction ('affective reaction'), which was not controlled rationally and could develop into emotions or passions.

De remediis ad utranque fortunam (1366) and *Secretum* (*c.* 1343) by Francesco Petrarch (1304–74) sought to provide a therapeutic means for the control of emotional turbulence. In chapter two of his *De remediis*, Petrarch offered a fully-fledged cure for the misery of the human condition. He followed the Stoic view that emotions should be suppressed, but at the same time he proposed the dignity of man as an effective consolation for fear of death, for despair, and bereavement. Petrarch argued that focus on the virtues and qualities of mankind could effectively stir us away from sadness and misery. More to the point, he considered eloquence in itself a healing device available to the few who could appreciate it.

The writings of Petrarch and Vives show how emotions were core business for humanists. Whether suppressed or encouraged, emotions were a keystone for the humanist textual community. Eloquence and reason were used to combat dangerous emotions such a shame or anger, but humanists also understood the importance of emotions in the pursuit of virtue: by affecting readers, authors move their hearts and led them towards the good.[7] Similarly, in his advice to an idealized ruler, Niccolò Machiavelli (1469–1527) stated that it was important for a leader to stir his subjects' emotions in order to achieve otherwise unattainable goals.[8]

The recognition of the value and effectiveness of emotions as key political, philosophical and historical means of persuasion went hand in hand with a strong sensitivity towards secular misery and unhappiness. For humanists, writing about emotions was a therapeutic exercise for themselves and the few who could appreciate the medicine (eloquence). Philosophy and eloquence provided opportunities for this textual community to find an effective medicine of the soul, while sharpening their reputations as learned and successful intellectuals. Following the death of his son Valerio, Venetian Jacopo Antonio Marcello (1399–1465) had received several consolatory orations from distinguished humanists. Unhappy with these gifts, in 1463 he commissioned another scholar to pen a response to these consolers. This response is an ambitious rebuttal of the arguments of the previous authors, and a strong defence of the legitimacy of Marcello's grief. As a result, Marcello's ghost-writer created a personal and sophisticated rhetoric of grief that brought fame to the grieving man.[9] Grief and fame may seem an odd pair for us today but they clearly made perfect sense in early modern Europe.

Another example helps to explain the inseparable connection between grief and fame in the humanists' view and writing about emotions. In his *Dialogus consolatorius* (Consolatory Dialogue) of 1438,[10] Giannozzo Manetti (1396–1459) wrote down in both Latin and vernacular a series of conversations he had had with two friends after the death of his four-year-old son Antonino. Manetti's aim to provide a useful and universal manual for the resolution of grief was matched by his own ambition. The quest for worldly fame and the search for timely eloquence return us to the pairing of grief and fame, and raise an important issue for the study of emotions in early modern period. George McClure argues that the study of consolatory humanist texts can shed light on the 'psychological functions of rhetoric and philosophy in Renaissance thought', and the connection between the history of ideas and the history of emotions.[11]

Recent studies point towards the need for historians to look more closely at what humanists say about emotions through their theoretical and non-theoretical texts. Understanding the relationship between theory and practice would allow us to discern 'the values – and with them the theories – of any period from the lived experience in the same period'.[12] In the humanists' texts dealing with emotions, the subjective and objective – as well as cognition and sensation – are difficult to separate. This is partly because body and soul were considered inseparable, and because the personal and the universal cannot be clearly demarcated in the humanist text. Historians of emotions have recently begun to compile collections of emotion words as a way to understand the emotional categories of past communities.[13] This is probably the most effective way to gauge the value given to specific emotions by a textual community such as the humanists. But the humanists' ambition for secular immortality stands between our understanding of past-lived emotions and mere representations of emotions. To paraphrase from a recent study of anger: are we really dealing with emotions at all, as we understand them today?[14] Perhaps the study of emotions in the early modern period (and not just representations) relies on the creation of new methodologies that can help us better understand the complex relationship between emotions and language.[15]

Further reading

Lagerlund, H. and M. Yrjönsuuri (eds), *Emotions and Choice from Boethius to Descartes* (Dordrecht: Kluwer, 2002)

—sheds light on the influence of Vives and Descartes in the early modern and modern history of emotions and brings to light theories of emotions put forward by largely ignored philosophers of the late medieval period.

McClure, G.W., *Sorrow and Consolation in Italian Humanism* (Princeton: Princeton University Press, 1991)

—a first comprehensive discussion of consolatory humanist literature, which invites more research on the study of the psychological function of rhetoric and philosophy in early modern thought.

Notes

1 See A. Rizzi, 'Violent Language in Early Fifteenth-century Italy: The Emotions of Invectives', in S. Broomhall and S. Finn (eds), *Violence and Emotion in Early Modern Europe* (Abington: Routledge, 2015), 145–58.
2 B. Stock, *The Implications of Literacy: Written Language and Models of Interpretation in the Eleventh and Twelfth Centuries* (Princeton: Princeton University Press 1983), 88–90.
3 L. Casini, 'Emotions in Renaissance Humanism: Juan Luis Vives' "De anima et vita" ', in H. Lagerlund and M. Yrjönsuuri (eds), *Emotions and Choice from Boethius to Descartes* (Dordrecht: Kluwer, 2002), 205–28.
4 Aristotle, *Nicomachean Ethics*, (trans. and ed.) D. Ross (London: Oxford University Press, 1954), 1106b, 21–3.
5 J.L. Vives, *The Passions of the Soul: The Third Book of De Anima et Vita*, (ed.) C.G. Noreña (Lewiston, N.Y.: E. Mellen Press, 1990), 1.
6 Casini, 'Emotions', 216.
7 G. Zak, *Petrarch's Humanism and the Care of the Self* (Cambridge: Cambridge University Press, 2010), 156–7.
8 G. Ruggiero, *Machiavelli in Love: Sex, Self, and Society in the Italian Renaissance* (Baltimore: Johns Hopkins University Press, 2007), 181–2.
9 G.W. McClure, *Sorrow and Consolation in Italian Humanism* (Princeton: Princeton University Press, 1991), 114–15.
10 G. Manetti, *Dialogus consolatorius*, (ed.) A. De Petris (Rome: Edizioni di Storia e Letteratura, 1983)
11 McClure, 'Art of mourning: autobiographical writings on the loss of a son in Italian humanist thought (1400–1461)', *Renaissance Quarterly* 39, 3 (1986), 440–75, here 440.
12 B.H. Rosenwein, *The Place of Renaissance Italy in the History of Emotions*, online at https://repository.library.georgetown.edu/handle/10822/707326, accessed 10 March 2015.
13 Rosenwein, *Emotional Communities in the Early Middle Ages* (Ithaca: Cornell University Press, 2006); I. Rosier-Catach, 'Discussions médiévales sur l'expression des affects', in D. Boquet and P. Nagy (eds), *Le sujet des emotions au Moyen Age* (Paris: Beauchesne, 2009), 201–23; S. Ferente, 'Metaphor, Emotions, and the Language of Politics in Late Medieval Italy. A Genoese "Lamento" of 1473', online at https://repository.library.georgetown.edu/handle/10822/707326, accessed 12 March 2015.
14 S.D. White. 'The Politics of Anger', in Rosenwein (ed.), *Anger's Past. The Social Use of an Emotion in the Middle Ages* (Ithaca: Cornell University Press, 1998), 127–52.
15 On the need for new methodologies, see S. Ferente, 'Storici ed emozioni', *Storica* 43/45 (2009), 371–92.

IV.23 Print media

Luc Racaut

The historiography surrounding early modern print often assumes that the emergence of print led to the rise of modern Western values: individualism, democracy and capitalism. Roger Chartier pioneered the history of emotions and the media with *Pratiques de la lecture* (1985), which emphasized the role that reading in private played in the development of individualism.[1] If this work taught us a great deal about intimate passions, thanks to diaries and first-hand accounts, the question of how collective emotions could be stirred by the media remained largely untouched. To get an insight into the role of print media in stirring emotions we have to go back to the Reformation: indeed contemporaries, chroniclers and crowned heads often ascribed its success to the manipulation of 'popular emotions' by reformers, notably in print.

The elite's first instinct was to suspect printing of stirring the passions of ordinary folk, to an extent that almost outweighed the benefits that it had brought to the Republic of Letters.

Protestantism is usually credited for democratizing Scripture, which was met with considerable resistance from the Catholic Church who assumed that the *illiterati* were incapable of making sense of the sacred texts. It is a commonplace of Whig historiography that the end of the monopoly of the Catholic Church on the Christian faith was universally welcomed from below as it allowed people to have a choice. If we take emotions into account, however, then it becomes clear that the emergence of the Protestant Reformation constituted for most a traumatic experience. The crisis of faith of individual reformers could be highly emotional: the father of the Protestant Reformation, Martin Luther (1483–1546), was himself wracked with pathological anxiety about his personal salvation that the discovery of the theological concept of the free gift of grace in Scripture supposedly cured. Following Jean Delumeau's pioneering work on fear, many historians of the Reformation have argued that the success of the Protestant Reformation lay precisely in the reassuring quality of this central message.[2] Irrespective of the inherent simplicity of the Lutheran message, it was not universally received and the Reformation was the starting point of a century and a half of religiously-motivated interpersonal violence. Owning forbidden books or woodcuts was dangerous and could lead to execution whereas many pamphlets advocated violence against the confessional enemy. The printed page as an object was perhaps as emotionally charged as the words that it contained, and was a source of perplexity and fear as much as enlightenment. The multiplication of vitriolic texts that fuelled and were fuelled by the confessional struggle was the origin of a moral panic amongst the elite that was ironically conveyed in pamphlets, cheap prints and woodcuts as well as books. This panic was heightened by the fact that the written word had considerably more power than it does today: it could be a force for good or evil, and its effect on the world was nothing short of magical.

The idea can be traced back to the medieval period where books were rare and mysterious objects that could be a source of awe for the illiterate majority and the distinction between the 'good book' and a book of spells was a difficult one to make. The words that granted salvation in the Eucharist were written in a book that only the priests could read, an act associated with the occult: *hocus pocus* is a bastardization of *hoc est corpus meum* 'this is my body', which were the words of consecration necessary for transubstantiation to take place. Contrary to popular belief, the Bible was no less magical for Protestants than for Catholics: a woodcut printed in Wittenberg in 1568 portrays Luther with both feet firmly planted in the ground holding a vernacular Bible as if a weapon, the invisible power of which unseats Pope Leo X (1475–1521) from his throne (*Lutherus Triumphans*). The printed page as an object in itself could have agency even if it was not read: illiterate French Protestants were executed for owning a Geneva Bible (easily recognizable by the printer's mark on the title page) that they had acquired as a token of their belonging to the Protestant faith, just as Catholics brought back memorabilia from pilgrimages. Before being a stimulus to the intellect and fostering critical thinking, printing held a strong emotional charge and elicited a variety of responses, from devotion and reverence to fear and anxiety. Long before viruses were discovered, the language of contagion was used to describe the way dangerous ideas could spread thanks in part to the dissemination of clandestine

Protestant books through illicit channels – Calvinist books were literally floated down the Rhone valley from Geneva to Lyon.

The irrational response of commoners to print media, by contrast to the measured consumption of books by the literate elite, follows the familiar hierarchy between reason and emotion that has been used to justify social differentiation since antiquity. This does not mean, however, that the literate elite were totally dispassionate about books: a Parisian printer once observed that on the occasion of a siege by Protestant troops he had to wield 'weapons instead of books' against them.[3] Books held no mysteries for this printer who supervised their manufacture from beginning to end and yet he still considered them to be endowed with spiritual power, just as *Lutherus Triumphans* above suggests. As Tatiana Debbagi Baranova has shown, pamphlets were not originally intended for public consumption but often deeply engaged the honour and reputation of their authors who used books to make a profession of faith for a limited audience.[4] These pamphlets were therefore very personal and appealed as much to the emotions as to the reason of their intended audience (usually a powerful patron). By contrast, pamphlet wars engaged their authors in a verbal (or scribal) joust in a vendetta that could substitute or supplement actual physical violence on a variety of scales (either interpersonal or actual wars in extreme cases). Thanks to the dissemination of print media, these pamphlet wars became accessible to a much larger portion of the population than ever before and 'public opinion' was increasingly solicited in defence or attack of a particular author's reputation and social standing.

Early modern print media also appealed to the intended audience's emotions directly, from the satirical woodcuts of the Lutheran Reformation to the lengthy compilations of the ordeals of Protestant or Catholic martyrs that were often illustrated with horrific woodcuts. The wars of religion were flooded with images of violence in various forms that were collected by humanists such as Pierre de L'Estoile (1546–1611) during the Holy Catholic League or informed the thoughts of Michel de Montaigne (1533–92) in his *Essais*. Although the term propaganda is heavily connoted, it is useful to describe the concerted efforts of networks of individuals involved in the Protestant and Catholic Reformations that were not necessarily or always orchestrated centrally by either Rome or Geneva. The French crown's response to religious propaganda and the state of religious pluralism that existed in France between 1562 and 1598 is particularly enlightening as it served as a blueprint for other countries. In a famous speech given to the Paris *Parlement* in January 1599, Henri IV (1553–1610) personally addressed the (largely Catholic-leaning) lawyers charged with ratifying the Edict of Nantes that brought the French Wars of Religion to an end. He presented himself as 'a good father' and mixed implicit threats with soft words in order to conciliate his former Catholic enemies on one hand and his former Protestant allies on the other. The violence of the wars of religion was referred to as *émotions populaires* (popular emotions) that he accused a portion of the ultra-Catholic intelligentsia of having deliberately stirred through the spoken and printed word. As a result, his successors Louis XIII (1601–43) and Louis XIV (1638–1715) tightened the grip of the state's censorship on print in order to prevent further 'popular emotions' and thus enshrined a neo-platonic dichotomy between popular emotion and elite reason in legislation. The history of emotions has an obvious contribution to make to the understanding of how print media affected their readership. Recent scholarship on printed collection of songs and *contrafactum* (new words put to the music of popular tunes), for instance, has demonstrated the role that music played in disseminating emotionally charged messages in the context of the religious wars on both sides of the confessional divide. An interesting avenue for future research includes the emotional charge associated with the material culture surrounding books, which clearly had symbolic value for their owners irrespective of their content.

Further reading

Karant-Nunn, S., *Reformation of Feeling: Shaping the Religious Emotions in Early Modern Germany* (Oxford University Press, 2010)

—demonstrates that the Lutheran Reformation in particular and the Protestant Reformation generally far from being a dry cerebral departure from medieval Christianity was, on the contrary, imbued with a powerful emotional message that was conveyed in print and in sermons.

Notes

1 R. Chartier, *Pratiques de la lecture* (Paris: Payot, 1985)
2 J. Delumeau, *La Peur en Occident (XIVe–XVIIIe siècles): Une cité assiégée* (Paris: Fayard, 1978)
3 L. Racaut, 'Nicolas Chesneau, Catholic printer in Paris during the French Wars of Religion', *The Historical Journal* 52, 1 (2009), 1–19.
4 T. Debbagi Baranova, *À Coups de Libelles: Une culture politique au temps des guerres de religion (1562–1598)* (Geneva: Droz, 2012)

IV.24 Antiquarianism

Alicia Marchant

The study of emotions and antiquarianism is an exciting and yet underexplored field of research. Recent scholarship has skirted around this important topic, considering various aspects of antiquarian practices, but not asking questions pertaining to the affective nature of these practices.[1] Driven by a deep curiosity and desire to explore, collect, document and display physical remains of the past, the practice of antiquarianism became increasingly popular in early modern Europe. The range of curious sought-after treasures of the past was limitless, and included ruins and ancient monuments, inscriptions, statues, books and manuscripts, and objects of everyday life such as coins and pots. Antiquaries amassed large personal collections, many of which were to form the basis of national institutions; the ancient manuscript collection of Sir Robert Cotton (*c.* 1570–1631), for instance, formed the core of the British Library's holdings. Others sought to create inventories of artefacts and monuments, producing maps and written accounts, bibliographical catalogues of objects and sketches of ruin-filled landscapes. There is a great diversity of scholarship that comes under the title of antiquarianism; indeed it is considered a forerunner to the modern academic fields of archaeology, heritage studies, museology (collection, curation and conservation) and topographical studies to name only a few.

While antiquarianism was practised all over early modern Europe, it particularly flourished in Britain where wealthy gentlemen drove this movement. The gentry provided patronage in support of antiquaries, and also, particularly from the eighteenth century, were themselves collectors and exhibitors of antiquities as a leisure pursuit.[2] For antiquaries, it was not only the aesthetic pleasure that these material objects generated that motivated their studies, but that they embodied moments of history that had broken through to resonate in the present; the material objects provided a portal to the past. The urge to engage with these objects was driven as much by a love of history as it was by a dissatisfaction with the present. Rose Macauley observed in Renaissance antiquaries a 'desire to build up the ancient ruins into their glorious first state, and to lament their ruin as wreckage of perfection'.[3] The past seemingly offered a far grander, richer and more sophisticated culture. Throughout early modern Europe it was the Roman empire and its material remains that were held in the highest regard as the idealized golden age of Europe. When English antiquary William Camden (1551–1623) started compiling a document of British antiquities, it was only the Roman features that he was going to survey, however, this quickly expanded to include all time periods.[4] In the preface to his *Britannia* (1586) Camden writes of the motivation for his composition: 'I would to restore antiquity to Britaine, and Britaine to its antiquity'.[5] Antiquaries, then, envisaged their practices as having restorative qualities: the long hidden and unvalued past could, through further study and discoveries, be restored and recovered; the disjoined past and the present could be reconnected.

A theoretical approach informed by the history of the emotions not only helps to identify the particular emotions associated with antiquarianism (like nostalgia, grief, happiness and fear), but also questions the work that these emotions do, highlighting, for instance, the personal and social motivations driving the practice of antiquarianism, its meanings and significance.[6] Although there were formal societies and groups, the practice of antiquarianism was mostly undertaken in private spaces and formed private collections. The great cabinets of curiosities (Kunstkabinett or Wunderkammer) were particularly popular in northern Europe in the early modern era, and housed illustrations, historic artefacts and objects of natural history. The collection of curiosities compiled by Ole Worm (1588–1654) contained many historical objects of his native Denmark, particularly ruinic inscriptions. A catalogue of the collection was produced after Worm's death as *Museum Wormianum*, which contains woodcuts of many objects and of the collection as a whole.[7] With the printing of catalogues, knowledge about specific collections became more accessible to a wider number of people. These catalogues were, along with the artefacts, circulated in Europe and beyond through networks of commerce and cross-cultural exchange. Early modern antiquarianism was dominated by educated and/or wealthy men, who found in the practice a way to engage in intellectual sociability and to formulate male emotional communities. There are some notable exceptions to this, such as Elizabeth Elstob (1683–1756) who specialized in Anglo-Saxon language and culture.

Emotion theory is crucial in the analysis of the nexus between antiquaries and the objects of their study, which is affective and corporeal in its practice. The narratives compiled in written texts or constructed through the display of collections focus on nostalgia and memory. Unlike other forms of historical practice in the early modern era, antiquarianism involved physical, embodied engagement with the materiality of the past through travel, excavation and cataloguing: ruins were walked around, and could be touched, breathed in, and smelt. This emphasis on the individual in the physical acquisition of artefacts, can also be seen in the text. Antiquarian historical writings were structured spatially according to the path in which the antiquarian encountered the many monuments, ruins and objects on a journey.

In popular literature and plays produced in early modern Europe, it is this full-bodied consumption of the past that is often picked up on, leading to unflattering caricatures of antiquarians. According to a description from 1698, an antiquary was 'a curious critic in old Coins, Stones and Inscriptions, in Worm-eaten Records and ancient Manuscripts, also one that affects and blindly dotes, on Relics, Ruins, old Customs Phrases and Fashions'.[8] This is a common image of the antiquary, an old man who suffers from extreme emotional excesses and 'blindly dotes' with an obsession so strong that it borders on madness. Another common image focuses on the material objects, depicting them as worthless, and riddled with decay and ruination; in a description by John Earle (1601–65) from 1628, he calls it an 'unnaturall disease' that an antiquary 'loves all things (as Dutchmen doe Cheese) the better for being mouldy and worme-eaten'.[9]

While such caricatures are to be taken with a grain of salt, they do speak to a notion of the relationship between the antiquary and the objects of their study as primarily affective, depending upon emotive historical narratives and an embodied engagement with the vestiges of a lost past in the ruins of the present. As a practice, however, antiquarianism was frequently considered (in both early modern times and today) to have no historical merit; lacking in objectivity and chronology, and with no apparent concern for wider historical context, early modern antiquaries were mocked and ridiculed. It is, however, these very points of criticism that make antiquarian texts so interesting. How and why such imagery of the antiquary developed opens up numerous possible points of inquiry. Antiquarianism and emotions offer exciting prospects for research in sensory histories and expressions of emotions related to specific material objects, as well as notions of the individual, collective and emotional communities.

Further reading

Marchant, A., 'A Landscape of Ruins: Decay and Emotion in Late Medieval and Early Modern Antiquarian Narratives,' in S. Broomhall (ed.), *Gender and Emotions in Medieval and Early Modern Europe: Destroying Order, Structuring Disorder* (Farnham: Ashgate, 2015), 109–25.

—considers the role of emotion in antiquarian texts of late medieval and early modern England, focusing particularly on the meaning of ruins and the narrative strategies used to communicate emotion.

Sweet, R.H., *Antiquaries: The Discovery of the Past in Eighteenth-Century Britain* (Hambledon: Bloomsbury, 2004)

—explores various aspects of antiquarian practice, examining the individuals who participated, the communities that they formed and the sorts of historical pasts that were the subjects of their study.

Woolf, D., *The Social Circulation of the Past: English Historical Culture, 1500–1730* (Oxford: Oxford University Press, 2003)

—provides a useful discussion that contextualizes antiquarianism within wider historiographical practices in early modern England.

Notes

1 One recent example that does consider the emotional practice of antiquarianism is A. Marchant, 'A Landscape of Ruins: Decay and Emotion in Late Medieval and Early Modern Antiquarian Narratives', in S. Broomhall (ed.), *Gender and Emotions in Medieval and Early Modern Europe: Destroying Order, Structuring Disorder* (Farnham: Ashgate, 2015) 109–25.
2 See D.R. Woolf, 'The dawn of the artefact: the antiquarian impulse in England 1500 to 1730', *Studies in Medievalism* 4 (1992), 5–35.
3 R. Macauley, *The Pleasure of Ruins* (New York: Walker, 1953), 192–3.
4 Woolf, 'Images of the Antiquary in Seventeenth-Century England', in S. Pearce (ed.), *Visions of Antiquity: The Society of Antiquaries of London 1707–2007* (London: Society of Antiquaries of London, 2007), 15.
5 W. Camden, 'Preface to the Reader', *Britannia: Or, a Chorographical Description of the Flourishing Kingdoms of England, Scotland, and Ireland, and the Islands Adjacent; From the Earliest Antiquity* (London, 1789), 6.
6 S. Ahmed, *The Cultural Politics of Emotion* (New York: Routledge, 2004), esp. 1–19.
7 O.P. Grell, 'In Search of True Knowledge: Ole Worm (1588–1654) and the New Philosophy', in P.H. Smith and B. Schmidt (eds), *Making Knowledge in Early Modern Europe: Practices, Objects, and Texts, 1400–1800* (Chicago: University of Chicago Press, 2007), 214–32.
8 *A New Dictionary of the Terms Ancient and Modern of the Canting Crew, in its Several Tribes, of Gypsies, Beggers, Thieves, Cheats, &c. with an Addition of Some Proverbs, Phrases, Figurative Speeches, &c* (London, 1698), 16.
9 J. Earle, *Micro-cosmographie. Or A peece of the World Discovered; in Essays and Characters* (London, 1628), sigs C1v–C2r.

IV.25 Medicine and science

Yasmin Haskell

Emotions have been the engine as well as the object of scientific and medical enquiry since antiquity. Indeed, before the rise of modern notions of scientific objectivity the emotional life of scholars and 'scientists' was itself a frequent object of medical scrutiny. While the emotional dimension is implicitly acknowledged in various studies of conduct and sociability in early modern knowledge cultures and communities, it is rarely their main focus.[1] Intellectual historians have also studied the passions in the writings of key early modern physicians and philosophers,[2] philosophical traditions such as Epicureanism and (neo-)Stoicism,[3] and eclectic discourses such as consolation and *medicina mentis* ('medicine of the mind').[4] Awareness of these contemporary learned conceptualizations of the passions is, conversely, indispensable for future research on the communities and cultures of early modern science and scholarship. In addition to intellectual history and history of science and medicine, social, cultural, legal, literary and art, historians have all contributed useful perspectives on, for example, pre-modern notions of 'mental health'.

Learned physicians of the early modern period paid lip service, at least, to the emotions, or 'passions of the soul', and readily acknowledged their role in health, in medical letters and treatises. Not only did physicians correspond with one another but also with astrologers, from whose charts they avidly gleaned information on human types and emotional dispositions. The connection between temperament, vice, disease, and emotion was complex. In so-called 'hypochondriac melancholy' – not to be confused with modern health anxiety – the patient's humours, unbalanced as a result of inborn complexion and/or vicious living, led to disorders of the organs 'below' (*hypo*) the 'cartilage of the ribs' (*chondria*), giving rise, quite literally, to disturbing vapours that caused physical and mental illness accompanied by emotions of fear, suspiciousness, sadness and sometimes even anger. Seventeenth-century Munich physician Malachias Geiger devoted a long treatise to this condition, thought to be epidemic (*Microcosmos Hypochondriacus*, 1652), but while 'hypochondriac' was the variety of melancholy most often discussed in late Renaissance medical literature, other kinds, including love and religious melancholy, were extensively analysed by Robert Burton (1577–1640) in his *Anatomy of Melancholy* (1621). French physician Jacques Ferrand (*c.* 1575–*c.* 1630) devoted an entire treatise to love melancholy (1610),[5] and 'greensickness' in pubescent girls was thought to have both physical and emotional causes.[6] Although the interplay of emotional and bodily health in such 'conditions' to some extent parallels modern assumptions about somatopsychic illness, the early modern faculty of the imagination is the elephant in the room; it was believed to play a crucial role in mediating the presumed effects of humours, vapours and demons.

At a time when psychiatry and psychology did not exist in anything like their current forms, then, 'medical' and 'scientific' understandings of the emotions must be sought not only in collections of physicians' case studies, observations and dissertations, or in the writings of moral philosophers, theologians and demonologists (often also physicians), but also in theorists of poetry, rhetoric, music, drama and art. Marsilio Ficino (1433–99), who sparked a Renaissance fashion for 'genial' melancholy (in which the condition is viewed as *pre*-condition for philosophical and artistic achievement), was physician, philosopher, priest *and* humanist translator and commentator of the works of Plato. In consequence of the last, he was also a major early modern theorist of love. The influence of Ficino's writings continued to be felt throughout the Renaissance, in learned literature, vernacular poetry and art. A less metaphysical vocabulary of the passions is transmitted via the striking illustrations of *De humana physiognomia* (1586) by the natural philosopher/magician Giambattista della Porta (*c.* 1535–1615), correlating human faces with those of animals. Della Porta's images influenced seventeenth-century French painter Charles Le Brun (1619–90) in his theory of expression of the passions, along with, of course, *Passions de l'âme* (1649) by René Descartes (1596–1650).

While the older medical language of the humours and spirits gradually gave way to other metaphors, such as those of machines and nerves, the assumption that a scholarly or scientific life could be bad for one's physical, mental and *emotional* health endured throughout the early modern period into the eighteenth century. Swiss physician Samuel-Auguste Tissot (1728–97) was scathing about the dangers of the intellectual life especially for the middle-aged and not-so-brilliant, in his inaugural oration as professor of medicine at the University of Lausanne, 'On the Health of the Learned' (1767).[7] Many satirical works on the vices and emotions of scholars were produced in the seventeenth and eighteenth centuries, especially in German-speaking lands.[8] The learned were said to be prone to envy and anger as well as the ubiquitous melancholy. The collecting and book cultures of the Renaissance and early modern 'Republic of Letters' spawned their own scholarly passions, such as curiosity and bibliomania.[9]

The Copernican revolution and the Renaissance encounter with the 'new world' brought new religious anxieties as well as new desires, intellectual and secular – even the possibility of worlds beyond ours, proclaimed by Giordano Bruno (1548–1600) among others. But if Bruno's hero, Lucretius, had sought to demystify the cosmos, 'wonder' had been regarded as an impetus to scientific discovery since Aristotle (*Metaphysics* 1. 982b) and remained an important emotion of encounter and enquiry from late antiquity through the Middle Ages, as in Augustine and Thomas Aquinas.[10] In the sixteenth century, Italian cosmologist and physician Girolamo Fracastoro (1478–1553), still professed 'wonder' both at the new world and at the new disease of syphilis in his influential eponymous poem on the venereal plague of the Renaissance. The emotion of wonder pervades the Baroque 'science' of seventeenth-century Jesuit polymath Athanasius Kircher (1602–80), who evoked it in word and image in his massive illustrated tomes on topics from optics to magnetism to seismology to music.

Advances in the science of electricity – demonstrated spectacularly, interpreted religiously and applied in healing, including sexual healing – stirred up emotions of attraction and repulsion and were celebrated or satirized in learned and popular literature.[11] Nor was the Linnaean revolution of the eighteenth century without passion: Carl von Linné (1707–78) was criticized for sexualizing plants and for his practice of naming plants after his friends – and his enemies. Together with specimens and scientific information we can observe the circulation of emotions in his wide-ranging correspondence.[12] Other rich sources for exploring the history of emotions in early modern science are the letters, diaries and reports of Jesuit missionaries and of Dutch, French and British explorers in Asia, the Americas and Australia. In addition to wonder and curiosity, 'sensibility' – roughly, a heightened sensitivity to both emotional and empirical stimuli – became a desirable quality for the scientist in the eighteenth century.[13]

The foregoing may give the impression that emotions in the fields of early modern science and medicine have already been well plotted, if not by historians of emotion *stricto sensu*. This is far from the case. There is scope for further careful study, for example, of the history of emotions/ disease concepts over the *longue durée*, in different discursive and confessional contexts, and different languages. The '(de-)motivational' emotions of enquiry and discovery, from 'wonder' and 'curiosity' to 'attention', 'distraction', 'interest', 'sloth' and 'boredom' might be tracked through various genres, from notebooks and diaries to correspondence. The very desirability and legitimacy of scientific knowledge was bound up with religion in the period in review so that passions for learning and science must often be read in the light (or shadow) of faith.[14] Along with religion, the lens of gender remains a useful one for surveying the emotions in early modern medicine and science: not just the distinctive physiologies, emotions and emotional capacities attributed to the different genders, but the role of women in science, and the legitimation or prohibition of certain (gendered) emotional styles in different cultures of knowledge.[15]

Further reading

Carrera, E. (ed.), *Emotions and Health 1200–1700* (Leiden: Brill, 2013)

—a good touchstone for recent work on the emotions in medieval and early modern medicine and faculty psychology.

Haskell, Y. (ed.), *Diseases of the Imagination and Imaginary Disease in the Early Modern Period* (Tunhout: Brepols, 2011)

—brings together essays that highlight the interdependence of perception, emotion and physical illness in 'scientific' and medical discourse from the fifteenth through eighteenth centuries.

Pickavé, M. and L. Shapiro (eds), *Emotion and Cognitive Life in Medieval and Early Modern Philosophy* (Oxford: Oxford University Press, 2012)

—reveals the important role played by the emotions in cognition in a series of major medieval and early modern philosophers, from Aquinas to Hume.

Notes

1 A. Goldgar, *Impolite Learning: Conduct and Community in the Republic of Letters 1680–1750* (New Haven: Yale University Press, 1995); S. Kivistö, *The Vices of Learning: Morality and Knowledge at Early Modern Universities* (Leiden: Brill, 2014)

2 S. James, *Passion and Action: The Emotions in Early Modern Philosophy* (Oxford: Oxford University Press, 1997); S. Gaukroger (ed.), *The Soft Underbelly of Reason: The Passions in the Seventeenth Century* (Abingdon: Routledge, 1998); G. Giglioni, 'Girolamo Cardano on the passions and their treatment', *Brunelliana e Campanelliana* 12, 1 (2006), 25–40.

3 J. Kraye, 'Ἀπ άθεια and Προπ άθειαι in early modern discussions of the passions: stoicism, Christianity and natural history', *Early Science and Medicine* 17, 1–2 (2012), 230–53.

4 A. Gowland, 'Consolations for Melancholy in Renaissance Humanism', *Society and Politics* 6, 1 (2012), 10–38; S. Corneanu, *Regimens of the Mind: Boyle, Locke, and the Early Modern* Cultura Animi *Tradition* (Chicago and London: University of Chicago Press, 2011)

5 Gowland, 'Consolations'.

6 According to Helen King, emotion, especially love, was considered a major cause of *chlorosis* after the eighteenth century, *The Disease of Virgins: Green Sickness, Chlorosis, and the Problems of Puberty* (London & New York: Routledge, 2004), 30.

7 Y. Haskell, '"Physician heal thyself!" Emotions and the Health of the Learned in Samuel Auguste André Tissot (1728–1797) and Gerard Nicolaas Heerkens (1726–1801)', in H.M. Lloyd (ed.), *The Discourse of Sensibility: The Knowing Body in the Enlightenment* (Dordrecht: Springer, 2013), 105–24.

8 Kivistö, *The Vices of Learning*; P. Hummel, *Moeurs érudites: Études sur la micrologie littéraire (Allemagne XVIe-XVIIIe siècles)* (Geneva: Droz, 2002)

9 N. Kenny, *The Uses of Curiosity in Early Modern France and Germany* (Oxford: Oxford University Press, 2003); R.J.W. Evans and A. Marr (eds), *Curiosity and Wonder from the Renaissance to the Enlightenment* (Aldershot: Ashgate, 2006)

10 L. Daston and K. Park, *Wonders and the Order of Nature: 1150–1750* (Cambridge, MA: The MIT Press, 2001); Evans and Marr (eds), *Curiosity and Wonder.*

11 For an overview, see P. Bertucci, 'Therapeutic Attractions: Early Applications of Electricity to the Art of Healing', in H.A. Whitaker, C.U.M. Smith and S. Finger (eds), *Brain, Mind and Medicine: Essays in Eighteenth-Century Neuroscience* (Boston: Springer, 2007), 271–83.

12 Available online: http://linnaeus.c18.net/Letters/searchtext.php.

13 J. Riskin, *Science in the Age of Sensibility: The Sentimental Empiricists of the French Enlightenment* (Chicago: Chicago University Press, 2002). See also A.C. Vila, *Enlightenment and Pathology: Sensibility in the Literature and Medicine of Eighteenth-Century France* (Baltimore: John Hopkins University Press, 1998)

14 See P. Harrison, *The Territories of Science and Religion* (The Gifford Lectures) (Chicago: University of Chicago Press, 2015)

15 See D.L. Opitz, S. Bergwik and B. Van Tiggelen (eds), *Domesticity in the Making of Modern Science* (London: Palgrave Macmillan, 2015)

IV.26 Baroque music

Jane W. Davidson and Alan Maddox

The term 'Baroque music' is a relatively modern one, having come into use only in the early twentieth century.[1] It is now typically considered to apply to Western art music of the period *c.* 1600 to *c.* 1750. In fact, interest in the underpinnings of musical performance practices from previous centuries did not emerge until the late nineteenth and early twentieth centuries. To that point, repertoire from the period was played very much in the same style as the contemporary music of the day. This can be demonstrated by listening to recordings of the *Messiah* by George Frideric Handel (1685–1759) made in the 1930s. The tempi are slow, the *legato* lines and *vibrato*-filled tones are shaped principally by the aesthetics and musical instruments that had been developed in the nineteenth century. Awareness of playing original seventeenth- and eighteenth-century instruments in the style current at the time when the music was composed, and applying period information about how to express musical and emotional ideas was scant. The dawn of interest in historical 'accuracy' is often attributed to Arnold Dometch's book of 1915, *The Interpretation of the Music of the XVIIth and XVIIIth Centuries*, which for the first time systematically drew on the many treatises on performance practice published during the Baroque period to demonstrate how different many aspects of performance had been in earlier times, and to advocate for a return to historical practices. In doing so, it raised many questions about how to approach historical ideology in expressive interpretation.

In subsequent decades, performances of Handel's oratorios – the only music of the entire period that has remained continuously in the repertoire since it was new – as well as a whole plethora of music from 1600 onwards, has changed immensely in how it is interpreted. Beginning in the 1960s and 1970s, a new generation of musicians such as Gustav Leonhardt, Nikolaus Harnoncourt and Christopher Hogwood established specialist Baroque ensembles playing on period instruments, and their influential recordings profoundly changed the accepted modes of performance for this repertoire. As a rule of thumb, tone has become lighter and tempi are quicker; timbres are more transparent and the music being articulated has an explicit focus on accessing the emotional meaning of the musical material through subtle note-by-note variation. This entry explores the matter of Baroque musical performance, in particular, it includes attempts at understanding of the role of emotions in the whole philosophy and practice of seventeenth- and eighteenth-century musical repertoire in Europe.

The first challenge facing any researcher who attempts to analyse texts from the past is how to fill those texts with appropriate significance and then translate this into meaningful action in our modern world context. Nowhere is this challenge more acute than in translating the signs and symbols of music into a performance. In the case of Baroque music, in the absence of sound recordings, the written score is the only mediating artefact to the music, and even the information notated in the score is very limited in comparison with scores of the nineteenth and twentieth centuries, carrying few explicit cues to performance practices of the period. In the case of the original manuscripts of Johann Sebastian Bach (1685–1750), for example, there are very few score indications relating to how the musical notes should be interpreted. For instance, there is rarely information about the dynamics (volume) or tempo (speed), and limited instruction relating to articulation, as this information was taken for granted by the musicians of the time. Even the actual notes (pitches and rhythms) were often not fully specified, as performers were expected to embellish their parts with added trills, appoggiaturas and other ornaments, according to their own taste and ability and for expressive effect. Further to this, many scores were only available to the musician in part form. That is, musicians often worked from single-line scores that were quickly copied and supplied no larger context. For example, opera singers' scores from this period contained only the notes and words of a particular character. There were no expressive markings and minimal cues from other characters' roles.

As in all symbolic forms of communication, codes for the delivery of emotionally charged music to the audience were communicated through compositional devices. These included dissonant harmonies employed to create tension, evoke anger, sadness, the pangs of love or to signal impending danger, as well as the precise use of harmonic shifts to indicate mood change. We can understand these by examining the musical devices deployed in context. For example, in the famous *Orfeo* by Claudio Monteverdi (1567–1643), one of the earliest operas of the Baroque period, contrasts in the harmony are used to underline the changing emotions. In Act 2, for instance, Orfeo's aria flicks between the Hypoionian (or 'cheerful mode') and Hypoaeolian mode (which was said to signify 'tears, sadness, solitude, calamities, and every kind of misery'). These 'meanings' were reported in period treatises about music such as *Istitutioni harmoniche* (1573) by Gioseffo Zarlino (1517–90).[2]

Musicologists with a keen interest in decoding documents found that the devices for expressing emotions were many: repetition or variation were seen to heighten affective content, timbre to reflect the nature of the character – evil being low and dark-hued, heroic being high-pitched and bright-toned. A conventional vocabulary of rhythmic devices and melodic shapes were also designed to reinforce the affective and descriptive elements of the words, for instance by representing sadness in slow-moving, descending melodies. In addition to these somewhat straightforward matters, rhetorical devices that related to vocal style and bodily postures and gestures were the means through which meaning was to be delivered in performance. These devices themselves varied tremendously across the period, and by the 1720s the kinds of ornaments and embellishments used to 'decorate' the works and so intensify their meaning were very different to those of the seventeenth century. Some of these expressive devices are 'built into' the structure of the composition and can be read from the score, while other aspects of unwritten or improvisatory performance practice can be gleaned from treatises which reflected these changes.

An overarching goal was for instrumental music to imitate the voice, so many of the expressive devices developed in vocal music to express particular semantic meanings were also carried across by analogy into untexted instrumental music, providing a rich vocabulary of rhetorical devices which were understood to convey meaning – particularly affective meaning – even in the absence of words.[3] One of the greatest recent interpreters and advocates of the art of musical rhetoric was the late Bruce Haynes whose discoveries led him to propose adopting the term 'rhetorical music' as a more apt designation for the period.[4]

The emergent history of 'Baroque music' reveals that interests in scholarship and performance have shifted and will probably continue to do so as further details of the period and its style are uncovered and performances are reimagined. Over the past thirty years, there has been a further significant change in the direction of work on Baroque music. Led by musicologist Richard Taruskin in the 1980s and 1990s, there was a strong challenge to the ideology that had dominated those decades focused on historical accuracy or 'authenticity'.[5] Taruskin and others argued strongly that performers could be informed by the score, historical treatises and other sources of information, but that these sources can never offer sufficient detail to recreate all of the necessary social and cultural, let alone historical conditions of an 'authentic' performance. It was in this new spirit of realization that the Historically Informed Performance (HIP) movement was founded under the leadership of performance scholars such as John Butt.[6] The whole approach brought with it a change of focus from textual accuracy (score-based) and an accompanying largely modernist concern with composers' intentions, to a much stronger focus on expressive and affective objectives and a re-imagining of the un-notated rhetorical practices through which expression was projected by musicians in performance.

Acknowledging that the gap between modern-day and historical understanding endures, the aims of the HIP movement demonstrate that we can begin to prepare a performance that may offer an interpretation that is not merely a dry 'museum art', but takes us closer to the historical intention of moving the affections.

Further reading

Donington, R., *The Interpretation of Early Music* (1963) (New York: Norton, 1992)
—regarded as a 'classic' source on collating and interpreting the historical evidence.

Wilson, N., *The Art of Re-Enchantment Making Early Music in the Modern Age* (New York: Oxford University Press, 2013)
—a recent contribution to the discourse on the philosophical and conceptual issues underpinning historically informed performance, which follows on from the works cited above by Richard Taruskin, John Butt and Bruce Haynes.

Notes

1 C. Sachs, 'Barokmusik', *Jahrbuch der Musikbibliothek Peters*. 26 (1919), 7–15.
2 J. Whenham, *The Cambridge Opera Handbook: Monteverdi's* Orfeo (Cambridge: Cambridge University Press, 1986), 56.
3 D. Bartel, *Musica Poetica: Musical-Rhetorical Figures in German Baroque Music* (Lincoln: University of Nebraska Press, 1997)
4 B. Haynes, *The End of Early Music: A Period Performer's History of Music* (Oxford: Oxford University Press, 2007), 12.
5 R. Taruskin, *Text and Act: Essays on Music and Performance* (Oxford: Oxford University Press, 1996)
6 J. Butt, *Playing with History* (Cambridge: Cambridge University Press, 2002)

IV.27 Baroque art

Stephanie S. Dickey

European artists of the Baroque era were deeply concerned with representing the passions and with eliciting strong emotional responses in viewers. Scholars have long recognized that a heightened emphasis on emotion distinguishes Baroque art from the Renaissance trends out of which it developed.[1] This concern is well-documented in literary sources such as the letters of the Flemish artist Peter Paul Rubens (1577–1640) and theoretical treatises by artists such as Karel van Mander (1548–1606) in the Netherlands, Giovanni Pietro Bellori (1613–96) in Italy and Charles Le Brun (1619–90) in France. Current scholarship enriches the study of literary and visual documents with research into the cultural circumstances in which works of art operated as well as the psychology of emotion and the powerful impact of visual imagery on the human mind.

While Baroque artists' approaches were grounded in strategies developed long before (the rhetorical theories of Quintilian and Aristotle, the expressive figural style of Raphael (1483–1520)), the visual culture of the seventeenth century was distinguished by the intensity, vivacity and theatricality of effects cultivated in all media. Exploration and scientific enquiry prompted fresh curiosity about both the physical world and the inner realm of the human psyche, and the art market expanded to embrace middle-class consumers as well as elite patrons. Advances in travel, trade and technology spread ideas and imagery across Europe and its colonial tributaries. In this new climate, the taste for emotionally engaging content and expression manifested itself in diverse ways.

Seventeenth-century theorists expected the visual arts to delight, instruct and move the spectator. Artists strove to suggest not only the complex interior life of the figures they depicted but also the transitoriness and mutability of emotions and their outward expression. Painters of narrative scenes (history and genre) had to rely on physical gesture and facial expression to communicate mood and motive while inspiring sympathetic reactions in viewers. To achieve this, they combined the demonstrative conventions of oratorical rhetoric and theatre with a new spirit of empirical analysis. The goal of art theoretical writings by authors such as Franciscus Junius (1589–1677) in 1638 and Charles Le Brun in 1688 was to develop convincing systems of representation, while treatises such as *Les passions de l'âme* (1649) by René Descartes (1596–1650) and *Leviathan* (1699) by Thomas Hobbes (1588–1679) had more philosophical aims, but their conclusions were similarly grounded in close observation of human behaviour. Junius, for instance, advised artists to search 'the eyes and countenances' of their contemporaries for 'the severall faces of anger, love, feare, hope, scorne, joy, confidence, and other perturbations of the mind'.[2]

The heightened emotional appeal of Baroque imagery produced both approbation and critique. Neo-Stoic philosophers strove to inure themselves from the physiological and psychological effects of viewing violent or erotic images, and conservative moralists fulminated against art's deceptive allure. Yet the widespread market for evocative subjects ranging from gruesome saintly martyrdoms to humorous scenes of daily life shows that seventeenth-century viewers found pleasure in images that probed the complex emotional currents of human interiority and sociability. The erotic power of the gaze was recognized and exploited throughout the period, gaining a particular resonance in the Rococo art of early eighteenth-century France, where emotions of joy and pleasure were cultivated.[3]

In southern Europe (especially Italy and Spain), the religious zeal of the Catholic Reformation prompted efforts to inspire and renew devotion by eliciting empathy for the mystical fervour and physical suffering of Jesus and other historical champions of the faith. Even Baroque architecture was calculated to prompt emotional responses in visitors as the severe geometry of the Renaissance gave way to undulating surfaces and lofty, richly decorated interiors punctuated by dramatic illumination. Structure and space, sculpture and painting worked together to create a total environment designed to inspire wonder as well as reverence.

A canonical example of all this is the decoration of the Cornaro Chapel in Santa Maria della Vittoria, Rome, by Gian Lorenzo Bernini (1598–1680) (see Figure IV.27.1). Known primarily as a gifted sculptor, Bernini functions here like the impresario of an opera, blending a variety of media to create a powerful, unified effect. Behind the altar, a classical aedicula splits open like the layers of an onion to admit bronze rays of divine radiance, augmented by natural light falling from a concealed window onto the floating, sculpted marble body of Saint Teresa of Avila (1515–82), the Spanish nun whose diary described in vividly sensual terms her mystical union with the divine. Her own words formed the inspiration for the scene, in which Teresa swoons in ecstasy as an angel prepares to pierce her heart, setting it aflame with love of God. One bare foot dangles helplessly, a subtly erotic touch but also a reminder that Teresa founded the order of the Discalced (unshod) Carmelites. Overhead, the dove of the Holy Spirit hovers above painted stucco clouds that seem to invade the space of the chapel, while on either side, members of the Cornaro family marvel at the action like box-seat holders at the theatre. Bernini's animated portraits commemorate the donors of the chapel while inviting the visitor to share in their reverential delight at the vision unfolding before their eyes.

In northern Europe (The Netherlands, Germany, England), where visual imagery was divorced from Protestant religious worship, an inventive range of subjects developed to serve a broad market for secular art. Here, too, emotional impact contributed to both moral instruction and visual pleasure as artists crafted naturalistic yet evocative representations of the visible world and of human characters captured in states of strong emotion or pensive introspection.

In the civic guard portrait by Rembrandt van Rijn (1606–69) known as *The Night Watch* (Figure IV.27.2), a conventionally static form is brought to life. Depicted as if in action rather than posing, Captain Frans Banning Cocq (1600–55) and his cohort of citizen volunteers are preparing to march. Their intent is more likely a celebratory parade than military action; the presence of excited children underfoot adds a note of festivity. Although the scene was composed in the studio, the artist's astute rendering of elements such as costumes, weaponry and body language creates a veristic effect. The emotions evoked here are decidedly secular and sociable: masculine bravado and camaraderie, civic pride in Amsterdam (then the mercantile capital of Europe), and patriotism for the new Dutch Republic. Following a trend fostered by his Italian predecessor, Michelangelo Merisi da Caravaggio (1571–1610), Rembrandt manipulates light and shade to dramatic effect. Viewers are caught up in the energy of the moment

Figure IV.27.1 Gian Lorenzo Bernini, *The Ecstasy of Saint Teresa,* 1645–1652. Mixed media. Rome, Cornaro Chapel, Santa Maria della Vittoria.

From *Bernini and the Art of Architecture,* Tod A. Marder (Abbeville Press, 1998).

Figure IV.27.2 Rembrandt van Rijn, *Civic Guard of District II under the Direction of Capt. Frans Banninck Cocq*, known as *The Night Watch*, 1642, oil on canvas, 379.5 × 453.5 cm. Amsterdam, Rijksmuseum.

as the troop seems ready to march straight out of the canvas and into our space.

Baroque artists and their public understood that emotions were closely linked with sensory experience. In a culture richly attuned to the associative connotations of material things, even everyday objects could carry emotional impact. Illusionistic effects that dissolved barriers between reality and fantasy worked to elicit desire, wonder and even revulsion. An allegorical still life by the Spanish painter Juan de Valdes Léal (1622–90) (Figure IV.27.3) greets visitors to the church of the Hospital de la Caridad in Seville with a chilling vision: the life-size figure of a skeleton tramples a chaotic pile of books, weapons, and other worldly goods. Lavish ecclesiastical trappings litter the table, while the album open on the floor illustrates a triumphal arch from the ceremonial entry of the Habsburg Cardinal-Infante Ferdinand of Austria (1609–41) into Antwerp in 1635, designed by Rubens.[4] These references testify that no one is immune to Death and Time, symbolized by the skeleton's attributes of scythe and coffin. Reaching out to snuff the candle, symbolic of life, the spectre's bony hand calls attention to the inscribed title, *In Ictu Oculi*, meaning 'in the blink of an eye' (1 Corinthians 15:52). The theme of *vanitas* or *memento mori,* reminding viewers that material possessions and earthly accomplishments are merely ephemeral, found international appeal in the Baroque era, as artists and their public brought a new self-awareness to the moral complexities of a period marked by unprecedented prosperity and cultural innovation.

As scholars continue to mine treatises and other sources for evidence of how emotions were understood and represented in early modern Europe, art historians are partnering with scientists to explore the psychological and even physiological effects of expressive visual imagery. Baroque artists strove not only to represent human interiority and emotional expression but also to prompt viewer responses ranging from adoration to horror. The techniques they employed to do so suggest an intuitive understanding of instinctual reactions that neuroscience is now beginning to elucidate.[5] In concert with increasingly nuanced studies of the social circumstances of art production and consumption in the early modern era, this line of enquiry sheds new light on the centrality of emotion in the visual language of the Baroque.

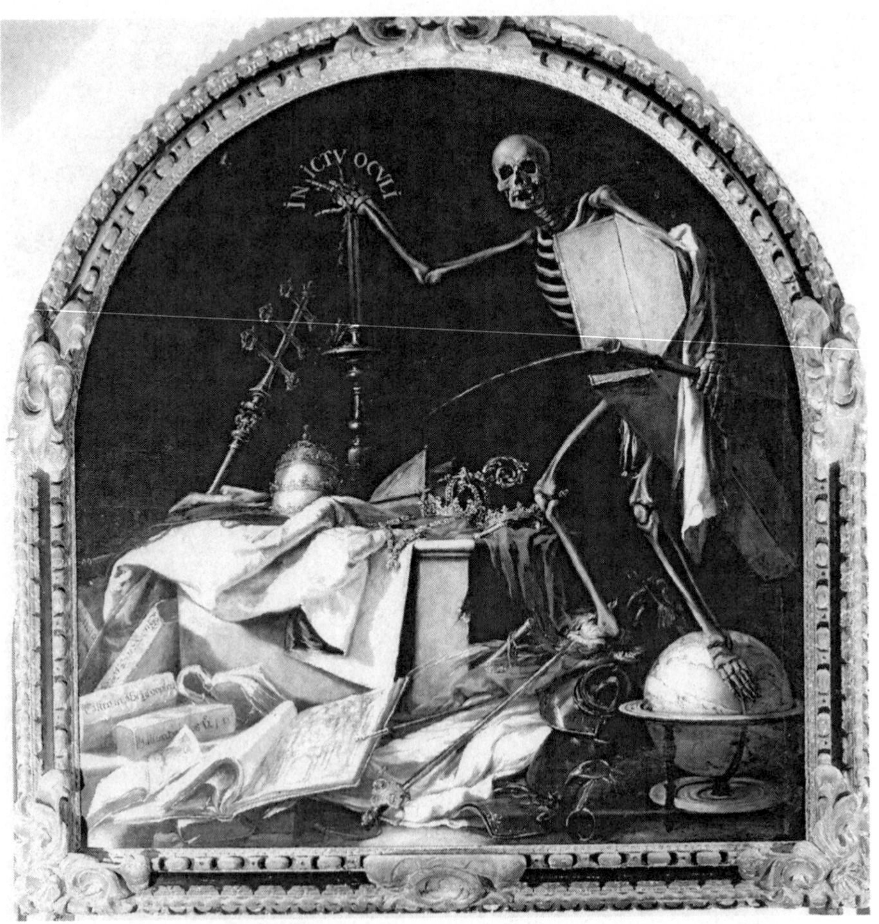

Figure IV.27.3 Juan de Valdés Leal, *In Ictu Oculi,* 1670–72. Oil on canvas, 220 × 216 cm. Seville, Hospital de la Caridad.

Further reading

Dickey, S.S. and H. Roodenburg (eds), *The Passions in the Arts of the Early Modern Netherlands* (Zwolle: Waanders, 2010)

—includes an introduction summarizing the current state of research on emotions in Northern Baroque art and essays that approach questions of emotional representation and response from a variety of methodological perspectives.

Martin, J.R., *Baroque* (New York: Harper & Row, 1977)

—remains fundamental for the study of basic trends in Baroque art. Chapter 3, 'The Passions of the Soul' (73–118), provides a clear overview of the representation of emotion.

Montagu, J., *The Expression of the Passions: The Origin and Influence of Charles Le Brun's 'Conférence sur l'expression générale et particulière'* (New Haven: Yale University Press, 1994)

—provides a scholarly analysis of the artistic theory of Charles Le Brun, whose efforts to describe and categorize emotional expression were highly influential for artists from the seventeenth to the nineteenth centuries.

Notes

1 See, for instance, J.R. Martin, *Baroque* (New York: Harper & Row, 1977), 73–118.

2 K. Aldrich, P. Fehl and R. Fehl (eds), *The Literature of Classical Art: Franciscus Junius, The Painting of the Ancients (1638)*, vol. 1 (Berkeley: University of California Press, 1991), 208. On Le Brun, see J. Montagu, *The Expression of the Passions: The Origin and Influence of Charles Le Brun's 'Conférence sur l'expression générale et particulière'* (New Haven: Yale University Press, 1994)

3 M. Morford, *Stoics and Neostoics: Rubens and the Circle of Lipsius* (Princeton: Princeton University Press, 1991); E.J. Sluijter, *Rembrandt and the Female Nude* (Amsterdam: Amsterdam University Press, 2006); G.A. Bailey, *Spiritual Rococo: Decor and Divinity from the Salons of Paris to the Missions of Patagonia* (Burlington: Ashgate, 2014)

4 See recently A.C. Knaap and M.C.J. Putnam (eds), *Art, Music and Spectacle in the Age of Rubens: The Pompa Introitus Ferdinandi* (Turnhout: Brepols, 2013)

5 See, for instance, the work of Ulrich Heinen on Rubens: U. Heinen and A. Thielemann (eds), *Rubens Passioni: Kultur der Leidenschaften im Baröck* (Göttingen: Vandenhoeck and Ruprecht, 2001); U. Heinen, 'Huygens, Rubens and Medusa: Reflecting the Passions in Paintings, with Some Considerations of Neuroscience in Art History', in S.S. Dickey and H. Roodenburg (eds), *The Passions in the Arts of the Early Modern Netherlands* (Zwolle: Waanders, 2010), 151–76.

IV.28 Enlightenment

Laura Mandell

During the last 15 years, much new work has been done concerning the relationship between Enlightenment rationality and emotions, using the methodologies developed in the field of cultural criticism. John Mullan's *Sentiment and Sociability* (1990), Annette Baier's *A Progress of Sentiments: Reflections on Hume's Treatise* (1991) and Adela Pinch's *Strange Fits of Passion* (1996) recognized the importance of emotion in the work of Enlightenment philosopher David Hume (1711–76), while G.J. Barker-Benfield's *Culture of Sensibility* (1992) described the centrality of emotions to the period generally.[1] By re-reading the major Enlightenment thinkers of the age, historians of emotion and critics of literary and cultural criticism have re-evaluated the role that emotions played in a culture championing rational thinking.

The basic principle of Enlightenment was articulated as early as the Royal Society's motto coined in the 1660s, *nullius in verba* (take nobody's word for it). In a 1784 essay that appeared in *Berlin Monthly* called 'What is Enlightenment?' (*Aufklarung* in German), Immanuel Kant (1724–1804) explicitly declared both the name 'Enlightenment' and its 'motto': *Sapere aude* (Dare to know!); 'Have the courage to use your own understanding'. Because of its emphasis on *thinking* rather than feeling, the Enlightenment has traditionally been called 'The Age of Reason', implicitly contrasted with a movement that occurred during the same time, 'The Age of Sensibility'. Thomas Dixon notes that the word 'emotion' is only first used toward the end of the period as a central 'psychological category' in the *Lectures on the Philosophy of the Human Mind*, by Thomas Brown (1778–1820) first published in 1820.[2] Nonetheless, the Enlightenment did in fact pay attention to 'passions', 'moral sentiments', 'sympathy', 'sensibility', 'affections', 'interest', and a host of other terms for what we now designate as emotions. The champion of Enlightenment thinking par excellence, Scottish philosopher Hume, was Brown's precursor in using the word 'emotion' in our modern sense,[3] and stated in regards to moral philosophy, 'Reason is, and ought only to be the slave of the passions, and can never pretend to any other office than to serve and obey them'.[4]

Hume drew his ideas from 'moral sense' philosophers Anthony Ashley-Cooper, the 3rd Earl of Shaftesbury (1671–1713) and Francis Hutcheson (1694–1746), who argued that humans have a moral sense akin to the other senses of perception, and external objects such as images of suffering humanity stimulate emotions prompting us to behave virtuously, with benevolence and kindness. Like Hume, another Scottish philosopher, Adam Smith (1723–90), fully developed out of moral sense philosophy the notion of 'sympathy' as a means of sensing what others feel: as Smith puts it repeatedly in his *Theory of Moral Sentiments* (1759), through sympathy we imagine what we would feel if in another's situation by 'bringing the case home to ourselves'.[5]

The moral sense school of philosophy stimulated and participated in the sensibility movement. Recent scholars have come to see sensibility as nothing distinct from empirical philosophy, the bulwark of Enlightenment.[6] In *The Poetics of Vacancy*, Kate Singer summarizes our current view that 'Enlightenment notions of embodied sensation' form 'the building block of both sensibility and empiricism'.[7] Thus John Locke (1632–1704) in his *Essay Concerning Human Understanding* (1690, 1700) describes how ideas are formed in the mind: sense impressions make themselves felt 'in some part of the Body, as produces some Perception in the Understanding'.[8] But if in Locke impressions always give rise to ideas, in Hume's early empirical work, some give rise directly to passions.

Hume, in his 1739 *Treatise of Human Understanding,* articulates a social theory of emotions in which they are communicated from person to person immediately:[9]

> [A]n idea of a sentiment or passion, may . . . be so inliven'd as to become the very sentiment or passion. . . . [T]he ideas of the affections of others are converted into the very impressions they represent, and . . . the passions arise in conformity to the images we form of them.[10]

As so adeptly explained by Pinch, Hume is describing sympathy here – an enlivening fellow-feeling – as a kind of transformer: seeing others in a passion is not simply to receive an idea of the impression but to feel it, to receive directly the impression, the feeling itself.[11]

The famous formulation by René Descartes (1596–1650), 'I think, therefore I am', best expresses rationality's central idea, leaving the human being captured by scepticism and solipsism. 'Sympathy' as articulated by Hume and Smith provides a way out of the prison of self: its central formulation might be, 'I feel, therefore *you are*'. A focus on the human mind as an instrument of reason and recipient of sensations and passions conditioned, and was conditioned by, this conjunction of empiricism (with its emphasis on sensation), rationalism (with its emphasis on the mind), and the 'moral sense' school's notions of sensibility and sympathy. Significantly, to speak of 'the' human mind or 'the' human understanding is inherently levelling. Locke's notion that there are 'no innate ideas' in the mind is politically revolutionary precisely because it means that the nobility do not inherit better ways of thinking and feeling from their bloodlines. Further, this interest in the psychology of feeling gave rise to a whole discourse of aesthetics, most famously explored by Edmund Burke (1729–97) in his *Philosophical Enquiry into the Origin of Our Ideas of the Sublime and Beautiful* (1757): how does literature affect the mind and feelings? Burke argues in his 'Introduction on Taste' that literature such as the epic poem *Paradise Lost* by John Milton (1608–74) is great because it produces in us a feeling of the sublime, as agreed upon those who have excellent taste.[12] The aesthetic feelings produced by great art are not, however, appreciated by those 'so continually [engaged] in the agitation of gross and merely sensual pleasures'.[13] People can define their own membership in a higher 'class' based upon how deeply and how much emotion they feel, indicating as it does both their virtue and their refinement; a highly emotional and very sensitive person participates in what Herman Melville would later call an 'aristocracy of feeling'.[14]

Eighteenth-century literature, art and even tourism were designed to 'strengthen' virtuous feelings.[15] The sentimental novels by Samuel Richardson (1689–1761), *Pamela* (1740), *Clarissa* (1748), and *Sir Charles Grandison* (1753), provide excellent examples. Where thinkers differed was on the question of how powerful such natural sensibility was on its own and to what extent it had to be shaped, preserved or educated. Because virtue, sensitivity and aristocracy were associated with sensitivity, the eighteenth century witnessed the rise of 'hyperbolic sentimentalism – [people] weeping, collapsing, exclaiming and pontificating'.[16] The range of outward displays of emotion and their meaning were visible in bourgeois tragedy, or 'tragédie larmoyante', such as *Le Fils Naturel* (1757) by Denis Diderot (1713–84). Via his theory of 'emotives': William M. Reddy describes how people who practised sentimentality by displaying emotion would, upon feeling something stir inside them, find their beliefs about emotionality confirmed.[17] Or, as Pinch puts it, feelings are both conventional and that which animates convention.[18] However, as both Lynn Festa and Reddy notice, these practices changed. *The Man of Feeling* (1771), a novel by Henry Mackenzie (1745–1831) produced at the height of the sensibility movement, could no longer by 1823 be read aloud without producing laughter in its audience.[19] Reddy credits this remarkable transformation in attitudes towards excessive displays of sensibility with people's desire to distance themselves from a sentimentality that fed the French Revolution. He concludes, 'In the late eighteenth century, reason and emotion were not seen as opposed forces; in the early nineteenth they were'.[20]

We have seen how interconnected rationality and sensibility were during the Enlightenment. Late twentieth-century historians and cultural studies critics are now fully exploring what has been reconceived as the Age of Sentimental Reason. Currently, critics such as Deidre Lynch are examining the role of media and its impact on emotion.[21] A further avenue of exploration might follow from new critiques of the Enlightenment focus on epistemology, upon human knowing as a superior mode of relationship among objects in the world. When the human mind is seen as one agent involved in myriad cosmic and natural relationships among many others, a path being explored by Graham Harman, Timothy Morton, and Jane Bennett, among others,[22] our understanding of interactions between emotion and reason change: can we see that change presaged or denied in Enlightenment thinking and practice?

Further reading

Barker-Benfield, G.J., *The Culture of Sensibility: Sex and Society in Eighteenth-Century Britain* (Chicago: University of Chicago Press, 1992)

—among the first to broach the mutually constitutive relationship between empiricism and sensibility, the idea that all knowledge comes to us via the senses, and the theory and practice of emotional sensitivity.

Van Sant, A.J., *Eighteenth-Century Sensibility and the Novel: The Senses in Social Context* (Cambridge: Cambridge University Press, 1993)

—examines how representations of emotion in novels connects to and influences Enlightenment discourses in the disciplines of science and psychology.

Notes

1 J. Mullan, *Sentiment and Sociability: The Language of Feeling in the Eighteenth Century* (Oxford: Clarendon Press, 1990); A.C. Baier, *A Progress of Sentiments: Reflections on Hume's Treatise* (Cambridge, MA: Harvard University Press, 1991); A. Pinch, *Strange Fits of Passion: Epistemologies of Emotion, Hume to Austen* (Stanford: Stanford University Press, 1996); G.J. Barker-Benfield, *The Culture of Sensibility: Sex and Society in Eighteenth-Century Britain* (Chicago: University of Chicago Press, 1992)

2 T.M. Dixon, *From Passions to Emotion: The Creation of a Secular Psychological Category* (New York: Cambridge University Press, 2003)

3 Ibid., 105. Brown read Hume carefully (102).

4 David Hume, *A Treatise of Human Nature* (1739) (ed.) L.A. Selby-Bigge. 2nd Edition, (ed.) P.H. Nidditch (Oxford: Clarendon Press, 1978), 415.

5 A. Smith, *The Theory of Moral Sentiments* (London, Edinburgh, 1759), 20; repeated 5, 7, 22, 28.

6 Barker-Benfield, *The Culture of Sensibility*; A.J. Van Sant, *Eighteenth-Century Sensibility and the Novel: The Senses in Social Context* (Cambridge: Cambridge University Press, 1993)

7 K. Singer, *Romantic Vacancy: The Poetics of Gender, Affect, and Radical Speculation* (book manuscript).

8 J. Locke, *Essay Concerning Human Understanding*, 4th Edition (1700), (ed.) P.H. Nidditch (Oxford: Clarendon Press, 1975), cited by book, chapter, and section: 2.1.23.

9 Mullan, *Sentiment and Sociability*, 35–6.

10 Hume, *A Treatise of Human Nature*, 319.

11 Pinch, *Strange Fits of Passion*,18, 25.

12 E. Burke, *Philosophical Enquiry into the Origin of Our Ideas of the Sublime and Beautiful* (1757), (ed.) J.T. Boulton (Notre Dame, IN: Univ. of Notre Dame Press 1958), 59.

13 Ibid., 24.

14 H. Melville, *Letter to Nathaniel Hawthorne* (1851), online at www.melville.org/letter3.htm, accessed 11 November 2015.

15 L. Festa, *Sentimental Figures of Empire in Eighteenth-Century Britain and France* (Baltimore: Johns Hopkins University Press, 2006), 44.

16 S.C. Maza, 'Luxury, morality, and social change: why there was no middle-class consciousness in prerevolutionary France', *Journal of Modern History* 69, 2 (1997), 199–229, quote 227.

17 W.M. Reddy, *The Navigation of Feeling: A Framework for the History of Emotions* (New York: Cambridge University Press, 2001), 3, 164, 105.

18 Pinch, *Strange Fits of Passion*, 48–9.

19 Festa, *Sentimental Figures*, 21.
20 Reddy, *Navigation*, 216.
21 D.S. Lynch, *Loving Literature: A Cultural History* (Chicago: University of Chicago Press, 2015); L. Mandell, *Breaking the Book: Print Humanities in the Digital Age* (Oxford: Wiley Blackwell, 2015)
22 G. Harman, *Towards Speculative Realism* (Washington, DC: Zero Books, 2010); T. Morton, *Hyperobjects* (Minneapolis: University of Minnesota Press, 2013); J. Bennett, *Vibrant Matter: A Political Ecology of Things* (Durham: Duke University Press, 2010)

IV.29 Romanticism

R.S. White

It has never been disputed that Romanticism in all art forms and across Europe was based on prioritizing emotions and imagination, and so all accounts of the movement and its authors make relevant comments on the importance of emotions. The definitions of poetry offered by William Wordsworth (1770–1850) as 'emotions recollected in tranquility' and 'the spontaneous overflow of powerful feelings' specify this, and the movement was a conscious reaction against neo-classical emotional restraint with its emphasis on aesthetic forms rather than feelings.[1] This entry summarizes some of the particular emotional states that were given priority in Romantic thought and poetry. The sources are largely literary, but Romanticism as broad movement covered all aspects of the arts, including music, and politics, since revolutions swept Europe and America in the period.

The dates usually taken to define Romanticism, from the 1780s to 1832, refer to historical events driven by political passions. The American War of Independence against England (1775–83) was one of several revolutions across the Western world, culminating in France in 1789. Despite reactionary governments in England, a general mood for political and social change was manifested by rising middle classes resenting their disenfranchisement and seeking to overthrow the dominance of aristocracies and monarchical systems. In 1832 partial but significant success was achieved in the enactment of the so-called Great Reform Act in England, extending suffrage to a wider section of the population (though still only men), and undermining the system of 'rotten boroughs' which had kept power in the hands of a wealthy few. Meanwhile, war between England and France was an ever-present reality between 1789 and 1815 (formally declared in 1802), eliciting from writers a range of emotive responses, both pro- and anti-war.

Collective, emotionally expressed arguments for change were advanced by writers such as Thomas Paine (1737–1809), Jean-Jacques Rousseau (1712–78), William Godwin (1756–1836) Mary Wollstonecraft (1759–97) and many others, all expressing a fervent desire for 'rights' – abolition of slavery, the right to vote, rights of women, children and animals. Creative writers became important agents for popularizing the ideas, compelling readers' emotional engagement with affecting narratives in novels, and poems expressing and eliciting strong feelings. Such a paradigm shift towards emotional engagement did not come overnight but instead had been building up for a century. Feelings became touchstones for morality and for political aspirations.

Romantic writers espoused the primacy of individual feelings and the creative imagination over coercive reason and authority. Wordsworth's long work, *The Prelude*, was subtitled by his sister Dorothy (1771–1855) *The Growth of a Poet's Mind* (1798, 1805, 1850), and it shows a concentration on the psychology of the imagination. Wordsworth and Samuel Taylor Coleridge (1772–1834) in their collaborative volume, *Lyrical Ballads* (1798, 1800), focused sympathetically on marginalized social outcasts such as the rural poor and the insane, and intensely visualized an emotionally healing relationship between nature and humanity. William Blake (1757–1827) wrote poems from a burning desire for social reform in cities which increasingly bore scars from 'dark satanic mills' of the Industrial Revolution. Percy Bysshe Shelley (1792–1822) argued that 'change within', based on guiding emotions such as love, fellow feeling, altruism and moral indignation, were necessary in forming a social conscience that could lead towards 'change without' in political revolution.

To offer a more nuanced sense of the diversity of emotions given fresh meanings in the Romantic period, we might look at two in particular, melancholy and sympathy. Melancholy pointed to a substantial legacy of meanings from the past, offering continuities and developments from medieval and ancient times, while sympathy indicated philosophical, political and psychological dimensions which pointed to modern times.

The primary meaning of melancholy in earlier times was medical, deriving from a belief that bodily and mental ailments were interconnected. Melancholy caused a wide spectrum of physical and emotional symptoms which we now call moods or pathologies, ranging from depression right through to mania. Even over-zealous religious faith could be as worrying a form of melancholy as 'green sickness' caused by love in young women.

Increasing importance of anatomy and surgery in medical training in the later decades of the eighteenth century indicated a separation of body and mind, leading to discrete professions, physicians for the body and others who concentrated on the mind and emotions. The split was accentuated by the rise of the public hospital system after 1800, resulting from power struggles within the medical profession. The word 'melancholy' increasingly became the 'writer's malady', associated with the kind of lonely creativity synonymous with Romantic poetry.

'Graveyard poetry' was one result. Typically, the poet would be meditating at twilight in a graveyard on life and death. The most famous example is the *Elegy Written in a Country Churchyard* (1751) by Thomas Gray (1716–71) an influential model for Romantics of the literary conventions of melancholy. In a state of 'lonely contemplation' the poet muses on the varied lives which had been led by all those who lie dead in the graveyard, from lowly nonentities to petty tyrants. These include an archetypally lovelorn young poet, described on his epitaph as one whom 'Melancholy marked . . . for her own': 'He gave to Misery all he had, a tear'.[2] The poet writing the elegy transparently envisages his own ultimate fate, and generalizes on the vanity of wishes when death comes to all.

Coleridge's poem, 'Dejection: An Ode' (written 1802) is written from a more psychologically based emotional state of 'dull pain': 'A grief without a pang, void, dark, and drear, / A stifled, drowsy, unimpassioned grief'. The poet can 'see, not feel' the beauty around him, and in this state of alienation he cannot 'hope from outward forms to win / The passion and the life, whose fountains are within'. The 'Ode' then follows a therapeutic path on 'wings of healing', as the poet strives to recapture lost 'Joy' through his 'shaping spirit of Imagination'.[3] The loosening of his 'viper thoughts' comes spontaneously, as a combination of love and identification with living things and natural processes, bringing about a peaceful closure to a poem which, in a suggestive phrase used by William Hazlitt (1778–1830) charts a 'logic of passion'. The pattern is enacted in the more familiar poem by Coleridge, 'The Rime of the Ancient Mariner', which has influenced the modern environmental, 'green' movement.

Graveyard poetry contributed to another increasingly fashionable genre, the Gothic novel, initiated in *The Castle of Otranto* (1764) by Horace Walpole (1717–97) as a medieval revival. The increasingly familiar, affective signs are visible, designed to stir readers' emotions: a ruined castle or gloomy manor house, a pervading atmosphere of foreboding apprehension, fear and horror. John Keats (1795–1821) fused melancholy and Gothic conventions in his narrative poems 'The Eve of St Agnes' and 'Isabella', and he also wrote an 'Ode on Melancholy'.

Another distinctively Romantic form of melancholy was stimulated by the epistolary, semi-autobiographical novel by the German writer, Johann Wolfgang von Goethe (1749–1832), *The Sorrows of Young Werther* (1774; trans. 1779), which swept Europe, causing a cult of youthful suicide for unrequited love. Lord Byron (1788–1824) became the first literary 'superstar' when he covered similar emotional terrain in *Manfred* (1816–17), depicting a Faust-like wanderer, and in *Childe Harold's Pilgrimage* (1812–18).

The Gothic genre was regarded as especially aimed at female readers, and some women became identified as exemplary writers into the Romantic age, such as Ann Radcliffe (1764–1823) (*The Mysteries of Udolpho* [1794]), poet and novelist Charlotte Smith (1749–1806) and Mary Shelley (1797–1851) (*Frankenstein* [1818]). However, it was also a woman, Jane Austen (1775–1817), who helped puncture the Gothic novel's hypnotic hold over credulous readers, in *Northanger Abbey* (1818), gently debunking the conventions. In similar vein, Thomas Love Peacock (1785–1866) in his hilarious novels *Headlong Hall* (1815) and *Nightmare Abbey* (1818), satirized his poetic friends, Coleridge, Shelley and Byron, for their self-conscious dedication to a pose of melancholia.

During the eighteenth century we also find an increasing emphasis on sympathy and benevolence, underpinned by philosophical, political and even economic arguments for altruism by Scottish Enlightenment writers such as David Hume (1711–76) and Adam Smith (1723–90). Such impulses were based on a stronger valuation of emotions themselves as part of a developing 'cult of sensibility'.

The later eighteenth century, leading up to Romanticism, is sometimes called 'the Age of Sensibility', and the French *Encyclopédie* in 1765 went so far as to claim that 'sensibility is the mother of humanity'. However, the word had a different and almost opposite meaning from our 'sensible'. Encapsulated in Rousseau's radical revision of the famous phrase of René Descartes (1596–1650), 'I think therefore I am' into 'I felt before I thought', sensibility referred to a strong awareness of the feelings of others. Acute empathy with suffering influenced public policy since ideally it drove people to make society more just and happy. It was popularized in 'sentimental' novels where (especially) heroines were prone to weep, faint and generally respond in an emotionally sympathetic way to the wrongs done to individuals. Examples are novels such as *Mary: A Fiction* (1788) and *Maria: or, The Wrongs of Women* (1798) by Mary Wollstonecraft (Mary Shelley's mother). Later, when blood was visibly shed in revolutionary action, sensibility came to be mistrusted as potentially leading to wrongs as much as rights, and again it was Jane Austen who gently criticized the cult in her *Sense and Sensibility* (1811). However, vestiges of the sentimental novel persisted into Victorian times, when Charles Dickens (1812–70) stirred readers' consciences through emotions, regarding issues like public education and child exploitation. It is a significant part of the lasting legacy of the Romantic movement, reflecting cyclical revivals of emotions as a basis for reform.

Since Romanticism is defined by its general prioritizing of emotions, the senses, sympathy and nature over reason, intellect, judgement and the city, future research will no doubt continue to consolidate the view that intense emotions were considered the most fundamental source of knowledge, and the basis for art and political demands.

Further reading

McCalman, I., J. Mee, G. Russell, C. Tuite, K. Fullagar and P. Hardy (eds), *An Oxford Companion to the Romantic Age: British Culture, 1776–1832* (Oxford: Oxford University Press, 1999)

—an invaluable reference work with chapters and entries on virtually every writer and aspect of emotions in the Romantic Age.

Parisot, E., *Graveyard Poetry: Religion, Aesthetics and the Mid-Eighteenth-Century Poetic Condition* (Farnham: Ashgate, 2013)

—examines the importance of melancholy in one of the poetic genres of early Romanticism.

White, R.S., *Natural Rights and the Birth of Romanticism in the 1790s* (London: Macmillan, 2005)

—examines the political and intellectual background to the revolutions in thought occurring in the 1790s, driven by a passion for equality and human rights as manifested, for example, in the campaigns for abolition of slavery and equal rights for women. Such changes in thought were as much a product of feeling-states like sensibility and sympathy as of rational debate.

Notes

1 The phrases are from Wordsworth's 'Preface' to *Lyrical Ballads* (1798) written by Wordsworth and Coleridge.

2 S. Greenblatt (ed.), *Norton Anthology of English Literature: The Restoration and the Eighteenth Century*, 9th Edn (New York: W. W. Norton, 2012), 305.

3 Greenblatt (ed.), *Norton Anthology of English Literature*, 479.

Beliefs

IV.30 Monastic communities

Claire Walker

There is little research in English dedicated to monasticism and emotions, despite the cloister presenting an obvious laboratory for exploring the relationship between early modern understandings of the passions and how they might inform communal living, religious ritual, meditative prayer and the contemplative apostolate. Most scholarship considers nuns, whose unruly passions were generally deemed to be in greater need of reform. The Council of Trent (1545–63) stipulated the strict enclosure of religious women, while acknowledging that male monastics might preach, teach and engage in other spiritual labour outside the cloister. Defined by claustration and contemplation, nuns were expected to embody virtue and chastity through the strict regulation of their passions and thereby serve as moral examples of perfection for society at large. Monks observed enclosure in monasteries and were tutored in emotional regulation, but teaching, preaching and missionary work required a different emotional repertoire to engage the hearts and minds of students, townsfolk and converts.

In prescriptive literature, monks and nuns alike were enjoined to embrace humility and subject themselves to the authority of their superiors and the rigour of their rule. The 1661 English Benedictine constitutions required the male novice to go to weekly confession and communion, and abstain from eating meat. He undertook training in Gregorian chant, spiritual exercises, mental prayer and the humanities, as well as being tested in humility and deportment.[1] The aspiring nun underwent a similar formation process, which required strict self-abnegation to unlearn secular habits, stifle personal desires and subjugate the passions. In the English Augustinian convent in Louvain, the novice mistress taught the aspiring nun 'to overcome her passions and imperfections, [and] to mortify all sensuall desires'.[2] Women evidently took such advice to heart. Teresa Bream (1590–1650) of the English Benedictines in Ghent was praised in her obituary for maintaining 'an absolute Command over her passions . . . she was never seen discomposed'.[3] Other women fell short of the requisite standard but were praised nonetheless for efforts to conquer unruly feelings. Ghent lay sister, Cecily Price (professed 1624) who died in 1630, 'was naturally Cholerick, Yet most Heroically combatted with her Passions'.[4]

The prescription for emotional restraint continued into the eighteenth century. The advice manual of Franciscan Michel-Ange Marin (1697–1767) admonished women to eschew affection for the secular realm, identifying three loci of worldly attachment: the 'exterior world' from which they were separated physically by cloister walls; the 'interior world' of the convent with its quotidian distractions; and the 'domestick world' of the body which harboured passions and defects.[5] Other monastic texts similarly excoriated the baser passions of pride, anger, sloth and lack of charity. Yet there is evidence that such ideals were not as rigidly policed as in the previous centuries. Geoffrey Scott has traced a relaxation in the austerity of monastic life for Benedictine monks, including punishments for those who fell short of prescribed behaviours.[6] The obituaries of English Franciscan nuns in Brussels suggest that sisters were acknowledged more than in the past for their musical, managerial and craft expertise, but adherence to emotional restraint remained important. Elizabeth Joseph Boucher (*c.* 1685–1736) was praised for her exemplary 'sweet & Aimable Conversation' and 'Singular Prudence'.[7]

Yet the prescribed emotional regime often belied the realities of cloistered communal living. Monastic and diocesan records detail internal dissension, inappropriate friendships and the manifold disruptions caused by those who failed to conquer their passions. Unwilling nuns, like the well-known Venetian, Arcangela Tarabotti (1604–52), wrote passionately about forced vocations at a time of soaring marriage dowries. Others retained intimate attachments with family and friends. Moreover, far from supporting absolute emotional restraint, many religious leaders ameliorated the rigour of monastic discipline with humour, music and theatrical performance. In 1618, Carmelite Ana de San Bartolomé (1549–1626) reported 'here there has been much gaiety, for I had [the nuns] doing all sorts of nonsense; and they made sport of Monsior de Beruel and his associates, . . . so that we were dying of laughter'.[8] Such performances were not just recreation. Theatre comprised an important pedagogical function in Jesuit formation. Jesuit performances engaged the emotions to inspire loyalty to the order and to prepare students for missionary careers and possible martyrdom. Elissa Weaver has uncovered a similar didactic function in convent theatre where nuns could learn how to talk, move and emote like the saints and holy women they acted.[9] Recent work on chronicle accounts of war and iconoclasm reveals how religious women framed their fear of anticipated and actual violence as martyrdom.[10] Likewise, from the early Renaissance through the Baroque, religious cloisters commissioned religious art to inspire affective piety.

Spirituality provided the key platform for emotional expression. The primary task for both nuns and monks was communal prayer. In the *Opus Dei*, plainsong required restraint in performance, but it was possible for individuals to derive emotional satisfaction; like Elizabeth Abraham Scarisbrick (*c.* 1705–33) of the Brussels Franciscans whose obituary noted that she 'took Great Delight in Singing the Divine Praises & Playing upon the Organ'.[11] Moreover such work might invoke an emotional response. Mary Joseph Petre (*c.* 1695–1734) had 'A most Angelicall Sweet Voice' and her determination to perform her choir duties when ill 'moved the Hearts of all that heard her to Devotion'.[12] Private prayer provided greater scope for emotional engagement through mystical contemplation. The early modern church was wary of mysticism. Many female cloisters had Jesuit spiritual supervision to ensure orthodoxy. Ignatian spirituality was designed for the active apostolate rather than the monastic environment. However, in the *Spiritual Exercises* Ignatius of Loyola (1491–1556) adapted late medieval affective piety, using the imagination to stimulate the passions. English Benedictine, Lucy Knatchbull (1584–1629), described how making the exercises 'settled my thoughts much in God'. This grounding became a springboard for visions and trances. After receiving the Eucharist, she felt her soul drawn into Christ's arms, upon which he gathered 'into himself the affections of my whole heart' and she almost fainted.[13]

Ignatian spirituality was not alone in employing the imagination. Some Teresian techniques used images to excite the senses, while others eschewed engagement of the passions. The meditation practised in the English Benedictine Congregation, propounded by the monk, Augustine Baker (1575–1641), encouraged mystical contemplation through annihilation of the self. The Cambrai nun, Gertrude More (1606–33), wrote that before learning Baker's method her heart had 'grown . . . as hard as a stone'.[14] Once tutored to overcome her passions and entered into a state of contemplation, More described divine union in distinctly emotive language: 'the more I sigh, the more I am delighted to sigh after *thee, whom* I would so fain enioy'.[15] She highlights the tension in monasticism regarding the emotions. Mysticism required subjugation of the passions to achieve the heightened sensibility necessary for divine union, but the ensuing mystical encounter was embodied and experienced through the emotions.

A consideration of monasticism through the lens of emotion reveals the degrees to which it both constrained and liberated monks and nuns in their quotidian lives and spiritual endeavours. Monasticism formally required both men and women to eschew affective ties to achieve closer union with God. The principal channel for emotional expression lay in spiritual devotion, where mystical union with Christ legitimated an outpouring of passionate feelings, words, tears and gestures. Yet from 1500 to 1800 there were subtle changes in the way emotional control and expression informed communal living. Regulations became more relaxed, and as the eighteenth century progressed there was a far greater emphasis on practical engagement than mystical contemplation for both nuns and monks. While there is little scholarship thus far that considers the insights an emotions history of monasticism might bring to our understanding of the field, the research that exists points to exciting possibilities for future investigation. More work on mysticism is necessary, and emotions could also offer new perspectives on internal and external monastic relationships, the structure and use of sacred space, liturgy and ritual and monastic politics.

Further reading

Hallett, N., *The Senses in Religious Communities, 1600–1800: Early Modern 'Convents of Pleasure'* (Farnham: Ashgate, 2013)

—Hallett's exploration of the senses in early modern female monasticism reveals the scope for further investigation of the area for women, but also with respect to monks, friars and male clergy.

Lux-Sterritt, L., 'Divine Love and the Negotiation of Emotions in Early Modern English Convents', in C. Bowden and J.E. Kelly (eds), *The English Convents in Exile, 1600–1800: Communities, Culture and Identity* (Farnham: Ashgate, 2013), 229–45.

—an introductory exploration of the significance of the emotions in female mysticism, which points to the tremendous potential for further research on the topic.

Walker, C., 'An Ordered Cloister? Dissenting Passions in Early Modern English Cloisters,' in S. Broomhall (ed.), *Gender and Emotions in Medieval and Early Modern Europe: Destroying Order, Structuring Disorder* (Farnham: Ashgate, 2015), 197–214.

—demonstrates the significance of emotional regulation in religious cloisters, but reveals how women found outlets for passionate expression, which ultimately served to maintain the emotional status quo.

Notes

1 G. Scott, 'A Long Exile,' in D. Rees (ed.), *Monks of England: The Benedictines in England from Augustine to the Present Day* (London: SPCK, 1987), 186.

2 Douai Abbey, Reading, St Monica's MS E4: 'Constitutions of the English Regular Canonesses of the Holy Order of St Augustine in the Convent of St Monica, Louvain' (1609), fol. 63.
3 'Obituary Notices of the Nuns of the English Benedictine Abbey of Ghent in Flanders, 1627–1811', in *Miscellanea XI* (London: Catholic Record Society, 1917), 47.
4 Ibid., 14.
5 M. Marin, *The Perfect Religious: A Work Designed for the Assistance of those who Aspire after Perfection in a Religious State* (Douai, 1762), in L. Lux-Sterritt (ed.), *English Convents in Exile, 1600–1800, vol. 2 Spirituality* (London: Pickering and Chatto, 2012), 85–6.
6 Scott, 'Long Exile', 193–6.
7 R. Trappes-Lomax (ed.), *English Franciscan Nuns 1619–1821 and the Friars Minor of the Same Province 1618–1761* (London: Catholic Record Society, 1917), 212.
8 E. Arenal and S. Schlau (eds), *Untold Sisters: Hispanic Nuns in their Own Words* (Albuquerque: University of New Mexico Press, 1989), 72–3.
9 E.B. Weaver, *Convent Theatre in Early Modern Italy: Spiritual Fun and Learning for Women* (Cambridge: Cambridge University Press, 2002), 61–75.
10 E. Kuijpers, '"O, Lord, Save us from shame": Narratives of Emotions in Convent Chronicles by Female Authors during the Dutch Revolt, 1566–1635' in S. Broomhall (ed.), *Gender and Emotions in Medieval and Early Modern Europe: Destroying Order, Structuring Disorder* (Farnham: Ashgate, 2015), 127–46.
11 *English Franciscan Nuns*, 211.
12 Ibid., 212.
13 T. Matthew, *The Life of Lady Lucy Knatchbull* (London: Sheed and Ward, 1931), 40–2.
14 G. More, *The Spiritual Exercises of the Most Vertuous and Religious D. Gertrude More of the Holy Order of S. Bennet* (Paris, 1658), 14.
15 Ibid., 154.

IV.31 The reformations

Susan C. Karant-Nunn

Although medievalists have long considered the Catholic emotional ideals for meditating on the suffering of Christ during Holy Week, the treatment of emotion within the Reformation context is a very recent phenomenon. We now realize that no human transaction is without its emotional dimensions. This is true of all groups and theologies that begged to differ with the predominant Roman Catholicism during the early sixteenth century, and whose differences have proved permanent. The Reformation in all its forms must be viewed against the backdrop of the emotional ideals of that Mother Church. In the fifteenth century, by means of art and the preached word, ecclesiastical leaders urged Christians, as a devotional act, to cultivate identity with the panoply of saints who had undergone martyrdom, and especially with the crucified Christ. All meditative roads led to Christ in his Passion, and the saints themselves were to remember that their own suffering did not attain the level of torment that the Saviour endured. Artists and preachers took on the obligation of *moving* their audiences to grief over the agony of these historic or legendary exemplars of devotion. Giorgio Vasari (1511–74) wrote of Fra Angelico (*c.* 1395–1455) that 'whenever he painted a Crucifixion the tears would stream down his face'.[1] Early in the following century, the Franciscan preacher in Germany Johannes Wild (1497–1554) declared that all hearts should melt as they recall Christ's wounds, blood, suffering and death.[2] The devout should break down and cry. Christ's individual wounds underwent separate sanctification and personification and became the objects of prayers themselves. The Counter-Reformation Church saw no diminution in its call to meditate upon the Passion.

Second only to her son in the degree of pain presented to her worshippers for contemplation was the Virgin Mary. From the late Middle Ages on through the sixteenth and seventeenth centuries, the mother of Jesus was depicted with swords piercing her heart as Simeon had foretold (Luke 2: 35). The devout were to recollect her suffering as Herod sought to kill her son, as his parents lost the boy Jesus in the temple, as his Jewish admirers turned away from him and as he underwent torture and died on the cross.

Art and architecture held out to the faithful the hope of joy, usually in the afterlife but sometimes, as in the *Ecstasy of Saint Teresa* by Gian Lorenzo Bernini (1598–1680), still on earth. More frequently, baroque depictions of the putto-filled heavens afforded a glimpse into the presence of God and of Christ, as the Son ascended to the Father, as Mary was assumed into reunion with her Son, or as Christ crowned his mother. Light-filled portraits of the blessed hereafter meant to elicit from even ordinary mortals the determination to exploit the sacramental theology of the church with its devotional templates, and to rise ultimately themselves. As Carlo Borromeo (1538–84) prescribed them, even precious building materials should inspire heavenly aspirations in those who marveled at them.

Nevertheless, early modern Catholicism remained acutely mindful of sin and the Devil. The horrors of hell were ever a reality, as imaginatively depicted by Hieronymus Bosch (*c.* 1450–1516), and prayers and pious acts continued to aim for the relief of souls in purgatory. The ascetic feats of members of new orders such as the Capuchin friars conveyed an emotional state of their own, one defined by a conviction of the inadequate suppression of the demands of the flesh. Ignatius of Loyola (1491–1556) relentlessly punished his body in an effort to prove worthy of salvation, as his long-unpublished 'Autobiography' shows.

The Wittenberg Reformer and those of his followers who subsequently occupied positions of authority in the emerging churches drastically modified their emotional prescriptions. As expressed in the altarpiece predella of the St Mary's Church (City Church) in Wittenberg, the emphasis was now on the atonement and on God's love for humanity. Theologians still believed in hellfire, but they stressed instead the consolation (*Trost*) that the heavenly Father held out to believers. The observances of Holy Week differed from preacher to preacher, with some continuing to describe the specific agonies of the Saviour, but others, including Martin Luther (1483–1546), preferred biblical brevity to marathons of elaboration, with their focus upon the loving endurance of God's Son for the expiation of sin and for human reconciliation with the Father. The prevailing clerical view was one of scorn for the emotional excesses of Catholic treatment. Christians should feel thankful release from the deserved penalties for their postlapsarian disfigurement through the Fall.

Many images of the Virgin and of the saints in their martyrdom disappeared from sanctuaries. Their removal, mainly not through iconoclasm, constituted a major toning down of emotional elicitation. Yet crucifixes remained in every church, displaying the bleeding, naked Christ upon the instrument of his bodily torment. Increasingly, as replacement of devotional objects became possible, the Lord was no longer suffering but was dead; his eyes were closed and did not engage the look of the worshipper below. His expression was exhausted but peaceful. Patrons no longer desired artists to include exaggerated bleeding and tendonal distention. Simultaneously, preachers encouraged sorrow for sin and confidence in God's compassion. Weeping, if done, was a matter for personal devotion.

Within prescribed forms of worship remained, and indeed expanded, music that eventually engaged the laity. Song, organs and bells, vernacular biblical passages and rites all may have drawn an emotional response, although we still know too little about its nature.

When evangelical clergy attended the dying, their message was similarly one encompassing regret for one's chronic transgressions and reliance on divine mercy in light of Christ's satisfaction. Again, the net assumption was that Jesus' sacrifice of himself should comfort the about-to-be decedent and his/her family.

Religious expression outside the churches was to be concentrated within the personal life of prayer and within domestic practice. Heartfelt conviction would, Luther preached in his *Hauspostille* (Georg Rörer version, published in Jena 1559), inevitably show itself in acts of loving kindness toward one's neighbours. Gone were the convivial processions of Corpus Christi and Rogation Days. Left in place, however, were post-wedding feasts and modest dances. The rootedness of the cult within social life and tradition was still recognizable even if reduced. The churches approved of constrained human enjoyment.

The Reformed Churches, taking their models from the Zwinglian in Zurich and, later, the Calvinist in Geneva, strove to remove all images from sites of worship. All the traditional signals to feel were cleansed from the churches and not encouraged at home. Even music was suspect, with the exception of a cappella and unison Psalms within Calvinism. The sentiments that Jean Calvin (1509–64) strove to arouse in his sermons are distinctly two: (1) awed recognition of the majesty of the Godhead; and (2) abject, unceasing self-incrimination for sin. Johann Salmuth (1552–1622), court preacher to the Reformed Saxon Elector Christian I (1560–91), blamed the prince's premature decease in 1591 on the sins of his subjects:

> We recognize and lament before your countenance that we are great transgressors and miserable sinners. Our sins are more than the [grains of] sand in the sea. We are raised out of sinful seed, and our mothers conceived us in sin. We have behaved unrighteously and have become godless; we did not obey your servants who in your holy name . . . preached repentance and forgiveness of sins to us.[3]

Such themes are representative of Calvinism in the Age of Orthodoxy, when all denominations tended toward discipline. God as well as His representatives on earth were often angry. It is hard to know how their hearers integrated such harsh messages into their image of themselves. It may be that citizens of Geneva were not keen on Calvin's preaching, which they saw as insulting them, but the Reformer had numerous avid followers in The Netherlands.[4] The sermon of the well-known Massachusetts

Puritan divine, Jonathan Edwards (1703–58), 'Sinners in the Hands of an Angry God', was quite in keeping with the mood of his day and his reference group.[5]

The Reformed conviction that the Holy Spirit worked upon the souls of the elect (and only the elect) as the Spirit-inspired Word was preached, if taken to heart, did introduce a note of sanctity into the otherwise cleansed environment. As the pastor mounted into the pulpit, he served as a mouthpiece of the divine.

Social life in Reformed parishes was meant to conform to biblical standards of piety. Games and dances, feasts and festivals were prohibited. In some parts of the Holy Roman Empire, the people resisted the thoroughness of these strictures. Likewise, in England and The Netherlands, because other persuasions were readily available, moral discipline could not be as consistent as in a city-state of uniform confession. Throughout Europe, folk beliefs persisted and afforded local mitigation of official rules.

Reformation scholars have only begun to explore the ways in which advocated feeling shifted in the transition from Catholic to Protestant ideals. Differences between and among reforming groups arose and helped to set them apart. Did Spiritualists advocate the display of feeling over those who emphasized the written, read and preached Word? Most challenging is, of course, to gain evidence of lay responses to models set out by clergy. How, for example, did listeners respond to Calvin's frequent disparagement, even condemnation of the lack of guilt displayed in their own lives? Someone may want to take up Calvin's own emotions as he confronted the seeming indifference of his neighbours.

Further reading

Bestul, T.H., *Texts of the Passion: Latin Devotional Literature and Medieval Society* (Philadelphia: University of Pennsylvania Press, 1996)

—relates written content to prevalent practices within society.

Karant-Nunn, S.C., *The Reformation of Feeling: Shaping the Religious Emotions in Early Modern Germany* (Oxford: Oxford University Press, 2010)

—an initial effort to draw attention to the emotional content of the Reformation's program of religious transformation.

Kreitzer, B., *Reforming Mary: Changing Images of the Virgin Mary in Lutheran Sermons of the Sixteenth Century* (Oxford: Oxford University Press, 2004)

—less about Mary's own purported feelings than about the Reformers' changed attitudes toward the Mother of God and toward their parishioners' entrenched veneration of her.

Notes

1 G. Vasari, *Lives of the Artists*, (trans.) G. Bull (Harmondsworth: Penguin, 1965), 206.

2 J. Wild, *Sacrosancta Passionis Saluatoris nostri Iesu Christi Hystoria* (Mainz, 1555), 517.

3 Sächsisches Hauptstaatsarchiv Dresden, Geheimes Archiv 10024, Loc.4382 / 10, elec. fol. 165r.

4 B. Gordon, *Calvin* (New Haven: Yale University Press, 2009), 138–40.

5 An on-line video contains the warning that the language is inappropriate for children under 13. Edwards preached to congregations that did contain children, however.

IV.32 Tolerance

Giovanni Tarantino

One of the most difficult obstacles to overcome in efforts to build a more inclusive society, which is able to adopt a curious, humble and respectful attitude towards diversity rather than responding with mistrust, fear, mockery and contempt, is the internalization of a stereotypical representation of religious alterity, or indeed of alterity as a whole. No history of tolerance can therefore disregard the psychological processes that forge the human propensity for prejudice.

Referring to circles in early eighteenth-century London where 'Churchmen and Dissenters, Believers and Unbelievers, Free-thinkers, Half-thinkers, and No-thinkers, all *most Christianly* meet together', the Scottish freethinker and Sinophile Thomas Gordon (*c.* 1691–1750) argued that 'this is the only way to work off their prejudices against each other: And if it don't make them *nominal*, it will make them *real* Christians'.[1] Not rarely, however, Gordon's use of irony to profanize salvation and encourage concord ended up sliding into a dismissive, and ultimately intolerant, demonization of the religious Other. Something not dissimilar can be found in contemporary public debate about religious difference in multicultural Western liberal democracies, where concerns about the emotional effects of hate speech and religious insult on the social and democratic fabric loom large.

A more effective argument for mutual tolerance, by contrast, seems to emerge from *Cérémonies et coutumes religieuses de tous les peuples du monde* (1723–37) by Jean-Frédéric Bernard (*c.* 1683–1744) and Bernard Picart (1673–1733). In this work, emphasis is placed on the supposed common psychological roots of all religious traditions, a more indulgent view is taken of human nature, and the culturally specific differences between various 'religious' traditions are highlighted and for the most part respectfully depicted. Bernard and Picart's literary and visual survey of the different Christian denominations and of world religions and beliefs seems to express the hope for peaceful coexistence between cultural diversities in society and the world, on the basis of a mutual and charitable recognition of the limits of human knowledge.[2]

The notion of a steady progression towards an enthusiastic embracing of liberties and freedoms, popularized chiefly and irresistibly by Enlightenment philosophy, has proved an influential narrative, but is now yielding to a more nuanced historical interpretation.[3] It has become more widely acknowledged that a practical philosophy of tolerance also existed, moulded more by contingencies than principles, which adopted the language of neighbourliness and commonality rather than that of religion and difference,[4] aptly summed up by the Dutch religious historian Willem Frijhoff as 'the ecumenicity of everyday life' (*omgangsoecumene*).[5]

The forced social promiscuity among groups forming part of different confessions or religions – mostly though not always in top-down publicly sanctioned or tolerated multi-confessional settings – not infrequently led to a profound rethink, individually and collectively, of rigid confessional distinctions, especially relating to purely exterior manifestations of faith. Sometimes this gave rise to spurts of tolerance (and a certain cultural relativism verging almost on religious indifference), and in other circumstances to very personal, eclectic wanderings and moving backwards and forwards between faiths and confessions.[6] Other tendencies were also at play though: when religious pluralism was tacitly accepted or even officially licensed, religious minorities often became worried that they might lose their identity and disappear, and instinctively began to differentiate themselves even more tangibly from their neighbours with diverging creeds of modes of worship. Moreover, until at least the early eighteenth century, the appeals for toleration were not infrequently tactical in nature, from which many of the formerly marginalized and oppressed backed away in haste when they themselves were granted institutional respectability.[7]

The growth of religious diversity thus took place in a setting, that of early modern Europe, riddled with contradiction. On the one hand there was the range of factors that fostered uniformity – confessionalization, exclusive identities, the ideal of orthodoxy, affective cartographies – while on the other there were discourses of tolerance and accommodation and, more relevantly, the actual practice of plurality, which enabled different religious communities to rub shoulders with each other, despite being antagonistic. As Alexandra Walsham notes, impulses such as enmity and amity, prejudice and benevolence, persistently coexisted in early modern society at large, and the relationship between them was 'cyclical rather than linear'.[8]

For the most part, people were reluctant to betray those with whom they shared bonds of affection and neighbourhood, not to mention ones of class loyalty, economic interest and kinship. As John Lockman (1698–1771), the English translator of Bernard and Picart's *Cérémonies* and an unflagging exposer of the violent proselytizing practices of the Roman Catholic Church, exclaimed: 'What kind of community must that be, whence gratitude, love, and a mutual forbearance with regard to human frailties, are banish'd!'[9] But it was one thing to display tolerance socially, quite another to accept it in ideological terms. As a result, the inclination to love, tolerate and embrace tended to be interwoven with other, conflicting impulses, for instance to despise, to shun and to victimize. The periodic flaring up of prejudice and violence can thus be interpreted as a channel adopted by individuals to psychologically deflect and assuage the guilt they felt about having dealings with people who insisted on subscribing to a 'false' creed.[10] In view of the fact that the status of minority groups was objectively precarious, and a good deal of uncertainty surrounded their rights, consideration needs to be given to the feelings – as evidenced in petitions, diaries and correspondence – arising from the concrete prospect of more stringently applied discriminatory legislation.

The real-life experiences of 'interconfessional conviviality' imply that the intellectual endeavours of those who argued the case for toleration did not occur in a social or cultural vacuum. But it was not until Pierre Bayle (1647–1706) that the assumed existence of an intrinsic link between being a believer and being a good citizen was seriously called into question, and the rights of the so-called erroneous conscience were acknowledged. No less significantly, John Locke (1632–1704), the Western philosopher most closely associated with toleration (albeit a 'thin' and exclusive variety), recognized that for a peaceful and productive discussion of religious issues, it was necessary to consider not just the substance but also the *manner* of disagreement, namely civility. *True* civility was not just a question of actions, but of dispositions – that is, the 'disposition of the *mind* not to offend others'. In practical terms, toleration was not just a matter of parading an 'outward respect', but of expressing *actual* 'respect', 'esteem' and even 'love'. To legislate against offence – whether to God or one's neighbour – was to authorize and encourage citizens to draw the civil sword against any ideological opponent. So in matters of civility, as in religion, popular instruction was best served not by legislative proscription but by education, and by the setting of a moral and emotional example.[11] Without doubt, it offers a seasonable lesson for our own age.

Studies of early modern ideas and practices of tolerance have generally concentrated on theological justifications for persecution, on the enduring divisions brought about by the Reformation, on the battle of ideas which saw humanists, Protestants or deists speaking out for liberty of conscience, or, no less interestingly, on the economic ill-effects caused by intolerance. Historians of emotions, in seeking to trace the background and development of modern psychological thinking, can make a significant contribution to a more complex understanding of the observable trends towards greater tolerance in Europe over the period by investigating the practical and affective local-level relations between people of differing faiths and by shedding light on both gaps and points of contact between patterns of intellectual history and those of social and cultural history.

Further reading

Linden, D. van der, *Experiencing Exile: Huguenot Refugees in the Dutch Republic, 1680–1700* (Farnham: Ashgate, 2015)

—in his seminal account of the experiences of ordinary Huguenot émigrés in the Dutch Republic, van der Linden considers exile memoirs that do not simply relate the terrible persecution suffered by Huguenots, but also their friendship with Catholic priests and neighbours.

Walsham, A., *Charitable Hatred: Tolerance and Intolerance in England, 1500–1700* (Manchester: Manchester University Press, 2006)

—in this authoritative investigation of 'confessional feelings' and attitudes to persecution in early modern England, Walsham argues that although the notions of tolerance and intolerance seem to imply a simple polarity, the relationship between them was highly complex and perhaps even interdependent.

Notes

1 T. Gordon, *Vindication of the Quakers, Or, An Answer to the Bishop of L[ichfield]'s Charge Against Them* (London, 1732), 17–18.

2 See L. Hunt, M.C. Jacob and W. Mijnhardt (eds), *Bernard Picart and the First Global Vision of Religion* (Los Angeles: Getty Research Institute, 2010).

3 A. Thomson, '(Why) Does the Enlightenment Matter?', *Diciottesimo Secolo* 1 (2016), 147–68.

4 W. Sheils, '"Getting On" and "Getting Along" in Parish and Town: Catholics and Their Neighbours in England', in B. Kaplan, B. Moore, H. van Nierop and J.S. Pollman (eds), *Catholic Communities in Protestant States: Britain and the Netherlands c. 1570–1720* (Manchester: Manchester University Press, 2009), 67–83.

5 W. Frijhoff, 'The Threshold of Toleration: Interconfessional Conviviality in Holland during the Early Modern Period', in his *Embodied Belief: Ten Essays on Religious Culture in Dutch History* (Hilversum: Uitgeverij Verloren 2002), 39–65, here 44.

6 See T.A. Mantecón, 'Isaac Nabrusch, Christian and Jew: A Pious Man at Life's Many Crossroads', in J. Sponholz and G.K. Waite (eds), *Exile and Religious Identity, 1500–1800*, (London: Pickering & Chatto, 2014), 81–96.

7 It has been shown that Huguenot refugees in the American colonies, despite their own experience of oppression, had no compunction about using slaves on their plantations, especially in South Carolina. See B. van Ruymbeke, *From New Babylon to Eden: The Huguenots and Their Migration to Colonial South America* (Columbia: University of South Carolina Press, 2006).

8 A. Walsham, *Charitable Hatred: Tolerance and Intolerance in England, 1500–1700* (Manchester: Manchester University Press, 2006), 231 and *passim*.

9 J. Lockman, *The Sufferings of John Coustos for Freemasonry and for His Refusing to Turn Roman Catholic in the Inquisition at Lisbon* (London, 1746), 173.
10 Walsham, *Charitable Hatred*, 280 and *passim*.
11 T.M. Bejan, 'John Locke on Toleration, (In)civility, and the Quest for Concord', *History of Political Thought*, 37, 3 (2016), 556–87.

IV.33 Protestant theology

Alec Ryrie

Early modern Protestant theology does not exactly have a reputation for emotional richness. The persistent stereotype is that Protestantism, especially Reformed / Calvinist Protestantism, was a highly intellectualized religion suspicious of emotional expression, and that it remained so until the emergence of Pietism and of evangelical revivalism in the eighteenth century. And the stereotype is true at least to this limited extent: these were religious traditions which took the emotions intensely seriously, which believed that a rightly ordered emotional life was essential to flourishing as a Christian, and which therefore set out to discipline and to channel the emotions accordingly. However, this was a matter of direction, not of suppression. Right emotions were to be encouraged and amplified. The stereotype is also misleading in two other important respects. First, the opposition between reason and emotion, or 'head' and 'heart', which has become so thoroughly conventional in the modern age, only began to emerge during the early modern period. Even those who accepted it did not treat it as a truism or as an absolute division. And second, the division between emotionally cold sixteenth- and seventeenth-century Protestants and their emotionally warm eighteenth-century descendants does not stand up to closer scrutiny. Chiefly with reference to the Anglophone world and to the Puritan tradition, this entry will survey the emotional assumptions and ambitions of Protestant theological writers through this period.

If theological texts do not seem like an obvious entry-point to emotional culture, that is again because of the persistence of the head-heart opposition. Early modern Protestants were slow to build up a library of explicitly devotional writing, which their Catholic opponents saw as a failing, but that criticism implied a division between theology and piety which Protestant writers and readers apparently rejected. Correct theology, they argued, ought to provoke the correct emotions, and was to some extent validated by doing so; and those correct emotions included a zealous desire to know God, his will and his Word, a desire which naturally drove the believer to theology.

Protestant theologians were well aware that this view cut against important parts of their classical inheritance. The Stoics, who had aspired to rise above passions altogether, had a formative influence on early Christian ethics and were enthusiastically revived in the Renaissance: Jean Calvin (1509–64) himself had cut his scholarly teeth on an edition of Seneca. Yet Protestant theologians lined up to denounce Stoic views of the emotions, whose ideal of absolute self-reliance was both unrealistic and potentially blasphemous. If Christ himself had wept in his Passion, Christians could hardly shun the emotions. Far from being an ideal, even an unattainable ideal, Stoic impassivity was for Protestant theologians a potentially lethal snare. For that way lay the terrible spiritual death which was described variously as coldness, dryness, dullness, hardness or deadness: a stony-hearted numbness whose sufferers felt nothing, and drifted insensate into the icy nothingness of utter alienation from God.

Throughout the period, perhaps the most urgent task of Protestant theology was to rouse people from this lethal slumber, and instead to provoke feeling. Exactly what feelings was a matter of some dispute. A widespread orthodoxy, from Martin Luther (1483–1546) to the English Puritans to the Pietists, held that the order of salvation must begin with fear, horror and despair for sin, in the same way that you must feel pain if you are to learn to snatch your hand from a fire. This was a preacher's truism throughout the early modern period and beyond it: the notorious 1741 sermon, *Sinners in the Hands of an Angry God*, by Jonathan Edwards (1703–58) is only the best-known example of this determination to use fear to waken sinners from their terrible 'security'. However, a growing body of experience suggested that gentler methods could sometimes work, and that it was possible for believers to bypass the depths of fear and despair and proceed directly to the more delightful emotions. This applied especially to women, whose conversion experiences were by convention gentler than men's, and to children, whose ability to attain genuine faith even at a young age was slowly becoming accepted. Baptists, Moravians and others began to explore theological alternatives of this kind.

Whether by the conventional emotional route or via a short cut, the believer was supposed eventually to attain a state of assurance. As originally postulated by Luther, this was a kind of existential certainty of salvation which transcended rational categories, but in practice it was hard to see what that meant if not an emotional state. The emotional experience of assurance – a settled certainty of being held within God's love – was evidently both immensely powerful and widely shared. It was not, however, as widespread or as persistent as many believers might have wished, and even those who experienced it found, paradoxically, that it came and went. In emotional terms, it seems best described as an experience which may have been ephemeral as a matter of crude chronological fact but whose qualities included the fact that it seemed enduring. Alongside this settled, peaceful experience sat a range of other, more dynamic and perhaps more attainable positive emotions, such as desire for God (a state which was itself desirable, and indeed believers were urged to cultivate the desire for desire) or joy (a matter of fleeting, transporting stabs of ecstasy). Underpinning all of these was the state which they called *zeal*, an intense earnestness which was the very antithesis of Stoic impassivity or of cold stony-heartedness. Some English theologians understood zeal to be a particular emotion, such as a composite of love and anger, but the consensus was that zeal was 'a high strain of all the affections', the state which every emotion attains when it is rightly directed and when its flame is fanned so that it becomes hottest, in which believers weep for their sinfulness and God's glory, and in which they blaze with a fervour so intense that joy and sorrow cannot be disentangled.[1]

It was this belief that assurance, joy and burning zeal ought to be normative for believers which produced one of Puritan theology's best-known emotional preoccupations, with despair. Those whose emotional experience did not live up to the theologians' billing might naturally be troubled, and when combined with the theology of predestination the result could indeed sometimes be a crushing despair. It remains a matter of dispute how serious a problem this in fact was.[2] It is clear, at least, that a great many Protestant pastors were concerned to relieve this problem, and that doing so was for many of them an intensely theological task. A 600-page commentary on one short book of the Bible, for example, might not sound like the most accessible source of spiritual comfort, but Luther's commentary on Galatians ran through seven editions in English in less than half a century, and that was before John Bunyan (1628–88) said: 'I do prefer this book . . . excepting the Holy Bible, before all books that I have ever seen, as most fit for a wounded conscience'.[3] English readers were particularly drawn to the theme, but it was writing on that theme which first won English theologians an international readership. William Perkins (1558–1602), England's first genuinely successful Protestant export, was distinguished by his subtle and – to use an anachronistic term – emotionally intelligent analysis of this problem. In particular, he observed, in a typically Protestant paradox, that for true believers, feelings of despair might actually be a sign of a deeper grace.

These themes did not make their way through to Pietism and the evangelical revivals of the eighteenth century entirely unchanged, but the sophisticated exploration of them by English Puritans and by other pastoral theologians in the Netherlands, Germany and elsewhere was decisive in shaping those later developments. So, in 1741, Jonathan Edwards denied the accusation that the emotionalism of the revivals was irrational. For those who suddenly realize that they are standing on the very brink of Hell to react with intense emotion is, he argued, entirely rational. It is those who are *not* terrified who are deluded. That insistence that emotional intensity and theological insight ought to belong together in theory, and do in fact reinforce one another in practice, is a thread which runs through Protestantism throughout the early modern period, and beyond.

It is a thread on which scholars are only now beginning seriously to pull. Some pioneering work has been done in this field, much of it interdisciplinary in nature, but much of the ground remains unbroken. The history of the emotions has the potential to open up the deep logic underpinning both the theological positions to which early modern people adhered, and the passion with which they adhered to them; and therefore to connect the history of ideas with the social and cultural history of religion in new ways. Whether we have either the sources or the methods to fulfil that potential remains to be seen.

Further reading

Karant-Nunn, S.C., *The Reformation of Feeling: Shaping the Religious Emotions in Early Modern Germany* (Oxford: Oxford University Press, 2010)

—a groundbreaking and subtle attempt to look at the Reformation era's religious emotions in cross-confessional comparison.

Ryrie, A., *Being Protestant in Reformation Britain* (Oxford: Oxford University Press, 2013)

—uses the history of the emotions to postulate that Protestantism in England and Scotland *c.* 1530–1640 was a dynamic, intensive and broad-based religious culture.

Ryrie, A. and T. Schwanda (eds), *Puritanism and Emotion in the Early Modern World* (Basingstoke: Palgrave, 2016)

—a collection of essays with a particular focus on the theological basis and significance of the emotions for English and American puritans.

Notes

1 W. Fenner, *A Treatise of the Affections; Or, The Soules Pulse* (London, 1642: Wing F707), 142; cf. S. Ward, *A Coal from the Altar, to Kindle the holy fire of Zeale* (London, 1615: RSTC 25039), 3–5.

2 For contrasting positions, see J. Stachniewski, *The Persecutory Imagination: English Puritanism and the Literature of Religious Despair* (Oxford: Clarendon Press, 1991); L. Dixon, *Practical Predestinarians in England c. 1590–1640* (Farnham: Ashgate, 2014).

3 J. Bunyan, *Grace Abounding to the Chief of Sinners* (London, 1666), para 130.

IV.34 Witchcraft

Jacqueline Van Gent

Early modern Europeans had no hesitation in associating the power of emotions with the social practice of witchcraft. Although magical practices, and their legal framing as the crime of witchcraft, varied widely across early modern Europe, the central role emotions played in them is consistent across countries. Despite earlier historical work on the emotional dynamics in witch crazes, which largely applied psychoanalytical frameworks, and productive theoretical impulses from anthropology, early modern European witchcraft and emotions remain surprisingly understudied.[1] The historical meanings of emotions, and their manifestations in tears, gestures and body language are an essential part of witchcraft beliefs, practices and witch trials in the early modern period.

Magical practices and witchcraft embodied the impact of emotional states, such as anger, envy or hate, on the health of other humans and of farm animals. Such anti-social emotions could therefore become visible on the bodies of their victims. These emotions had literally a material impact on households and communities. In magical rituals, body fluids (such as milk or blood) and body parts (such as hair) acted as transmitter of powerful emotions, resulting in harm or in healing. Milk magic was a common form of witchcraft whereby the milk of the neighbour's cows was redirected to one's own. A visible sign of cows being bewitched was that their remaining milk turned into blood, and the cow sickened or died. Here the emotion attributed to this malevolent practice was envy.

In witchcraft, emotions had a strong somatic character and could be transmitted in magical rituals through body fluids and body parts. Demonological treatises and published witchcraft pamphlets often represented witches as incapable of expressing certain emotions, such as sympathy. In many respects these depictions are very reductionist because they do not allow space to consider the ambivalent nature of magical practitioners and the ambivalent emotions surrounding magical rituals. Magical practitioners such as healers equally relied on the power of emotions in their healing rituals; here compassion, love or empathy constituted the driving emotional forces.

Not all witchcraft and sorcery included or even needed a devil. In particular the many court trials outside of witch hunts allow us to see a more nuanced picture of everyday magic and its emotional dynamics. Magic was not exclusively linked to anti-social feelings with which the Devil is usually associated (greed, envy, revenge, sexual transgression). Instead magical practices, and their emotional economies, extended to include many other supernatural beings with whom people had an emotional association: nature spirits, and spirits identified as house guardians, Catholic Saints were likewise evoked (even in Protestant northern Europe), fairies, wood-nymphs and spirits dwelling in water were all approached for help in magical rituals. A mixture of Christian and non-Christian beliefs and emotions was enacted in benevolent as well as malevolent magic. Emotions of hope, despair or gratitude often surrounded healing rituals and expressions of empathy and compassion could be attributed to magical healers or sorcerers.

Witchcraft has traditionally been linked to negative intentions and emotions such as fear, anger and envy. Witches' use of magic for personal gain and at the expense of other members of the community, were understood to be caused by anti-social emotions such as envy.

Not everything connected to magic was loaded with negative feelings though. Magic, as many cases outside the witch crazes show, was equally employed in protection rituals, for finding treasures, healing or in winning someone's love.[2] These acts showed compassion; so for example when a healer helped mothers to restore the health of their children.

When considering the full spectrum of magical practices in early modern Europe – healing, love magic, finding lost treasurers, detecting thieves, malevolent magic – it becomes apparent how central emotions are to a discussion of witchcraft. Apart from fear and envy already mentioned, guilt, grief but also joy, intimacy, trust and hope form part of the emotional register of these magical practices.

The figure of the witch was associated with socially transgressing emotions as well as with the inability to control her or his emotions in socially and gender appropriate ways. Witches' inability (and deliberate disinterest) in controlling their emotions and desires (anger, rage, lust, envy and resentment) resulted in socially disruptive activities: illness, death, storms and other destructive weather. In witchcraft, anti-social emotions could lead to social chaos.

Secular courts, where trials concerning witchcraft were conducted, formed important social spaces for public emotional performances. Accusations and counter accusations wove families, kinship and local authorities such as the minister or priest into a web of emotional claims and counter claims. If torture was employed, largely during the intensive persecutions of the so called witch hunts, the pain inflicted on the accused was believed to bring the truth to light. The correct emotional and somatic display of guilt and repentance in words and gestures (such as weeping) was expected by secular and religious authorities, as well as the wider local community.

In the demonological literature, popularized by pamphlets and broadsheets, the witch became the personification of the most socially damaging emotions – envious, resentful, spiteful and unlimited in her thirst for revenge – this was supposed to instil fear and a readiness for violent punishment of such a witch in the audience.[3]

Men and women practised witchcraft, were accused of witchcraft and involved in practices or in trials as witnesses. While there is a predominance in women as accused witches in witch crazes, trials outside these intense periods of persecutions, reveal that men were also accused of doing malevolent or benevolent magic.[4] Even Catholic priests or Protestant ministers could be accused in some cases. Recent studies also reveal for other European countries that many more men were accused of witchcraft than historians previously assumed, which raises the question of a possibly gendered emotional repertoire of male and female witches as an interesting research area for the future.

The performance of gendered emotions was an important part of witchcraft discourses and of social regulations of moral behaviour. By asking about the power dimensions of emotional performances – who could express what kind of emotion to whom – we are able to understand gendered agency in a new light. In early modern Europe, women were not permitted to express anger in public. Women's speech was deemed dangerous and forceful because it reflected their supposed inability to control their emotions; it was 'heated speech' which could turn quickly into fatal curses. Thus women transgressing the gender code and speaking out angrily towards neighbours and family could easily run the risk of being accused of witchcraft and socially reprimanded.

Gendered differences in emotional expectations and meanings can also be seen in love magic. Love magic has been discussed as a field of witchcraft, but what exactly 'love' meant to historical players is a new question, and one that allows us to see interesting gender differences. Women who practised love magic usually admitted that they had hoped to achieve a binding promise of marriage (sometimes because they had fallen pregnant) from a man, something that was very important to their social honour as women. Men, on the other hand, were usually not interested in securing a marriage, but in winning sexual favours.

The lens of historical emotions allows us to consider witchcraft practices, beliefs and persecutions in a new light. The perspective of emotions and witchcraft also allows us to address wider questions of embodiment and personhood in the early modern period. Magical self-transcendence, soul journeys and body metamorphosis expressed a cultural concept of a person that contrasts fundamentally with the Enlightenment's philosophical ideal of humans as rational and autonomous subjects. The prominent role emotions played in witchcraft highlights this contrast between the Enlightenment ideal and early modern practices of personhood.

Emotions were of vital importance in both healing and harmful magic because they formed a bridge between the individual and society. Early modern witchcraft cases demonstrate how emotions could signify the embodied nature of the self: emotions could be transmitted by blood or become visible as rash on the skin. Anger and envy were the key emotions associated with harmful witchcraft and were frequently employed as metaphors for magical acts and for the power of the self. Neither the abolishment of witchcraft as a legal crime nor the Enlightenment argumentation for a more rational human being did hail the end of witchcraft beliefs. Instead, social dynamics of local communities with strong kinship obligations and close-knit household organizations continued to regulate conflict through emotions and magical rituals. In contrast to early witchcraft histories which were singularly preoccupied with emotions of fear, more recent witchcraft studies are offering a more nuanced reading of the wide spectrum of emotions and their social implications associated with magical practices. Future avenues to be explored in this field could include gendered emotions and witchcraft, the emotional dynamics of witchcraft outside of witch crazes, the meaning of emotions and witchcraft in culturally diverse societies and their possible transformations in colonial contexts.[5]

Further reading

Geschiere, P., *Witchcraft, Intimacy and Trust: Africa in Comparison* (Chicago: The University of Chicago Press, 2013)

—explores the emotional strategies of African societies, which is a useful framework also for early modern historical studies.

Ginzburg, C., *The Night Battles: Witchcraft & Agrarian Cults in the Sixteenth & Seventeenth Centuries* (1966), (trans) J. and A.C. Tedeschi (Baltimore: Johns Hopkins University Press, 1992)

—remains an important work depicting the very moment of historical changes in emotional regimes in interpreting early modern magic.

Van Gent, J., *Magic, Body and the Self in Eighteenth-Century Sweden* (Leiden: Brill, 2009)

—demonstrates the endurance of magical practices, both benevolent and malevolent, grounded in perceptions of an interconnected body, self and spiritual cosmos.

Notes

1 For psychoanalytic approaches, see L. Roper, *Witch Craze: Terror and Fantasy in Baroque Germany* (New Haven: Yale University Press, 2004); for an earlier anthropological framework, M. Stephen, 'Witchcraft, grief, and the ambivalence of emotions', *American Ethnologist* 26, 3 (1999), 690–710.

2 For a recent publication on everyday magic, see K.A. Edwards (ed.), *Everyday Magic in Early Modern Europe* (Farnham: Ashgate 2015)

3 For published English pamphlets see P. Elmer (ed.), *English Witchcraft 1560–1736*, 6 vols (London: Pickering and Chatto, 2003)

4 E.J. Kent, *Cases of Male Witchcraft in Old and New England, 1592–1692* (Turnhout: Brepols, 2013)

5 I. Gareis, *The Oxford Handbook of Witchcraft in Early Modern Europe and Colonial America* (Oxford: Oxford University Press 2013)

IV.35 Wonders of nature

Jennifer Spinks

Early modern Europe was filled with reports of the marvels of the physical world. Sources from the period tell us today about the birth of 'monstrous' children and animals, of comets, of terrible storms, of extraordinary battle scenes that appeared in the sky and other prodigious wonders. These phenomena tested the limits of the natural world and often formed part of an apocalyptic worldview underpinned by Protestant and Catholic reform. Anxiety, fear, angry polemic, religious awe and eager curiosity formed some of the dominant emotional modes that shaped visual and textual, print and manuscript reports of signs of the disordered natural world. While the expression, incitement and sometimes the management of emotions are central to these sources, scholarship to date has tended to consider such issues in implicit rather than explicit ways. This discussion excavates material relevant to the history of emotions from existing studies, including some of the most recent scholarship which is more directly reflective of the emotional turn in historical research.

In their ground-breaking book *Wonders and the Order of Nature 1150–1750*, Lorraine Daston and Katharine Park demonstrated the co-existence of explanatory systems for and attitudes towards wonders and marvels, in which fear and pleasure were amongst the many possible responses to extraordinary natural phenomena, and religious and secularizing explanations co-existed.[1] Recent studies focused more specifically on the sixteenth and seventeenth centuries have particularly emphasized the pivotal role of religious reform in shaping contemporary readings of providence, prodigies and the disordered Book of Nature; readings in which polemical representations were common and emotions ran high.[2] In addition to marvelous phenomena as varied as health-giving springs, 'monstrous births', and wonder-working jewels, it is also increasingly clear that reports of terrifying disasters such as earthquakes and floods and even acts of violence were frequently a corollary of early modern understandings of prodigies.[3] The emotional range was equally broad, encompassing but not limited to pleasure, pathos and terror. Analyses of print culture as ways of understanding the formation and transmission of ideas and attitudes have been particularly central to scholarship on this material, in which polemical and emotionally-charged publications aimed at wide audiences take centre stage.

Printed pamphlets, broadsheets and 'wonder books' as well as manuscript collections recording the same types of stories are all inherently rich sources for thinking about the emotions in early modern Europe. Periods of crisis around warfare and religious conflict are crucial, for some of the most important waves of prodigy culture chronologically map onto key events in the German Reformation, the French Wars of Religion, and the English Civil War. The confessionally-driven emotional dimensions of these sources both reflected and sought to shape the emotions of communities in crisis through image and text. They are thus ideal for examining from the perspective of the history of emotions, which has done so much to prompt new ways of thinking about the formation and testing of early modern identities.

Some of the most emotionally-rich sources concern 'monstrous births', as contemporaries generally called them. Anger and anxiety were expressed through the polemical reports of, for example, such Reformation and Counter-Reformation staples as the Monk Calf and Papal Ass, written about by Philipp Melanchthon (1497–1560) and Martin Luther (1483–1546) in 1523, and regularly recycled across the century.[4] The tonsure-like bald patch and the preaching gesture of the Monk Calf led Luther to characterize it as a deformed monk that gave visible form to the ills of Catholicism. In the same publication his fellow reformer Melanchthon provided an exceptionally detailed argument for how the 'womanish' belly, diabolical rear end, cloven hoof, ass' head, and other physical feature of the Papal Ass likewise could all be read as signs of Rome's degeneracy. The language of their texts epitomized vernacular Reformation polemic, which sought to intensify responses of disgust, anger and scorn in readers already sympathetic to the Lutheran cause – or to needle and provoke Catholic enemies inflamed by the direct attack on Rome.

While Lutheran reformers wrote polemically about the Monk Calf and Papal Ass as signs of the degeneracy of the papacy in Rome, Catholic authors would turn the creatures into cyphers for Lutherans in later examples of printed propaganda. The Monk Calf, for example, would be reinvented as Luther himself in a French publication later in the sixteenth century, presented as a bodily manifestation of fleshy weakness and perversion. These qualities were exemplified through Luther's marriage to former nun Katharina von Bora (1499–1552), as one hardline French Catholic author wrote in an illustrated Latin publication later translated into French and very widely distributed (Figure IV.35.1). Material like this utilized extraordinary natural phenomena as a starting point. But – as the sideways attack here on Luther's marriage demonstrates – it also went straight to fault-lines between Lutherans and Catholics that were fundamentally concerned with the ordinary religious rituals and daily lives of Christians across western Europe.

Examining reports of the wonders of the natural world through the lens of the history of the emotions reminds us that cases of human monstrous births were generally deployed to tap into common experiences and communal patterns of life around events like birth, marriage and death. Such reports were not always fearful and inflammatory; they could also elicit pity and sadness. 'Monstrous' infants almost always died as soon as they were born, underlining their role as signs but also adding pathos to reports. Appearing before the Reformation, reports of conjoined twins born in Ertingen in 1512 stressed in one publication the heart-tugging scene of conjoined twin girls curled up to sleep, while another printed broadsheet recorded how their father was saddened. Whether he felt this emotion in the wake of their deaths or upon beholding the deformities that would kill them is left unsaid.[5] Moments of household intimacy such as these were parlayed into rapidly-produced verses and often roughly-hewn images for wide audiences.

Such children and animals were only one type of the many wondrous natural signs that formed part of the prodigy culture of the early modern world. Others were more threatening: fear-inspiring prodigies came from the skies overhead in the form of comets, fiery signs, and terrible storms and weather patterns. In a particularly rich source for the emotional significance of such events, nuns at the abbey of Beaumont-lès-Tours recorded in a diary the local, communal emotional responses to phenomena such as terrifying hail storms and wheat that shed blood.[6]

Individual broadsheets, pamphlets, books and diaries recorded signs of the disordered natural world as parts of a larger pattern. They were signs of the times and evidence of God's providence, and as such demanded careful and pious scrutiny and a moral response. Many longer book-length works from this period, particularly those by Lutherans, presented an apocalyptic world view that was often increasingly pessimistic and fearful in outlook.[7] Terrible natural events might afflict an external religious enemy, as in the case of an earthquake in Constantinople in 1556 that was widely reported in Europe. They could also strike within the heart of a community as signs of an angry God, or as 'loving' warnings to avoid worse to come. They could be joyful advents as well as terrifying warnings of the coming Last Days. While events that disordered the natural world were rare and exceptional, they were part of a pattern that underpinned the flow of daily life, even if – like the emotions they aroused – they lay at the more extreme end of the spectrum of human experience. Recent and forthcoming work increasingly provides richer analyses and narratives of the ways that early modern people expressed and managed their emotions in the face of the wonders of the disordered world.

Further reading

Soergel, P.M., *Miracles and the Protestant Imagination: The Evangelical Wonder Book in Reformation Germany* (Oxford: Oxford University Press, 2012)

—Sorgel's closely-focused study opens up important broader lines of thought for considering wondrous phenomena and their relationship to pessimism understood in religious terms.

TRACTATVS

que ſynceritate ſplendorem reſtitue. Ecce vt miſera incedit tota Gallia ſanguine ſuffuſa & lachrymis. Vide Domine humilitatem illius & laborem, & dimitte vniuerſa delicta illius, dirige greſſus ſuos in ſemitis tuis, vt non moueantur veſtigia eius à cætero: ſed in ſemitis mãdatorum tuorum perpetuò perſeueret. Aſininum ſummi frigoris ſemen, omninò deſtrue, vt igne perfectæ charitatis accenſi, diſsipatis erroribus ac impietatibus vniuerſis, ac eliſa omni inimicorum tuorum audacia, Eccleſia tua ſecura tibi ſeruiat libertate per Chriſtum Dominum noſtrum. Amen.

De monſtro vitulo-monacho Lutheri temporibus nato, circa annum domini. 1523.

Figure IV.35.1 Anonymous artist, Luther as the Monk Calf, woodcut, in Arnaud Sorbin, *Tractatus de monstris* (Paris: Hierome de Marnef and Guillaume Cavellat, 1570).

Special Collections, Baillieu Library, the University of Melbourne. Shelfmark 29a/29.

Spinks, J. and C. Zika (eds), *Disaster, Death and the Emotions in the Shadow of the Apocalypse, 1400–1700* (Houndsmills: Palgrave Macmillan, 2016)
—new edited collection that offers a broad range of case studies from across Europe that explicitly address the experience of disaster within the framework of the history of emotions.
Walsham, A. *Providence in Early Modern England* (Oxford: Oxford University Press, 1999)
—classic study unpacks pivotal dimensions of the emotionally-rich ways in which early modern people understood and represented God's providence as evident in extraordinary events.

Notes

I acknowledge the support of an Australian Research Council Postdoctoral Fellowship and an Arts and Humanities Research Council UK Early Career Fellowship (grant number AH/L015013/1).

1 L. Daston and K. Park, *Wonders and the Order of Nature 1150–1750* (New York: Zone Books, 1998).
2 See, for example, A. Walsham, *Providence in Early Modern England* (Oxford: Oxford University Press, 1999); J. Spinks, *Monstrous Births and Visual Culture in Sixteenth-Century Germany* (London: Pickering and Chatto, 2009); P.M. Soergel, *Miracles and the Protestant Imagination: The Evangelical Wonder Book in Reformation Germany* (Oxford: Oxford University Press, 2012)
3 J. Spinks and C. Zika (eds), *Disaster, Death and the Emotions in the Shadow of the Apocalypse, 1400–1700* (Houndsmills: Palgrave Macmillan, 2016)
4 Spinks, *Monstrous Births*, 59–79.
5 Ibid., 42–9.
6 S. Broomhall, 'Disorder in the Natural World: The Perspectives of the Sixteenth-Century Provincial Convent', in J. Spinks and D. Eichberger (eds), *Religion, the Supernatural and Visual Culture in Early Modern Europe: An Album Amicorum for Charles Zika* (Leiden: Brill, 2015), 240–59.
7 Soergel, *Miracles and the Protestant Imagination.*

IV.36 Racial othering – Jews

François Soyer

Anti-Judaism and anti-Semitism, and the murderous fears and hatred that they have unleashed, form an integral part of the history of Europe from antiquity and the medieval period up to the present day. Surprisingly, however, they have not yet been specifically analysed within the broader framework of the history of emotions. This omission is striking as the subject has a clear emotional dimension and large numbers of monographs that have been published on the religious, cultural, political and economic aspects of the persecutions of Jews in European history. An examination of emotions and emotional language in the anti-Jewish propaganda produced in early modern Europe offers an interesting, and hitherto ignored, opportunity to further our understanding of this phenomenon.

The prominent historian of modern anti-Semitism, Jacob Katz, perceived anti-Jewish propaganda produced during the early modern period as an extension of the ideas 'rooted in the medieval world, in which theology dominated thought and in which the affairs of the Jews – their law, character and actions – were judged in the light of theology'.[1] Such a view, whilst not wrong, overlooks the impact of the early modern printing revolution as well as the gradual emergence of a new and expanding lay readership. During this period increasing numbers of anti-Jewish polemics began to appear in vernacular languages and their authors were compelled to frame their arguments in a manner better suited to pander to a lay readership. The early modern period also witnessed the growth of the modern European state system and the process of 'confessionalization' which, amongst other things, led to renewed anxieties about the status of religious minorities (not just Jews but minorities from different Christian denominations as well, such as Catholics living under Protestant rule) within the body politic in European states that still based their legitimacy upon a state religion. The immediate consequence of this shift was the appearance of a virulent polemical literature that endeavoured to promote fear and hatred of Jews amongst the lay population by presenting Jews as an existential threat to all Christians and sought to pressure the secular and ecclesiastical authorities to take measures against the Jews (usually persecutory legal measures or expulsions). As Sara Ahmed has emphasized, narratives seeking to demonize others work by 'generating a subject that is endangered by imagined others whose proximity threatens not only to take something away from the subject . . . but to take the place of the subject'.[2]

No scientific theory of race existed in this period but there was a noticeable difference between polemics written in the Iberian Peninsula and those in the rest of Europe. Many Spanish and Portuguese polemicists insisted upon presenting the hatred for Christianity of the Jews, or more accurately of *conversos*, the descendants of converted Jews, as a quasi-biological phenomenon over which the individuals concerned appeared to have little control. The notion that the Jews/*conversos* passed on their faith and anti-Christian hatred to successive generations through their 'blood' in a hereditary manner was widespread in the Iberian World. The *Repertorium Inquisitorium* – a Spanish manual for inquisitors printed in Valencia in 1494 and Venice in 1575 – explicitly states that 'the Jews transmit the perfidy of the Old Law [of Moses] to each other from father to son, through the blood'.[3]

In central Europe and Italy, hostility against Jews did not adopt such proto-racialist overtones but remained largely based in theology and the belief formulated by medieval mendicant polemicists that Jews taught anti-Christian beliefs to their children through their Rabbinical 'doctrine'. The Italian author Hadrianus Finus (1431–1517), for instance, commented in his Latin polemic (1538) that Jews inculcated a hatred of Christ to their children through their education.[4] Similarly, Martin Luther (1483–1546) complained in 1543 that the Jews taught, urged and trained their children from infancy to remain bitter, virulent and wrathful enemies of the Christians. The language used in some texts does come perilously close to formulating a proto-racialized vision of the transmission of Jewish beliefs, and therefore anti-Christian hatred. In a short pamphlet printed in 1510, the German printer Hieronymus Holtzel (fl. 1500–1525), for instance, clearly described a Jew attacking a consecrated host as acting 'out of a congenital Jewish hate and envy' (*daraus auß håssigem judischem angeboren neydt*).[5]

The dehumanization of the figure of the Jews insisted on representing them as collectively consumed by the emotion of hate: a 'hatred' of Jesus Christ logically led them to entertain a burning and vengeful 'hatred' of all Christians. The image of the hating Jew effectively allowed early modern polemicists to turn the tables on Jews. The Jews are transformed from a minority persecuted by Christians to a minority persecuting Christians. A powerful narrative of Christian victimhood was thus created in polemical propaganda produced in Central and Eastern Europe as well as in the Mediterranean area. Moreover, this emotional dimension in anti-Jewish polemics also contrasted the 'rational' faith of Christians with the irrational – read emotional – rejection of Christianity by Jews. The hatred that the Jews feel for Christianity and Christians leads them into uncontrollable fits of rage and violence against Christians.

The term 'hatred' is an emotion that appears in the vast majority of early modern anti-Jewish polemics. The Jewish convert to Catholicism Johannes Pfefferkorn (1469–*c.* 1522/3) declaimed in his *Judenfeind* (1509) that Jews would seize any opportunity to mock or kill Christians for 'they hate the sign of the cross' and 'they hate Christians much more than any other nations'.[6] Likewise, Martin Luther asked the rhetorical question in his 1543 opus *On the Jews and their Lies*: 'How, then, do we incur such terrible anger, envy, and hatred [from the Jews]?'[7] Similarly, in southern Europe, the Portuguese Vicente da Costa Mattos (fl. 1620s) loudly proclaimed to his readers in 1621 that 'a hatred of Christians is innate to Jews' and the Spanish friar Francisco de Torrejoncillo (d. 1704), writing in the late 1660s and early 1670s, wondered 'who will be up to the task of revealing the loathing and hatred in which the Jews hold our Catholic Faith as well as us [Christians]?'[8]

Christian polemicists and scholars in both northern and southern Europe pointed their readers to Jewish religious texts, and the purported evidence contained therein, to justify the image of the 'hating Jews'. The works of early modern Jewish converts to Christianity in Germany and the Mediterranean, written by men who presented themselves as 'experts' on Judaism and wrote with an obviously partisan agenda, contributed greatly to this phenomenon. In the context of the Holy Roman Empire, the neophytes Victor von Karben (1442–1515) and Antonius Margaritha (*c.* 1492–1542) accused the Jews of cursing Christians and Christianity in their respective books *Judenbüchlein* (A little book on Jews), printed in Latin in 1508 and translated into German in 1550, and *Der Gantz Jüdisch Glaub* (The Whole Jewish Belief), in 1530. Although the works of converts were often directed at unbaptized Jews (and aiming to convert them) or intended to provide quasi-ethnographical information about Jews and Judaism to interested Christians, they were also repositories of useful information for polemicists. The influence of such works can be found in the writings of men such as the famous German Hebraist Johannes Buxtorf (1564–1629), who noted the Jewish hatred of Christians in his work and went so far as to write an unfinished work explicitly entitled *Aus was Ursachen die Juden andere völker alzeit gehasst und veracht haben* (The Reasons why Jews have always Hated and Despised Other Peoples).[9] Johannes Eisenmenger (1654–1704), dedicated an entire chapter of his influential 1700 opus *Entdecktes Judenthum* (Judaism Revealed) to the subject of 'the Jewish hatred against all [Gentile] peoples'.[10]

The notion that the Talmud explicitly taught the Jews to hate non-Jews endured in both Catholic and Protestant Europe. The Italian Jesuit Giovanni Pietro Pinamonti (1632–1703), who authored a book entitled *La Sinagoga disingannata* in the second half of the seventeenth century (1694, later translated into Portuguese and Spanish), insisted that the rational judgement and free will of the Jews was clouded by their 'passions' (*passioni*). These passions were provoked by the Talmud and teachings of Rabbis since abhorrence of Christians was 'one of the precepts most taught in the Talmud'. The 'Talmudists' are accused of holding the hatred of Gentiles as a 'saintly thing' and that no individual was worthy to become a Rabbi unless he 'cherished it in his bosom'.[11]

The multifaceted nature of anti-Jewish propaganda in early modern Europe therefore clearly offers interesting research perspectives in the history of emotions for scholars. Its use of highly charged emotional rhetoric and vocabulary to inspire fear and hatred of Jews as an essential 'other' must be studied in detail if the reasons for the success of this propaganda are to be fully understood by historians.

Further reading

Deutsch, Y., *Judaism in Christian Eyes: Ethnographic Descriptions of Jews and Judaism in Early Modern Europe* (Oxford: Oxford University Press, 2012)

—offers the first comprehensive analysis of Christian ethnographic studies of Jews in the early modern period, primarily those produced in German.

Hering Torres, M., M.E. Martínez and D. Nirenberg (eds), *Race and Blood in the Iberian World* (Münster: Lit Verlag, 2012)

—the edited essays collected in this work explore racial discrimination in the early modern Iberian world in all of its cultural, historical and ideological patterns.

Kaplan, D., 'Jews in early modern Europe: the sixteenth and seventeenth centuries', *History Compass* 10, 2 (2012), 191–206.

—offers a concise yet thorough overview of the status of Jews across Europe between 1500 and 1700.

Notes

1 J. Katz, *From Prejudice to Destruction: Anti-Semitism, 1700–1933* (Cambridge, MA, Harvard University Press, 1980), 23.
2 S. Ahmed, *The Cultural Politics of Emotion* (New York: Routledge, 2004), 43.
3 L. Sala-Molins (ed.), *Le dictionnaire des inquisiteurs (Valence 1494)* (Paris: Éditions Galilée, 1981), 78.
4 H. Finus, *In iudaeos flagellum ex sacris scripturis excerptum* (Venice, 1538), fol. 405v.
5 H. Holtzel, *Ein wunderbarlich Geschichte Wye dye Merckischen Juden das hochwirdige Sacrament gekaufft, vnd zu martern sich vnderstanden* (Nuremberg, 1510)
6 E. Rummel, *The Case Against Johann Reuchlin: Religious and Social Controversy in Sixteenth-Century Germany* (Toronto: University of Toronto Press, 2002), 55–6.
7 *Luther's Works, Volume 47: The Christian in Society IV*, (eds) F. Sherman and H.T. Lehman (Philadelphia: Fortress Press, 1971), 267.
8 V. da Costa Mattos, *Breve Discurso contra a Heretica Perfidia do Iudaismo* (Lisbon, 1623), fol. 140r; F. de Torrejoncillo, *Centinela contra Judíos puesta en la Torre de la Iglesia de Dios* (Pamplona, 1691), 141.
9 S.G. Burnett, *From Christian Hebraism to Jewish Studies: Johannes Buxtorf (1564–1629) and Hebrew Learning in the Seventeenth Century* (Leiden: E. J. Brill, 1996), 91–3.
10 J. Eisenmenger, *Entdecktes Judenthum* (Frankfort, 1700).
11 G.P. Pinamonti, *La Sinagoga disingannata overo via facile à mostrare a qualunque ebreo la falsità della sua seta* (Bologna, 1694), 23–4 and 65–6.

IV.37 Muslim 'others'

Audrey Calefas-Strebelle

On 26 August 1635, Sultan Murad IV (1612–40) ordered the execution of his brother Beyazid (d.1635) following weeks of palace rumours and intrigue. Among and around the splendours of the palace of Topkapi, with its precious gold-threaded carpets and bejewelled caftans and turbans, ran rivers of blood. Newspapers, magazines and travel logs relayed news of the killing, first in France and then all over Europe. The French ambassador Philippe de Harley, Comte de Césy (1582–1652) related it directly to the court.[1] Everywhere reactions were those of fear, repulsion, horror and stupefaction, but also fascination and awe, as was typical for events at the Ottoman court. Whatever the reaction, it was always highly emotive. Even authors who were usually regarded as measured and objective offered descriptions loaded with emotion.

Until now and following Edward Said, the representation of Muslim otherness has been influenced by *orientalism,* as this work generated a large corpus of research along post-colonial lines. Looking at Muslim Otherness through the lens of emotions is a relatively new perspective.[2] The role of emotions in the perception of the Turk in early modern France relies on first-hand sources such as travel logs, letters received directly from the Muslim Orient and accounts of the visits of ambassadors or envoys from Muslim empires and states, and from second-hand sources such as novels and plays. The emotional state of such authors and witnesses was very influential for the circulation of ideas and impressions about the Muslim Other. Emotional responses to Muslim otherness were influenced by the national, religious and sociological background of the writers, and also by historical events such as wars and political or economic alliances. For instance, the official friendship of France with the Ottoman Empire, beginning in 1535 with the signing of political and economic contracts, would shape the emotional response to the Turk in French sources differently, seen in a better light than in other European sources. Michel de Montaigne (1533–92) and Jean Bodin (1530–96), for example, were great admirers of the Ottomans' army, of its discipline and order, especially in comparison with the violence and abuses committed by the French army during the wars of religion. However, the general European relationship to the Muslim Other was one of fear and awe.

For Westerners, the Muslim Other comprised all Muslim peoples including those from the Iberian Peninsula, the Barbary Coast and the Ottoman, Safavid and Mughal Empires. The Muslim Other is referred in European texts from 1500 to 1800 as the 'Moor', the 'Turk', the 'Mahommetan', the 'Arab', and the 'Persian'. But interest in Turks was more acute than for any other Muslims, and they generated the strongest emotional responses: Turks had been terrorizing Europe since the crusades, and with the fall of Constantinople (1453) the Ottoman Empire camped at the gates of Europe and would not cease to be a threat for two centuries, until its defeat at the unsuccessful second siege of Vienna in 1683. For Europe, the Turk was a fierce, and a most feared and hated, enemy.

Texts from the period nurtured a fear of the Turks with such rhetorical means as the use of blood-dripping vocabulary, vivid enumerations and graphic images that evoked terror and left a long-lasting impression on readers' memories. In the 1659 *Relations Extraordinaires*, a volume of news' compilation published yearly by Theophraste Renaudot (1586–1653), one can read: 'Not a day goes by without he [Sultan Mehmet IV] having fifty heads chopped off, as many men strangled and as many impaled. So much so that this city can truthfully be called a cemetery'.[3] The effect of listing the means of massacre – strangling, beheading, impalement – alongside the image of a cemetery was intended to strike the imagination with horror, and induce a strong reaction of repulsion.

Next in the contest for most terrifying was the Moor. The fear he elicited was related to the Barbary Coast pirates who sailed and pillaged as far as England, capturing women and children to be sold on the slave markets of the Ottoman Empire. An entire literature from captives exists, the Barbary Captivity Narrative, relating in pathetic detail the terrible conditions of bondage. This was designed to elicit pity and compassion in the reader, who might sometimes be moved to contribute to the ransom of a captive.

Descriptions of the cruelty of the sultans and 'the ferocity of the nation'[4] gained a dramatic dimension in theatre. In *Bajazet* (1672) by Jean Racine (1639–99) and other 'Turkish' or 'Oriental' plays, the characters delight in cruelty. Displaying the horrors of the Ottoman Empire induced the audience into a cathartic purge of their own violent repulsions. Court society in Europe, in the process of being pacified, was supposed to find a channel for violence and emotion. Readers and audiences exposed to representations of the great bloodshed occurring in the Ottoman Empire experienced by proxy the *cruor*, or delight in seeing blood being shed. The repressed and internalized violent emotions of the members of the new court society found a symbolic release in the castigation of the Muslim Other.

But European society felt not only horror or repulsion in relation to the Turk. Fascination at the immense wealth, mixed with fear and awe at the might displayed in magnificent ceremonies, stirred the emotions just as much. The opulence and marvel of the Great Mughal was described in emphatic terms by two English ambassadors: Edward Terry (1590–1660) and Thomas Roe (1581–1644).[5] Antoine Galland (1646–1715) was so impressed by all these sumptuous wonders – the silk, the feathers, the enormous jewels and precious stones, the richly dressed court and numerous retinue in livery – that he would fill the pages of the *Thousand and One Nights* with them: 'The grand signor appeared to my eyes so full of Glory and majesty that I was bedazzled'.[6]

One area of the palace was the focus of intense European interest: the harem. Emotions ran high for authors, as Charles-Louis de Secondat, Baron de Montesquieu (1689–1755) drew parallels with slavery, Richard Knolles (1545–1610) blamed lechery on religious hypocrisy and Michel Baudier (1589–1645) condemned amoral sexual practices at length and in detail.[7] But, behind the cries of offended modesty and decency, European men were transfixed by these descriptions of life in the harem, where they imagined lascivious bathing, rampant sodomy and lesbianism and scenes of unbridled sexuality that were far from reality but reflected the unsatisfied lust and sexual fantasies of a repressive society. Lady Mary Wortley Montagu (1689–1762) was an exception. She visited the harem and affirmed that the bathhouse was a social place and not a den of debauchery, and saw the women as the only free people in the empire.[8] The eroticization of the harem was a male emotional construct, which would blossom as a new genre in eighteenth-century literature.

The figure of the Muslim Other was almost always presented as an emotional being, driven by lust, violence and jealousy. Even those shown in a positive light, such as Uzbek, the 'wise' Persian friend of relativism and scepticism in the *Persian Letters*,[9] or Othello, the noble and generous Moorish general, cannot but be overcome by their passions. They are both consumed by overwhelming jealousy. The fear of their wives' infidelity and their inability to reason with themselves led them almost inevitably to crime. Following Aristotle, Bodin and Nicolas Boileau (1636–1711), Montesquieu claimed that climate influences character, passions and emotional states.[10] According to his climate theory people in hot climates were 'hot-tempered', they had particular sensitivities, and exhibited strong passions and sexual behaviours. Their violent passions and emotional states produced all manner of crimes. For Europeans, these violent emotions were perceived as a source of dangerous instability and feared as potentially damaging to the public peace. The harsh emotional regime established by court society in Europe and the pressure to restrain emotion have been influential in the depiction of the Muslim Other as an 'emotional being'. By projecting a certain emotional state onto the Muslim Other, it became representative of foreign and inappropriate behaviours. The projection of violent emotions, outbursts of violence, of life in a state of constant fear and indulgence in lasciviousness onto the Muslim world served as a controlling and censoring device for unwanted displays of emotions in Europe. Thus emotions played an important role in framing the identity of the Muslim Other and in defining, by antithesis, European identity. Emotions also played a crucial role in framing the colonial gaze and Europe's 'emotional' categorizations of Otherness. However, the field could yet be enriched by cross-cultural analysis from a finer and more detailed analysis of Muslim otherness, recognizing that the emotional appreciation of the Muslim Other depends on their origin and the point of view, for instance, of Spaniards, Germans, English or French.

Further reading

Blanks, D. and M. Frassetto (eds), *Western Views of Islam in Medieval and Early Modern Europe: Perception of Other* (New York: St Martin's Press, 1999)

—essays analyse the reactions of medieval and early European writers toward Islamic religion and culture. The novelty of this volume is the collaboration between historians and literary scholars, and the analysis of the perception of the Muslim Other across Europe from historical and literary material that sometimes reveals a difference of views.

Curtis, M., *Orientalism and Islam, European Thinkers on Oriental Despotism in the Middle East and India* (Cambridge: Cambridge University Press, 2009)

—provides an historical analysis of the perception of Oriental despotism and Oriental society, and the conflicted emotions toward them, by European political writers.

Said, E., *Orientalism* (New York: Vintage books, 1979)

—in spite of the controversy over Said's thesis, *Orientalism* remains an unavoidable book that changed the view on the Orientalist discourse, and on the perception of Muslim Otherness. Later research on Orientalism still positions itself *vis à vis* Said's book.

Notes

1. P. de Harley, J. Racine, First preface of *Bajazet* in *Complete Plays*, (trans.) G.A. Argent, 5 vols (University Park: The Pennsylvania State University Press, 2011), 2: 29.
2. Two researchers affiliated with the Australian Research Council Centre of Excellence for the History of Emotions, François Soyer and Mirko Sardelic, are working respectively on fear and hatred of the 'other' in southern Europe and on the role of emotions in contacts between Eurasian cultures.
3. *Recueil des gazetes, nouvelles, relations extraordinaires et autres récits des choses remarquables advenues* 155 (1659), 1239–44.
4. Racine, *Bajazet,* second preface, 29.
5. E. Terry, *A Voyage to East India* (1655; repr., London, 1777); T. Roe, *The Embassy of Sir Thomas Roe to the Court of the Great Mughal, 1615–1619,* (ed.) W. Foster, 2 vols (London: The Hakluyt Society, 1899)
6. A. Galland, *Voyage à Constantinople, 1672–1673,* (ed.) C. Schefer (Paris: Maisonneuve et Larose, 2002), 121–43. Author's translation.
7. R. Knolles, *The General History of the Turks,* 3rd Edition (London: Islip, 1621); M. Baudier, *General History of the Harem and of the Court of the Grand Turk,* (trans.) E. Grimeston (London, 1635)
8. M.W. Montagu, *The Turkish Embassy Letters,* (ed.) M. Jack (London: Virago, 1994)
9. B. de Montesquieu, *Persian Letters,* (ed.) C.J. Betts (London: Penguin, 1973)
10. Montesquieu, *The Spirit of Laws,* (ed.) D.W. Carrithers (Berkeley: University of California Press, 1977)

The world beyond Europe

IV.38 Global trading companies

Jacqueline Van Gent

Only very recently have emotions come to be considered in the study of global trading companies. These new works utilize primary sources such as letters, travelogues and company instructions to East India Company employees, diaries, company reports, ship registers and increasingly also ambassadorial reports of Asian diplomats. Most historical studies of global trading companies discuss their activities in terms of economic or political networks and material consumption of mainly Asian goods.[1] And yet mercantile enterprises were, perhaps surprisingly, driven by emotional judgements and had to devise affective management strategies in their encounters with people and cultures outside Europe. The desire for luxury goods from outside Europe fuelled the establishment of trading empires and in the emotional imagination of early modern Europeans Asia, Africa and the Americas became locations for the acquisition of almost unlimited wealth. These 'New Worlds' became spaces for emotional projections of fear and anxiety (expressed in cannibalism stories), sexual desire and greed. Goods and objects returning to Europe were met by strong affective responses, ranging from the admiration of diplomatic gifts by Asian and African rulers to the concern about the effect of colonial foodstuff like coffee or tobacco on the health of Europeans or the effects an uncontrolled consumption of luxury goods like silk might have on the social order.

European trading companies were established to build global trade exchanges with the Americas, and Africa (so-called West India Companies) as well as Asia and Australia. These global trading companies could be large and long-term enterprises such as Danish Asiatic Company (1730–79), Dutch East India Company (VOC) (1602–1798), Swedish East India Company (1731–1813), French East India Company (1664–1769) or much smaller and short-lived companies such as the Portuguese Company (1628–33). These were more than just mercantile enterprises, which brought highly desired luxury goods to Europe or engaged in the cross-Atlantic slave trade. They simultaneously acted as significant political and social players, and exercised significant power in their respective overseas trading ports and colonial territories. The members of these trading companies – from the director to supercargoes and ordinary seamen – had their own hopes and anxieties during the long voyages and their sometimes lengthy stays at one of the trading posts overseas.

The archives of global trading companies offer significant opportunities to explore emotional styles and meanings at many social levels. In their different social interactions within and outside of these companies, their social behaviour and decision making was influenced by many emotions such as aspiration, desire and even greed but also guided by hope, anxiety, fear or sorrow and scorn. We find regularly expressions of frustration and anger concerning miscommunication or simply disinterest of potential foreign trading partners. Envy and competition between European trading nations influenced their political manoeuvres as much as admiration or distain for non-European societies and the desire for lucrative commodities and high profits.[2]

One of the most important aims of trading companies was the establishment of relationships of trust or friendship with foreign rulers and merchants to gain their permission to establish trading posts. This was best achieved by participating in public rituals that expressed respect and loyalty towards Asian rulers, often linked to ostentatious gift giving which was acknowledged as tribute. Detailed journals, reports and eyewitness accounts, like those of Johan Nieuhof (1618–72), describe the experiences, fears and hopes of East India Company employees at the imperial court in China.[3]

Diplomatic skills were equally important in negotiating European contact with societies where social stratification was less visible to the European eye such as the Khoikhoi in South Africa or indigenous people in Australia. Here the hopes of VOC men to establish favourable trade relations were often disappointed because indigenous people did not always find them desirable. At the same time violence against local people was used to reinforce European interests, to facilitate slave trade and to crush rebellions. Massacres of local people were often part of the rule of East India Companies and cruelty towards slaves, or captured prisoners of war, was common.

Competition, envy and suspicion between European powers were very strong because the Asian market was lucrative and produced high profits. The order, possession and display of its commodities in Europe was an effective social strategy to signal pride in status and exclusive social standing. As status markers they also carried considerable social anxieties: their social circulation was regulated by prohibitions (for example for lower classes to wear silk) to secure social exclusion. In the eighteenth century, public discourse increasingly associated the consumption of Asian luxury goods with wastefulness, folly and female excessiveness but in social practice objects like silk, tea, coffee and porcelain became status symbols for royal and aristocratic families, and later also for middle-class men and women.[4]

An important aspect of accessing the goods brought by global trading companies was the establishment of elite networks and patronage, relationships which extended the existing relations of 'strategic affection' which bound patrons and clients together. Supercargoes were directly responsible for the management of cargo and, importantly, they arranged for private orders of cargo that was not publicly auctioned off. This enabled them to build intimate and strong patronage networks with elite clients. For example armorial porcelain services were directly commissioned by the European elite via the East India Company supercargoes from Canton. These services expressed social success, standing and upward mobility and they separated nobility from non-nobility. Thus armorial porcelain became an affective material device to display pride in aristocratic lineage. Asian porcelain was also a popular diplomatic gift to secure royal patronage. In early modern societies, gifts carried the implicit duty to return favours and appealed to the status and honour of the receiver and this reciprocal nature of gifts reemphasized the strategic affection which was the essence of early modern patronage relations.[5]

The role of global trading companies as political agents placed them unavoidably in situations of conflict, resentment and violence. In the massacre of Amboyna (1623) on Ambon Island (today Maluku, Indonesia), Indonesians working for the English East India Company were killed by Dutch VOC members for suspected treason. Suspicions, hatred and fear fuelled such escalations, and sorrow, grief and guilt accompany such actions but often remain less visible in the colonial archives. Grief and sorrow about the loss of fellow Europeans, for example as result of the not too infrequent shipwrecks are more readily expressed. A sustained and public use of violence was part and parcel of slave trade which was facilitated by almost all European trading companies. Doubt, shame or rejection of this violence was rarely expressed in official documents but can be found in private letters, diaries or travelogues.[6]

Most male employees of trading companies travelled without their families and often associated with local women, often in long-term relationships and with resulting children who were only rarely taken back to Europe. These colonial households reflect intimacy and affection, but also patriarchal rule and subordination of women, children and servants. There was increasing anxiety in Europe about European men being too much influenced by the Asian cultures in which they lived with local companions. Sons were sometimes sent back to Europe for their education but the affectionate attachment to local women was rarely acknowledged back home, despite the women's often considerable power in the colonies.[7]

Love, affection, fear and longing were expressed more readily in the letters between the men working for trading companies and the families they had left behind at home. A rare insight into the emotional lives of ordinary sailors and their families are possible in the surviving letters of Dutch VOC seamen, which were captured by the English during the seventeenth and eighteenth centuries. These 'Sailing Letters' are a valuable source for the everyday lives, hopes and emotions of ordinary Dutch women, children and men who wrote to their loved ones in times of separation during their travels.[8]

Scholars are only beginning to apply the perspective of historical emotions to global trading companies. Where the role of emotions has been considered, new dimensions on cultural motivations, social practices and attitudes to mercantile and political encounters emerge. In the future, new avenues in the field of global trading companies might be explored for example in the study of emotional responses to trading goods, affective networks that were created as part of trading companies' activities both in Europe and outside of Europe, and a comparison of the 'emotional geographies' formed by European merchants in their encounters with an early modern global world.

Further reading

Broomhall, S., 'Shipwrecks, Sorrow, Shame, and the Great Southland: The Use of Emotions in Seventeenth-Century Dutch East India Company Communicative Ritual', in M.L. Bailey and K. Barclay (eds), *Emotion, Ritual and Power in Europe, 1200–1920: Family, State and Church* (Houndmills: Palgrave, 2016)

—argues for a stronger consideration of the VOC as an imagined emotional community and the ways in which this community ritualized emotions.

Van Gent, J., 'Linnaeus' tea cup: masculinities, affective networks and Chinese porcelain in eighteenth-century Sweden', in J. Van Gent and R. Toivo (eds), Special Issue: 'Gender, Objects and Emotions in Scandinavian History', *Journal of Scandinavian History* 41 (2016)

—explores the emotions associated with gendered patronage and social status in relation to the Swedish East India Company.

Notes

1 See, for a recent example, M. Berg (ed.) with F. Gottman, H. Hodacs and C. Nierstrasz, *Goods from the East, 1600–1800: Trading Eurasia* (Houndmills: Palgrave Macmillan, 2015)
2 S. Broomhall, 'Shipwrecks, Sorrow, Shame, and the Great Southland: The Use of Emotions in Seventeenth-Century Dutch East India Company Communicative Ritual', in M.L. Bailey and K. Barclay (eds), *Emotion, Ritual and Power in Europe, 1200–1920: Family, State and Church* (Houndmills: Palgrave, 2016); A. Clulow, *The Company and the Shogun: The Dutch Encounter with Tokugawa Japan* (New York: Columbia University Press, 2014)
3 J. Nieuhof, *Het gezantschap der Neederlandtsche Oost-Indische Compagnie aan den groten Tatarischen cham* (Amsterdam, 1665)
4 On gendered use of Chinese porcelain and emotions, see for example J. Van Gent, 'Linnaeus' tea cup: masculinities, affective networks and Chinese porcelain in eighteenth-century Sweden', in J. Van Gent and R. Toivo (eds), Special Issue: 'Gender, Objects and Emotions in Scandinavian History', *Journal of Scandinavian History* 41, 3 (2016), 388–409; S. Broomhall and J. Van Gent, 'The Gendered Political Agency of Porcelain among Early Modern Dynasties', in J. Daybell and S. Norrhem (eds), *Gender and Political Culture in Early Modern Europe* (London: Routledge, 2016)
5 This has been recently argued for diplomatic gifts by M. Auwers, 'The gift of Rubens: rethinking the concept of gift-giving in early modern diplomacy', *European History Quarterly* 43, 3 (2013), 421–41; M. Jansson, 'Measured reciprocity: English ambassadorial gift exchange in the 17th and 18th centuries', *Journal of Early Modern History* 9, 3/4 (2005), 348–70.
6 See for example the travelogue of the Swedish naturalist and abolitionist A. Sparrman, *A Voyage to the Cape of Good Hope, towards the Antarctic Polar Circle, and Round the World: But Chiefly into the Country of the Hottentots and Caffres, from the Year 1772 to 1776* (London, 1789)
7 L. Blussé, *Bitter Bonds: A Colonial Divorce Drama of the Seventeenth Century*, (trans.) D. Webb (Princeton: Markus Wiener Publishers, 2002)
8 See the 'Letters as Loot project' at the University of Leiden, online at www.brievenalsbuit.nl/.

IV.39 Amerindian and African slaves

Giuseppe Marcocci

Slavery was a global characteristic of the early modern world and played a central role in European colonialism. In particular, the construction of overseas empires in the Atlantic world – the specific area considered here – was accompanied by massive recourse to Amerindian and African slave labour. The history of emotions may contribute to rethinking this dramatic phenomenon of subjugation and exploitation, by exploring in detail cultural and social dynamics that have often been relegated to the background in favour of economic and demographic macro-analyses. For a long time, indeed, Amerindian and African slaves and their descendants, who were often the fruit of unions with persons of different origin (though this did not give them their freedom), have been seen as a silent presence in the early modern Atlantic world, whose thoughts and feelings it was, by definition, impossible to know. This has traditionally been due to the scarcity of written sources with which historians can hear the direct voice of subaltern groups that lived in the past.

The history of emotions approach is ideally placed to retrieve tensions and expressions of inner movements as witnessed by sources and, so, reach a less schematic, timeless vision of the affective interactions in the context of power relations between slave-owners, masters and slaves, as well as of the emotional reactions of the slaves themselves. When the chronicler Gomes Eanes de Zurara (*c.* 1410–73/4) described the first raids the Portuguese carried out in the mid-fifteenth century on the West African coast, he also dealt with the emotional impact when African slaves were first portioned out in Portugal. Zurara confessed to shedding some 'tears' at the sight, underlining the slaves' 'humanity that maketh mine to weep in pity for their sufferings'. At the same time, however, his careful description of their exterior displays of 'sadness' (lowered gaze, copious tears, sighs, cries, beating their faces and singing ritual songs of lamentation) is set alongside the 'pleasure' with which Prince Henry (1394–1460), the promoter of the expeditions, solemnly seated on his imposing horse, considered the future salvation of their souls, thanks to their conversion to Christianity.[1] The history of emotions' approach helps us grasp the dynamics of the complex tensions that surrounded the religious justification of the origins of the Atlantic trade.

Around a century later, the Dominican Bartolomé de las Casas (*c.* 1484–1566) also drew on the vocabulary of emotions in denouncing the violence with which the Spanish conquistadors destroyed the social order in the New World and reduced the surviving Amerindians to slavery, driving them to flee in terror towards the interior and sometimes to kill themselves, simply to escape the torment, weeping and cries of pain.[2] While such denunciations led the Spanish crown to ban the enslavement of Amerindians (1542), slavery was not abandoned in the rest of America, where, from the late sixteenth century onwards, increasing numbers of Africans began to arrive to work in the plantations and mines, undergoing the most harsh ill-treatment, which has left a trace in popular tales and songs that express their feelings and the suffering their living conditions brought them. Africans disembarked after a terrible Atlantic crossing on board the slave-ships. As soon as the ship set sail, fear of death, anxiety and dismay were the lot of these men in chains, as they crossed the ocean for weeks toward an unknown destination. In those days there were already the first critics of the trade, like the Dominican Tomás de Mercado (*c.* 1525–75), who described in detail the physical afflictions of the slaves, transported 'naked, being allowed to die of thirst and hunger', breathing in the foulest smells. More recently, scholars have drawn attention to the human dimension of this experience, to the emotions felt and expressed inside the ships, where both death and the risk of shipwreck were equally common.[3]

Amerindians continued to share the fate of African slaves in Brazil, as in the Antilles and North America. The result was a connected and partly shared history, but there was also the transfer across the ocean of the beliefs and cultural practices of many African places, mainly those on the west coast, which reproduced with some modifications aspects of their original way of life registered in oral traditions and objects that, thanks to anthropology and archaeology, can once again reflect some of the emotions experienced by the slaves centuries ago. These were mainly ones of grief and suffering. Sometimes they changed to the rage and courage that were necessary for the attempts at rebellion that studded the history of Amerindian and African slaves in the New World, as is witnessed by the continual episodes of escape, which in Latin America sometimes culminated in the creation of citadels of fugitives (*quilombos, palenques*). An emotional regime was imposed there that differed from that of colonial society. Sometimes revolts took place at sea. What happened on board the ship *Amistad* (1839) is at the centre of a recent documentary that explores the emotional traces of a mutiny.[4]

The history of emotions is a valid tool for penetrating the inner world of the slaves. It offers better results than studies of the iconography of pictorial depictions, which often tend to reproduce the viewpoint of the society of the colonists more than that of the slaves. It is a way of preserving an echo of the voices of the latter, especially before their first autobiographical writings, such as *The Interesting Narrative of the Life of Olaudah Equiano* (1789), describing the vicissitudes and emotions in the life of an ex-slave of Igbo origin.[5] Our exploration of the emotional dynamics that surrounded the Amerindian and African slavery is only in the initial stages. However, if more attention is paid to cross-cultural affectivity in the multiple ways slaves interacted with their ever-changing social context, this will renew conventional views of a tragic phenomenon, which so deeply marked the history of the relationship between early modern Europe and the world.

Further reading

Curto, J.C. and P.E. Lovejoy (eds), *Enslaving Connections: Changing Cultures of Africa and Brazil During the Era of Slavery* (Amherst, NY: Humanity Books, 2004)

—although more generally focused on cultural history, provides a number of descriptions of affective contexts which make it an important contribution for the history of emotions.

Rediker, M., *The Slave Ship: A Human History* (New York: Viking, 2007)

—a most fascinating account of the lives, deaths and terrors of the enslaved sailing aboard the ships that brought them from the coast of Africa across the Atlantic to the Americas.

Restall, M. (ed.), *Beyond Black and Red: African-Native Relations in Colonial Latin America* (Albuquerque: University of New Mexico Press, 2005)

—the first book to deal specifically with the multiple relations between Africans and Amerindians in colonial Latin America, including key points to better understand their emotional aspect, including mixed marriages, cultural exchanges and labour.

Notes

1 G.E. da Zurara, *The Chronicle of the Discovery and Conquest of Guinea* (eds) C.R. Beazley and E. Prestage (London: Hakluyt Society, 1896), vol. 1, 80–3. Zurara completed his chronicle in 1453.

2 B. de las Casas, *The Tears of the Indians* (London, 1656). The title of John Phillips' English translation of the work, first published in Spanish in 1552, is emblematic.

3 T. de Mercado, *Suma de Tratos y Contratos* (Seville, 1571), fol. 109r.

4 See *Ghost of Amistad: In the Footsteps of the Rebels*, made in Sierra Leone by T. Buba drawing on the book by M. Rediker, *The Amistad Rebellion: An Atlantic Odyssey of Slavery and Freedom* (New York: Viking, 2012)

5 V. Carretta, *Equiano, the African: Biography of a Self-made Man* (Athens: University of Georgia Press, 2005)

IV.40 Missionary Catholicism

Peter A. Goddard

Jean Delumeau's *Sin and Fear*, first published in 1983, and in English 1990, demonstrated on a broad scale that powerful emotional currents animated religious actions in the early modern period. Delumeau's insight that a 'pastoral of fear' pushed believer and non-believer alike into acceptance of new forms of religiosity is especially useful in the history of early modern evangelization. A defining element of early modern Catholicism is the mission: the effort, led by specialized religious orders, to convert to a renovated belief system the non-Christian – often the non-European – or the religiously-different – European Protestants, specifically. The Council of Trent (1545–63) set out a corrected form of religious observance, and, in competition with Protestant models of piety, a deeper understanding of both conversion and everyday religious practice. Missionary orders, notably the Society of Jesus (the 'Jesuits') and various Franciscan orders, carried this renewed pastoral program to the ends of what Europeans knew of the world.

Early modern Catholicism was characterized by 'affective piety', religious observance which aimed to produce a bodily and sentimental response to religious assertions. Affective piety is evident in the enormous corpus of pastoral writing – and coextensive ritual apparatus – on the 'Passion', or incomprehensible suffering, of Christ on the cross in the late medieval world. Reformed Catholicism carried forth this emphasis on pain, sadness, joy, remorse and guilt into the modern world; it differed from Protestant observance in bodily dimension – believers continued to act out and feel the demands of faith, from fasting, kneeling prayer, to pilgrimage and hair shirt – whereas Protestantism generally favoured an abstract asceticism over widely-emoted religious expression. Of course Catholicism and Protestantism differed on other grounds, but the focus here is on emotions, and their role in religious conversion. In a competitive religious landscape, Catholic missions deployed a tactile, textured, sensual and moving, but also often brash, confrontational and iconoclastic program – 'spiritual conquest', to use a Franciscan expression – to win converts.

The embrace of affective piety over more abstract and intellectualized forms took place however in a vocabulary which precedes modern emotionology. Early modern writers – Protestant and Catholic alike – employed the language of the 'passions' to describe the bodily-experience pulls and pushes of feelings and instinctive urges. This way of viewing emotions derives from Aristotle, and was widely-used in Scholastic approaches to perception and experience of life. Among early modern Jesuits and Franciscans, and indeed every other Catholic mission order that this author has been able to survey, Aristotelian language of higher and lower – angelic and animal, soul and body, reason and its opposite – dominated. In the Aristotelian view, as translated for early modern practitioners, bodily-origins of feeling were 'natural' – an unavoidable consequence of one's bipartite self – but, crucially, in need of control and regulation. Over time, religious conversion, in the Catholic world, came to be seen as the imposition of what Catholic writers understood as 'Order', and, conversely, non-

Christian practice, while it might be admirable in its resemblance to pre-Christian antiquity, was, at root, in thrall to the disorder of the unchecked passions. Christianity promised to harness these unruly forces, and direct them to proper ends of reverence and devotion.

At same time, Catholic theorists in the aftermath of the Reformation – leading examples here include Nicolas Coeffeteau (1574–1623), in his 1620 *Tableau des Passions humaines* (Portrait of the Passions) and Jean-François Senault (*c.* 1599–72), in *De l'Usage des Passions* (The Use of the Passions) (1641) – had another target for their renovated Aristotelian program of emotional management. European elites, educated and libertine, embraced of the writings of the Stoics, including Seneca, the great pagan beacon of detachment and equanimity. For the Catholic vanguard, Stoicism led such elites inevitably to Protestantism or even paganism – which was worse? – denoted pride as well as folly. For as Catholic intellectuals knew, emotions – the passions – were part of life – far from the Stoic characterization of emotion as illness – and even the most enlightened person felt these forces course through his or her life. The issue was not to deny the passions, but rather to channel them into productive engagement. Coeffeteau and others provided a positive evaluation of emotions, and saw in the uncontrolled elements of behaviour promising grounds for the action of God's grace. Against the self-sufficiency of the Stoics, Catholic missionaries believed that peoples whose lives were governed by the appetites and aversions could be elevated, changed and Christianized only through a higher, supernatural power.

There was no single early modern Catholic mission: a proliferation of religious orders, and different national mandates, as well as widely varying target populations, who, according to an Aristotelian stadial model, occupied different rungs on the ladder of civilization, meant that a wide range of techniques were developed, ranging from *il modo soave* (the gentle way) – which Alessandro Valignano proposed for the Japanese mission in the 1580s – to what Delumeau has described as *la pastorale de la peur* (pastoral of fear) that we encounter in the French Jesuits' extensive mission program in Canada in the middle part of the seventeenth century. 'The gentle way' presupposed minimal disruption to the custom patterns of observance, and indeed Catholic missionaries believed that 'civilized' pagans, such as the Chinese or Japanese, already demonstrated mastery of the 'lower' self, and showed the high levels of interdependence and restraint that constituted 'order'. The confrontational approach was reserved for the inhabitants of the Americas who lived outside and in Aristotelian terms, prior to, 'civilization'. Missions to these people demonstrate the full onslaught of a program of affective piety, with an understanding of emotional management at the centre. Jesuits in New France asserted that 'fear is the forerunner of faith in the Barbarian mind': attempts to terrify, and then to assuage, and to cut through resistance by appealing directly to the emotions, lay at the heart of the conversion program among these New World peoples.

Early modern missions to the Americans – be they to Peru, to Paraguay, to Mexico, Florida or Canada – rarely produced the utopias which early modern theorists promoted. Mass conversions led by Franciscans in the Mexican valley in 1520s introduced a bare patina of Christian observance; later missionaries worked to 'deracinate' traditional religious practices and supplant them, through syncretic mechanisms, with Christian rites. The same process was followed in many other mission fields. In Canada, Jesuits, who dominated mission activity, replacing Franciscans who opened the mission in the early decades of the seventeenth century, saw mission as an educational venture, one which, starting with the youth, would produce new kinds of believers. Missions first to Algonquian boreal hunter-gatherers and then to the horticulturalist, palisaded-village dwelling Wendat and Haudenosaunee, coincided with significant change in the St Lawrence River/Great Lakes basin, as epidemic disease produced unprecedented population declines, and Haudenosaunee, or Iroquoian peoples to the south of the Great Lakes launched wars of incorporation to restock their villages and take over the rich borderlands of the expanding European presence. As such, war, disease, dislocation and despair pervaded New France. Jesuits thrust themselves into this lugubrious environment, and found that a grim and terrifying message of perdition resonated among peoples facing civilizational collapse, or at least made sense of the Jesuits' often stymied efforts. In addition to the catechism – learning by repetition – of children and willing adults, the chief means of acquiring converts was through death-bed confession; the newest members of the church were often the newly dead.

In such difficult circumstances, propitious to millennial fervour and rally against the Devil, the understanding and indeed 'usage', or manipulation, of emotions is apparent. Images, song and speech emphasized the suffering of the crucified Christ; converts wept in pity and remorse, for their own sins and those of their benighted people. We may identify *intégrisme* – or 'fundamentalism' in this approach: the convert, shocked and awed by a message of divine power as well as individual sinfulness, launches into a 'new life' of identification with the suffering Christ, thereby over-coming the resistance posed by her own culture and fellows. Conversion produced – and was equated with – dramatic and convulsive emotional heights. Emphasis, in Jesuit and Franciscan accounts, on the emotional character of conversion also reflected a weak link in the form of linguistic understanding: expressions in body and face were easier, it seemed, to read, than the speech or other ritual gesture of the new convert.

Emotion, known as 'passion', was understood by Catholic missionaries as a universal vulnerability in humanity, and, as such, ideal locus for the application of divine power. Emotional manipulation – through fear, sorrow, love and relief – opened the convert to the full set of teachings that would produce the Christian life of continence and order. Early modern Catholic emotionology, to give it a modern label, conferred advantage, if that is what is was, in global mission. The centrality of emotions in communication, including those between the early modern missionary and the convert or the unbeliever, offer historians a new way to understand the conversion project, and the expansion of Christianity in the early modern world.

Further reading

Delumeau, J., *Sin and Fear. The Emergence of a Western Guilt Culture, 13th–18th Centuries,* (trans.) E. Nicholson (New York: St. Martin's Press, 1990)

—an important study of the weight of feeling in both pre- and post-Reformation thinking and pastoral action.

Karant-Nunn, S.C., *The Reformation of Feeling* (Oxford: Oxford University Press, 2010)

—shows divergence in Catholic and Protestant treatments of emotion and affection through study of early modern German sermon literature.

Müller, M., *'These Savage Beasts become Domestick': The Discourse of the Passions in Early Modern England, with Special Reference to Non-fictional Texts* (Trier: Wissenschaftlicher Verlag, 2003)

—finds evidence of emotional intelligence, and a positive appraisal of emotions, in English literature; an emerging awareness of the positive value of the passions appears widespread in early modern thinking.

IV.41 Protestant global missions

Jacqueline Van Gent

Emotions played a vital role in the proselytizing efforts of global Protestant missions in the early modern period. The range of suitable sources is indeed very wide: there are official sources produced by missions as institutions, such as reports from the mission fields and mission diaries, private letters written by missionaries and sometimes by indigenous converts, mission journals, memoirs and auto/biographies of missionaries and converts.[1] Emerging scholarly work explores these sources for a comparison of the emotional experiences of missionaries and of indigenous converts.[2] The leading Protestant mission societies, such as the Moravian Church, had a strong Pietist background, which privileged personal emotional experiences over knowledge of the Scripture. Culturally accepted emotions can be held to constitute 'emotional styles', as William M. Reddy has argued, where social norms of emotions are promoted and group members are socialized accordingly, and where transgressions or non-compliance are usually punished.[3] One could argue that indigenous local cultures and Protestant mission societies had distinct 'emotional styles' which differed significantly, and potential converts, actual converts and those who 'relapsed' needed to be continually reminded of and socialized into the emotional styles of 'their' mission society. Thus, Protestant missions constituted 'emotional communities', in the sense that Barbara H. Rosenwein has suggested, as groups of people who share emotional norms.[4] In the context of early modern colonial expansion, a number of questions arise about the power imbalance between indigenous converts and missionaries and how this difference influenced the nature of such an emotional community.

Religious conversions on Protestant missions were a long and drawn-out process encompassing religious, social and emotional changes. Formal conversions of indigenous people to Christianity constituted only a very small part of a much broader social process aimed at modifying converts' social and moral behaviour. The performance of 'appropriate' emotions was taken by missionaries as a reliable external indicator of successful internal conversion or, at least, a readiness for baptism. Conversion rituals fostered the display of emotions such as joy, but also terror, shame and guilt associated with spiritual transformations. Indigenous converts were expected to demonstrate sincerity of their new beliefs in 'appropriate' emotional behaviour. This entry will discuss how historical meanings of emotions were negotiated as part of a global outreach of Protestant missions.

Protestant missions started in a more global fashion in the eighteenth century. There were earlier attempts by the Lutheran churches in Scandinavia to missionize Saami people, but these remained localized northern attempts as part of the state church. The Halle mission, under the political patronage of the Danish king, was the first official attempt to missionize outside of Europe. This enterprise remained restricted to a few stations in India. Methodists were reluctant to missionize (until the 1780s). The most important and fastest growing Protestant mission organization in the eighteenth century became the Moravian Church. Owing to their intensive missionary activities, the Moravians had built up an impressive geographical presence around the Atlantic rim, spanning Greenland to South Africa by the mid-eighteenth century.

The conversion of indigenous people was intended to fundamentally reshape their identities, moral systems and their behaviour, and emotions were to play a vital role in aligning converts with Moravians, and – ideally – in integrating them into the Moravians' emotional community, which was built at the local and at the global level. From the beginning of the Moravian evangelical outreach in the 1730s, Moravian missionaries developed a very distinct set of rituals, language and behaviour to create a distinct Moravian identity and establish an 'imagined community'[5] which had a specific emotional style. This community was centred on the love of Christ and his suffering, which had to be experienced individually by each believer in an 'awakening' moment, causing a 'moved heart', and the desire to change their spiritual path by handing over their heart to Christ.[6] The Moravians thus developed an elaborate 'religion of the heart' (*Herzensreligion*) where the convert and believer comprehended the Christian message internally and the heart was conceptualized as the spiritual centre and the seat of all feelings.[7] The state of the heart reflected the spiritual state of the believer in images of movement or bodily heat: a strong believer had a 'warm', 'moved' or 'melted' heart, those who were untouched by the Moravian message were identified as possessing 'cold' or 'unmoved' hearts. The internalization of Christ's suffering was expressed in the state of the heart: the heart could be 'warm', 'alive' or 'moved'.

Part of the conversion process was the close observation and the frequent discussion of the state of the convert's heart, to ascertain if their heart signalled a readiness for baptism. Moravian missionaries encouraged potential candidates for baptism to report about the state of their hearts and to record their observations regularly in their diaries, reports and letters. In a closely related trope, tears, which were believed to flow from the heart, similarly conveyed spiritual messages; tears and the ritual of weeping acquired specific social meanings and interpretations as part of the conversion process, which reinforced power differences between Moravian missionaries and indigenous converts.

Indigenous converts to the Moravian Church had to negotiate emotions as part of the conversion process and of belonging to the mission community. This was part of a much deeper, inherently colonial dilemma, where missionaries sought to promote a shared understanding of spiritual love and the experience of Christ's suffering, while also maintaining social distance and superiority by reinforcing shame and patriarchal obedience. Emotions became thus an important part of a wider colonial socialization process, and were indeed tools of social affiliation.[8] The socialization into particular emotional styles or even into emotional communities is a life-long process, where belonging needs to be re-affirmed and which does not take place without conflict, resistance and contradiction – just like conversion. At Protestant missions, conversion into another belief system was thus strongly associated with a conversion into another emotional style and community.

Importantly, Moravian missions were a product of colonial encounters and their inherent social conflicts and Moravian emotional practices reflected these social hierarchies and the kind of bonding with indigenous converts envisaged by Moravians was not free from coercion and social control.[9] At the same time there was an expectation of emotional attachments on both sides.

The study of historical emotions in the mission project of Protestant churches allows us to gain a more nuanced understanding of the processes of religious, social and moral changes that are part of proselytization. The way emotions were expected to be changed and performed brings the attention to power relations. This is particularly obvious in understanding the agency of indigenous people and their responses to Protestant missions. Their behaviour ranged from indifference, to resistance or acquiring leadership positions in the Moravian church as local evangelists and later as ministers.

Indigenous converts negotiated their belonging to the emotional community of Moravians in careful expressions of shared religious identity, symbols and emotions. The spirituality of Moravians was strongly Christocentric, with an awakening experience, and a strong emotional and somatic identification with Christ's suffering and his wounds, at the core of Moravian identity. Part of this negotiation of belonging to an emotional community was the reordering of social hierarchies, which were, as recent scholarship has shown, facilitated to a significant degree by emotions. In the context of Moravian conversions of indigenous people, emotions such as love were used simultaneously as means of social bonding and as tools of social distancing and coercion and frontier violence, which formed an important part of the social and emotional context of Protestant missions, needs to be taken into consideration. At the same time, a perspective on emotions and their contagious nature, might help us to understand why people from so many different cultures chose to join Protestant missions. The Protestant message, translated always into the vernacular, of Christ's suffering might have struck a strong emotional chord with the experiences of social disruptions in these communities.

The field of Protestant missions and emotions is expanding fast and produces exciting new work that allows for a deeper understanding of mission encounters and the agency of indigenous people. Future areas for enquiry may include the gendered and embodied nature of emotions on Protestant missions, the different emotional dynamics in specific historical mission situations and the use of emotional performances as social tools of intervention by indigenous people.

Further reading

McLisky, C., K. Vallgårda and D. Midena (eds), *Emotions and Christian Missions: Historical Perspectives* (Basingstoke: Palgrave Macmillan, 2015)

—provides a good overview of emerging themes in the field.

Scheer, M. and P. Eitler, 'Emotionsgeschichte als Körpergeschichte. Eine heuristische Perspektive auf religöse Konversionen im 19. Und 20. Jahrhundert', *Geschichte und Gesellschaft* 35, 2 (2009), 282–313.

—does not strictly discuss early modern missions, but remains a key text on embodied emotions and religious conversions.

Van Gent, J. and S. Young (eds), Special Issue: 'Emotions and Conversion', *Journal of Religious History* 39, 4 (2015)

—several articles in this collection discuss the emotions of indigenous people as well as of missionaries and pay attention to the central role emotions play in processes of religious change.

Notes

1 For a discussion of emotions and indigenous converts' letters see J. Van Gent, 'Sarah and her sisters: identity, letters and emotions in the early modern Atlantic World', *Journal of Religious History* 38, 1 (2014), 71–90.

2 For example, C. McLisky, K. Vallgårda and D. Midena (eds), *Emotions and Christian Missions: Historical Perspectives* (Basingstoke: Palgrave Macmillan, 2015); J. Van Gent and S. Young (eds), Special Issue: 'Emotions and Conversion', *Journal of Religious History* 39, 4 (2015)

3 W.M. Reddy, *The Navigation of Feeling: A Framework for the History of Emotions* (Cambridge: Cambridge University Press, 2001). Reddy further develops his concept of 'emotional styles' in his recent book *The Making of Romantic Love* (Chicago: University of Chicago Press, 2012)

4 The concept of 'emotional community' has been developed by B.H. Rosenwein. See her article 'Worrying about emotions in history', *American Historical Review* 107, 3 (2002), 821–45; see also Rosenwein, *Emotional Communities in the Middle Ages* (Ithaca: Cornell University Press, 2006); and more recently, 'Theories of Change in the History of Emotions,' in *A History of Emotions, 1200–1800*, (ed.) J. Liliequist (London: Pickering & Chatto, 2012), 7–20.

5 B. Anderson, *Imagined Communities* (1983; London: Verso, 2006)

6 J. Van Gent, 'Gendered Power and Emotions: The Religious Revival Movement in Herrnhut in 1727', in S. Broomhall (eds.), *Destroying Order, Structuring Disorder: Gender and Emotions in Medieval and Early Modern Europe* (Farnham: Ashgate, 2015), 233–47.

7 C.D. Atwood, 'Understanding Zinzendorf's blood and wounds theology', *Journal of Moravian History* 1 (2006), 31–47.

8 For a very useful discussion on how emotions link the individual to the social sphere, see J. Bourke, 'Fear and anxiety: writing about emotions in modern history', *History Workshop Journal* 55, 1 (2003), 111–33.

9 J. Van Gent, 'Moravian Memoirs and the Emotional Salience of Conversion Rituals', in M.L. Bailey and K. Barclay (eds), *Emotion, Ritual and Power in Europe, 1200–1920: Family, State and Church* (Houndmills: Palgrave Macmillan, 2016)

IV.42 Colonialism

Donna Merwick

'Colonialism' is a deceptive word. It conjures up something highly systematic. It points to empires rationally pre-planned and, with equally clear reasoning, successfully maintained. At home in the metropolitan, 'colonialism' asserts itself in majestic buildings, in variants of The Colonial Office or The Ministry of Colonial Affairs. Within such self-assertive artefacts of hegemony are hard-headed men who can supposedly master the patterning of multidimensional projects of control. They will, for example, see to it that naval commanders, are given detailed instructions: where to rendezvous on the outward voyage (ordinarily at an island); when to open secret instructions; how to make for the naval facilities that are their destinations; when and how to set a course for home. Administrators must organize the sending of military personnel, munitions-makers, hydrographers and surveyors, sail makers. Abroad, colonial officials will be expected to create spaces manifesting the 'know-how' of rule.[1] They'll need intelligence and cunning to work out the control of both natives and their own European populations.

Consider for a moment some of the demands of the early modern Dutch seaborne empire. By 1650, East India Company ships were disgorging tons of exotic spices as well as chests loaded with gemstones and diamonds, rosewood and silks. At mid-century in Amsterdam, company directors were overseeing work going on in warehouses and shipbuilding establishments that effectively controlled the sprawling waterfront. In the eighteenth century alone, clerks in the general pay office in Batavia (Jakarta in Indonesia) were writing about 2,275,000 pages of correspondence, at least half of it destined for the Amsterdam offices and other chambers of the company. Back in Amsterdam, the company's splendid *Oostindisch Huis* contained an audit office composing a clearing office, pay office and chief accountant's rooms. In a reception office, the cashier and his assistants handled silver and gold to be sent to Asia. Bookkeepers also worked in the warehouses where accountants and clerks oversaw matters regarding shipbuilding and the fitting out of the company's overseas fleets.[2]

It would seem reasonable, then, to think that the total control visible to the directors in the geography of its presence in Amsterdam would be present also in its far wider transoceanic endeavours. 'Colonialism' encourages that thinking. But if we disallow 'colonialism's' power to limit our investigations and, instead, study more closely the 'colonial lives' that gave existential reality to long-distance adventuring, we discover that such projects called up every aspect of the human condition. From the East India Company directors down the social scale to the wharfies, brothel-owners and carters of Amsterdam's maritime culture, across to country folk who made it to the seaport and set sail on the giant ships, and their wives who negotiated (often fruitlessly) to collect their wages, a range of emotions gave shape to the vast overseas enterprises.

Historical evidence discloses a gap between the hegemonic ambitions of company directors (or elsewhere, royally-appointed ministers), and the day-to-day lives of distant administrators and their subjects.[3] There, all were prepared – to one degree or another – to make overseas existence work. But equally all lived with fear and uncertainty, fright at their ignorance of natives who kept themselves in shadows, distrust of superiors and themselves. They had entered an uncertain geographical space but an uncertain emotional space as well.

Each of western Europe's peoples who sailed for the new worlds transported distinctive cultural formations and emotional values. The Portuguese, English, Spanish, Dutch and French performed different cultural traits governing social hierarchies, epistemic systems, racial and religious divisions, and ardently defended (if scarcely defined) categorizations regarding land-ownership. Even those 'certainties' that were shared, such as the Christian gospel, were embedded – always emotionally – in specific traditional narratives.[4]

In 1987, Simon Schama published a brilliant study in which he isolated a paradoxical but nonetheless dominant set of Dutch emotions aroused by the overseas enterprises undertaken during the Golden Age. He examined not only the process by which overseas treasures were beginning to flow into the Netherlands but also reconstructed the anxieties aroused by the sudden 'superabundance' that Dutch people began to experience and fear. Clergymen, artists such as Johannes Vermeer (1632–75), poets such as Joost van den Vondel (1587–1679), political pamphleteers, even some of Holland's highest authorities, all became troubled polemicists. The Netherlands was, they pleaded, a notably stable society. Now it was being destabilized – and by the greed resulting from the unexpected availability of riches. To combat worldly vanity, they half-heartedly made the effort to 'moralize materialism'.[5] But they continued to worry about fetishizing commodities and reports of Dutch overseas behaviour. Searching for Dutch identity in its excesses, they expressed alarm: this is not us.

Benjamin Schmidt furthered Schama's argument, identifying the Dutch way of estimating their own overseas experience by triangulating it with that of the Spanish and the native Americans whom both European powers were encountering and – in the case of the Spanish – brutally subordinating. They found the natives to be innocent victims of Spanish perfidy, the same treachery that they believed was theirs at the hands of the Spanish against whom they had so recently and successfully rebelled. Mercilessly, the Dutch took a discursive position against the conquistadors as tyrannical monsters. The propaganda triumphed because its emotional power had more than a ready audience. But unforgiving too – or, better said, dismayed and shamed – were the Dutch when they began to receive reliable reports of their own overseas atrocities.[6]

In 1621, the West India Company received a charter bestowing exclusive rights to govern and trade within its legally discovered territories. The company's directors at home as well as its overseas officials imagined small but fortified alongshore enclaves that would allow them presence – a powerful trading presence – but not dominion.[7] Neither extensive landownership nor the founding of settler societies were their *desiderata*. As traders they needed the emotions of transients toward the natives: depersonalization, employment of the tactics of wheeling-and-dealing, non-entanglement in native cultures, such as religious practices. Tactics to keep exchanges – and corporate profits – unproblematic.

Peter Stuyvesant (*c.* 1612–72) served as the company's Director-General of New Netherland (present-day New York) from 1647 to 1664. His papers reveal something about the range of emotions that propelled the province forward from its beginnings until its fall to the English in 1664.[8] These emotions arose from two sources worth considering. First, the company directors were determined to put in place ordinances mandating the peaceful contact of its people with the indigenous populations. They realized that the Dutch populace at home were unsympathetic to any evidence of violence toward the Amerindians. This required restraint: the enactment of local legislation imposing geographical separation in times of tension; watchful waiting; quelling any colonist's urge to retaliate to native provocations; punishing anyone for maltreating natives; invoking diplomacy, even if each participant knew the others were play-acting. Stuyvesant fully agreed with the policy and enforced it as rigorously as the proximity of a slowly increasing European population and resistant natives would allow. For example, in 1655 and 1660, some colonists were demanding aggressive military action as revenge against natives. On both occasions, he and his council heatedly debated the possibility of a just war. Twice they rejected it because local Dutch men had initiated the hostilities.[9]

Second, the language of the correspondence between Stuyvesant and the directors offers evidence of an uneasy and at times confrontational relationship. In their extensive correspondence with Stuyvesant, the directors adhered meticulously to the protocols governing proper businessmen's letters. There was no release of emotion, no blustering, no willingness to enter into the necessarily demeaning arguments about policy directives or (as they generally were) already-settled decisions. But Stuyvesant was like the company's other overseas employees: he did not trust them. So, when he was reassigned from his company post in the Caribbean to be Director-General in New Netherland, he carefully arranged to take copies of his correspondence with him. Similar officials would not have been surprised – nor would the directors have been. For the most part, his correspondence also adhered to the unspoken codes of businessmen's letter writing. Emotions, as everyone expected, were cautiously suppressed.

But occasionally words and phrases rose to the surface, like flotsam on the sea's surface betraying much larger wreckage hidden below. In the early 1660s, Stuyvesant wrote to the directors in undisguised anger: the province needed stronger defences than the company was willing to provide – despite the near-certainty of its immanent loss to the English. Later and after his unavoidable surrender of the province, the directors recalled him to trial in Holland for his 'neglect or treachery'.[10] When they washed their hands of him in the course of it, he wrote of his sense of abandonment and humiliation. A friend consoled him: 'I cannot imagine on what pretext the loss of the country can be laid to your charge'.[11]

In all of this we, as historians, are only now focusing squarely on emotions. As late nineteenth- and twentieth-century historians embraced the need to make the research and writing-up of history more scientific, more objective, they succumbed to the prevailing and powerfully value-laden dichotomy drawn between the rational and the emotional. It would be a mistake to reverse the assignment of values while retaining the dualism. Women and men living out their colonial lives in the sixteenth and seventeenth centuries would have been bewildered at such philosophical abstractions and just got on with being – forgive another abstraction – holistically human.

Further reading

Merwick, D., *The Shame and the Sorrow: Dutch-Amerindian Encounters in New Netherland* (Philadelphia: University of Pennsylvania Press, 2006)

—describes how the seventeenth-century Netherlanders' intentions of being tolerant, pluralistic and anti-militaristic overseas were vitiated by their experiences of contact and rule in North America.

Merwick, D., *Stuyvesant Bound: An Essay on Loss Across Time* (Philadelphia: University of Pennsylvania Press, 2013)

—explores the structures of feeling and reason available to a seventeenth-century Dutch man – as administrator, Calvinist believer and official who surrendered New Netherland to the English in 1664.

Stoler, A.L., *Along the Archival Grain: Epistemic Anxieties and Colonial Common Sense* (Princeton: Princeton University Press, 2009)

—foregrounds the anxieties of Dutch men and women involved in overseas expansion in the Indies. Hers is a brilliant and key work in this field.

Notes

1 A.L. Stoler, *Along the Archival Grain: Epistemic Anxieties and Colonial Common Sense* (Princeton: Princeton University Press, 2009), 2.
2 D. Merwick, 'A genre of their own: Kiliaen van Rensselaer as guide to the reading and writing practices of early modern businessmen', *William and Mary Quarterly* 3rd Ser., LXV, 4 (2008), 683.
3 Stoler, *Along the Archival Grain*, 1.
4 See L. Gregerson and S. Juster (eds), *Empires of God: Religious Encounters in the Early Modern Atlantic* (Philadelphia: University of Pennsylvania Press, 2011)
5 S. Schama, *The Embarrassment of Riches: An Interpretation of Dutch Culture in the Golden Age* (New York: Alfred A. Knopf, 1987), xi, 4, 8, 49.
6 B. Schmidt, *The Dutch Imagination and the New World, 1570–1670* (Cambridge: Cambridge University Press, 2001). See also Merwick, *The Shame and the Sorrow: Dutch-Amerindian Encounters in New Netherland* (Philadelphia: University of Pennsylvania Press, 2006)
7 F. Jennings quoted in Merwick, *The Shame and the Sorrow*, 264.
8 See Merwick, *Stuyvesant Bound: An Essay on Loss Across Time* (Philadelphia: University of Pennsylvania Press, 2013)

9 Merwick, *The Shame and the Sorrow*, 50, 120, 175, 230, on a just war, 218–34 and see 252–56. Further on deterrence, see Merwick, *Stuyvesant Bound*, 34–56. Even in 1664, the population numbered only between 9,000 and 10,000.
10 Merwick, *Stuyvesant Bound*, 117.
11 Ibid., 117, 120, see chapters 8 and 9.

IV.43 Theories of empire

Nicole Eustace

In the first decades of the twenty-first century, critical studies of empire have begun to incorporate the approaches and questions of emotions history. Much of this work on the 'intimate history of empire' has been focused on the nineteenth- and twentieth-century imperial projects of the United States and Britain. However, the very latest work has begun to broaden out geographically, to include debates on emotion and civility amongst imperial powers originating in the Middle East and Asia, and to reach back chronologically, to look at the early modern origins of modern imperial uses of emotion.[1]

From the earliest days of English and Scottish colonization in the British Atlantic, to the Age of Enlightenment, British commentators took strength from classical theories that justified the seizure of alien lands and peoples on the basis of the supposedly superior civilization of the imperialists. Sixteenth-century colonizers measured civilization by the practice of agriculture, while eighteenth-century ones turned to polite culture as the distinguishing feature of civilization. Over the centuries that spanned this shift, from tilling soil to cultivating sentiment, unprecedented levels of violence added ever-increasing urgency to the project of claiming morality for civility.[2]

During the sixteenth-century, while Spain established a significant empire on the other side of the Atlantic – the inhabitants of the British Isles practised the process of colonization in their home waters. By the 1560s, early English invaders of Ireland imagined that they could act as latter-day Romans, arguing that, 'among all the nations of the world, they that be politic and civil do master the rest'. For early English imperialists, language, law and faith defined the essence of civilization, the means 'whereby the Romans conquered and kept long time a great part of the world'. They soon added manure as the true ground civility, claiming that Ireland 'lacketh only inhabitants, manurance, and pollicie', and explaining that civility 'encreaseth more by keeping men occupyed in Tyllage, than by idle following of heards'. The English imagined active settlers filling idle and empty lands; despite praise for Romans who 'conquered', violence played little overtly acknowledged part in plans for possession.[3]

Early English advocates of imperialism consistently emphasized the civil above the martial in a bid to differentiate their colonial ambitions from those of their rivals, the Spanish. By 1583, the year the English first reached North America, they could read in translation the moral condemnation of Spain's Atlantic empire handed down by the Spanish priest Bartolomé de las Casas (*c.* 1484–1566). Published in London as *The Spanish Colonie,* the very first page of the book announced that it documented 'Spanish cruelties and tyrannies, perpetrated in . . . the newe founde worlde'. If Roman precedents enticed the English with the possibility of keeping 'a great part of the world' for themselves, social critics in Catholic Spain were already complicating the moral claims of imperialists. For the English to distinguish themselves in the Atlantic, it seemed they would have to counter Spanish 'cruelty and tyranny' with benevolence and liberty.[4]

The Scots, like the early English, preferred describing imperialism as a benign process of natural growth. Setting his sights on unincorporated areas of Scotland in 1598, James VI (1566–1625) recommended 'planting colonies among them . . . that within a short time may reforme and civilize the best inclined among them'. He furthered the botanical allusion to colonization as 'planting' when he advised 'rooting out or transporting the barbarous and stubborne sort and planting civilitie in their rooms'.[5] Whatever violence was implied in the notion of pulling out human weeds, the abiding image remained the peaceful project of planting a garden of civility.

Nevertheless, building a British Atlantic Empire proved to be bloody beyond all reckoning. The English first set sail on the Atlantic in military expeditions. By 1607, the first permanent colony would be established at Jamestown – only to be followed two years later by the first full-scale war between the English and the land's original inhabitants. The first Powhatan War, as that conflict became known, began in 1609 and lasted until 1614. By 1619, the English colonists had taken possession of their first shipment of enslaved Africans and the unbroken history of British Atlantic aggression only increased from there.[6]

In the seventeenth century, boasts of superior civility continued, now with the new problem of reconciling such claims with nearly a century's history of depravity. John Locke (1632–1704), creator of a constitution for the new colony of Carolina, played a prominent part in this process. By the time Locke published his *Two Treatises of Government* in 1689, the English no longer claimed that their colonizing activities would necessarily extend the reach of civility to all. Instead, Locke satisfied himself with describing what he called 'civil society' among the English alone. 'Civil society being a state of peace, amongst those who are of it', he declared, 'the state of war is excluded by the umpirage, which they have provided in their legislative [bodies]'. Linking English liberty to the strength of its representative legislature, Locke reserved the state of peace for those who were already within civil society; amongst those who were not 'of it' the state of war might rule.[7]

While Locke is more often credited as a political than as a moral philosopher, his *Two Treatises* (1690) represents something of a turning point in English ideas about the links between emotion and civility. For, in explaining the power of the legislature to ensure English peace, Locke made explicit reference to the role of sympathy in civility, saying: 'it is in their legislative [aspect], that the members of a commonwealth are united, and combined together into one coherent living body . . . from hence the several members have their mutual influence, sympathy, and connexion'. In Locke's vision, only those inside civil society enjoyed the peace that came with union through sympathy.[8]

The English soon elevated sympathy to the *sine qua non* of morality and civility. Writing on sympathy in 1759, in the midst of the Seven Years War (a worldwide struggle for empire), Adam Smith (1723–90) opined, 'Among civilized nations, the virtues which are founded upon humanity are more cultivated. . . . Among savages and barbarians, it is quite otherwise. [The] savage . . . can expect from his countrymen no sympathy'. In Smith's *Theory of Moral Sentiments* (1759), civility advanced humanity itself. As he explained, 'Before we can feel much for others, we must in some measure be at ease ourselves . . . and all savages are too much occupied with their own wants and necessities to give much attention to those of another person'. While Smith did assert that 'savages' had virtues other than humanity (such as strength), he damned them with faint praise. By the time the Scotsman Henry Home (1696–1782), Lord Kames, added his opinion in 1778 that, 'the principles of morality are little understood among savages: and if they arrive at maturity among enlightened nations, it is by slow degrees', the attitude that sympathy defined the superior morality of civility had attained the status of conventional wisdom.[9]

From the earliest days of English and Scottish colonialism, commentators had insisted on the connection between civility and mastery. Yet from the first, the British had also evinced discomfort with the 'cruelty and tyranny' of empire. Over two centuries of violence – that enabled vast profits from seized lands and forced labour – the British developed an ever more urgent need to ease their conscience by associating civility with morality. They came to claim that the heightened emotional sensitivities of Europeans gave them the advanced moral standing to assert control over the lives and lands of 'savages'. The rise of the culture of moral sensibility did not merely coincide with the modern age of empire; it actively helped underwrite it.

The history of empire and the history of emotion have only just begun to intersect; vast areas prime for scholarly exploration remain. From studies of European ideologies of civility, such as that sketched briefly here, to work that explores the affective and material experience of colonialism; from comparative research on the emotional cultures of myriad colonial societies to studies that analyse the role of emotional negotiations in the imposition and contestation of imperial power, the possibilities for new scholarship are almost unlimited.

Further reading

Eustace, N., E. Lean, J. Livingston, J. Plamper, W.H. Reddy and B.H. Rosenwein, 'AHR conversation: the historical study of emotions', *American Historical Review* 117, 5 (2012), 1487–531.

—provides an overview of debates on methods and approach in the history of emotion by scholars specializing in several fields and periods.

Stoler, A.L., 'Tense and tender ties: the politics of comparison in North American history and (post) colonial studies', *The Journal of American History* 88, 3 (2001), 829–65.

—helped initiate scholarly conversations on the colonial studies and intimate history.

Plamper, J., *The History of Emotion: An Introduction* (Oxford: Oxford University Press, 2012)

—provides a synthesis of current scholarly approaches to the study of emotion across the disciplines, while also providing an intellectual history of the rise of emotion as a domain of scholarship.

Notes

1 See N. Eustace, 'The sentimental paradox: humanity and violence on the Pennsylvania frontier', *The William and Mary Quarterly* 65, 1 (2008), 29–64; T. Ballantyne and A.M. Burton (eds), *Moving Subjects: Gender, Mobility, and Intimacy in an Age of Global Empire* (Urbana: University of Illinois Press, 2009); M. Pernau, H. Jordheim, O. Bashkin, C. Bailey, O. Benesch, J. Ifversen, M. Kia, R. Majumdar, A.C.

Messner, M. Park, E. Saada, M. Singh and E. Wigen, *Civilizing Emotions: Concepts in Nineteenth-Century Asia and Europe* (Oxford: Oxford University Press, 2015)

2 On Roman imperial inspiration, see A. Pagden, *Lords of All the World: Ideologies of Empire in Spain, Britain and France c. 1500–c. 1800* (New Haven: Yale University Press, 1995), esp. 11–28.

3 T. Smith, *Discourse of the Commonweal of this Realm of England* (1549); Smith to William Cecil, 7 November 1565; and Smith, *A Letter sent by I.B. Gentleman* (1572) as quoted in D. Armitage, *The Ideological Origins of the British Empire* (Cambridge: Harvard University Press, 2000), 49, 50, 56.

4 B. de las Casas, *The Spanish Colonie, or Briefe Chronicle of the Acts and Gestes of the Spaniards in the West Indies*, (trans.) M.M.S. (London, 1583). On the 'black legend,' see, K. Ordahl Kupperman, *Providence Island, 1630–1641: The Other Puritan Colony* (Cambridge: Cambridge University Press, 1995), 93.

5 James VI, *Basilikon Doron* (Edinburgh, 1598), as cited in Armitage, *Ideological Origins*, 56.

6 See K. Donegan, *Seasons of Misery: Catastrophe and Colonial Settlement in Early America* (Philadelphia: University of Pennsylvania Press, 2013)

7 J. Locke, 'The Second Treatise' (1690), in P. Laslett (ed.), *Locke: Two Treatises of Government* (Cambridge: Cambridge University Press, 1988), 407.

8 Ibid., 407.

9 A. Smith, 'Of the Influence of Custom and Fashion upon Approbation', (1759) in K. Haakonssen (ed.), *Adam Smith: The Theory of Moral Sentiments* (Cambridge: Cambridge University Press, 2002), 239–240; H. Home, Lord Kames, *Sketches of the History of Man* (London, 1778), as cited in K. Wilson, *The Island Race: Englishness, Empire and Gender in the Eighteenth Century* (London: Routledge, 2003), 10. On Smith as imperial critic, see J. Pitts, *A Turn to Empire: The Rise of Imperial Liberalism in Britain and France* (Princeton: Princeton University Press, 2005)

IV.44 Indigenous/European encounters

Maria Nugent

Scholars of cross-cultural encounters and exchanges between European maritime explorers and indigenous people have rarely failed to notice the emotions that such interactions produced. But only recently have there been efforts to theorize the work of emotion and affect within cross-cultural relations in the context of expanding European exploration. While work that engages explicitly with contemporary theories of affect is in its infancy, it is proving to be particularly productive, both for re-interpreting certain interactions or specific voyages and for questioning well-worn assumptions about European exploration as a predominantly 'rational' and 'intellectual' enterprise.[1]

The seventeenth and eighteenth centuries were a period of intense maritime activity and exploration in the South Seas, undertaken mainly by Dutch, French and British expeditions, and the resulting expansive archives brim with descriptions of encounters when Indigenous people were confronted by European strangers coming into their domains from the sea. Early contact situations could provoke a giddying array of emotions on both sides – and generated a good deal of second guessing about what inner states were expressed through certain bodily demeanours, gestures, stances, sounds, actions and reactions. As European explorers and travellers sought to use an emotional repertoire instrumentally to manage and choreograph an encounter, such as by attempting to mollify a tense moment by making peaceable gestures or by seeking to instil fear through a show of force, they usually struggled to interpret accurately the feelings of the people with whom they sought to make contact, sometimes with fatal results. All such situations required on the spot improvisation, hypothesizing and other forms of interpretive effort. But travellers could not always tell a welcoming from a hostile reception. When in late April 1770, the British navigator Lieutenant James Cook (1728–79), in command of the *Endeavour* voyage, landed for the first time on the east coast of New Holland (now Australia) the mood of interactions with the indigenous people encountered swung from apparent indifference to impatient assault. Initially, the people on shore were observed to behave as though unfazed by the ship's presence – 'to all appearance totaly unmoved at us'.[2] This gave the British sailors hope, confidence even, that they could venture ashore without causing ruction. However, as the landing party of armed men approached in boats, two men came down to the water's edge. The British were unsure if their actions were of welcome or repulsion.[3] They later ascribed to them negative emotions: their language was loud and harsh, their manner disputatious and menacing, their response unwelcoming and resolute. This first meeting, marked by violence, was the start of a week-long encounter in which feelings and moods would swing on both sides between suspicion, curiosity, courage, fear, humility, bluster, sympathy and confusion.

Every encounter between indigenous people and European voyagers was a unique event, with its own potential for relations to develop or disintegrate, for knowledge to be gained or lost, and for transformation of different kinds in all parties to an encounter to occur. Relations developed responsively and reactively rather than being predictable effects of predetermined actions. These exchanges, in turn, 'produced feelings, often divergent, through their subjects'.[4] Recognizing the 'affective economies', in Sara Ahmed's terms,[5] of embodied encounters has inspired approaches to writing histories of European exploration that capture the dynamism and contingency of multifaceted interactions between indigenous people and European voyagers. One approach evident in recent scholarship involves writing close-grained narratives of embodied encounters in particular times and places, and which are alert to the ways in which reactions on both sides produced affects – and effects – in others. Adopting this interpretive method for studying the *Endeavour*'s stay at Botany Bay in 1770, for instance, provokes questions about the consequences of the landing party's interpretation of the indigenous men's reactions as hostile and surly, which they used to rationalize their decision to meet it with violence. How did this initial assessment influence the ways in which relations subsequently developed – or failed to develop – during the expedition's stay? Had their mood and behaviour been interpreted otherwise by the Europeans, might the situation have unfolded differently?[6]

Focusing on the affective dimensions of the 'frictions' of cross-cultural encounter is part of a broader move away from reading European textual and visual sources as representations of the imputed emotional states of indigenous people to instead asking questions about what emotions do – what they produced or enabled – in contact situations. Among the most fruitful work is that which tracks ideas of affective bonds, such as friendship or romantic love, which are assumed to be 'universal', or at the very least shared and commensurable across cultures. Vanessa Smith, for instance, has examined friendship (or *taio*) in late eighteenth-century European/indigenous encounters in the Pacific. With this focus, new historical understandings of intercultural interactions are opened up, particularly as it reveals the 'emotional significances' which ideas – and ideals – of friendship held for eighteenth-century Europeans and the Pacific islanders they encountered. In the process, Smith's study exposes the emotional investments, so often overlooked, involved in making contact and getting intimate with 'others'.[7]

This mode of interpretation is not always easy, especially when it comes to interpreting indigenous people's feelings towards European voyagers. For many situations, the only sources are those authored by Europeans themselves, and they are often frustratingly oblique, less than disinterested, or lacking in detail. Many, however, do include quite detailed descriptions of the emotional displays of indigenous people because, like embodied experience more generally, they were considered a means for revealing truths about the 'other'. Other evidence of the affective economies of European/indigenous encounters is less obvious but no less revealing. The names given to places sometimes preserved the prevailing mood of relations, such as Friendly Cove or Savage Island, so much so that European maps produced in the context of exploration might be read as representing an affective geography. Moreover, as Bronwen Douglas has argued, Europeans' perceptions of the initial responses they received from indigenous people could filter into their assessments about the local population more generally and seep into scientific discourses about race.[8]

Closely and carefully read, the written and visual archives of exploration do provide some rich evidence of indigenous people's feelings towards the Europeans who crossed into their countries. Voyager descriptions of dealings with indigenous people can be thought of, as anthropologist Peter Sutton suggests, 'stories about feeling'.[9] His discussion of the records of Dutch-Aboriginal encounters in the Cape York region in north-east Australia between 1606 and 1756 highlights evidence of indigenous people's aggression towards intruding outsiders, feelings of grief for kidnapped kin, and displays of indifference as various responses to the presence of strangers, all of which Sutton contextualizes and interprets in relation to Aboriginal people's philosophies of *relatedness* to people and place. Later ethnographic accounts are a key resource for this line of analysis, but interpretations that attempt to reconstruct indigenous people's perspectives of Europeans and their actions remain, necessarily, speculative. Indeed, there are serious limits on what can be said with certainty. The inner states of indigenous peoples are often as opaque to us now as they were to European observers and chroniclers at the time. Given this, it is worth asking questions about the stakes involved in pursuing these lines of inquiry. What do we hope to gain in terms of historical understandings by exploring emotions in encounters between Europeans and indigenous people? And, moreover, does the presumption to know and understand what indigenous people felt and thought when confronted by Europeans risk replicating the usually unequal power relations that shaped those encounters? These are difficult questions to answer, but vital ones to ask.

If nothing more, attention to emotions and affect in studies of cross-cultural encounters between European explorers and indigenous people has helped to unsettle a familiar mode of analysis which relies on altogether too simplistic notions of power and difference. Rather, the best of the new work begins with an assumption of 'no metaphysical division'[10] between people who met on 'beaches' (to use Greg Dening's celebrated metaphor). From that premise, it proceeds to understand relations, desires and feelings as having 'discrete valences [which] are created between subjects in particular contexts of contact'.[11] If this seems like a path leading to multiplying particularities and the proliferation of idiosyncratic studies of interaction within broader histories of encounter and exchange, then that is something to be embraced rather than eschewed.

Further reading

Broomhall, S., 'Emotional encounters: indigenous peoples in the Dutch East India Company's interactions with the South lands', *Australian Historical Studies* 45, 3 (2014), 350–67.

—provides a model for applying a history of emotions approach to studying the Dutch East India Company (VOC) in Australia in ways that unsettle orthodox explanations that give precedence to commercial contexts and motives over the influence of interpersonal interactions between the Dutch and indigenous people.

Smith, V., *Intimate Strangers: Friendship, Exchange and Pacific Encounters* (Cambridge: Cambridge University Press, 2010)

—explores the politics of friendship in the history of cross-cultural encounters and relations between British and indigenous people in the Pacific. Literary in focus, it is one of the few recent historical treatments in the field to give prominence to affect, emotions and desires in interpreting contexts of contact.

Sutton, P., 'Stories About Feeling: Dutch-Australian Contact in Cape York Peninsula, 1606–1756', in P. Veth, P. Sutton and M. Neale (eds), *Strangers on the Shore: Early Coastal Contacts in Australia* (Canberra: NMA Press, 2008), 35–59.

—employs ethnographic insights to reinterpret the fragmentary archive of descriptions of encounters between indigenous people and Dutch voyages in north-east Australia, and to theorize about the meanings of those interactions through the prism of local philosophies of relatedness between people and place.

Notes

1 S. Konishi, *The Aboriginal Male in the Enlightenment World* (London: Pickering and Chatto, 2012)

2 J. Banks' Journal, daily entries, 28 April 1770, online at http://southseas.nla.gov.au/journals/banks/17700428.html, accessed 14 July 2015.

3 M. Nugent, *Captain Cook Was Here* (Melbourne: Cambridge University Press, 2009)

4 S. Broomhall, 'Emotional encounters: Indigenous peoples in the Dutch East India Company's interactions with the South Lands', *Australian Historical Studies* 45, 3 (2014), 351.

5 S. Ahmed, *The Cultural Politics of Emotion* (Routledge: London, 2004), 8.

6 Nugent, *Captain Cook Was Here.*

7 V. Smith, *Intimate Strangers: Friendship, Exchange and Pacific Encounters* (Cambridge: Cambridge University Press, 2010). See also S. Konishi, 'François Péron and the Tasmanians: An Unrequited Romance', in M. Hannah and I. Macfarlane (eds), *Transgressions: Critical Australian Indigenous Histories* (Canberra: ANU e-Press, 2007), 1–18.

8 B. Douglas, 'Naming places: voyagers, toponyms, and local presence in the fifth part of the world, 1500–1700', *Journal of Historical Geography* 45 (2014), 12–24.

9 P. Sutton, 'Stories About Feeling: Dutch-Australian Contact in Cape York Peninsula, 1606–1756', in P. Veth, P. Sutton and M. Neale (eds), *Strangers on the Shore: Early Coastal Contacts in Australia* (Canberra: NMA Press, 2008), 35–59.

10 J. Lamb, *Preserving the Self in the South Seas 1680–1840* (Chicago: Chicago University Press, 2001) cited in Smith, *Intimate Strangers*, 15.

11 Smith, *Intimate Strangers*, 15.

The non-human world

IV.45 Relations with the divine

Phyllis Mack

'Religion is heart work.'

Mary Fletcher, Scripture Notes[1]

In the 1740s and on into the late eighteenth century, Protestant Christianity was transformed from a religion known by its sacraments, theologies and official hierarchies, into communities of readers, talkers and singers. Meeting in informal groups as well as in church, they practised an evangelical Christianity grounded in biblical knowledge, solitary prayer, and communal life and worship; shaped, above all, by a new emphasis on the emotions as the basis of spiritual knowledge. 'We are all governed by our feelings', wrote the Victorian reformer Elizabeth Fry (1780–1845):

> Now the reason why religion is far more likely to keep you in the path of virtue, than any theoretical plan is, that you feel it, and your heart is wrapt up in it; it acts as a furnace on your character, it refines it, it purifies it; whereas principles of your own making are without kindling to make the fire hot enough to answer its purpose.[2]

Historians have long been aware of the emotional substratum of the evangelical movement and the spiritual dimension of artistic concepts like the sublime. Less well studied is the artistic education of the senses in order to enhance spiritual perception. We normally think of the Reformation as anti-art, focused on the pulpit rather than the ornate communion altar or decorated statues of saints, and we imagine pious Protestants mulling over sermons and religious texts rather than fine-tuning their aesthetic sensibilities through their engagement with poetry or music. In fact, religious leaders were intensely interested in different kinds of artistic media – paintings, music, poetry, decorative clothing – and they offered their adherents what amounted to an education in spiritual aesthetics: that is, a way of looking, listening and singing that would refine sensory and emotional perception and open new pathways for apprehension of the divine. Artistic creativity and performance were thus not simply ends in themselves; they might be experienced as both modes of worship and agents of self-transformation.

For at least two contemporary religious communities, Methodists and Moravians, artistic engagement was not just an act of piety or a celebration of God's grandeur; it was an attempt to tune into a divine frequency and establish a three-way communication between God, the individual and the congregation. The Methodist leader John Wesley (1703–91) and the Moravian leader Nikolaus Ludwig von Zinzendorf (1700–60) not only encouraged emotional responses to sermons and liturgy in their respective movements; they also taught new modes of perception, a new relationship to art as holding the potential for self-transformation and a more profound understanding of the meaning of Jesus's death.[3]

But the importance of hymn-singing was not only to teach religious values or heighten the drama of Jesus's sacrifice. Wesley's main edition of published hymns was organized to move the worshipper through stages of spiritual development, incorporating such mundane experiences as nursing a sick child or attending a tea party. Beginning with the terror of divine judgement, the hymns depicted the pain and humiliation of those convinced of sin, the sinner struggling toward rebirth, the horror of backsliding and a final deathbed epiphany. Wesley was also fascinated by the psychological effects of different kinds of music. In his view, simple melodies had profoundly affected the nervous systems of ancient peoples, but this effect had been diluted by the addition of complicated harmony and counterpoint in modern composition. Wesley wanted hymns to be like the songs of simple Celtic peasants, where the melody 'is not only heard but felt by all those . . . whose taste is not biased (I might say corrupted) by listening to counterpoint and complicated music'.[4] The new hymns, most of them composed by his brother Charles (1707–88) were thus both powerful and dangerous: not only might they allow the listener to be swept away by the music rather than the message; they might also inflate the egoism of the singer.

> Still let us on our guard be found,
> And watch against the power of sound
> With sacred jealousy;
> Lest haply sense should damp our zeal,
> And music's charms bewitch and steal
> Our heart away from thee.[5]

Zinzendorf's use of hymns and overall goals was similar to those of the Methodists, but he advocated 'a more cheerful, contemplative spirituality in which one's gaze was directed away from interior states towards the concrete and sensual apprehension of Christ suffering on the cross . . . an understanding of salvation in which no legal preparation was necessary, but only a childlike trust and radical identification with the love of the dying Jesus'.

> Powerful wounds of Jesus, So moist, so gory, bleed on my heart
> so that I may remain brave and like the wounds.
> . . .
> Purple wounds of Jesus, You are so succulent, whatever comes near
> becomes like wounds and flows with blood.
> Juicy wounds of Jesus, Whoever sharpens the pen and with it pierces you
> just a little, licks and tastes it.
> Warm wounds of Jesus, In no pillow can a little child feel itself so secure
> before cold air.

> Soft wounds of Jesus, I like lying calm, gentle, and quiet and warm. What should I do? I crawl to you.[6]

These images are particularly fascinating because they were built not only around traditional themes of sinfulness and punishment, but on the miracles of birth, infancy and erotic love. For the Moravian worshipper, Jesus's tortured body was not horrific; it was a place of gestation and rebirth, a celebration of mutual love and joy.

While Moravian worshippers were quietly ecstatic, sinking into contemplation and silent ecstasy as they perceived themselves enveloped by Jesus' bloody womb, Methodists were noisily demonstrative as they were urged to gird their loins and become active in the service of God. Indeed, Wesley opposed not only the eroticism of Moravian hymns and the 'fondling' language of some hymns by his brother Charles; he also opposed what he called 'nambi-pambical' writing about a 'meek' or 'gentle' feminine Jesus. Wesley edited out many of Charles's more morbid verses that expressed the worshipper's despair and longing for death. And while some hymns depicted the suffering Christ as vulnerable and in need of the believer's pity, the image of blood (used 800 times in the later hymns) was far more often a redemptive image of cleansing and renewal. Moravians described their ecstatic and passive contemplation, 'conjugal penetration of our bloody husband'; Methodists, in contrast, sang in full voice of the blood of the atonement, the blood that renews the sinner and imbues him with the strength to achieve the goal of sanctification:

> Soldiers of Christ, arise,
> And put your armor on,
> Strong in the strength which God supplies
> Through His eternal Son; . . .
> From strength to strength go on;
> Wrestle and fight and pray;
> Tread all the powers of darkness down,
> And win the well-fought day.[7]

The hymns of Methodists and Moravians suggest the extraordinarily wide range of views and practices relating to the emotions in eighteenth-century Protestantism. Indeed it is hard to imagine a stronger contrast than that between the relatively pallid lyrics of a Methodist hymn to be sung while drinking tea with Moravian pain-filled ecstasies, or the Moravians' 'stillness' viewed alongside the Methodists' 'enthusiasm'.

There were many other modes of religious belief and behaviour, like the cult of relics and extreme physical self-mortification that were rejected by the denizens of the Enlightenment. Yet many worshippers sought and found what they perceived as a direct, emotional experience of the supernatural and the sacred. Unlike the spectacular and melodramatic art and pageantry of the Baroque church, which dazzled the passive viewer and induced a kind of self-alienation, hymn-singing or the contemplation of a painting hung in a gallery or private house both reflected and stimulated the singer's or viewer's individuality, his or her personal sensibility and emotions – a goal that was profoundly in tune with the Enlightenment emphasis on sensibility.

In her path-breaking study of evangelicalism in modern America, T.M. Luhrmann describes the role of discipline and conscious effort in developing what evangelicals believe is the capacity to talk with God and to literally hear His voice.[8] The process involves learning to focus on the sounds and voices inside one's own head, being especially attentive to those voices whose counsel feels both authentic and ethical. This surely works as a description of efforts of eighteenth-century Protestants, whether Methodists or Moravians, to attune themselves to God's voice in their hearts. They tried to feel the emotions of physical ecstasy, the bliss of infancy, the calm security of an obedient child ready for bed. The Age of Enlightenment thus marked the beginning of a transition from the culture of pre-modern Europe, where God was assumed to exist even though He did not always appear, to our own modern Western world, where doubt of God's existence and the desire to hear His voice survive with equal intensity.

The contemporary study of emotion and religion breaks new ground in thinking about religious affect, most obviously in challenging the earlier tendency of historians to view religious emotions as forms of hysteria. This mindset was especially true in the cases involving religious women, where the prevalent attitude has been to interpret female writing and behaviour as a reflection of social or sexual frustration. Current writing aims to discern more complex and subtle practices and feelings, while giving full respect to the seriousness of religious discipline and expression.

Further reading

Hindmarsh, D.B., *The Evangelical Conversion Narrative: Spiritual Autobiography in Early Modern England* (New York: Oxford University Press, 2005)

—a tightly-focused study of a single genre of religious writing in eighteenth-century England: spiritual autobiography. Hindmarsh argues that the conversion process was, in fact, several processes that occurred at different moments in the life of an individual. The focus here is on religion, not as a single epiphany or an example of collective behaviour, but on the changing dynamic of religious sensibility and practice.

Mack, P., *Heart Religion in the British Enlightenment: Gender and Emotion in Early Methodism* (Cambridge: Cambridge University Press, 2008)

—seeks to understand both elite and popular religion in the eighteenth century, focusing less on theology or socio-economic processes, as the way emotions became central to both the practice of religion and philosophical reflections on the subject.

Thomas, K., *Religion and the Decline of Magic* (London: Weidenfeld and Nicholson, 1971)

—this classic study of popular religion, magic and witchcraft sets out the terms of the debate on the modernization of religion in the seventeenth and eighteenth centuries.

Notes

1 M. Fletcher's scripture notes, manuscript, Fletcher-Tooth Collection, John Rylands Library, The University of Manchester.

2 *Memoir of the Life of Elizabeth Fry* (edited by her daughters) 2 vols (Montclair, NJ: Patterson Smith, 1974), vol. 1, 46.

3 On Methodists, see D.B. Hindmarsh, *The Evangelical Conversion Narrative: Spiritual Autobiography in Early Modern England* (Oxford: Oxford University Press, 2005), chapter 5, 162–92.

4 J. Wesley, 'Thoughts on the Power of Music', *The Works of the Reverend John Wesley*, vol. 15 (London, 1812), 360–63.

5 J. Wesley, 'A Collection of Hymns,' no. 196, *The Works of John Wesley: A Collection of Hymns for the Use of the People Called Methodists* (Oxford: Clarendon Press, 1983), 63.

6 N. von Zinzendorf, 'Litany of the Wounds of the Husband', (1700–1760) cited in C.D. Atwood, *Community of the Cross: Moravian Piety in Colonial Bethlehem* (University Park, PA: The Pennsylvania State University Press, 2004), 1.

7 C. Wesley, 'Soldiers of Christ, Arise,' (1749), in D.L. Jeffrey (ed.), *A Burning and a Shining Light: English Spirituality in the Age of Wesley* (Grand Rapids, MI: William B. Eerdmans, 1987), 273.

8 T.M. Luhrmann, *When God Talks Back: Understanding the American Evangelical Relationship with God* (New York: A. Knopf, 2012)

IV.46 The Devil and demons

Laura Kounine

In the early modern period emotions were not considered products of the unconscious, but were rather interpreted, experienced and expressed in the context of one's relationship to God and to the Devil. This was an age in which people could sink into deep melancholy, suffer overwhelming despair or confess to the crime of witchcraft because they believed they were afflicted by, or in relationship with, the Devil. The way in which people thought about themselves in relation to the supernatural, and in particular to the Devil and demons, has been considered in a number of different historical terrains: in intellectual thought; the history of madness; religious history; and in witchcraft scholarship. This entry synthesizes some of these approaches while also offering new research as a way to engage with emotions in the context of early modern beliefs about the Devil. It will examine three key ways in which a relationship with the Devil or demons was understood in the early modern period: first, in the context of witchcraft; second, in the context of demonological writings and third, in the context of emotions that were specifically understood as diabolical afflictions.

The early modern period, an age of fierce confessional strife, was marked by an intense preoccupation with, and fear of, the Devil. This can be seen most powerfully in the ferocious witch-hunts that swept Europe, perhaps the most startling phenomenon of the early modern period. Witchcraft was a highly emotional crime: it directly centred on the belief that one person's emotions of envy, hate and anger could cause physical harm to other people and animals. Witchcraft in continental Europe – while allowing for great local and regional variation in practice – was premised on the diabolical pact; that is, the alleged pact, sealed with sexual intercourse, between the witch and the Devil.[1] The focus on the diabolical pact made early modern witchcraft both distinctly gendered and also highly emotionalized; it also made the crime fundamentally an act of apostasy rather than an act of malefice.

The Holy Roman Empire was the heartland of the witch-craze, with approximately 23,000 executions for the crime, which reached their peak in the late sixteenth and early seventeenth centuries. Around three-quarters of those tried for witchcraft were women. Witchcraft was thus primarily, but not exclusively, considered to be a female crime.[2] A recent emphasis in the vast historiography on the early modern witch-hunts is on the emotional self-representation of the witch. Witchcraft confessions, as documented in the often highly rich trial records that survive in early modern Germany, can offer access to the emotional landscape of those women (and men) put on trial for the crime of witchcraft. As the work of Lyndal Roper has demonstrated, women on trial for witchcraft in early modern Germany, who were often old and poor, invested their confessions with powerful fantasies and emotions.[3] Central to the diabolical pact was a story of courtship and seduction. The Devil was often disguised as a handsome, well-dressed man, although sometimes with tell-tale signs of his diabolical nature such as cloven feet. He seduced women with promises of money and power, and sometimes even promised marriage. Yet as soon as the woman had sex with him, he immediately disappeared, and his gifts of money turned to dirt. Sex with the Devil was cold and hard, lacking the male 'heat' necessary for fertility.[4] These courtship narratives, which are repeated throughout witchcraft confessions, reveal powerful – gendered – fantasies and emotions of hope, desire, envy, power, and often, disappointment.

The Devil and demons were also prominent in early modern intellectual thought, in particular in the growing genre of demonologies that flourished in this period.[5] These texts were academic studies on demonism, magic and witchcraft, and focused on the Devil or demons in plural. The *Malleus maleficarum* (1486), written by Heinrich Kramer (*c.* 1430–1505), is the most famous of early modern demonological treatises. For Kramer, the chief reason why witches were women was because 'everything is governed by carnal lusting, which is insatiable in them'.[6] Women, according to Kramer, lacked intelligence, which meant that they were more likely to renounce the faith; and they were driven by passions and 'irregular desires' which meant that they inflicted acts of vengeance.[7] According to this argument, witches were female, and this was due to their unbridled passions, which made them specifically prone to the temptations of the Devil.

The late sixteenth century witnessed the peak not only of witch persecutions, but also of demonological texts, from writers such as Jean Bodin (1530–96), Nicolas Remy (1530–1616), Martin Del Rio (1551–1608) and Peter Binsfeld (*c.* 1545–98). These texts were written by learned men, often jurists, and were widely circulated. The *Demonolatry* (1595) by Remy, for instance, was one of the most successful demonologies in the Holy Roman Empire at the turn of the seventeenth century. Where the *Malleus maleficarum* focused on the lustfulness of women to explain why they were prone to witchcraft, Remy's *Demonolatry* also conceived of the relationship between the Devil and the witch as an emotional relationship, but it was premised on the notion of a violent Devil, driven by jealousy and anger, to explain why people – both men and women – could fall prey to witchcraft.

In his *Demonolatry*, Remy writes: 'Namely that the evil fiend those / whom he cannot move through good / frequently knows how to bring them into danger and to frighten them'.[8] Remy later recounts the story of Kuno Gugnot, who 'numerous times had been beaten almost to death by him [the demon] / because he had either too late / or sometimes not even at all appeared at their gathering [Sabbath]'.[9] Although Remy still believed that women were more prone to the temptations and deceits of the Devil, his treatise underlines the frailty of human nature, and the violent force of the Devil, to show how the crime of witchcraft could befall any human.

Finally, not all those who thought themselves to be in relationship with the Devil were necessarily considered to be a witch. Indeed, temptations by the Devil could afflict any person, particularly in early modern Lutheran thought. Martin Luther (1483–1546) considered himself to be constantly in battle with the Devil, and he understood such assaults or temptations (*Anfechtungen*) to be a necessary step in the path to salvation: they were a symbol of piety and a mark of being spiritually alive. The emotion of despair, *Verzweiflung*, was especially paramount for Lutherans. In order to become closer to God, one first had to overcome the Devil. This understanding was meant to provide consolation for those afflicted with such thoughts, since Luther held out the hope that 'whoever suffers from the devil here will not suffer from him yonder'. Yet, as Luther himself acknowledged, this was slim consolation for anyone caught in a deep depression.[10]

The fact that Luther held that despair was a necessary step on the path to salvation, a stage in which believers could well fall victim to demonic temptation and religious melancholy, has led Erik Midelfort to suggest that 'sixteenth-century Lutheran culture positively expected that some anguished souls would fall into despair and perhaps try to commit suicide'.[11] Despair, therefore, when experienced in the correct measure, was considered a healthy state of being: it reminded the believer of their inherent and utter sinfulness. However, it could easily tip over into suicidal despair, where the believer began to doubt their own salvation. Indeed, David Lederer suggests that, in early modern Germany, despair, along with demonic possession and raving madness, was one of the most serious spiritual afflictions.[12]

These examples demonstrate the importance of the Devil in the early modern worldview. The Devil was theorized in early modern intellectual thought; he was integral to witchcraft confessions; and he plagued ordinary people in their everyday lives. In all these ways, crucially, the relationship with the Devil was imagined in highly emotionalized terms: he could seduce women with promises of love and power; he could compel men and women through violence and fear; and he could taunt people with their sinfulness through despair and temptations. This entry has shown the inroads that thinking with emotions has made – and continues to make – in understanding early modern beliefs about the Devil and demons. There is still work to be done by placing emotions centre-stage in examining how people at all levels of society conceptualized themselves in relation with the supernatural, how this was confessionally charged, and how this changed over time.

Further reading

Clark, S., *Thinking with Demons: The Idea of Witchcraft in Early Modern Europe* (Oxford: Oxford University Press, 1997)

—magisterial study on early modern demonology that surveys all the published works on witchcraft from the fifteenth to the early eighteenth century, and remains the key work in this field.

Lederer, D., *Madness, Religion and the State in Early Modern Europe* (Cambridge: Cambridge University Press, 2006)

—study of spiritual psychic in early modern Bavaria that sheds light on the history of madness, the emergence of psychiatry and how people understood the soul in the context of the Counter-Reformation.

Roper, L., *Witch Craze: Terror and Fantasy in Baroque Germany* (New Haven: Yale University Press, 2004)

—examines the psychological landscape of the early modern German witch-hunts, with a focus on the emotional dynamics of interrogation, torture and confession, as well as exploring the cultural imagination that made old women particularly susceptible to accusations of witchcraft.

Notes

1 B.P. Levack, *The Oxford Handbook of Witchcraft in Early Modern Europe and Colonial America* (Oxford: Oxford University Press, 2013)
2 L. Kounine, 'The gendering of witchcraft: defence strategies of men and women in German witchcraft trials', *German History* 31, 3 (2013), 295–317.
3 L. Roper, *Witch Craze: Terror and fantasy in Baroque Germany* (New Haven: Yale University Press, 2004)
4 Ibid. See also U. Rublack, 'Interior States and Sexuality in Early Modern Germany', in S. Spector, H. Puff and D. Herzog (eds), *After the History of Sexuality: German Geneologies with and Beyond Foucault* (New York: Berghahn, 2013), 43–62, here 49.
5 S. Clark, *Thinking with Demons: The Idea of Witchcraft in Early Modern Europe* (Oxford: Oxford University Press, 1997)
6 H. Kramer, *The Hammer of Witches: A Complete Translation of the Malleus Maleficarum*, (trans.) C.S. Mackay (Cambridge: Cambridge University Press, 2009), 122.
7 R. Schulte, *Man as Witch: Male Witches in Central Europe*, (trans.) L. Froome-Döring (Basingstoke: Palgrave, 2009), 99.
8 N. Remy, *Daemonolatria. Das ist Von Vnholden und Zauber Geistern* (Frankfurt, 1598), 4.
9 Ibid., 96. This will be further developed in my forthcoming book, provisionally entitled: *Imagining the Witch: Emotions, Gender and Selfhood in Early Modern Germany*.
10 Luther quoted in H.C.E. Midelfort, *A History of Madness in Sixteenth-Century Germany* (Stanford: Stanford University Press, 1999), 106.
11 Ibid., 12.
12 D. Lederer, *Madness, Religion and the State in Early Modern Europe* (Cambridge: Cambridge University Press, 2006), 170–2.

IV.47 Ghosts, fairies and the world of spirits

Julian Goodare

The early modern world was an uncanny place, rather like J.R.R. Tolkien's 'Middle-Earth', in which humans might expect to encounter various kinds of non-human beings. Even the actual phrase 'Middle-Earth' was sometimes used, meaning the world between heaven and hell. This entry introduces the emotions that the common people might feel when they encountered ghosts, fairies or other 'spirits'. These encounters might be in stories, but for some people the encounter with spirits was a matter of direct and sometimes terrifying experience. The history of emotions is a new field of scholarship, and no scholarly works have been devoted specifically to the role of emotions in understanding early modern people's relationships with spirits, but what follows will attempt to outline a way in which the topic can be approached.

There are two main ways in which early modern 'spirits' can be classified: by form, and by moral function. A formal classification divides spirits broadly into three types: ghosts, the spirits of dead humans; angels and demons, Christianity's minor deities; and nature spirits, associated with the natural world. A classification by moral function is also threefold: good spirits, including angels; bad spirits, including demons; and ambivalent spirits, including most nature spirits and ghosts, which might be beneficial but could also be harmful. This moral classification was of immediate relevance to someone encountering a spirit. Was it a good spirit or a bad spirit? Would it help you or harm you? Could you negotiate with it? It may have been particularly important to negotiate with bad spirits. The most characteristic emotion that spirits evoked in people was fear.

Spirits were usually thought of as humanoid, with personalities and emotions to which humans could relate. This was particularly notable for nature spirits such as fairies. (There were also magical animals like dragons, and even magical plants; the mandrake plant, the root of which can resemble a human body, was thought to have human characteristics.) But, as well as being *like* humans, nature spirits were also and simultaneously *unlike* them. This like-but-unlike quality is captured in descriptions of spirits that appeared human in front but were hollow, or fiery, from the back. Depictions of mermaids as half-woman-half-fish derive from attempts to represent a water spirit that was *both* a woman *and* a fish simultaneously. The like-but-unlike pattern allowed the human imagination to expand, populating the world with human-like beings that reflected light back onto the human condition.

Nature spirits appeared in endless variety of form and name. In English we have 'fairy', 'elf', 'goblin', 'imp', 'puck', 'brownie' and many others. Many books on fairies classify these almost in the way that bird books classify birds – appearance, habitat and so on. This can be misleading unless we remember that the focus of study should not be on the fairies themselves, but on the humans who believe in fairies or experience encounters with fairies.

While folk belief recognized nature spirits as real, elite authors were sceptical. There were no fairies in the Bible, nor in the main intellectual traditions of natural philosophy. So elite authors explained fairies away; if someone reported seeing a fairy, it must really have been a demon. There *were* demons in the Bible, and demons were deceptive. Elite authors sometimes related fairies instead to the nature spirits of the classical world – nymphs, dryads, fauns and sirens. These, indeed, could also be understood as demons. As for ghosts, some churchmen accepted reports of these, though Protestant theologians often denied that ghosts could return. By the eighteenth century, the decline of elite demonology meant that ghosts and fairies were no longer reinterpreted as demons; instead they became 'vulgar superstitions'.

Relationships with ghosts, fairies and other spirits occurred in various ways. Many nature spirits were associated with wild places – forests, lakes, hills – separate from the community's safe, cultivated land. Miners sometimes encountered underground spirits. In Germany, a noted mining region, these were called *kobolds*.

There were stories and ballads about spirits, such as the stories of a relationship between a male human and a female water-spirit. Typically they married and had children, but she returned to the water when he broke a taboo. Another typical story told of a demonic encounter in which the peasant hero outwitted the demon through trickery. Although these were 'stories', they were assumed to represent reality, just as modern novels are assumed to represent real human behaviour.

There were rituals connecting people to spirits or protecting people from them. When a person was dying it was common to open a window to let the dead person's spirit depart. People might ward fairies off with a horseshoe over the door, or placate them with offerings of milk or ale. Prayers or rituals for good health could address God or the saints, but might also address fairies.

Some people took part in collective rituals with spirits. The Sicilian *donas de fuera* (ladies from outside) was a cult in which the human members entered trances and flew out in spirit with fairies. Together they conducted joyful nocturnal processions and visited houses for feasting and dancing. The human members of the cult used their fairy connection to become magical practitioners, curing their neighbours' fairy-induced illnesses.[1]

Witches in some regions were believed to have a spirit companion. This was often a toad, lizard or cat that lived with the witch and was sent out to commit magical harm. This belief was found in most detail in Hungary and England; in Hungary the animal was called a *lidérc*, in England it was called a 'familiar'. The word 'familiar' came from the biblical phrase 'familiar spirit', understood to mean a demon assigned personally to the witch. The idea of a personal demon was also common in northern Germany, Scandinavia and Russia.[2]

Many ghost beliefs and stories were connected with death and bereavement, a time of strong emotions. Ghosts varied in their manifestation, with a slow change occurring during the early modern period. Medieval ghosts were usually thought of as solidly physical, and sometimes bloodstained. This was related to the idea of the returning physical body after death, sometimes called a 'revenant'. In the sixteenth century, people began to report airy or translucent white ghosts, and these eventually became the most common type. There were also poltergeists ('noisy ghosts'), heard but not seen.[3] Vampires, known in south-eastern Europe, were related to revenants, and could attack humans. As well as corpses returning as vampires, living people could also be thought to be vampires through inheritance. There were preventative rituals against vampires and returning ghosts, such as burying a body face down.

Ghosts evoked fear, but the wandering ghost could also be pitied for its inability to reach heaven. A ghost usually returned for a purpose. Often it had unfinished business on earth, such as an unpaid debt, or – more gruesomely – a murder to be avenged. Ghosts in stage plays almost always sought vengeance. More positively, some ghosts might reveal buried treasure. Many hopeful treasure-seekers ritually summoned the aid of ghosts – or of demons, which might also prove to be guardians of treasure.

A final type of spirit encounter occurred in connection with childbirth and parenthood. Parenthood, like bereavement, evokes strong emotions. There was a group of beliefs concerning 'changelings': the idea that fairies would steal a child and replace it with a fairy impostor. This fake infant might demand large quantities of food but remain ill-nourished and miserable. Such beliefs could readily thrive among inexperienced and desperate parents. A Swedish ritual to protect a child from being stolen was to place a psalm-book below its head, a typical manifestation of popular Protestant Christianity.

Ultimately, the reality behind spirit encounters, if there was such a thing as 'reality' here, may be sought via psychology. Some people experience hallucinations, often in the form of hearing voices speaking to them; this is currently experienced by about five per cent of the population. Visual hallucinations – seeing things that are not there – also occur. Some 'fantasy-prone' people have difficulty distinguishing fantasies from reality. Finally there is the sleep disorder known as sleep paralysis, in which the sufferer wakes up unable to move, and often feels a strange presence threatening or assaulting them. These encounters, sometimes vivid and terrifying, demand explanations, and people interpret them in terms of the culture with which they are familiar; sleep paralysis today gives rise to reports of abduction by aliens.[4] When someone in early modern times heard a disembodied voice or experienced a threatening nocturnal presence, they were likely to think that it was a spirit of some kind. Historians can thus recognize that spirit encounters were experienced as real. The dreamlike culture of ghosts, fairies and other spirits has much to contribute to the history of emotions.

Further reading

Harte, J., *Explore Fairy Traditions* (Loughborough: Heart of Albion, 2004)
—a brief study arguing helpfully for a focus on the human relationship with fairies.

Rose, C., *Spirits, Fairies, Gnomes, and Goblins: An Encyclopedia of the Little People* (Santa Barbara, Calif.: ABC-Clio, 1998)
—uses the classificatory approach criticized by Harte, but contains much useful information.

Warner, M., *No Go the Bogeyman: Scaring, Lulling and Making Mock* (London: Chatto & Windus, 1998)
—not entirely about spirits, but contains material relevant to the history of emotions.

Notes

1 G. Henningsen, '"The Ladies from Outside": An Archaic Pattern of the Witches' Sabbath', in B. Ankarloo and G. Henningsen (eds), *Early Modern European Witchcraft: Centres and Peripheries* (Oxford: Clarendon, 1990), 191–215.

2 É. Pócs, *Between the Living and the Dead: A Perspective on Witches and Seers in the Early Modern Age*, (trans.) S. Rédey and M. Webb (Budapest: Central European University Press, 1999)

3 O. Davies, *The Haunted: A Social History of Ghosts* (Basingstoke: Palgrave Macmillan, 2007)

4 Davies, 'The nightmare experience, sleep paralysis, and witchcraft accusations', *Folklore*, 114, 2 (2003), 181–203.

IV.48 Working animals

Louise Hill Curth

There are many different types of academics representing a range of disciplines who are interested in studying human-animal relationships in the past. In order to discuss the relationship between working animals and emotions, it is necessary to begin by defining the term 'animal'. While historical understandings did include biological factors, the major focus was on their inability to think or reason. A key influence on the early modern definition was Aristotle's *Scala Naturae*, or 'Ladder of Nature', which classified non-human animals according to their reasoning abilities. In the early modern period, 'cattle', which was the contemporary generic term for domesticated animals, were divided according to whether they were 'greater' or 'lesser' creatures. The former category included larger and more important animals such as horses, oxen, cows, calves, sheep, goats, hogs and working dogs. Lesser cattle encompassed a variety of birds including geese, peacocks, ducks and chickens, as well as deer and conies (rabbits).

Unlike wild animals, domesticated animals had many virtues, the most important being the value they could bring for humans. *The Historie of Foure-Footed Beastes* by Edward Toppsell (*c.* 1572–1625) divided working animals in terms of the purposes they served. They were classified depending on whether they produced 'marchandize' or by-products, or laboured. The first category covered 'cattell of all sorts' who were bred for 'fatting, feeding and felling' and those who produced 'butter and cheese'. It also included animals whose wool could be gathered while they were alive, or who provided leather and/or skin with 'their haire and wooll upon them for garments' once they were dead. The second group included various types of 'cattell' who were valuable for their 'travile and plowing and carriage', as well as for riding for sport or in wartime.[1]

Regardless of the type of animal in question, however, they could only provide benefits for humans if they were in a state of at least relative health. This meant that owners made some effort to ensure that they provided their animals with both preventative and remedial health care. Early modern principles of what constituted health or illness were based on the inseparable relationship between mind and body. This was an orthodox, traditional, dualistic mind–body system based on ancient Greek ideas. Commonly referred to as 'classical', 'Hippo-Galenic', 'Galenic' or simply as the 'humoral' theory, this model was based on the idea that all living beings contained four fundamental elements, qualities or humours. *De natura hominis*, which was part of the *Hippocratic Corpus*, discussed how these four 'liquid Substance[s]' had very different qualities in terms of their 'nature', taste, colour and purpose. Sweet tasting blood, which provided the body with fuel, was of a 'temperate' and 'mean thickness'. Watery, white and 'unsavoury' phlegm tempered the blood and making the 'Joynts slippery' while clear, watery 'subacid' black bile helped to move blood through the body. Thin and 'fiery' yellow bile, which played a major role in the emotion of anger, was best known for thinning phlegm'.[2]

Although all living creatures had a unique combination of humours, there were general principles that applied to all. For example, despite the humours being constantly in flux, health could be defined as being when the four humours within the body were in 'relative' balance. Despite the fact that all living creatures had a discrete combination of humours, it was believed that all had one dominant humour which shaped and defined their 'constitution' or 'complexion'. This would help to determine the types of diseases to which they would be most susceptible, their general character, the healthiest type of food and lifestyle and their emotional state. Although all individuals' underlying humoral characteristics were thought to change as they aged, their main 'complexion' was determined by the 'science of the stars' and the position of the planets at the time of their birth. 'Fiery' animals whose predominant humour was yellow bile, for example, had a choleric constitution that made them quick to anger. Choleric animals were easily identifiable through both physical and behavioural characteristics. These included the colour of their fur or hide and also its texture, which would be very dry, hard and/or rough. Melancholic animals, on the other hand, had a predominance of black bile which made them prone to nightmares and 'ravings' (similar to what would now be called 'mania'). As with choleric animals, their constitution could be identified by a brown/earthy colour and cold, dry fur or hide.

Although it was impossible to change one's innate humoral balance, it was possible to try to manipulate facets of it, including one's emotions, through what might now be called a 'healthy lifestyle'. This was linked to a tripartite system comprising three basic types of phenomena: the 'naturals', 'non-naturals' and 'contra-naturals'. The naturals were linked to the four elements of earth, air, fire and water that manifested in the body as the four humours. While the naturals played a major role in the lives of living creatures, contra-naturals contributed to sickness and death. As the use of 'contra' suggests, these were factors that went against or opposed the naturals discussed above. While neither naturals nor contra-naturals could be influenced, the opposite was true of the non-naturals which consisted of air (relating to the state of the air as in 'foul' and weather conditions), food and drink, sleep, exercise, evacuations and emotions or 'passions of the mind'.

However, while it would have been recognized that adherence to all the 'non-naturals' would benefit animals, it was simply not practical. In addition, it seems likely that human concern for this differed according to the type of animal in question. Although historically all animals were expected to provide services for humans, as Keith Thomas has pointed out, only horses – 'the most noble of animal creatures' – fulfilled a range of practical, moral and aesthetic purposes. The lifestyle of horses, which were the most valuable and important members of the domesticated animal kingdom, probably received the most attention. They were also thought to be able to experience the widest range of emotions, including hate, anger, joy, love, sorrow and fear. Such claims were often linked to stories such as the horse owned by 'Nicomedes a King' who 'so intirely loved him' that after his master died he refused to eat 'till he dyed', as well.[3]

This particularly held true when considering the final 'non-natural', emotions. According to early modern thought, 'passions' were linked to, or 'generated' in, the spirit or soul and manifested as physical symptoms. Excess passions and emotions whether positive or negative, as with all the non-naturals, could result in disease. Emotions such as sadness could 'straiten and presse the heart, weaken the spirits . . . [affecting] the digestion of the meats [generic term for food]'. Fear and hatred could 'strike such a Damp upon the Spirits that it puts the Body into the most dismal Disorders' through diverting 'the vital heat from the circumference to the centre' of the animal. Anger, on the other hand, 'inflammeth the blood' and could lead to an imbalance in the choleric humour. Together, they were likely to result in the 'kindeling of fiery Fevers'. The same was true of violence, which 'the nature of the Horse abhoreth'.[4] While horses were thought to have the greatest range of feelings, all working animals were understood to be able to experience emotions.

Although there has been a growing academic interest in the history of human emotions in recent times, that of working animals has lagged far behind. A similar pattern can be seen in the evolution of the social history of medicine over the past few decades. Until fairly recently, this has mirrored Western society's prevailing anthropocentric view of our world. While the term 'medical history' is still generally considered to refer to human health and illness, there are now a growing number of academics interested in the experience of animals in the past. It seems likely that a similar pattern will emerge, in time, within the study of domesticated, working animals and their emotions.

Further reading

Curth, L.H., *The Care of Brute Beasts: A Social and Cultural Study of Veterinary Medicine in Early Modern England* (Leiden: Brill 2010)
—the first academic monograph on the health and illness of early modern animals.
Curth, L.H., A *Plaine and Easie Waie to Remedie a Horse: Equine Medicine in Early Modern England* (Leiden: Brill, 2013)
—academic monograph on the health and illness of early modern horses.
Thomas, K., *Man and the Natural World: Changing Attitudes in England 1500–1800* (Oxford: Pantheon Books, 1983)
—this classic text focuses on the prevailing anthropocentric world view of early modern England and the resulting impact this had on human-animal relationship.

Notes

1 E. Toppsell, *The Historie of Foure-Footed Beastes* (London, 1607), sig. A3v.
2 J. Pechey, *A Plain Introduction to the Art of Physick* (London, 1697), 11; J. S., *A Short Compendium of Chirurgery* (London, 1678), 15.
3 R. Almond, *The English Horsman* [sic] (London, 1673), 2–3.
4 T. Venner, *Via recta ad vitam longam* (London, 1620), 302–3; W. Vaughan, *Directions for Health* (London, 1612), 240; N. Culpeper, *Galen's Art of Physick* (London, 1657), 132; J. Blagrave, *Epitome of the Art of Husbandry* (London, 1675), 206; W. Gibson, *The Farrier's New Guide* (London, 1722), 121.

IV.49 Familiars

Charlotte-Rose Millar

Familiar spirits, devils in animal form, are one of the most distinctive features of English witchcraft. These creatures often appeared as domestic or common animals such as dogs, cats, rats, toads, chickens or ferrets. The origins of familiar spirits remain a matter of speculation. They have been described as both a form of household fairy, hobgoblin, sprite or elf and as a folklorized version of the types of demons conjured by medieval magicians. These ideas, when combined with older beliefs about the Devil's ability to take animal form, may all have contributed to the popular construction of the familiar as a tangible, animalistic and demonic creature. This entry focuses on three points: the way in which the familiar performed the role of the Devil; the way in which the familiar introduced a personal element to English witchcraft; and the different ways in which accused witches formed emotional bonds with their familiar spirits. Given its centrality to English witchcraft, there is surprisingly little historical scholarship on the familiar spirit. Those who have considered the familiar in relation to a witch's emotions, through the use of pamphlet sources and trial records, tend to focus on the domestic or anti-maternal elements of this relationship.[1] But this analysis can be taken further. I would argue that familiar spirits performed a dual role: they acted as devils and they represented external expressions and embodiments of witches' internal thoughts and feelings. Through a personal relationship with the witch, a familiar became a conduit for the witch's internal desires.

Before we expand on the emotional connection between witch and familiar, we must ask: how does the familiar perform the role of the Devil? In early modern Europe accused witches were commonly believed to form a pact with the Devil. Typically, the witch gave the Devil his (or more commonly her) soul and, in return, the Devil assured the witch that she should never want and gave her the power to take revenge on her enemies. In England, this pact was nearly always made through a familiar spirit who was believed to be both the Devil himself and an agent of the same. These creatures either declared their demonic nature themselves (such as the ferret with fiery eyes who introduced himself as Satan) or were described as such by pamphleteers, magistrates, accused witches or supposed victims.[2] After an exchange of promises, familiars sucked blood from the witch to complete the pact. From the 1560s until the 1640s, these creatures appeared almost exclusively in animal form.

In entering into a demonic pact with a witch, familiars created a personal bond between themselves and their mistresses. For some accused witches, such as the man who wanted revenge on the person who stole his purse, or the woman who was overwhelmed by the discords of her children, the pact (and their relationship) with their familiar was instigated by their inability to control overwhelming emotions.[3] At the moment that these men and women expressed extreme anger, frustration or hatred the Devil appeared to them. In the man's case, the Devil appeared as a black, shaggy, bear-like creature that had paws like a bear but was no bigger than a rabbit; for the woman, the Devil took the form of an iron-grey rat. These animalistic devils are described as lying in wait to prey on those who are unable to successfully regulate their emotions.

For most witches, even if uncontrolled emotions did not precipitate a familiar's appearance, strong emotions such as anger, greed or a desire for love or revenge led them to make an agreement with a familiar spirit. Once this pact was made, witches and familiars developed strong emotional bonds which often evolved over decades. The form that these emotional attachments took differed depending on the person. For many English witches their relationship with the Devil involved sexual activity. Margaret Flower (1619), for example, confessed that her black spotted dog sucked 'within the inward parts of her secrets'; whereas Mary Trembles (1682) claimed that her demonic lover (who took the shape of a lion) had carnal knowledge of her body and then sucked her secret parts.[4] These intimate relationships were often described by the accused in affectionate and pleasurable terms.

For other accused, their bond with their familiar was described in maternal or familial terms. Elizabeth Clarke (1645) confessed that she slept with a man-like Devil but described her animalistic familiars as her children.[5] Elizabeth, a poor, lame woman, constructed a demonic family in which she had a lover and children. Elizabeth is one of the very few witches who described their familiars as their children. Many more suckled their familiars at their breast – an action that has both maternal and sexual connotations, and is undeniably intimate. Male witches (approximately 10 per cent of the accused in England) were also believed to form deep attachments to these creatures. John Bysack (1648) confessed that he had six snail familiars (all of whom he named) which sucked blood from teats on his right side. John confessed that 'he oftentimes arose out of his bed, and made a fire, and lay down by it to let [the snails] suck his blood'.[6] This cosy description of John suckling little creatures next to a warm fire reminds us that the relationship between witch and familiar was often described by pamphleteers as well as by witnesses, accusers and the accused witches themselves, in emotional, interpersonal and intimate terms.

The above cases highlight how the pact between witch and devil was generated and sustained by emotion. In many witchcraft narratives, witches drew on this bond to act upon their desires. Accused witch Mother Sutton (1613) provides a key example. On hearing that her son had been struck by a neighbour, Mother Sutton commanded her two familiars, Dick and Jude, to 'strike' and 'torment' him.[7] In her confession, Mother Sutton explains that she first allowed Dick and Jude to suck her thighs and then, after this reinforcement of their bond, commanded them to act on her feelings of anger and her desire to harm her son's attacker.

For the vast majority of accused, interactions with familiar spirits were overwhelmingly positive.[8] By looking at how accused witches, witnesses, supposed victims, magistrates and pamphleteers described the relationship between witch and familiar spirit, and the uniformity in which they labelled anger, vengeance and envy as key emotional drivers, we can explore how witchcraft was imagined as a crime motivated by strong, often uncontrolled emotions. Witches were not believed by accusers and pamphleteers to enter into pacts with the Devil out of any rational motivation; they did so because of hatred, envy, lust and love. In examining the familiar/witch relationship, we can better understand accused witches' motivations for performing (or confessing) to acts of witchcraft and gain an insight into their greatest hatreds, jealousies, fears and desires. It is not possible to understand witchcraft allegations without an understanding of the emotions that drove them. Further work on the different influences in witchcraft accusations, such as those from pamphleteers, accusers, witnesses and victims, and the types of emotions that they emphasized and their own emotional motivations would increase our understanding of the precise ways in which emotions were drawn upon in witchcraft accusations.

Further reading

Macfarlane, A., *Witchcraft in Tudor and Stuart England: A Regional and Comparative Study* (London: Routledge, 1970 and 1991).

—despite its age, Macfarlane's study of revenge as a key motivator for witchcraft acts remains one of the most important works in the field.

Millar, C.-R., 'Sleeping with Devils: The Sexual Witch in Seventeenth-Century England', in V. Bladen and M. Harmes (eds), *Supernatural and Secular Power in Early Modern England* (Farnham, Surrey: Ashgate, 2015), 207–32.

—moves away from previous scholarship on English witchcraft as asexual and instead highlights the intimate, sexualized relationships that witches were believed to enjoy with their familiar spirits.

Wilby, E., *Cunning Folk and Familiar Spirits: Shamanistic Visionary Traditions in Early Modern Witchcraft and Magic* (Brighton: Sussex Academic, 2005)

—Wilby's exploration of the 'working relationship' between witch and familiar represents one of the first attempts to understand the emotional dynamics of this liaison.

Notes

1 D. Purkiss, 'Women's stories of witchcraft in early modern England: the house, the body, the child', *Gender and History* 7, 3 (1995), 408–32; D. Willis, *Malevolent Nurture: Witch-Hunting and Maternal Power in Early Modern England* (Ithaca: Cornell University Press, 1995)

2 Anon., *The Apprehension and Confession* (London, 1589), sig. B1r-v.
3 J. Davenport, *The Witches of Huntingdon* (London, 1646), 3 and 9.
4 Anon., *The Wonderful Discoverie* (London, 1619) sig. G1 r; Anon., *A True and Impartial Relation* (London, 1682), 34. Dates in text refer to when these witches' stories were circulated in print.
5 H.F., *A True and Exact Relation* (London, 1645), 3–4.
6 J. Stearne, *A Confirmation and Discovery of Witchcraft* (London, 1648), 41.
7 Anon., *Witches Apprehended* (London, 1613), sig. C1 v.
8 For rare examples of witches who fear their familiars, see Elizabeth Sawyer's fear that her Devil would tear her to pieces (H. Goodcole, *The wonderfull discoverie* (London, 1621) sig. C4 v), Temperance Lloyd's fear of the same (Anon., *A True and Impartial Relation* (London, 1682), 19) and Mother Bennet's battle with two familiars who attempted to thrust her into a burning oven after she refused to give them her soul (W.W., *A True and Just Recorde* (London, 1582), sig. B8 r).

IV.50 Vermin

Lucinda Cole

The affective and cognitive capacities of medium and large mammals – especially elephants, apes and dogs – were vigorously debated in the early modern period, and animal studies scholars have carefully mined seventeenth- and eighteenth-century natural philosophy for proof that, both before and after René Descartes (1596–1650) and his 'beast machine', warm-blooded animals were, like humans, thought to respond to the world through feeling and rudimentary forms of intellection.[1] Research on the emotional being of worms, insects, amphibians and small mammals, however, is still in its early stages.[2] This lack of attention is partly because these so-called 'vermin' – any animal that populates rapidly and, in so doing, is a potential threat to the comfort or food supplies of human beings – tend to be regarded in groups, rather than as individuals, as part of packs, hives or swarms. Yet early modern natural philosophers, from Francis Bacon (1561–1626) on, argued that the lower creatures – insects, spiders and worms – share a complex sensory system with humans. Bacon claims in *Sylva Sylvarum* (1670), that 'Insecta have Voluntary Motion, and therefore Imagination', a belief he supports by the evidence of ants going 'forwards to their Hills' and bees who 'admirably know the way, from a Flowry Heath, two or three Miles off, to their Hives', proving that 'though their Spirit be diffused, yet there is a Seat of their Senses in their Head'.[3] By 'spirit' Bacon means the animals spirits that, as George Rousseau argues, were in the forefront 'of all theories explaining life' between 1400 and 1800.[4] Bacon's 'Seat of the Senses', the brain, housed or served as a kind of switchyard for the animal spirits, whose presence and movement constituted what early modern natural philosophers, following Aristotle's *De Anima*, called the corporeal, brute or sensitive soul. The driving assumption within this tradition was that the corporeal soul, shared among all living creatures, was responsible for autonomic functions as well as memory, imagination and certain forms of intellection. From this perspective, even the lowest and most abject forms of animal life can be said to have emotion – defined here as feeling and instinct – and, with it, agency.

That so-called vermin had what we might recognize as emotions, then, was not really a question within the neo-Aristotelian tradition, in which all animals shared a 'sensitive soul' shot through with 'animal spirits'. Even Descartes would grant to vermin and other animals sensations: 'I deny sensation in no animal, in so far as it depends on a bodily organ'.[5] The more immediate question for natural philosophy was to what extent one could assume thought, reason and therefore an incorporeal soul in non-human animals. By virtue of that debate, however, lasting assumptions about the emotional lives of vermin would be formed.

In attempting to distinguish between the brute, sensitive or corporeal soul and its more ethereal counterpart, natural philosophers were compelled to posit theories about the essence of 'life' and how it might be differentially distributed across the animal kingdom. Early neurological studies, such as those by Thomas Willis (1621–75), posit a vital principle, endowed by God and best described as a kind of heat. In his 1672 treatise *De Anima Brutorum* (*Two Discourses Concerning the Soul of Brutes Which is that of the Vital and Sensitive of Man)*, Willis, admitting that the 'proper essence' of the animal spirits is a matter 'hard to be unfolded', suggests these 'Spirits sent from the Flame of Blood' might best be likened 'to the Rays of Light, at least to them Interwoven with the Element and the Air'.[6] Enkindling is merely a metaphor, he admits, for the functioning of a corporeal soul 'which cannot be perceived by our Senses, but is only known by its Effects, and Operations'. Animal spirits 'leave no Foot-steps of themselves'.[7] Yet one can surmise their presence and dissemination by cutting a worm, an eel or a snake into pieces and watching the pieces 'move themselves for a time'[8]; its continued movement suggests the corporeal soul both exists and is spread throughout the entire body. The motions of the dying worm, then, make visible the presence of vanishing animal spirits.

Allied with this careful and largely figural assumption about the nature of life was confidence that, whatever 'life' was, humans had the greatest share of it. Willis placed living creatures into three classes according to the 'Various Constitution of the Vital Humour': those without blood (insects, certain fishes, oysters, lobsters and crabs); those with 'less perfect' or frigid blood (earthworms, some fish, frogs, serpents, lizards); and those of 'more perfect' or hot blood (fowls and four-footed beasts). Each class of animals, in his view, had varying concentrations of the 'vital' liquor, and thus different kinds of corporeal souls, with the soul of hot-blooded brutes being 'a Rule or Square, by which others more inferior ought to be measured, and as the same actuating the humane body'.[9]

In arguing for a difference between classes of animals based on the presence and motion of animal spirits in the blood, Willis created a structural, neuroanatomical basis for the uneven distribution of 'life' across species. Worms, oysters and lobsters speak the truth for early modern science not by demonstrating their similarities to humans, as do dogs, cats and foxes, but by manifesting their quiet, cold difference. In this sense, vermin provide a neurological (and largely figural) grounding for the ancient Great Chain of Being, even as their 'false fire', their appearance of 'life', could be used to establish the infinitely more complex emotional being of humans and of creatures higher up on the Chain. Indeed, Willis admits, given their comparative complex neurological systems, some hot-blooded animals could have incorporeal souls; he can 'be a little solicitious, for [the souls of] the almost infinite multitude of the more perfect Beasts, which have liv'd, and do live'.[10] Without denying that vermin have neurological systems (and thus sensitive 'souls'), Willis reframes vermin as different from other creatures, primarily in terms of four related issues: their proximity to 'heat', as we have seen, their tendency to reproduce rapidly, their low place on a food chain, their short lives and their historical role in Christian theology. Produced 'daily', the *insecta* serve largely as 'Food to other Creatures', even as they multiply and swarm in their roles as instruments of 'Divine Punishment'. In Willis's view, then, when considered as a group, vermin are largely instrumental beings, called into existence beyond the regimes of human counting and calculation. Because their sheer number boggles the mind, it is impossible 'to be Conceived' how these creatures could be either 'immaterial' or 'immortal'.

In such passages, the father of neuroanatomy reimagines vermin as members of a group, as a series of swarms. This perception governs English literature, where vermin – which, as we have seen, share a nervous system with other creatures – are far more likely to be imagined as part of a distasteful and destructive population than they are to be treated in their singularity. Any similarities between flies, insects, snakes and the 'more perfect' creatures are eclipsed in the name of a religious narrative – the story of Exodus – preceding Willis's neurological experiments, and perhaps helping to shape them. From this still-familiar religious perspective, 'vermin' do not feel but inflict suffering in terms of pestilence, disease and famine. Assimilated to apocalyptic stories and regarded as unmarked members of a natural or God-given plague, vermin will be depicted, in early modern literature, as frogs raining from the sky, as plagues of lice swarming over bodies, as locusts eating their way through newly planted fields. Vermin contribute materially to dearth, famine and disease, but perhaps more importantly they contribute discursively to ethical and political systems which build on fears of scarcity and contagion.

The history of emotions requires interdisciplinary research that recognizes the role played by natural philosophy in describing the source and contours of feeling. Such interdisciplinary analysis, however, must be extended beyond the human realm to the affective capacities of nonhuman animals. Animal studies has, within the past twenty years, been partially successful in exposing the anthropocentric nature of much research on affect. In order to complete that historical project, it is probably necessary to look beyond companion animals and livestock – those creatures who love and serve us – to the zoological outcasts with whom identification is rarely possible or desired.

Further reading

Brown, L., *Homeless Dogs and Melancholy Apes: Humans and Other Animals in the Modern Literary Imagination* (Ithaca: Cornell University Press, 2010)

—focusing on depictions of the human-animal relationship, Brown explores how the experience of interspecies intimacy (primarily through dogs and other complex mammals) helps create the possibility of human identification across race, class and other categories of difference.

Cole, L., *Imperfect Creatures: Vermin, Literature, and the Sciences of Life, 1600–1740* (Ann Arbor: University of Michigan Press, 2016)

—focusing on depictions of vermin and other animals usually not thought to be included on Noah's Ark, this book examines the emotions of fear and loathing and their place in the development of strategies of fear, containment and population control.

Thomas, K., *Man and the Natural World: Changing Attitudes in England, 1500–1800* (London: Allen Lane, 1983)
—Thomas's wide-ranging analysis of debates within literature and natural philosophy about the nature and status of nonhuman animals remains foundational.

Notes

1 Foundational historical studies on this topic include K. Thomas, *Man and the Natural World: Changing Attitudes in England, 1500–1800* (London: Allen Lane, 1983); E. Fudge, *Perceiving Animals: Humans and Beasts in Early Modern Culture* (Urbana: University of Illinois Press, 2002); K. Raber and T.J. Tucker (eds), *The Culture of the Horse: Status, Discipline, and Identity in the Early Modern World* (New York: Palgrave, 2005); Fudge, *Brutal Reasoning: Animals, Rationality, and Humanity in Early Modern England* (Ithaca: Cornell University Press, 2006); L. Brown, *Homeless Dogs and Melancholy Apes: Humans and Other Animals in the Modern Literary Imagination* (Ithaca: Cornell University Press, 2010)
2 See L. Cole, *Imperfect Creatures: Vermin, Literature, and the Sciences of Life, 1600–1740* (Ann Arbor: University of Michigan Press, 2016) for an extended description of why animals lower on the Great Chain of Being have been mostly ignored by scholars of the early modern period.
3 F. Bacon, *Sylva Sylvarum: Or, The Natural History in Ten Centuries, in The Works of Francis Bacon*, (eds) J. Spedding, R.L. Ellis and D.D. Heath (New York: Garrett Press, 1968), 177.
4 See G. Rousseau, 'Nerves, Spirits, and Fibres: Towards Defining the Origins of Sensibility', in his *Nervous Acts: Essays on Literature, Culture, and Sensibility* (Basingstoke: Palgrave Macmillan, 2004), 160–84.
5 J. Cottingham, '"Brute to the brutes?": Descartes' treatment of animals', *Philosophy* 53, 206 (1978), 557.
6 T. Willis, *Two Discourses Concerning the Soul of Brutes Which Is that of the Vital and Sensitive of Man* (London, 1683), 23.
7 Ibid., 6.
8 Ibid., 5.
9 Ibid., 18.
10 Ibid., 4.

IV.51 Nature

Grace Moore

The early modern period marked a shift in attitudes towards and perceptions of nature and while a number of excellent ecological studies of the Renaissance have appeared over the past decade, there is still a great deal of work to be done to connect the history of emotions to environmental history. Scholarship is emerging on affective relations to place in the contemporary world and, given the growing significance of emotions theory to early modernists, it is only a matter of time before environmental research interests in place, nostalgia and memory are consolidated through an 'emotions' methodology.[1]

For the people of the early modern period, the environment was a highly emotional issue. The legalized enclosure of land and more systematic approaches to its management coincided with increased urbanization and a perception that the countryside was in jeopardy. As Malcolm Hebron has noted, 'The early modern sense of nature . . . involved a sense of alienation', tied to a growing sense of longing for the natural world.[2] According to Hebron, the traditional idea of a Chain of Being (a divinely-ordered hierarchy wherein all living matter had a pre-determined place, with humanity at the top and animals, insects and plants below) was increasingly regarded as a less-than-adequate model for understanding and engaging with the natural world. Hebron convincingly suggests that it was at this time that Europeans began to reconfigure their relationship towards nature, and to engage with it on an emotional level.

In his classic study of the shift from an agricultural economy towards a capitalist one, *The Country and the City* (1973), Raymond Williams commented that for the English, 'country life has many meanings', signalling the plurality of responses that it can evoke.[3] Simon Schama emphasizes further the connections between landscape and memory in his anthropocentric study of the same name, noting that nature is often annexed by culture, to which it can become subordinate.[4] Increasingly, the management of land involved re-shaping it, whether that was through the rise of the 'landscaped' garden – whose cultivation was viewed as an 'improvement' on nature – or the more systematic planting and felling of forests, which Oliver Rackham reminds us, occurred in response to the 'Little Ice Age', and the need to burn wood for warmth.[5] Furthermore, he notes that the over-felling of trees by sixteenth-century industrialists generated great anger within both politicians and the wider public, who saw the woodlands as areas to be cherished, not destroyed.

Discourses of 'mastery' had long underpinned ideas of land-ownership, and planting and ordering – whether in a small flower garden, or a large forest – was seen as evidence of human authority over nature. For the affluent, gardening was about decoration and artistry, rather than subsistence, and a passion for re-shaping plant life came to be seen as a sign of refinement. As Jennifer Munroe, among many others, has noted, nature was frequently represented as feminine (and therefore subject to masculine authority) and the arrangement of a 'disorderly' environment often involved power struggles – sometimes between human notions of order and the natural, at others between men and women and their ideas of the aesthetic.[6]

More broadly, in mapping notions of husbandry and the historical roots of recent ecological crises Lynn White, Jr. noted the ways in which the Bible has been historically invoked to authorize the perception of animals and plants as 'resources'.[7] There are, White argues, many points of origin for the exploitation of both land and animals and he demonstrates the role of technologies (exemplified by the invention of the scratch-plough) in facilitating this dominance over the natural world. It was, however, in the period between 1500 and 1800 that perceptions of human relations with nature began to shift and become more complicated. Alongside the movement towards industrialism came a new consideration for nature that was tied to a sense of its endangerment. As Keith Thomas has expressed it, relations between human beings and non-human species were reconfigured at this time, leading to a very strong interest in the natural world, along with concerns about our relationship to it which, Thomas argues, 'we have inherited in magnified form'.[8]

There may seem to be tensions between Thomas' assertion of fascination and Hebron's arguments that humans became increasingly alienated from the environment. However, these two perspectives did not sit in opposition to one another, with the growth of cities leading to a yearning for an unspoiled countryside and its comparatively simple way of life. Attitudes towards nature (particularly animals) became increasingly sentimental, yet living creatures were still perceived to have been placed on earth to serve man. *Paradise Lost* (1667) by John Milton, for example, both licences the idea of human dominion over the earth, while at the same time celebrating the cultivation of the land through the figure of Eve, whom Leah Marcus has described as a 'proto ecologist'.[9]

People of the early modern period struggled with a number of ecological concerns that are familiar to us today, and their emotional responses show that they shared some of our concerns about the world around them. There are reports of London smog, caused by the burning of soft coal, from the late medieval period onwards. The writer and gardener, John Evelyn (1620–1706), wrote emphatically about the causes and effects of air pollution in *Fumifugium* (1661) in which he petitioned Charles II (1630–85) to abandon the burning of coal in favour of burning wood, while at the same time arguing that industries causing pollution should be removed from city centres. Evelyn's later publication, *Sylva* (1664), attempted to encourage the planting of trees, but still very much with the view of wood as a resource to be exploited – in this case for ship-building – rather than in the interests of conservation.

As Terry Gifford points out, early modern poetry and drama often drew upon classical pastoral traditions, bringing gardens, forests and the weather into focus. While literary scholars have conventionally interpreted these subjects on an allegorical level, the rise of the environmental humanities has led to their reinterpretation. As Gifford expresses it in relation to William Shakespeare's plays, 'What have been regarded . . . as symbolic or allegorical references to nature . . . are now being understood as actually referencing real environmental concerns for forest resources, urban pollution, or issues about food sources and ethics'.[10] Even when early modern writing focuses on the urban, it is often, as Ken Hiltner notes, punctuated by a yearning for the rural that is tinged with nostalgia and regret. Trade with America involved travellers returning with tales of vast unspoiled woodlands and unexplored wildernesses, which provided a point of contrast with the hedgerow boundaries and carefully arranged trees that signified a European landscape under control. Then, as now, the countryside was associated with innocence, and the city with corruption, and bucolic settings are likely to have pointed to a growing sense of their endangerment.

Beyond the use of trees as commodities, one of the more contentious and emotional aspects of the early modern engagement with the natural world was through a sequence of Enclosure (or 'Inclosure') Acts, dating from 1604 onwards. This legislation sought to privatize what had previously been regarded as common land, to be shared and farmed by all people, but particularly the peasantry. While forests were celebrated as magical arcadias in Renaissance poetry and plays, which harked back to a classical model of the pastoral, in reality the communal countryside was becoming a thing of the past. Monastic lands were redistributed and arable areas were subsumed into private ownership. At the same time, hunting became increasingly gentrified, mutating from an act of necessity into a sport, while legislation like the Black Act of 1724 (which made it a capital offence to stalk deer in royal forests) sought to protect game and to criminalize those in need. Suzanne J. Walker has emphasized the great cruelty of the early modern hunt, capturing the emotions surrounding the chase with an insightful analysis of how animals were disembodied in accounts, before being rendered mere 'meat' on capture. It was thus that valorization of the hunt could continue to sit alongside a growing sense of compassion towards those animals who were increasingly domesticated, such as dogs and cats.[11]

The contradictions surrounding early modern relations with the natural world reflect a diverse society at a point of transition. Nature was an emotional issue regardless of whether one believed in its exploitation or conservation, while its fragility and finitude were beginning to become apparent. These are concerns that resonate today and scholars in the environmental humanities are increasingly interested in historical points of origin for the Anthropocene. Through bringing the history of emotions together with environmental history and ecocritical theory, we stand to learn a great deal about issues of custodianship and environmental destruction, which may in turn feed into more contemporary understandings of our affective responses to the world around us.

Further reading

Daston, L. and K. Park, *Wonders and the Order of Nature, 1150–1750* (New York: Zone Books, 2001)
—a compelling study of enthusiasm, wonder and their role in advancing discoveries about the natural world.

Knight, L., *Of Books and Botany in Early Modern England: Sixteenth-Century Plants and Print Culture* (Farnham: Ashgate, 2009)
—an ecocritical analysis of the connections between plants and prose in early modern writing.

Thomas, K., *Man and the Natural World: Changing Attitudes in England, 1500–1800* (Harmondsworth: Penguin, 1983)
—a classic and wide-ranging examination of human interactions with nature in the pre-industrial age.

Notes

1. See, for example T.K. Davidson, O. Park and R. Shields (eds), *Ecologies of Affect: Placing Nostalgia, Desire, and Hope* (Waterloo, ON: Wilfred Laurier Press, 2011) and the work of Jennifer Ladino for examples of how scholars of contemporary literature and culture are bringing environmental concerns together with emotions and affect theory.
2. M. Hebron, *Key Concepts in Renaissance Literature* (Basingstoke: Palgrave Macmillan, 2008), 231.
3. R. Williams, *The Country and the City* (1973) (London: Bloomsbury, 1993), 4.
4. S. Schama, *Landscape and Memory* (London: Harper Collins, 1995), 12.
5. See J. Munroe, *Gender and the Garden in Early Modern English Literature* (Farnham: Ashgate, 2008) for an account of gardening as improvement, and the spatial politics that were played out in the design and care of gardens. See O. Rackham, *Trees and Woodland in the British Landscape: The Complete History of Britain* (1976) (London: Phoenix Press, 1990) for an overview of woodland management, particularly 75–105.
6. Munroe's 'Introduction' provides a thorough contextualization of the politics underpinning garden space, in *Gender and the Garden*.
7. L. White, Jr., 'The Historical Roots of Our Ecological Crisis': www.uvm.edu/~gflomenh/ENV-NGO-PA395/articles/Lynn-White.pdf, accessed 19 April 2016
8. K. Thomas, *Man and the Natural World: Changing Attitudes in England, 1500–1800* (Harmondsworth: Penguin, 1983), 15
9. L. Marcus, 'Ecocriticism and vitalism in *Paradise Lost*', *Milton Quarterly* 49, 2 (2015), 96.
10. T. Gifford, 'Pastoral, Anti-Pastoral, and Post-Pastoral', in L. Westling (ed.), *The Cambridge Companion to Literature and the Environment* (Cambridge: Cambridge University Press, 2014), 20.
11. See S.J. Walker, 'Making and Breaking the Stag: The Construction of the Animal in the Early Modern Hunting Treatise', in K.A.E. Enenkel and P.J. Smith, *Early Modern Zoology: The Construction of Animals in Science, Literature, and the Visual Arts* (Leiden: Brill, 2007), 317–37.

IV.52 Landscape

Anthony Colantuono

Heirs to a hauntingly fragmented vision of the ancient and medieval Mediterranean countryside, the artists and writers of early modern Europe viewed their contemporary landscape through the lens of literary and historical knowledge – and through humanistic protocols of emotional response. The poetics of the ancient bucolic or pastoral (especially the *Idylls* of Theocritus and the *Eclogues* of Virgil) governed the most important of these protocols. The bucolic *locus amoenus* was the scene of human experience in all its breadth – the painful trials of love, the endless yearning for fulfillment and (in the spirit of the pastoral elegy) the mournful complaints of mortality and loss.[1] The plaintive, 'tender' quality of sentiment that commentators perceived in the ancient bucolics thus partakes both of nature's beauty and of the pitiful status of humanity within it, combining seemingly antithetical sentiments into a single emotional experience.

The early modern recovery of pastoral poetry entailed a creative transformation of this emotional paradox. In his *Arcadia*, probably composed around 1480–85 and first published in 1504, the Neapolitan poet Jacopo Sannazzaro (*c.* 1456–1530) synthesized a new, vernacular version of the ancient pastoral landscape. Through a complex mixture of poetry and prose, Sannazzaro's alter ego, Sincero, tells of his unrequited love and self-banishment to the Arcadian countryside. Every feature of the landscape reminds him of the lost object of his affection, embodying both happiness and sorrow. Sannazzaro attributes emotions to the non-human landscape elements themselves. His mountains possess the quality of 'pride'; his trees can choose to be 'courteous'; and nature herself experiences 'delight' in forming its many wonders. Through such rhetorical distortions, Sannazzaro transforms nature into an emotionally conscious being, which somehow shares in Sincero's sentiments of bittersweet regret.

Sannazzaro's sentient landscape is thought to have inspired extraordinary developments in sixteenth-century Venetian landscape painting.[2] Such works as the *Concert Champêtre* attributed to Giorgione (Giorgio Barbarelli da Castelfranco) (*c.* 1477/8–1510) and/or Titian (Tiziano Vecellio) (*c.* 1488/1490–1576) seem to capture a similar quality of sentiment with their dense forests, soft shadows, overcast skies and trickling streams – at once seductively lovely and yet somehow mournful (Figure IV.52.1). The *Concert* portrays four principal human figures whose presence underscores this sentimental quality through the mime of the human figure. The two nude females are nymphs – the one pouring water into the fountain personifying the source of water, and the other holding a flute to personify the winds. This natural music inspires the lute and recorder played by the two human males. Just as the shepherd tending his flocks at the right hints at a quasi-Arcadian landscape, the artist's personification of natural forces recalls the thematics and mood of the ancient pastoral landscape as reconstituted by Sannazzaro.

Building upon the poetical innovations of Giovanni Battista Guarini (1538–1612) and Torquato Tasso (1544–95), the seventeenth century witnessed a remarkable efflorescence of literary landscape, still rooted in the emotional binaries of the ancient

Figure IV.52.1 Giorgione and Titian, *Concert Champêtre*, *c*. 1509, Oil on canvas, 105 cm × 137 cm.

Musée du Louvre, Paris, Photo: Erich Lessing/Art Resource, NY.

pastoral. In a brilliant essay, Ezio Raimondi examined the theme of landscape in the *Carmina* (1658) and *Poesie* (1664) of the Italian poet and nobleman Don Virginio Cesarini (d. 1624). Cesarini postures himself in a mode of moralistic reverie, contemplating a desolate countryside replete with ancient ruins as well as the obligatory forests, fields and streams. Introducing his poetry, Cesarini asserts that from this meditation on nature springs a counterpoint of fear (*pavor*) and joy (*gaudium*) – a sentimental antithesis that resounds through the poems themselves. Raimondi traces this notion to St Augustine and likewise to Tasso's chivalric epic *Gerusalemme Liberata* (1581).[3] The element of 'horror' or 'terror' omnipresent in the seventeenth-century landscape – that is, in the human response to nature's grandeur, unpredictable power or wildness – later came to be associated with the aesthetic concept of 'the sublime' in Romantic landscape painting. Yet it is crucial to understand that this novel application of the term 'sublime' is in some ways foreshadowed by the emotional construct of 'fear-as-pleasure' already established in the seventeenth-century poetics of landscape.

The seventeenth-century painter Nicolas Poussin (1594–1665) theorized what he called the *maniera magnifica* in painting – a pictorial analog of the ancient rhetorical theorist Longinus' 'magnificent' or 'sublime' manner. For Poussin, this 'magnificence' consisted primarily in the pictorial subject being portrayed, and it is no surprise that even in his landscapes, the artist often selected subjects that juxtapose nature's serene beauty with a display of its most profound terrors. In a passage of his *Dialogues des Morts* concerning Poussin's *Landscape with a Man Killed by a Snake* (Figure IV.52.2), the French theologian and writer François de Salignac de la Mothe Fénelon (1651–1715) identifies fear itself as the actual subject of the painting. Poussin's landscape portrays a male figure discovering a dead man in a landscape, with the frightful snake that killed him still nearby, and a woman who cannot yet see the body itself, but sees the man's terrified reaction. Explaining how each figure expresses its own species of fear, Fénelon asks: 'Is it not true that these various expressions of fear and surprise constitute a kind of game that both touches and pleases [the beholder]?'[4] Fénelon rightly perceived that the emotion of fear is here juxtaposed not merely with the sweetness of nature's beauty but also with a species of neo-Aristotelian cognitive pleasure. The surprise experienced by the figures discovering the dead man is mirrored by the beholder's process of understanding, the contemplation of each figure bringing its own deductive revelation.

It is not improbable that fear itself should have been the intended subject of Poussin's landscape. Basing his pictorial theory on Tasso's heroic poetics, the artist conceived of painting as a form of epideictic rhetoric, whose primary purpose was to demonstrate his power to move the beholder through the vivid portrayal of the *affetti* or passions. But seventeenth-century pictorial theory also required that every formal element should contribute to this affect – even including the landscape or architectural setting. In Poussin's 'classic' strain of landscape painting, built upon a model established by Annibale Carracci (1560–1609) and his pupil Domenichino (Domenico Zampieri) (1581–1641),[5] one often finds the suggestion of an omniscient, divine consciousness residing within nature, judging all human actions: for example, in Poussin's *Landscape*

Figure IV.52.2 Nicolas Poussin, *Landscape with a Man Killed by a Snake*, *c.* 1648, oil on canvas, 118.2 × 197.8 cm.

National Gallery, London, UK, Photo: © National Gallery, London/Art Resource, NY.

with the Burial of Phocion (1648), a weeping tree in the foreground seems to mourn over the unjustly executed Athenian statesman. Seventeenth-century painters including Salvator Rosa (1615–73) and the Dutch artist Jacob van Ruisdael (1628–82) similarly structured their landscape images around the exposition of powerful emotions, often linked with moral themes. In Rosa's *Landscape with the Fable of the Dishonest Woodsman* (Figure IV.52.3), a dark wood with its strangely agitated vegetation seems to figure Mercury's – and nature's own – disapproval of the woodsman's unabashed lies and greed. These artists generally portrayed very small figures in the vastness of the landscape – a formulation that bespeaks both the pathetic insignificance of humanity and the implication that even in our ignorance we are, unwittingly, integral to some grand design. Carracci's most famous essay in this genre, his *Flight into Egypt*, places the privileged beholder in a position to see and be awed by the vastness of this divine plan – in this instance that of Salvation – and by the revelation of humanity's place within it. The great seventeenth-century landscapist Claude Lorrain (*c.* 1600–82) likewise essayed a similar sense of awe in such compositions as his *Seascape with the Embarkation of St. Ursula* (1641), where the figures are dwarfed by the magnificent beauty of a distant, atmospherically enshrouded sun – a divine light about to reveal the as yet unforeseen mystery of the virgin handmaidens' gruesome martyrdom.

Yet the emotional content of all landscape is ultimately in the mind of the beholder. For example, the meditations of Cardinal Federico Borromeo (1564–1631) upon landscape paintings by Paul Bril (1554–1626) and Jan Bruegel the Elder (1568–1625) show that he often perceived and responded with awe to God's presence in the pictorial landscape – to the wonders of divine love and munificence – even where the paintings

Figure IV.52.3 Salvator Rosa, *Landscape with the Fable of the Dishonest Woodsman*, after 1649, oil on canvas, 125.7 × 202.1 cm.

Photo: National Gallery, London/Art Resource, NY.

themselves offered no hint of a religious subject.[6] In the end, the non-human world of landscape has no emotions except for those brought by the beholder.

The exploration of landscape as emotional experience in early modernity is plainly in its infancy. Even if the natural landscape may pertain to a non-human and non-sentient world, the artificial landscapes found in early modern literary and pictorial representations are products of the human mind, and on an imaginative plane could indeed embody the experience of human emotions. Grounded in ancient models (especially in Virgil's *Eclogues* and *Georgics*), Tasso's and Guarini's visions of a living, emotionally conscious landscape – and their pictorial analogs – surely merit further study as expressions of the new political/affective, natural-philosophical and spiritual parameters of early modern experience.

Further reading

Walford, E.J., *Jacob van Ruisdael and the Perception of Landscape* (New Haven: Yale University Press, 1992) —posed new questions about the presence of religious sentiment in Ruisdael's seemingly 'secular' landscapes. This interpretative model may have much broader applicability in the criticism of early modern landscape painting.

Notes

1 G. Norlin, 'The conventions of the pastoral elegy', *The American Journal of Philology* 32, 3 (1911), 294–312.

2 M. Tanner, 'Ubi sunt: an elegiac topos in the Fête Champêtre', in *Giorgione: atti del Convegno internazionale di studio per il 5° centenario della nascita* (Castelfranco Veneto, 29–31 maggio 1978), (ed. Banca Popolare di Asolo e Montebelluna) ([Venice]: Comitato per le celebrazioni giorgenesche / Stamperia di Venezia, 1979), 61–6.

3 E. Raimondi, 'Paesaggi e rovine nella poesia d'un "virtuoso"', in *Anatomie secentesche* (Pisa: Nistri-Lischi, 1966), 45–6.

4 F. de Salignac de la Mothe Fénelon, *Dialogues des morts, composés pour l'éducation d'un prince*, (ed.) J. Le Brun (Paris: Gallimard/Pléiade, 1983), I, 434.

5 G. Careri, *La fabbrica degli affetti: la Gerusalemme liberata dai Carracci a Tiepolo* (Milan: Il Saggiatore, 2010), 79–82.

6 P.M. Jones, 'Federico Borromeo as a patron of landscapes and still lifes: Christian optimism in Italy ca. 1600', *The Art Bulletin* 70, 2 (1988), 266–8.

Select bibliography

Alberti, F. Bound (ed.), *Medicine, Emotion and Disease, 1700–1950* (Basingstoke: Palgrave Macmillan, 2006)

Alberti, F. Bound, 'Bodies, hearts, and minds: why emotions matter to historians of science and medicine', *Isis* 100, 4 (2009), 798–810.

Alberti, F. Bound, *Matters of the Heart: History, Medicine and Emotion* (Oxford: Oxford University Press, 2010)

Altbauer-Rudnik, M., 'Love, madness and social order: Love melancholy in France and England in the late sixteenth and early seventeenth centuries', *Gesnerus* 63 (2006), 33–45.

Arab, R., M. Dowd and A. Zucker (eds), *Historical Affects and the Early Modern Theater* (New York: Routledge, 2015)

Bähr, A., 'Remembering Fear. The Fear of Violence and the Violence of Fear in Seventeenth-Century War Memories', in E. Kuijpers, J.S. Pollmann, J. Müller and J. van der Steen (eds), *Memory before Modernity. Practices of Memory in Early Modern Europe* (Leiden: Brill, 2013), 269–82.

Baier, A.C., *A Progress of Sentiments: Reflections on Hume's Treatise* (Cambridge, MA: Harvard University Press, 1991)

Bailey, J., *Unquiet Lives. Marriage and Marriage Breakdown in England, 1660–1800* (Cambridge: Cambridge University Press, 2003)

Bailey, J., *Parenting in England 1760–1830: Emotions, Identities, and Generation* (Oxford, Oxford University Press, 2012)

Bailey, M.L. and K. Barclay (eds), *Emotion, Ritual and Power in Europe, 1200–1920: Family, State and Church* (Houndmills: Palgrave Macmillan, 2016)

Bamford, K. and N.J. Miller (eds), *Maternity and Romance Narratives in Early Modern England* (Farnham: Ashgate, 2015)

Barclay, K., *Love, Intimacy and Power: Marriage and Patriarchy in Scotland, 1650–1850* (Manchester: Manchester University Press, 2011)

Barclay, K., 'Intimacy and the life-cycle in the marital relationships of the Scottish elite during the long-eighteenth century', *Women's History Review* 20, 2 (2011), 189–206.

Barclay, K., 'Love and Courtship in Eighteenth-Century Scotland', in *Women in Eighteenth-Century Scotland: Public, Intellectual and Private Lives* (eds) K. Barclay and D. Simonton (Farnham: Ashgate, 2013), 37–54.

Barclay, K., 'Natural Affection, Children, and Family Inheritance Practices in the Long Eighteenth Century', in *Children and Youth in Premodern Scotland* (eds) E. Ewan and J. Nugent (Woodbridge: Boydell and Brewer, 2015), 136–51.

Barclay, K., 'Gossip, Intimacy and the Early Modern Scottish Household', in C. Walker and H. Kerr (eds), *Fama and Her Sisters: Gossip in Early Modern Europe* (Turnhout: Brepols, 2015), 187–207.

Barclay, K. (ed.) 'Section: Intimacy and Emotion', in *The Routledge History Handbook of Gender and the Urban Experience* (gen. ed.) D. Simonton (London: Routledge, 2016)

Barclay, K. and K. Reynolds with C. Rawnsley (eds), *Death, Emotion and Childhood in Premodern Europe* (Houndmills: Palgrave Macmillan, 2016)

Barker, E., *Greuze and the Painting of Sentiment* (Cambridge: Cambridge University Press, 2005)

Barker-Benfield, G.J., *The Culture of Sensibility: Sex and Society in Eighteenth-Century Britain* (Chicago: University of Chicago Press, 1992)

Ben-Amos, I.K., 'Reciprocal bonding: parents and their offspring in early modern England', *Journal of Family History* 25, 3 (2000), 291–312.

Billig, M., *The Hidden Roots of Critical Psychology: Understanding the Impact of Locke, Shaftesbury and Reid* (London: Sage, 2008)

Bos, J., 'The decline of character: humoral psychology in ancient and early modern medicine', *History of Human Sciences* 22, 3 (2009), 29–50.

Braddick, M.J. and J. Innes (eds), *Suffering and Happiness in Early Modern England* (Oxford: Oxford University Press, 2016)

Broomhall, S. (ed.), *Emotions in the Households, 1200–1900* (Basingstoke: Palgrave Macmillan, 2008)

Broomhall, S., 'Disturbing Memories: Narrating Experiences and Emotions of Distressing Events in the French Wars of Religion', in E. Kuijpers, J. Pollmann, J. Müller and J. van der Steen (eds), *Memory before Modernity. Practices of Memory in Early Modern Europe* (Leiden: Brill, 2013), 251–67.

Broomhall, S., 'Reasons and identities to remember: composing personal accounts of religious violence in sixteenth-century France', *French History* 27, 1 (2013), 1–20.

Broomhall, S., 'Emotional encounters: indigenous peoples in the Dutch East India Company's interactions with the South Lands', *Australian Historical Studies* 45, 3 (2014), 350–67.

Broomhall, S., '"Quite indifferent to these things": the role of emotions and conversion in the Dutch East India Company's interactions with the South Lands', *Journal of Religious History* 39, 4 (2015), 524–44.

Broomhall, S., '"My daughter, my dear": the correspondence of Catherine de Medici and Elisabeth de Valois', *Women's History Review* 24, 4 (2015), 548–69.

Broomhall, S. (ed.), *Destroying Order, Structuring Disorder: Gender and Emotions in Medieval and Early Modern Europe* (Farnham: Ashgate, 2015)

Broomhall, S., (ed.) *Ordering Emotions in Europe, 1100–1800* (Leiden: Brill, 2015)

Broomhall, S. (ed.), *Spaces for Feeling: Emotions and Sociabilities in Britain, 1650–1850* (London: Routledge, 2015)

Broomhall, S. (ed.) *Authority, Gender and Emotions in Late Medieval and Early Modern England* (Basingstoke: Palgrave Macmillan, 2015)

Broomhall, S., 'Dishes, Coins and Pipes: The Epistemological and Emotional Power of VOC Material Culture in Australia', in A. Gerritsen and G. Riello (eds), *The Global Lives of Things: Material Culture of Connections in the Early Modern World* (Abingdon: Routledge, 2016), 145–61.

Broomhall, S., 'Tears on silk: cross-cultural emotional performances among Japanese-born Christians in Seventeenth-Century Batavia', *Pakistan Journal of Historical Studies* 1, 1 (2016), 18–42.

Broomhall, S., 'Feeling Divine Nature: Natural History, Emotions and Bernard Palissy's Knowledge Practice', in R. Garrod, P.J. Smith and C. Murphy (eds), *Natural History in Early Modern France: The Poetics of an Epistemic Genre* (Leiden: Brill, 2017)

Broomhall, S., 'Fire, Smoke and Ashes: Communications of Power and Emotions by Dutch East India Company Crews on the Australian continent', in G. Moore (ed.), *Fire Stories* (New York: Punctum Books, 2017)

Broomhall, S. and S. Finn (eds), *Violence and Emotions in Early Modern Europe* (Abingdon: Routledge, 2015)

Broomhall, S. and J. Van Gent, 'Corresponding affections: emotional exchange among siblings in the Nassau Family', *Journal of Family History* 34, 2 (2009) 143–65.

Broomhall, S. and J. Van Gent, 'Converted relationships: re-negotiating family status after religious conversion in the Nassau dynasty', *Journal of Social History* 47, 3 (2014), 647–72.

Brown, L., *Homeless Dogs and Melancholy Apes: Humans and Other Animals in the Modern Literary Imagination* (Ithaca: Cornell University Press, 2010)

Capp, B., '"Jesus wept" but did the Englishman? Masculinity and emotion in early modern England', *Past & Present*, 224, 1 (2014), 75–108.

Careri, G., *La fabbrica degli affetti: la Gerusalemme liberata dai Carracci a Tiepolo* (Milan: Il Saggiatore, 2010)

Carrera, E., 'Pasión and afección in Teresa of Avila and Francisco de Osuna', *Bulletin of Spanish Studies* 84, 2 (2007), 175–91.

Carrera, E., 'The emotions in sixteenth-century Spanish spirituality', *Journal of Religious History* 31, 3 (2007), 235–52.

Carrera, E., 'Lovesickness and the therapy of desire: Aquinas, cancionero Poetry and Teresa of Avila's *Muero porque no muero*', *Bulletin of Hispanic Studies* 86, 6 (2009), 729–42.

Carrera, E., Special Issue: 'Madness and Melancholy in Sixteenth- and Seventeenth-century Spain', *Bulletin of Spanish Studies*, 87, 8 (2010)

Carrera, E., 'The social dimension of shame in Cervantes's *La fuerza de la sangre* (1613)', *Perífrasis: Revista de Literatura, Teoría y Crítica* 4, 7 (2013), 19–36.

Carrera, E. (ed.), *Emotions and Health, 1200–1700* (Leiden: Brill, 2013)

Carrera, E., 'Embodied cognition and empathy in Cervantes's *El celoso extremeño* (1613)', *Hispania* 97, 1 (2014), 113–24.

Champion, M. and A. Lynch (eds), *Understanding Emotions in Early Europe* (Turnhout: Brepols, 2015)

Clarke, D., '"Formed into Words by Your Divided Lips": Women, Rhetoric and the Ovidian Tradition', in D. Clarke and E. Clarke (eds), *This Double Voice: Gendered Writing in Early Modern England* (Houndsmills: Palgrave Macmillan, 2000), 61–87.

Cockcroft, R., *Rhetorical Affect in Early Modern Literature: Renaissance Passions Reconsidered* (Basingstoke: Palgrave Macmillan, 2003)

Colantuono, A., 'Titian's tender infants: on the imitation of Venetian painting in Baroque Rome', *I Tatti Studies* 3 (1989), 207–34.

Cole, L. '(Anti)feminist sympathies: the politics of relationship in Smith, Wollstonecraft and More', *ELH* 58, 1 (1991), 107–40.

Cole, L., 'Distinguishing friendships: Pope's *Epistle to a Lady* in/and literary history', *The Eighteenth Century: Theory and Interpretation* 34 (1993), 169–92.

Cole, L. *Imperfect Creatures: Vermin, Literature, and Sciences of Life, 1600–1740* (Ann Arbor: University of Michigan Press, 2016)

Colwell, T.M., 'Gesture, Emotion, and Humanity: Depictions of Mélusine in the Upton House Bearsted Fragments', in J. Rider and J. Friedman (eds), *The Inner Life of Women in Medieval Romance Literature* (New York: Palgrave, 2011), 107–27.

Cummings, B. and F. Sierhuis (eds), *Passions and Subjectivity in Early Modern Culture* (Farnham: Ashgate, 2013)

Davidson, J.W. and R. Prince (eds), *Singing Emotions: Voices from History* (Perth: Australian Research Council Centre of Excellence for the History of Emotions, 2012)

Daybell, J., 'Social negotiations in correspondence between mothers and daughters in Tudor and early Stuart England', *Women's History Review* 24, 4 (2015), 502–27.

DeJean, J., '(Love) letters: Madeleine de Scudery and the epistolary impulse', *Eighteenth-Century Fiction* 22, 3 (2010), 399–414.

Delumeau, J., *Sin and Fear: The Emergence of a Western Guilt Culture, 13th–18th Centuries*, (trans.) E. Nicholson (New York: St. Martin's Press, 1990)

Dermineur, E.M., 'Trust, norms of cooperation and the rural credit market in eighteenth-century France', *Journal of Interdisciplinary History* 45, 4 (2015), 485–506.

Dickey, S.S. and H. Roodenburg (eds), *The Passions in the Arts of the Early Modern Netherlands* (Zwolle: Waanders, 2010)

Dijkhuizen, J.F. van and K.A.E. Enenkel (eds), *The Sense of Suffering: Constructions of Physical Pain in Early Modern Culture* (Leiden, Brill, 2009)

Dixon, T., *From Passions to Emotions: The Creation of a Secular Psychological Category* (Cambridge: Cambridge University Press, 2003)

Dixon, T., '"Emotion": the history of a keyword in crisis', *Emotion Review* 4, 4 (2012), 338–44.

Dixon, T., 'Enthusiasm delineated: varieties of weeping in eighteenth-century Britain', *Litteraria Pragensia: Studies in Literature and Culture* 22 (2012), 59–81.

Dixon, T., *Weeping Britannia: Portrait of a Nation in Tears* (Oxford: Oxford University Press, 2015)

Dolan, A. and S. Holloway (eds), Special Issue: 'Emotional Textiles', *Textile: The Journal of Cloth and Culture* 14, 2 (2016)

Donegan, K., *Seasons of Misery: Catastrophe and Colonial Settlement in Early America* (Philadelphia: University of Pennsylvania Press, 2013)

Downes, S., A. Lynch and K. O'Loughlin (eds), *Emotions and War: Medieval to Romantic Literature* (Houndmills: Palgrave Macmillan, 2015)

Drew, D., *The Melancholy Assemblage: Affect and Epistemology in the English Renaissance* (New York, Fordham University Press, 2013)

Dülmen, R. van, *Theatre of Horror: Crime and Punishment in Early Modern Germany*, (trans.) E. Neu (Cambridge: Polity, 1990)

Eckstein, N.A. 'Mapping Fear: Plague and Perception in Florence and Tuscany', in N. Terpstra and C. Rose (eds), *Mapping Space, Sense, and Movement in Florence: Historical GIS and the Early Modern City* (London: Routledge, 2016), 169–186.

Enenkel, K.A.E. and A. Traninger (eds), *Discourses of Anger in the Early Modern Period* (Leiden: Brill, 2015)

Enterline, L., *Shakespeare's Schoolroom: Rhetoric, Discipline, Emotion* (Philadelphia: University of Pennsylvania Press, 2012)

Eustace, N., '"The cornerstone of a copious work": love and power in eighteenth-century courtship', *Journal of Social History* 34, 3 (2001), 518–45.

Eustace, N., *Passion is the Gale: Emotion, Power and the Coming of the American Revolution* (Chapel Hill: University of North Carolina Press, 2008)

Eustace, N., 'The sentimental paradox: humanity and violence on the Pennsylvania frontier', *The William and Mary Quarterly* 65, 1 (2008), 29–64.

Eustace, N., E. Lean, J. Livingston, J. Plamper, W.H. Reddy and B.H. Rosenwein, 'AHR conversation: the historical study of emotions', *American Historical Review* 117, 5 (2012), 1487–531.

Evans, J. and C. Meehan (eds), *Perceptions of Pregnancy from the 17th Century to the 20th Century* (Basingstoke: Palgrave Macmillan, 2016)

Evans, R.J.W. and A. Marr (eds), *Curiosity and Wonder from the Renaissance to the Enlightenment* (Aldershot: Ashgate, 2006)

Finuzzi, V. and R. Schwartz (eds), *Desire in the Renaissance: Psychoanalysis and Literature* (Princeton: Princeton University Press, 1994)

Fontaine, L., *The Moral Economy: Poverty, Credit, and Trust in Early Modern Europe* (New York: Cambridge University Press, 2014)

Frevert, U., C. Bailey, P. Eitler, B. Gammerl, B. Hitzer, M. Pernau, M. Scheer, A. Schmidt and N. Verheyen, *Emotional Lexicons: Continuity and Change in the Vocabulary of Feeling 1700–2000* (Oxford: Oxford University Press, 2014)

Friedland, P., *Seeing Justice Done: The Age of Spectacular Capital Punishment in France* (Oxford: Oxford University Press, 2012)

Frye, N., 'Varieties of eighteenth-century sensibility', *Eighteenth-Century Studies* 24, 2 (1990–1), 157–72.

Garrod, R. and Y. Haskell (eds), *Changing Heart: Performing Jesuit Emotions Between Europe, Asia and the Americas* (Leiden: Brill, 2016)

Gaukroger, Stephen (ed.), *The Soft Underbelly of Reason: The Passions in the Seventeenth Century* (London: Routledge, 1998)

Giglioni, G., 'Girolamo Cardano on the passions and their treatment', *Brunelliana e Campanelliana* 12, 1 (2006), 25–40.

Gill, A. McCue and S. Rolfe Prodan (eds), *Friendship and Sociability in Premodern Europe: Contexts, Concepts, and Expressions* (Toronto: University of Toronto Press, 2014)

Goring, P., *The Rhetoric of Sensibility in Eighteenth-Century Culture* (Cambridge: Cambridge University Press, 2005)

Gowland, A., *The Worlds of Renaissance Melancholy: Robert Burton in Context* (Cambridge: Cambridge University Press, 2006)

Gowland, A., 'Consolations for melancholy in Renaissance humanism', *Society and Politics* 6, 1 (2012), 10–38.

Grace, P., *Affectionate Authorities: Fathers and Fatherly Roles in Late Medieval Basel* (Aldershot: Ashgate, 2015)

Harvey, K., 'What Mary Toft felt: language, emotions and the body', *History Workshop Journal* 80, 1 (2015), 33–51.

Haskell, Y. (ed.), *Diseases of the Imagination and Imaginary Disease in the Early Modern Period* (Tunhout: Brepols, 2011)

Haskell, Y., '"Physician Heal Thyself!" Emotions and the Health of the Learned in Samuel Auguste André Tissot (1728–1797) and Gerard Nicolaas Heerkens (1726–1801)', in H.M. Lloyd (ed.), *The Discourse of Sensibility: The Knowing Body in the Enlightenment* (Dordrecht: Springer, 2013), 105–24.

Haskell, Y., 'The Passion(s) of Jesuit Latin', in P. Ford, J. Bloemendal and C. Fantazzi (eds), *Encyclopedia of the Neo-Latin World* (Leiden: Brill, 2014), 775–88.

Heinen, U. and A. Thielemann (eds), *Rubens Passioni: Kultur der Leidenschaften im Baröck* (Göttingen: Vandenhoeck and Ruprecht, 2001)

Helgerson, R., 'Weeping for Jane Shore', *The South Atlantic Quarterly* 98, 3 (1999), 451–76.

Hillman, J. (ed.), Special Issue: 'Appetite for Discovery: Sense and Sentiment in the Early Modern World', *Historical Reflections* 41, 2 (2015)

Hindle, S., 'Dependency, shame and belonging: badging the deserving poor, *c.* 1550–1760', *Cultural and Social History* 1, 1 (2004), 6–35.

Hirschman, A.O., *The Passions and the Interests: Political Arguments for Capitalism before its Triumph* (New Jersey: Princeton University Press, 1977)

Ibbett, K., 'Pity, compassion, commiseration: theories of theatrical relatedness', *Seventeenth-Century French Studies* 30, 2 (2008), 196–208.

James, C., 'What's love got to do with it? Dynastic politics and motherhood in the letters of Eleonora of Aragon and her daughters', *Women's History Review* 24, 4 (2015), 528–47.

James, S., *Passion and Action: The Emotions in Seventeenth-Century Philosophy* (Oxford: Clarendon Press, 1997)

Jardine, L., 'Pedagogy and the Technology of Textual Affect: Erasmus's Familiar Letters and Shakespeare's *King Lear*', in J. Raven, H. Small and N. Tadmor (eds), *The Practice and Representation of Reading in Early Modern England* (Cambridge: Cambridge University Press, 1996), 77–101.

Jarzebowski, C., 'Gotteskinder: Einige Überlegungen zu Alter, Geschlecht und Emotionen in der europäischen Geschichte der Kindheit, 1450–1800', *Troja. Jahrbuch für Renaissancemusik* (2013), 27–53.

Jarzebowski, C., 'Das gefressene Herz. Emotionen und Gewalt in transepochaler Perspektive', in C. Jarzebowski and A. Kwaschik (eds), *Performing Emotions: Zum Verständnis von Politik und Emotion in der Frühen Neuzeit und in der Moderne* (Göttingen: V&R unipres, 2013), 94–112.

Jarzebowski, C., 'The Meaning of Love: Emotion and Kinship in Sixteenth-Century Incest Discourses,' in D. Luebke and M. Lindemann (eds), *Mixed Marriages: Transgressive Unions in Germany from the Reformation to the Enlightenment* (Oxford: Bergahn Books, 2014), 166–83.

Jarzebowski, C., 'Tangendo: Überlegungen zur frühneuzeitlichen Sinnes- und Emotionengeschichte', in A. Brendecke (ed.), *Praktiken der Frühen Neuzeit. Akteure – Handlungen – Artefakte* (Köln: Böhlau, 2015), 398–411.

Jarzebowski, C., '"My Heart Belongs to Daddy!" Emotion and Narration in Early Modern Self-Narratives', in H. Flam and J. Kleres (eds), *Methods and Emotions. Interdisciplinary Perspectives* (New York: Routledge, 2015), 248–58.

Jarzebowski, C. and T.M. Safley (eds), *Childhood and Emotion across Cultures 1450–1800* (London: Routledge, 2014)

Johnson, T., 'Blood, Tears and Xavier Water: Popular Religion in the Eighteenth-Century Upper Palatinate', in R.W. Scribner and T. Johnson (eds), *Popular Religion in Germany and Central Europe, 1400–1800*, (Houndmills: Palgrave Macmillan, 1996), 183–202.

Jones, C., *The Smile Revolution in Eighteenth-Century Paris* (Oxford: Oxford University Press, 2014)

Kahn, V., *Wayward Contracts: The Crisis of Political Obligation in England, 1640–1674* (Princeton: Princeton University Press, 2004)

Kahn, V., N. Saccamano and D. Coli (eds), *Politics and the Passions, 1500–1850* (Princeton: Princeton University Press, 2006)

Kambaskovic, D. (ed.), *Conjunctions: Body and Mind from Plato to Descartes* (New York: Springer, 2014)

Kambaskovic-Sawers, D., 'The Two Faces of Love in Western Philosophy', in S. Scollay (ed.), *Love and Devotion: From Persia and Beyond* (Melbourne: MacMillan Art Publishing in association with State Library of Victoria and the Bodleian Library, 2012), 141–50.

Karant-Nunn, S.C., '"Christians' Mourning and Lament Should not be Like the Heathens": The Suppression of Religious Emotion in the Reformation', in J.M. Headley, H.J. Hillerbrand and A.J. Papalas (eds), *Confessionalization in Europe, 1555–1700: Essays in Honor and Memory of Bodo Nischan* (Aldershot: Ashgate, 2004), 107–30.

Karant-Nunn, S.C., *The Reformation of Feeling: Shaping the Religious Emotions in Early Modern Germany* (Oxford: Oxford University Press, 2010)

Kauffman, L.S., *Discourses of Desire: Gender, Genre, and Epistolary Fictions* (Ithaca: Cornell University Press, 1986)

Kennedy, G., *Just Anger: Representing Women's Anger in Early Modern England* (Carbondale: Southern Illinois Press, 2000)

Kerr, H., D. Lemmings and R. Phiddian (eds), *Passions, Sympathy and Print Culture: Public Opinion and Emotional Authenticity in Eighteenth-Century Britain* (Basingstoke: Palgrave Macmillan, 2015)

King, E.L., 'Affect contagion in John Donne's *Deaths Duell*', *SEL Studies in English Literature 1500–1900* 56, 1 (2016), 111–30.

Konishi, S., 'Early encounters in aboriginal place: the role of emotions in French readings of indigenous sites', *Australian Aboriginal Studies* 2 (2015), 12–23.

Kounine, L. and M. Ostling (eds), *Emotions in the History of Witchcraft: Unbridled Passions* (Basingstoke: Palgrave, 2016)

Kraye, J., Ἀπ ἀθεια and Προπ ἀθειαι in early modern discussions of the passions: stoicism, christianity and natural history', *Early Science and Medicine* 17, 1–2 (2012), 230–53.

Kuijpers, E., 'The Creation and Development of Social Memories of Traumatic Events: The Oudewater Massacre of 1575', in M. Linden and K. Rutkowski (eds), *Hurting Memories: Remembering as a Pathogenic Process in Individuals and Societies* (London: Elsevier, 2013), 191–201.

Kuijpers, E. and J.S. Pollmann, 'Why Remember Terror? Memories of Violence in the Dutch Revolt', in J. Ohlmeyer and M. Ó Siochrú (eds), *Ireland 1641: Contexts and Reactions* (Manchester: Manchester University Press, 2013), 176–96.

Kuijpers, E. and C. van der Haven (eds), *Battlefield Emotions 1500–1850: Practices, Experience, Imagination* (Basingstoke: Palgrave MacMillan, 2016)

Lagerlund, H. and M. Yrjönsuuri (eds), *Emotions and Choice from Boethius to Descartes* (Dordrecht: Kluwer, 2002)

Lansing, C., *Passion and Order: Restraint of Grief in the Medieval Italian Communes* (Ithaca: Cornell University Press, 2008)

Lawrence-King, A., 'Il palpitar del core: The Heart-Beat of the "First Opera" ', in D. Crispin and B. Gilmore (eds), *Artistic Experimentation in Music: An Anthology* (Leuven: Leuven University Press, 2014), 157–66.

Lederer, D., 'The myth of the all-destructive war: afterthoughts on German suffering, 1618–1648', *German History* 29, 3 (2011), 380–403.

Leemans, I. and E. Hagen, 'Een "vuurige aandoening van het hart": Drift en geestdrift in het Nederlandse theater en de Nationale Vergadering, 1780–1800', *Tijdschrift voor Geschiedenis* 126, 4 (2013), 530–47.

Leemans, I., J.M. van der Zwaan, I. Maks, E. Kuijpers, and K. Steenbergh, 'Mining embodied emotions: a comparative analysis of sentiment and emotion in Dutch texts, 1600–1800', *Digital Humanities Quarterly* (2016)

Lefebvre, G., *The Great Fear of 1789: Rural Panic in Revolutionary France*, (trans.) J.A. White (Princeton: Princeton University Press, 2014)

Lemmings, D. and C. Walker (eds), *Moral Panics, the Media and the Law in Early Modern England* (Basingstoke: Palgrave Macmillan, 2009)

Lemmings, D. and A. Brooks (eds), *Emotions and Social Change: Historical and Sociological Perspectives* (New York: Routledge, 2014)

Liliequist, J. (ed.), *A History of Emotions, 1200–1800* (London: Pickering and Chatto, 2012)

Liliequist, J., 'From Honour to Virtue: The Shifting Social Logics of Masculinity and Honour in Early Modern Sweden', in C. Strange, R. Cripp and C.E. Forth (eds), *Honour, Violence and Emotions in History* (London: Bloomsbury, 2014), 45–68.

Lux-Sterritt, L., 'Divine Love and the Negotiation of Emotions in Early Modern English Convents', in C. Bowden and J.E. Kelly (eds), *The English Convents in Exile, 1600–1800: Communities, Culture and Identity* (Farnham: Ashgate, 2013), 229–45.

McClary, S. (ed.), *Structures of Feeling in Seventeenth-Century Expressive Culture* (Toronto: University of Toronto Press, 2012)

McClure, G.W., 'Art of mourning: autobiographical writings on the loss of a son in Italian humanist thought (1400–1461)', *Renaissance Quarterly* 39, 3 (1986), 440–75.

McClure, G.W., *Sorrow and Consolation in Italian Humanism* (Princeton: Princeton University Press, 1991)

McGann, J., *Poetics of Sensibility: A Revolution in Literary Style* (Oxford: Clarendon Press, 1998)

Mack, P., *Heart Religion in the British Enlightenment: Gender and Emotion in Early Methodism* (Cambridge: Cambridge University Press, 2008)

McLisky, C., K. Vållgarda and D. Midena (eds), *Emotions and Christian Missions* (Basingstoke: Palgrave Macmillan, 2015)

McNamara, R.F. and U. McIlvenna, Special Issue: 'Medieval and Early Modern Emotional Responses to Death and Dying', *Parergon* 31, 2 (2014)

Maddern, P. and A. Lynch (eds), *Venus and Mars: Engendering Love and War in Medieval and Early Modern Europe* (Nedlands: University of Western Australia Press, 1995)

Maddern, P., J. McEwan and A.M. Scott (eds), *Performing Emotions in the Medieval and Early Modern World* (Turnhout: Brepols, 2017)

Marchant, A. (ed.), *Historicising Heritage and Emotions: The Affective Histories of Blood, Stone and Land from Medieval Britain to Colonial Australia* (London: Routledge, 2016)

Marotti, A., ' "Love is not love": Elizabethan sonnet sequences and the social order', *English Literary History* 49, 2 (1982), 396–428.

Meek, R. and E. Sullivan (eds), *The Renaissance of Emotions* (Manchester: Manchester University Press, 2015)

Merwick, D., *The Shame and the Sorrow: Dutch-Amerindian Encounters in New Netherland* (Philadelphia: University of Pennsylvania Press, 2006)

Merwick, D., *Stuyvesant Bound: An Essay on Loss Across Time* (Philadelphia: University of Pennsylvania Press, 2013)

Montagu, J., *The Expression of the Passions: The Origin and Influence of Charles Le Brun's 'Conférence sur l'expression générale et particulière'* (New Haven: Yale University Press, 1994)

Muir, E., *Mad Blood Stirring: Vendetta and Factions in Friuli during the Renaissance* (Baltimore: Johns Hopkins University Press, 1993)

Mullan, J., *Sentiment and Sociability: The Language of Feeling in the Eighteenth Century* (Oxford: Clarendon Press, 1990)

Mullaney, S., 'Affective Technologies: Toward an Emotional Logic of the Elizabethan Stage', in M. Floyd-Wilson and G. Sullivan (eds), *Environment and Embodiment in Early Modern England* (Basingstoke: Palgrave Macmillan, 2006), 71–89.

Mullaney, S., *The Reformation of Emotions in the Age of Shakespeare* (Chicago: University of Chicago Press, 2015)

Müller, M., *'These Savage Beasts Become Domestick': The Discourse of the Passions in Early Modern England, with Special Reference to Non-fictional Texts* (Trier: Wissenschaftlicher Verlag, 2003)

Murphy, T., ' "Woful childe of parents rage": suicide of children and adolescents in early modern England', *Sixteenth Century Journal* 17, 3 (1986), 259–70.

Naphy, W.G. and P. Roberts (eds), *Fear in Early Modern Society* (Manchester: Manchester University Press, 1997)

Newton, H., *The Sick Child in Early Modern England, 1580–1720* (Oxford: Oxford University Press, 2012)

Parisot, E., *Graveyard Poetry: Religion, Aesthetics and the Mid-Eighteenth-Century Poetic Condition* (Farnham: Ashgate, 2013)

Paster, G.K., K. Rowe and M. Floyd-Wilson (eds) *Reading the Early Modern Passions: Essays in the Cultural History of Emotions* (Philadelphia: University of Pennsylvania Press, 2004)

Percival, M., *The Appearance of Character: Physiognomy and Facial Expression in Eighteenth-Century France* (Leeds: Modern Humanities Research Association, 1999)

Percival, M., *Fragonard and the Fantasy Figure: Painting the Imagination* (Aldershot: Ashgate, 2012)

Percival, M. and G. Tytler (eds), *Physiognomy in Profile: Lavater's Impact on European Culture* (Newark: University of Delaware Press, 2005)

Perfetti, L. (ed.), *The Representation of Women's Emotions in Medieval and Early Modern Culture* (Gainesville: University Press of Florida, 2005)

Pickavé, M. and L. Shapiro (eds), *Emotion and Cognitive Life in Medieval and Early Modern Philosophy* (Oxford: Oxford University Press, 2012)

Pinch, A., *Strange Fits of Passion: Epistemologies of Emotion, Hume to Austen* (Stanford: Stanford University Press, 1996)

Pollock, L., 'Anger and the negotiation of relationships in early modern England', *The Historical Journal* 47, 3 (2004), 567–90.

Pollock, L.A., *Forgotten Children: Parent-Child Relations from 1500 to 1900* (Cambridge: Cambridge University Press, 1983)

Pollock, L.A., 'The practice of kindness in early modern elite society', *Past & Present*, 211, 1 (2011), 121–58.

Prince, R. (ed.), *Grief and Joy: Emotions in the Music of the 18th Century* (Perth: Australian Research Council Centre of Excellence for the History of Emotions, 2012)

Pucci, S., 'Snapshots of family intimacy in the French eighteenth century: the case of *Paul et Virginie*', *Eighteenth-Century Culture* 35 (2008), 89–118.

Racaut, L., *Hatred in Print: Catholic Propaganda and Protestant Identity during the French Wars of Religion* (Farnham: Ashgate, 2002)

Raeburn, G.D., 'Death, superstition, and common society following the Scottish Reformation', *Mortality* 21, 1 (2016), 36–51.

Reddy, W.M., *The Navigation of Feeling: A Framework for the History of Emotions* (Cambridge: Cambridge University Press, 2001)

Reddy, W.M., *The Making of Romantic Love: Longing and Sexuality in Europe, South Asia, and Japan, 900–1200* (Chicago: Chicago University Press, 2012)

Ricciardelli, F. and A. Zorzi (eds), *Emotions, Passions, and Power in Renaissance Italy* (Amsterdam: University of Amsterdam, 2015)

Riskin, J., *Science in the Age of Sensibility: The Sentimental Empiricists of the French Enlightenment* (Chicago: University of Chicago Press, 2002)

Rittgers, R.K., 'Grief and consolation in early modern Lutheran devotion: the case of Johannes Christoph Oelhafen's *Pious Meditations on the Most Sorrowful Bereavement* (1619)', *Church History* 81, 3 (2012), 601–30.

Romney, S.S., *New Netherland Connections: Intimate Networks and Atlantic Ties in Seventeenth-Century America* (Chapel Hill: University of North Carolina Press, 2014)

Roodenburg, H., 'Empathy in the making: crafting the believers' emotions in the late medieval low countries', *BMGN – Low Countries Historical Review* 129, 2 (2014), 42–62.

Roodenburg, H. (ed.), *A Cultural History of the Senses in the Renaissance* (London: Bloomsbury, 2014)

Roodenburg, H. and C. Santing (eds), Special Issue: 'Batavian Phlegm? The Dutch and their Emotions in Pre-Modern Times', *BMGN – Low Countries Review* 129, 2 (2014)

Roper, L., '"Evil imaginings and fantasies": child-witches and the end of the witch craze', *Past & Present* 167 (2000), 107–39.

Roper, L., *Witch Craze: Terror and Fantasy in Baroque Germany* (New Haven: Yale University Press, 2004)

Rosenwein, B.H., *Generations of Feeling: A History of Emotions, 600–1700* (Cambridge: Cambridge University Press, 2015)

Rousseau, G., *Nervous Acts: Essays on Literature, Culture, and Sensibility* (Basingstoke: Palgrave, 2004)

Rublack, U., 'Fluxes: the early modern body and the emotions', *History Workshop Journal* 53, 1 (2002), 1–16.

Ruggiero, G., *Machiavelli in Love: Sex, Self, and Society in the Italian Renaissance* (Baltimore: The John Hopkins University Press, 2007)

Russell, G. and C. Tuite (eds), *Romantic Sociability: Social Networks and Literary Culture in Britain, 1770–1840* (Cambridge: Cambridge University Press, 2006)

Ryrie, A. and J. Martin (eds), *Private and Domestic Devotion in Early Modern England* (Aldershot, Ashgate, 2012)

Ryrie, A., *Being Protestant in Reformation Britain* (Oxford: Oxford University Press, 2013)

Ryrie, A. and T. Schwanda (eds), *Puritanism and Emotion in the Early Modern World* (Basingstoke: Palgrave, 2016)

Sanchez, M., *Erotic Subjects: The Sexuality of Politics in Early Modern English Literature* (Oxford: Oxford University Press, 2011)

Schiesari, J., *The Gendering of Melancholia: Feminism, Psychoanalysis, and the Symbolics of Loss in Renaissance Literature* (Ithaca: Cornell University Press, 1992)

Schliesser, E. (ed.), *Sympathy: A History* (Oxford: Oxford University Press, 2015)

Schmitter, A.M., '17th and 18th Century Theories of Emotions', in E.N. Zalta (ed.), *The Stanford Encyclopedia of Philosophy* (2014). Online at http:plato.stanford.edu/archives/spr2014/entries/emotions-17th18th/

Schneider, G., 'Affecting correspondence: body, behaviour, and the textualization of emotion in early modern English letters', *Prose Studies*, 23, 3 (2000), 31–62.

Shaw, P., *Suffering and Sentiment in Romantic Military Art* (Farnham: Ashgate, 2013)

Siegel, P., 'Christianity and the Religion of Love in *Romeo and Juliet*', *Shakespeare Quarterly* 12 (1961), 164–82.

Smith, V., *Intimate Strangers: Friendship, Exchange and Pacific Encounters* (Cambridge: Cambridge University Press, 2010)

Solomon, J.R., 'You've Got to Have Soul: Understanding the Passions in Early Modern Culture', in S. Pender and N.S. Struever (eds), *Rhetoric and Medicine in Early Modern Europe* (Farnham: Ashgate, 2012), 195–228.

Spinks, J. and C. Zika (eds), *Disaster, Death and the Emotions in the Shadow of the Apocalypse, 1400–1700* (Basingstoke: Palgrave Macmillan, 2016)

Stachniewski, J., *The Persecutory Imagination: English Puritanism and the Literature of Religious Despair* (Oxford: Clarendon Press, 1991)

Stephen, M., 'Witchcraft, grief, and the ambivalence of emotions', *American Ethnologist* 26, 3 (1999), 690–710.

Stoyle, M., 'Memories of the maimed: the testimony of Charles I's former soldiers, 1660–1730', *History* 88, 290 (2003), 204–26.

Styles, J., 'Objects of Emotion: The London Foundling Hospital Tokens, 1741–60', in A. Gerritsen and G. Riello (eds), *Writing Material Culture History* (London: Bloomsbury, 2015), 165–72.

Styles, J., *Threads of Feeling: The London Foundling Hospital's Textile Tokens, 1740–1770* (London: The Foundling Museum, 2010)

Sullivan, E., 'The history of the emotions: past, present, future', *Cultural History* 2, 1 (2013), 93–102.

Sullivan, E., *Beyond Melancholy: Sadness and Selfhood in Renaissance England* (Oxford: Oxford University Press, 2016)

Sutton, P., 'Stories about Feeling: Dutch-Australian Contact in Cape York Peninsula, 1606–1756', in P. Veth, P. Sutton and M. Neale (eds), *Strangers on the Shore: Early Coastal Contacts in Australia* (Canberra: NMA Press, 2008), 35–59.

Tarantino, G., 'Mapping religion (and emotions) in the Protestant Valleys of Piedmont', *ASDIWAL: Revue Genevoise d'Anthropologie et d'Histoire des Religions* 9 (2014), 91–105.

Tarantino, G., 'Disaster, emotions and cultures: the unexpected wink of Shiba Kokan (1738–1818)', *Rivista Storica Italiana* 128, 1 (2016)

Tatlock, L. (ed.), *Enduring Loss in Early Modern Germany: Cross Disciplinary Perspectives* (Leiden: Brill, 2010)

Todd, J., *Sensibility: An Introduction* (London: Methuen, 1986)

Toivo, R., 'Parent-abuse in early modern Finland: structures and emotions', *Journal of Family History* 41, 3 (2016), 255–70.

Toivo, R. and J. Van Gent (eds), Special Issue: 'Gender, Objects and Emotions in Scandinavian History', *Journal of Scandinavian History* 41, 3 (2016)

Trevor, D., *The Poetics of Melancholy in Early Modern England* (Cambridge: Cambridge University Press, 2005)

Trexler, R.C., 'In search of father: the experience of abandonment in the recollections of Giovanni di Pagolo Morelli', *History of Childhood Quarterly* 3, 2 (1975), 225–52.

Trigg, S., 'Delicious, tender Chaucer: Coleridge, emotion and affect,' in A.S. Monnet and A. Langlotz (eds), Special Issue: 'Emotion, Affect, Sentiment: The Language and Aesthetics of Feeling', *Swiss Papers in English Language and Literature* 30 (2014), 1–66.

Trigg, S., '"Language in Her Eye": The Expressive Face of Criseyde/Cressida', in A.J. Johnston, R. West-Pavlov and E. Kempf (eds), *Love, History and Emotion in Chaucer and Shakespeare: Troilus and Criseyde and Troilus and Cressida* (Manchester: Manchester University Press, 2016), 94–108.

Van Gent, J., 'Sarah and her sisters: identity, letters and emotions in the early modern Atlantic world,' *Journal of Religious History* 38, 1 (2014), 71–90.

Van Gent, J. and S. Young (eds), Special Issue: 'Emotions and Conversion', *Journal of Religious History* 39, 4 (2015)

Van Sant, A.J., *Eighteenth-Century Sensibility and the Novel: The Senses in Social Context* (Cambridge: Cambridge University Press, 1993)

Vaught, J.C. (ed.), *Masculinity and Emotion in Early Modern English Literature* (Aldershot: Ashgate, 2008)

Vila, A.C., *Enlightenment and Pathology: Sensibility in the Literature and Medicine of Eighteenth-Century France* (Baltimore: Johns Hopkins University Press, 1998)

Walsh, L., 'The expressive face: manifestations of sensibility in eighteenth-century French art', *Art History* 19, 4 (1996), 523–50.

Walsham, A., *Charitable Hatred: Tolerance and Intolerance in England, 1500–1700* (Manchester: Manchester University Press, 2006)

Watanabe-O'Kelly, H., '"Mit offentlich-ausgebrochenen Liebes=Thränen" – How and why early modern festival books depict emotions', *History of Emotions – Insights into Research*, (November 2014) www.history-of-emotions.mpg.de/en/texte/mit-offentlich-ausgebrochenen-liebesthranen-how-and-why-early-modern-festival-books-depict-emotions

Weisser, O., 'Grieved and disordered: gender and emotion in early modern patient narratives', *Journal of Medieval and Early Modern Studies* 43, 2 (2013), 247–73.

White, R.S., *Natural Rights and the Birth of Romanticism in the 1790s* (London: Macmillan, 2005)

White, R.S., '"False Friends": Affective Semantics in Shakespeare', *Shakespeare* 8 (2012), 286–99.

White, R.S., 'Emotional landscapes: romantic travels in Scotland', *Keats-Shelley Review* 27, 2 (2013), 76–90.

White, R.S. 'Smiles that conceal, smiles that reveal', *Shakespeare*, 10 (2015), 1–14.

White, R.S., *Shakespeare's Cinema of Love* (Manchester: Manchester University Press, 2016)

White, R.S., M. Houlahan and K. O'Loughlin (eds), *Shakespeare and Emotions – Inheritances, Enactments, Legacies* (Basingstoke: Palgrave Macmillan, 2015)

Index

Acerbi, Alberto 30
Adams, Thomas 55
Adams, Tracy 225–8
Adamson, John 181
Addison, Joseph 67
administrative records 15, 304, 309, 313–8
admiration 35, 75–7, 203, 234, 304–5
adoration 231, 268
Aebischer, Pascale 95
Aemilie Juliane, countess of Schwarzburg-Rudolstadt 212–14
affect theories 10–13
affection(s) xxxvi, 33–4, 49, 106, 158, 170, 173–6, 270, 278, 288, 305–6; holy 67–70
affective economies 18–19, 325; fields 18, 131; value 19
affiliation 65, 185, 314
agency 17–18, 55, 71, 167, 184–5, 212, 252, 292, 315, 343
Ahmed, Sara 13, 18–20, 66, 131–2, 257, 298, 300, 324, 326
Ahrendt, Rebekah 230
Aikin, Judith 212, 214
Akkerman, F. 217
Alberti, Fay Bound 167, 207
Alberti, Leon Battista 38–9
Aldrich, Keith 269
Alembert, Jean le Rond d' 29–30
Alighieri, Dante 54, 89
Allen, Christopher 74–7
Allen, Michael J. 140
Almond, Robert 340
Altbauer-Rudnik, Michal 55, 355
altruism 274–5
amazement 29, 34
ambition 10, 56, 248, 250, 287, 317, 320
Anabaptists 186, 190
Anderson, Benedict 316
Anderson, Emily 230
Anderson, Rune S. 238
Angelico, Fra 280–1
anger 3, 9, 14, 28–9, 35, 40, 51–2, 72, 82, *82,* 102, 105, 110, 123, 156, 158–9, 170–1, 175, 186–8, 192–3, 202, 206, 211–2, 218, 230, 235, 237, 240, 242–3, 246, 249–50, 258–9, 262, 264, 278, 282, 288, 290–4, 299, 305, 319, 331–2, 338–9, 341–2, 347 see also choleric, rage
anger, divine 69, 143, 179, 207, 288, 284, 295
anguish 58, 79, 90, 95–7, 153, 239, 333
animal, emotions of 13, 337–40, 343–5; emotions towards xxxvii, 18, 45, 47, 141, 206, 239–40, 242–3, 258, 273, 290, 293, 295, 331, 335, 337–40, 347–9; spirits 24, 166, 343–4
Ankarloo, Bengt 337
Annales school 132, 242
Anne of Austria, queen consort of France 46, 180
anthropology xxxviii, 7, 10, 14, 17, 19, 290, 293, 308, 325
anticipation 67, 164, 212
antiquarianism 105, 125, 254–7
Antonio, Amy 56
anxiety 34, 56, 58, 60, 75, 110, 112, 122–3, 133, 138, 143, 210–3, 221, 224, 245, 252, 258–9, 293–4, 298, 304–6, 308, 317, 319
apathy 188
apocalyptic thought 104, 143, 184, 189–91, 293, 295, 345
Appadurai, Arjun 139
apprehension 138, 211–3, 275; of the divine 327–8
Aquinas, Thomas 37, 67, 70–1, 259–60
Arab, Ronda 9, 355
archaeology 5, 17–18, 136, 234, 254, 308
architecture 20–1, 83, 152, 229–32, 234–5, 265, 281, 329, 352
archives 99, 102–4, 109, 118, 124–7, 156, 165, 189, 191, 229, 234, 304–6, 323, 325–6

d'Arcy, Sing 230–35
Arellano, Jerónimo 19, 20
Arenal, Electa 280
Arendt, Hannah 63
Ariès, Philippe 214, 244–5, 247
Arikha, Noga 41
Aristotle 24, 38, 42, 62, 71, 93–4, 225, 227, 249, 251, 259, 264, 302, 310–11, 337, 343–4, 352
arrogance 51–2, 66, 248
ars moriendi 221, 223
'art objects' 17
art 8–9, 13, 15, 17, 19, 41, 44, 46–7, 73–7, 81–5, 118, 129–30, 133, 140–52, 205, 218, 223, 228, 231, 235, 239, 241, 258, 264–9, 271, 273–4, 276, 278, 280–2, 327–31, 350–4, see also architecture, devotional objects, maps, sculpture, textiles
art academies 74–7, 81, 83, 85, 150
art theory, early modern 38, 41, 44, 74–7, 81–5, 258, 264–5, 269
Ascham, Roger 96, 99–100
asceticism 72, 281, 310
Asciesi, Gabriele d' 239
Asciesi, Guglielmo d' 239
Ascoli, Albert R. 91
Ashley, Robert 39
aspiration 305
associationism 24–5
Aston, Margaret 160
astonishment 34, 75–6, 83
atmosphere, emotional 11, 18, 114
atonement 281, 329
attunement 18–19
Atwood, Craig D. 191, 316, 330
audience engagement, as beholders, buyers, collectors, readers, viewers, listeners 26, 37, 40–1, 43–4, 81–2, 84, 89, 90–2, 94–8, 101, 103–6, 119, 128–9, 130, 133–4, 140–1, 143–7, 149–50, 155–6, 158, 160, 169, 170, 172, 175–6, 184, 193–5, 197, 203, 228–30, 234, 240, 242, 248–9, 253, 255, 262, 264–5, 267–8, 271, 273, 275–6, 280, 283, 287, 289, 291, 294–5, 297–9, 301–2, 318, 327–9, 352–4
Augustine of Hippo 67, 70–1, 184, 259, 351
Austen, Jane 275–6
Austin, Gilbert *170*, 171, 173
autobiographies and self-narratives 29, 103, 125, 139, 169, 191, 199, 202–3, 209, 216, 243, 281, 309, 330 see also memoirs
Auwers, Michael 307
Avicenna 42
awe 17, 127, 129, 179–80, 193, 203, 252, 282, 293, 301–2, 312, 353
Bach, Johann Sebastian 174, 262
Bacon, Francis 34, 343, 346
Bähr, Andreas 202, 204, 355
Baier, Annette 269, 272, 355
Bailey, Christian xxxviii, 35, 322, 358
Bailey, Gauvin Alexander 118, 121, 230–1, 269
Bailey see Begiato (Bailey), Joanne
Bailey, Merridee L. 17, 99–102, 108–11, 220, 306–7, 316, 355[FA1]
Baker, Augustine 279
ballads 195–6, 274, 335
Ballantyne, Tony 322
ballet 179, 228
Bamford, Karen 16, 355
Bandes, Susan A. 195
Banks, Joseph 326
Banning Cocq, Frans 265, *267*
baptism 115, 117, 137, 158, 216, 313–4
Baptists 288
Barbauld, Anna Laetitia 80
Barclay, Katie 14–17, 20–3, 114, 204, 208, 210, 217–20, 244–7, 306–7, 316, 355
Bardi, Giovanni de' 174
Barish, Jonas 225–7
Barker, Emma 85, 355
Barker-Benfield, G.J. 168, 269, 272, 355
Barnes, Diana G. 89–91, 95–8
Barnett, Dene 172–3
Baroque, art 264–9, 278, 281, 329; music 174–5, 261–3; theatre 172
Barrie, David G. 114
Bartel, Dietrich 176, 263
Bartelink, G.J.M. 217
Bartolozzi, Francesco 84, *84*
Bashkin, Orit 322
Baskerville, Hannibal 125
Baskerville, Mary 125
Bate, Jonathan 98
battlefields 221, 235–8
Baudier, Michel 302
Baxandall, Michael 146
Baydala, Angelina 26–7
Bayle, Pierre 285
Beattie, J.M. 114
Beatty, Heather R. 167
Beaufort, Margaret 133
beauty 54, 83–4, 146, 148, 150, 271, 275, 350, 352–3
Beazley, Charles R. 309
Begiato (Bailey), Joanne 102, 208, 211–14, 356
Behn, Aphra 73
Bejan, Teresa M. 287
Bellay, Joachim du 89–90
Bellori, Giovanni Pietro 264

Bellotti, Pietro 148
belonging 20, 137, 140, 202, 314–5
Bembo, Pietro 54, 89–90
Ben-Amos, Ilana K. 217, 356
Benedict, Philip 205
Benesch, Oleg 322
benevolence 62–3, 79, 270, 275, 285, 321
Bennett, Jane 18, 20, 272–3
Benserade, Isaac de 181
Bentham, Jeremy 73
Bentley, R. Alexander 30
bereavement, see grief
Bercé, Yves-Marie 188
Berg, Maxine 307
Bergwik, Staffan 260
Berkowitz, Leonard 27
Berlant, Lauren 11–13, 64
Bernard, Jean-Frédéric 284
Bernini, Gian Lorenzo 265, *266*, 281
Bertucci, Paola 260
Bestul, Thomas H. 283
Betts, C.J. 303
Beveridge, David 208
Bevington, David 61
Beza, Théodore 206, 208
Bible 34, 43, 68, 81, 103–4, 125, 128, 133, 141, 161, 189–90, 203, 252, 282, 289, 335–7, 347
Billig, Michael 27, 356
Binding, Paul 132
Binsfeld, Peter 332
biographies 125, 139, 191, 223, 313
Birdwell-Pheasant, Donna 23
birth 46, 115, 117, 133, 143, 158, 167, 211–5, 293–5, 329, 336, 338
Bladen, Victoria 342
Blagrave, Joseph 340
Blair, Rhonda L. 61
Blake, William 274
Blandy, Mary 194
Blanks, David 303
Bloch, Marc 43
Bloemendal, J. 217, 358
blood 35, 39, 40–1, 44, 46–7, 58, 143, 166, 195, 197, 212, 215, 240, 244–6, 271, 276, 281, 290, 292, 295, 298, 300–2, 328–9, 336, 338–9, 341–2, 343–4
blushing 11, 79, 151
Blussé, Leonard 307
Boccaccio, Giovanni 89
Bodin, Jean 301–2, 332
body, the and corporeal 10, 12–5, 19, 21, 24, 26, 28–9, 33–4, 38–40, 43, 46–9, 58, 60, 67–9, 71, 78–80, 83, 100, 106, 119–20, 122, 134, 138, 141, 150, 153, 156, 162, 165–73, 185, 193, 196–7, 212, 220, 239, 250, 252, 255, 265, 270, 274, 277, 281, 290, 292–3, 298, 310, 312, 321, 329, 335–6, 338–9, 341, 343–4 see also blushing, brain, clothing, eye, face, gesture, hair, hand, heart, smile, pregnancy, nervous system, voice
Boehler, Jean-Michel 243, 244
Boerhaave, Herman 107–8
Boiger, Michael xxxviii, 26–7
Boileau, Nicolas 302
Bolton, Edmund 65, 67
books 46–7, 96, 109–10, 122, 125, 130–5, 140–1, 162, 166, 252–4, 259, 267, 295, 336 see also prints, print media
Bora, Katharina von 294
boredom 259
Borromeo, Carlo 281
Borromeo, Federico 353
Boquet, Damien xxxviii, 38–9, 251
Bos, Jacques 27, 356
Bosch, Hieronymous 281
Bosq, Jacques du 96–7
Bouchard, Gérard 244
Boucher Elizabeth Joseph 278
Bourdieu, Pierre 5, 12, 48–9, 226
Bourke, Joanna 316
Bowden, Caroline 279, 360
Braddick, Michael J. 185–8, 356
Bradshaigh, Dorothy 78
Bradshaw, John 180
brain, relationship with emotions 24, 40, 42, 45, 58, 100, 106, 166–7, 343 see also mind
Bream, Teresa 277
Breen, Katharine 48, 50
Brendecke, Arndt 359
Breton, Nicholas 96–7
Brewer, J.S. 155
Brewer, John 66
Bright, Timothie 41, 55, 58, 60–1
Bril, Paul 353
Brinsley, John 48–50
broadsheets 140–6, 291, 294–5
Broce, Gerald 224
Brodey, Inger 79–80
Brooks, Ann 227, 360
Broomhall, Susan xxxvi–iii, 6, 10, 15–16, 19, 23, 26, 67, 105, 108, 114, 123–4, 145–6, 192, 202, 204–5, 214, 246, 251, 256–7, 279–80, 297, 306–7, 316, 326, 356
Brown, Judith 195, 198
Brown, Laura 345–6, 356
Brown, Thomas 270, 272
Bruce, George 238
Bruegel the Elder, Jan 353

Brundage, James A. 117
Bruno, Giordano 54, 259
Bry, Theodor de 144, 146
Buba, Tony 309
Bull, Ida 247
Bulwer, John *169*, 171, 173
Bunyan, John 5, 289–90
burial practices 197, 206
Burke, Edmund 83, 271–2
Burnett, Stephen 300
Burton, Antoinette 322
Burton, Robert 5, 41, 52, 55–8, *57*, 60–1, 258
Butler, Judith 14–16
Butt, John 263
Buxtorf, Johannes 299
Byrd, William 173
Byron, Lord George Gordon 275
Bysack, John 341

Cabantous, Alain 243–4
Caferro, William 240–1
Calefas-Strebelle, Audrey 300–3
Calvin, Jean 173, 206, 282–3, 287
Calvinists 43, 138, 159, 203, 224, 253, 282, 287, 319
Camden, William 255, 257
Campbell, Lily B. 91
Campbell-Orr, Clarissa 181
Campion, Henri de 107
Canning, Joseph 205
Capellanus, Andreas 54
Capern, Amanda L. 202
Capp, Bernard 356
Caravaggio, Michelangelo Merisi da 147, 265
Careri, Giovanni 354, 356
Carracci, Annibale 352–3
Carrera, Elena 43–4, 260, 356-7
Carretta, Vincent 309
Carriera, Rosalba 148
Carrithers, David W. 303
Casas, Bartolomé de las 308–9, 321, 323
Casini, Lorenzo 251
Castellio, Sebastian 206
Castello, Alberto da 160
Castiglione, Baldassare 225, 227
Catherine de Medici, queen of France 213
Catholic emotional practices 68, 118–21, 138, 141, 152–3, 156, 159–60, 173, 203, 216, 218, 220, 222, 224, 231–2, 252–3, 265, 280–1, 285, 294, 310–12, 312
Cavaillé, Jean-Pierre 227
Cavalcanti, Bartolomeo 168
Cawdrey, Robert 61, 64
ceremonies, 181, 302; coronation 179; entries 267; marriage 217, 219; mourning 222
Ceruti, Giacomo 148
Cesarini, Don Virginio 351
Chai, Jean Julia 39
Chakravarti, Ananya 118–21
Chambers, Robert 207
Champion, Michael 357
charity 15, 99, 121, 162, 180, 200, 202, 278
Charland, Louis C. 26, 27
Charles I of England, Scotland, Ireland 180, 183
Charles II of England, Scotland, Ireland 348
Charles V, Holy Roman Emperor 179–80
Charleton, Walter 68, 70
Chartier, Roger 251, 254
Chaucer, Geoffrey 54, 89
Chaytor, Miranda 247
cheer 66, 92, 160, 262, 328
Cherso, Francesco Patrizi da 54
childhood 70, 99, 101, 214–17
children 16, 45–7, 53, 70, 99–102, 106–7, 122, 125–6, 148–51, 164, 167, 194, 208–12, 214–7, 219, 246, 249, 265, 273, 276, 283, 288, 291, 293, 295, 298, 302, 306, 312, 328, 336, 341 see also maternal, parental, paternal emotions
Chipps Smith, Jeffrey 146
choleric 35, 39–40, 58, 73, 277, 338–9 see also anger, humoral theory
Chomedey, Jérôme 39
Christian I, elector of Saxony 282
chronicles 6, 29, 97, 102–5, 202, 204, 239, 251, 278, 308
church interiors 8, 151, 156, 180, 230–5, 267, 281–2, 329
Churchill, Wendy 168
Churchyard, Thomas 89, 91
Cicero 38, 44, 71, 95–7, 168–9, 182
civic culture 110, 182, 184, 186, 225, 238–41, 265
civil war, English 9, 65, 90, 125, 294
civility 66, 95, 98, 226, 285–7, 320–2
Cixous, Hélène 16
Clark, Stuart 333–4
Clarke, Danielle 91, 98, 357
Clarke, Elizabeth 91, 98, 357
climate, meteorological 72, 302
clothing 11, 18, 92, 104, 138, 147–51, 161–6, *163*, 180, 193, 197, 237, 265, 302, 304–5, 327, 338
Clulow, Adam 307
Cockcroft, Robert 357
Cody, Lisa 213
Coeffeteau, Nicolas 311

coercion, forms of 8, 65, 200, 274, 314–15
Cohn Jr, Samuel K. 205, 207–8, 241
Colantuono, Anthony 350–4, 357
Cole, Lucinda 343–6, 357
Coleridge, Samuel Taylor 274–6
Coli, Daniela 73, 185, 359
collecting 9, 19, 104, 121, 124, 126–7, 148, 253–5, 258–9
colonialism 9, 47, 118, 120, 127, 129, 231, 264, 286, 292, 303–4, 306–9, 313–4, 316–22
Colwell, Tania M. 7–10, 357
commemoration see memory
companies, trading and banking 109, 124, 304–7, 316–19, 326
compassion 35, 61–4, 110, 141, 156, 193–5, 197, 207, 237, 242, 282, 290–1, 302, 349 see also mercy
confession, legal 47, 112–3, 195, 332–3, 341–2; sacrament of 118, 120, 191, 195, 197, 277, 312
consumerism 109, 111, 264, 304–5
contagion, emotional 63, 66, 80, 92, 94, 252, 315
contemplation 74–7, 156, 220, 222, 274, 277–9, 281, 328–9, 352
Cottingham, John 346
conversion 118–20, 191, 231, 288, 298–9, 308, 310–16, 330
conviviality 65–6, 222, 282, 285
Cook, James 324
Coole, Diana 185
Cooper, Tracy E. 235
Copertino, Giuseppe di 47
Corelli, Arcangelo 174
Corens, Liesbeth 104–5
Corneanu, Sorana 260
Corneille, Pierre 93–4
Cornelison, Sally J. 160
Corrigan, John 120
Corsi, Jacopo 174
Costa Mattos, Vicente da 299–300
Cotgrave, Randle 37, 39
Cotton, Sir Robert 254
Couchman, Jane 124
Couperin, François 174
courage 51–2, 80, 180, 237, 270, 308, 324
courts, church and secular 23, 113–7, 126, 139, 192–3, 199–202, 209–10, 216, 242–3, 290–1; elite 23, 65, 83, 90, 162, 173, 180–2, 213, 225–8, 301–3, 305
courtship 114, 137, 164, 332
cowardice 204, 237
Cozens, Alexander 84, *84*
Crabb, Ann 124
craftwork 130, 135–8, 161–2, 196, 278
Cranach workshop *143*
Crane, Mary Thomas 13
Crawford, Patricia 115–7
credit 109–11, 199–202, 225
Crespi, Giuseppe Maria 148
Crick, Bernard 185
crime, see law
Cripp, Robert 360
Crispin, Daria 360
Crowston, Clare H. 202
cruelty 46, 197–8, 203, 239, 305, 321–2, 348 see also punishment, violence
Crystal, David 35
Cuffe, Henry 197–8
Cullen, William 106
Culpeper, Nicholas 340
Cummings, Brian 357
curiosity 72, 100, 126, 129, 146, 155, 254–6, 259, 264, 284, 293, 324
Curth, Louise Hill 337–40
Curtis, Michael 303
Curto, José C. 309
Cusick, Suzanne G. 176

Dahlberg, Charles 56
Dale, Sharon 104
Dalgleish, Tim 30
dance 66, 144, 228–9, 231, 282–3, 336 see also ballet
Daniel, Samuel 54
Darcy, Eamon 204
Darnton, Robert 98
Daston, Lorraine 260, 293–4, 297, 349
data set mining 27–30
Davenport, John 343
David, Jacques-Louis 83–4
Davidson, Jane W. 23–7, 168–73, 173–6, 261–3, 357
Davidson, Tonya K. 349
Davies, Owen 337
Davis, Natalie Zemon 113–14, 125, 127, 244
Daybell, James 123, 124–7, 307, 357
death 16, 55, 107, 113, 115, 117, 133, 138, 141, 147, 151–5, 166, 180, 183, 191, 193–7, 205–6, 210–12, 215–16, 218, 220–4, 234–5, 239, 245, 249–50, 255, 267, 274, 281–2, 288, 291, 295, 308–9, 312, 328–9, 332, 334–6, 338–9, 344–5, 350, 352 see also archives, ceremonies, grief, monuments, Passion of Christ, plague, procession, punishment, ritual
Debbagi Baranova, Tatiana 253–4
debt, see indebtedness
DeJean, Joan 97–8, 357
dejection 56, 60, 274

Dekker, Rudolf 217
Dekker, Thomas 109
Deleuze, Gilles 13, 15–16
Del Rio, Martin 332
Delumeau, Jean 70, 252, 254, 310–12, 357
DeMause, Lloyd 214–15, 217
demons 210, 258, 331–6, 340–1
Demosthenes 168
Dening, Greg 326
Dermineur, Elise M. 199–202, 242–44, 357
Derrida, Jacques 124, 127
Descartes, René 24, 42, 45, 62, 71–3, 75, 225, 228, 250, 258, 264, 271, 275, 343–4
Desceliers, Pierre 129, *130*
De Selincourt, E. 188
Deseure, Brecht 105
desire 24–5, 49, 53–5, 72, 76, 89, 92, 97–8, 109, 111, 117, 146, 149, 151, 267, 287–8, 304–5, 332, 341–2
desires 10–11, 15, 115, 129, 135, 150–1, 165, 259, 277, 291, 326, 332, 341–2
despair 60, 221–2, 224, 249, 288–9, 291, 312, 329, 331, 333
Deutsch, Helen 213
Deutsch, Yaacov 300
Devereux, Penelope, Lady Riche 90
Devereux, Robert, earl of Essex 197
devil(s) 53, 55, 141, 144, 212, 220, 281, 290–1, 312, 314, 340–3 see also demons
devotion 35, 49, 71, 103, 119–20, 134, 140–1, 179, 239, 252, 265, 278–82, 311
devotional texts 46, 119, 136, 212, 240, 287; objects 138, 141, 156–61, 281–2
Dhere, Ramchandra C. 121
diaries 8–9, 67, 69, 105–7, 109, 125, 161, 166, 189, 202, 209, 218, 229, 236, 239, 251, 259, 265, 285, 295, 304, 306, 313–4
Dickens, Charles 276
Dickey, Stephanie S. 44, 45, 264–9, 357
Diderot, Denis 29, 82, 92, 94, 211, 271
Dijkhuizen, Jan Frans van 358
disability 212, 237
disappointment 305, 332
disaster, natural 143, 293–7
discouragement 75
disgust 28, 140–1, 145, 193–4, 211, 229, 294
disinterest 72, 291, 305, 325
dismay 308, 318
distain 305
distrust 317
Dixon, Leif, 290
Dixon, Thomas xxxviii, 37–8, 70, 167, 270, 272, 357
Dolan, Alice 164–5, 357
Dolan, Frances 116–7
Dolven, Jeffrey 50
Domański, J. 217
Domenichino, Domenico Zampieri 352
domestic experience, 22, 114, 135–40, 282, 341 see also family, household, violence
Dometch, Arnold 261
Donegan, Kathleen 323, 357
Donington, Robert 263
Donne, John 222
Doody, Margaret A. 98
Dorsten, Jan A. van 91
doubt 222, 306, 330, 333
Douglas, Bronwen 325–6
Dowd, Michelle 9, 355
Downame, John 40–1
Downes, Stephanie 91, 132–35, 204, 238, 357
drama 6, 8–10, 13, 29–30, 34, 40, 58, 62, 64, 82, 92–5, 223, 228, 230, 258, 302, 348
Drayton, Michael 54, 97
dread 212
Drew, Daniel 13, 357
Duby, Georges 55
Duindam, Jeroen 226–7
Du Laurens, André 41
Dülmen, Richard van 198, 358
Dürer, Albrecht *59*, 60
Dutton, Richard 95
duty 35, 68, 179, 185, 194, 208, 210

Earle, John 256–7
Easton, Timothy 140
Eastop, Dinah 164
Ebreo, Leone 54
Eckstein, Nicholas A. 238–41, 358
economic and trade processes 66, 108–11, 199–202, 218–9, 242–3, 246, 275, 285–6, 301, 304–7, 308, 318 see also credit, indebtedness
economic records 108–11, 304
ecstasy 69, 184, 265, 288, 329–30
Edson, Evelyn 132
education see pedagogy
Edward IV of England 89
Edwards, Jonathan 283, 288–9
Egginton, William 225, 227
ego-documents see autobiographies, diaries, letters
Ekman, Paul 28, 30
Eichberger, Dagmar 297
Eisenmenger, Johannes 299–300
Eitler, Pascal xxxviii, 35, 315, 358
elegies 90, 222, 274, 350
Eleonora of Aragon 122
Elferen, Isabella van 230
Elias, Norbert 3, 6, 43, 226–7

Elisabeth de Valois, queen of Spain 213
Elizabeth I of England 9, 23, 152–5, 162, 180
Ellis, Robert L. 346
Elmer, Peter 108, 293
eloquence 89, 97, 248–50
Elster, Jon 199, 202
Elstob, Elizabeth 255
elves 210, 334–7, 340
Elyot, Thomas 61
embodiment see body
embroidery 19, *159,* 160–2, *163* see also textiles
emotion, early modern meaning of 33, 36–9
emotion induction, theories of 25
emotional community 3–6, 21, 29, 65, 115–16, 152, 156, 209, 255–6, 306, 313–5; geographies 21, 129, 306 ; regimes 5, 7–10, 65, 97, 113, 129, 187, 209, 215, 227, 278, 293, 303, 309
emotives 7–10, 15, 271
empathy 94, 141, 186–7, 239, 243, 265, 275, 290–1
empire see colonialism
Enenkel, Karl A.E. 349, 357–8
Engelhardt Mathiassen, Tove 164–5
Enlightenment 79, 81–2, 181, 186, 197, 269–73, 275, 284, 292, 320, 329–30
enmity 285
Enterline, Lynn 48–50, 56, 101–2, 358
enthusiasm 35, 72, 191, 329, 349
envy 72, 109, 123, 127, 200, 212, 243, 259, 290–2, 298–9, 305, 331–2, 342
epistolary literature 95–8, 275, 302
epitaphs 3, 153, 222, 274
Erasmus, Desiderius 96, 99–101, 215, 217, 222, 248
Ermath, Elizabeth 15–16
erotic 55–6, 147, 151, 185, 190, 264–5, 302, 329 see also lust, sexual desire, sexuality
Equiano, Olaudah 309
Equicola, Mario 54, 56
Erskine, Thomas 193-4
eschatology 104, 189
Este, Hercule d', duke of Ferrara 131
Este, Isabelle d', marchioness of Mantua 122, 124
etiquette 226
Eustace, Nicole xxxviii, 9, 10, 220, 320–3, 358
Evans, Jennifer 213, 358
Evans, Richard J. 198
Evans, Robert J.W. 260, 358
Evelyn, John 107, 108, 348
Ewan, Elizabeth 355
execution see punishment
exploration 259, 264, 323–6
eye 264, 282

face 75–7, 81–5, 122, 141, 146–51, 153, 171, 225, 229, 239, 258, 264, 282, 308, 312
fainting 193, 275, 278
fairies 291, 334–7, 340
Falkeid, Unn 91
familiars 336, 340–3
family 3, 9, 21, 66, 90, 103–4, 106, 113, 115, 119, 121–7, 133, 138–9, 143–4, 152, 164, 196–7, 200, 203, 208–12, 216, 218–9, 235, 243–7, 265, 278, 282, 291–2, 305–6, 341 see also children, domestic violence, household, marriage
fanaticism 35, 190
Fantazzi, Charles 358
Fantoni, Marcello 241
fascination 17, 301–2, 347
Fasli, Maria 30
fasting 47, 207, 310
Faulkner, Thomas C. 61
Favret, Mary A. 205
fear 22, 28, 36, 46, 49, 54, 58, 60, 62, 67, 69–70, 72, 75–6, 81, 90, 100, 104–7, 110, 112–3, 115, 127, 129, 133, 138, 140, 145, 155, 157, 160, 166, 179, 182–7, 188, 194–6, 200, 202–3, 205–7, 210–13, 216, 221, 237, 243, 249, 252, 255, 258, 264, 275, 278, 284, 288, 291–5, 297–8, 300–6, 308, 310–12, 317, 324, 331, 333, 335–6, 339, 342–3, 345, 351–2
Febvre, Lucien 43, 132, 134–5
feeling rules 4, 193
Fehl, Philipp 269
Fehl, Raina 269
Fehleison, Jill R. 120
fellow-feeling 61–4, 78, 270, 274
Fenner, William 290
Féraud, Jean-François 64
Ferber, Michael 80
Ferente, Serena 251
Ferdinand of Austria, Cardinal-Infante 267
Ferraguto, Mark 230
Ferrand, Jacques 41, 55, 258
Fenton, Geffray 36–9
Festa, Lynn 271–2
Ficino, Marsilio 41, 54, 60, 258
Fielding, Henry 194
Fielding, Sarah 73
Filatkina, Natalia 161
Finger, Stanley 260
Finn, Margo 110–1
Finn, Sarah 145–6, 251, 356
Finus, Hadrianus 298, 300

Finuzzi, Valeria 56, 358
Fisher, Kate 213
Flam, Helena 359
Flather, Amanda J. 23
Flaxman, John 83
Fletcher, Mary 327, 330
Fletcher, Phineas 55
Flohr Sørensen, Tim 18–20
Florio, John 36–9
Flower, Margaret 341
Floyd-Wilson, Mary 12–13, 64, 73, 91, 94, 361
Fontaine, Laurence 200–1, 358
Forbes, Robert 238
Ford, Philip 358
Fordyce, David 79–80
forest, emotions towards 243
Forestier, Georges 95
Forth, Christopher E. 360
fortitude 89, 187
Fortunatus, Venantius 4
Foster, William 303
Foucault, Michel 5, 79
Fouquet, Nicolas 74
Fracastoro, Girolamo 259
Fragonard, Jean-Honoré 149, 151
Franceschi, Franco 241
Frassetto, Michael 303
Frederick II (the Great), King of Prussia 180
Freedman, Paul 244
Frescobaldi, Girolamo 174–6
Freud, Sigmund 53, 226
Frevert, Ute xxxviii, 35, 111, 181, 358
Fried, Michael 150–1
Friedland, Paul 198, 358
Friedman, Jamie 357
friendship 64–5, 89, 95–7, 104, 106–7, 113, 126, 150, 162, 164, 181, 200, 245–6, 250, 259, 275, 278, 286, 301, 305, 319, 324–6
Frijhoff, Willem 284, 286
Frost, Samantha 185
frustration 55, 305, 330, 341
Fry, Elizabeth 327
Frye, Northrop 79–80, 358
Frykholm, Gunilla 173
Fudge, Erica 346
Fullager, Kate 276
Fuller, Thomas 155
Furetière, Antoine 62, 64

Gaimster, David 139
Gainsborough, Thomas 150
Galen 40, 42
Galilei, Vincenzo 176
Galland, Antoine 302–3
Gammerl, Benno xxxviii, 35, 358
Gandolfi, Gaetano 148
Gandolfi, Ubaldo 148
Garber, Marjorie 61, 64
Gardiner, Julie 140
Gareis, Iris 293
Garnett, Philip 30
Garrido, Sandra 23–7
Garrod, Raphaele 356, 358
Gatrell, V.A.C. 114, 198
Gaukroger, Stephen 77, 260, 358
Geertz, Clifford 240–1
Gelderen, Martin van 185
Gelfand, Toby 26
Geiger, Malachius 258
Gell, Alfred 17–20, 135, 140
Gerritsen, Anne 19, 165, 356, 363
Geschiere, Peter 293
gesture 11, 14–15, 36, 38, 44, 77, 82, 92, 141, 168–73, 193, 199–201, 229, 243, 262, 264, 279, 290–1, 308, 312, 323–4
Gesualdo, Carol 174
ghosts 334–7
Gibson, William 340
Giddens, Anthony 21, 23, 111
Gifford, Terry 348–9
gift giving 131, 133, 137, 139, 160, 162, 164, 225, 246, 250, 304–5
Giglioni, Guido 260, 358
Gill, Amyrose McCue 67, 358
Gilmore, Bob 360
Ginzburg, Carlo 293
Giorgione Barbarelli da Castelfranco 147, 149, 350, *351*
Girolamo, Francesco di 47
Goddard, Peter A. 310–12
Godwin, William 273
Goertz, Hans-Jürgen 191
Goethe, Johann Wolfgang von 83, 275
Goffman, Erving 14–16
Goldgar, Anne 260
Gómez, Maricarmen 172
Gonzaga, Francesco 122, 124
Goodare, Julian 334–7
Goodcole, Henry 343
Gordon, Bernard de 55
Gordon, Bruce 283
Gordon, Daniel 66, 67
Gordon, Thomas 284, 286
Goring, Paul 80, 358
Gothic genre 275
Gottmann, Felicia 307
Goubert, Pierre 181
Gower, John 51, 53
Gowland, Angus 60, 260, 358
Grace, Philip 209–10, 358
Graeber, David 201–2

gratitude 95–6, 179, 211, 213, 220, 285, 291
graveyards 223, 274–5
Gray, Catharine 91, 182–5
Gray, Thomas 274
Grayson, Cecil 39
greed 73, 109, 242, 291, 304–5, 317, 341, 353
Greenblatt, Stephen 41–2, 94, 276
greensickness 41, 55, 258, 274
Greenwald, Jordan 13
Gregerson, Linda 319
Gregg, Melissa 13
Gregory the Great, Pope 4–5
Gregory of Tours 4
Gregory, Brad S. 205
Grell, Ole Peter 108, 257
Greuze, Jean-Baptiste 82, *82*, 85, 150
Greyerz, Kaspar von 204
grief 17, 37–8, 44–5, 51, 61, 67, 78, 89–90, 92, 104, 107, 141, 155–7, 160–2, 164, 166, *169*, 171, 180, 184, 202–3, 206, 215–6, 218, 222, 224, 234–6, 239–41, 249–50, 255, 274, 280, 291, 306, 308, 325, 336
Grimou, Alexis 149
Gritten, Anthony 173
Gross, Daniel M. 73
Guarini, Giovanni Battista 350, 354
Guattari, Félix 13
Guevara, Antonio de 36–7, 39
Guicciardini, Francesco 36, 39
guilds 109–10
Guillaume, Xavier 238
Guillotin, Joseph-Ignace 197
guilt 47, 68, 70, 104, 113, 203–4, 240, 283, 285, 291, 306, 310, 313
Guterry, Jean de 39

Haakonssen, Knud 64, 323
Hagen, Edwina 360
hair 40, 122, 144, 162, *162*, 290, 310, 338
Hall, Marcia B. 235
Hallett, Nicky 279
Halpern, Richard 50
Hamling, Tara 135–40, 160
hand 29, 134, 138, 152, 156–8, *169*, 171, 196, 267
Händel, Georg Friedrich 174, 261
Hanley, Ryan P. 63
Hannah, Mark 326
Hannan, Leonie 23
happiness 28, 33, 79, 107, 153, 170, 188, 207, 255, 275, 350
Hardy, Patsy 276
Hardy, Thomas 193–4
Harley, J.B. 132
Harley, Philippe de, comte de Césy 301, 303
Harman, Graham 272–3
Harmes, Barbara 56
Harmes, Marcus 56, 342
Harms, Wolfgang 146
Harnoncourt, Nikolaus 261
Harris, Oliver J.T. 18, 19, 20
Harrison, Peter 260
Harte, Jeremy 337
Hartman, George 167
Harvey, Brian 128
Harvey, Gabriel 91
Harvey, Karen 165–8, 358
Harvey, William 166
Haskell, Yasmin 77, 257–60, 358
Hastings, Henry, Lord 90
hatred 72, 76, 80, 170, 192, 200, 202–3, 212, 237, 240–1, 284, 290, 297–301, 306, 331, 339, 341–2
Haven, Cornelis van der 205, 238, 360
Hawthorne, Nathaniel 272
Hayes, Catherine 193
Haynes, Bruce 262–3
Hazlitt, William 275
Headley, John. M. 359
heart 44, 51, 54, 67–8, 76, 79–80, 90, 103, 122, 141, 155, 161, 166, 174–5, 180, 184, 196, 213, 215, 222, 240, 249, 265, 278–9, 281, 288, 314, 327–8, 330, 339
Heath, Douglas D. 346
Hebron, Malcolm 346–7, 349
Heesakkers, C.L. 217
Heiligensetzer, Lorenz 204
Heinen, Ulrich 269, 359
Heinsius, Daniel 228
Helgerson, Richard 91, 359
Heller-Roazen, Daniel 44
Henderson, Lindsay 56
Henningsen, Gustav 337
Henri II of France 130
Henri IV of France 253
Henry (the Navigator) of Portugal 308
Henry VII of England 65, 134
Henry Stuart, Prince of Wales 155
Herbert, George 222
Herbert, William 58
Herdman, Emma 205
Hering Torres, Max S. 300
heritage studies 29, 236–7, 254 see also memory
heroism 89, 103, 152, 203, 232, 236, 262, 277
Herzog, Dagmar 334
Hill, Helga 172
Hillerbrand, Hans Joachim 359
Hillman, Jennifer 359

Hiltner, Ken 348
Hindle, Steve 165, 359
Hindmarsh, D. Bruce 330
Hippocrates 39
Hirschfelder, Dagmar 151
Hirschman, Albert O. 111, 359
hissing 229
Historically Informed Performance 229, 263
Histories, early modern 9, 97, 102–5, 202–5, 251–2
Hitchcock, Tim 114
Hitzer, Bettina xxxviii, 35, 358
Hobbes, Thomas 61–4, 72, 184–5, 264
Hobgood, Allison P. 230
Hodacs, Hanna 307
Hogwood, Christopher 261
Hollander, John 91
Holloway, Sally 161–5, 357
Holt, Maria C. 120–1
Holtzel, Hieronymus 298, 300
Home, Henry, Lord Kames 322–3
Hone, Nathaniel 149
honour 29, 55, 97, 104, 111, 164, 196, 198, 200–4, 208–10, 237, 240, 243, 253, 292, 305
Hoogstraten, Samuel van 44
hope 45–6, 49, 90, 105, 135, 138, 155, 161–2, 164, 184, 186–8, 202, 211, 222, 224, 264, 291, 305, 324, 332
Hope, Tony 27
Horace 44, 89, 93
horror 196, 235, 268, 275, 288, 301–2, 328, 351
hospitality 137
Houlahan, Mark 364
Houlbrooke, Ralph 222, 224
household 9, 20–23, 109, 116, 130, 135–40, 208–10, 214, 218–9, 242–7, 282, 290, 292, 295, 306, 340; objects 128, 135–41, 159 see also domestic violence, family
Howard, Henry, earl of Northampton 152, 155
Howard, Jean E. 94
Howard, Sharon 213–14
Hoxby, Blair 229–30
Huizinga, Johan 43
Hull, Clark L. 27
Hultquist, Aleksondra 71–3
humanism 71–2, 96, 99, 152, 174–5, 184, 222, 225, 248–51, 253, 258, 286, 350
Hume, David 25, 63, 64–67, 71–3, 78, 80, 260, 269–72, 275
humiliation 140–1, 164, 198, 200–1, 203, 240, 319, 328 see also shame
humility 95, 175, 184, 277, 324 see also piety
Hummel, Pascale 260
humour 114, 141, 278 see also laughter
humoral theory 10, 13, 24, 33–4, 39–43, 52, 58, 60, 72–3, 93, 100, 166, 207, 258, 338–9, 344
Hunt, Arnold 45
Hunt, Lynn 186–8, 286
Hunter, John 46, 48, 166
Hurley, Erin 94
Hutcheson, Francis 72, 270
Hutchinson, Thomas 188
Hutton, Ronald 140
hymns 191, 328–30
hypochondria 258 see also melancholy
hysteria 38, 107, 330

Ibbett, Katherine 61–4, 359
identity 14–17, 20, 22–3, 58, 64–5, 73, 101, 117, 125–7, 151, 184–5, 203–6, 213, 217, 236, 237, 243, 246, 280, 285, 294, 303, 314–5, 317
Ifversen, Jan 322
illness 24, 33, 40, 53, 56, 58–9, 68, 70, 105–8, 166, 237, 258, 260, 291, 311, 336, 338–40 see also madness, medicine, melancholy, pain, plague, suffering
indebtedness 199–202
indifference 283, 285, 315, 324–5
Indigenous peoples, emotions of 118–20, 129, 190, 305, 313–16, 318, 323–7
indignation 35, 104, 114, 186–7, 189, 274
individualism 109, 111, 201, 251
infanticide 195, 208
injustice 110, 186, 191, 202, 236
Innes, George 236
Innes, Joanna 188, 356
interdisciplinarity xxxvii, 13
interest 61–2, 77, 115, 182–4, 259, 270, 285
interiority 22, 121, 225–6, 265, 268
intimacy 4, 16, 96, 104, 116–7, 122–3, 126, 150, 167, 191, 219, 222, 232, 244–6, 278, 291, 295, 305–6, 320, 322, 325, 341–2, 345

Jack, Malcolm 303
Jackson, Edward 197
Jacob, Christian 132
Jacob, Margaret 286
Jaeger, C. Stephen 227–8
James VI and I 152, 179, 206, 208, 321, 323
James, Carolyn 121–4, 359
James, Leighton 205
James, Susan 260, 359
Jardine, Lisa 98, 359
Jarzebowski, Claudia 214–17, 220, 359

jealousy, sexual and other 35, 171, 218–9, 243, 302, 328, 332, 342
Jeffrey, David L. 331
Jesuits 118–21, 156, 168, 259, 278, 299, 310–8
Jews 164, 281, 297–300
jewels 150, 221, *221*, 294, 302
Jodelle, Étienne 54
Johann Georg IV, Elector of Saxony 179
Johnson, Samuel 22, 34
Johnson, Trevor 160, 359
Johnston, Andrew 363
Johnston, Pamela 160
Jones, Colin 359
Jones, Pamela M. 354
Jonge, H.J. de 217
Jonson, Ben 61, 73, 95
Jordheim, Helge 322
Jossa, Stefano 91
Josselin, Ralph 68–70
joy 4, 24, 28, 55, 67–9, 72, 78–9, 83, 102, 105, 156–7, 180, 184, 202, 211, 213, 220, 222, 235, 264–5, 275, 281, 288, 291, 295, 310, 313, 329, 336, 339, 351
judicial sources see law
Juneja, Moncia 146
Junius, Franciscus 44, 264
Juslin, Patrik N. 25–7
Juster, Susan 319

Kahn, Victoria 73, 184–5, 359
Kambaskovic, Danijela 39–42, 53–6, 359
Kamuf, Peggy 98
Kant, Immanuel 71, 270
Kaplan, Benjamin 286, 300
Karant-Nunn, Susan 6, 8, 10, 45, 120, 224, 280–3, 289, 312, 359
Karantonis, Pamela 230
Karben, Victor von 299
Katajala-Peltomaa, Sari 210
Katz, Jacob 297, 300
Kauffman, Linda S. 98, 359
Keats, John 275
Kelly, James E. 279, 360
Kemp, Martin 39
Kempf, Elisabeth 363
Kendon, Adam 172–3
Kennedy, Gwynne 359
Kenny, Neil 260
Kent, Dale V. 241
Kent, Eliza J. 293
Kermode, Frank 91
Kerr, Heather 246, 355, 360
Kerr, John 26
Kesson, Andy 93, 95
Ketelaar, Eric 127
Kia, Mana 322
Kiessling, Nicolas K. 61
King, Elaine C. 173
King, Emily L. 360
King, Helen 260
King, Peter 114
Kircher, Athanasius 259
kissing 23, 134, 141, 160
Kivistö, Sari 260
Klapisch-Zuber, Christiane 56
Klein, Lisa M. 162, 165
Kleine-Engel, Ane 161
Kleres, Jochem 359
Klibansky, Raymond 61
Klötzer, Ralf 192
Knatchbull, Lucy 278
Knecht, Ross 48–50
Knight, Leah 349
Knolles, Richard 302–3
Knott, Sarah 220
Konishi, Shino 326, 360
Koslofsky, Craig 222, 224
Kounine, Laura 331–34, 360
Kramer, Heinrich 332, 334
Kraye, Jill 260, 360
Kreitzer, Beth 283
Krieken, Robert van 226–7
Kuijpers, Erika 6, 30, 102–5, 202–5, 238, 280, 355–6, 360
Kupperman, Karen Ordahl 323
Kwaschik, Anne 359

Labbie, Erin F. 205
La Bruyère, Jean de 242, 244
Ladino, Jennifer 349
Lagerlund, Henrik 250–1, 360
Lamb, Jonathan 326
lament 96–7, 103–4, 203, 222, 255, 282, 308
Lampos, Vasileios 30
Lancre, Pierre de 144, *145*, 146
Landau, David W. 146
landscape 20–1, 83, 150, 254, 347–8, 350–4
Lange, Bettina 195
Langlotz, Andreas 363
Lansing, Carol 241, 360
Laslett, Peter 247, 323
Lassus, Orlande de 173
laughter 14, 100, 130, 207, 211, 229, 271, 278
Lavater, Johann Kaspar 83
Laven, Mary 156–61
law 40, 45, 47–8, 72, 103, 112–7, 162, 179–83, 192–201, 203, 209, 218, 243, 290, 292, 297–8, 302, 320, 331–2, 342, 348 see also injustice, punishment
Lawrence-King, Andrew 360

Lawence-Zúñiga, Denise 23
Lazar, Benjamin 172
Léal, Juan de Vales, 267, *268*
Lean, Eugenia xxxviii, 322, 358
Le Brun, Charles 74–7, *74*, *76*, 81–3, 85, 258, 264, 269
Le Brun, Jacques 354
Lederer, David 205, 333–4, 360
Lediard, Thomas 228
Leemans, Inger 27–30, 360
Lefebvre, Georges 205, 360
Lefebvre, Henri 20–1, 23
Lehmann, Hartmut 205
Lehmann, Helmut T. 300
Leibniz, Hottfried Wilhelm von 71
Leiden, Jan van 190
Lemmings, David 114, 192–5, 227, 360
Lemnius, Levinus 56
Leo X 252
Leonhardt, Gustav 261
Le Roy, Louis 37
Le Roy Ladurie, Emmanuel 244
L'Estoile, Pierre de 253
letters 5, 8–9, 29, 36–7, 62, 65, 78–9, 89, 95, 97, 103, 105–6, 109–10, 113, 118, 121–7, 138, 161, 166, 189, 194, 202, 209–10, 212–3, 216, 218, 225, 229, 236, 257, 259, 264, 285, 301–2, 304, 306, 313–4, 317–8
see also epistolary literature
Levack, Brian P. 334
Levine, Laura 94
Leys, Ruth 12–13
Lidman, Satu 210
Lievens, Jan 147–8
Liliequist, Jonas 209–10, 230, 316, 360
Liljeström, Simon 27
Lindemann, Mary 41, 220, 359
Linden, David van der 286
Linden, Michael 238, 360
Linné, Carl von 259
listeners, see audience engagement
liturgy 173, 189–91, 223, 231–2, 234, 279, 328
Liu, Bing 30
Livingston, Julie xxxviii, 322, 358
Llewellyn, Nigel 155
Lloyd, Henry Martyn 260, 358
Locke, John 25, 72, 79, 80, 99, 100–1, 185, 270–2, 285, 321, 323
Lockman, John 285, 287
Lomazzo, Gian Paolo 38, 39
Longinus 351
Lope de Vega, Félix 93–5
Lord Smail, Daniel 201–2
Lorrain, Claude 353
Lorris, Guillaume de 53
Louis XIII of France 162, 180, 253
Louis XIV of France 46, 74, 179–81, 226, 253
Louis-Courvoisier, Micheline 168
love 7, 16, 29, 33, 35, 45, 49, 53–6, 62, 66–9, 72, 76, 79–80, 83, 89–91, 95–7, 100, 107, 117, 119–20, 122–3, 134–5, 138, 140, 150, 159, 161–2, 164, 179–82, 184–5, 194, 200, 202, 204, 208–10, 215–6, 218–20, 242–3, 245–6, 255–6, 258, 260, 262, 264–5, 274–5, 285–6, 288, 290–2, 306, 312, 314–5, 324, 328–9, 333, 339, 341–2, 345, 350
love, divine 69, 179, 216, 281, 288, 353
love sickness 40–1, 55
Lovejoy, Paul E. 309
loyalty 7, 40, 53, 114, 155, 182, 246, 278, 285, 305
Loyola, Ignatius of 47, 278–9, 281
Lucius Junius Brutus 183
Lucretius 259
Luebke, David M. 220, 359
Luhrmann, T.M. 329, 331
Lully, Jean-Baptiste 174
Lundh, Christer 247
Lundqvist, Lars-Olov 27
lust 54–5, 144, 291, 302, 332, 342
Luther, Martin 72, 173, 189–90, 220, 222, 248, 252, 281–2, 288–9, 294–5, *296*, 298–9, 333
Lutherans 8, 141, 294–5, 333
Lux-Sterritt, Laurence 279–80, 360
Lyly, John 93
Lynch, Andrew 3–6, 91, 204, 238, 357, 361
Lynch, Deidre 272–3
Lyne, Raphael 91
Lynn, John A. 238

Macauley, Rose 255, 257
McCalman, Iain 276
McClary, Susan 176, 360
McClure, George W. 250–1, 360
McConachie, Bruce 94
MacCulloch, Diarmaid 192
McEwan, Joanne 112–4, 361
Macfarlane, Alan 342
Macfarlane, Ingereth 326
McGann, Jerome J. 79–80, 360
Machiavelli, Niccolò 72–3, 182–5, 249
McIlvenna, Una 195–8, 223–4, 361
Mack, Phyllis 327–31, 360
Mackenzie, Henry 271
McLisky, Claire 120–1, 192, 315–16, 360
McNamara, Rebecca 223–4, 361
Macrobius 53, 56
McTavish, Lianne 213

Maddern, Philippa 217, 361
Maddox, Alan 168–76, 261–3
madness 53, 55, 58, 256, 274, 331, 333, 338
Magellan, Ferdinand 129
magic 17, 151, 197, 210, 252, 258, 290–7, 330, 332, 334–7, 340, 348
Magnusson, Lynne 98
Mahiet, Damen 230
Majumdar, Rochona 322
Maks, Isa 30, 360
Malebranche, Nicolas 71
Mandell, Laura 269–73
Mander, Karel van 264
Manetti, Giannozzo 250–1
Mangy, Thomas 138, *138*
Mannerism, in art and music 174
Manoff, Marlene 127
Mantecón, Tomás 286
maps 127–32, 254, 325
Marais, Marin 174
Maravall, José Antonio 235
Marcello, Jacopo Antonio 249–50
Marchant, Alicia 127–32, 235–8, 254–7, 361
Marcocci, Giuseppe 307–9
Marcus, Leah 348–9
Marenzio, Luca 174
Margaret Tudor, Queen of Scots 134
Margaritha, Antonius 299
Margey, Annaleigh 204
Maria Theresia, Empress and 'King' of Hungary 180–1
Marin, Michel-Ange 277, 280
Marotti, Arthur 90–1, 361
Marr, Alexander 260, 358
marriage and the conjugal 29, 45, 54–5, 92, 115–7, 122–3, 126, 133, 137, 139, 160, 164, 180, 190, 201, 208, 210, 217–20, 245–6, 249, 278, 282, 292, 294–5, 309, 329, 332, 335 see also family, household
Marschke, Benjamin 204
Martelli, Carlo 239
Martin, Henri-Jean 135
Martin, Jessica 140, 362
Martin, J.R. 269
Martínez, María Elena 300
martyrs 46–7, 153, 155, 187, 197, 203, 221, 253, 264, 278, 280–1, 353
Marvell, Andrew 90–1
Mary, mother of Jesus Christ 141, 158, 239, 281, 283
Mary Stuart, Queen of Scots 152, *153*, 153–5
masculinity 22, 60, 89, 97, 101, 183, 204, 209–10, 265, 347
massacre 9, 187, 203, 206, 235, 301, 305–6
Massey, Doreen 22–3
Massey-Westropp, Jeanette 172–3
Massumi, Brian 11, 13
materiality 17–21, 23, 97, 125–7, 132–4, 135–40, 156–65, 254–6, 302
maternal, emotions 16, 126, 141, 158–9, 162, 179–80, 211–2, 215, 281, 283, 287, 291, 341 see also parental
Matheson, Peter 192
Matikainen, Olli 210
Matt, Susan J. 30, 109, 111, 135
Mattheson, Johann 176
Matthew, Sir Tobie 280
Mauriceau, François 211
Mauser, Wolfram 182
Maximilian I, Holy Roman Emperor 143
Maza, Sarah C. 272
medicine 24, 35, 39, 41, 46–7, 52–3, 55, 58, 60, 72, 94, 105–8, 166–7, 207, 211–5, 236, 249, 257–60, 274, 339 see also humoral theory, pain, suffering
Medick, Hans 204–5
Mee, Jon 276
Meehan, Ciara 213, 358
Meek, Richard 13, 94–5, 120, 361
Mégret, Frédéric 236, 238
Mehmet IV, Sultan 301
Mei, Girolamo 175
melancholy 5, 13, 24, 34–5, 39–41, 51–2, 55–61, 72, 80, 92, 100, 107, 207, 222, 237, 258–9, 274–6, 331, 333, 338
Melanchthon, Philipp 294
Melville, Herman 271–2
memento mori 138, 221, *221*, 267
memoirs 102–5, 180, 202, 204, 216, 225, 286, 313 see also autobiographies
memory 42–3, 46, 68, 103–4, 124–7, 139, 151–2, 155, 159, 202–3, 216, 235–7, 239, 252, 255, 265, 301, 343, 346–7 see also archives, chronicles, heritage, histories, nostalgia
Mendelson, Sara 115–7
Ménestrier, Claude-François 228
Mennonites 44, 203
Merback, Mitchell B. 48
Mercado, Tomás de 308–9
Mercator, Geraldus 129
merchants 108–11, 122, 239, 265, 304–6
Mercier, Philip 149
mercy 68, 107, 113, 153, 156, 193, 221, 282 see also compassion
Merwick, Donna 316–20, 361
Mesquita, Batja xxxviii, 27
Messerli, Alfred 146
Messner, Angelika C. 323
Methodists 313, 327–30
Meun, Jean de 53

Midelfort, Erik 333–4
Midena, Daniel 120–1, 315–6, 360
migrants and migration 21, 36–7, 186–8
Mihalcea, Rada 30
Mijnhardt, Wijnand 286
milk 215, 290, 336
Millar, Charlotte-Rose 115–7, 340–3
Miller, Naomi J. 16, 355
Miller, Nicholas 139
Milton, John 184–5, 271, 348
mind 10–13, 24, 26, 33–4, 36–40, 43, 51–3, 58, 60, 62–3, 66, 68, 75, 78–81, 90, 103, 106, 120, 165, 171, 175, 211, 214–5, 220–1, 257, 264, 270–2, 274, 285, 311, 338–9, 354
missions 118–21, 156, 189–90, 231, 259, 277–8, 310–16
modes in art 38, 83, 85
Moibanus, Ambrosius 101
monarchies 9, 23, 179–83, 234, 273
monastic communities 3–4, 56, 102, 141, 277–80, 294 see also nuns
Monnet, Agnieszka 363
Montagu, Jennifer 38, 77, 85, 269, 361
Montagu, Lady Mary Wortley 302–3
Montaigne, Michel de 37, 185, 253, 301
Montesquieu, Secondat, Charles-Louis de, baron de 302–3
Monteverdi, Claudio 174–5, 262–3
Montgomery, Scott B. 160
Montmorency, Anne, Duke of 130
monuments 151–5, 223, 234, 254, 256
mood 49, 50–3, 94, 138, 165, 262, 264, 274, 324
Moore, Bob 286
Moore, Grace 346–9, 356
moral economy 80, 199–202; panic 193–4, 252; sentiments 63, 270, 322
morality and moral frameworks 64, 68, 72–3, 79, 81–2, 107, 109–10, 115, 130, 141, 144, 159–60, 182, 185, 200–1, 203, 218, 236, 248–9, 264–5, 270–1, 274, 277, 283, 286, 292, 295, 302, 313–4, 320–2, 334–5, 339, 353
Moravians 189–92, 288, 313–5, 327–30
More, Gertrude 279–80
More, Thomas 101
Morelli, Giovanni 239–40
Morford, Mark 269
Morland, Henry 149
Morillon, Claude 181
Morrall, Andrew 161
Morse, Margaret A. 161
mortality, see death
Mortimer, Geoff 204
Morton, Timothy 272–3
Moscoso, Javier 45–8
Mothe Fénelon, François de Salignac de la 352
Moulinier-Brogi, Laurence xxxviii,
mourning see grief
Mozart, Wolfgang Amadeus 229
Muecke, Frances 77
Muir, Edward 240–1, 361
Mulcaster, Richard 99, 100, 102
Muldrew, Craig 110–11
Mullan, John 269, 272, 361
Mullaney, Stephen 6, 93–4, 361
Müller, Johannes 105, 204, 356
Müller, Marion 312, 361
Münch, Brigit Ulrike 161
Munroe, Jennifer 347, 349
Müntzer, Johann 181
Müntzer, Thomas 189–90
Murata, Margaret 172
Muratori, Ludovico Antonio 230
murder 113, 143, 193–5, 221, 239, 297, 336
Murphy, Catherine 356
Murphy, Elaine 204
Murphy, Terence R. 361
Musacchio, Jacqueline 160
music 8, 15, 26, 44, 69, 72, 83, 147, 149–50, 173–6, 228–31, 234, 253–4, 258, 273, 278, 282, 327–8, 350; Baroque 261–3; composition 173–6, 228–30, 261, 263, 265, 328; Romantic 273 see also ballads, song, opera, oratorio, voice
Muslims 119, 300–3
Murad IV, Sultan 300
mysticism 47, 189, 191, 265, 278–9

Nagy, Piroska xxxviii, 38, 39, 251
Naphy, William G. 361
Nassau dynasty 123
Nassau, Frederik Hendrik, Prince of Orange *223*
natural world, the 52, 243, 291, 293–7, 334–5, 337–54
Neale, A.V. 217
Neale, Margo 326, 363
Neher, Gabriele 161
neighbours 3, 53, 110, 114–6, 138, 186, 205, 209, 216, 220, 282–6, 290, 292, 336, 342
Nelson, John C. 56
Nelson, Kathleen 172
Neoplatonism 26, 41, 53–4, 60, 174, 253
Neostoicism 62, 89–90, 107, 222, 248–9, 257, 264, 283–4, 287–8, 307, 311
nerves and nervous system 24, 42, 166–7, 258, 328, 345
neuroscience xxxviii, 38, 268
newspapers see press media

Newton, Hannah 16–7, 67–70, 80, 167, 361
Newton, Isaac 25, 80
Nicot, Jean 62, 64
Nidditch, P.H. 272
Nierop, Henk van 286
Nierstrasz, Chris 307
Nieuhof, Johan 305, 307
Nirenberg, David 300
Noah Harari, Yuval 105
nonchalance 225
Norbrook, David 185
Noreña, Carlos G. 251
Norlin, George 354
Norrhem, Svante 307
nostalgia 155, 237, 255, 346, 348
Novetzke, Christian Lee 121
Nowell-Smith, Geoffrey 135
Nugent, Janay 355
Nugent, Maria 323-6
nuns 6, 16, 46, 56, 265, 277–80, 294–5
Nussbaum, Martha 63–4

object-oriented ontology 18
obsession 35, 41, 256
O'Connell, Michael 94
Ohlmeyer, Jane 205, 238, 360
O'Loughlin, Katrina 64–7, 78–80, 91, 204, 238, 357, 364
opera 168, 175, 181, 228–30, 262–3, 265,
Opie, John 149
Opitz, Donald K. 260
oratorio 261
oration 38, 43, 80, 168–9, 171, 175, 180, 225, 250, 258, 260, 264 see also eloquence
organ, musical instrument, 175, 234, 278, 282
Ormerod, David 91
Ortelius, Abraham *128*, 129–31
Ó Siochrú, Micheál 205, 238, 360
Ostling, Michael 360
Overton, Richard 55
Ovid 89, 95–7
Owens, Samantha 228–30

Pagden, Anthony 323
pain 28, 45–8, 55–6, 60, 62–3, 79, 81, 95, 107, 156–8, 160, 166–7, 195–8, 203, 210–2, 235, 237, 239, 274, 281, 288, 291, 308, 310, 328–9, 350
Paine, Thomas 273
painting 42, 44, 47, 74–7, 81–5, 130, 141, 146–51, 234, 239, 265, 327, 329, 350–4
Palestrina, Giovanni Pierluigi da 173
Palisca, Claude 176
pamphlets 9, 47, 140–6, 194, 203, 252–3, 290, 294–5, 298, 317, 340–2 see also prints, print media
Panofsky, Erwin 61
Papalas, Anthony J. 359
Pardo, Osvaldo F. 120–1
Paré, Ambroise 43, 45
parental emotions 16, 53, 70, 96, 99–100, 102, 167, 208–10, 211–17, 239, 249, 281, 336
Parisot, Eric 276, 361
parish 99, 115–8, 155, 164, 283
Park, Katharine 260, 293–4, 297, 349
Park, Myoung-kyu 323
Park, Ondine 349
Parker, Rozsika 161, 165
Parshall, Peter 146
Parsons, Robert 64–5, 67
Pascal, Blaise 25
Passion of Christ 35, 43, 47, 71, 141, 220, 280–1, 288, 310
passions xxxvi, 10–11, 13, 24–6, 33–8, 41, 43, 47–55, 58, 63, 66–8, 70–8, 80–1, 90–1, 97–9, 101–2, 106, 111, 118, 153, 165, 170–2, 175, 182–5, 187, 191, 197, 220, 228–30, 248–9, 251–2, 257–9, 264, 270–1, 273–6, 277–80, 287, 289, 299, 302, 310–12, 332, 339, 352
Paster, Gail Kern 12–13, 40–1, 64, 73, 91, 361
paternal emotions 179, 210, 239, 253, 295
pathos 49, 148, 294–5
patriotism 89, 193, 204, 265
patronage 130–1,152, 234, 248, 253, 305–6
Patterson, Annabel 98
Peacock, Thomas Love 275
Pearce, Susan 257
Peasants' War, German 186, 190, 242
Pechey, John 340
pedagogy 45, 47–50, 73, 81, 93, 96, 99–102, 126, 150, 168, 173, 175, 209, 214–15, 225, 227, 231, 248, 276–7, 286, 298–9, 306, 311–12, 327–8
penance 47
Pender, Stephen 44, 363
penitence 140, 192, 197
Pennebaker, James W. 28
Pepys, Samuel 106
Perfetti, Lisa 361
performance, emotional 9–10, 14–16, 21–3, 38, 65–6, 92, 119–21, 133, 156, 161, 179, 184, 188, 193, 200, 210, 225, 231, 234, 236–7, 240, 291–2, 313, 315, 317; musical and theatrical 26, 92, 94, 168–76, 196, 228–31, 234, 261–3, 278, 327
performativity 7–8, 14–17, 50, 198, 236

Perkins, William 289
Pernau, Margrit xxxviii, 35, 322, 358
Perrucci, Andrea 172, 175–6
Personal writings 125, 166 see also autobiographies, letters, diaries
persuasion 38, 146, 175, 235, 249
pessimism 295
Peters, Kate 104
Petit, Pierre 55
petitions, charitable 121, 202 legal 112–13, 285
Percival, Melissa 146–51, 361
Petrarch, Francesco 54, 89–90, 96–7, 249
Petre, Mary Joseph 278
Petterson, Christina 185–8
Petty, Lady Elizabeth 126
Petty, Charles 126
Petty, Sir William 126
Peucker, Paul 192
Pfefferkorn, Johannes 299
Phaire, Thomas 217
phenomenology 11, 18, 44
Phiddian, Robert 360
Phillips, John 309
Phillips, Mark 241
physiological see body
phlegm and phlegmatic 35, 39–40, 58, 166, 338
Piazzetta, Giambattista 150
Picart, Bernard 284
Pietism 189, 287–9, 313
piety 8, 35, 95, 118, 138, 152–3160, 180, 184, 241, 278, 283, 287, 310–11, 327, 333
Pickavé, Martin 260, 361
Pickren, Wade E. 27
pilgrimage 107, 152, 186, 252, 310
Pilloud, Séverine 168
Pinamonti, Giovanni Pietro 299–300
Pinch, Adela 80, 269–72, 361
Pitts, Jennifer 323
pity 35, 61–3, 66, 72, 110, 113, 186–8, 194, 239, 295, 302, 308, 312, 329
plague 104, 107, 156, 205–8, 345
Plamper, Jan xxxviii, 5, 6, 10, 322, 358
Plantagenet, Arthur, Lord Lisle, 126
Plato 53–4, 55
pleasure 28, 41, 62, 64, 69, 80–1, 100, 109, 127, 132, 144, 255, 264–5, 294, 308, 351–2
Plett, Heinrich F. 45
Plutchick, Robert 28
Pócs, Éva 337
poetry 51, 53–5, 58–9, 73, 79, 89–91, 97, 119, 139, 151, 174, 179, 180–4, 222, 230, 258–9, 271, 273–6, 317, 327, 348, 350–1
Polanyi, Karl 199, 202
Poll-van de Lisdonk, M.L. van 217
Pollock, Linda 123–4, 361
Pollman, Judith S. 105, 204–5, 238, 286, 355–6, 360
Polo, Marco 130
Pontara, Johanna Ethernersson 230
Pope, Alexander 73
Porta, Giambattista della 258
portraits 44, 143, 146–7, 150, 181, 265, 281
Potter, Ursula 56
Poussin, Nicolas 75, *75*, 351–2, *352*
Power, Eileen 56
Power, Mick J. 30
Praetorius, Michael 174
prayer 43, 72, 107, 133–4, 138, 141, 152–3, 157, 179, 196, 207, 212–13, 221–2, 239, 277–8, 281–2, 310, 327, 329, 336
preaching 6, 8, 42–4, 156, 189, 240, 277, 280–3, 288, 294
pregnancy 113, 158, 211–14, 292 see also birth
prejudice 284–5
Prentiss, Karen 121
press see print
Prestage, Edgar 309
Price, Cecily 277
pride 72, 100, 104, 127, 131, 135, 155, 235, 237, 265, 278, 305, 311, 350
Prince, Kathryn 92–5
Prince, Rebekah 357, 362
prints 75–6, 140–46, 150, 203, 251–4, 293–5
print media and processes 47, 130, 132–4, 138, 140–46, 193–4, 203, 251–5, 293–5, 297–9
Priscian 49
processions 156–7, 160, 180, *223*, 237, 282, 278, 336
prophetic 182, 184
protective objects 136–7, 159, 164; rituals 212, 291, 335–6
protests 38, 183, 206, 239–40
Protestant emotional practices 8, 43, 55, 68, 70, 118, 138, 141, 152–3, 155–6, 159–60, 203, 206, 212, 216, 218, 220–2, 224, 252–4, 265, 282, 286–90, 291–2, 294–5, 310, 312, 313–16, 327–31, 333, 335–6
psychoanalysis 10, 24, 60, 101, 290
psychological approaches xxxviii, 7, 10–12, 23–9, 33, 38, 71, 94, 215, 226, 239, 258, 260, 270, 272, 286, 336
Pucci, Suzanne R. 247, 362
Puff, Helmut 334
punishment 46–7, 49, 100, 104, 110, 113–14, 143, 152–3, 179, 183, 189–90,

192–8, 203, 207, 212, 252, 278, 281, 291, 300, 313, 318, 329, 331, 345 see also law
Purcell, Henry 174
Purcell, Stephen 94
Purchas, Samuel *154*
Puritanism 22, 43, 68, 283, 287–90
Purkiss, Diane 342
Putnam, Michael C.J. 269

Quantz, Johann Joachim 175–6
Quietism 77
Quintilian 38, 169, 264
Quiviger, Francis 44

Raber, Karen 346
Racaut, Luc 205, 251–4, 362
race 16, 246, 297–300, 317, 325, 345
Racine, Jean 302–3
Rackham, Oliver 347, 349
Radcliffe, Ann 275
radical formations 189–2
Raeburn, Gordon S. 205–8, 362
rage 229, 237, 239–40, 291, 299, 308 see also anger
Raimondi, Ezio 351, 354
Rameau, Jean-Philippe 174
Ramsden, Betty 212
Randles, Sarah 17–20
Raoux, Jean 149
rape 69, 203
Raphael, Raffaello Sanzio da Urbino, 264
Raven, James 98, 359
Rawnsley, Ciara 16–17, 52, 93, 95, 355
Ray, Meredith K. 98
readers, see audience engagement
Rebellion, Münster 189–91
reciprocity 11, 64, 69, 78, 109–10, 179, 180, 305
Reddy, William M. xxxvi, xxxviii, 5–10, 15–16, 26–7, 55–6, 187–8, 219–20, 226–7, 241, 271–2, 313, 316, 322, 358, 362
Rediker, Marcus 309
Rees, Daniel 279
Reformation, Hussite 190
Reformation, Radical 189–92
Reformations 6, 8, 141, 145, 155, 173, 180, 186–7, 191, 220, 224, 231–2, 234, 243, 252–4, 265, 280–3, 286, 289, 290, 294, 311–12, 327, 333
refugees 191, 286
regret 72, 282, 348, 350
Reid, Thomas 25
Reinis, Austra 224
relics 18, 46, 107, 156, 162, 256, 329
Rembrandt van Rijn 44, *147*, 147–8, 149, 265, *267*
remorse 140–1, 195, 310, 312 see also repentance, penitence
Remy, Nicolas 332, 334
Renaudot, Theophraste 301
Renshaw, Sal 16
repentance 46, 197, 207, 282, 291 see also remorse, penitence
Republics 182–5
repulsion 190, 259, 301–2, 324
resentment 80, 200, 243, 291, 306
resilience 204
resistance 311
Restall, Matthew 309
restraint 43, 83, 90–1, 101, 187, 207, 222, 226, 241, 273, 277–8, 303, 311, 318
reverence 239, 252, 265, 311
Revolt, Dutch 186, 203–4
Revolution, American 9, 186, 273; French 8, 162, 186–7, 226, 271, 273
Revolutions, political 185–8, 189, 204, 273–4
Reynolds, Joshua 149–50
Reynolds, Kim 16, 355
rhetoric 43–4, 62, 81, 83, 95–6, 98, 101, 103–6, 122–3, 125–6, 168–76, 199–201, 210, 223, 225, 229, 231, 242–3, 248, 250, 258, 262–4, 300–1, 350–2 see also oration
Ribera, Jusepe de 148
Ricciardelli, Fabrizio 227, 241, 362
Richardson, Catherine 135, 139–40
Richardson, Samuel 78, 80, 97, 271
Rider, Jeff 357
ridicule 141, 256
Riello, Giorgio 19, 165, 356, 363
rights, discourse of 9, 186–8, 198, 218, 273, 276, 285
riot see protests
Risi, Clemens 230
Riskin, Jessica 79, 80, 260, 362
Rittgers, Ronald K. 220, 362
ritual 3, 8, 16, 22, 119, 133–4, 144, 156, 160, 164, 180–1, 191, 197–8, 209, 217, 220, 222, 225–6, 240–1, 277, 280, 290–2, 295, 305–6, 308, 310, 312–14, 335–6
Rizzi, Andrea 248–51
Roberts, Penny 205, 361
Rococo, art 265
Roe, Thomas 302–3
Roebling, Irmgard 182
Roeck, Bernd 205
Rogers, Timothy 68–70
Rohr, Julius Bernhard von 181
Rolfe Prodan, Sarah 67, 358
Romanticism 25, 79, 204, 273–6, 351

Romney, Susannah S. 362
Ronsard, Pierre 54
Roodenburg, Herman 42–5, 269, 357, 362
Roper, Lyndal 115, 117, 167–8, 217, 293, 332–4, 362
Rore, Cipriano de 174
Rosa, Salvator 353, *353*
Rose, Carol 337, 358
Rosenwein, Barbara H. xxxvi, xxxviii, 3–6, 10, 38–9, 43, 45, 67, 110–11, 115–7, 144, 147, 152, 155, 160, 227–8, 241, 244, 251, 313, 316, 322, 358, 362
Rosier-Catach, Irène 251
Ross, David 251
Rotari, Pietro 150
Roth, John D. 192
Rousseau, George 343, 346, 362
Rousseau, Jean-Jacques 62, 72–3, 83, 99, 101–2, 214, 273, 275
Rowe, Katherine 12–13, 64, 73, 91, 361
Royce, Jacalyn 93, 95
Rubens, Peter Paul 147, 150, 264, 267, 269
Rublack, Ulinka 113–14, 168, 211, 213, 334, 362
Rudy, Kathryn M. 134–5, 160
Ruggiero, Guido 251, 362
Ruisdael, Jacob van 353–4
Rummel, Erika 300
Runeson, Sverker 173
Russell, Gillian 65, 67, 276, 362
Russell, James A. 25, 27
Rutherford, Alexandra 27
Rutkowski, Krzysztof 238, 360
Ruymbeke, Bertrand van 286
Ryrie, Alec 45, 70, 140, 224, 287–90, 362

Saada, Emmanuelle 323
Sabean, David W. 244
Sabor, Peter 98
Saccamano, Neil 73, 185, 359
Sachs, Curt 263
Sackville, Edward, earl of Dorset 125
sadness 28, 33, 58, 60, 72, 104, 196, 207, 222, 235, 237, 239, 249, 258, 262, 295, 308, 310, 339
Safley, Thomas M. 217, 359
Said, Edward 301, 303
saints 69, 119–20, 141, 156, 232, 234, 264–5, 278, 280–1, 291, 327, 336
St Clare Byrne, Muriel 127
Saint-Gelais, Octavien de 89
Sala-Molins, Louis 300
Sales, François de Saint 77
Salmela, Mikko 188
Salmuth, Johann 282
Samothrakis, Spyridon 30
San Bartolomé, Ana de 278
Sanchez, Melissa E. 185, 362
Sandberg, Brian 205
Sannazzaro, Jacopo 350
sanguine 35, 39–40
Santerre, Jean-Baptiste 149
Santing, Catrien 362
Sardelic, Mirko 303
Saxl, Fritz 61
Scarlatti, Alessandro 174
Scarlatti, Domenico 174
Scarisbrick, Elizabeth Abraham 278
scepticism 271, 302, 335
Schama, Simon 188, 317, 319, 347, 349
Scheer, Monique xxxviii, 10, 12–4, 35, 43, 45, 315, 358
Schefer, Charles 303
Scheidt, Samuel 174
Schein, Johann Hermann 174
Schenk, Gerrit Jasper 146
Scheve, Christian von 188
Schlau, Stacey 280
Schiesari, Juliana 60, 362
Schlechte, Monika 181
Schliesser, Eric 63, 362
Schmidt, Anne xxxviii, 35, 358
Schmidt, Benjamin 257, 317, 319
Schmitter, Amy 26, 27, 362
Schneider, Gary 121–4, 362
Schoch, Rainer 146
Scholz Williams, Gerhild 146
schools see pedagogy
Schulte, Rolf 334
Schütz, Heinrich 174
Schwanda, Tom 289, 362
Schwartz, Regina 56, 358
science, early modern 24–5, 41, 68, 71, 79–81, 83, 85, 126, 129, 166, 182, 245, 257–60, 264, 335, 338, 343–6, 272, 354
Scodel, Joshua 224
Scollay, Susan 359
scorn 264, 294, 305
Scott, Anne M. 361
Scott, Geoffrey 278–80
Scott, James C. 202, 244
Scott, Paul H. 238
Scribner, Robert W. 145–6, 160, 359
Scudéry, Madeleine de 97
sculpture 44, 47, 74, 76, 81, 83, 153, 157, 234, 265
Seigworth, Gregory J. 13
Selby-Bigge, Lewis A. 272
Senault, Jean-François 68, 70, 311
Seneca 71, 287, 311
senses 25, 42–5, 54, 68, 119–20, 161, 231, 235, 270, 272, 276, 279, 327, 343–4

sensibility 33, 35, 78–82, 85, 166, 181, 197–8, 259, 269–72, 275–6, 279, 322, 327, 329–30
sentimentalism and sentimentality 8, 63, 78–80, 85, 151, 226, 271
sermons 8–9, 43, 67, 109, 111, 118, 156, 189, 215, 221–4, 231, 254, 282, 288, 312, 327–8
Serralta, Frédéric 95
servants and service 41, 126, 150–1, 206, 208–9, 245–6, 306
sexual behaviours 54, 115–17, 160, 190, 203, 211, 218, 220, 226, 245, 291–2, 302, 331–2, 341
sexual desire 33, 35, 54–5, 147, 151, 185, 190, 259, 264–5, 302, 304, 329–30
Sévigné, Marie de Rabutin-Chantal, Madame de 106
Shaftesbury, Anthony Ashley-Cooper, third Earl 72, 270
Shakespeare, William 5, 9, 26, 29, 34–6, 40–2, 51–4, 92–4, 109, 221, 348
shame 29, 35, 95, 100, 104–5, 110, 113–14, 141, 164, 171, 195–8, 200, 202–4, 240, 249, 306, 313–14, 318–9
Shapiro, Lisa 260, 361
Shaw, Philip 205, 362
Sheils, W.J. 286
Shelley, Mary 275–6
Shelley, Percy Bysshe 274–5
Shemek, Donna 124
Shepard, Alexandra 110–11
Shepherd, Rupert 161
Sherlock, Peter 151–5, 220–4
Sherman, Franklin 300
Sherman, William H. 133–4
Shields, Rob 349
Shirley, Anne 133
shock 207–8
Shore, Jane 89
Shorter, Edward 215, 217–8, 220
Shuger, Debora 43, 45
Sidney, Mary, Countess of Pembroke 133
Sidney, Philip 54–5, 89–91, 133–5
Siegel, Paul N. 56, 362
Sierhuis, Freya 357
Sievernich, G. 146
Silver, Larry 146
Silverman, Lisa 48
Simons, Patricia 36–9
Simonton, Deborah 355
sin 53, 55, 60, 75, 103, 107, 115, 141, 160, 191, 195–8, 203–4, 207, 218, 220–2, 239, 281–3, 288, 312, 328–9, 333
Singer, Kate 270, 272
Singh, Jyostna 9
Singh, Mohinder 323
Skeyne, Gilbert 208
Skinner, Quentin 185
slavery 66, 182–3, 273, 276, 286, 302, 304–6, 307–10, 321
Sloboda, John 27
sloth 150, 259, 278
Sluijter, Eric Jan 269
Small, Helen 98, 359
smile 52, 146, 150, 166
Smith, Adam 63, 64, 270–2, 275, 322–3
Smith, Ann *159,* 160
Smith, C.U.M. 260
Smith, Charlotte 275
Smith, Greg M. 53
Smith, J.C. 91
Smith, Pamela H. 257
Smith, Paul J. 349, 356
Smith, Sir Thomas 323
Smith, Vanessa 324–6, 363
Snyder Jon R. 227
Soárez, Cypriano 168–9, 172
sociability 62, 64–7, 137, 245, 255, 257, 265
social status 22, 41, 46, 58–9, 66, 81, 102, 106, 112, 134–5, 148, 187, 196–8, 200–1, 219, 236, 239–40, 243, 253, 264, 271, 273, 285, 305–6, 317, 345
sociality 64–7, 236
Soergel, Philip M. 295, 297
solace 159
solidarity 62, 186, 200–1, 222
solipsism 271
Solomon, Julie R. 44, 363
song 66, 68–9, 119, 197, 253, 278, 282, 308, 312, 328 see also voice
Soni, Vivasvan 63–4
Sonnenfels, Joseph von 181
Sorbin, Arnaud *296*
sorrow 24, 41, 51, 56, 60, 63, 66, 79, 102, 106, 135, 141, *142,* 153, 156–7, 162, 171, 193, 220, 222, 275, 282, 288, 305–6, 312, 339, 350 see also sadness
soul 23, 38, 60, 68, 166, 193, 202, 216, 236, 246, 274, 277, 288, 304, 306, 342, 344–5
Soyer, François 297–300, 303
Sparrman, Anders 307
Spector, Scott 334
Spedding, James 346
Spenser, Edmund 5, 54, 89, 91
Spinks, Jennifer 105, 146, 204–5, 293–97, 363
Spinoza, Baruch 11, 24, 72
Sponholz, Jesse 286
Stachniewski, John 290, 363
Staines, John 64
Stanislavki, Konstantin 94

Stayer, James 192
Stearne, John 343
Stearns, Carol Z. 5–6
Stearns, Peter 5–6, 10, 30
Steen, Jasper van der 105, 204–5, 355–6
Steenbergh, Kristine 30, 230, 360
Steggle, Matthew 230
Stephen, Michele 293, 363
Stephens, Thomas 119, 121
Steward, James 69–70
Stewart, Anne 27
'sticky' objects 19, 131
Stock, Brian 4, 6, 251
Stolberg, Michael 108
Stoler, Ann L. 319, 322
Stone, Lawrence 218, 220
Storace, Giovani Vincenzo 240
Stoyle, Mark 204, 238, 363
Strange, Carolyn 360
Strapparava, Carlo 30
Strocchia, Sharon 224
Struever, Nancy S. 44, 363
Stuart Mill, John 110
Stuyvesant, Peter 318
Styles, John 162–5, 363
sublime 327, 351
suffering 5–6, 43, 45–9, 53–6, 58, 61–3, 69, 71, 104, 107, 141, 155, 158, 167, *169*, 185–8, 195–8, 203, 200, 204, 210, 212, 237, 256, 265, 270, 275, 280–3, 286, 288, 308, 310, 312, 314–15, 328–9, 331, 336, 345
suicide 33, 222, 275, 333
Sullivan, Erin 13, 33, 35, 56–61, 94–5, 120, 363
Sullivan, Garrett A. 94, 361
surprise 28, 34, 75–6, 129, 166, 171, 212, 352
suspicion 115, 212, 258, 305–6, 324
Sutton, Peter 325–6, 363
Sweerts, Michiel 148, *148*, 150
Sweet, Rosemary 105, 256
Symonds, Dominic 230
sympathy 61, 63, 66, 72–3, 78–9, 90, 96, 121, 123, 156, 193–4, 203, 264, 270–1, 274–6, 290, 321–2, 324

Tacitus 187
Tadmor, Naomi 98, 246–7, 359
Tallon, Andrew 118, 120
Tan, Jacinta 27
Tanner, Marie 354
Tarabotti, Arcangela 96, 98, 278
Tarantino, Giovanni 284–7, 363
Tarlow, Sarah 17–18, 20
Tartini, Giuseppe 176
Taruskin, Richard 176, 263
Tasso, Torquato 54, 58, 350–2, 354
Tatlock, Lynne 205, 363
Tawney, R.H. 110–11
Taylor, Barbara 220
Taylor, Gary 36, 52
tears 11, 79, 82, 90, 92, 96–7, 152, 160, 166, 180, 197, 222, 229, 262, 274, 279, 281, 290, 308, 314 see also weeping
Telemann, Georg Philipp 174, 228
Teo, Thomas 26
Teresa of Avila, St 265, *266*
Terpstra, Nicholas 191, 198, 358
Terrall, Mary 213
terror 17, 75, 83, 113, 171, 183, 205, 212, 294, 301, 308–9, 313, 328, 351–2
Terry, Edward 302–3
Terry-Fritsch, Allie 205
Testelin, Henri 75–7, *76*
testimonies 112–3, 115, 124, 136, 199–200, 202, 222, 243
textiles 160–5, 302, 304–5 see also clothing, embroidery
theatre 6, 9, 62, 65–6, 80, 82, 93–4, 172, 175, 228–32, 264–5, 278, 302 see also drama, music
Theibault, John 205
Theocritus 350
Thielemann, Andreas 269, 359
Thirty Years War 202–3, 216
Thomas of Erfurt 49
Thomas, Keith 330, 339–40, 346–7, 349
Thompson, E.P. 111, 200, 202
Thornton, Alice 166, 212
Tiepolo, Giambattista 148–9, *149*
Tilmouth, Christopher 185
Tissot, Samuel-Auguste 166, 258
Titian, Tiziano Vecelli 147, 149, 350, *351*
Todd, Janet 80, 363
Toft, Mary 167
Toivo, Raisa Maria 208–10, 306–7, 363
tolerance 284–6, 319
Tolkien, J. R.R. 334
Tomes, Nancy 114
Tomkins, Silvan 26
Toppsell, Edward 338, 340
torment 38, 46–7, 55, 58, 220, 280, 282, 308, 342
Torrejoncillo, Francisco de 299–300
Toscano, Alberto 192
Tosi, Pierfrancesco 175–6
touch 42, 122, 134, 141, 181, 211, 256 see also senses
Toulalan, Sarah 213
Trapman, J. 217
Trappes-Lomax, Richard 280

Traub, Valerie 23
Traut, Wolf 141, *142*
Treitler, Leo 172, 176
Trembles, Mary 341
Trevor, Douglas 41, 363
Trexler, Richard 239, 241, 363
Trigg, Stephanie 10–13, 363
Trumbach, Randolph 220
Trust 110, 287, 301
Tuck, Richard 188
Tucker, Treva J. 346
Tuite, Clara 65, 67, 276, 362
Tuke, Thomas 69–70
Turberville, George 89
Turner, Henry S. 229
Turner, Vicki 16
Tytler, Graeme 361

Ulbrich, Claudia 204
urban space 22, 29, 236 see also civic culture

Valignano, Alessandro 311
Vållgarda, Karen 120–1, 315–6, 360
Van Eck, Caroline 17, 19–20
Van Gent, Jacqueline 123–4, 192, 290–3, 304–7, 313–16, 356, 363
Van Sant, Anne Jessie 272, 363
Van Tiggelen, Brigitte 260
Vasari, Giorgio 280–1, 283
Västfjall, Daniel 27
Vaughan, William 61, 340
Vaught, Jennifer C. 363
Vecchio, Silvana 56
Venegas, Alejo de 47
vengeance and revenge 72, 153, 192–3, 291, 318, 332, 336, 341–2
Venner, Thomas 106
Venner, Tobias 340
Verdi Webster, Susan 157, 160
Vergerio, Pietro Paulo 100
Verheyen, Nina xxxviii, 35, 358
Vermeer, Johannes 130, 317
Vesalius, Andreas 42
Veth, Peter 326, 363
viewers, see audience engagement
Vickery, Amanda 161, 165, 214
Victoria, Tomás Luis de 173
viewers, see audience engagement
Vila, Anne 260, 363
village 66, 115–6, 156, 205, 209, 242–4, 312
Villani, Giovanni 239–40
Vinci, Leonardo da 38–9
violence 36–7, 43, 47, 51, 55, 69, 83, 107, 114, 153, 175, 183, 194, 202–6, 208–11, 216, 218, 226–7, 229, 235–43, 248, 252–3, 264, 278, 285, 291, 294, 299, 301–3, 305–6, 308, 315, 318, 320–2, 324, 332–3, 339
Virgil 89, 350, 354
virtue 53–5, 63, 73, 97, 99–100, 144, 152–3, 155, 160, 166, 183, 212, 249, 270–1, 277, 322, 327
Vivaldi, Antonio 174
Vives, Juan Luis 249–51
voice, singing 44, 93, 122, 169–72, 175–6, 262, 278
Volter, Christophe 211
Vondel, Joost van den 317
Vuori, Juha A. 238

Wade, Mary R. 91
Waite, Gary K. 286
Walford, E. John 354
Walker, Claire 10, 16–17, 195, 246, 277–80, 355, 360
Walker, Suzanne J. 348–9
Walkington, Thomas 40–2
Wallis, H.R.E. 217
Walpole, Horace 275
Walsh, Linda 81–5, 363
Walsh, Richard T.G. 26
Walsham, Alexandra 105, 161, 285–6, 293, 363
Walter of Brienne 239
war 6, 37, 47, 90, 102–4, 129, 136, 180, 202–5, 216, 235–8, 253–5, 273, 278, 294, 301, 305, 312, 318, 321, 338 see civil war, revolution, Thirty Years War, violence
Wars of Religion, French 186, 203–4, 253, 294, 301
Ward, Samuel 290
Warner, Marina 337
Watanabe-O'Kelly, Helen 179–82, 364
Watt, Tessa 146
Weaver, Elissa 278, 280
Weber, Max 43, 110–11,
weddings 160, 180, 282 see also marriage
weeping 23, 44, 100, 156, 171, 193, 222, 239, 271, 275, 282, 288, 291, 308, 314 see also tears
Weiss, Piero 176
Weisser, Olivia 168, 364
Welch, Ellen R. 230
Wells, Stanley 36, 52
Wesley, Charles 328–9, 331
Wesley, John 328–30
West-Pavlov, Russell 363
Westling, Louise 349
Weston, Robert L. 105–8

Weststeijn, Thijs 45
Westwater, Lynn L. 98
wet nurses 215
Whenham, John 263
Whitaker, Harry 260
White Jr, Lynn 347, 349
White, Stephen D. 251
White, Paul 91
White, R.S. 26, 33–6, 50–3, 93, 95, 273–6, 364
Whyman, Susan E. 66–7
Wieck, Roger S. 146
Wiesner-Hanks, Merry 23
Wigen, Einar 322–3
Wilby, Emma 342
Wild, Johannes 281, 283
Wilkes, Thomas 229
William, Duke of Cumberland 236
Williams, Raymond 347, 349
Williams Lewin, Alison 104
Willet, Laura 91
Willis, Deborah 342
Willis, Thomas 24, 344–6
Wills 105, 136, 139, 154, 182, 223
Wilson, Adrian 213
Wilson, Kathleen 323
Wilson, Nick 263
Wilson, Peter 205
Winckelmann, Johann Joachim 83
Winchester, Barbara 127
Winston-Allen, Anne 105
Winter, Jay 205
witchcraft 9, 112, 144–5, *145*, 166, 210, 216–7, 243, 290–3, 330–4, 336, 340–3 see also familiars, magic, supernatural
Wither, Geroge 182–5
Wollstonecraft, Mary 73, 273, 276
wonder 35, 72, 81, 89, 102, 127, 129, 140, 152, 155, 234, 259, 265, 267, 293–7, 302, 349, 353 see also awe
wondrous, the 141, *144*, 295
Woodford, Robert 69–70
Woodward, David 128, 132
Woolf, Daniel R. 256–7
Wootton, David 135
Wordsworth, Dorothy 274
Wordsworth, William 187–8, 273–4
Worm, Ole 255
Wortham, Christopher 91
Wrath, see anger
Wright, Thomas 13
Wrightson, Keith 65, 67, 220
Wunderkammer 19, 255
Wunderli, Richard 224
Wyatt, Thomas 54, 90–1
Wyckoff, Elizabeth 146

Young, Spencer 315–6, 363
Yrjönsuuri, Mikko 250–1, 360

Zak, Gur 251
Zalta, Edward N. 26, 362
Zarlino, Gioseffo 262
zeal 35, 265, 287–8, 328
Ziarnko, Jan 144–5, *145*
Zika, Charles 105, 140–6, 204–5, 297, 363
Zinzendorf, Nicolaus Ludwig von 190, 316, 328, 330
Zorzi, Andrea 227, 362
Zucker, Adam 9, 355
Županov, Ines G. 121
Zurara, Gomes Eanes de 308–9
Zwaan, Janneke M. van der 30, 360
Zweig, Stefan 208